THE GOOD MAIL OR

Noelle Walsh was the editor of *Good Housekeeping* for four years and is the author of *The Good Deal Directory*, *The Good Deal Directory Guide to Bringing Up Baby on a Budget* and *The Good Deal Directory Guide to a Wonderful Wedding that Won't Cost a Fortune*. She is also a consumer journalist for the *Daily Mail*, ES magazine and the *Daily Telegraph*, and makes regular TV and radio appearances as a bargain shopping expert.

Also by the same author

The Good Deal Directory Guide
to Bringing Up Baby on a Budget

The Good Deal Directory Guide
to a Wonderful Wedding that Won't
Cost a Fortune

THE GOOD
Mail Order
GUIDE

Everything you need to know about ordering top-quality goods from the comfort of your living room

NOELLE WALSH

MACMILLAN

First published in Great Britain
in 1994 as *The Virgin Home Shopping Handbook*
by Virgin Books.

First published 1996 by Macmillan
an imprint of Macmillan General Books
25 Eccleston Place, London, SW1W 9NF
and Basingstoke

Associated companies throughout the world

ISBN 0-333-65238X

Copyright © Noelle Walsh 1996

The right of author to be identified as the
author of this work has been asserted by her in accordance
with the Copyright, Designs and Patents Act 1988.

Although every effort has been made to ensure the accuracy of
the information in this book, neither the Author nor the Publisher
can accept responsibility for any errors it may contain.

The Author and Publisher do not assume and hereby disclaim
any liability to any party for any loss or damage caused by errors
or omissions in *The Good Mail Order Guide*, whether such errors
or omissions result from negligence, accident, or any other cause.

The Publisher cannot give guarantees regarding goods or firms,
nor deal with complaints. Inclusion in this book does not imply
endorsement.

All rights reserved. No reproduction, copy or transmission
of this publication may be made without written permission.
No paragraph of this publication may be reproduced, copied
or transmitted save with written permission or in accordance
with the provisions of the Copyright Act 1956 (as amended).
Any person who does any unauthorized act in relation to
this publication may be liable to criminal prosecution
and civil claims for damages.

9 8 7 6 5 4 3 2 1

A CIP catalogue record for this book is available
from the British Library

Typeset by Spottiswoode Ballantyne Printers Limited
Printed by Mackays of Chatham Plc, Chatham, Kent.

CONTENTS

vii	**Introduction**
1	**How Mail Order Works**
	Methods of Payment
3	**Your Rights**
	Consumer Legislation
	Codes of Practice
	Guarantees
	Mail Order Preference Service
5	**Complaining**
7	**Mail Order Tips**
8	**Goods Prevented from Being Sent by Royal Mail**
9	**Useful Addresses**
11	**Entries**
	Accessories/Jewellery
	Art & Art Materials
	Baby Products
	Books
	Charities
	Clothes
	Collectables
	Computers
	DIY Supplies
	Electrical Appliances

CONTENTS

Electronics
Flowers
Food & Drink
Footwear
Furniture
Gadgets
Gardening
General Catalogues
Gifts
Health & Beauty
Hobbies & Crafts
Home
Kitchenware
Luggage
Medical & Scientific
Museums
Musical Instruments
Office Equipment
Optical
Outdoor (including Camping)
Pets
Photographic
Recordings
Software
Sports Equipment
Sportswear
Stationery
Toys
Travel
Watches & Clocks

544 **Index**

INTRODUCTION

Mail-order shopping is on the threshold of the biggest change in its history, making the term 'mail order' rather a misnomer. At the moment, people order by telephone and by post, with some purchases taking place via the Internet and pilot schemes such as television/telephone link-ups. But with the growth of on-line, interactive and television shopping, plus catalogue distribution through CD-Rom, a gradual change will take place that will become the norm as younger, computer-literate generations enter their earning-power years. Mail-order research company Verdict predicts that home shopping in general will increase its share of retail sales from 3.9% to more than 8% in the next 15 years, although the growth will be in on-line shopping at the expense of the catalogues. This is also true of the European market, according to financial reports, where most of the 21% rise in the mail-order market over the next 10 years will come from electronic shopping as it wins an increasing share of home-shopping sales. Customers in the next century will be able to shop when and where they want, not at a time, place or speed that retailers have dictated. And they don't have to carry their purchases home. For the purposes of this book, however, we are mainly concerned with the traditional forms of mail-order shopping: via a catalogue or brochure which you can touch, feel and flick through.

The top 6 companies – Great Universal Stores (GUS), Littlewoods, Freemans, Grattan, Empire Stores and Next – dominate the industry, accounting for approximately 95% of the market by value. Which only leaves 5% for the other 1,600-plus companies to fight over. The battle is for a share of a £6 billion market and the figures for operating in this area are similarly huge: GUS despatches more than 9 million catalogues a year; Freemans receives more than a quarter of a million orders a week; Littlewoods accepts at least £3 million worth of orders a day, according to a 1994 survey on home shopping by research company Key Note.

But while the big companies still dominate – even in Europe 47% of the market is dominated by 4 main players: Otto Versand and Quelle in

Germany, La Redoute in France (and since 1995 in the UK), and Great Universal Stores in Britain — they have taken note of the niche targeting of smaller companies dedicated to one particular type of customer.

The top-selling companies have all launched smaller spin-offs. GUS has 5 main catalogues — Great Universal, Choice, Family Album, Marshall Ward and Kays — as well as supplementary titles — Fashion Extra, Marshall Ward Direct, Fashion Update and First Needs. Littlewoods produces 6 main catalogues, plus two direct-mail brochures — All Of Us, for people with a credit limit, and Index Extra which doesn't use agents and therefore discounts the goods. Freemans has One to One, an experimental direct catalogue which does away with the agent, as well as undertaking trials of a CD-i version of its catalogue in conjunction with Philips.

Moreover, in 1995 GUS launched a Shoppers Universe electronic home-shopping service on Microsoft Net. MSN is a service which is available to customers with the Windows 95 package and features 10 stores offering over 1,000 products and services from GUS. Freemans and Littlewoods are also investigating interactive and on-line shopping.

Other changes in mail order are taking place. For example, there is a bourgeoisification of mail order — the market is booming with middle-class people who would never have thought of buying by post in the past, the customer who wants to buy Cotswold pottery from the original maker, for example.

Credit terms plus convenience, speed and service are what attract the traditional customer to the large catalogues. The new middle-class customers like the fact that they are able to buy stylish, unusual or original products which are often impossible to find elsewhere and which are delivered within a few days. For example, companies offering such diverse products as vegan perfumes, cat statues, personalised calendars, fruit presses, instant patios, antiquarian cookery books and reversible clothes for children.

The recession has caused a dramatic change in the way we shop. Those of us who are in work, work harder and have less time so anything that can be done quickly and on the phone is a godsend. Those of us with more time usually have less money so we try to avoid the temptation of the high street, turning instead to the credit facilities and competitive prices of many of the larger mail-order companies. Mail-order companies have been quick to respond to the recession, improving their catalogues, launching new smaller brochures aimed at smaller groups, inviting top designers to work for them, buying their own delivery vans and investing in new technology so they can provide a better service.

There are certain areas which are doing better than others in home shopping: by the year 2000, it has been estimated that 10–15% of food sales will be made by mail order, according to Prospects for Home Shopping in Europe, a *Financial Times* Retail Report.

HOW MAIL ORDER WORKS

The vast majority of catalogues are free but some specialist companies do make a charge in order to deter the 'catalogue collector'. Printing and distributing a catalogue is expensive and businesses cannot afford to hand them out free to people unlikely to order. In cases where a charge is made, the price of the catalogue is usually refundable against the first order.

When you order either a catalogue or goods your name will generally be kept on a computer database. This customer list is a valuable resource for the company. Not only can they mail you new catalogues and special offers but they can also sell your name to other, similar businesses. This selling of mailing lists is highly profitable.

Under current UK legislation it is quite legal to keep and sell customer details as long as the company is registered with the Data Protection Registrar and the customer has been given the opportunity to opt out. However, you can have your name removed from such lists by applying to an agency called the Mail Order Preference Scheme (*see* Useful Addresses, page 9).

When a company receives your order it may fulfil it on the same day or put it in a pile. It should only bank the cheque or process the credit card once the order is sent. So if you have been waiting some time for an item to arrive, check your bank account or credit card statement to make sure that your money has not already been deducted.

Most reputable companies will have some form of insurance for goods in transit. This will cover both the loss of items – and things do occasionally simply disappear – and breakages. It is nevertheless worth checking before you part with money just how comprehensive the cover is.

If the goods are not satisfactory you can usually return them but you often have to pay the postage both ways – unless you can argue that the goods are faulty. Always keep the original packaging in case you do have to send something back.

METHODS OF PAYMENT

Most companies accept a number of ways of paying: cheque, postal order, credit card, Switch, Delta and stage payment for the big catalogue companies. Credit card is by far the most flexible since it can be dictated over the phone, sent by fax or mailed. The two cards mostly widely accepted are Visa and Mastercard. Diners Club and American Express are less popular since they can be more complicated and expensive for the merchant to process.

Some people are reluctant to give their credit card details over the phone in case they get charged for items they never ordered. It is unlikely that a reputable supplier will misuse your card since if there is any hint of fraud their merchant privileges are removed and their business suffers.

If there has been fraudulent use of a card, the supplier is responsible not you. They will therefore have to reimburse the money in full and suffer the loss themselves. To minimise fraud always check your credit card bill as soon as it arrives and BEFORE paying it. If you find an item which you have not authorised, contact the credit card company immediately and ask for 'proof of purchase'. You might like to settle the remainder of the bill along with a letter explaining why you are withholding the disputed amount.

The credit card company will then contact the supplier and ask for further information. It is the supplier's responsibility to prove that it was indeed a genuine order. They will need to produce either the original, signed voucher or, in the case of a phone order, your full name and address as well as details of what you ordered and when. If they are unable to provide these you will not be charged.

YOUR RIGHTS

You have the same statutory rights when you buy through mail order as when you buy from a shop. Goods should be delivered within a reasonable time, usually 28 days or as specified in the catalogue or advertisement. If the goods do not turn up you can cancel the order and ask for your money back. But if you agree to allow the seller extra time, you cannot cancel until that time is up.

The law allows you a reasonable amount of time to examine the goods. Do this as soon as you can, and if they are faulty, send them back immediately with a note explaining the problem. Keep a copy of your note. It is also advisable to get a proof of postage certificate from the Post Office. When receiving goods from a courier or by special delivery which you have not been able to check in the presence of the delivery person, write alongside your signature that you have not been able to check them before signing.

If you order through an advertisement, read it thoroughly before placing an order and keep a copy. Always note the advertiser's name and address, where and when the ad appeared, when you posted your order and any other details such as charges for postage and packing.

If ordering from a book or record club, make sure you know what commitment you are making. Find out exactly what you have to buy and over how long in order to qualify for the introductory offer, if there is one.

Most newspapers and magazines have mail order protection schemes. These cover you if you sent payment in advance for goods in response to an advertisement, and the firm goes out of business before you get the goods or a refund. If your purchase is over £100, buy with a credit card which will give you added protection. The credit card company become equally liable for any claim you have against the trader. For example, if the goods are not delivered or are not what you ordered, you may be able to claim from the credit card company. These rights do not apply to debit cards (Delta, Switch) or charge cards (where you must pay all you owe within a few weeks of receiving the account). Moreover, many mail-order companies belong to trade associations which may also offer ways of resolving problems. Look for a trade association logo in ads or catalogues. (*See* Useful Addresses, page 9.)

If you receive goods through the post that you have not ordered, you should write to the firm explaining that you do not want them. If they are not collected within 30 days, they become yours. If you do not write to the company, put the goods to one side, unused. After 6 months, they will become yours. A firm which demands payment for unsolicited goods could be breaking the law. If you come across this problem, contact your local trading standards officer.

There is a growth in the number of companies selling goods by telephone. If you would like to reduce the number of sales calls you receive, contact your telephone company and ask to register with the Telephone Preference Service (*see* page 10). If you regularly receive unwanted calls from the same company, write and ask it to stop, which it is legally obliged to do.

COMPLAINING

If you are in any way dissatisfied you should, of course, complain. The following are some strategies to adopt which will help win your case.

- Keep the receipt. It may seem obvious but the simple receipt is a powerful ally. It proves what you bought, when, from whom and for how much. But not all receipts are created equal. Do not accept one that simply reads: 'Goods, £32'. Insist on details. It should denote the date, the name and address of the supplier and a brief description of the goods.

  If the company won't send you such a receipt (which in itself should ring alarm bells) write the details in yourself at the time. And then keep the receipt for at least a year.

- Keep copies of all correspondence, including faxes.

- Keep a record of phone calls. If you can't record conversations (most answering machines have this facility) then do write down what was said. Keep a note of the name of the person you spoke to and at what time.

- If complaining by phone or fax, send a hard copy to confirm and place the matter on record.

- When ordering write 'Time is of the essence' on the order form. This somewhat archaic phrase ensures that the delivery date you have agreed with the supplier (i.e. the one often written on the form itself) becomes legally binding. In its absence the delivery date has no legal standing.

- If returning a faulty item do so as quickly as possible. Delay may result in losing the right to a complete refund and only having recourse to compensation, which may mean a replacement or repair only.

- If you have a complaint, contact the retailer in person, preferably by phone, and let them know the nature of the problem. If that doesn't yield the proper response, write a letter to include:

    - the problem
    - the date of purchase
    - a copy of the receipt
    - a copy of cancelled cheque, or itemised credit card bill
    - what you would consider a fair and equitable settlement
    - a date by which you would like a response.

If this still fails to elicit a satisfactory response, contact your local Office of Fair Trading (*see* page 10) or Citizens Advice Bureau.

MAIL ORDER TIPS

Nearly all catalogues have simple-to-follow order forms but there are a number of tips worth noting.

- It is often better to call or fax your order since this gets a quicker response. It is also useful to speak to someone in case the price has changed, the item is no longer available and so on.

- If ordering over the phone, fill in the form as if you were mailing it. You can then read off the information in the correct order for the sales assistant to take down and thereby save phone time and eliminate errors.

- If writing, make sure your address is clear and always write in capitals. Faxed handwriting can come out 'bitty' so be sure to write clearly in a bold, dark colour and never use pencil.

- When ordering by credit card make each number clear – it is easy to confuse 0 with 9 and 7 with 1. Write 1s as straight lines and do not put a slash through the middle of a 7 as this can get confused with a 3. Write zeros as 0 not ø.

- Split up the credit card number into a series of digits rather than one long number which can be misread. And of course do not forget to include the expiry date of the card, written as a number not as a full date, e.g. 11/94 rather than November 94.

GOODS PROHIBITED FROM BEING SENT BY ROYAL MAIL

Pathological Specimens – e.g. blood, urine, semen etc; unless by an authorised person (doctor, vet, etc.)
Illegal Drugs
Poisons – any substance which could harm an employee
Living Creatures – with certain exceptions
Radioactive Materials
Compressed Gases
Oxidising Material
Corrosives
Asbestos
Flammable Liquids
Flammable Solids
Paints, Varnishes, Enamels, etc.
Matches
Obscene Materials
Counterfeit Currency & Stamps
Perishable Goods

Aerosols and lighters are allowed in certain circumstances. For a copy of the full regulations contact your local Customer Service Centre (see telephone book) or pick up a copy of 'Prohibited & Restricted Goods' from any Post Office.

USEFUL ADDRESSES

Advertising Standards Authority
Brook House
2–16 Torrington Place
London
WC1E 7HN

The British Direct Marketing Association
Grosvenor Gardens House
Grosvenor Gardens
London
SW1W 0BS

Consumers Association
2 Marylebone Road
London
NW1 4DF
TEL: 0171 486 5544

Direct Marketing Association
Haymarket House
1 Oxendon Street
London SW1Y 4EE
TEL: 0171 321 2525

Mail Order Protection Scheme
16 Tooks Court
London
EC4A 1LB
TEL: 0171 405 6806

USEFUL ADDRESSES

The Mail Order Traders' Association of Great Britain
100 Old Hall Street
Liverpool
L3 9TD
TEL: 0151 227 4181

The Mailing/Telephone Preference Service
FREEPOST 22
London
W1E 7EZ
TEL: 0171 738 1625
British Telecom: 0800 398893
Mercury: 0500 398893

The Office of Fair Trading
Publications Department
PO Box 2
Central Way
Feltham
Middlesex TW14 0TG
TEL: 0181 398 3405
Consumer information line: 0345 224499

Periodical Publishers Asscociation
Imperial House
15–19 Kingsway
London
WC2B 6UN

Accessories/Jewellery

AVON COSMETICS LTD
Earlstrees Road
Industrial Estate
Corby
Northants
NORTHAMPTONSHIRE
NN17 4AZ
Telephone
0800 663664

Cosmetics and jewellery
Established in the UK in 1959, Avon is probably best known for its direct-selling methods and distinctive dingdong trademark. Now available through mail order, it has considerably expanded its range to include jewellery, haircare products, CDs and videos, giftware, lingerie and handbags in addition to its original cosmetics and skincare products.

While prices remain very reasonable with lipstick from £1.79 and eau de toilette sprays from £4.99, there are often added incentives to purchase, with free extras or reduced-price jewellery.
Catalogue Catalogue, Colour, 127 pages, Free **Postal charges** £1.95 **Delivery** Royal Mail **Methods of Payment** Postal Order, Credit Card, Switch, Cheque

BANANA BARN
Street Farm
Stinchcombe
Dursley
Gloucestershire
GL11 6AW
Telephone
01453 544276
Fax
same

Navajo North American Indian jewellery
Norman and Linda Sellers developed this business from their own interest in creating a wildlife garden. Their catalogue is packed with information. Did you know that hedgehogs are a natural controller of slugs? A Hedgehog House costs £34.50. Banana Barn sells bird-feeders and badger mix, bat boxes and dormouse boxes, wildflower seeds and flowering lawn mix. Through their fascination with fossils and crystals another part of the business grew up. They also sell Navajo and Zuni jewellery hand-crafted from turquoise and silver.

ACCESSORIES/JEWELLERY

BRUFORD & HEMING LTD
28 Conduit Street
New Bond Street
London
W1R 9TA
Telephone
0171 629 4289
Fax
0171 493 5879

Catalogue Annually, A5, Catalogue, Colour and B/W, 50 pages, Free **Postal charges** £2.50 for orders up to £15 **Delivery** Royal Mail, Parcelforce **Methods of Payment** Cheque, Credit Card

Silverware

While they are renowned for their fine antique silver and jewellery, Bruford & Heming produce a catalogue that features only newly produced silver items, all fully hallmarked. Gift items include photograph frames (from £20), small perfume bottles (from £43), silver bookmarks (from £11) and cutlery sets (from £1,200).

New and antique jewellery is displayed in an additional colour brochure, arranged according to price. An antique five-stone rhodolite garnet half-hoop ring (Chester 1878) will set you back £320, or for £1,530 you could buy a ruby, diamond and rock crystal Art Deco-style brooch.

Catalogue A5, Catalogue, Colour, 36 pages, Free **Postal charges** Free **Delivery** Royal Mail **Methods of Payment** Cheque, Credit Card, American Express

C & T EYEWEAR LTD
PO Box 41
Teddington
Middlesex
TW11 05X
Telephone
0181 943 4815
Fax
0181 977 1717

Ray-Ban sunglasses

C&T offer 40% off the retail price for genuine Bausch & Lomb Ray-Ban sunglasses. Recently these have once again become fashion items, usually with prices to match.

The leaflet pictorially displays their extensive range of glasses, ranging from the Wayfarer Black G-15 to The General II Gold RB-50. Every pair of Ray-Ban glasses sold has a one-year guarantee and prices include a soft or hard case, depending on model. All frames are adjustable.

Catalogue, A4, Catalogue, Colour, 4 pages, Free

CAIRNCROSS OF PERTH
18 St John Street
Perth
Scotland
PH1 5SR
Telephone
01738 624367
Fax
01738 643913

Jewellery
Quality colour photographs display the beautiful Cairncross range of Scottish river pearl jewellery. The pearls are fished from the rivers Spey, Esk, Connan and Tay as they have been for generations, and set with semi-precious stones in 18 and 9car-gold. Sloeberry brooch, £200; amethyst cluster earrings, £290; single Scottish pearl drop on a chain, from £160.

Catalogue Annually, A5, Catalogue, Colour, 10 pages, Free **Postal charges** Varies with item **Delivery** Royal Mail **Methods of Payment** Cheque

CARELL LEATHER
Hembury Cottage
Buckland Filleigh
Beaworthy
North Devon
EX21 5PH
Telephone
01409 281433

Leather goods
Have you ever longed for an old-fashioned Gladstone bag or a no-nonsense bridle handbag? This North Devon company has the answer with its range of leather bags and cases in various sizes and colours. Commissions and restoration work are undertaken. Gladstone bag, from £388; briefcase, from £155; handbag, from £100.

Catalogue Annually, A4, Leaflets, Colour and B/W, 2 pages, Free **Postal charges** Varies with item **Delivery** Royal Mail **Methods of Payment** Cheque, Postal Order, Credit Card

CELTIA
Hill House
Mount Pleasant
Framlingham
Suffolk
IP13 9HJ
Telephone
01728 723039
Fax
01728 723039

Jewellery
Celtia are gold- and silversmiths producing handcrafted original designs in the Celtic style. There are knots symbolising long life and eternal friendship, fish symbolising Christianity, birds symbolising freedom of spirit and serpents symbolising fertility.

Sterling silver earrings are £19.45 per pair for the 'Little Dragon' style; a 9car-gold 'Bird' brooch costs £43.50 and a sterling silver 'Serpent' ring costs £17.50. Commissions are undertaken.

ACCESSORIES/JEWELLERY

THE CLIVEDON COLLECTION
Witham Friary
Frome
Somerset
BA11 5HH
Telephone
01749 850728
Fax
01749 850729

Catalogue A5, Brochure, Colour, 6 pages, Free **Postal charges** £3.00 **Delivery** Royal Mail **Methods of Payment** Cheque, Credit Card, Switch

Badges, keyrings and models

Clivedon claim to be the manufacturers of the world's finest aviation giftwear including tie bars, cufflinks, pendants, earrings, keyrings, badges and bookmarks in the shape of famous aeroplanes. They take great care to ensure that all their models are accurate reproductions. There is a minimum mail order of £10. Badges start at £4, tie bars and money clips cost £8.50, cufflinks £16 and keyrings £6. Baseball caps range from £4 to £7. Other ranges, including animals and cars, are also available.

Catalogue A4, Catalogue, Colour, 18 pages, Free **Postal charges** UK: Order value £10.00-£25.00, add £1.50; £26.00-£50.00, add £3.00; £51.00-£100.00, add £6.00; over £100.00, add £10.00. **Delivery** Royal Mail **Methods of Payment** Cheque, Credit Card

THE COACH STORE
8 Sloane Street
London
SW1X 9LE
Telephone
0171 235 1507
Fax
0171 235 3556

Fine leather handbags and accessories

Coach offers simple but attractive gift ideas for both men and women including leather handbags (from £64), wallets and purses (from £55), brief cases, waist pouches, cosmetic cases, belts and organisers. Every item is made from fine leather with gold-plated clutches, buttons and poppers, and is available in a variety of colours.

Catalogue Annually, A5, Catalogue, Colour, 58 pages, Free **Postal charges** £3.50 **Delivery** Royal Mail, Parcelforce **Methods of Payment** Cheque, Postal Order, Credit Card, American Express

CORRYMOOR MOHAIR

Westcountry Mohair
Corrymoor Farm
Stockland
Honiton
Devon
EX19 9DY

Mohair socks

The Corrymoor flock of pedigree Angora goats are large and deep-bodied with exceptionally fine, lustrous, kemp-free mohair fleeces. Kemp is the short, thick fibre which makes poor quality mohair itchy. The Corrymoor farm is worked to exacting organic standards without the use of artificial fertiliser and sprays. Corrymoor goats are shorn twice a year and the fleeces graded to ensure that only the best quality is used for the socks. The socks come in four varieties: the Sportsman – short, plain-knit lightweight sock ideal for town and everyday wear; Countryman – short, stretch-rib sock with cushion sole perfect for cold fee and hard wear; the Woodlander – knee-length sock with turnover top, stretch rib and cushion sole, ideal for walking and climbing; and the Highlander, a knee-length ribbed stocking with traditional patterned turnover top, the perfect dress and shooting stocking. Sizes are small (4–7), medium (8–10) and large (11–13).

Catalogue Sixth A4, Leafets, Colour and B/W, 8 pages, Free **Postal charges** 50p for one pair; 40p each for 2–7 pairs; free with 8 pairs or more **Methods of Payment** Credit Card, Cheque, Postal Order

JAMES SMITH & SONS

Hazelwood House
53 New Oxford Street
London
WC1A 1BL
Telephone
0171 836 4731

Umbrellas and sticks

James Smith established his umbrella shop in 1830 and it remains the world's most famous even today. The shop itself has changed little over the years, umbrellas are still displayed in specially woven baskets, repairs are carried out on the premises and from here quintessentially English brollies and sticks of all descriptions are sent around the world. Solid Stick Umbrella with hickory crook, £79.50; Country Umbrella, men's large, £65.75, ladies', £54.50; Alpine Stick, £34.50.

ACCESSORIES/JEWELLERY

Catalogue Annually, A5, Catalogue, Colour, 12 pages, Free **Postal charges** Varies with item **Delivery** Royal Mail, Parcelforce **Methods of Payment** Cheque, Credit Card

NUMERO VERDE
Bennett House
1 High Street
Edgware
Middlesex
HA8 7DE
Telephone
0181 958 3999
Fax
0181 958 1759

Leather goods and silk scarves

Numero Verde offers a sumptuous range of co-ordinated purses, wallets and accessories crafted from smooth Italian leather at affordable prices. The items come in a variety of shapes and sizes: women's double-sided purse wallet, £21.99; men's flap wallet, £18.99; key case, £9.99. To complement the leatherware, Numero Verde's catalogue also contains elegant, long silk chiffon scarves, £24.99, and generous square silk twill scarves, £39.99.

Catalogue Annually, A5, Catalogue, Colour, 8 pages, Free **Postal charges** £1.50; 24-hour delivery, £10 **Delivery** Royal Mail, Parcelforce **Methods of Payment** Cheque, Postal Order, Credit Card

OGDEN OF HARROGATE LTD
38 James Street
Harrogate
North Yorkshire
HG1 1RQ
Telephone
01423 504123
Fax
01423 522283

Jewellery, watches, silverware and gifts

Ogden of Harrogate is a well-established family business offering an extensive selection of jewellery and silverware, watches and clocks. Its range includes antique and secondhand items in addition to traditional and modern designs. Prices from £65 to £23,500. The company's craftsmen offer a design, re-design, alteration and repair service. A valuation service is also available.

Catalogue Annually, A5, Brochure, Colour, 31 pages, Free **Postal charges** £5 approx. **Methods of Payment** Cheque, Credit Card, American Express, Diners Club

RAFFIATAT
80 Hotham Road
Putney
London
SW15 1QP

Handmade plaited raffia hats

A RaffiaTat is a modern interpretation of the classic straw hat reminiscent of times past. They are entirely hand-crafted from natural fibres with a luxurious hand-finished silk lining, and each hat

ACCESSORIES/JEWELLERY

Telephone
0181 785 2753

is unique. A choice of 16 styles is available ranging from the classic Breton and Pollyanna through those inspired by the past such as the Raj and Flapper to the ethnically influenced Cossack and Fez, the Casual Beach and the chic Chocolate Box. Hats range from £75.

Catalogue Third A4, Leaflets, Colour and B/W, 4 pages, Free **Postal charges** Free **Methods of Payment** Cheque, Postal Order

SALLY GRAFTON DESIGN
3 Victoria Road
Sevenoaks
Kent
TN13 1YB
Telephone
01732 460929
Fax
01732 460162

Gold and silver jewellery in flower designs

The colour catalogue shows exquisite flowers sculpted in gold and silver. The flowers are made into earrings, pendants, brooches, necklets, stickpins and tie-tacks. Some pieces are set with pearls, rubies or sapphires, and there is also a good selection of chains. All the jewellery is hallmarked sterling silver, 9car or 18car-gold, and carries a full money-back guarantee. The flowers currently featured are fuchsias (a popular design with moving droplets), narcissus (beautifully detailed three-dimensional flower), rose (classic-bloomed shape), primroses (small and delicately shaped), clematis (pretty, open-work design with complementary elegant leaf forms), and wild rose (a tiny detailed flower).

Catalogue Annually, A4 folder, Catalogue, Colour, 6 pages pages, Free **Postal charges** £1.50 for silver; £4 for gold; £5 for overseas. **Delivery** Insured post **Methods of Payment** Cheque, Postal Order, Credit Card

SILVER DIRECT
PO Box 925
Shaftesbury
Dorset
SP7 9RA
Telephone
01747 828977

Silver jewellery and gift items

Silver Direct operates on the principle that the finest-quality silver becomes affordable when bought direct. 9car-gold and graduated pearl drop earrings cost £118 (average retail price, £135); sterling silver and gilt champagne cufflinks cost £65 (average retail price, £79); and a silver-

Fax
01747 828961

plated travelling corkscrew costs £35 (average retail price, £40). Postage and VAT are included and all their products are boxed and ready for presentation.

Catalogue Annually, A5, Catalogue, Colour, 8 pages, Free **Postal charges** Free **Delivery** Parcelforce, Royal Mail **Methods of Payment** Cheque, Postal Order, Credit Card, Switch

SPENCER THORN JEWELLERS
Belle Vue
Bude
Cornwall
EX23 8JY
Telephone
01288 353905
Fax
01288 353905

Napkin hooks

Described as 'the essential dress accessory', the Diner's Napkin Hook is as practical as it is unusual. Designed to hang from a shirt or blouse button, or between the shirt overlap, or even from the collar, these stylish jewellery items are bound to be the subject of conversation at the dinner table. The napkin hooks are crafted in hallmarked sterling silver and available in a variety of designs: Original, Crown and Hinged. Prices, which include VAT and postage and packing, vary from £29.50 (Original) to £39.50 (Hinged). Both versions can be hand-engraved with up to three initials at £3.25 per letter. The Crown model in silver is £33 and is also available in polished brass with silver detail for £15.95.

Catalogue Annually, A4, Leaflets, B/W, 1 page, Free **Postal charges** Free **Delivery** Royal Mail **Methods of Payment** Cheque, Credit Card, American Express, Switch

Art & Art Materials

ALEC TIRANTI
70 High Street
Theale
Reading
Berkshire
RG7 5AR
Telephone
01734 302775
Fax
01734 323487

Materials for sculpture
Alec Tiranti sells an extensive range of tools, materials and equipment for modelling, wood-carving and sculpture and stocks a variety of books and technical booklets on the various techniques. Extra-fine stainless steel modelling tool, £6.52; carver's A punch, £2.47; high-speed cutter, £6.94.
Catalogue Annually, A5, Catalogue, B/W, 104 pages, Free **Postal charges** Varies with item **Delivery** Royal Mail, Parcelforce, Courier **Methods of Payment** Cheque, Postal Order, Credit Card

ART ROOM
Witney
Oxfordshire
OX8 6BH
Telephone
01993 770445
Fax
01993 700749

Fine art pictures and gifts
Enjoy the work of famous artists without having to pay auction-house prices. Art Room specialises in framed prints and gifts. Vincent Van Gogh's 'Irises' on a blue mount with a gilt frame costs £24.95; Turner's 'The Grand Canal, Venice', framed in a gilt moulding, costs £69.95; mugs decorated with Monet paintings, £6.95 each; Macke napkins, £2.75 a pack.
Catalogue Bi-annually, A4, Catalogue, Colour, 31 pages, Free **Postal charges** £2.95 **Delivery** Parcelforce **Methods of Payment** Cheque, Postal Order, Credit Card, Switch, American Express, Diners Club

THE ART VENEERS CO LTD
Industrial Estate
Mildenhall
IP28 7AY
Suffolk
IP28 7AY
Telephone
01638 712550
Fax
01638 712330

Decorative veneers
This interesting catalogue tells you everything you need to know about veneering. As well as the veneers themselves it shows inlay bandings, inlay motifs, knobs and handles, hinges and marquetry tools. There's a booklist at the back including titles such as 'Cabinet Making for Beginners' and 'Practical Veneering' both by Charles H. Hayward. There's also a useful glossary and information on health and safety.

Catalogue Annually, A5, Catalogue, Colour and B/W, 104 pages, Free **Postal charges** Varies with item **Delivery** Parcelforce, Courier **Methods of Payment** Cheque, Postal Order, Credit Card, COD

ARTAGRAPH REPRODUCTION TECHNOLOGY LTD
Evrite House
Haden Road
Cradley Heath
West Midlands
B64 6ES
Telephone
01384 66042
Fax
01384 410127

Reproduction art
Artagraph is a process which ensures not just perfect colour, but a faithful recreation of the surface texture of the original painting. Brush strokes, tiny flaws, cracks and fissures are all there to see and touch. Artagraph has 50 popular paintings in stock, all framed, although you can choose your own frame if you don't like the stock frames. They also have a special limited collection available which covers pictures from The Hermitage Museum in St Petersburg, Russia. Artists include Monet, Gauguin, Cezanne, Van Gogh, Matisse and Turner.

Catalogue Third A4, Leaflets, Colour, 6 pages, Free **Methods of Payment** Cheque, Postal Order, Credit Card, American Express, Switch, Diners Club

ARTISTA STUDIO PUBLICATIONS
PO Box 42
Etchingham
East Sussex
TN19 7BQ

Oil paintings of country scenes
These good-quality hand-printed lithographic limited editions are reproduced from oil paintings by Anthony Richard Tiffin, and are numbered, hallmarked and signed individually by the artist. Accompanied by a descriptive certificate of

ART & ART MATERIALS

Telephone
01435 882542
Fax
01435 812117

authenticity, the traditional country scenes include 'Picnic at Partridge Green' (£35) and 'Heavy Horses Ploughing in Sussex' (£29.50).

Catalogue A4, Leaflets, Colour and B/W, 6 pages, Free **Postal charges** Free **Delivery** Royal Mail **Methods of Payment** Cheque, Postal Order, Credit Card

BOW ART (PRINTS BY POST)
PO Box 6471
London
E3 5UB
Telephone
01225 892009
Fax
01225 892009

Pictures
Bow Art specialises in reproductions of fine art. Their new series of works by Modern British Painters includes two prints by Eric Ravilious: 'Tea at Furlongs' and 'Interior at Furlongs', painted in 1939 while Ravilious was staying with friends near Lewes in Sussex. These two editions are printed on acid-free paper with light-fast inks. Price: £34.50 each. All prints are supplied unframed.

Catalogue A5, Leaflets, Colour, 1 page, Free **Postal charges** £2.00 (UK); £6.00 (Europe and Eire); £9.00 (rest of world) for up to 4 prints. **Delivery** Parcelforce **Methods of Payment** Cheque, Postal Order

THE BRUTON STREET GALLERY
28 Bruton Street
London
W1X 7DB
Telephone
0171 499 9747
Fax
0171 409 7867

Paintings
The Bruton Street Gallery produces superb catalogues for its exhibitions, containing colour photographs of the work for sale and a write-up about the artist.

Catalogue Bi-monthly, A5, Catalogue, Colour, 28 pages, Free **Postal charges** Varies with item **Delivery** Parcelforce **Methods of Payment** Cheque, Credit Card

CARRSON ARTISTIC PRODUCTS
66 Old Park Avenue
Canterbury
Kent
CT1 1DN

Decorative butterflies
Giant and not-so-giant butterflies to grace your home. Carrson supplies a range of hand-crafted decorative butterflies from a jumbo 24in-wing-span Swallowtail (£46) which comes with sturdy aluminium brackets to fix to your garden wall or

Telephone
01227 459076

onto a stake in your flower bed, to 2.5in assorted indoor life-size stick-on butterflies (£1.25 for five) to brighten pot plants and pelmets. Magnets are also available.

Catalogue Annually, A4, Leaflets, Colour and B/W, 3 pages, Free **Postal charges** £1 **Delivery** Royal Mail **Methods of Payment** Cheque, Postal Order

CCA GALLERIES
8 Dover Street
London
W1X 3PJ
Telephone
0171 499 6701
Fax
0171 409 3555

Limited edition signed original prints

CCA Galleries, formerly Christies Contemporary Art, is one of the leading publishers of original etchings, lithographs and screenprints in Europe. Its catalogue features work by a variety of contemporary artists, including young printmakers and respected names such as John Piper and Donald Hamilton Fraser. Each print is numbered and signed by the artist. This exclusivity, thankfully, is not reflected in the cost. Prices start from £75 unframed and rise to £2,350. The full range can be viewed at its galleries in Mayfair, Cambridge, Oxford, Bath and Farnham. They have an exciting exhibition programme which includes paintings and sculpture by their successful stable of artists.

Catalogue Quarterly, A4, Catalogue, Colour, 24 pages, Free **Postal charges** Varies with item **Delivery** Parcelforce, Courier, UPS **Methods of Payment** Cheque, Stage Payments, Credit Card, American Express, Diners Club, Postal Order

CHROMACOLOUR INTERNATIONAL
Cartoon House
16 Grange Mills
Weir Road
Balham
London
SW12 0NE

Materials and equipment for artists and animators

If you are an artist, professional animator or enthusiastic amateur, this is the catalogue for you. It features Chromacolour's extensive range including Chroma Artists Colours, animation cell paints, brushes, animation paper, drawing discs, technical pens and commercial punches. There are

Telephone
0181 675 8422
Fax
0181 675 8499

books and videos for all levels. Chroma Artists Colours from £2.49; animation paint, from £4.41/100ml; animation paper, from £33 a box with discounts on multiples; storyboards from £3.90; cell crayons, from 47p. Prices exclude VAT.

Catalogue Annually, A4, Catalogue, Colour and B/W, 30 pages, Free **Postal charges** Varies with item **Delivery** Courier, In-house delivery **Methods of Payment** Cheque, Credit Card, American Express, Diners Club

THE COMPLEAT STENCILLER
The Saddle Room
Capesthorne Hall
Macclesfield
Cheshire
SK11 9JY
Telephone
01625 860970
Fax
01625 860970

Stencils
American Traditional Stencils are the largest manufacturer of solid brass and laser cut stencils in the world. They also supply paints, crayons, brushes, tools and instructions for embossing; electric heat pens and cutting knives; marbling, colourwash and liming kits; and dolls' house stencils. On receipt of £1, they will send their mail-order list of craft books and products. Their full-colour catalogue which shows multi-layer stencils, some 5ft long, is available on receipt of £6.

Catalogue Annually, A4, Catalogue, Colour, 30 pages, Free **Postal charges** £2.00 **Delivery** Parcelforce, Royal Mail **Methods of Payment** Cheque, Credit Card, Postal Order

THE CONNAUGHT HERITAGE
Unit 6 Leaside Business Centre
Millmarsh Lane
Brimsdown
Enfield
Middlesex
EN3 7BJ
Telephone
0181 805 8899
Fax
0171 236 6063

Art gifts
The Connaught Heritage offers beautiful handcrafted mirrors, pictures and flower pots. These come in various designs: Shell, Classic, Sunflower, Tartan, Paper Rose and Gingham. There's also a set of six cameos of musical instruments handcrafted from an original design by artist Emma Daniels. The series is called Musical Moments and the cameos measure 7 in × 6 in (17.8 cm × 15.2 cm).

Catalogue A4, Leaflets, Colour, 4 pages, Free **Postal charges** £10.00 **Delivery** Parcelforce **Methods of Payment** Cheque

COPPELIA DECORATIVE STENCILS
Newton Villa
Ashfield Crescent
Ross-on-Wye
Herefordshire
HR9 5PH
Telephone
01989 566838
Fax
01989 768345

Stencils

Coppelia's attractive stencils and stencil borders include an 'Oriental' collection with ginger jar (£18.95, pre-cut), fan dish (£8.95) and willow-pattern plate (£8.95). The 'Conservatory' collection includes a climbing clematis (life-size), an arranged urn and a delphinium (£15.95 each). The borders include 'Deco sunray' and 'Alpine strawberries' (£11.95 each). Stencil brushes are also available in sizes 4, 6 and 8 from £2.50.

Catalogue A4, Catalogue, Colour, 7 pages, Free **Postal charges** UK: £1.50; overseas: £5.00. **Delivery** Royal Mail, Parcelforce **Methods of Payment** Cheque

CRAFT DEPOT
1 Canvin Court
Somerton Business Park
Somerton
Somerset
TA11 6SB
Telephone
01458 274727
Fax
01458 272932

Arts and crafts supplies

This catalogue features an enormous range of materials for the craftsperson. There are dolls to dress, chairs to seat, animals to make, clocks to assemble and jewellery to fashion, plus needlecraft supplies, items for woodcraft and a large selection of craft books. Safety cat eyes, £1.32 for six pairs; brooch pins, 72p for 12; three wooden trays for stencilling, £19.95.

Catalogue Annually, A4, Catalogue, B/W, 72 pages, £3 **Postal charges** Varies with item **Delivery** Royal Mail, Parcelforce **Methods of Payment** Cheque, Credit Card

THE ENGLISH STAMP COMPANY
Sunnydown
Worth Matravers
Dorset
BH19 3JP
Telephone
01929 439117
Fax
01929 439150

Interior design stamps

The English Stamp Company sells devices to 'decorate with stamps'. This does not mean covering your wall with 25p stamps, but using special devices to make impressions on flat surfaces. All you need is a stamp, a roller applicator and some stamp paint. A 2in 'Moon' stamp costs £6.95; 4in 'Fleur de Lys', £12.95. Paint is from £2.95 and a roller £2.95. Complete kits are £22.95.

ART & ART MATERIALS

F. FRITH & CO.
Netherhamptom
Salisbury
Wiltshire
SP2 8PU
Telephone
01722 744666

Catalogue A5, Catalogue, Colour and B/W, 16 pages, Free **Postal charges** Free **Delivery** Royal Mail, Parcelforce **Methods of Payment** Cheque, Postal Order, Switch, Credit Card

3-D Picture Sculpture

The country's leading specialist in the art of Picture Sculpture. There are many products included in this catalogue including a new floral art collection, the chance to arrange your own floral bouquet in Picture Sculpture. Craft Packs from £2.40, print Packs from £3.00, picture sculpture prints from 40p, and tools and accessories from craft knives to a set of shaping tools. Frith's also have a frame for every print in their collection. Truly delightful 3-D prints from cats to flowers. **Catalogue** Annually, A4, Catalogue, Colour and B/W, 18 pages, Free **Postal charges** Varies with item **Delivery** Courier **Methods of Payment** Cheque, Credit Card

LAWRENCE & TURNER
Imperial House
FREEPOST (GL217)
Cheltenham
Gloucestershire
GL50 2BR
Telephone
01242 515222
Fax
01242 238201

Fine art reproductions

Owners of a gallery in Cheltenham, they have produced their first mail-order catalogue. By and large it shows the less well-known works of the great art collections. The reverse of each picture bears a hand-numbered and signed Certificate of Authentication from the gallery declaring the print to be a faithful reproduction of the original. When you purchase all 6 framed pictures in a single payment, the price is just £395 – effectively giving you 6 pictures for the price of 5. Examples include Turner's 'Venice', limited edition of 5,000; Turner's 'Rivers of France'; Pierre-Joseph Redoute's 'The Romance of the Rose'; Georg Dionysius Ehret's 'Rare Plants and Butterflies'; Rossetti's 'Waterwillow' and 'Study for Daydream'. You can see the works of art in the catalogue at the gallery in Lypiatt Road, Cheltenham.

Catalogue A4, Catalogue, Colour, 24 pages **Postal charges** Free **Delivery** Special carrier **Methods of Payment** Cheque, Postal Order, Credit Card, American Express, Diners Club, Switch

LOCKETTS
8–9 Charnham Lane
Hungerford
Berkshire
RG17 0EY
Telephone
01488 685256
Fax
01488 681101

Photograph albums and frames

A comprehensive range of photograph frames and albums. Photograph albums with a marbled cover and plain cover are available from £39; also visitors books at £54.50 and address and scrap books. Photograph frames in leather, bevelled glass, coloured wood, lacquer and wood, at prices from £16.75 to £61.85 dependent upon size and finish.

Catalogue Annually, A4, Brochure, Colour, 14 pages, Free **Postal charges** 1 frame – £4, 2 or more frames – £6, orders over £250 free **Delivery** Courier **Methods of Payment** Cheque, Postal Order, Credit Card

MERLE'S STUDIO
Branscombe
Devon
EX12 3AY
Telephone
01297 680322

Prints, 3-D decoupage and sculpture

Merle's studio stocks a wide range of prints for decoupage. The subjects include flowers, animals, children, whimsical scenes and elegant fashion prints. They are generally sold in sets of five (Fruits by Bob Pohl, £2.25 a set), and two instructional videos are available (£16.95 each).

Catalogue Annually, A5, Catalogue, B/W, 52 pages, Free **Postal charges** Varies with item **Delivery** Royal Mail **Methods of Payment** Cheque

NATIONAL GALLERY PUBLICATIONS
Freepost
Helston
Cornwall
TR13 0YY
Telephone
01209 831888

Cards, posters, prints

A must for art lovers, this is a beautifully produced catalogue. All sales help to support the nation's art collections in the National Gallery in London. A stationery range is based on works by Impressionist and Renaissance artists, and there are also jigsaws, social journals, desk accessories, calendars, wrapping paper and greetings cards. All feature

Fax
01209 831995

reproductions of one or more famous paintings from the gallery. There is also a good selection of fine art books, including those based on special exhibitions held at the gallery.

Catalogue A4, Catalogue, Colour, 32 pages, Free **Postal charges** Under £10, £2.50; over £10, £4.95 **Delivery** Parcelforce and TNT **Methods of Payment** Cheque, Postal Order, Credit Card, American Express

RICHARD WADE ETCHINGS
52 Main Road
Norton in Hales
Market Drayton
Shropshire
TF9 4AT
Telephone
01630 657942

Etchings

The vital ingredient in Richard Wade's very attractive etchings is character. Rural scenes depicting country kitchens and farm animals and nostalgic motoring scenes feature prominently in his collection. All prints are sold unframed. Printed on Sanders Waterford paper with 2–3in margins, all editions are limited to 200. 'Home Sweet Home' (3in × 2in) is priced at £24 and 'Abandoned Alvis' (4in × 3in) at £25.

Catalogue A5, Brochure, Colour, 1 page, Free **Postal charges** Add £3.00 to UK orders; £5.00 to overseas orders. **Delivery** Royal Mail **Methods of Payment** Cheque

SMITCRAFT
Unit 1
Eastern Road
Aldershot
Hampshire
GU12 4TE
Telephone
01252 342626
Fax
01252 311700

Arts and crafts materials

This must be one of the most comprehensive handicraft catalogues. Whether a professional or amateur, you will find this catalogue brimming over with materials and kits at competitive prices. There is everything you need for cane seating and basket making, picture framing, marquetry, creative jewellery, leatherwork, Christmas decorations, floral work, toy making, rug making, sewing, knitting, needlework, model making, plus brushes and paints and more. You can buy a dolls' house kit for £43.95, a fort kit for £33.95. Traced embroidery kit with threads and frame, £3.70. Prices exclude VAT.

Catalogue Annually, A4, Catalogue, Colour, 158 pages,

ART & ART MATERIALS

Free **Postal charges** £4.50 plus VAT for orders up to £50; free to mainland UK for orders of more than £50 **Delivery** Royal Mail, Parcelforce, Courier **Methods of Payment** Cheque, Credit Card

STENCIL ESSENTIALS
Madhatters Emporium
26 High Street
Otford
Kent
TN14 5PQ
Telephone
01959 525578
Fax
01959 522778

Stencils and paints

Stencil Essentials supplies original stencils either cut from clear acetate or as designs for you to cut. They can be used as borders or individual motifs, on walls, curtains, furniture, trays, bins or boxes. Prices from £5 to £8. Stencils can also be designed and cut for you, and a heat pen for use on acetate is available (£19.95). The company also stocks two ranges of paints, Jo Sonjas' acrylics and old-fashioned milk paint.

Catalogue Annually, A4, Catalogue, Colour and B/W, 8 pages, Free **Postal charges** Free **Delivery** Royal Mail, Parcelforce **Methods of Payment** Cheque

THE STENCIL FACTORY
105 Upgate
Louth
Lincolnshire
LN11 9HF
Telephone
01507 600948
Fax
same

Stencils

This brochure contains a range of hand-cut stencils for decorating walls and furniture. Most of the stencils are laser-cut from Mylar which can be used over and over again, and are coded according to difficulty of use. There are stencils for borders, eg 'Toadstools' (11 x 3in, £7.50) and 'Eight Pointed Stars' (9 x 3in, £5). There are corner stencils, 'Fishy' stencils ideal for bathrooms, 'In the Country' stencils and a range of children's stencils (eg 'Steam Train', 13 × 3in, £8.50).

Catalogue Bi-annually, A4, Brochure, B/W, 17 pages, Free **Postal charges** Free **Delivery** Royal Mail **Methods of Payment** Cheque

TOMAS SETH & COMPANY
Holly House
Castle Hill

Artists' colours and accessories

Jo Sonja's acrylic artists' colours are tough and flexible, suitable for painting on paper, canvas, board, wood, metals, glass and ceramics and some

Hartley
Kent
DA3 7BH
Telephone
01474 705077
Fax
01474 703093

plastics. This brochure gives advice on palette set-up, working with the paint and cleaning up as well as how to paint onto the various mediums. Jo Sonja's tubes of paint cost £2.68 each, stencils £3.30 per pack, colour selectors £16.50 and books such as 'The Art of Folk Painting', £10.25.

Catalogue A4, Brochure, Colour, 8 pages, Free **Postal charges** Add £3.00 on orders under £70.00. **Delivery** Royal Mail **Methods of Payment** Cheque, Postal Order

Baby Products

THE BED-SIDE-BED COMPANY
98 Woodlands Avenue
Wanstead
London
E11 3QY
Telephone
0181 989 8683
Fax
0181 989 4006

Convertible Cots
The Bed-Side-Bed is an ingenious cot with three sides enabling it to be placed alongside an adult's bed. The baby has the reassurance of sleeping next to mum, on the same level, and the independence of his or her own cot, while the parents have their own space without the fear of hurting their baby. The cot is made from beech. It comes with a fourth side and can easily be converted into a child's bed. Price, £249.95

Catalogue Annually, Third A4, Catalogue, Colour, 2 pages, Free **Postal charges** Free **Delivery** Courier **Methods of Payment** Cheque, Postal Order

THE BETTER BABY SLING COMPANY
60 Sumatra Road
London
NW6 1PR
Telephone
0171 433 3727

Baby slings
This versatile baby carrier is designed to cradle the baby close to its mother's body in the most natural way. It goes on and comes off easily, allows for discreet breastfeeding, can be used from newborn up to 30lb toddler size and does not cause shoulder ache or back strain. It comes in a choice of three patterned cotton fabrics and costs £24.95 including an instructional video or £21.75 without the video.

Catalogue Third A4, Leaflets, B/W, 3 pages, Free **Postal charges** Free **Delivery** Parcelforce **Methods of Payment** Cheque, Postal Order, Credit Card

CHARLOTTE
40 Connaught Road
Norwich
Norfolk
NR2 3BP
Telephone
01603 627448

Cot blankets

'Charlotte' is a small one-woman craft business in Norwich. Her cot blankets are handframed in pure new wool, cotton or a wool/alpaca mix and can be personalised with the child's first names, month and year of birth.

The blankets are double thickness and reversible, with a different design on the back. The cotton blankets are quilted using a fine layer of wadding. Measuring 24in × 34in or 24in × 32in, prices start at £24.00. An unusual and original christening gift.

Catalogue A4, Brochure, Colour, 1 page, Free **Postal charges** £2.50 **Delivery** Royal Mail **Methods of Payment** Cheque

CABOODLE BAGS
20 Priory Road
Davington
Faversham
Kent
ME13 7EJ
Telephone
01795 590664

Baby bags

The Caboodle Bag is a bag for mothers with young babies who have to carry a lot of equipment – nappies, food, clean clothes, wipes and lotions. Designed by a mum who knows the problems, it will carry all necessary equipment and its many features have been carefully thought out. It has a separate changing mat, pockets for 'grubby stuff', a detachable shoulder strap, bottle pockets and see-through inside pockets. The company also produce a Wellington boot bag and a range of Caboodle Bags: a baby bag, baby carrier, out-and-about bag, and a shopper to go on the pushchair.

Catalogue Updated regularly, A5, Leaflets, Colour, 4 pages, Free **Postal charges** Under £20, £2; over £20, £3 **Delivery** Royal Mail **Methods of Payment** Cheque, Postal Order, Credit Card

CHAUSON COMPANY
3 Grasslands
Smallfield

All-in-one nappies made of structured fibres

Mikey diaper is a genuine all-in-one. Its use of specially structured fibres makes it remarkably

Horley
HR6 9NU
Telephone
01342 844910

absorbent and its special waterproof shell breathes, keeping baby cool and comfortable.

DAISY DIAPERS
3 Arun Grove
Taunton
Somerset
TA1 2NR
Telephone
01923 253484

Cotton towelling nappies
Daisy Diapers are made from layers of soft cotton towelling, shaped to grow with your baby. Gently elasticated around the legs, with generous fasteners for a comfortable and secure fit. Trial pack of one nappy, one insert and one silk liner, £5.90.

ESSENTIAL WELL BEING
PO Box 160
Wokingham
Berkshire
RG11 3YX
Telephone
01734 791737

Aromatherapy products for mothers and babies
Essential Well Being has developed a range of aromatherapy products containing oils known to be safe for use during pregnancy, labour, and for new mothers and babies. The products can be purchased individually or gift-wrapped, making ideal presents. Tiredness Bath Oil for mothers-to-be, £7.25/100ml; Tummy Tightener Lotion for new mothers, £7.25/100ml; Baby Fretfulness Lotion, £4.99/100ml. Several packs are available including a Labour Day Pack, £14.99, and a Baby Pack, £9.99.
Catalogue Annually, Third A4, Leaflets, B/W, 2 pages, Free **Postal charges** £1.75 **Delivery** Royal Mail **Methods of Payment** Cheque, Postal Order

FIRSTBORN
32 Bloomfield Avenue
Bath
BA2 3AB
Telephone
01225 422586

Pure wool knitted Wunderpants
Firstborn make and supply pure-wool, knitted Wunderpants which can be used with their large, flat-weave muslin nappies or any quick-release nappy. They are available ready-made and in easy-to-knit kits. Trial pack of one Wunderpant and one 100% cotton square is £9.75.

BABY PRODUCTS

THE GREAT LITTLE TRADING COMPANY
134 Lots Road
London
SW10 0RJ
Telephone
0171 376 3337
Fax
0171 352 2615

Practical products for parents and kids.
The Great Little Trading Company is a new mail-order catalogue designed for children aged 0 to 6. From nappy bags (£35.99) to home first-aid kits (£34.99) the catalogue is full of useful gadgets, toys and babycare equipment – all intended to make life as a parent as easy as possible.
Catalogue Annually, A5, Catalogue, Colour, 24 pages, Free **Postal charges** £3.95 (free with orders over £75) **Methods of Payment** Cheque, Postal Order, Credit Card

INDISPOSABLES
131 Milner Road
Brighton
East Sussex
BN2 4BR
Telephone
01273 688212

Re-usable cotton babywear and nappies
Super-absorbent, machine-washable cotton fitted nappies, pants, swimwear, trainers and liners. A trial pack which includes two quick-release nappies, one pant, four paper liners costs £14.55 for the small pack (up to 20lb), £15 for the large pack (up to 30lb) and there are also extra small and extra large sizes. You can order any quantity you require.
Catalogue A4, Brochure, Colour, 4 pages, Free **Postal charges** Varies with item **Delivery** Royal Mail **Methods of Payment** Cheque, Postal Order

INFANT ISLE PRODUCTS
Sir Frank Whittle
Business Centre
Great Central Way
Rugby
Warwickshire
CV21 3XH
Telephone
01788 537893
Fax
01788 576017

Baby products
Infant Isle's aim is to produce useful, entertaining and unusual items such as the 40in × 50in splat mat (£7.99), a hard-wearing, flexible PVC mat designed for placing under the highchair at meal times or for messy play sessions or bath time. Then, for storing all those masterpieces your child brings home from nursery, there's an eye-catching artwork folder (£5.99) in a robust laminated fluted cardboard with an integral handle and Velcro fastening. Also made from laminated fluted cardboard is the video storage box (£4.99) which comes in the shape of a house with integral carrying handle.

BABY PRODUCTS

Catalogue Leaflets, Colour pages, Free **Postal charges** Postage and packing for one item: £1.50; for two items: £2.00; for three or more items: £2.50; for orders over £50, free. **Delivery** Royal Mail **Methods of Payment** Cheque, Postal Order, Credit Card

J R PRODUCTIONS
60 Swan Street
Sileby
Leicestershire
LE12 7NW
Telephone
01509 816787

Cotton Tails terry towelling nappies

JR Productions sell Cotton Tails – soft, absorbent and comfy terry-towelling nappies with gently elasticated legs and Velcro fastenings. Night-time inserts for increased absorbency and separate pull-on waterproof pants are also available. A trial pack of one nappy and one night-timer costs £5.

Delivery Royal Mail **Methods of Payment** Cheque, Postal Order

JOJO
134 Lots Road
London
SW10 0RJ
Telephone
0171 351 4112
Fax
0171 352 7089

Maternity and babywear and nursery equipment

JoJo offers bright, fun beachwear, comfortable separates, city suits and smart dresses for mothers-to-be. Easy-fit jacket, £34.99, and matching trousers, £26.99; grandad top, £18.99; wrap skirt, £18.99, and matching bandeau, £5.99; print dress, £39.99. It also offers babywear essentials for 0–24 months (leggings with feet, £4.99; shorts £5.99; dungarees, £8.99) and a limited range of nursery equipment including baby carriers, £18.99; changing bags, £15.99; table seats, £21.99; bouncy chairs, £18.99; and a Torben cot, £129.

Catalogue Bi-annually, A4, Catalogue, Colour, 24 pages, Free **Postal charges** Varies with item **Delivery** Royal Mail, Parcelforce **Methods of Payment** Cheque, Postal Order, Credit Card

KIDDYCARE
Easter Lawrenceton
Forres
Moray

Continental nursery products

Here's a way to keep your baby cosy: an ingenious continental sleeping bag, with or without sleeves, in winter or summer weight. Kiddycare offers an

BABY PRODUCTS

Scotland
IV36 ORL
Telephone
01309 674646
Fax
01309 676007

appealing range of nursery products in cheerful colours, from cot sets to highchair cushions and you can even purchase the material by the metre to make your own co-ordinating items. Quilted sleeping bag with sleeves, £32.95; duvet cover and pillowcase, £29.95; generous quilted changing mat, £24.95; material per metre, £9.50.

Catalogue Annually, A4, Catalogue, Colour, 11 pages, Free **Postal charges** £2 **Delivery** Royal Mail **Methods of Payment** Cheque, Postal Order, Credit Card

KOOSHIES
12 Thornton Place
London
W1H 1FL
Telephone
0171 637 1020

Classic, all-in-one nappy with cotton outer

State-of-the-art terry nappy, shaped, patterned and fitted with waterproofs for a modern mother who cares about the environment. Trail pack of one item from £3.95 for the wrap to £6 for the ultra.

Catalogue Quarterly, A4, Brochure, Colour, 16 pages, Free **Postal charges** Varies with item **Delivery** Royal Mail, Parcelforce **Methods of Payment** Cheque, Postal Order, Credit Card, American Express, Switch

KRUCIAL KIDS
56A Woodford Avenue
Ilford
Essex
1G2 6XF
Telephone
0181 550 4933
Fax
0181 551 4927

Toys and maternity lingerie

Krucial Kids distributes innovative play-stations and activity centres made by the award-winning Canadian firm Educo International. Called Supermaze, these mazes of rigid coloured wires bent into intriguing shapes, threaded with coloured balls and set into smooth wooden bases offer hours of entertainment. Prices from £45. Krucial Kids sells Wimmer-Ferguson toys from America, too, and distributes the Bellybra, designed to relieve weight strain on the lower back and abdomen during pregnancy, from £34.99.

Catalogue Annually, A4, Catalogue, Colour, 8 pages, Free **Postal charges** Free **Delivery** Royal Mail, Parcelforce **Methods of Payment** Cheque, Postal Order

BABY PRODUCTS

MOTHERCARE HOME SHOPPING
Cherry Tree Road
Watford
Hertfordshire
WD2 5SH
Telephone
01923 240365
Fax
01923 244757

Baby products
Mothercare Home Shopping Catalogue is the ultimate in everything for expectant mothers, babies and toddlers, from rattles and toys to highchairs, cots and prams. Creams, soaps and talc also on sale. It takes the headache out of shopping as Mothercare will not only deliver in the UK but overseas as well.

Catalogue Annually, A4, Catalogue, Colour, 79 pages, 50p **Postal charges** Orders under £200, £3; over £200, free **Delivery** In-house delivery **Methods of Payment** Cheque, Postal Order, Credit Card American Express

NATIONAL ASSOCIATION OF NAPPY SERVICES (NANS)
St George House
Hill Street
Birmingham
West Midlands
B5 4AN
Telephone
0121 693 4949

UK-wide nappy-laundering service
NANS members offer UK-wide delivery and collection of freshly laundered cotton nappies for home and carers. Phone or write to find out where your local service is.

Methods of Payment Cheque, Postal Order

NATURE'S BABY
PO Box 2995
London
NW2 1DW
Telephone
0181 905 5661

Cloth nappies and baby accessories
If the disposable-nappy mountain's effects on the environment concerns you, then take a look at Bumkins, an American, plastics-free, nappy system. Colourful, machine-washable, quick-drying nappy covers (from £5.25) are used with cotton flannel fold-over nappies (£12.99 for six). There is an all-in-one cloth nappy, too (from £6.99), featuring a silky waterproofed polyester shell and easy-grip closures, which can be used with extra-absorbency inserts (£5.99 for three).

Catalogue Annually, A4, Leaflets, Colour and B/W, 4 pages, Free **Postal charges** Varies with item **Delivery** Royal Mail **Methods of Payment** Cheque

NATURE'S NAPPIES
Unit 9
Northern Court
Baseford
Nottingham
Nottinghamshire
NG6 OVJ
Telephone
0800 137 344

Nappy-laundering service
Nature's Nappies provide, launder to Health Authority standards, collect and deliver cotton nappies to Nottinghamshire, Derbyshire, Staffordshire, Leicestershire and Birmingham areas.

NCT MATERNITY SALES
Burnfield Avenue
Glasgow
Scotland
G46 7TL
Telephone
0141 633 5552
Fax
0141 633 5677

Mother and baby wear, gifts
The National Childbirth Trust publishes two catalogues: one concentrating on well-designed antenatal and postnatal bras and nighties, swimsuits, baby carriers, baby gowns and rompers, and the other on stationery, gifts and safety products. Its merchandise combines the latest technical and medical considerations with the lifestyles and tastes of the mothers it aims to serve and has been developed with the help of the many mothers who attend NCT antenatal classes nationwide. Mava 2 bra, £15.50; nightie, £11.75; romper, £4.75; Sleepyhead car rest, £16.95; colouring-in cards, £2.50. All profits are covenanted to the Trust.

Catalogue Annually, A5, Catalogue, Colour, 12 pages, Free **Postal charges** Varies with item **Delivery** Royal Mail, Parcelforce **Methods of Payment** Cheque, Postal Order, Credit Card

POPPY
44 High Street
Yarm
Cleveland
TS15 9AE
Telephone
01642 790000
Fax
01642 788235

Children's clothes, bedding and gifts
This delightful catalogue contains a selection of cotton printed clothes for babies and children, with co-ordinated caps (£13.99), floppy hats, headbands, bows and duffel bags. There is something for every occasion and children will delight in choosing which way round to wear the reversible jacket (from £33.99) and whether to wear the smock over the petticoat (from £53.99 a

set), or just the petticoat as a sun-dress. Poppy also stocks an enchanting range of co-ordinated wallpapers (£11.95/roll), fabrics (£11.95/m), bedding (cot quilt, £33.95) and gifts (bookends, clocks, lamps) for children's nurseries, in pastels and primaries.

Catalogue Annually, A4, Catalogue, Colour, 8 pages, Free **Postal charges** Varies with item **Delivery** Royal Mail **Methods of Payment** Cheque, Credit Card

SARAH DEEM
Studio 6
50 Belsize Square
London
NW3 4HN
Telephone
0171 794 8821

Christening gowns

All the gowns in this brochure are intended as heirlooms. The main christening-gown collection consists of extremely intricate designs, using large amounts of fine lace and hand-embroidery. Swiss cotton is used for this superior collection and silk ribbon is used for sleeve ties on most gowns. Matching bonnets are also available. Each christening gown is made to order and it is possible to create a christening gown from a wedding dress or existing antique lace etc. Prices, which include matching petticoat/lining, are from approximately £280. Matching bootees are available in either cotton or silk at £24 per pair.

Catalogue Annually, A5, Brochure, Colour, 12 pages, Free **Postal charges** Varies with item **Delivery** Royal Mail **Methods of Payment** Cheque

SCHMIDT NATURAL CLOTHING
155 Tuffley Lane
Gloucester
Gloucestershire
GL4 ONZ
Telephone
01452 416016

Children's underwear and nappies in natural fibres

Underwear, socks, tights and nappies made of 100% natural fibres such as wool, silk and cotton, for babies, children and adults. Also natural toiletries and deodorant stones. The main emphasis is on natural fibres which are not chemically treated.

Catalogue A4, Catalogue, B/W, 30 pages, Free **Postal charges** Free **Delivery** Royal Mail, Parcelforce **Methods of Payment** Cheque, Postal Order

SQUIDGY THINGS LTD
195 New Kings Road
London
SW6 4SR
Telephone
01374 560151
Fax
01374 560152

Baby clothes and accessories
A distinctive collection of colourful designer nursery products from a Moses basket (£124.99) to co-ordinated nappy stackers (£34.99). With a choice of fabric ranges for each item, your individual preferences can be indulged.

Catalogue Annually, A3, Catalogue, Colour, 15 pages, Free **Postal charges** Postage & Packing, £3.95 per order **Delivery** Royal Mail **Methods of Payment** Cheque, Postal Order, Credit Card

STORK TALK (MIDLANDS) LTD
16a Birkdale Close
Manners Industrial Estate
Ilkeston
Derbyshire
DE7 8YA
Telephone
0115 9306700
Fax
0115 9304700

Prams, pushchairs, cots and highchairs
Stork Talk have been selling Silver Cross products for over a decade and now offer the opportunity to have them delivered direct to your door. All their prices include VAT at 17.5% and all goods are brand-new straight from the manufacturer and are covered by a full warranty. Highchairs from £49.99, Cots from £115 (mattress £29.99), babywalker £31.99, lobster pot playpen £49.99, pushchairs from £130, steel-bodied prams from £229.

Catalogue Annually, A4, Brochure, Colour, 26 pages, Free **Postal charges** £5 total per order to any address in mainland Britain **Delivery** In-house delivery **Methods of Payment** Cheque, Postal Order, Credit Card

THIMBELINA
7 Acremead Road
Wheatley
Oxfordshire
OX33 1NZ
Telephone
01865 872549

Christening gowns, dresses and rompers
Hand-made, traditional-style christening outfits are the speciality of Thimbelina. The garments are well presented with clear pen-and-ink diagrams, and helpful fabric swatches are included. Each piece is beautifully made and evidently designed as a family heirloom. Christening gowns, including matching bonnet and hand-made lined box, £115 to £235. The range also includes rompers (from £44.50), short frocks (from £44.50) and a sailor suit (from £59.50) in a range of fabrics.

BABY PRODUCTS

Catalogue Annually, A4, Catalogue, B/W, 10 pages, Free **Postal charges** Varies with item **Delivery** Royal Mail, Parcelforce **Methods of Payment** Cheque

THIZ BAGS
36 Radnor Road
Twickenham
London
TW1 4NQ
Telephone
0181 744 9262
Fax
0181 744 3151

Designer nursery bags

Pretty nursery bags and children's rucksacks made from Designers Guild and Anna French fabrics and featuring cats, teddies, flowers, yachts, big dots and stripes and checks. All are made in 100% washable cotton with strong, white, waterproof lining and packed in their own drawstring bag. The range includes the Thiz Bag, the Alzo Bag, the Rucksac, the Duffle Bag, changing mat, classic sponge bag, pillows, cot bumpers, cot quilts and teddy bears. Prices range from £9.50 up to about £40.

Catalogue Bi-annually, A4, Catalogue, Colour, 4 pages, Free **Postal charges** £2 on orders under £50

WILKES & WEAVER
Offa House
Offa Street
Hereford
Hereford and Worcester
HR1 2LH
Telephone
01432 268018
Fax
same

Pure wool and cotton mattresses for babies and children

Wilkes & Weaver make a range of traditional children's bed, cot, crib and Moses-basket mattresses using natural cotton and wool (from £49). You are asked to supply measurements and templates of cribs and baskets. It offers a full range of adult bedding, too. Wilkes & Weaver also supply mattresses at a discount for the Bed-Side-Bed (see page 30), an ingenious three-sided cot from the Bed-Side-Bed Co which is designed to be placed beside an adult's bed.

Catalogue Annually, Third A4, Leaflets, Colour, 10 pages, Free **Postal charges** Varies with item **Delivery** Royal Mail, Parcelforce **Methods of Payment** Cheque, Credit Card

ZORBIT BABYCARE
Wholesale Promotions
4 Dales Park Drive
Worsley Road
Swinton
Manchester
M27 OPF
Telephone
0161 728 2784

Terry nappies
Zorbit terry nappies in four qualities of increasing absorbency: budget, popular, superior and supreme. Supreme costs £21.50 for a pack of 12; superior, £18.95; popular, £16.95.
Delivery Royal Mail **Methods of Payment** Cheque, Postal Order

Books

ADMIRALTY CHARTS
Hydrographic Office
Taunton
Somerset
TA1 2DN
Telephone
01823 337900
Fax
01823 323753

Charts and publications
Phone the Hydrographic Office and they will give you the name of your nearest agent who will send out Admiralty charts and publications by mail order. With their reputation for excellence, Admiralty charts have been used by navigators worldwide for nearly 200 years. This particular leaflet advertises a range of products designed exclusively for the Small Craft user, whether in sail or power. The charts are selected Admiralty charts that have been modified to meet the needs of this kind of user.

The charts arrive folded to a convenient size (215 x 355 mm) for ease of storage and include a wealth of supplementary information derived from Admiralty nautical publications.

Products included are Tidal Stream Atlases at £5.20 each and Tide Tables for Yachtsmen at £4.00 each.

Catalogue A4, Catalogue, Colour and B/W, 16 pages

ANTIQUARIAN COOKERY BOOKS
10 The Plantation
Blackheath
London
SE3 0AB
Telephone
0181 852 7807

Antiquarian cookery books and other cookery items
Liz Seeber stocks several hundred antiquarian cookery books and sells other items such as collectible menus, leaflets, cookery magazines and original manuscripts, both English and foreign. Also stocked are antiquarian books on wine, beer, cocktails and other drinks. Liz's regularly updated stocklist provides detailed descriptions. Prices

Fax
0181 318 4675

from £2 to several hundred pounds. **Catalogue** Fortnightly, A4, Brochure, B/W, 54 pages, Free **Postal charges** Varies with item **Delivery** By arrangement **Methods of Payment** Credit Card, Cheque, Postal Order

APPLAUSE THEATRE BOOKS
406 Vale Road
Tonbridge
Kent
TN9 1XR
Telephone
01732 357755
Fax
01732 770219

Theatrical books

This catalogue is packed with texts, critiques and books on acting, music and theatre history. Each book has a brief, informed review and can be obtained through high street book shops as well as by mail order direct from Applause.

A Chorus Line, the book of the musical, is £19.99; Brecht's *Antigone* is £5.95; and *The End of Acting* by Richard Hornby is £15.99. Inspection copies may be obtained without charge, if proof is given of a classroom order of ten or more copies.

Catalogue Annually, Catalogue, B/W, 62 pages, Free **Postal charges** Books are sent second-class mail. For titles under £7.00, add 60p per book; for titles between £7.00–£9.99, add £1.00 per book. For titles over £10.00, add £1.50 per book. Orders over £30.00, free. **Delivery** Royal Mail **Methods of Payment** Cheque, Credit Card, American Express, Postal Order

BAGS OF BOOKS
1 South Street
Lewes
East Sussex
BN7 2BT
Telephone
01273 479320
Fax
same

Spoken-word tapes

Catering for 2–16 year olds, Bags of Books supply spoken-word cassettes to schools, libraries and individual mail-order customers. Some of these recordings are unabridged and can be used with a book for reading along. This increases a child's knowledge of a text and develops listening skills. Books to go with tapes and book and tape packs are also available.

Matilda by Roald Dahl is £7.49 for two tapes plus £3.99 for the accompanying book. *Asterix the Gladiator* is £7.99 for the tape and £3.99 for the book.

Catalogue A4, Catalogue, B/W, 22 pages, £1.00 **Postal charges** For orders under £16.00, add £2.00; £16.00–£25.00, add £3.75; £25.00–£50.00, add £4.75. **Delivery** Royal Mail **Methods of Payment** Cheque, Credit Card

BCA
Guild House
Farnsby Street
Swindon
Wiltshire
SN1 5XD
Telephone
01793 548100

Books, music and home-computer software

This is the largest book club operator in the UK and clubs that you can join run by BCA include: World Books, Literary Guild, Quality Paperbacks Direct (QPD), Mystery and Thriller Guild, Arts Guild, Home and Garden Guild, Science and Nature Book Club, Executive World, The History Guild, The Ancient and Medieval History Book Club, Military and Aviation Book Society, Railway Book Club, Fantasy and Science Fiction Book Club, Children's Book of the Month Club. Music clubs are Music Direct and the Home Computer Club offer software products.

Introductory offers are advertised in the press and by direct mail with products priced between £0.50 and £2.00 each. Having joined, you then receive a catalogue either monthly, bi-monthly or quarterly depending on the club. You are required to order a minimum number (exact number dependent on the club) in the first year, these and other membership details will be noted in the introductory offer.

The catalogues show each product with a colour picture of the cover, a short description, size, number of pages, name of publisher, book club price and recommended retail price. Books and software are offered for at least 25% below the publisher's price (not including postage and packing). Music products do not have a rigid discount structure. Each catalogue has an editor's choice which is sent automatically unless you tick a box on the order form and return within 10 days. If you pay by credit card you still have to post your order.

BIBLIOPHILE BOOKS

5 Thomas Road
London
E14 7BN
Telephone
0171 515 9222
Fax
0171 538 4115

Books

This company offers a vast selection of hardback books at half the publisher's price or less. Bibliophile publish 10 catalogues a year, each with over 700 titles. There is no membership fee and no commitment to purchase. All the books are in mint condition, and many out of print and likely to increase in value.

Prices are excellent, with a 1991 *Macmillan Encyclopaedia* of 1,336 pages for £12.95 instead of £24.95; and *The Complete Works of William Shakespeare* for a mere £5.99. Schools and libraries may be invoiced.

Catalogue A3, Catalogue, Colour and B/W, 19 pages, Free **Postal charges** £2.00 **Delivery** Parcelforce **Methods of Payment** Cheque, Postal Order, Credit Card, American Express

BLACKWELL'S EXTRA

International Mail Order
Book Service
50 Broad Street
Oxford
Oxfordshire
OX1 3BQ
Telephone
01865 792792
Fax
01865 261355

Books

Blackwell's is, of course, something of an institution. Famed not only in Oxford but throughout the world as a supplier of books to libraries, universities and institutions. But it also has an extensive mail-order arm for the private book-buyer and will send books anywhere in the world. Readers may join their mailing list and, by indicating what areas they are interested in, receive regular information on relevant books. An excellent way of keeping up-to-date without having to commit to a book club. The service is now available on the Internet. Customers can access and order over 150,000 titles, get information on over 80 Blackwell's bookshops, look up Blackwell's Book of the Month and exchange second-hand books. The e-mail address is: blackwells.extra@blackwell.co.uk. The Internet address is: http://www.blackwell.co.uk/bookshops/ Outside office hours (Mon–Fri 8.30am–5.30pm), there is an answerphone on +44(0) 1865 261381. Blackwell's also take Blackwell's Personal Account Card.

Catalogue Monthly, Colour and B/W, Free **Postal charges** Varies with item **Delivery** Royal Mail, Courier **Methods of Payment** Cheque, Postal Order, Credit Card, American Express

THE BOOKWORM CLUB
Heffers Booksellers
20 Trinity Street
Cambridge
Cambridgeshire
CB2 3NG
Telephone
01223 568650
Fax
01223 568591

Children's book club

This club is aimed at schools, not individuals, though groups of parents or PTA members can get together and join. Children choose from 2 leaflets: The Bookworm Club, for 7 to 13-year-olds, and The Early Worm for under-8s. Books are sold at the full published price, but 10% of the value of the total order is refunded to the organiser. Each catalogue contains 30 to 40 books to choose from with additional teachers' notes. Prices range from £1.99 to £5.99.

Catalogue Bi-monthly, A4, Catalogue, Colour, 8 pages, Free **Postal charges** Varies with item **Delivery** Royal Mail, Parcelforce **Methods of Payment** Cheque

BOOKS FOR CHILDREN
PO Box 413
Uxbridge
Middlesex
UB11 DX
Telephone
0181 606 3030

Children's book club

The monthly magazine is divided into four sections: under 5s; 4 to 7-year-olds; 7 to 10-year-olds; and 10 years and above. The first pages are devoted to the recommended selection for each of the 4 different age groups. Each of the other books on offer has a colour picture of the cover, name of author, short description, number of pages, size, whether colour or black and white, a reference number, name of publisher, and original price as well as discounted club price. There is usually an introductory offer such as 8 books for £1.99 plus p&p.

You pay within 10 days of receipt of order, which arrives within 8 weeks, but you can make an additional order in the meantime. Most of the books have to be bought in pairs or sets, and prices are usually over £5. You automatically receive the recommended title for the relevant age group unless you cross the box when you send back your invoice. Publishers include Dorling Kindersley, Hodder & Stoughton, Heinemann, Hamlyn and Oxford University Press. Prices range from £5.99 to £24.95 for a video.

COMICS BY POST
4 Springfield
Woodsetts
Worksop
Nottinghamshire
S81 8QD
Telephone
01909 569428

Comics and books
This interesting company specialises in comics, but not the sort that a modern child would buy – these are strictly for collectors. As well as Beanos and Dandys from 1940 onwards, they stock annuals such as Judy (1965, £6) and Dennis the Menace (1960, £20). They also stock a considerable amount of material on Rupert Bear, including a good selection of annuals and original artwork cells (£47 each). Comic prices start at £10 and rise according to rarity.

Catalogue Annually, A5, Catalogue, Colour and B/W, 12 pages, Free **Postal charges** Free **Delivery** Royal Mail **Methods of Payment** Cheque, Postal Order, Credit Card, Switch

DILLONS DIRECT
PO Box 192
Epping
Essex
CM16 6YB
Telephone
0171 636 1577
Fax
0171 580 7680

Books
Dillons offers a bookstore by post with hundreds of different titles in categories as diverse as biographies, crime fiction, fiction, literature, craft, reference, and art ... the list is endless. There is also a range of lower-priced books with up to 25% off.

Dillons bookstores are sited throughout Britain and therefore delivery is quick and easy. Books can be ordered at any time in any quantity with no limits on the numbers purchased. Most of the Dillons stores will send out books by post. Any

book can be ordered by this method and they will put your name on a mailing list for new catalogues.
Catalogue Quarterly, A4, Catalogue, Colour, 77 pages, Free **Postal charges** Orders up to £35, add £3; orders over £35, free **Delivery** In-house delivery **Methods of Payment** Cheque, Postal Order, Credit Card, American Express

DISNEY BOOK CLUB
Grolier
PO Box 75
Norwich
Norfolk
NR5 9QQ
Telephone
01603 740400
Fax
01603 740 401

Children's book club
Disney Book Club operates by direct mail and has no catalogue. Members are offered two books every month, chosen by the club, and have 10 days in which to accept or reject them. There is usually an introductory offer such as 4 free books and another non-book gift. The minimum order is 6 books a year, plus the introductory trial offer. Book characters are taken from the Disney video image, which means instant recognition from most children: Beauty and the Beast, Cinderella, 101 Dalmations. All books cost £2.50 each.
Catalogue by direct mail

EDDINGTON HOOK LTD
PO Box 239
Tunbridge Wells
Kent
TN4 0YQ
Telephone
01892 517439
Fax
01892 549481

Tertiary education books
Supplies Open University and specialist books for students, by mail order. Also stocks books required for National Extension College for overseas students and catering books. The Open University magazine prints lists of this company's books from which students can choose.
Catalogue Leaflets, Free

FREE ASSOCIATION BOOKS
39–41 North Road
London
N7 9RQ
Telephone
0171 609 5646

Books
Free Association Books strive to publish books that are not just a good read, but a challenging one, too. Its list covers psychoanalysis, social studies, child and adolescent psychotherapy, and includes *Femininities, Masculinities, Sexualities* by Nancy Chodorow (£8.95), *In the Best Interests of the Child*

Fax
0171 700 0330

by Ivor Gabor and Jane Aldridge (£15.95), and *Clinical Klein* by Bob Hinshelwood (£16.95).
Catalogue Annually, A5, Catalogue, B/W, 32 pages, Free **Postal charges** £2 for the first book, £1 for each additional book **Delivery** Royal Mail **Methods of Payment** Cheque, Credit Card, American Express

THE GOOD BOOK GUIDE
24 Seward Street
LONDON
EC1V 3GB
Telephone
0171 490 9900
Fax
0171 490 9908

Books, videos and audios

The Good Book Guide is an independent organisation, twice winner of the Queen's Award for Export, offering readers unbiased selections of the most interesting new titles from the UK with a worldwide ordering service. The monthly magazine contains special features, profiles and interviews with top writers, editors and critics but it is only available on subscription.
Catalogue Monthly, Catalogue, Colour and B/W, 23 pages, Free **Postal charges** UK: 1st class, add 20% (minimum £3.00); 2nd class, add £2.95 per order **Delivery** Royal Mail **Methods of Payment** Cheque, Credit Card, Postal Order, American Express, Diners Club

GUILD OF MASTER CRAFTSMEN PUBLICATIONS LTD
Castle Place
166 High Street
Lewes
East Sussex
BN7 1XU
Telephone
01273 477374
Fax
01273 478606

Books, magazines and videos

This catalogue features a wide range of woodworking and craft books and videos. Books include *Making Wooden Toys and Games* (£14.95) and *Making Collector Plates on Your Scroll Saw* (£9.95). Videos include *Traditional Upholstery Workshop*, a set of 2 videos by David James for £23.45. There are also magazines on wood turning and wood carving.
Catalogue Annually, A4, Catalogue, Colour, 14 pages, Free **Postal charges** Add £2.50 for the first book or video and an additional £1.00 per book thereafter or 50p per video. **Delivery** Parcelforce **Methods of Payment** Cheque, Credit Card, American Express, Diners Club

HAWK BOOKS
Suite 309
Canalot Studios
222 Kensal Road
London
W10 5BN
Telephone
0181 969 8091
Fax
0181 968 9012

Childrens books and T-shirts

Dan Dare and Billy Bunter fans will be pleased to learn that Hawk Books has this corner of the market sewn up. There are several Dan Dare adventures to choose from including *Dan Dare Volume 7: Reign of the Robots* which costs £18.95. The spirit of Billy Bunter lives on in Hawk's new series of collectors' titles. The Fat Owl has no choice but to go hiking with the Famous Five during the summer hols in Billy Bunter the Hiker, £14.95. Dan Dare, the Mekon and Billy Bunter are also featured on T-shirts (£12). A must for enthusiasts.

Catalogue Quarterly, A4, Catalogue, Colour, 4 pages, Free **Postal charges** £2.50 for orders up to £25; free for orders of more than £25 **Delivery** Royal Mail, Parcelforce **Methods of Payment** Cheque, Credit Card, American Express, Postal Order

HOLLYWOOD SCRIPTS
Enterprise House
Cathles Road
London
SW12 9LD
Telephone
0181 673 3192
Fax
0181 675 1432

Film scripts and books

This unique mail-order company sells genuine Hollywood film scripts, both classics and new releases. Scripts are from £18 to £22. They also sell unproduced screenplays, TV scripts (from £10) and books on screenwriting and cinema. *Waiting for the Boat: On Writing for Television* by Dennis Potter is £5.99. *Writing Screenplays that Sell* by Michael Hague is £9.99. An invaluable resource for film buffs.

Catalogue Annually, A4, Catalogue, Colour, 15 pages, Free **Postal charges** For scripts (UK), free; £3.00 overseas. For books (UK), add £2.00; £3.00 overseas **Delivery** Royal Mail **Methods of Payment** Cheque, Postal Order, Credit Card, American Express, Diners Club, Switch

BOOKS

INTERNATIONAL VIDEO NETWORK LTD
Freepost
Snowdon Drive
Winterhill
Milton Keynes
Buckinghamshire
MK6 1BR
Telephone
0800 227722
Fax
0181 995 7871

Travel videos
Now you can not only shop from your armchair but also travel! The Video Travel Library includes several different series of films showing locations from around the world. 'Video Visits' concentrates on exotic, romantic, and interesting destinations, while 'Fodor's travel videos' are indispensable preparation for your own travel, with useful hints on language, currency, accommodation, transport and customs.

'Video Expeditions' combine stunning scenery from some of the world's most remote spots with adventure and action, while 'The Endangered World' series charts the progress of animal conservation in Africa. The catalogue also includes films on the underground railways of the world's great cities along with the Readers Digest collection of travel and natural history videos. Tapes range from £9.99 to £12.99.

Catalogue Bi-annually, A5, Catalogue, Colour, 31 pages, Free

LETTERBOX LIBRARY
2nd Floor
Leroy House
436 Essex Road
London
N1 3QP
Telephone
0171 226 1633
Fax
0171 226 1768

Children's non-sexist, non-racist book club
Run by a women's co-operative, Letterbox offers non-sexist, non-racist, multi-cultural books for children up to the age of 14. Books are selected from mainstream as well as alternative and overseas publishers, tested on schoolchildren and sold at discounts of between 10 to 25%. The catalogue contains a wealth of titles including picture books, stories from around the world and reference books, each described in detail. You can join for a one-off fee of £5 and an undertaking to buy 3 books within the first year.

Catalogue Annually, A5, Catalogue, Colour, 24 pages, Free **Postal charges** Varies with item **Delivery** Royal Mail, Parcelforce **Methods of Payment** Cheque, Credit Card

LISTENING POST
Greatness Lane
Sevenoaks
Kent
TN14 5BQ
Telephone
01732 743732
Fax
01959 565557

Audio books
A comprehensive selection of audio books narrated by well known celebrities such as Derek Jacobi with *I, Claudius*; Christopher Lee narrating Edgar Allan Poe's *Tales of Horror*, and comedy classics from radio such as *Beyond the Fringe*. Prices range from £7.99 to £9.99.
Catalogue Annually, A5, Catalogue, Colour, 22 pages, Free **Postal charges** If order less than £20 add £1.50 **Delivery** Royal Mail **Methods of Payment** Cheque, Postal Order, Credit Card

MUSIC SALES LIMITED
Newmarket Road
Bury St Edmunds
Suffolk
IP33 3YB
Telephone
01284 702600
Fax
01284 768301

Sheet music
Music Sales specialises in the sale of musical arrangements for a variety of instruments, including vocals, in all styles. The full range is divided into 11 catalogues including piano, keyboard and organ, instrumental, guitar, video, CD-Rom, groups and personalities and educational. All styles of music are covered from Phil Collins and Bob Dylan to musicals such as *Guys and Dolls* and *Cats*, jazz and classical masterpieces. There are BBC Music Guides and Teach Yourself books, in fact everything for the musician.
Catalogue Annually, A4, Catalogue, Colour, 56 pages, Free **Postal charges** Varies with item **Delivery** Royal Mail **Methods of Payment** Cheque, Postal Order, Credit Card

MY ADVENTURE BOOKS
PO Box 569
Bristol
Avon
BS99 1QA
Telephone
0117 9639160

Personalised children's books
My Adventure Books are personalised for your child so he or she becomes the star in every story. The name of your child and other personal details are printed on almost every page. Each book has 30 pages of full colour illustrations. The 8 titles include: *My Birthday Land Adventure*, and *My Topsy-Turvy Adventure*. The books cost £7.90 each

BOOKS

Fax
0117 9639709

(£6.95 plus 95p postage and packing).
Catalogue A5, Leaflets, Colour, 1 page, Free **Postal charges** Add 95p postage and handling per book **Delivery** Royal Mail **Methods of Payment** Cheque, Postal Order, Credit Card

NATIONAL MARITIME MUSEUM
Romney Road
Greenwich
London
SE10 9NF
Telephone
0181 312 6700
Fax
0181 312 6700

Maritime books

A vast array of maritime titles from the undoubted experts in the field – the National Maritime Museum. The range has something for everyone in love with the sea. The books in this catalogue can bring the sea to life for even the most committed land-lubber. The collection contains books detailing the story of the *Titanic*, many explaining the technical wizardry involved in keeping today's Navy ship-shape, as well as a set of books telling you everything you could ever want to know about knots.
Catalogue Annually, A5, Catalogue, Colour, 11 pages, Free **Delivery** Royal Mail **Methods of Payment** Cheque, Postal Order, Credit Card, Switch

NICK HERN BOOKS
14 Larden Road
London
W3 7ST
Telephone
0181 740 9539
Fax
0181 746 2006

Theatrical books

Nick Hern books was founded as an imprint in 1988. It has now emerged as a fully fledged independent publisher of theatrical works.

A Year at the Court, written by arts journalist Christine Eccles, recalls the 12 months ending April 1992 that she spent as a 'fly on the wall' at the Royal Court theatre. During this time, Caryl Churchill's *Top Girl* was revived; Ariel Dorfman's *Death and the Maiden* was brought out of the studio and onto the main stage; and preparations were underway for Timberlake Wertenbaker's *Three Birds Alighting on a Field*. This fascinating account costs £17.99.
Catalogue Annually, Third A4, Catalogue, B/W, 24 pages pages, Free **Postal charges** Add 20% of sub-total

Delivery Royal Mail **Methods of Payment** Cheque, Postal Order, Credit Card

OTTAKAR'S
23 Cricklade Street
Cirencester
Gloucestershire

Books

Find the right book to give someone and they will love it for life, so the saying goes. At Ottakar's a wide variety of book titles are available from Arts & Music to Food & Drink. Books are also available on audio or CD-Rom. Children's books such as *A Message for Santa* for age 4+ at £8.99 and *Just William at Christmas* for age 8+ at £9.99 make wonderful Christmas presents. Autobiographies such as those by Margaret Thatcher and Colin Powell are priced from £20. The catalogue does not contain a telephone number.

Catalogue Annually, A5, Catalogue, Colour, 40 pages, Free **Postal charges** Varies with item **Delivery** Royal Mail **Methods of Payment** Cheque, Credit Card

PILGRIM BY POST
48 Culver Street
Newent
Gloucestershire
GL18 1DA
Telephone
01531 821075

New world music and books

Pilgrim produce the kind of material that graces every New Ager's home. Tapes to inspire meditation and relaxation range from *Spirit of the Rainforest* by Terry Oldfield: flute and pan pipes (£7.50), to *Earth Healer* by Medwyn Goodall (£7.50).

Pilgrim also produce books dealing with all the obvious subjects, from holistic health and healing to relaxation, meditation and astrology. Jessica Macbeth's *Moon Over Water* (£7.20) describes meditation techniques; *The Birth Chart Book* (£2.95) by Bill and Eileen Anderton shows you how to get the best from your birth chart.

Catalogue A5, Catalogue, Colour, 11 pages, Free **Postal charges** Free **Delivery** Royal Mail **Methods of Payment** Postal Order, Credit Card, Cheque

POSTSCRIPT

24 Langroyd Road
London
SW17 7PL
Telephone
0181 767 7421
Fax
0181 682 0280

Bargain books

PostScript is a family-run business dealing in bargain books; that is, publishers' overstocks. This enables them to sell at extremely low prices, well under half the normal charge and sometimes much less. They publish excellent monthly catalogues of around 32 pages, divided into subject areas with each book receiving a helpful and informative description. Areas include reference, history, social history, 20th century, science, art & architecture, biography, militaria, cookery, travel and much more. They also issue a separate 16-page academic catalogue offering more scholarly and learned titles, including psychology, philosophy, literature, history and politics. Catalogues are free of charge. You can telephone out of office hours on 0181 682 0280 or fax your order on the same number.

Catalogue 8–10 times a year, A5, Catalogue, B/W, 32 pages, Free **Postal charges** UK & Eire – £2.50, overseas P&P £2.50 + £2.00 per book **Delivery** Parcelforce **Methods of Payment** Cheque, Postal Order, Credit Card, Switch

PUFFIN BOOK CLUB

Freepost
27 Wrights Lane
London
W8 5TZ
Telephone
0171 938 2200
Fax
0171 416 3086

Children's book club

Aimed at schools, not individuals. Nevertheless, groups of parents or even NCT groups can join the club. Three magazines, each targeting different age groups, are mailed out 7 times a year, based on school terms. *Fledgling* magazine is aimed at those under 6; *Flight* is for 6 to 9 year olds; and *Post* is for 9 to 13 year olds. The magazines contain puzzles, colouring pages, activity ideas and poems.

Each age group also receives a colour leaflet with book availability and there are teachers' notes with additional special book offers and ideas. There is no minimum order, but the introductory offer which allows you to keep 50% of the value of your first order encourages a big order.

The organiser orders the required number of leaflets for each of the 3 reading ages, collates the different orders and then chooses one free book for every 10 paid for. The organiser can also order one each of all the new titles at a 25% discount so that the group can see before they order. These are non-returnable. The leaflets contain colour pictures of covers and some inside pages with price and a short description. Prices range from £1.99 to £4.99.

Catalogue A4, Brochure, Colour, 28 pages

RED HOUSE BOOKS LTD
Windrush Park
Witney
Oxford
Oxfordshire
OX8 5YF
Telephone
01993 779959

Children's books

Specialising in children's books, The Red House covers educational material, practical activity books, and fiction. It also offers a wide range of adult titles and some audio cassettes and videos. The books are a mixture of hardback and paperback and grouped according to age in the children's catalogue. There are excellent savings to be made: almost every book is discounted, some with as much as 50 per cent off the retail price.

Catalogue Monthly, A4, Catalogue, Colour, 16 pages (Children's), 8 pages (Adult), Free **Postal charges** Add 10% for orders under £30; for orders over £30, add £3.00; outside the UK add 20% for postage **Delivery** White Arrow **Methods of Payment** Cheque, Postal Order, Credit Card

RUNNING HEADS INTERNATIONAL
82 East Dulwich Grove
London
SE22 8TW
Telephone
0171 738 4096

Consumer guides

Running Heads is a small publisher who produce and distribute a range of consumer guides. One title, *The Deregulated Phone Book* is an invaluable guide to getting cheap phone calls. Apparently it is now possible to use systems other than BT or Mercury and save a considerable amount in the

BOOKS

Fax same

process. They also distribute a sister publication to *The Good Mail Order Guide*, called *The Global Shopper*. This comprehensive guide to international mail order means you can now shop the whole world.

Catalogue By advertising **Postal charges** Varies with item

SCHOLASTIC BOOK CLUBS
Westfield Road
Southam
Leamington Spa
Warwickshire
CV33 OJH
Telephone
01926 813910
Fax
01926 815574

Children's book club

Aimed at schools, Scholastic's 4 book clubs cater for children from 3 to 12. Each group has their own newsletter and teacher's notes outlining the choice of about 30 books from a range of publishers. Packs will not be sent to private addresses, but local nursery, playgroups or NCT groups can band together and join. Substantial discounts are offered plus incentives for schools and organisers, including free books and vouchers. *The Oxford Children's Book of Science*, £12.95 (RRP £14.99); *The Marmalade Pony*, £1.95 (RRP £2.50).

Catalogue Monthly, A4, Catalogue, Colour, 4 pages, Free **Delivery** Royal Mail, Parcelforce **Methods of Payment** Cheque, Postal Order

SCOPE INTERNATIONAL LTD
Forestside House
Forestside
Rowlands Castle
Hampshire
PO9 6EE
Telephone
01705 631751
Fax
01705 631322

Self-help books

The Scope Reports are a series of 14 books which offer advice on how to become a tax-exile, obtain second passports legally, enjoy visa-free travel, make a million in 3 years and create your own bank secrecy. Most of these reports are written by international entrepreneur, Dr. W.G. Hill, and can be purchased individually for £60 each or £465 for all 14.

Catalogue A4, Catalogue, B/W, 11 pages, Free **Delivery** Courier, Royal Mail **Methods of Payment** Diners Club, American Express, Credit Card, Cheque

SHIRE BOOKS
Cromwell House
Church Street
Princes Risborough
Buckinghamshire
HP27 9AA
Telephone
01844 344301
Fax
01844 347080

Books
The concept behind Shire Books is to offer books at low prices on subjects on which there is very little information in print. With over 900 books published, some 500 of which are in print and described in this catalogue, Shire has established itself as a publisher of authoritative but inexpensive material on unusual and specialised subjects. Books on antiques, archaeology, architecture and Egyptology to garden history, rural crafts and walking are just some of the many titles on offer. Books range in price from £2.25 to £5.99.
Catalogue Quarterly, A5, Brochure, Colour and B/W, 47 pages **Postal charges** Orders less than £6, add £1 P&P. Orders over £6, free **Delivery** Royal Mail **Methods of Payment** Cheque, Postal Order, Credit Card

THE SOFTBACK PREVIEW
PO Box 415
Uxbridge
Middlesex
UB1 1DZ
Telephone
0181 606 3111

Book club
The Softback Preview is different from most other book clubs in that you are under no obligation to buy from them. Every 4 weeks you'll receive a copy of their magazine to see whether there's anything new you fancy. As an introductory offer, you're entitled to any 3 books from their catalogue for only £1 each. *An Anthropologist on Mars* by Oliver Sacks cost £8.99; *Great Housewives of Art* by Sally Swain was £8.98; and *Rushing to Paradise* by J. G. Ballard was £7.99 as we went to press.
Catalogue Quarterly, Third A4, Catalogue, Colour and B/W, 37 pages, Free **Postal charges** £2.25 **Delivery** Parcelforce **Methods of Payment** Cheque, Credit Card

SWEET & MAXWELL LTD
South Quay Plaza
183 Marsh Wall
London
E14 9FT

Books on law, business and tax
Sweet & Maxwell publish high-quality, law-based information for professionals, academics and students. Key titles in their current catalogue include *Child Custody and Abduction* (£30), *UK Environmental Law* (£125), *European Community Law*

BOOKS

Telephone
0171 538 8686
Fax
0171 538 9508

(£49) and *Company Structures* (£48). Any book or books with a value in excess of £40.00 may be sent on 28 days' approval in response to a written request using a firm's letterhead. Prices are net, and trade discounts are available.
Catalogue Annually, A5, Catalogue, B/W, 128 pages, Free **Postal charges** Free if payment is sent with order **Delivery** Royal Mail **Methods of Payment** Cheque, Credit Card, American Express, Diners Club

THE TALKING BOOK CLUB
PO Box 993
London
SW6 4UW
Telephone
0171 731 6262
Fax
0171 736 0162

Books on cassette
The Talking Book Club offers a comprehensive range of books on tape including fiction, non-fiction, classics, biography, humour, thrillers, romance, travel and children's books. Ideal for those with impaired sight, and just the thing to listen to on long journeys, or while ironing or decorating. Both full-length and abridged versions are available. It costs £7.50 to enrol, plus from £1.25 for a fortnight's hire per title. With 2000 books to choose from and 400 titles being added every year, you won't have time to get bored.
Catalogue Bi-monthly, A4, Catalogue, Colour and B/W, 100 pages, Free **Postal charges** 8 cassettes or less £1.95, 10 cassettes or more £2.55. When ordering 2 or more titles, total cost £2.95. **Delivery** Royal Mail **Methods of Payment** Cheque, Credit Card

THE TALKING BOOK SHOP
11 Wigmore Street
London
W1H 9LB
Telephone
0171 491 4117
Fax
0171 629 1966

Books on cassette
This catalogue contains over 600 titles in a broad variety of categories which have been chosen from a stock of over 3000 titles. Audio books on tape make ideal gifts and they will gift wrap your order for you. Authors include John Le Carré, Jeffrey Archer, Agatha Christie and Ruth Rendell. Classics are also catered for by Charles Dickens, Jane Austen, Thomas Hardy and Robert Louis Stevenson. Every taste is catered for at reasonable prices. *Kidnapped*

by Robert Louis Stevenson, £7.99 for 2 cassettes; *The Forsyte Saga* by John Galsworthy, 6 cassettes for £25. Childrens titles include *The Chronicles of Narnia*, *The Wind in the Willows* and *The Roald Dahl Collection*. Just relax in the car or in your own armchair and enjoy books on tape.

Catalogue Quarterly, A4, Catalogue, Colour, 62 pages, £3 **Postal charges** £1.50 for any number of cassettes up to a retail value of £35 **Delivery** Royal Mail **Methods of Payment** Cheque, Credit Card

WATERSTONE'S MAILING SERVICE
4/5 Milsom Street
Bath
Avon
BA1 1DA
Telephone
01225 448595
Fax
01225 444732/420591

Books
From the high street shops of the same name comes this catalogue that selects and reviews the 'best' of recently published books. There is also an introduction to the Waterstone's 'Signed First Editions Club', which enables you to buy signed books at normal retail prices. Among the latest titles as we went to press, *Therapy* by David Lodge is priced at £15.99; *The Garden Designer* by Robin Williams and *As it Seemed to Me* by John Cole are each priced at £20.

Catalogue Bi-annually, A4, Catalogue, Colour, 14 pages, Free **Postal charges** UK: £1.25 for one paperback; £2.50 for two paperbacks; £3.00 for orders up to £35.00; orders over £35.00, free **Delivery** Royal Mail **Methods of Payment** Cheque, Credit Card, American Express

WHICH? BOOKS
Freepost
Hertford
Hertfordshire
SG14 1YB

Books
The Which? Book catalogue contains a choice of over 40 items, including new books and many new and updated editions of their best-selling titles. The catalogue is divided into 5 easy-to-find sections: Leisure, Around the House, Your Garden, Health and Reference. There are new editions of *The Good Food Guide* and *The Which Hotel Guide* which make superb gifts. *The Good Bed & Breakfast Guide* is 672 pages for £13.99.

BOOKS

Catalogue Annually, A4, Catalogue, Colour, 14 pages, Free **Postal charges** Free **Delivery** Royal Mail **Methods of Payment** Cheque, Postal Order

Charities

ACTIONAID TRADING PROMOTIONS
Nancegollan
Helston
Cornwall
TR13 OTT
Telephone
01209 831456

Stationery and gifts
Actionaid is a registered charity working in 20 countries with some of the world's poorest children, families and communities to make lasting improvements in health and education to their standard of living. Its well-produced catalogue features an attractive selection of cards, wrapping paper and gifts, including a Nefertiti silk scarf, £35.95; aromatherapy bath oil set, £8.95; silver filigree brooch, £17.99; Hasseena rug, £10.95; and T-shirts from £9.95.
Catalogue Annually, A5, Catalogue, Colour, 20 pages, Free **Postal charges** Up to £5, £1.50; £5.01 to £75, £3.75; £75.01 and over, free **Delivery** Royal Mail, Parcelforce **Methods of Payment** Credit Card, Switch, Cheque, Postal Order

ANIMAL HEALTH TRUST
PO Box 5
Newmarket
Suffolk
CB8 7DW
Telephone
01638 661111
Fax
01638 665789

Christmas cards and gifts
The Animal Health Trust produces a one-sheet leaflet featuring on one side its range of Christmas cards. These come in just 3 designs – all with animals of course – and cost from £1.85 for 5 or £4 for a pack of 10, depending on the design. The other side has colour photographs of promotional clothes. These include T-shirts, rugby sweatshirts and silk ties. All are printed with the Trust's logo and, of course, proceeds go towards their work. There are also some other items such as mugs, teddy bears, yo-yos and bottle stoppers.
Catalogue Leaflets, Colour, 2 pages, Free **Delivery** Royal

CHARITIES

Mail **Methods of Payment** Cheque, Postal Order, Credit Card

THE ANIMAL WELFARE TRUST
Tylers Way
Watford by-Pass
Watford
Hertfordshire
WD2 8HQ
Telephone
0181 950 8215
Fax
0181 420 4454

Gifts
The Animal Welfare Trust is a registered charity founded in 1971 to care for and re-home dogs, cats and other animals which would otherwise be abandoned, left to stray or put to sleep. The catalogue offers a range of gifts, the proceeds of which are used to assist in the upkeep of the Trust's Animal Rescue Centre. Pack of 10 Christmas cards with envelopes, £2.50; soft toys, £2.50; PVC apron, £5.50; duck door wedge, £6.25; sweatshirt with logo, £16.99.

Catalogue Annually, A4, Brochure, Colour, 6 pages, Free **Postal charges** Varies with item **Delivery** Royal Mail, Parcelforce **Methods of Payment** Cheque, Postal Order, Credit Card

BRITISH RED CROSS
Freepost
PO Box 38
Burton-on-Trent
Staffordshire
DE14 1BR
Telephone
01283 510111

Gifts and clothes
This is a charity catalogue, with the usual diverse range of goods, many of which are of ethnic origin. You can buy an entire set of tableware for 4, including cutlery, napkins and place mats for £29.99 or a pack of assorted birthday cards for £3.99. Products are clearly illustrated and range from stationery and office accessories, which can be personalised, to sweatshirts and T-shirts with flora or fauna motifs. Some worthwhile bargains are to be found.

CANCER RESEARCH CAMPAIGN
6–10 Cambridge Terrace
Regents Park
London
NW1 4JL

Gifts and cards
Each purchase from this catalogue makes a direct contribution to the Campaign's work. There is a diverse range of gifts including a 'Floating Whale Plug' and a 'Fish Design Waistcoat', T-shirts, and holdalls. The easy tick-off order form makes sure you waste no time choosing between those gift-

Telephone
01283 506444

card sets or the wealth of personalised pens, pencils and even luggage straps.

Catalogue Annually, A4, Catalogue, Colour, 32 pages, Free **Postal charges** Varies with item **Delivery** Royal Mail **Methods of Payment** Cheque, Postal Order, Credit Card

CARE CARDS by JONES WILLIAMS
PO Box 170
Spartan Road
Bradford
Yorkshire
BD12 0RX
Telephone
01274 531834
Fax
01274 531829

Christmas cards and calendars

By purchasing Care Cards you will help to support 20 major British Charities, from the British Diabetic Association to the Stroke Association, all very worthwhile causes. Cards range from Christmas classics such as Father Christmas, £40.30 for 25 cards, to Westminster Abbey, £35.10 for 25 cards. Some beautiful cards and calendars to choose from, catering for all tastes. You can order and then pay on invoice.

Catalogue Annually, A3, Brochure, Colour, 22 pages, Free **Postal charges** £4.95 **Delivery** Royal Mail **Methods of Payment** Cheque, Credit Card, Switch, Postal Order

THE CATS PROTECTION LEAGUE
17 Kings Road
Horsham
West Sussex
RH13 5PN
Telephone
01403 261947
Fax
01403 218414

Gifts

If you're a feline fan, there's something here for you! 'Catty' items include leather bookmarks in various colours (40p), dustpics (special adhesive brushes that pick up fur (£2), and balloons with the Cats' Protection League logo (£1 per dozen). Sweatshirts and T-shirts also bearing the logo range in price from £4.50 (T-shirts) and £9.50 (sweatshirts).

Catalogue A5, Catalogue, Colour, 8 pages, Free **Postal charges** Total value up to £1, add 30p; total value up to £5, add 80p; total value over £5, add £1.30. **Delivery** Royal Mail **Methods of Payment** Cheque

COMPASSION IN WORLD FARMING

Charles House
5A Charles Street
Petersfield
Hampshire
GU32 3EH
Telephone
01730 264208
Fax
01730 260791

Gifts

Profits from the Compassion in World Farming catalogue go directly towards funding its campaigns for farm animals. The products offered are well-designed and good quality. Free-range T-shirt, £11.99; A World of Difference for Farm Animals mug, £3.99; campaign window stickers, £1.50; recycled pens, 99p.

Catalogue Annually, A5, Catalogue, Colour, 8 pages, Free **Postal charges** £2.50 for orders up to £50; free for orders of more than £50 **Delivery** Royal Mail, Parcelforce **Methods of Payment** Cheque, Postal Order, Credit Card

COUNTRYWIDE WORKSHOPS CHARITABLE TRUST

47 Fisherton Street
Salisbury
Wiltshire
SP2 7SU
Telephone
01722 326886
Fax
01722 411092

Clothes, gifts, furniture and toys

Countrywide Workshops is a charitable trust whose aim is to create work for disabled people by selling the goods they make and encouraging their abilities. This catalogue contains a selection of beautifully made products from both home-workers and sheltered workshops. Made-to-measure skirts in Welsh wool, from £45; leather handbag, £41.25; hand-engraved glasses, from £22.50 for a set of 6 liqueur tumblers; hand-shaped nursery ark with 18 animals, £69.50; shoebag with ballet or trainer motif, £4.70; teddy clock, £16.50; bunkbeds, £305; and for the garden, a wooden slatted composter, £35.75.

Catalogue Quarterly, A5, Catalogue, Colour, 40 pages, Free **Postal charges** Free **Delivery** Royal Mail, Parcelforce **Methods of Payment** Cheque, Postal Order, Credit Card

ENVIRONMENTAL INVESTIGATION AGENCY

2 Pear Tree Court
London
EC1R 0DS

Gifts

The Environmental Investigation Agency is a small organisation with limited resources, but it is doing its bit for animal protection and conservation. The catalogue includes a great range of gifts, most of which have some connection with the

Telephone
0171 490 7040

animal world. There's a dolphin paperknife in handcrafted pewter for £16.95; packs of 12 picture postcards of wildlife, printed on 100% recycled card, for £2.95. And there are designer-label T-shirts for £14.95 with wildlife logos.

Catalogue Annually, Catalogue, Colour, 15 pages, Free **Postal charges** UK: orders up to £25.00, add £2.50; over £25.00, add £3.50. Overseas: add £5.00 + 15% of order value **Delivery** Parcelforce **Methods of Payment** Cheque, Postal Order, Credit Card

FELINE ADVISORY BUREAU (FAB)
c/o Mrs D.W. Savage
Middle Coombe Farm
Huish Champflower
Taunton
Somerset
TA4 2HG
Telephone
01984 624683
Fax
same

Gifts, clothing and stationery

The Feline Advisory Bureau is a registered charity for the benefit of these furry animals. Its small selection of products will delight any cat-lover: kitten-covered drinks tray, £7; notepaper, £1.50 a pack; T-shirt with cat logo, £6.75. You can also brush up your knowledge of 'Feline Behaviour Therapy' or learn 'How to Talk to Your Cat' from its range of books and videos.

Catalogue Annually, A5, Catalogue, Colour, 8 pages, Free **Postal charges** Varies with item **Methods of Payment** Cheque

GREAT ORMOND STREET LTD
PO Box 20
Tanners Lane
Barkingside
Ilford
Essex
IG6 1QQ
Telephone
01268 288577
Fax
01268 520230

General gifts

Support the most famous children's hospital in the world by purchasing from this catalogue. Everything from Christmas cards, decorations, toiletries, jewellery, toys and games to gentlemen's gifts and personalised stationery. Fine bone china classic boxed mug with hospital logo £8.99. Classic logo sweatshirt from £9.99 for child's size. There is a shop at the hospital which is open 7 days a week, selling a fuller range of their logo merchandise. Other gifts include a Victorian-style nightdress, £25.99, and housecoat, £28.99, both in 100% cotton.

Catalogue Annually, A4, Catalogue, Colour, 15 pages, Free **Postal charges** Varies with item **Delivery** Royal Mail **Methods of Payment** Cheque, Postal Order, Credit Card

CHARITIES

HELP THE AGED (MAIL ORDER) LTD
PO Box 28
London
N18 3HG
Telephone
0181 803 6861
Fax
0181 884 0148

Gifts and cards
Help the Aged's catalogue is quite eclectic in its choice of practical and well-priced goods. Profits go towards improving the quality of life of elderly people, for instance by buying minibuses to give the housebound the opportunity of going out, and funding hospices and day centres. From the catalogue, you can buy a wall trellis, £7.99; extending garden loppers, £16.99; easy kneeler, £33.99; Nature's Best supplements, from £3.50; personal aids such as a pair of colour-coded tap turners, £5.50; and an extendable travel bag, £12.99.
Catalogue Bi-annually, A4, Catalogue, Colour, 32 pages, Free **Postal charges** Free P&P for orders over £10 **Delivery** Royal Mail, Parcelforce **Methods of Payment** Cheque, Credit Card

THE HOME FARM TRUST
Merchant's House
Wapping Road
Bristol
Avon
BS1 4RW
Telephone
0117 927 3746
Fax
0117 922 5938

Christmas cards and gifts
The Home Farm Trust is a charity which provides residential care for hundreds of people with learning disabilities, helping them to lead full lives, attend college courses and take employment. Its catalogue contains attractive and well-designed Christmas cards (from £2.20 for a pack of 10), a Build Yourself Advent Stable (£3.95), calendars, tea towels and wrapping paper.
Catalogue Annually, A5, Catalogue, Colour, 12 pages, Free **Postal charges** £1.65 for orders up to £6; £3.10 for orders of more than £6 **Delivery** Royal Mail **Methods of Payment** Cheque, Postal Order, Credit Card

THE INTERNATIONAL PRIMATE PROTECTION LEAGUE
116 Judd Street
London
WC1H 9NS

Hampers for pets
IPPL was founded as a registered charity in 1974 to foil animal smugglers and has succeeded in the prosecution of many traffickers. It also contributes towards the care in sanctuaries of confiscated and abandoned primates which cannot be returned to

Telephone
0171 837 7227
Fax
0171 278 3317

the wild. Show your pets how much you love them by buying a gift hamper full of treats (from £12 for a dog, rabbit/hamster, cat, or budgie/canary hamper). Profits go towards primate welfare.
Catalogue Annually, Third A4, Brochure, Colour, 2 pages, Free **Postal charges** Varies with item **Delivery** Royal Mail, Parcelforce **Methods of Payment** Cheque, Postal Order, Credit Card

LEUKAEMIA RESEARCH FUND/LRF TRADING
Yorke Road
Croxley Green
Rickmansworth
Hertfordshire
WD3 3TP
Telephone
01923 779181
Fax
01923 896745

Gifts and stationery

Profits from the sale of goods in this catalogue are covenanted entirely to the Leukaemia Research Fund, a registered charity. It offers an attractive range of Christmas cards, some with Welsh greetings, from £2.40 for a pack of 10; wrapping paper; stocking fillers; and gifts (book light, £3.45; games set, £2.95).
Catalogue Annually, A5, Catalogue, Colour, 32 pages, Free **Postal charges** Varies with item **Delivery** Royal Mail, Parcelforce **Methods of Payment** Cheque, Postal Order, Credit Card

MENCAP LTD
PO Box 36
Burton upon Trent
Staffordshire
DE14 3LQ

Christmas cards and gifts

A wide range of Christmas cards, wrapping paper, festive tea towels, glass, star candles, tartan napkins, wreaths, indoor mini lights, Christmas tree bows, jungle tent, tiddly frogs, Beatrix Potter clock, balloon kit, beaded jug covers, piggy party tea towel, can safe, mustard kit, paisley scarf, jet brooch, aromatherapy soaps, Victorian bootscraper, gardener's gloves, golfer's gift caddy, duck doorstop and frog-and-leaf sundial.
Catalogue Annually, A4, Catalogue, Colour, 36 pages, Free **Postal charges** up to £69.99, £3.35; £70 and over, free **Delivery** Royal Mail **Methods of Payment** Cheque, Postal Order, Credit Card, Switch

CHARITIES

NATIONAL ANTI-VIVISECTION SOCIETY
261 Goldhawk Road
London
W12 9PE
Telephone
0181 846 9777
Fax
0181 846 9712

T-shirts and other items

The National Anti-Vivisection Society campaigns against medicines being tested on animals and organises a 'Lab Animal Week' each year to raise awareness of this issue. Their merchandise includes T-shirts bearing various messages, such as 'Rats, run for cover' and 'Unlock the Labs' (£8 each) and there's a silver padlock badge that can be worn to show your support for the anti-vivisection cause (£1 each). There are also mugs, baseball caps, pens and books.

Catalogue Annually, A5, Brochure, Colour, 6 pages, Free **Postal charges** Orders up to £10.00, add £1.90; up to £30.00, add £2.90; orders over £30.00, free **Delivery** Parcelforce **Methods of Payment** Cheque, Postal Order, Credit Card

NATIONAL CANINE DEFENCE LEAGUE
17 Wakley Street
London
EC1V 7LT
Telephone
0171 837 0006
Fax
0171 833 2701

Gifts, stationery and pet products

This registered charity's catalogue is devoted to products for dog and animal lovers alike. You can buy a Scotty door mat for £23.95, a neat carry loo for £4.50, a furry cat's cradle to hook over a radiator for £15.95, doggy Christmas cards for £1.95 for a pack of 10, ear wipes for £1.75, grooming products for your pet and sweatshirts for yourself, as well as books and animal bedding.

Catalogue Annually, A4, Catalogue, Colour, 8 pages, Free **Postal charges** Varies with item **Delivery** Royal Mail, Parcelforce **Methods of Payment** Cheque, Postal Order, Credit Card

NOTTING HILL HOUSING TRUST
Aspen House
1 Gayford Road
London
W12 9BY

Gifts

The Notting Hill Housing Trust provides homes for people in desperate need, such as families who live in bed-and-breakfast accommodation. Its Christmas catalogue helps to raise funds for its work and contains a sophisticated selection of gifts and items for the home. There are colourful check

Telephone
0181 563 4888
Fax
0181 563 4899

tablecloths (£12.99) and chenille throws (£29.99), a metal Christmas-tree candle-holder (£12.99), opaque glass vases (£14.99), a verdigris coat rack, £14.99, and ivory pyramid candles, 99p.

Catalogue Annually, A2, Catalogue, Colour, 16 pages, Free **Postal charges** £3.50 **Methods of Payment** Cheque, Postal Order, Credit Card

NSPCC TRADING COMPANY LTD
Quality & Style by Mail
PO Box 39
Burton upon Trent
Staffordshire
DE14 1BR
Telephone
01283 506101

Household and gift items

The many attractive and original items in this catalogue include a wooden chopping board with a built-in extra: a smooth sliding drawer with compartments for your knives and small kitchen implements. The timber is from managed forests and the price is £29.99. There's also a traditionally crafted wooden cheese board with wire cutter decorated with a Victorian-style ceramic tile (£16.99); a garden hammock made of tough plaited jute (£19.99); duvet sets from £14.99; a jumbo teapot (£19.99) and over-size cups and saucers (£14.99). Every purchase helps the NSPCC. The NSPCC also produce an annual Stocking Fillas brochure with over 350 stocking filler and party toy ideas, many under £1.

Catalogue Bi-annually, A4, Catalogue, Colour, 40 pages, Free **Postal charges** Goods value up to £69.99, add £3.35; goods value £70 and over, free. **Delivery** Royal Mail **Methods of Payment** Switch, Credit Card, Cheque, Postal Order

OXFAM TRADING
PO Box 72
Bicester
Oxfordshire
OX6 7LT
Telephone
01869 245 011

Gifts from around the world

A colourful publication containing hand-crafted products from around the world. Oxfam has done much to encourage and promote the skills of third-world producers, ensuring they are paid properly for their work and giving grants to strengthen their businesses. The catalogue contains

Fax
01869 247 348

an attractive selection of exotic home-ware, clothes, jewellery, stationery and foods with descriptions of the craft skills and countries of origin. Embroidered bedcover from Bangladesh, £75; Mexican rug, £125; Thai shirt, £6.95; child's white dress from El Salvador, £12.95.

Catalogue Bi-annually, A4, Catalogue, Colour, 32 pages, Free **Postal charges** £2.95 **Delivery** Royal Mail, Parcelforce, Courier **Methods of Payment** Cheque, Postal Order, Credit Card

RNLI (SALES) LTD
Freepost BH1654
Poole
Dorset
BH15 1BR
Telephone
01202 669777
Fax
01202 672262

General gifts

This catalogue is produced almost entirely by RNLI personnel and every penny of profit from your purchases is used to help in life-saving work. New products and nautical gifts plus a host of items for indoors and out, leisure and travel, house, garden, garage, etc. From Christmas cards depicting a lifeboat crew from a painting by Thomas Rose Miles, £3.45 for a pack of 10, to a Dalvey cabin clock for £39.95. A wide choice of gifts for all the family in this catalogue to benefit a worthwhile cause.

Catalogue Annually, A4, Catalogue, Colour, 48 pages, Free **Postal charges** £2.99 **Delivery** Royal Mail **Methods of Payment** Cheque, Postal Order, Credit Card, Switch

RSPB
The Lodge
Sandy
Bedfordshire
SG19 2DL
Telephone
01767 680551
Fax
01767 692365

Gifts

The Royal Society for the Protection of Birds is the largest voluntary wildlife conservation organisation in Europe. One way in which they raise vital funds to further their work is to produce 2 catalogues a year. The autumn/winter catalogue includes Christmas cards, calendars and gifts, in addition to the product range found in the spring/summer catalogue. Items include a Wren garden tap, £11.99; barn owl sweatshirt, £17.50; open-fronted nest box, £19.99; catwatch sensor, £15.95; and hanging feeder, £2.95.

Catalogue Bi-annually, A4, Catalogue, Colour, 32 pages, Free **Postal charges** Goods value up to £74.99 add £3.35; goods value £75.00 and over, free. **Delivery** Royal Mail **Methods of Payment** Cheque, Postal Order, Credit Card Switch

RSPCA TRADING LTD
Freepost
PO Box 38
Burton on Trent
Staffordshire
DE14 1BR
Telephone
01283 506125

Gifts

A comprehensive catalogue of quality gifts, household items, cards and clothes which supports a well-known charity. Choose from a colourful bone china cafetière, £49.95, with mugs to match, set of three £14.99, to a set of wildlife birthday cards, 2 packs for £3.75.

Catalogue Bi-annually, A4, Catalogue, Colour, 40 pages, Free **Postal charges** Up to £69.99, £3.35; £70 and over, free **Methods of Payment** Cheque, Postal Order

SAVE THE CHILDREN
PO Box 40
Burton upon Trent
Staffordshire
DE14 3LQ
Telephone
01283 506500

Gifts and household items

This catalogue has some attractive and original gift ideas. There's a natural wildlife garden kit for £8.99, a cast-iron boot-scraper for £9.99, a Panama hat for £29.99 and an antique book chess set for £39.95. Household items include pretty duvet sets (e.g. the Belinda patchwork design, from £14.99), 10-piece cotton towel bales for £24.95, and a 2-tier non-stick steamer for £19.99.

Catalogue Bi-annually, A4, Catalogue, Colour, 39 pages, Free **Postal charges** Up to £69.99, add £3.35; £70.00 and over, free **Delivery** Royal Mail **Methods of Payment** Cheque, Postal Order, Credit Card, American Express, Switch

SCOPE CENTRAL TRADING LIMITED
Freepost
PO Box 66
Burton upon Trent

Cards and gifts for Christmas

A selection of Christmas cards, gift-wrapping paper, printed Christmas tapes, gift label dispenser, curling ribbons, a selection of calendars, gifts and stocking fillers from £2.99 such as a Noah's Ark

Staffordshire
DE14 1BR
Telephone
01283 506506

rug, magnet building set, activity ring, soft blocks, name jigsaws, child's single duvet set, personalised pencil box, personalised pen watch, golfer's caddy kit, CD cleaning systems, cricket-ball clock, golf-bag towel, gorilla T-shirt, poppy peg-bag, turtle shoe brush, chopping board, mini-cake gift pack, kittens sandwich tray, hot toddy glasses, natural wood fruit bowl, Victorian Santa tins, bath mats, whale shower curtain, cosmetics bag, towel bales, crackers, candles, and zodiac signs tea towel. Scope is the charity for people with cerebral palsy.

Catalogue Annually, A5, Catalogue, Colour, 36 pages, Free **Postal charges** Up to £70, £3.35; £70 and over, free **Methods of Payment** Switch, Credit Card, Cheque, Postal Order

THE STROKE ASSOCIATION (TRADING) LTD
20 Halcyon Court
St Margarets Way
Huntingdon
Cambridgeshire
PE18 6DG
Telephone
01480 413280
Fax
01480 435330

Gifts and cards

The Stroke Association deals with research, advice, prevention, welfare and rehabilitation for stroke sufferers and their families. For over 21 years the charity has produced card and gift catalogues, and 100% of the profit is covenanted towards their work. The catalogue features a wide range of greetings cards as well as novelty gifts and household gadgets. Lap trays are £14.99; ladies' totes gloves are £7.99 and the Bee tea-towel and peg-bag cost £3.50 and £6.50 respectively.

Catalogue Bi-annually, A5, Catalogue, Colour, 11 pages, Free **Postal charges** Goods up to £24.99, add £2.55; goods from £25.00-£74.99, add £3.55; goods over £75, free **Delivery** Royal Mail **Methods of Payment** Cheque, Postal Order, Credit Card

UNICEF
Unit 1
Rignals Lane
Chelmsford
Essex
CM2 8TU

Cards, gifts and games

UNICEF was formed in 1946 to help children all over the world to lead fuller, richer and healthier lives. The charity works closely with local communities to help them to plan and support basic services such as health care, safe water

Telephone
01245 478266
Fax
01245 477394

supplies, sanitation, nutrition, education and training. The UNICEF catalogue offers a comprehensive selection of cards, gifts, wrapping paper, fashion items, stationery sets and children's puzzles, calendars and games, manufactured from recycled products wherever possible. Box of 10 cards and envelopes, £4.95; stationery set, £11.95; children's T-shirt, £7.50; jigsaw, £4.75.

Catalogue Annually, A5, Catalogue, Colour, 35 pages, Free **Postal charges** Varies with item **Delivery** Royal Mail, Parcelforce **Methods of Payment** Cheque, Credit Card

UNIVERSITIES FEDERATION FOR ANIMAL WELFARE (UFAW)
8 Hamilton Close
South Mimms
Potters Bar
Hertfordshire
EN6 3QD
Telephone
01707 658202
Fax
01707 649279

Animal welfare publications, Christmas cards and gifts

UFAW is an organisation working to improve the welfare of animals in zoos, laboratories, on farms, with pets and in the wild. It provides funds for education, brings together experts to offer advice internationally and produces a wide range of books, leaflets and videos on the subject. Prices from 50p to £50. It also offers a selection of low-cost Christmas cards and gifts from 75p to £12.50.

Catalogue Annually, A5, Catalogue, Colour and B/W, 12 pages, Free **Postal charges** Free **Delivery** Royal Mail **Methods of Payment** Cheque, Postal Order

WOMANKIND WORLDWIDE
122 Whitechapel High Street
London
E1 7PT
Telephone
0171 247 3436

Gifts

Womankind Worldwide is a development agency dedicated to supporting women's groups and organisations in developing countries to overcome poverty, to educate, to ensure better health and to give women more control over their own lives. The gift catalogue includes colourful Christmas cards in the form of a handmade patchwork banner made by a group of Peruvian women (£4.00 for 10 cards and envelopes), and mugs and T-shirts bearing the Womankind logo.

Catalogue Annually, A6, Catalogue, Colour, 8 pages, Free **Postal charges** £1.95 **Delivery** Royal Mail, Parcelforce **Methods of Payment** Cheque, Postal Order, Credit Card

WOOD GREEN ANIMAL SHELTERS
London Road
Godmanchester
Cambridgeshire
PE18 8LJ
Telephone
01480 831390

Gifts

This animal charity offers gifts ranging from hand-painted porcelain cord pulls of a black and white cat and a frog for £2.25 to kitten door stops for £6.99, and PVC shoulderbags with a doggy design for £6.25. There is also a range of books, T-shirts and stationery.

Catalogue Bi-annually, A4, Brochure, Colour, 4 pages, Free **Postal charges** Orders up to £6.99, add £1.75; £7.00–£15.99, add £2.75; £16.00–£24.99, add £3.75; £25.00–£49.99, add £4.75, £50.00 and over, add £5.75. **Delivery** Parcelforce **Methods of Payment** Cheque, Postal Order, Credit Card

WORLD WILDLIFE FUND UK LTD
PO Box 49
Burton upon Trent
Staffordshire
DE14 3LP
Telephone
01283 506105
Fax
01283 506310

Gifts with animal motifs

This catalogue contributes directly to WWF's many projects and campaigns (such as the creation of a whale sanctuary around Antarctica) that help to save wildlife and wild habitats throughout the world. Cotton T-shirts and sweatshirts with attractive animal motifs, such as the Red-eyed Tree Frog T-shirt (£11.99) and the cowl-necked Snow Leopard sweatshirt (£29.99) abound, as do other gift items, such as the WWF Parker rollerball pen (£5.99); Noah's Ark cotton rug (38in x 24in, £12.99); and the Hedgerow stationery set (£4.99).

Catalogue Bi-annually, A4, Catalogue, Colour, 23 pages, Free **Postal charges** Up to £69.99, add £3.35; £70.00 and over, free **Delivery** Royal Mail **Methods of Payment** Cheque, Postal Order, Credit Card, Switch

Clothes

A. GARSTANG & CO
9 Wellington Street
St Johns
Blackburn
Lancashire
BB2 6BP
Telephone
01254 59357
Fax
01254 261057

Made-to-measure shirts and blouses

Garstang has been in business for more than 60 years and is a major supplier of shirts to Jermyn Street in London. This is where you can have a shirt tailored to your exact needs as every order is hand-cut and -sewn to your instructions. Spare collars and cuffs can be supplied, too, and a repair service is available. There is a wide choice of fabrics including cotton, poly/cotton, wool/cotton, Viyella and silk, and swatches are sent with the brochure, along with an easy-to-follow measuring guide. Shirts and blouses from £40.40; spare collars from £5.25; pyjamas from £52.50 (pure silk, £109.50).

Catalogue Annually, A4, Leaflets, Colour and B/W, 5 pages, Free **Postal charges** £1.25 per shirt (maximum £3.50) **Delivery** Royal Mail **Methods of Payment** Cheque, Postal Order, Credit Card

ACORN
Crichton House
Pathead
Midlothian
Scotland
EH37 5UX
Telephone
01875 320352
Fax
same

Woollen clothing for women and men

Acorn makes clothes to last, using a wool which is dense but soft and which shrugs off wind and rain to keep you warm. These are classic clothes: waistcoats and jackets with matching or contrasting braid, tartan skirts, pin-tucked blouses and co-ordinating hats. The three-quarter coat looks just as good over a ball-dress or jeans (£170); jacket, £118; blouse, £34; men's waistcoat, £95.

Catalogue Annually, A5, Catalogue, Colour and B/W, 5 pages, Free **Postal charges** Varies with item **Delivery**

Royal Mail, Parcelforce **Methods of Payment** Cheque, Credit Card, American Express

ALAFOSS OF ICELAND
203 Main Road
Emsworth
Hampshire
PO10 8EZ
Telephone
01243 379337
Fax
01243 378498

Icelandic knitwear
Icelandic sheep have two coats of wool, a long, glossy outer layer and a finer, silky lower layer. Spun together this wool produces a soft, hard-wearing yarn and a durable garment which will keep its shape and last for years. Alafoss even includes a grooming brush for each sweater to maintain the texture of the wool. Traditional Icelandic colours and patterns prevail. Prices from £59.95 for a gloriously warm sweater to £147.50 for a cosy coat.

Catalogue Annually, A4, Catalogue, Colour, 8 pages, Free **Postal charges** £2.95 **Delivery** Royal Mail, Parcelforce **Methods of Payment** Cheque, Postal Order, Credit Card

ALLEN GRAY
PO Box 114
Wallington
Surrey
SM6 7QJ
Telephone
0181 207 1997
Fax
0181 207 4554

Classic menswear
Not a wide range of clothing but some good brand names here among the 10 or so items shown: Farah trousers, Lyle & Scott sweaters (some with a touch of cashmere), Pringle sweaters and Van Heusen shirts.

Catalogue Annually, Third A4, Catalogue, Colour, 6 pages, Free **Postal charges** 1 item, £2.50; 2 or more items, £3.00. **Delivery** Royal Mail **Methods of Payment** Cheque, Credit Card, American Express

ANKARET CRESSWELL
Wykeham
Scarborough
North Yorkshire
YO13 9QB
Telephone
01723 864406

Woollen garments for women and men
Ankaret Cresswell is a small firm producing well-made clothes in 100% pure wool, including lightweight fabrics. The styles are classic separates in plain and tartan twill and a smart jacquard. Women's boxy jacket, £125; fluted skirt, £97.50; gent's sports coat £225.

Fax
01723 864041

Catalogue Annually, A4, Catalogue, Colour, 8 pages, Free **Postal charges** Varies with item **Delivery** Royal Mail, Parcelforce **Methods of Payment** Cheque, Credit Card

ANNABEL LEE
PO Box 97
Banbury
Oxfordshire
OX16 7ER
Telephone
01280 850052
Fax
01280 850002

Women's blouses
Classic, feminine blouses in several designs and a number of different patterns. Annabel Lee offers striped, checked and tartan shirts, blouses with a pie-crust collar or soft, rolled neckline, and pretty prints in cotton or polyester from £35.50 to £40.90. Silk blouses cost £29.95. To top it all, there's an elegant cotton-linen mix, striped waistcoat (£35.60).

Catalogue Quarterly, A5, Catalogue, Colour, 14 pages, Free **Postal charges** £1.50 **Delivery** Royal Mail **Methods of Payment** Cheque, Credit Card

ARTIGIANO
PO Box 1
Yarmouth
Isle of Wight
PO41 0US
Telephone
01983 531 881
Fax
01983 531 726

Italian fashion by mail
Artigiano sells top-quality Italian fashion by mail. But most importantly they offer good value by dealing direct with the factories. A navy wool and cashmere blazer is £139, with navy flannel Italian cut trousers for £55. A selection of blue shirts in different patterns and shades, £37, and in sorbet colours, £39. A black flowing wool crêpe long wrap skirt £79. All clothes sizes 10–16 and in beautiful classic Italian designs.

Catalogue Quarterly, A5, Brochure, Colour, 23 pages, Free **Postal charges** £3.95 **Delivery** Royal Mail **Methods of Payment** Cheque, Postal Order, Credit Card, American Express

ATLAS KINGSIZE
197–199 Cricklewood
Broadway
London
NW2 3HS

Clothes for the larger man
As well as a comprehensive range of kingsize suits, blazers, formal and casual jackets, Atlas Kingsize also carry a large selection of knitwear and casual shirts up to size 6XL. Belts (up to 60in waist),

CLOTHES

Telephone
0181 452 0541
Fax
0181 450 9292

socks (to fit up to shoe size 16) and kingsize braces are also available. The taller man is also catered for (up to 38in inside leg).

Long-sleeved formal shirts in polyester and cotton (18in–21in collar) cost £15.99; sweatshirts and joggers from £19.99 each; stonewashed denim jeans (40in–60in waist) cost from £25.99 a pair.

Catalogue A4, Brochure, Colour, 2 pages, Free **Postal charges** For orders over £100.00, free; otherwise, add £3.50. **Delivery** Royal Mail **Methods of Payment** Cheque, Postal Order, Credit Card, American Express

BEETLEBUG
Broadway Studios
28 Tooting High Street
London
SW17 0RG
Telephone
0181 682 2389

Children's clothes aged 0–8 years

This new collection is imaginative, combining style and practicality with a chic European influence and fun, bright colours. The Autumn/Winter 1995 range for children aged 0–8 years, for example, was humorous, featuring a series of tactile animal and insect characters that fascinate children. All 100% cotton, machine-washable and endorsed by the eczema society as suitable for children with sensitive skins. Cable polo-neck jumpers start at £25.50, and cardigans at £25.

Catalogue Annually, A5, Catalogue, Colour, 12 pages, Free **Postal charges** £1.50 **Delivery** Royal Mail **Methods of Payment** Cheque, Postal Order, Credit Card

BENETTON DIRECT
Bolton
Lancashire
BL3 6AX
Telephone
0345 012012

Casual clothes for women, men and children

This well-known high street name has launched its first home-shopping catalogue. Now, instead of searching through all those neatly stacked piles of clothes in the stores, you can select your Benetton sweatshirts, polos, knitwear, denims, dresses and accessories at home from its neatly presented catalogue. Vest top, £12; denim jacket, £37; woollen roll-neck sweater, £22; men's chinos,

£37; jeans, £25; checked shirt, £25; kids' leggings, £12.

Catalogue Bi-annually, A4, Catalogue, Colour, 55 pages, Free **Postal charges** £2.95 **Delivery** Royal Mail, Parcelforce **Methods of Payment** Cheque, Postal Order, Credit Card, Switch

BIRKETT & PHILLIPS
1 Mill Buildings
Lea Bridge
Matlock
Derbyshire
DE4 5AG
Telephone
01629 534331
Fax
01629 534691

Underwear, outerwear and nightwear in natural fabrics

Birkett & Phillips have been trading in natural fabrics by mail order since 1920. They carry many reputable lines including knitwear and underwear by John Smedley and nightwear by Brettles. Smedley's merino wool knitwear is both fashionable and beautifully made in a range of plain colours: long skirt, £62.50; sweater with scoop neck, £65; men's classic shirt with three-buttoned front, £64; turtle-neck pullover, £55. Smedley's sea island cotton body, £30; men's briefs, £22.25. Cosijamas from £24.

Catalogue Annually, A5, Catalogue, Colour, 32 pages, Free **Postal charges** £2.50 **Delivery** Royal Mail **Methods of Payment** Cheque, Credit Card, Postal Order

BLOOMING MARVELLOUS LTD
PO Box 12F
Chessington
Surrey
KT9 2LS
Telephone
0181 391 4822
Fax
0181 397 0493

Maternity and childrenswear

Blooming Marvellous is the largest specialist mail-order maternity-wear company in the UK. Judy and Vivienne started the business 11 years ago when they were frustrated at the lack of choice in the shops. Now they have over 250 exclusive styles including wrap-over skirts (£28.99), Chino trousers (£24.99), polo shirts (£16.99), waistcoats (£16.99), and swimwear (£19.99).

Designed in fun prints for ages 0–11 years, their mix-and-match range of childrenswear co-ordinates with the maternity range and is designed to make your child stand out in a crowd. Sample prices: dresses from £14.99, sweatshirts from

£12.99, trackpants from £10.99 and leggings from £8.99, all of which seem excellent prices for the quality of merchandise.

Catalogue Quarterly, A4, Catalogue, Colour, 44 pages, Free **Postal charges** Varies according to value of order **Delivery** Royal Mail, Parcelforce **Methods of Payment** Cheque, Postal Order, Credit Card, Switch

BODEN
4 Pembroke Buildings
Cumberland Park
Scrubs Lane
London
NW10 6RE
Telephone
0181 964 2662
Fax
0181 964 2598

Men's and women's casual clothing

Johnnie Boden started this business 3 years ago because he couldn't find the clothes he wanted on the high street. Good quality and hard-wearing, all his garments are made from natural fibres. Unisex cotton T-shirts in white or grey with breast pocket are priced at £15.00; original twill shirts in red, green or blue, £36; drill jackets, £66; Boden original trousers, in orange, bottle, brick and khaki, £42. Women's French-collar cardigans in a linen/cotton mix, £52.

Catalogue Bi-annually, A5, Catalogue, Colour, 87 pages, Free **Postal charges** £4.00 **Delivery** Royal Mail **Methods of Payment** Cheque, Credit Card

BODY AWARE
Erskine House
Union Street
Trowbridge
Wiltshire
BA14 8RY
Telephone
01225 774164
Fax
01225 774452

Men's underwear and swimwear

The Body Aware range of underwear for men is the most up-to-date catalogue of its type. It features underwear and swimwear by European designers in styles that enhance the male anatomy yet feel good to wear, in sizes from S to XXL. Zip boxer, £18.50; form-fitting unitard, £16; leather short, £17; chamois leather thong, £15.50; swim trunk, £15.50; silk satin boxer, £15; swim bikini, £13.95; rubber brief, £11.50.

Catalogue Annually, A5, Catalogue, Colour, 24 pages, Free **Postal charges** £1.20 **Methods of Payment** Cheque, Postal Order, Credit Card

CLOTHES

BRAVISSIMO
PO Box 670
Oxford
Oxfordshire
OX2 8RD
Telephone
0181 744 2852
Fax
0181 287 9779

Women's underwear
The Bravissimo Mail Order Magazine was born out of the frustrating experiences of two big-bosomed women who could not find a good selection of bras in their size. They resolved to make it possible for women like themselves to have as much choice as other women. Bravissimo offers a range of pretty and stylish lingerie in cup sizes C–HH. Styles include underwired and softcup bras, sports bras, bodies and basques, strapless and backless bras. Also included is a selection of bra-sized bikinis and swimsuits in cup sizes C–FF. The magazine is a godsend to any woman who has found that shops don't cater for her size. In one customer's words, 'I was very impressed with your catalogue and I no longer feel abnormal – you have boosted my self-confidence no end!'

Catalogue Bi-annually, A4, Brochure, Colour, 20 pages, Free **Postal charges** £2 **Delivery** Royal Mail **Methods of Payment** Cheque, Postal Order, Credit Card, COD

THE BRETON SHIRT COMPANY
PO Box 15
Brampton
Cumbria
CA8 1RB
Telephone
016977 41936
Fax
016977 41937

Breton shirts
This colourful catalogue features a number of variations on the basic idea – the traditional French jersey. There is a seafarer sweatshirt in fleecy cotton, a three-buttoned polo shirt and a regatta shirt with collar, as well as the original style (£16.95) and children's versions, too. All are made from unbleached cotton in traditional blue and white stripes. Caps, shorts and Aran sweaters are also available. T-shirt, £14.50; seafarer, £22.95; Monty beret, £10.95; long-sleeved children's Breton, £7.95.

Catalogue Annually, A5, Catalogue, Colour, 8 pages, Free **Postal charges** Varies with item **Delivery** Royal Mail **Methods of Payment** Cheque, Postal Order, Credit Card, American Express

BRORA

7a Filmer Road Studios
75 Filmer Road
London
SW6 7JF
Telephone
0171 731 7672
Fax
0171 731 7704

Knitwear, rugs and blankets

Brora is the name of a village in Sutherland where the oldest tweed mill in Scotland, Hunters of Brora, has been based since it was established in 1901. The catalogue contains an attractive selection of quality knitwear (ladies' and men's cashmere jumpers, from £125). There are wraps (lambswool serape, £55); cotton dressing gowns (from £65); pyjamas (from £50); bed blankets (£65); tartan rugs (£55); tweed caps (£35); and loden jackets (£145).

Catalogue Bi-monthly, A4, Catalogue, Colour, 16 pages, Free **Postal charges** Varies with item **Delivery** Royal Mail, Parcelforce **Methods of Payment** Cheque, Credit Card, Switch

BUBBLES CHILDRENS CLOTHES

38 Holcombe Lane
Bathampton
Bath
Avon
BA2 6UL
Telephone
01225 466835

Children's clothes

All Bubbles' clothes are made in England from 100% machine-washable cotton to a high standard and are suitable for both girls and boys. The brochure illustrates Bubbles' summer collection of exclusive children's clothes for 0–8 year olds, featuring unique appliqué designs. Prices for Navy Boat Dungarees start from £19.95, for a Tartan Duck Pinafore from £28.95, and for Clown shorts from £13.95.

Catalogue Bi-annually, A5, Catalogue, Colour, 6 pages, Free **Postal charges** 1–2 items, £1.50; 3–4 items, £2; 5 or more items, £2.50 **Delivery** Royal Mail **Methods of Payment** Cheque

BUMPS N' BABES

38 Southbourne Road
Southbourne
Bournemouth
Hampshire
BH6 5AE

Maternity wear

Bumps n' Babes offers affordable clothing that is comfortable and practical and will accommodate your bump from the early days right through your pregnancy. The size range is from 6 to 34 and each garment comes in 3 lengths.

There's a completely adjustable jumpsuit with

CLOTHES

Telephone
01202 428866

shoulder and side ties in navy/white stripe polyester/cotton for £29.99, and a shaped bodiced cotton-mix dress with short sleeves in navy and white polka-dot for £39.99. They also offer one or 2 items for children up to 5 years old.

Catalogue A4, Catalogue, Colour, 8 pages, Free **Postal charges** Add £1.50 for 1 garment; £3.00 for 2 garments; £5.00 for 3–4 garments; and £7.00 for 5 or more garments **Delivery** Royal Mail **Methods of Payment** Cheque, Postal Order

BURBERRYS
18–22 Haymarket
London
SW1Y 4DQ
Telephone
0171 930 7803
Fax
0171 839 2418

Clothes, accessories, food and gifts

Burberrys of London provide a wide range of tailored clothes for both adults and children. All the merchandise in the catalogue is available from their stores in the United Kingdom or direct through mail order. Other goods on offer are toys (£25.00 for a teddy bear), knitwear, raincoats (£405.00), umbrellas, luggage, fragrances and watches (£325.00). There are also food hampers on offer containing jams, whisky, biscuits, chocolate, etc.

If you order clothes, the Burberrys visiting-tailor service will see that you have them made to measure and cut to your size and style. All gifts are gift-wrapped on request at no extra charge and you can even have your raincoat monogrammed with your own initials.

Catalogue Bi-annually, A4, Catalogue, Colour and B/W, 20 pages pages, £2.00 **Postal charges** For UK orders £3.50 **Delivery** In-house delivery **Methods of Payment** Cheque, Postal Order, Credit Card, American Express, Diners Club, Switch

CALIFORNIAN KIDS
36 Wadham Avenue
Walthamstow
London

Children's clothes

Californian Kids sell American designer-label clothes for ages 0–6 years. They do not produce a catalogue because many of the items are one-offs

E17 4HT
Telephone
0181 523 1944

and others are only stocked in small quantities. The company specialises in Oshkosh, with a basic line of dungarees from £18.50. Most of the stock is sold well below shop prices.

A new line called B.U.M. consists of jog pants (£14.50), sweat-tops (£16.50), hooded dresses, and zip-up hooded tops, all made in 100% cotton in America. They also stock items by Levi's and Reebok.

Catalogue Bi-annually, A4, By Advertising, B/W, 3 pages, Free **Postal charges** £2.00 for orders under £20.00; £2.50 for orders between £20.00–£30.00; and £3.00 for orders over £30.00 **Delivery** Parcelforce **Methods of Payment** Cheque

CARADOC
Mor Brook Barn
Morville
Near Bridgnorth
Shropshire
WV16 5NR
Telephone
01746 714275
Fax
same

Country clothes

Caradoc produces a range of all-year activity clothing and traditional country clothing for both men and women. Many of the garments have been developed to the company's own specifications and are not available elsewhere. Caradoc's range of clothing includes shooting jackets in Derby tweed with matching waistcoats. Also shirts, sweaters, breeches and trousers. Lighter wear is offered in the form of cotton casuals and a range of lightweight waterproofs.

Catalogue Annually, A5, Catalogue, Colour, 14 pages, Free **Postal charges** Varies with item **Delivery** Royal Mail **Methods of Payment** Cheque, Postal Order, Credit Card, Switch

CARLSEN
8 Heath Drive
Sutton
Surrey
SM2 5RP
Telephone
0181 642 9266

Quality knitwear in natural fibres

Carlsen is a knitwear company specialising in quality knitwear in natural fibres for children. Their knitwear is hand-framed and hand-finished, and even the buttons are dyed to match each season's colours. The knitwear is generously sized and is also available in adult sizes. In addition to the designs illustrated in their brochure they can also produce plain cardigans and sweaters.

Catalogue Annually, A5, Brochure, Colour, 3 pages, Free **Postal charges** £2 **Delivery** Royal Mail **Methods of Payment** Cheque, Postal Order, Credit Card

THE CASHMERE STORE LTD
Units 1 and 2
Canongate Venture
New Street
Edinburgh
Scotland
EH8 0LH
Telephone
0131 557 5855
Fax
0131 557 9796

Cashmere clothes for men and women

The Cashmere Store celebrates its 10th anniversary this year and, due to overwhelming demand for its range of Scottish cashmere knitwear, has greatly improved its mail-order service by moving it to a new despatch warehouse. Beautifully soft pure cashmere stoles cost £165; the 'Parisienne' cardigan/jacket with contrasting black trim and gilt buttons costs £179; men's slipover in wine or navy blue costs £109; and the unisex duffel coat made from 52% cashmere cloth costs £159.

Catalogue Annually, A4, Catalogue, Colour, 27 pages, Free **Postal charges** £2.50 for UK; £6.50 for Europe; £15.00 for Rest of World **Delivery** Royal Mail, Courier **Methods of Payment** Cheque, Credit Card, Diners Club, American Express

CAVENAGH LTD
5 The Coda Centre
189 Munster Road
London
SW6 5AW
Telephone
0171 610 3004
Fax
0171 610 2119

Men's and ladies' quality shirts and ties

Cavenagh sells top-quality, cotton, Oxford classic shirts both through its retail outlet in Fulham and by mail order. The shirts, for men and women, are constructed from two-fold poplin. The men's shirts, which go up to collar size 17½, have removable collar bones, split yokes and double cuffs and start at £29.50 (ladies' versions, £28). Printed silk ties start at £21.

Catalogue Bi-annually, A5, Catalogue, Colour, 10 pages, Free **Postal charges** For orders under £75.00, add £4.00. For orders over £75.00, add £6.00. **Delivery** Royal Mail **Methods of Payment** Cheque, Credit Card, American Express

CHARLES TYRWHITT SHIRTS
298–300 Munster Road
London
SW6 6BH
Telephone
0171 386 9900
Fax
0171 386 0027

Shirts
This small company manufactures quality cotton poplin shirts for men and women in plain colours, stripes, herringbones and ginghams. There are three collar styles: classic, cut-away and button-down. Models include celebrities such as Gavin Hastings and Lucinda Green. The shirts are priced at around £30 and there is a sleeve alteration service for £5. There is also a selection of cuff-links, ties, boxer shorts, waistcoats and polo shirts.

Catalogue Annually, A5, Catalogue, Colour, 24 pages, Free **Postal charges** UK: £3.50; Europe: £5.00; rest of world, £10.00 **Delivery** Royal Mail **Methods of Payment** Credit Card, American Express, Diners Club, Cheque, Postal Order, Switch

CLAIRE (INT) LTD
No 29 The Bank
Barnard Castle
County Durham
DL12 8PL
Telephone
01833 637325
Fax
same

Designer clothes for women
Claire's unique 'Wardrobe' collection of stylish womenswear includes flowing handknitted skirts and wraps, sweaters with elaborate stitch detail, tailored suits, polo-necks and neat feminine T-shirts. Every garment is made in 100% cotton and is machine-washable. A made-to-measure service is available.

Designed to flatter all shapes, the distinctive cowl-neck polo sweater comes with or without a side vent and costs £75. It can be teamed with a mini skirt (£36), an A-line skirt (£120), or leggings (£49).

Catalogue Annually, A4, Catalogue, Colour, 15 pages, £1.50 but credited with your order **Postal charges** Postage, packing and insurance: £3.50 (1 or 2 garments); £4.50 (3 or more garments) **Delivery** Royal Mail **Methods of Payment** Cheque, Credit Card

CLIFFORD JAMES

High Street
Ripley
Woking
Surrey
GU23 6AF
Telephone
01282 443333

Footwear and clothing for warmth and comfort

Clifford James has a shop and a mail-order service offering items such as Therm-O-Boots, the Husky real suede leather ankle boot, the Challenger thermal-lined waterproof zip boots, Frosties lined luxury real leather zip boots, Relaxer real leather comfort shoe, Galaxy velour wedge comfort slippers, Cosytoze pure sheepskin slippers, Hotter Dew high-quality leather comfort shoes, pigskin gloves, Eskimo natural wool lined leather shoes, Fiji lightweight leisure comfort shoes, thermal socks, winter warmer country socks, thermal underwear, classic wax jackets, waterproof jackets, Pac-A-Macs, men's brogues, and Marathon leather walking shoes. There is also a separate catalogue offering a wide range of men's and women's shoes, leisure shoes and slippers. There is a £2 Parcelforce charge for cash-on-delivery orders.

Catalogue Quarterly, A5, Catalogue, Colour and B/W, 48 pages **Postal charges** Free **Delivery** Parcelforce **Methods of Payment** Cheque, Postal Order, COD, Credit Card, Switch

COCOON COATS

Lomond Industrial Estate
Alexandria
Dunbartonshire
Scotland
G83 0TL
Telephone
01389 755511
Fax
same

Coats and jackets

Cocoon coats are elegant yet practical and generously cut so they can be worn over a suit or chunky jumper. They are made in 60% cotton/40% nylon and are water-resistant, machine-washable, crease-resistant, and comfortable to wear. They all have optional detachable linings in Viyella wool plaids. The classic trenchcoat costs from £220 (detachable lining, £75). The short ladies' jacket has good ventilating construction and a hood concealed in the collar and costs from £145. There is also a range of hats such as the 'Tammy' for £15.

CLOTHES

THE COLLAR COMPANY
Halls Farm
Silchester
Berkshire
RG7 2NH
Telephone
01256 881894
Fax
same

CORDINGS BY MAIL
Freepost
10 Fleming Road
Newbury
Berkshire
RG13 2DE
Telephone
01635 565021
Fax
01635 41678

Catalogue Annually, A4, Catalogue, Colour, 16 pages, Free **Postal charges** £4.00 **Delivery** Parcelforce **Methods of Payment** Cheque, Credit Card, American Express, Postal Order

Ladies' shirts, jumpers, gloves and scarves

The Collar Company offers a selection of colourful, individual shirt styles in four different sizes (small, medium, large and extra large). Each style has an appropriate name: for example, 'St Andrews' has a flattering high neck with two small pleats around the neck and a fly buttoned front (£36.75). 'Grandad' is a grandad-style casual shirt in pure cotton with contrasting collar and cuffs (£30.75). Cardigans are also on offer in a variety of vibrant colours (from £62.75).

Catalogue Bi-annually, A5, Catalogue, Colour, 14 pages, Free **Postal charges** £2.00 **Delivery** Royal Mail **Methods of Payment** Cheque, Credit Card

Classic English country clothes

Established in 1839 as weatherproofers and gentlemen's outfitters, Cordings are still selling high-quality, traditional country clothes. Everything is made in the British Isles, using only the best quality materials. The range includes a good selection of Tattersall check shirts (£52), hunt vests (£95), silk ties (£39), and webbing belts (£19). Their Keepers tweed field coat costs £285, and cotton drill trousers £54.

Catalogue Annually, A5, Catalogue, Colour, 20 pages, Free **Postal charges** Add £5.00 for UK orders. For next day delivery, add an additional £5.00 **Delivery** Royal Mail **Methods of Payment** Cheque, Credit Card, American Express, Diners Club

COTSWOLD COLLECTIONS
2 Queens Circus
Cheltenham
Gloucestershire
GL50 1RX
Telephone
01242 226262
Fax
01242 226252

Classic women's clothing

Cotswold Collections offers a range of stylish, smart clothes in silk, cotton and easy-care blends. The designs are, classic, well cut and reasonably priced. Eyelet blouse, £29.95; gingham skirt, £39.95; drill trousers, £34.95; unisex cotton cable sweater, £26.95.

Catalogue Quarterly, A4, Catalogue, Colour, 24 pages **Postal charges** £2.95 on orders below £150; free on orders above **Delivery** Royal Mail, Parcelforce **Methods of Payment** Cheque, Credit Card, American Express

COTTON MOON
Freepost (SE8265)
PO Box 280
London
SE3 8BR
Telephone
0181 319 8315
Fax
0181 319 8345

Children's clothes

Cotton Moon produces 100% cotton, comfort clothing for boys and girls aged from 12 months to 7 years. Their philosophy is that children's clothing should be easy to wear, easy to care for, fun and good value. They cut their clothes generously so they're comfortable and have plenty of room for growth. The general style is American, with many of the garments designed and manufactured by Cotton Moon in the USA. The range is fully colour co-ordinated and includes everyday play wear as well as items for special occasions plus matching socks, tights, hats and hairbands. They also offer 100% cotton, knitted cardigans and jumpers. Prices range from £7.25 for hats, £15.95 for trousers, and £21.95 for dresses.

Catalogue Bi-annually, Third A4, Catalogue, Colour, 14 pages, Free **Postal charges** £2.50; free for orders of more than £75 **Delivery** Royal Mail **Methods of Payment** Postal Order, Credit Card, Switch, Cheque

COTTON TRADERS DIRECT
PO Box 42
Altrincham

Leisurewear for men and women

Managed by ex-England International Rugby star Fran Cotton, Cotton Traders has made its name supplying the British public with top-quality

CLOTHES

Cheshire
WA14 1SD
Telephone
0161 926 8185

leisurewear at good-value prices. Every item is designed to give you more for less – finer fabrics, better features and longer life at good prices. Roll-necks, £9.99 or 3 for £24.99; short-sleeved pique shirt, £12.99; men's chinos, £19.99; Oxford shirts, from £15.99; floral dress, £29.99. Often there are special offers such as a barn jacket reduced from £79.99 to £59.99.

Catalogue Quarterly, A4, Catalogue, Colour, 24 pages, Free **Postal charges** Varies with item **Delivery** Royal Mail, Parcelforce **Methods of Payment** Cheque, Postal Order, Credit Card, American Express

COTTONTAIL
Unit 2
Tweedvale Mill West
Walkerburn
Peebleshire
Scotland
EH43 6AN
Telephone
01896 870 482
Fax
01896 870 483

Children's clothes

Cottontail sells beautifully made, traditional clothes for children from 3 months to 12 years old. These include dresses, pinafores and skirts in pretty cotton prints. There are also trews, shorts, cardigans, rompers and bloomers as well as baby wear, swimwear, night dresses and gowns, cricket sweaters and waterproof jackets. Seersucker romper, £21.95; smocked dress from £44.50; ruched swimsuit, £19.25; boy's Oxford shirt, from £18.95; cricket sweater from £27.50; drill shorts from £15.25.

Catalogue Quarterly, A5, Catalogue, Colour, 24 pages, Free **Postal charges** Varies with item **Delivery** Royal Mail **Methods of Payment** Cheque, Credit Card

THE COUNTRY SHOP
Easdale
By Oban
Argyll
Scotland
PA34 4RF
Telephone
01852 300349

Scottish country clothes and accessories

The Country Shop aims to sell things of good quality that are appropriate to the rural West Highlands of Scotland. As well as welcoming visitors to their shop and tearoom in the lovely village of Easdale from April to October, they can offer a growing range of original and exclusive items for purchase by mail order. The unisex Inverness Cape costs £57.75; the West Highland

Fax same

Rug backed with a tough waterproof cloth and strong webbing carrying straps costs £35.00; the Wax Cotton Hat in green or navy costs £28.75.

Catalogue A5, Leaflets, Colour and B/W, 4 pages, Free **Postal charges** £3.50 **Delivery** Parcelforce **Methods of Payment** Cheque, Postal Order, American Express

CROFTERS TRADITIONAL KNITWEAR
Middleton Road
Salisbury
Wiltshire
SP2 7AY
Telephone
01722 412864

Pure wool Guernsey knitwear

The popularity of the traditional Guernsey has burgeoned in recent years and its qualities have now been reproduced into a number of other styles. Crofters make Guernsey cardigans (£55.50) and gilets (£49.50), as well as crew necks (£45.95) and V-necks (from £45.94), hats (£8.50) and scarves (£18.50). The colour range is Navy Blue, Scarlet, Aran, Denim, Suffolk Nep, Grape, Aqua Green, and Bottle, and all the garments are made from 100% pure new wool which is oiled to give it a measure of weather protection.

Catalogue A5, Brochure, B/W, 6 pages, Free **Postal charges** Orders up to £35.00, add £3.00; orders up to £55.00, add £3.50; orders up to £85.00, add £4.00, free **Delivery** Parcelforce **Methods of Payment** Cheque, Postal Order, COD

DALE STREET MAIL ORDER HOLIDAY SHOP
PO Box 123
Manchester
Greater Manchester
M99 1HS
Telephone
0161 236 2233

Summer clothes

The Holiday Shop catalogue, an off-shoot of the larger Classic Combination mail-order catalogue, offers a wide selection of value-for-money clothes for the summer. Cotton embroidered blouse, £11.99; rib top, £7.99; drop-waist dress, £18.99; acrylic cardigan, £14.99.

Catalogue Annually, A5, Catalogue, Colour, 24 pages, Free **Postal charges** Free **Delivery** Royal Mail, Parcelforce **Methods of Payment** Cheque, Credit Card, Switch

CLOTHES

DAMART
Bowling Green Mills
Bingley X
West Yorkshire
BD97 1AD
Telephone
01274 510000
Fax
01274 568234

Thermolactyl clothing

Damart specialises in Thermolactyl clothing for men and women. Its underwear is beautifully soft and light, giving maximum warmth from the minimum weight of fabric. Women's short-sleeved jersey vest in Thermolactyl and Modal, £11.99; Finesse fancy-knit briefs, £6.99; floral camibrief (body), £13.99. Men's interlock short-sleeved vest, £12.99. Damart also stocks lambswool/Thermolactyl sweaters, cord jackets, gloves, slippers, duvets and rugs, in fact everything you need to keep warm.

Catalogue Annually, A4, Catalogue, Colour, 76 pages, Free **Postal charges** £1.50 **Delivery** Royal Mail, Parcelforce, Courier **Methods of Payment** Cheque, Postal Order, Credit Card

DAVID NIEPER
Saulgrove House
Somercotes
Derby
Derbyshire
DE55 9BR
Telephone
01773 836000
Fax
01773 520246

Lingerie, leisureware, blouses

Nieper specialises in traditional, romantic lingerie. The collection includes cotton camisoles (£18.95), polyester satin slips (from £29.95), cotton and polyester nightdresses (from £29.95) and wraps. There's a good choice of bras from Triumph, Lejaby and other well-known manufacturers.

Among the blouses is a pure silk crêpe de Chine design with a colourful pansy pattern for £85.75. For a small extra charge, goods can be sent in a gift box.

Catalogue Annually, Third A4, Catalogue, Colour, 31 pages, Free **Postal charges** UK: £2.75; Europe: £7.50; rest of world: £14.50 or £19.50. **Delivery** Royal Mail **Methods of Payment** Cheque, Credit Card, Switch, American Express, Diners Club

DAXON
PO Box 129
Ashford

General clothing for women

Daxon stock sizes 10–38 by mail order. From daywear to shoes and slippers sizes 3½ to 8 and with

CLOTHES

Kent
TN23 1XW
Telephone
01233 631177

a price range to suit all pockets. An embroidered shirt in various colours in 9 sizes £29.99, dresses from £21.99 and leggings from £11.99. Lingerie and dressings gowns are also featured. Bras in sizes 32B to 46D are available. Daxon also stock larger sizes for men up to 52in chest and 52in waist.
Catalogue Bi-annually, A5, Brochure, Colour, 31 pages, Free **Postal charges** £1.45 **Delivery** Royal Mail **Methods of Payment** Cheque, Postal Order, Credit Card Switch

DEANES
Rodd Estate
Shepperton
Middlesex
TW17 8AB
Telephone
01932 252266
Fax
01932 252444

Women's clothes

There is something to suit every size and shape in this catalogue, with sizes from 12 to 30 in regular and shorter lengths. Deanes has been supplying women's clothing for 25 years and offers an extensive range of reasonably-priced classic garments: a Jacquard two-piece in polyester/acrylic costs £29.50; a spring shirtwaister in polyester print, £19.95; blazer £27.95; poly/cotton nightie, £12.50.
Catalogue Quarterly, A5, Catalogue, Colour, 24 pages, Free **Postal charges** £1.95 for one item; £2.45 for multiple orders **Delivery** Royal Mail, Parcelforce **Methods of Payment** Credit Card, Cheque, Postal Order

DELIA MARKETING
24 Craven Park Road
London
NW10 4AB
Telephone
0181 965 8707
Fax
0181 965 4261

Women's lingerie

The Delia Collection is a popular mail-order service for women's underwear. A well-designed catalogue and a useful measuring guide make choosing easy. There is a comprehensive range of bras in sizes from 30in to 56in, and up to HH and J cups, from well-known manufacturers. Other lingerie items include pants, bodyshapers, sports bras, nursing bras, swimwear, corsets, petticoats, night attire and thermal wear. Advice is also offered to those who have had mastectomies. Triumph Doreen bra, £17.99; Silhouette bodyshaper, £28.99.

CLOTHES

Catalogue Annually, A4, Catalogue, Colour, 32 pages, Free **Postal charges** £2 **Delivery** Royal Mail **Methods of Payment** Cheque, Postal Order, Credit Card, Switch, American Express

DENNY ANDREWS
Clock House Workshop
Coleshill
Nr Swindon
Wiltshire
SN6 7PT
Telephone
01793 762476

Clothes, bedspreads and duvet covers

Denny Andrews supplies comfortable clothes in traditional styles from India, Wales and Ireland. Materials include pure cotton, silk or wool which is hand-embroidered or block-printed. There are shirts and waistcoats, dresses and full swirly skirts, kaftans, kimonos, nightgowns and trousers in various Indian shapes. Shirts, overalls, aprons, bedlinen and a great deal else feature – get the catalogue and see! Loose cotton dress, £34; kimonos, from £30; nightshirt, £21; harem-style trousers, £23; Indian shorts, £4.50.

Catalogue Annually, A5, Catalogue, Colour and B/W, 28 pages, Free **Postal charges** Varies with item **Delivery** Royal Mail, Parcelforce **Methods of Payment** Cheque, Credit Card

DESIGNER DISCOUNT CLUB
PO Box 40
Stourport on Severn
Worcestershire
DY13 8YW
Telephone
0990 143153

Designer women's clothes

If you love designer clothes, but can't afford or justify the cost, this is the catalogue for you. The Club has travelled through Germany and Italy visiting well-known manufacturers and obtaining the best discounts without sacrificing quality or styling. The result is a range of classic clothes with discounts of 50 to 80%. Ethnic-print shirt dress, RRP £149, Club price £69; linen/viscose double-breasted jacket, RRP £145, Club price £69.99; crêpe de Chine viscose skirt, RRP £125, Club price £49.

Catalogue Annually, A4, Catalogue, Colour, 20 pages, Free **Postal charges** £2.50 **Delivery** Royal Mail, Parcelforce **Methods of Payment** Cheque, Credit Card, Switch

DONALDSON'S OF CRIEFF
14 West High Street
Crieff
Tayside
Scotland
PH7 4DL
Telephone
01764 653303
Fax
01764 654303

Scottish tartan clothing for the family

Donaldson's is a family business as can be seen in the brochure where Tilda Donaldson is pictured sporting a pair of tartan trousers and cashmere sweater, and Kim, her great grand-daughter, is dressed in a snug tartan jacket. Skirts, kilts, trousers, waistcoats, plus twos and accessories including bow ties, tammies, stoles and scarves, can be made up from any of several hundred tartans (individual samples are available). Straight skirt, £45; hostess kilt, £99; gent's trousers, £95; child's padded jacket, £45; tartan by the yard, £22.50/yd.

Catalogue Annually, Third A4, Brochure, Colour and B/W, 6 pages, Free **Postal charges** Free **Delivery** Royal Mail, Parcelforce **Methods of Payment** Cheque, Postal Order, Credit Card

THE DUFFLECOAT COMPANY
140 Battersea Park Road
London
SW11 4NB
Telephone
0171 498 8811
Fax
0171 498 0990

Duffle coats

The perfect antidote to chilly winter weather, a cosy duffle coat. These handsome, long-lasting coats are made in England by Gloverall. Available in red, navy, camel, conifer, charcoal and teal, they cost £129.95 (children's sizes from £59.50 in navy only). Also from the same address: Norfolk Rainwear offers classic raincoats for men and women in stone with a check lining for £69.95; and Panama hats are available from The Genuine Panama Hat Company, from £29.95.

Catalogue Annually, A5, Catalogue, Colour, 12 pages, Free **Postal charges** £3 **Delivery** Royal Mail, Parcelforce **Methods of Payment** Cheque, Credit Card

DUNN & CO
FREEPOST
Swansea
West Glamorgan
Wales

Men's clothing

This well-established men's outfitters offers an extensive selection of classic clothes in its mail-order catalogue. Dunn & Co prides itself on personal service and on recognising that customers

SA5 5ZZ
Telephone
0800 378755
Fax
01792 580617

come in many different sizes. Its suits, jackets, casuals and knitwear are available from 38in to 54in chest; shirts from 14.5in to 20in collar; and trousers from 32in to 54in waist. Danimac walking coat, £85; Dunn & Co pure wool trouser, £50; check shirt, £19.99; Pringle pullover, £49.99; two-piece wool suit, £172.

Catalogue Bi-annually, A4, Catalogue, Colour, 47 pages, Free **Postal charges** Varies with item **Delivery** Royal Mail, Parcelforce **Methods of Payment** Cheque, American Express, Diners Club, Credit Card

ELEANOR HOUSE
PO Box 49
Stroud
Gloucestershire
GL6 8YA
Telephone
01453 884192

Children's clothes

Eleanor House's catalogue features a beautiful range of chic children's clothing from 3 months to 12 years (although the majority of designs stop at 8 years). A number of outfits come from France. For babies, a two-piece suit in padded cotton with a sheep print, from £37; for girls, a high-waisted scarlet dress in sweatshirt fabric, from £21; for boys, brushed cotton pull-on trousers with zip, from £26. There are co-ordinating shirts, polos, hats and tights, too, and a superb range of knitwear: cable denim jumpers, from £39; Scottie dog cardigan, from £55.

Catalogue Bi-annually, A4, Catalogue, Colour, 16 pages, Free **Postal charges** Add £3 **Delivery** Royal Mail, Parcelforce **Methods of Payment** Cheque, Credit Card

ELGAR SHIRTS
Nortonthorpe Mill
Wakefield Road
Scissett
Huddersfield
West Yorkshire
HD8 9FB
Telephone
01484 866284

Moleskin clothes for men and women

Moleskin is a soft, but hardwearing cotton fabric that is warm and comfortable and is ideal for outdoor activities. Elgar use it to make shirts (£47), waistcoats with silky backs (£37), and trousers (£47) in country colours. It also sells corduroy shirts (£40.50) and a heavy eight-wale corduroy skeet jacket (£45). A made-to-measure service is available.

CLOTHES

Fax
01484 865684

Catalogue Annually, A4, Catalogue, Colour, 4 pages, Free **Postal charges** Free **Delivery** Royal Mail **Methods of Payment** Cheque, Postal Order, Credit Card

EMPORIO ARMANI
191 Brompton Road
London
SW10
Telephone
0171 823 8818

Designer clothes and underwear

The Emporio Armani catalogue is more a work of art with wonderful black and white A3 photos illustrating clothes. There is a separate A5 black and white catalogue for underwear, again wonderfully photographed. Floral dress £250, bodysuit in black £35, and even sunglasses from £79. A variety of clothes for men and women in the latest fashions. Worth getting the catalogue at £3 just for the wonderful photos, which you could frame. Catalogues can be obtained from any of the shops by personal visit or by phone.

Catalogue Bi-annually, A3, Catalogue, B/W, 139 pages, £3 **Postal charges** Varies with item **Delivery** In-house delivery **Methods of Payment** Postal Order, Cheque, Credit Card

ENGLISH NATURALS
Erskine House
Union Street
Trowbridge
Wiltshire
BA14 8RY
Telephone
01225 774140
Fax
01225 774452

Lingerie

English Naturals' lingerie collection includes a pretty satin demi-cup bra (£12.99, sizes 34B, C–36B, C, D) and matching French knickers trimmed in translucent chiffon (£7.50, sizes S/M/L/XL). Pyjamas in softest satin charmeuse cost £39.95 and a satin charmeuse teddy with front lacing in dusky rose or ice mint costs £22.95.

There's even something for him: silk charmeuse boxer shorts for £14.95 and a hand-painted silk waistcoat for £55. There's also a gift-wrap service for £2 extra.

Catalogue Bi-annually, A4, Catalogue, Colour, 12 pages, Free **Postal charges** £1.20 **Delivery** Royal Mail **Methods of Payment** Cheque, Postal Order, Credit Card

ERIC HILL
High Street
Bramley
Guildford
Surrey
GU5 0HQ
Telephone
01483 898222
Fax
01483 892876

Women's clothing

Eric Hill's illustrated catalogue contains an extensive selection of classical dresses, separates and nightwear for women, many items of which are also available from its Bramley shop. There is something for everyone here, with sizes up to 26 in a number of styles, and several special offers. Cotton jersey dress, £84.95; two-piece acrylic knitted suit with fully-lined, pleated skirt, £107; cotton tartan pyjamas, £46.50.

Our last catalogue arrived with a large leaflet from Finn Karelia with a small range of blouses, tapered trousers, waistcoats and matching skirts and blouson type jackets.

Catalogue Quarterly, A5, Catalogue, Colour, 34 pages, Free **Postal charges** Free **Delivery** Royal Mail, Parcelforce **Methods of Payment** Cheque, Postal Order, Credit Card

FASHION WORLD
PO Box 123
China Lane
Manchester
Greater Manchester
M1 8BH
Telephone
0161 236 5511
Fax
0161 238 2626

Women's clothes and shoes

Fashion World are a fashion mail order company specialising in womenswear with some children's wear as well. Everything is available in sizes 12 to 26 and they give a guarantee of a full refund or replacement for any item if you are not happy with your purchase. The full range of clothing is covered from separates, dresses and swimwear to lingerie, nightwear and footwear.

Catalogue Bi-annually, A4, Catalogue, Colour, 186 pages, Free **Postal charges** Free **Delivery** In-house delivery **Methods of Payment** Cheque, Postal Order, Switch, Credit Card

FINE FIGURES
8 Nazeing Glassworks Estate
Nazeing New Road
Broxbourne
Herfordshire
EN10 6SF

Clothes for larger women

Fine Figures produce a good range of dresses and separates in sizes 16 to 36. The catalogue comes with swatches of cotton, viscose, polyester and linen-mix fabric attached. Dresses start at £53.75, skirts and trousers at £32. There's a stylish loose

Telephone
01992 442974
Fax
same

unlined jacket for £49 and a short-sleeved top for £18.

The affiliated Three Jay & Company produce waterproof rainwear and travel/sports bags. Their high protection raincoat for men and women costs from £78 to £96.

Catalogue A4, Brochure, Colour and B/W, 4 pages, Free **Postal charges** Up to £20.00, add £2.50; £21.00–£40.00, add £3.00; £41.00–£80.00, add £3.50; over £80.00, add £4.00. **Delivery** Royal Mail, Parcelforce **Methods of Payment** Cheque, Credit Card, Postal Order

FLAMBOROUGH MARINE
The Manor House
Flamborough
Bridlington
East Yorkshire
YO15 1PD
Telephone
01262 850943

Traditional knitwear and authentic fisherman's sweaters

Flamborough Marine offers intricately patterned, hand-knitted Ganseys, the traditional fishermen's sweaters. They are still knitted in one piece on five steel needles, as they have been for centuries, using a tightly-spun five-ply worsted wool known as Seamen's Iron, and they are ideal for outdoor activities. Available in a choice of patterns and colours, a Gansey costs from £45 for children and from £110 for adults. Kits are available, price from £41.25.

Catalogue Annually, A4, Catalogue, Colour and B/W, 11 pages **Postal charges** £3.20 **Delivery** Royal Mail, Parcelforce **Methods of Payment** Cheque, Postal Order, Credit Card, American Express

FOLEY & FOLEY
Unit 1
1A Philip Walk
London
SE15 3NH
Telephone
0171 639 4807
Fax
0171 277 5563

Shirts for men and women

Foley & Foley is a small family firm which has been making quality shirts for 20 years. Most are traditional two-fold cotton business shirts, but there is a small range for women. They are available in collar sizes from 14½in to 17½in (ladies 10–18) with single or double cuffs, classic or button-down collars, and feature pearl buttons and long tails. Colours are plain or stripes, with some tartans for women, price £36.50 each.

Catalogue Annually, A5, Catalogue, Colour, 12 pages, Free **Postal charges** Free **Delivery** Royal Mail **Methods of Payment** Cheque, Credit Card, American Express

FUN-GAREES
Flapsdown
Top Farm
Elsham
Brigg
Humberside
DN20 ONX
Telephone
01652 688712

Children's clothes

Fun-garees offers a wonderful range of bright cotton children's clothes at reasonable prices. Each season features a choice of about four fabrics and co-ordinating sweatshirts, T-shirts and hats. You choose the colour combination. Sizes up to age 6, larger sizes on request. T-shirts, £4.99; skating skirt, £12.99; reversible sundress with shoulder ties, £20.99; long dungarees, £17.99.

Catalogue Bi-annually, A5, Catalogue, Colour, 4 pages, Free **Postal charges** £1 per garment; free on orders of more than £100 **Delivery** Royal Mail, Parcelforce **Methods of Payment** Credit Card, Cheque

GALE CLASSIC CLOTHES
Dill House
69 Priory Street
Corsham
Wiltshire
SN13 0AS
Telephone
01249 712241
Fax
same

Traditional children's clothes

Gale's clothes are intended for children from birth to 6 years. All the garments are individually made from natural fibre fabrics. The range includes matinée coats, daygowns, smocked dresses, rompers, breeches, dungarees, pinafores, sailor suits and christening gowns. An infant daygown costs from £69.10 while a romper for an 18-month-old baby is £49.40. Deep-smocked dresses for 4-year-olds are £74.70 while a christening gown/coat is £105.50.

Catalogue A5, Catalogue, B/W, 16 pages, Free **Postal charges** UK orders under £100.00, add £4.00. Overseas orders, add £4.00 **Delivery** Parcelforce **Methods of Payment** Cheque, Postal Order

GOLLY GOSH DESIGNS LTD
Monkhurst Farm
Sandy Cross Lane
Heathfield
East Sussex
TN32 5JW
Telephone
01435 867307
Fax
01435 865731

Classic children's clothes

Jenny Grubb started Golly Gosh in 1987 on her own at home and it has proved so successful that she has now joined together with a team of helpers so that she can get on with creating new designs, such as Jacamanda, an exclusive 'limited edition' collection. All the clothes are 100% cotton unless otherwise specified and will wash and wear well. Accessories include socks, belts, hairbands and scrunchies. Golly Gosh has recently also added designs for older children aged 7–14 years to its collection which ranges from babies. There are girls' and boys' ranges, with the fabric in the boys' shirts and shorts matching that of the girls' dresses and skirts.

Catalogue Quarterly, A4, Brochure, Colour, 16 pages, Free **Postal charges** £3.95; orders over £200, free **Delivery** Royal Mail, Parcelforce **Methods of Payment** Cheque, Postal Order, Credit Card, COD

THE GRANDFATHER SHIRT COMPANY
10 Willan Drive
Portrush
Co Antrim
Northern Ireland
BT56 8PU
Telephone
01265 823697

Gleneske shirts

The Grandfather Shirt Company specialises in Gleneske Original Irish Grandfather shirts. For generations, the Gleneske shirt has been a traditional part of everyday life in rural Ireland; 100% cotton, fully shrunk with fast colours, the Gleneske offers warmth, comfort and durability. It is probably as fashionable as it is practical. The shirts are also available for children.

GRATTAN PLC
Ingleby Road
Bradford
West Yorkshire
BD99 2FP
Telephone
01274 575511

Women's wear

Class '95 was Grattan's first high-quality fashion catalogue offering women luxurious silks and fashionable linen mixes at affordable prices. There was a linen-mix trouser suit in navy with white maritime ribbon trim for £119.99; a sleeveless double-breasted denim dress with hemline vents for £49.99; and a glamorous navy and white off-

Fax
01274 574497

the-shoulder sweater for £29.99. After you have obtained your customer number, the easiest way to order is by telephoning 0345 444333. Credit terms are available.

Catalogue Bi-annually, Catalogue, Colour, 43 pages, Free **Postal charges** Free **Delivery** Royal Mail, Parcelforce **Methods of Payment** Credit Card, Cheque, Postal Order

'GRIZZLY BEAR' KIDDIES WEAR
Elmhurst House
Bradley Lane
Bradley
Staffordshire
ST18 9DN
Telephone
01785 780126

Girls' wear from 0–8 years

'Grizzly Bear' design and manufacture quality garments for little girls aged 0–8 years. The 'Goldilocks' designer collection is a range of pretty dresses and separates for that extra special occasion Only the highest quality fabrics and trims are used bought mainly from UK suppliers. Their pretty floral prints for sun dresses, playsuits, skirts and smocks are complimented by matching hats. Prices range from a 'Goldilocks' hat £12.95 to a lemon fruit print suit at £43.95.

Catalogue Bi-annually, A4, Brochure, Colour, 8 pages, Free **Postal charges** £2.50 **Delivery** Royal Mail **Methods of Payment** Cheque, Postal Order

HANRO DIRECT
PO Box 5
Olney
Buckinghamshire
MK46 5LE
Telephone
01234 241499
Fax
01234 240158

Underwear

Hanro Direct uses fine-quality cotton yarn, sometimes with Lycra, to produce a range of well-made up-to-the-minute underwear for women. Choose from briefs (from £11), vests (from £18.50), crop-top bras (from £12) and bodies (from £20), in white or black and, in some designs, blush. For chilly days, Hanro also offers a range of lingerie in merino wool and silk: vest, £29.50; ankle-length brief, £52.50.

Catalogue Annually, A4, Catalogue, Colour and B/W, 10 pages, Free **Postal charges** £2.50; free for orders of more than £150 **Delivery** Royal Mail **Methods of Payment** Credit Card, Cheque

HAWKSHEAD COUNTRYWEAR

Rothay Road
Ambleside
Cumbria
LA22 0HQ
Telephone
01539 434000
Fax
01539 431100

Classic casualwear for men and women

An established Lake District company, Hawkshead focuses on well-designed countrywear for women and men. Choose from everyday shorts, T-shirts and jumpers, or smarter dresses, blouses, trousers and jackets, and an attractive range of footwear. Ladies' Microfibre jacket, £39; white cotton blouse, £15; cotton-rich trousers, £19; cotton crew-neck jumper, £19; men's Strollabout leather lace-up shoes, £32.

Catalogue Quarterly, A4, Catalogue, Colour, 48 pages, Free **Postal charges** £2.95 **Delivery** Royal Mail, Parcelforce **Methods of Payment** Cheque, Postal Order, Credit Card, Switch

HERBERT JOHNSON

30 New Bond Street
London
W1Y 9HD
Telephone
0171 408 1174
Fax
0171 495 3655

Traditional headwear and accessories

This is where you will find those sartorial necessities of the sporting and social calendar: bowler hats, Homburgs, racing Trilbys, Scottish tweed hats and caps, Panamas, cashmere scarves and couture millinery, all exquisitely made from the finest materials. Herbert Johnson supplies royalty and regiments and has been known to fit out Inspector Clouseau and Indiana Jones. Bowler hat, £135; silk top hat, from £495; wide brim Fedora, £140; Panama, from £55; French beret, £20.

Catalogue Annually, A5, Catalogue, Colour, 12 pages, Free **Postal charges** Varies with item **Delivery** Royal Mail **Methods of Payment** Cheque, Credit Card, American Express, Diners Club

HERITAGE CASHMERE LTD

8 Hirst Lane
Mirfield
West Yorkshire
WF14 8NS

Cashmere products

Cashmere by Heritage is a unique concept whereby the company purchases the finest Chinese raw material to produce a superb garment at the keenest price. All the knitwear and accessories are expertly manufactured in Scotland and

Telephone
01924 490044
Fax
01924 492637

renowned for their quality. The ladies' two-ply 100% cashmere cardigan and men's two-ply 100% cashmere crew and V-neck pullovers all cost £99. Any two of these cost £175. There's also a ladies' cashmere stole in camel or black, 75in x 28in, for £85; and scarves, 12in x 55in, for £25.

Catalogue A5, Catalogue, Colour, 6 pages, Free **Postal charges** £4.50 for knitwear orders, £1.50 for gloves, scarves and socks **Delivery** Parcelforce **Methods of Payment** Cheque, Credit Card, Switch

HIGGINBOTHAM
PO Box 121
Diss
Norfolk
IP21 4JN
Telephone
01379 668833

Nightwear for men and women

Higginbotham offers pyjamas, nightshirts, kimonos and dressing gowns, made from the finest cotton poplin and based on patterns that have been used for generations. Available in stripe colours of red/white, blue/white, green/red on white, and white on blue. Prices range from £45 for a woman's nightshirt to £75 for a man's dressing gown.

Catalogue Annually, A4, Brochure, Colour, 3 pages, Free **Postal charges** £3 **Delivery** Royal Mail **Methods of Payment** Cheque, Postal Order, Credit Card, Switch

HIGH AND MIGHTY
The Old School House
High Street
Hungerford
Berkshire
RG17 0NF
Telephone
0800 521542
Fax
01488 684912

Clothes for big or tall men

The High and Mighty catalogue brings well-made, fashionable clothes and designer names within reach of big and tall men. For the business executive and man about town the collection is classic and elegant. Chinos, jeans and shorts also feature. Navy cotton/polyester jacket, £159, and matching trousers, £69; plain shirt, £19.95; linen-mix waistcoat, £55.

Catalogue Bi-annually, A4, Catalogue, Colour, 16 pages, Free **Postal charges** £3.30 for orders up to £60; £5 on orders of more than £60 **Delivery** Royal Mail, Parcelforce **Methods of Payment** Cheque, Credit Card, American Express, Diners Club

HIT THE SAC
Clark House
Ashmansworth
Newbury
Berkshire
RG15 9SJ
Telephone
01635 254444

Nightwear for the 9–14s
Are your children tired of toon characters on their pyjamas? Hit the Sac is a new company producing nightwear for the fashion-conscious rising teens – a group long overlooked by the clothes world. Their stylish unisex designs are made from 100% cotton jersey and are practical and comfortable as well as being suitably sophisticated! The T-shirt style Midnight Arch and long-sleeved Doc Tops designs are available with a choice of bottoms: Jams (short) or Bags (long) and in a choice of colours: teal or navy.

Catalogue A4, Leaflets, Colour, 1 page, Free **Postal charges** UK £1.50; Europe £2.50 **Delivery** Royal Mail **Methods of Payment** Cheque

HOME SHOPPING DIRECT
53 Dale Street
Manchester
M60 6ES
Telephone
0161 2365511

Ladies' fashions
A complete range of ladies' fashion and underwear in sizes 12 to 26. This catalogue contains a wide range of up-to-the-minute fashions with longline waistcoats from £21.99 to beachwear to fit sizes up to 18, swimsuits from £19.99. Pack of 2 big tops (T-shirts) for £10.99.

Catalogue Bi-annually, Third A4, Brochure, Colour, 48 pages, Free **Postal charges** Free **Methods of Payment** Cheque, Postal Order, Credit Card Switch

JACAMANDA
Monkhurst Farm
Sandy Cross Lane
Heathfield
East Sussex
TN21 8QR
Telephone
01435 867307
Fax
01435 865731

Children's clothes
Jacamanda uses, as much as possible, the Best of British in classic designs and quality and pays attention to detail and the best materials. They try to supply garments in 100% cotton or pure wool. High-quality classic clothes for children such as a smocked dress for ages 2–10 years £38.95, a hardwearing tweed jacket for boys age 5–14 years £69.95, corduroy trousers for boys age 2–14 years £25.95.

Catalogue Bi-annually, A4, Brochure, Colour, 7 pages, Free **Postal charges** £3.95, orders over £200 free **Delivery** Royal Mail **Methods of Payment** Credit Card, Cheque, Postal Order, American Express

JAKE
19 Cleaver Street
London
SE11 4DP
Telephone
0171 735 7577
Fax
0171 582 2876

Ladies' clothes

Jake mail-order is a well-known name to Sunday-magazine readers, who will recognise the stylish ads offering up-to-the-minute, stylish clothes at reasonable prices. The outfits are not high fashion, but neither are they boring – Jake offers classic clothes in the latest fabrics and designs almost as soon as the catwalks have heralded a new way of dressing.

You will always look smart and well-dressed in a Jake outfit and the catalogue offers a well-balanced selection from jeans, dresses and shirts to jackets, silk scarves and skirts. They also have jewellery and belts for sale. Sizes range from 10–16 with a body measurement chart included to help you.

Catalogue Quarterly, A4, Catalogue, Colour, 20 pages, Free **Delivery** Royal Mail **Methods of Payment** Cheque, Postal Order, Credit Card

JAMES MEADE
FREEPOST (SN 1676)
Andover
Hampshire
SP10 3JL
Telephone
01264 333222
Fax
01264 363200

Classic women's clothing

James Meade boasts 'Jermyn Street quality at affordable prices'. The catalogue features shirts in a choice of sleeve lengths, blouses, skirts, trousers, knitwear, nightdresses and accessories in classic styles and quality fabrics. White poplin shirt, £29.50; Egyptian cotton twill shirt, £45; silk blouse with wrap collar, £79.50; wool crêpe pleated skirt, £75; Liberty print viscose dress, £89.50; tartan cardigan, £69.50.

Catalogue Quarterly, A4, Catalogue, Colour, 24 pages, Free **Postal charges** £2 **Delivery** Royal Mail **Methods of Payment** Cheque, Credit Card

JANET REGER
2 Beauchamp Place
London
SW3 1NG
Telephone
0171 584 9360
Fax
0171 581 7946

Lingerie and nightwear

Janet Reger is famous for her luxurious and covetable lingerie and this catalogue shows it off to its best advantage. Descriptions with sizes and colour availability are shown on the same page as the garments, which range from wired bras, mini slips, suspender belts, briefs and G-strings to pyjamas, nightdresses and robes. Prices range from £3.50 for a pair of stockings to £499 for a Hayworth coat in silk satin. Briefs cost from £32; a wired bra is £53.

Catalogue Annually, A4, Catalogue, Colour and B/W, 24 pages, Free **Postal charges** £5 **Delivery** Royal Mail **Methods of Payment** Cheque, Postal Order, Credit Card, American Express

JEAN JERRARD
Designer House
Lime Street
Bingley
Yorkshire
BD97 1AD
Telephone
01274 566666

Clothes and accessories

The Jean Jerrard catalogue offers a wide range of practical, reasonably priced clothes, leisure wear, lingerie and accessories for men and women who are fuller figured or under 5'2" tall. Sizes go from 12 up to 30 and the colours are bright and attractive (two-piece caramel suit, £44.99, floral tie-back dress, £19.99), but garments in the larger sizes (24 to 28) are more expensive.

Catalogue Quarterly, A4, Catalogue, Colour, 120 pages
Methods of Payment Cheque, Postal Order, Credit Card

JOHN BROCKLEHURST
Bridge Street
Bakewell
Derbyshire
DE45 1DS
Telephone
01629 812089
Fax
01629 814777

Men's clothes

John Brocklehurst specialises in quality, traditional British clothing for men. The look is mostly 'gentleman farmer' with plenty of checked shirts, cord trousers and sports jackets. There is also a range of high-class leather footwear, waistcoats and even plus-twos. Prices are good for this quality, with shirts from £9.95 (three for £27.90); twill trousers £69.95; corduroys £47.50; and weatherproof brogues, £105.

CLOTHES

Catalogue Quarterly, A4, Catalogue, Colour, 28 pages, Free **Postal charges** Varies with item **Delivery** Parcelforce, Courier **Methods of Payment** Cheque, Postal Order, Credit Card, American Express

JOHNSTONS OF ELGIN
Newmill
Elgin
Moray
IV30 2AF
Telephone
01343 554040
Fax
01343 554080

Cashmere wool clothing
The finest of cashmere garments with ladies' round-neck cable sweater £199, men's V-necked cardigan £139 and a beautiful fine 100% cashmere stole at £125. These traditionally knitted designs will enhance any discerning buyer's wardrobe.
Catalogue Annually, A4, Catalogue, Colour, 15 pages, Free **Postal charges** UK £3 **Methods of Payment** Cheque, Switch, Credit Card, American Express, Postal Order

JOJO
134 Lots Road
London
SW10 0RJ
Telephone
0171 351 4112
Fax
0171 352 7089

Maternity and babywear and nursery equipment
JoJo offers bright, fun beachwear, comfortable separates, city suits and smart dresses, for mothers-to-be. Easy-fit jacket, £34.99, and matching trousers, £26.99; grandad top, £18.99; wrap skirt, £18.99, and matching bandeau, £5.99; print dress, £39.99. It also offers babywear essentials for 0-24 months (leggings with feet, £4.99; shorts £5.99; dungarees, £8.99) and a limited range of nursery equipment including baby carriers, £18.99; changing bags, £15.99; table seats, £21.99; bouncy chairs, £18.99; and a Torben cot, £129.
Catalogue Bi-annually, A4, Catalogue, Colour, 24 pages, Free **Postal charges** For orders up to £24.99, add £1.95; for orders over £25, add £2.95 **Delivery** Royal Mail, Parcelforce **Methods of Payment** Cheque, Postal Order, Credit Card

JOLI JOLIE
De Bertrands
La Fosse
St Martin's

Children's clothes
These classic, easy-to-wear styles are handmade in pure cottons and pure wools for children aged from 2 years. Fabrics include seersucker tartans,

Guernsey
Channel Islands
GY4 6EE
Telephone
01481 36977
Fax
01481 65757

navy poplin and plain twills. Each item is individually handmade to order. The pinafore dress has a high-cut crossover front and buttons on the shoulders and sides (from £25.60). Trousers and shorts have double pleats and optional braces (from £14.40) and the popular full swing skirt has an elasticated waist and sideseam pockets (from £14.40).

Catalogue A5, Leaflets, Colour, 4 pages, Free **Postal charges** UK and Eire: for orders up to £50.00; add £1.50; for orders over £50.00, add £3.00. **Delivery** Parcelforce **Methods of Payment** Cheque, Postal Order

JOLLIMAN
FREEPOST (BR1414)
Worthing
West Sussex
BN11 3BR
Telephone
01903 202944
Fax
01903 209926

Men's clothing

Jolliman's clothes are conservative, well-made and perhaps best suited to those 30-plus. Many items are manufactured in Britain and these are indicated in the catalogue by Union Jacks. There is a good range of trousers and shirts as well as sweaters, slippers and socks, underwear, dressing gowns and pyjamas. For outdoors there are fleeces, waterproof jackets and hats. Rustic quilted jacket, £24.99; cord trousers, from £26.99; worsted trousers, from £25.99; poly/cotton shirt, £11.98 for two (Spring saver). For women, there are slacks from £11.99.

Catalogue Quarterly, A5, Catalogue, Colour, 36 pages, Free **Postal charges** £2.49 **Delivery** Royal Mail **Methods of Payment** Cheque, Postal Order, COD, Credit Card

JUDITH GLUE
25 Broad Street
Kirkwall
Orkney
Scotland
KW15 1DH
Telephone
01856 876263

Orkney knitwear and high quality gifts, crafts

Living and working in the remote Orkney islands in Scotland, Judith designs and manufactures a range of knitwear based on Orkney's rich archaeological heritage and landscape. The Shetland, Donegal, sloppy Joe sweater starts at £46.80. The Hebridean patchwork tweed jacket costs £189.95 and the enormous fleecy lined 'puffin'

Fax
01856 874225

sweatshirt costs £29.95. To complement the knitwear collection there are mugs, brooches (the tartan sheep brooch costs £8.50), and malt whiskies.

Catalogue Annually, A4, Catalogue, Colour, 46 pages, Free **Postal charges** Under £20.00, add £1.75; £20.00-£85.00, add £3.85; over £85.00, free. UK only **Delivery** Royal Mail **Methods of Payment** Cheque, Credit Card, American Express, Switch

KENT & CAREY
Camberwell Business Centre
Lomond Grove
Camberwell
London
SE5 7HN
Telephone
0171 703 1948

Children's clothes

Kent & Carey last year joined forces with The General Clothing Company, which also makes clothes for children. Nightwear features prominently in K&C's tasteful collection of children's wear. The Seashore range includes a dressing gown lined in terry towelling (from £41.90). The floral rosebud short-sleeved nightdress in 100% cotton jersey starts at £27.90; the boys' short pyjamas start at £27.90 (long, £29.90). The 'Sleepycozy' continental sleeping bag for babies aged 3–24 months, approved by the Cot Death Society, is available in a choice of designs and costs from £39.95.

Catalogue Bi-annually, A4, Catalogue, Colour, 6 pages, Free **Postal charges** Orders excluding robes, add £3.00; orders including robes, add £7.00 **Delivery** Royal Mail, Parcelforce **Methods of Payment** Cheque, Credit Card

KIDS' STUFF
10 Hensmans Hill
Clifton
Bristol
Avon
BS8 4PE
Telephone
0117 970 6095

Children's clothes

Kids' Stuff has a great range of comfortable, co-ordinated, good-value casual clothes that will stand up to all those washes. Plain T-shirts, from £5.70 for a one-year old to £8.10 for an 11–12 year old; leggings from £4.50; cycle shorts from £4.90; pinafore dresses from £11; striped trousers from £11.60. Trendy youngsters will also be able to sleep easy and in the smartest of company – not only are colourful print, cotton jersey pyjamas on offer (from £10.50) but teddy gets to wear a matching pair, too (£3.20; or with bear, £9.20).

Catalogue Bi-annually, A5, Catalogue, Colour, 16 pages, Free **Postal charges** Free **Delivery** Royal Mail, Parcelforce **Methods of Payment** Cheque, Postal Order, Credit Card

KINGS OF MAIDENHEAD
18 Ray Street
Maidenhead
Berkshire
SL6 8PW
Telephone
01628 29283
Fax
same

Barbour country clothing

Kings of Maidenhead are Barbour specialists. J. Barbour & Sons have been manufacturing the world's best outdoor clothing for nearly a century. Their now familiar range of clothing consists of 16 specially designed waxed coats as well as trousers, jumpers, socks, boots and other accessories. They offer the 'Border' jacket for £139.95, the 'Pennine shooting waistcoat' for £36.95 and a Loden coat for £285.00.

Catalogue A6, Catalogue, Colour, 82 pages, Free **Postal charges** Orders up to £29.99, add £3.50; orders over £30.00, free **Delivery** Royal Mail **Methods of Payment** Cheque, Credit Card, American Express, Postal Order

THE KINGSHILL COLLECTION LTD
The British Designer Collections
FREEPOST
Great Missenden
Buckinghamshire
HP16 0BR
Telephone
01494 890555
Fax
01494 866003

British designer fashion

Kingshill's line-up of designer names both national and international – Jean Muir Studio, Caroline Charles, Bellville Sassoon, Amanda Wakeley, Paul Costelloe, Betty Jackson, Roland Klein, Paddy Campbell, Georgina von Etzdorf, Ben de Lisi, English Eccentrics, Joseph, and Tomasz Starzewski – is very impressive indeed. As is their catalogue: a hardcover brochure with stylish photographs showing covetable clothes. Each designer is pictured at the front of their section and items are often shown worn in more than one way.

There is also a fabulous array of accessories and jewellery from top labels such as Georgina von Etzdorf, Anya Hindmarch, Shakira Caine, Mulberry, Farah Lister and Annabel Jones. Prices are in line with the profile of the famous designers' names. For example, Amanda Wakeley cashmere and cotton V-neck sweater with satin cuffs, £278.00; Jean Muir navy blue wool crêpe unlined tapered trousers with elasticated waist, £196.00.

Kingshill have also recently produced a gift brochure with beautiful gifts selected by Jane Churchill; a Diffusion catalogue with 90 pages of designer fashions, still straight from the catwalks and the designers' collections; and a small men's catalogue. The emphasis in Diffusion is more on casual and businesswear while still carrying some evening wear. Designers include Paul Costelloe Dressage range, Caroline Charles jeans, Jaeger London, Browns Own Label, Benny Ong, Artwork, Joseph Basics, Ally Capellino Hearts of Oak and John Smedley. The men's catalogue features classic sweaters, cords and outerwear from Mulberry, Kent & Curwen, Sam Browne, Tom Scott and John Smedley and quirky cufflinks from Tateossian.

Catalogue Bi-annually, 22.5x25mm, Catalogue, Colour, 134 pages, £5 **Postal charges** £5; Saturday, £5 extra; free over £500 **Delivery** Royal Mail **Methods of Payment** Cheque, Postal Order, Credit Card, American Express, Switch

KINLOCH ANDERSON
Highland Dress Shop
Commercial Street/Dock Street
Leith
Edinburgh
Scotland
EH6 6EY
Telephone
0131 555 1390

Highland dress

Established since 1868, Kinloch Anderson have three royal warrants. The Kinloch Anderson kilt is made to measure and contains seven or eight yards of the best quality Worsted (from £260) or Fine Saxony (from £240) cloth. There is an extensive selection of tartans in modern, ancient and reproduction or muted colourings for day wear and evening wear. A man's kilt jacket for day

Fax
0131 555 1392

wear costs from £145 and for evening wear from £235. Accessories such as sporrans, kilt pins, and skean dhus are also available.

Catalogue Annually, A5, Catalogue, Colour, 10 pages, Free **Postal charges** Varies with item **Delivery** Parcelforce **Methods of Payment** Cheque, Credit Card, Diners Club, American Express

KRUCIAL KIDS
56A Woodford Avenue
Ilford
Essex
1G2 6XF
Telephone
0181 550 4933
Fax
0181 551 4927

Maternity lingerie and toys

Krucial Kids distributes the Bellybra, designed to relieve weight strain on the lower back and abdomen during pregnancy. Price from £34.99. It also sells innovative play-stations and activity centres for children, made by the award-winning Canadian firm Educo International. Called Supermaze, these mazes of rigid coloured wires bent into intriguing shapes, threaded with coloured balls and set into smooth wooden bases offer hours of entertainment. Price from £45. It distributes Wimmer-Ferguson toys from America, too.

Catalogue Annually, A4, Catalogue, Colour, 8 pages, Free **Postal charges** Free **Delivery** Royal Mail, Parcelforce **Methods of Payment** Cheque, Postal Order

LA REDOUTE
PO Box 777
Wakefield
Yorkshire
WF2 8XZ
Telephone
0500 777 777

General clothes catalogue

La Redoute offers clothes for all the family, very up-to-the-minute and with a French flair, all in continental sizes but with a chart at the back of the catalogue for conversion to English sizes. Ladies', gent's, children's and baby clothes are all featured, from outerwear to underwear and shoes. A reefer jacket in a variety of colours and sizes for ladies for £79.99; Naf Naf underwear for children, packs of 2 vest tops from £6.99, cotton/polyester shirts for men £12.99, all in plain colours. Bonpoint, Petit Boy, A L'heure Anglaise, Rendery, Donna di Cuori are just some of the names that feature in this catalogue.

Catalogue Annually, A4, Catalogue, Colour, 642 pages, Free **Postal charges** Free **Delivery** In-house delivery **Methods of Payment** Postal Order, Cheque, Credit Card Switch

LAETITIA ALLEN LTD
26 Adam and Eve Mews
London
W8 6UJ
Telephone
0171 221 0140
Fax
0171 221 0626

Lingerie
Launched in 1993, this collection is available exclusively by mail order. Laetitia Allen commissions her designs from British designers and sources easy-care fabrics both here and in Europe. All the designs are flattering, comfortable and made with meticulous attention to detail. Items arrive beautifully packaged and a special gift wrap, together with a card, is available for a modest charge. Orders are usually despatched on the day they are received, with next-day delivery offered as an option.

Catalogue Bi-annually, Catalogue, Colour, 16 pages pages, Free **Postal charges** P & P £2.50; optional 24-hour delivery £10; optional gift wrap £3 **Methods of Payment** Cheque, Postal Order, Credit Card, American Express

LANDS' END DIRECT MERCHANTS
Pillings Road
Oakham
Rutland
Leicestershire
LE15 6NY
Telephone
0800 220106
Fax
01572 722554

Clothes
Lands' End Direct Merchants UK Ltd is a wholly-owned subsidiary of an American company and has quality as its number one priority. The clothes are simple, well-made classics and include swimwear (from £36 for women, £22.50 for men), 100% cotton square rigger shorts for men (£24), and the cotton jersey-knit 'Skort', a supremely comfortable cross between shorts and a skirt that has an elasticated waistband and two onseam pockets (£21). For girls, there's a cotton 'Super-T dress' from £14 and colourful cotton shorts for boys and girls from £10.

**LAURA ASHLEY
BY POST**
PO Box 5
Newtown
Powys
SY16 1WW
Telephone
0800 868 100
Fax
01686 621273

Catalogue Bi-annually, A4, Catalogue, Colour, 83 pages, Free **Postal charges** £2.95 **Delivery** Royal Mail **Methods of Payment** Cheque, Postal Order, Credit Card, American Express

Clothes

Laura Ashley have shops all round the world but also offer a mail-order service. The fashion catalogue features T-shirts, dresses, trousers, leggings, wrap-over skirts, shorts and jumpers, as well as shoes, belts and socks. Woven espradilles cost £9.95; cotton crew-neck T-shirt, £9.95; casual printed trousers, £29.95; printed swimsuit, £19.95; 100% cotton button-through indigo twill dress, £64.95. The Winter 1995 48-page catalogue featured velvet close-fitting tops, taffeta skirts, merino jumpers, knit swing dresses, embroidered cardigans, nightwear, and a small range of Christmas gifts.

There is also a Laura Ashley Home catalogue, which costs £3.50 from the same address and telephone number.

Catalogue Quarterly, A4, Catalogue, Colour, 91 pages, £1.50 **Postal charges** Up to £150.00, add £2.95; over £150.00, free **Delivery** Parcelforce **Methods of Payment** Cheque, Postal Order, Credit Card, American Express

LITTLE ELEFANT KIRI
493 Fulham Palace Road
London
SW6 6SU
Telephone
0171 610 6830

Individually styled childrenswear

In business for more than five years by mail order, Little Elefant Kiri also has a shop at the same address. All the girls' and boys' outfits are made using the best quality fabrics sourced from a variety of European countries. They range from 6 months to 10 years and although there isn't a large selection, they include everything from flower dresses, a cord pinny with matching hat, Peter Pan shirts and tartan trousers to reversible winter coats, rosebud blouses, dungarees, dressing gowns and pyjamas. Prices are reasonable and quality of manufacture good.

Catalogue Bi-annually, A4, Catalogue, Colour, 12 pages, Free **Postal charges** £2.50 **Delivery** Royal Mail **Methods of Payment** Switch, Credit Card, Postal Order, Cheque

LITTLE TREASURES
10 Braemar Crescent
Leigh-on-Sea
Essex
SS9 3RL
Telephone
01702 559005

Women's and children's clothes

Little Treasures provides individually handmade traditional clothes and a range of co-ordinating cotton knitwear for children. It has recently been joined by its Treasures range of womenswear, so mothers, too, can buy the beautifully made frilled blouses and tiered skirts for themselves. Little girl's floral, tartan or gingham dress with pique collar, from £28 (sizes 2–12 years); boy's breeches, from £16 (18 months–6 years); baby romper, from £26; Guernsey cotton sweater, from £22.50 children, £56 adult.

Catalogue Bi-annually, A5, Catalogue, Colour, 16 pages, Free **Postal charges** £2 for orders up to £75; £4 for orders up to £150; free on orders of more than £150 **Delivery** Royal Mail **Methods of Payment** Cheque, Postal Order, Credit Card

LONG TALL SALLY
Unit B
Pioneers Industrial Park
Beddington Farm Road
Croydon
Surrey
CR0 4XB
Telephone
0181 689 9000

Fashionable clothes for tall women

Careful attention to cut, design and proportion ensure that everything in Long Tall Sally's collection will fit women over 5ft 9in tall. Up-to-date styles, colours and fabrics are featured in their seasonal fashion catalogues, while everyday items such as trousers, jeans and classic suiting are available from the Essentials range. Sizes range from 10 to 22 and prices are competitive with leading fashion houses. Prices start at £59.95 for a classic gaberdine jacket; £29.95 for extra-long jeans. The collection includes casualwear, co-ordinates and separates as well as dresses, coats, swimwear and eveningwear.

Catalogue Quarterly, A4, Catalogue, Colour, 21 pages, Free **Postal charges** Orders up to £30, £1.95; over £30, £2.95; over £150, free **Delivery** Royal Mail, Parcelforce **Methods of Payment** Cheque, Credit Card, American Express, Diners Club, Postal Order, Switch

MacCULLOCH & WALLIS LTD
PO Box W1A 2DX
Dering Street
London
W1A 2DX
Telephone
0171 409 3506
Fax
0171 409 2481

Bridal wear
MacCulloch & Wallis have been in business since 1902, selling fabrics and silks. They now offer a unique service by mail – silk wedding dress kits. For just £99, you get the pattern, the silk ivory dupion, the lining and all the necessary haberdashery. All five styles are simple yet stunning. Tulle veiling is also available at £3 per metre.

Catalogue Catalogue, Colour, 9 pages, Free **Postal charges** Free **Delivery** Royal Mail **Methods of Payment** Cheque, Credit Card

MADE IN AMERICA
Unit 5B
Hathaway Retail Park
Chippenham
Wiltshire
SN15 1JG
Telephone
01249 447558
Fax
01249 446142

American clothes, foods and gifts
Made In America's catalogue contains all things American from casual sportswear to ceramic mugs featuring different breeds of dogs. Clothes include Oshkosh for children (dungarees, £19.99) and a men's Golden Bear brown leather bomber jacket (£350). You can order a mailbox complete with mounting post for £19.99, or a life-size cardboard cut-out of a Star Trek character for £24.99. And for those who yearn for an American breakfast, try Albers Quick Grits, £1.91, Betty Crocker's wild blueberry muffin mix, £6.75, and maple syrup, £1.69.

Catalogue Bi-annually, A5, Catalogue, B/W, 6 pages, Free **Postal charges** Varies with item **Delivery** Royal Mail, Parcelforce **Methods of Payment** Cheque, Postal Order, Credit Card

MAVERICK MAIL ORDER
Mill House
Brookend Street
Ross-on-Wye
Herefordshire
HR9 7EG
Telephone
01989 768650
Fax
01989 768563

Country clothes for women, men and children
The Maverick catalogue contains a collection of essential country clothing from British manufacturers, selected for quality, style and practicality. This is where you will find a Musto Highland jacket for men, £270; women's corduroy breeches, £49; and for children an indispensable tartan duvet waistcoat from £30.
Catalogue Annually, A4, Catalogue, Colour, 15 pages, Free **Postal charges** Free **Delivery** Royal Mail, Parcelforce **Methods of Payment** Cheque, Credit Card

MIDNIGHT LADY
20–24 Cardigan Street
Luton
Bedfordshire
LU1 1RR
Telephone
01582 391854
Fax
01582 454022

Sexy lingerie
Midnight Lady produces three catalogues, each offering different varieties of exotic lingerie. As they say, 'No girl knows how daring she will be' – until she sees this collection of raunchy garments. Suspender tights, £2.40; briefs, open crotch, £8.25; six-strap suspender belt, £11.70; bra, quarter cup, £14.55; stretch dress, £22.80.
Catalogue Annually, A4, Catalogue, Colour, 12 pages, Free **Postal charges** Free **Delivery** Royal Mail **Methods of Payment** Cheque, Credit Card

MONCKTON LTD
FREEPOST TY297
Pitlochry
PH17 2BR
Telephone
0500 633232
Fax
01882 633319

Shirts and accessories for men
Monckton make traditional Jermyn Street shirts with real pearl buttons, in a range of plain colours, classic stripes and more adventurous stripes. By buying in bulk, 6 shirts can be purchased for £29 each instead of £35 for a single purchase. This company also supplies silk ties from £22.95, socks from £7, cuff links from £30.95. Additional to their range for more informal occasions are boxer shorts at 3 pairs for £21.95 and pyjamas at £95.
Catalogue Annually, A5, Brochure, Colour, 16 pages, Free **Postal charges** £3.50 **Delivery** Royal Mail **Methods of Payment** Cheque, Postal Order, Credit Card, Switch

MUJI

26 Great Marlborough Street
London
W1V 1HL
Telephone
0171 494 1197
Fax
0171 494 1193

Stationery, clothes and accessories

For the minimalist look, Muji's catalogue of simply and effectively designed products is the one. Muji opened in Tokyo in 1983 and now has four shops in the UK selling a range of functional, uncluttered stationery, household goods, furniture, clothes, belts, bags and watches. Clever cardboard storage drawers, from £7.95; acrylic magazine holder, £10.95; plastic cosmetic bottle, 95p; zinc box, £22.50; cotton T-shirt, £9.50; nylon bucket bag, from £14.95; sofa, £475.

Catalogue Annually, A3, Catalogue, Colour, 8 pages, Free **Postal charges** Varies with item **Delivery** Royal Mail, Parcelforce **Methods of Payment** Cheque, Credit Card, American Express, Diners Club

MUMS2BE

3 Mortlake Terrace
Mortlake Road
Kew
Richmond
Surrey
TW9 3DT
Telephone
0181 332 6506

Maternity clothes

The stock at Mums2Be is tailored for the fashion conscious. A large collection of maternity clothes including many international labels, Blooming, Page Boy and Beuf Lune to name but a few. There is also a hire section which is invaluable for those special occasions. Outfits include ballgowns and suits for weddings. Black evening dress to buy £69.50, velour two-piece £93.50, Prince of Wales jacket £90 and matching skirt £49.50.

Catalogue Annually, A5, Brochure, Colour, 3 pages, Free **Postal charges** Free **Delivery** Royal Mail **Methods of Payment** Cheque, Postal Order, Credit Card

MYERSCOUGH-JONES OF LEIGH

8 Lonsdale Avenue
Leigh
Lancashire
WN7 3UE
Telephone
01942 674836

Lingerie

Myerscough-Jones are specialists in underwear by post. The underwear on show here is not of the glamour type, but is more practical if not entirely conservative. There's still room for a selection of 'Fantasie Lingerie'; the Renaissance collection includes an underwired bra (up to size 36E) to make the most of your credentials for just £15.50.

There are also high-legged briefs for £8.25 and a full brief for the same price. Vests cost from £17.95 and boxer panties from £14.25. There's also something called a 'Cosytop', with a 'V' neck and long sleeves, which costs from £14.95.

Catalogue A5, Leaflets, B/W, 16 pages, Free **Postal charges** Varies with item **Delivery** In-house delivery **Methods of Payment** Credit Card, Cheque, Postal Order

N. PEAL
37 Burlington Arcade
London
W1V 9AE
Telephone
0800 220 222
Fax
0171 734 1345

Cashmere collection for women and men

N. Peal is famous for its cashmere clothes and this catalogue brings together some of the popular items from its Burlington Arcade shop in London. There are tunics, cardigans, waistcoats, capes and dresses for women, and sweaters, cardigans and waistcoats for men. Women's classic cashmere mock-turtle sweater, £165; long-ribbed funnel neck dress (30% cashmere/70% wool), £195, and matching mid-calf length waistcoat, £225. Men's six-ply cashmere turtle sweater, £670.

Catalogue Quarterly, A4, Catalogue, Colour, 16 pages, Free **Postal charges** £5 **Delivery** Royal Mail, Parcelforce **Methods of Payment** Diners Club, Cheque, Credit Card, American Express, Postal Order

NATURAL FACT LTD
192 Kings Road
Chelsea
London
SW3 5UX
Telephone
0171 352 4283
Fax
0171 352 3337

Environmentally friendly clothes

Natural Fact's fashion garments come in a rich, natural cream – the colour of the original raw combed cotton yarn. Nothing is added or changed. Most of the clothing is designed to fit both men and women and comes in sizes small, medium, large and extra large. The heavyweight towelling robe is priced at £49.99; nightshirt, £19.99; sweatshirt, £19.99; shoestring body (£12.99) and boxer shorts (£9.99).

The new baby range includes a romper suit made from organic cotton (from £14.99), terry-towelling bunny and whale toys (from £12.99), and baby toiletries.

Catalogue A5, Catalogue, Colour, 14 pages, Free **Postal charges** For orders of £5.00 to £20.00, add £2.00; for orders over £20.00, add £3.00. Minimum order, £5.00 **Delivery** Royal Mail **Methods of Payment** Cheque, Credit Card

NCT MATERNITY SALES
Burnfield Avenue
Glasgow
Scotland
G46 7TL
Telephone
0141 633 5552
Fax
0141 633 5677

Mother and baby wear, gifts

The National Childbirth Trust publishes two catalogues: one concentrating on well-designed antenatal and postnatal bras and nighties, swimsuits, baby carriers, baby gowns and rompers, and the other on stationery, gifts and safety products. Its merchandise combines the latest technical and medical considerations with the lifestyles and tastes of the mothers it aims to serve and has been developed with the help of the many mothers who attend NCT antenatal classes nationwide. Mava 2 bra, £15.50; nightie, £11.75; romper, £4.75; Sleepyhead car rest, £16.95; colouring-in cards, £2.50. All profits are covenanted to the Trust.

Catalogue Annually, A5, Catalogue, Colour, 12 pages, Free **Postal charges** Varies with item **Delivery** Royal Mail, Parcelforce **Methods of Payment** Cheque, Postal Order, Credit Card

NEXT DIRECTORY
PO Box 299
Leicester
Leicestershire
LE5 5GH
Telephone
0345 100 500
Fax
0116 2738749

Men's, women's and children's clothes

The Next Directory was in the forefront of the transformation of British mail order and remains one of the most stylish ways to order clothes through the post. The catalogue itself is a well-designed hardback featuring ranges available in the high street shops. For women, a double-breasted blazer costs £99; pleated skirt, £49.99; Next brand briefs (two-pack), £9.99. For men, a suit costs £99.99 for a navy gabardine jacket and

£49.99 for the matching trousers. There is also a selection of children's wear: blue stone-washed denims for a 6 to 9-month-old baby, £8.99; lightweight jacket from £19.99. A must for any serious catalogue shopper.

Catalogue Bi-annually, A4, Catalogue, Colour, 387 pages, £3 **Postal charges** £2.50 **Delivery** Courier, Parcelforce, In-house delivery **Methods of Payment** Cheque, Stage Payments, Credit Card, American Express, Diners Club

NICOLA JANE
Lagness
Chichester
West Sussex
PO20 6LW
Telephone
01243 268686
Fax
01243 268886

Mastectomy wear

Coming to terms with breast cancer is daunting, but Nicola Jane can help you to look good with its comprehensive range of attractive, fashionable, quality mastectomy wear. The catalogue features swimsuits, bras and prostheses. Fully-trained staff are only a phone call away to offer help and advice. Swimsuits from £34.95; bras from £13.99; lightweight prosthesis, £14.99; Trulife Supreme silicone prosthesis, £92.

Catalogue Annually, A4, Catalogue, Colour, 16 pages **Postal charges** Varies with item **Delivery** Royal Mail, Parcelforce **Methods of Payment** Cheque, Postal Order, Credit Card

NIGHTINGALES
Meadowcraft Mill
Bury Road
Rochdale
Lancashire
OL11 4AU
Telephone
01706 620850
Fax
01706 620838

Women's clothes

Nightingales sells a collection of dresses, suits, skirts, blouses, evening and night wear combining exclusive British-made designs with quality, at excellent prices. Viscose/linen lined jacket, £32.99; strappy little black dress, £28.99; button-through print dress, £27.99; camisole, £9.99, and matching skirt, £15.99; cotton blouse, £14.99; pretty cotton nightdresses, from £17.99.

Catalogue Quarterly, A5, Catalogue, Colour, 32 pages, Free **Postal charges** Please add, for 1 item £1.99; for 2

items £2.99; for 3 or more items £3.99; a donation from every order received will go to Romanian orphanage project **Delivery** Royal Mail, Parcelforce **Methods of Payment** Cheque, Postal Order, Credit Card

NORFOLK HEADWEAR
140 Battersea Park Road
London
SW11 4NB
Telephone
0171 498 2099

Headwear
The Norfolk Intrepid is the ultimate outdoor hat which has been expedition tested. Made in the UK from 100% cotton, its brass gauzed eyelets keep you cool and keep bugs out! Priced at £28.50 it knocks the spots off other hats.
Catalogue Annually, A4, Leaflets, Colour, 2 pages, Free **Postal charges** £1.45 **Delivery** Royal Mail **Methods of Payment** Cheque, Postal Order, Credit Card, American Express

NORTHAMPTON FOOTWEAR DISTRIBUTORS
Summerhouse Road
Moulton Park
Northampton
Northamptonshire
NN3 1WD
Telephone
01604 790827

Shoes and boots
Northampton Footwear produce a comprehensive range of men's and women's budget footwear. There's everything here, from trainers and slippers to boots, brogues and high-heeled shoes. Their men's 'Nubuck Suede Hiking Boot' has a strong ridged rubber sole, burgundy panels at the back and hook-and-eye lacing. Sizes range from 7 to 13. Men's slippers are available in dark brown plain bri-nylon or check cord material.
Catalogue Quarterly, A4, Leaflets, Colour, 4 pages, Free **Postal charges** £6 **Delivery** Royal Mail **Methods of Payment** Cheque, Postal Order

ORKNEY ANGORA
Isle of Sanday
Orkney
Scotland
KW17 2AZ
Telephone
01857 600421

Angora thermal clothing
Orkney Angora is a family-run, croft-based business situated on one of Orkney's most northerly isles. It offers high-quality, natural-fibre thermal clothing produced from the wool of angora rabbits. A wide range of items is available including sweaters, socks and snoods, back-warmers and long johns. Angora/lambswool

CLOTHES

Fax
same

sweater in a choice of colours, £59.50; cardigan, £65; waistcoat, £45; thermal socks, from £6.99 children, £11.99 adults; shoulder-warmer, from £16.95; balaclava, from £7.99.

Catalogue Annually, A5, Catalogue, Colour and B/W, 28 pages, Free **Postal charges** £1 **Delivery** Royal Mail **Methods of Payment** Cheque, Credit Card, Postal Order

THE ORVIS COMPANY INC
The Mill
Nether Wallop
Stockbridge
Hampshire
SO20 8ES
Telephone
01264 783283
Fax
01264 783277

Clothing, fly fishing equipment and gifts

Although most of this catalogue is devoted to fishing tackle, there is a substantial section featuring casual country clothes for men and women and a gift section which includes luggage, watches and dog beds. Established since 1856, Orvis offer quality goods. Their salmon rods start at £295; kit bags from £79; disc drag reels from £23.00. Twenty flies for unknown waters cost £9.50; fly boxes from £6. Waders with integrated boot design start at £110. There are also fleece neck cushions, alarm clocks, waterproof rugs, log carriers, pewter hair brushes, cartridge cufflinks, folding magnifiers, travellers' watches, brass thermometers, loo-roll holders, pewter wine stoppers, wine racks, bellows, wall egg racks, giraffe alphabet puzzles, dog and cat angels, bear in a bag, Advent tree calendar, fleece dog toys, peanut feeders, stereo electronic earmuffs, cracker throwers, binoculars, plus a wide range of clothing for men and women.

Catalogue Bi-annually, A4, Catalogue, Colour, 67 pages, Free **Postal charges** Flies, leaders and toppets, add £2.00; all other goods, add £3.75 **Delivery** Royal Mail **Methods of Payment** Cheque, Postal Order, Credit Card, American Express

OSBORNE'S BIG MAN'S SHOP
Fore Street

Outsize menswear and shoes

Osborne's sell clothes for big and tall men, going up to 70in chest/waist, 40in inside leg and 23in

Beer
Devon
EX12 3JB
Telephone
01297 20700/23481
Fax
01297 23738

collar. They can provide dinner and formal suits in mix-and-match fittings both at their shops and by mail order. A 54–56in poly/wool mix suit costs £126.75; Club Casual Extra Tall trousers, £31; and Double Two King shirts in poly/cotton, from £24.60.

They also stock shoes, sports coats, blazers, leisure jackets and trousers and have an extensive range of formal and leisure shirts along with fancy waistcoats, workwear and underwear.

Catalogue Annually, A4, Catalogue, Colour, 31 pages, Free **Postal charges** £3.45; COD orders, £2.00 **Delivery** Royal Mail **Methods of Payment** Cheque, Postal Order, Credit Card, Switch

THE OXFORD HAT COMPANY
Avenue Three
The Covered Market
Oxford
Oxfordshire
OX1 3DY
Telephone
01865 200844/510721

Hats
A simple range of hats for any occasion. The Oxford Hat Company produces seven deep-crowned designs, with medium or wide, turned-up or flat brims, in hessian, linen or silk and decorated with bows, fabric flowers or a swathe of raffia and antique roses. They are as versatile as they are robust and will team equally well with a formal outfit or a sundress. Prices £22.50 to £39.95. You can even send your own fabric – about half a metre is needed.

Catalogue Bi-annually, Third A4, Brochure, Colour, 2 pages, Free **Postal charges** £1.50 per hat **Delivery** Royal Mail **Methods of Payment** Cheque, Credit Card

PAKEMAN CATTO & CARTER
No 5 The Market Place
Cirencester
Gloucestershire
GL7 2NX
Telephone
01285 641113

Traditional gentlemen's clothing
Pakeman Catto & Carter have been tailors since 1863 and are one of the few still to be found outside London's Savile Row. Their shop in Cirencester stocks their full range of gentlemen's clothing from shoes to hats, jackets and dressing gowns. Their catalogue contains an enticing selection of their best garments, including mole-

Fax
01285 641114

skin trousers, £52.50; waistcoats, £65; shirts, £39.50; pyjamas, £45; fishermen's sweaters, £42.50; and a range of belts, socks, ties and caps.
Catalogue Bi-annually, A5, Catalogue, Colour, 23 pages, Free **Postal charges** £3 **Delivery** Royal Mail, Parcelforce **Methods of Payment** Cheque, Credit Card, American Express

PALOMA DESIGNS
26 Liston Road
London
SW4 0DF
Telephone
0171 720 4283
Fax
0171 498 3553

Outdoor clothing

Paloma's stylish detachable sleeved jackets are water-resistant, breathable, lightweight and windproof, and are designed to give warmth without weight. They can be machine-washed and tumble-dried with no danger of shrinkage or loss of colour. A hood is concealed in the back collar of the jacket, behind a Velcro tab. Available in a choice of 5 colourways, the jackets start at £50 for children (2–4 years) and £76 for adults.
Catalogue A4, Leaflets, Colour, 1 page, Free **Postal charges** Add £4.00 for 1 garment; £6.50 for 2 garments; £9.00 for 3 garments **Delivery** Royal Mail **Methods of Payment** Cheque, Postal Order

PAMANDRA
17 Kings Avenue
St Johns
Redhill
Surrey
RH1 6QH
Telephone
01737 770815

Silk underwear

Surely nothing beats silk underwear for comfort. Pamandra sells an extensive range of bras, briefs, camisoles, French knickers, nightgowns, slips and suspenders in beautiful silks and satin, some decorated with embroidery or edged with lace. Sizes generally 10–18, but up to 22 in some designs and larger by arrangement. Annette Chinese silk with embroidery: bra (full cup), £49.95; French knickers, £45.99; negligee, £125.50.
Catalogue Annually, Third A4, Leaflets, Colour, 14 pages, Free **Postal charges** Free **Delivery** Royal Mail **Methods of Payment** Cheque, Postal Order

PATRA SELECTIONS
1–5 Nant Road
London
NW2 2AL
Telephone
0181 209 1112
Fax
0181 458 3207

Silk clothes, knitwear, underwear and nightwear
Patra specialises in machine-washable (30°C) silk clothing for women with a few styles for men. Designs are classic. Pure silk shirt, unisex, £31.95; floral skirt, £33.95; sweater, £36.95; trousers, £37.95; striped pyjamas, £49.95; silk briefs, £5.50 women, £7.50 men.
Catalogue Bi-annually, A5, Catalogue, Colour, 46 pages, Free **Postal charges** Free **Delivery** Royal Mail, Parcelforce **Methods of Payment** Cheque, Postal Order, Credit Card

PENNY PLAIN
10 Marlborough Crescent
Newcastle upon Tyne
Tyne and Wear
NE1 4EE
Telephone
0191 232 1124
Fax
0191 222 0316

Clothes for the individualist in cotton, linen, silk and wool
Penny Plain makes exclusive clothes that are designed to look good and to last. Founded in 1981 by Gillian Banyard and Christine Kerr, theirs is a largely natural-fibres catalogue – cottons, linens, silks and wool. Their range of ladies' separates, leisure wear and knitwear comes in sizes 10–22. Bali shirt, £49.94, and matching skirt, £69.95; classic linen shirt/jacket, £69.95; silk dress, £129; suede jacket, £235.
Catalogue Bi-annually, A4, Catalogue, Colour, 32 pages, Free **Postal charges** Varies with item **Delivery** Royal Mail, Parcelforce **Methods of Payment** Cheque, Postal Order, Credit Card, Switch

PERUVIAN CONNECTION
3 Manor Farm Barns
Nettlebed
Henley-on-Thames
Oxfordshire
RG9 5DA
Telephone
0800 550000
Fax
01491 642174

Art-knit from the Andes
In business for over 19 years, Peruvian Connection produces an art-knit collection for each season, from original designs that are then made by hand in the Andes. They use precious luxury yarns of alpaca and Peruvian pima cotton, rare gems of the fibre world. Each one of their original pieces takes an Andean knitter with a lifetime of experience up to a month to complete. The complexity of stitches and patterns they use in their designs would daunt most knitters. The

texture that results is unmistakably handmade. Each piece is as beautiful inside as it is outside, with every strand of yarn worked back into the fabric. Their aim is to create a collection of art knits you won't find outside of a single piece in a knitter's home studio or a thousand-dollar sweater in a European designer's atelier. The range includes sweaters, coats, waistcoats and cardigans for women and men, photographed in both still life and on models in situ. The order form is in the middle of the catalogue. Gift-wrapping in a forest green gift box is available for £3. There is a sizing chart on the order form.

Catalogue A4, Catalogue, Colour, 40 pages, Free **Postal charges** £4 per order **Methods of Payment** Cheque, Postal Order, Credit Card, American Express

PICTURE WEAR ORIGINALS
PO Box 79
Bury St Edmunds
Suffolk
IP29 4AE
Telephone
01284 735220
Fax
same

Children's clothes

These appealing brightly-coloured cotton children's clothes are designed by Alison Jump. Animals are the central theme, with plain primary co-ordinates for ages from 3 months to 6 years. Reversible jackets in cotton drill with animal print, £33; wrapover pinafore, £24.95; baby suits, £15; long shorts, £9.50.

Catalogue Annually, A4, Leaflets, Colour, 3 pages, Free **Postal charges** Varies with item **Delivery** Royal Mail **Methods of Payment** Cheque

POPPERS BY POST
Poppers (93) Ltd
PO Box 8
Fishguard
Dyfed
Wales
SA65 9YA
Telephone
01348 875156

Children's appliqued jackets

Appliquéed jackets and trousers made from top-quality fabrics such as 100% cotton corduroy and 65% poly/35% cotton with co-ordinating trim and appliqué and a winterweight padding that keeps kids really snug. They stand up to machine washing at 40°C and can be tumble-dried. There are lots of bright colours with different applique designs: dog, carousel horse, snail, racing car, jack

Fax
same

in box, Noah's ark, elephant, polar bear and Suzy Snowdrop. Cody padded trousers are available to match the jackets. The clothes fit ages 3 months up to 8 years, both boys and girls. There are retail outlets in Fishguard and Haverfordwest with further ranges of reversible pinafores, dungarees and dresses.

Catalogue A5, Catalogue, Colour, 6 pages, Free **Postal charges** £2.50 **Delivery** Royal Mail **Methods of Payment** Cheque, Postal Order, Credit Card

POPPY
44 High Street
Yarm
Cleveland
TS15 9AE
Telephone
01642 790000
Fax
01642 788235

Children's clothes, bedding and gifts

This delightful catalogue contains a selection of cotton printed clothes for babies and children with co-ordinated caps (£13.99), floppy hats, headbands, bows and duffel bags. There is something for every occasion and children will delight in choosing which way round to wear the reversible jacket (from £33.99) and whether to wear the smock over the petticoat (from £53.99 a set), or just the petticoat as a sun dress. Poppy also stocks an enchanting range of co-ordinated wallpapers (£11.95/roll), fabrics (£11.95/m), bedding (cot quilt, £33.95) and gifts (bookends, clocks, lamps) for children's nurseries, in pastels and primaries.

Catalogue Annually, A4, Catalogue, Colour, 8 pages, Free **Postal charges** Varies with item **Delivery** Royal Mail **Methods of Payment** Cheque, Credit Card

PRINGLE OF SCOTLAND
42 Garden Walk
Metro Centre
Gateshead
Tyne & Wear
TD9 7AL
Telephone
0191 4932727

Golf clothing for women and men

Pringle is famous for its distinctive golfing sweaters, but it also sells quality sports shirts, shorts, trousers, scarves and umbrellas. The colourful catalogue includes the Nick Faldo Collection, Ladies' Golf and Sports Classic Collections. Knitwear from £44.95; shirts from 28.95; Trophy umbrella, £22.95.

Fax
same

Catalogue Bi-annually, A4, Catalogue, Colour, 36 pages, Free **Postal charges** Varies with item **Delivery** Royal Mail **Methods of Payment** Cheque, Credit Card, Switch, American Express

R. NEWBOLD
7–8 Langley Court
Covent Garden
London
WC2E 9JY
Telephone
0171 240 5068
Fax
0171 379 0241

Men's clothing

R. Newbold's exceptionally stylish catalogue features a small but interesting range of men's clothing based on historical designs. There is a classic shirt with deep double cuff and generous tail, a high-button jacket, miner's trousers, a selection of jackets and a check shirt as manufactured by R. Newbold for the General Post Office. **Catalogue** Annually, A4, Catalogue, Colour and B/W, 20 pages, Free **Postal charges** Varies with item **Delivery** Royal Mail, Parcelforce **Methods of Payment** Cheque, Credit Card

RACHEL GRIMMER LTD
2 Princes Square
Harrogate
North Yorkshire
HG1 1LX
Telephone
01423 524236

Designer knitwear

Bold colours and patterns and original designs are the hallmarks of Rachel Grimmer's knitwear. Although measurements are given in standard lengths and sizes, adaptations to suit the customer's needs can be made. Designed to last a lifetime, the garments are made from wool, cotton, silk and chenille. There are 10 basic shapes including the buttoned waistcoat (£210), the raglan-sleeved button-to-neck cardigan (£225), and the 44in-51in long coat/cardigan which costs £325.
Catalogue Annually, A4, Catalogue, Colour, 22 pages, Free **Postal charges** For orders up to and including £250.00, add £6.00; orders over £250.00, free **Delivery** Royal Mail **Methods of Payment** Cheque, Postal Order, Credit Card

RACHEL RILEY
La Roche Froissard
Gennes 49350
France

Children's clothes

Rachel Riley's classic children's clothes are made in France out of cotton or wool fabrics. The Liberty lawn flowers ruched bathing suit with skirt

Telephone
00 33 41380493
Fax
00 33 41380220

and halter-neck costs from £35; 'Provencal' dress from £38. For boys, short trousers are from £18, shirts from £22, and Oxford lawn pyjamas from £26. Other items include romper suits, shoes, hats and anoraks.

Catalogue Bi-annually, A5, Catalogue, Colour, 24 pages, Free **Postal charges** £4.00 France; £5.00 rest of Europe; £9.00 elsewhere **Delivery** Royal Mail **Methods of Payment** Cheque, Credit Card

RACING GREEN
PO Box 100
Morley
Leeds
West Yorkshire
LS27 0BX
Telephone
0345 331177
Fax
0113 2382465

Clothes for women and men
A nineties' success story: Racing Green has carved a successful niche for itself selling relaxed, stylish, well-made clothes for men and women, clothes that will take you to the city office, the country or the beach. The fabrics are predominantly natural – cotton, linen and wool – with leather shoes, silk ties and straw hats. Typical products are the short-sleeve polo shirts, £17; cotton twill jeans, £32; twill dress, £30; chambray shirts, £27; swimsuits, from £20, and trunks from £18; men's navy poplin jacket, £99, and matching trousers, £39.

Catalogue Quarterly, A4, Catalogue, Colour, 84 pages, Free **Postal charges** £3 **Delivery** Royal Mail, Parcelforce **Methods of Payment** Cheque, Credit Card, American Express, Postal Order

REDISCOVERED ORIGINALS
Whitehouse Street
Leeds
West Yorkshire
LS10 1AD
Telephone
0113 2432323
Fax
0113 2467797

Clothes for men and women
Comfortable, well-made, work-a-day clothes in natural fabrics at sensible prices. Rediscovered Originals have scoured the world to bring you denim jeans for men and women (£19.98); the Wool Grower's Pullover (£34); grandad shirts (£12.50) and check shirts (17.50); Harry's wool felt hat (£26.98); a full-length suede skirt (£119); Drizza-Bone Stockman's Coat (£119); and the ultimate hip-hugging Boxer Briefs (£6.98).

Catalogue Quarterly, A5, Catalogue, Colour, 32 pages,

CLOTHES

Free **Postal charges** £1.95 for orders up to £20; £2.95 for orders of more than £20 **Delivery** Royal Mail, Parcelforce **Methods of Payment** Cheque, Postal Order, Credit Card, Switch

ROBERT NORFOLK
Dualfold Ltd
677 Gatwick Road
Crawley
West Sussex
RH10 2RD
Telephone
01293 407300
Fax
01293 407310

Casual clothes

Robert Norfolk produce a range of elegant, co-ordinated separates. Specialising in sweatshirts with various motifs from sporting to animals, they cater principally for women and children. Most of the products are made from 100% cotton and come in small, medium and large. Adult sweatshirts start at £14.95 and long-sleeved polo shirts at £27.95. For children, the Mickey and Minnie sweatshirt costs £12.95; T-shirt, £8.95; leggings, £8.95.

Catalogue Bi-annually, A4, Catalogue, Colour, 31 pages, Free **Postal charges** £2.95 **Delivery** Royal Mail **Methods of Payment** Cheque, Postal Order, Credit Card

ROHAN DESIGNS
30 Maryland Road
Tongwell
Milton Keynes
Buckinghamshire
MK15 8HN
Telephone
01908 618888
Fax
01909 211209

Outdoor clothing

Rohan Designs has for some time been one of the market leaders in outdoor clothing. Its lightweight, durable garments are easy to care for and ingeniously designed. Thinking of going up in a Microlight, white-water rafting or mountain trekking? 'Bags' are the answer. Practical, windproof, light, cool, durable trousers, with double seat and knees, six pockets (four zipped) and expansion panels, and all for £42. Other products include the Grand Tour jacket, £115; globetrotter shorts, £35; and a selection of boots, shoes and backpacks.

Catalogue Bi-annually, A4, Catalogue, Colour, 22 pages, Free **Postal charges** £3 **Delivery** Royal Mail, Courier **Methods of Payment** Cheque, Postal Order, Credit Card, American Express

ROSIE NIEPER
12 Munster Road
Teddington
Middlesex
TW11 9LL
Telephone
0181 977 2863

Women's and children's T-shirts and Sweatshirts
A unique collection of outrageous T-shirt and sweatshirt designs which include logos drawn by children such as jellyfish, urchins, whales, etc, as well as cat aerobics. Prices range from £10.99 to £19.99, babies unbleached cotton T-shirts £11.99. Colourful and unusual.
Catalogue Bi-annually, A4, Brochure, Colour, 21 pages, Free **Postal charges** Free **Delivery** Royal Mail **Methods of Payment** Cheque, Credit Card

ROSIE POCKETT
Trenowan
49 Pendarves Road
Camborne
Cornwall
TR14 7QJ
Telephone
01209 713065

Children's clothes and accessories
Rosie Pockett is a family business specialising in traditional clothes for little girls and boys. Made to a high standard, using 100% cotton and striking fabrics, a Blackwatch tartan dress costs from £26.99; floral print pinafore from £17.50; reversible cord trousers from £15; shirts £12.99; and baby dresses and jumpsuits from £16.50. There are anoraks from £19.99 and bodywarmers from £15.50, plus hats, brooches and Rosie the Mouse (£1.99). Sizes mainly from 6 months to 7 years, with some items for 0–6 months and others up to 12 years.
Catalogue Bi-annually, A5, Catalogue, Colour and B/W, 8 pages **Postal charges** Varies with item **Delivery** Royal Mail **Methods of Payment** Cheque, Postal Order, Credit Card

ROWLAND'S
PO Box 1784
Bradford-on-Avon
BA15 2YW
Telephone
01225 865000
Fax
01225 864828

Men's and women's clothing
Rowland's is a privately owned company that believes firmly in the importance of customer service. Their catalogue contains clothing from Austria and Scotland. Tartan pleated skirts and tartan trousers are among some of the clothes featured, skirts £59.50 and fully lined, trousers £54.50. Austrian cardigan in 100% wool in bottle green and black for £79.50. Ruffle blouses in white and blue/white stripes £39.50. An

CLOTHES

Austrian evening skirt with velvet trim and narrow lace border at the hem for £109.00. Navy Loden jacket for £149.50. Men's garments feature mainly shirts, jumpers, ties and corduroy trousers priced at £49.50. Beautifully made and classic designs are a feature in this catalogue.

They also have shops in Bath, Chichester, Salisbury and Farnham.

Catalogue Bi-annually, A4, Catalogue, Colour, 35 pages, Free **Postal charges** Varies with item **Delivery** Royal Mail **Methods of Payment** Cheque, Postal Order, Credit Card, American Express

---

THE SCOTCH HOUSE
2 Brompton Road
Knightsbridge
London
SW1X 7PB
Telephone
0171 581 2151
Fax
0171 589 1583

Clothes

The Scotch House offers a wide range of beautifully made clothes, mainly woollen, with a Scottish feel. Cashmere and lambswool are the main fabrics, but the company also uses Fair Isle and merino. Tartan features prominently not only in the clothes but also in the various gift items: pens, china, jewellery and other accessories. The Scotch House has half a dozen branches: three in London (one on Brompton Road and two on Regent Street), one in Glasgow, one in Edinburgh and one at Terminal 4, Heathrow Airport.

Catalogue A4, Catalogue, Colour, 24 pages, Free **Postal charges** Postal charges for UK orders, £3.50. Postal charges will be added to orders mailed overseas. **Delivery** Royal Mail **Methods of Payment** Cheque, American Express, Diners Club, Credit Card

---

SECRET LOOKS
9 Swan Lane
Norwich
Norfolk
NR2 1HZ
Telephone
01603 616322

Lace underwear

This range contains lingerie from some of the country's top designers, including Charnos, Gossard and Triumph, as well as four of Secret Looks' own collections.

Catalogue A4, Catalogue, Colour, 8 pages, Free **Postal charges** £2 **Delivery** Royal Mail **Methods of Payment**

Fax
01603 617686

Cheque, Postal Order, Credit Card, Switch, American Express

SELECTIVE MARKETPLACE
Belton Road West
Loughborough
Leicestershire
LE11 0XL
Telephone
01509 235 235
Fax
01509 262 202

Women's clothes
Offering a range of exclusive styles in sizes from 12–24, this catalogue provides an excellent choice of women's clothes at competitive prices. The garments come in a range of fabrics and are generously cut to ensure they are comfortable as well as smart. Many styles are carefully tailored to be particularly flattering to the fuller figure. Among the items are a linen/cotton-mix suit, jacket from £39.95, skirt from £32.95 and trousers from £32.95; and a cotton jersey shirt in a range of colours, £16.95.

Catalogue Quarterly, A4, Catalogue, Colour, 32 pages, Free **Postal charges** Varies with item **Delivery** Royal Mail, Parcelforce **Methods of Payment** Cheque, Postal Order, Credit Card

SELFRIDGES SELECTION
Admail 70
Oxford Street
London
W1E 3YZ
Telephone
0800 101 101
Fax
0171 820 2979

Women's clothes
With the Selfridges Selection catalogue you can choose your wardrobe at home from this well-known London store and save yourself a trip to the West End. The latest designs from famous names, including Betty Barclay, Jacques Vert and Windsmoor, are pictured alongside Selfridges' own collection, offering something for every occasion from leisure and casual wear (Jantzen's swimsuit, £39.95; Betty Barclay gingham shirt, £59.95, and trousers, £63), to formal (jacket, £129, and matching short skirt, £49.95), with coats and showerproof jackets. There is a small collection of men's leisure wear.

Catalogue Annually, A4, Catalogue, Colour, 67 pages, Free **Postal charges** Free on first order **Delivery** Royal Mail, Parcelforce **Methods of Payment** Cheque, Postal Order, Credit Card, American Express, Diners Club

SEYMOURS OF BRADFORD
136 Sunbridge Road
Bradford
West Yorkshire
BD1 2QG
Telephone
01274 726520
Fax
01274 735911

Shirts, blouses and pyjamas
Seymours have specialised in traditional, made-to-measure shirts, blouses and pyjamas for 65 years. Each garment is exclusively hand-cut and individually sewn by Seymours' own seamstresses according to each customer's measurements, and choice of style and cloth. Free sample swatches showing over 400 superb designs taken from the world's finest fabrics are available to choose from. Any size can be made. Shirts and blouses start at £39.95 for polyester/cotton fabrics. Garments in 100% cotton begin at £43.35; wool/cotton blends at £57.15; and pure silk at £79.50.

Catalogue Annually, A4, Leaflets, Colour, 4 pages, Free **Postal charges** Varies with item **Methods of Payment** Cheque, Postal Order

SHALLOTS
The Onion Skins
Shelton Lodge
Nr Newark
Nottinghamshire
NG23 5JJ
Telephone
01949 850335
Fax
01949 850714

Children's clothes
Shallots produce appliqué and embroidered clothes for babies and children, each worked individually by skilled embroiderers. Colourfast and machine-washable, the sweatshirts are made out of 75% cotton fleece and have a design on the front and the back. Their catalogue comes with an appliquéed sample and designs include 'Fishes', 'Clown', 'Toadstool mouse' and 'Tractor'. There's a choice of bright colours and prices range from £14.50 to £19.50. Tabards, leggings, shorts, T-shirts and joggers are also available.

Catalogue A5, Brochure, Colour, 7 pages, Free **Postal charges** UK: Up to £50.00, add £1.50; £50.01-£100.00, add £2.50; over £100.00, free. Europe: £4.00; Rest of World, £5.00 **Delivery** Royal Mail **Methods of Payment** Cheque, Postal Order, Credit Card

SHETLAND KNITWEAR ASSOCIATES

31 King Harald Street
Lerwick
Shetland
Scotland
ZE1 0EQ
Telephone
01595 692746
Fax
same

Hand knitted and hand-frame knitted Shetlands knitwear

This company only sells the real thing, genuine Shetland knitwear made in the islands themselves by the world-renowned knitters. The range includes traditional Fair Isle and lace as well contemporary designs. All the items are either hand or hand-frame knitted and made to last. Women's lambswool turtle-neck, £41.25; Fernbank sweater from the island of Yell, £155; tartan cardigan, £94.

Catalogue Annually, A5, Catalogue, Colour, 11 pages, Free **Postal charges** £1.80 per sweater, £0.90 per accessory/jewellery **Delivery** Royal Mail **Methods of Payment** Cheque, Credit Card, Postal Order

SPARKLERS SHIRTS

Eythorne House
Eythorne
Dover
Kent
CT15 4BE
Telephone
01304 830424
Fax
01304 831506

Ladies' shirts

Sparklers was started 10 years ago by two sisters aiming to provide quality shirts in fine fabrics and simple designs. The shirts are all 100% cotton or silk and a card of sample swatches is included with their catalogue. Prices are around the £40 mark.

Catalogue Bi-annually, A5, Catalogue, Colour and B/W, 12 pages, Free **Postal charges** £1.50 **Delivery** Parcelforce **Methods of Payment** Cheque, Credit Card

ST ANDREWS WOOLLEN MILL

The Golf Links
St Andrews
Fife
Scotland
KY16 9JH
Telephone
01334 472366
Fax
01344 476416

Men's and women's woollen clothing

The St Andrews Woollen Mill, located at the famous golf links in Scotland, creates cashmere clothing in a variety of classic styles. It sells lambswool sweaters, Shetland knitwear, travel rugs, children's kilts and tartans by the yard. Its stock is much wider than shown in the catalogue and its staff are always happy to discuss with you what is available. Ladies' round-neck cashmere pullover, £115; men's V-neck 2-ply cashmere cardigan, £195; wool worsted tartan, £19.95/yd.

Catalogue Annually, Third A4, Brochure, Colour, 4 pages, Free **Postal charges** Varies with item **Delivery** Royal Mail **Methods of Payment** Cheque, Credit Card, American Express

START SMART
Woodgate Manor Farm
Woodgate
Bromsgrove
Worcestershire
B60 4HG
Telephone
01527 821760
Fax
01527 821275

Children's clothes

Start Smart offers a wide range of children's clothes, aimed at the younger child up to age 10. The range of designs is extensive and modern, including Bermuda shorts and culottes, as well as classical dresses and romper suits. Not only is the selection of styles very broad, but the choice of colours is also wide. Swimwear for girls is available, both in one-piece and bikinis, and sun-hats too. The hand-framed knitwear in machine-washable cotton is also available, as is machine-washable anti-tickle wool knitwear. As with other items, the selection of these jumpers is also wide.

Catalogue Bi-annually, A5, Catalogue, Colour, 8 pages, Free **Postal charges** £2.50 **Delivery** Royal Mail **Methods of Payment** Cheque, Postal Order, Credit Card

SULIS
Westfield Industrial Estate
Midsomer Norton
Bath
Avon
BA3 4BH
Telephone
01761 410107
Fax
01761 410108

Silk clothes for women

Sulis offers a range of simple, unfussy silk clothes in a variety of colours. There are nightdresses from £40; luxurious silk satin pyjamas, £70; cosy silk nightshirts from £24; camisole, £14; and briefs from £6. For outerwear, a medium-weight silk jersey polo costs £28 and a long-sleeved top £35.

Catalogue Annually, A5, Catalogue, Colour, 16 pages, Free **Postal charges** £1 **Delivery** Royal Mail, Parcelforce **Methods of Payment** Cheque, Postal Order, Credit Card, Switch

SUSAN J
Units 4 & 5,
Hale Trading Estate

Classic clothes for women

Susan J offers a choice of styles in an extensive range of marvellous fabrics and colours. An added

Lower Church Lane
Tipton
West Midlands
DY4 7PQ
Telephone
0121 557 3200
Fax
0121 557 5262

advantage is being able to choose a shorter or longer sleeve, body, trouser or skirt length, for a fully proportioned fit. There's an elegant long-sleeved blouse with wide revers and side splits in cotton lawn for £59; a fully lined tailored coatdress in tropical silk for £149 (£89 in all other fabrics); and a tailored waistcoat available in silk or wool for £79, or panache microfibre for £49.

Catalogue A4, Catalogue, Colour, 7 pages, Free **Postal charges** £3.50; orders over £150.00, free **Delivery** Royal Mail, Parcelforce **Methods of Payment** Cheque, Credit Card, Postal Order

SWALEDALE WOOLLENS LTD
Strawbeck
Muker
Richmond
North Yorkshire
DL11 6QG
Telephone
01748 886251
Fax
same

Woollen clothing

When Swaledale Woollens was founded 20 years ago, it revived the ancient craft of hand-knitting and crochet work in the Dales. Today, a wide variety of knitwear is produced in the homes of local people. Their work and other Dales woollen products using the Swaledale and Wensleydale sheep wool can be delivered by mail order from the firm's unique cottage shop in Muker, Upper Swaledale. Prices for most items range between £35 and £50.

Catalogue Bi-annually, A4, Catalogue, Colour, 8 pages, Free **Postal charges** Varies with item **Delivery** Parcelforce, Royal Mail **Methods of Payment** Cheque, Postal Order, Credit Card, American Express

T M LEWIN & SONS
106 Jermyn Street
London
SW1Y 6EQ
Telephone
0171 839 1664
Fax
0171 839 7791

Quality shirts and ties for men and women

T M Lewin & Sons of Jermyn Street began making fine-quality shirts and ties in 1898 and are still the leading specialists in corporate, club and regimental ties. Shirts are made from the finest quality two-fold poplin or pinpoint Oxford cotton, giving a luxurious feel and comfortable fit. All are generously cut and available in a range of

sleeve lengths. There are also two collar styles to choose from and a choice of double or button cuffs. The quality silk ties and shirts are designed and produced in Lewin's own factory. Dress accessories, such as cuff links, braces, handkerchiefs and collar stiffeners are also available, along with a selection of cotton and silk blouses, night attire, jewellery and capes for women. Men's shirts start at around £42.50, ties at £25. Blouses for women start at £39/£50 and capes from £52.50.
Catalogue A4, Brochure, Colour, 8 pages, Free **Postal charges** £3 within the UK **Delivery** Royal Mail **Methods of Payment** Cheque, Credit Card, American Express, Switch, Postal Order

TARQUIN
PO Box 187
Bristol
BS99 7GD
Telephone
0117 962 3905

Costumes, wigs and make-up

Family company offering a wide range of dancewear and fitness wear for children and adults. They also supply a range of outfits, wigs and masks together with any 'props' for shows, events and special occasions such as Halloween. There are sweatpants, letoards, ballet bags, cycle shorts, leggings, footless tights, stirrup tights and catsuits in different designs, all of which are shown in colour photos and by line drawings. The masks include Dracula with attached cape, the Devil with attached cape, monster/werewolf, vampire, vampire bat, old man with glasses, old lady with glasses, skull with attached hood, all made in adult sizes from rubber and with real hair where applicable. All are full overhead masks with eye and mouth holes. There are also eye-only masks attached by adjustable elastic behind the head, ideal for children and adults: black panthers, leopards, Persian cats, harlequins, highwayman/burglar and sequinned masks. Dressing-up wear includes a witch dress and hat, a clown, wildcat, bunny, Miss M Mouse outfit, caveman, cave-

CLOTHES

woman, pirate man and lady, monk, Arab sheik, nun, French maid, rag doll, prisoner lady, and saint hat which lights up. The wigs include one for a witch, punk, schoolgirl, hippy male and female, grandma, Tina Turner, Father Christmas, panto dame, southern belle, Affro and bald head. Prices seem very reasonable.

Catalogue A4, Leaflets, Colour and B/W, 15 pages, Free **Postal charges** Under £30, £1.50; otherwise free **Delivery** Royal Mail **Methods of Payment** Postal Order, Cheque

---

TARTAN LANDSCAPES
20 St Cuthbert Street
Kirkcudbright
Dumfries and Galloway
Scotland
DG6 4HZ
Telephone
01557 330371
Fax
01557 331572

Tartan waistcoats, children's kilts and scarves

Based in Kirkcudbright, south-west Scotland, this company specialises in tartan waistcoats using pure wool cloth produced in Scotland. All the waistcoats are individually tailored and are available in 10 of the most popular tartans. The company carries a range of 400 tartans which can be supplied at short notice. It also makes ties and bow ties, scarves, self-fringed wraps, caps, knee rugs, table settings, cushion covers and children's kilts. Men's and women's waistcoats, £41.50; ties, £14; children's kilts, from £18.50.

Catalogue Annually, A5, Leaflets, B/W, 3 pages, Free **Postal charges** Free **Delivery** Royal Mail **Methods of Payment** Cheque, Credit Card

---

THOMAS PINK
85 Jermyn Street
London
SW1
Telephone
0171 498 3882
Fax
0171 622 2803

Exclusive shirts for men

If there is an occasion on which you need to dress to impress, then contact Thomas Pink. *The Times* said they were *the* place to buy shirts in London today and one look at their catalogue will show you why.

They maintain a stock of classic shirts in a range of the most popular fabrics and also have a limited range of exclusive designs which change month by month. Every shirt shows the painstaking attention to detail which has won the company such a good reputation. Their best-selling shirts are £42.50, while silk ties are £24 and cufflinks are from between £5 and £44.

Catalogue Quarterly, A5, Leaflets, Colour, 4 pages, Free **Postal charges** Add £4 for UK, £12 for overseas **Delivery** Royal Mail **Methods of Payment** Cheque, Postal Order, Credit Card, American Express, Diners Club

TOWN & COUNTRY MANNER
Penrith Estate
Penrith
Cumbria
CA11 9EQ
Telephone
01768 899111
Fax
01768 899222

Classic clothes for men and women
This small family-owned company's policy is to support small British manufacturing companies by buying British. Their classic clothes are offered at very reasonable prices. The men's sports gilet with lots of pockets is £19.99; the traditional country quilted bodywarmer is £12.99; tartan ladies' waistcoats are £29.99; casual men's cord trousers, £14.99; and sheepskin slippers, £24.99.

Catalogue Bi-annually, A4, Catalogue, Colour, 11 pages, Free **Postal charges** £2.95 for orders up to £25.00; between £25.00 and £75.00, add £3.95; over £75.00, free. **Delivery** Parcelforce **Methods of Payment** Cheque, Postal Order, Credit Card

TRAVELLING LIGHT
Morland
Penrith
Cumbria
CA10 3AZ
Telephone
01931 714488
Fax
01931 714555

Hot-weather clothing for men and women
Travelling Light is the only company in the UK to specialise in hot-weather clothing all the year round. The clothes are co-ordinated, smart and practical, designed for travel, safaris, cruises and the beach. Each item is made in the UK from top-quality fabrics. It also offers a made-to-measure service and stocks a range of useful travel accessories. Men's safari jacket, £62.95; women's Ambassa dress comprising shirt £49.95, top £39.95, and skirt £59.95, teamed with Silke jacket, £105.

Catalogue Bi-annually, A4, Catalogue, Colour, 48 pages, Free **Postal charges** £3.25, 2nd class; £5.95, first class; £15, overnight **Delivery** Royal Mail, Parcelforce, Courier **Methods of Payment** Credit Card, Cheque, Postal Order

TUF CLOTHING COMPANY
Lodge Road
Kingswood
Bristol
Avon
BS15 1JX
Telephone
01179 611811
Fax
01179 674574

Work clothes
Now part of TUF Work and Safety Wear, TUF Clothing Company have a royal warrant. Made from top-quality fabrics with strong fastenings and reinforced stitching, the garments are practical, comfortable and stylish. The smart boilersuit is available in polyester/cotton or 100% cotton and costs £22.50; the nylon quilted bodywarmer is £9.50; and the waterproof Portland jacket with reflective strip costs £55.00. All prices are exclusive of VAT. They also offer company name badges embroidered or sewn on free of charge.
Catalogue Annually, A4, Catalogue, Colour, 23 pages, Free **Postal charges** £3.75; orders over £250.00, free **Delivery** Royal Mail **Methods of Payment** Cheque, Credit Card

UNLIMITED COLOUR COMPANY
Lairg
Sutherland
Scotland
IV27 4EH
Telephone
01549 402485

Knitwear
Polly Hoad's knitwear is stunningly original. Her black and white Mayan Coat made from soft spun cheviot wool costs £260. Her Valencia Jumper in multi-coloured soft 4-ply wool costs £180 and her Ripples Jacket in multi-yarn silk/cotton costs £270. She selects her multi yarns for colour and texture combining cotton, silk, wools, bouclé, hand spun, etc., using up to 25 different yarns in one garment.
Catalogue A4, Catalogue, Colour and B/W, 18 pages, £2.50 refundable against first order **Postal charges** £3.00 per item **Delivery** Parcelforce **Methods of Payment** Cheque, Credit Card

WEALTH OF NATIONS
Unit 28
The Talina Centre
Bagleys Lane
London
SW6 2BW

Clothes from around the world
The Wealth of Nations pocket-sized catalogues gather together traditional, elegant clothes that have been worn in their countries of origin for thousands of years, but still look superb today. The director, Julia Woodham-Smith, ensures that all her clothes are made to Fair Trading Standards by

CLOTHES

Telephone
0171 371 5333
Fax
0171 371 5398

visiting every manufacturer and factory. Cheongsam silk dress, £125; Chinese cadre suit, £95; silk shift, £38; Welsh hedger's waistcoat, £55; Guatemalan shirt, £45; little spinners' smock (ages 2–8), £18.

Catalogue Bi-annually, A6, Catalogue, Colour, 62 pages, Free **Postal charges** £2.95 **Delivery** Royal Mail **Methods of Payment** Cheque, Postal Order, Credit Card, American Express

WEARITE
Park View Works
257 West Green Road
London
N15 5EG
Telephone
0181 802 3399
Fax
0181 809 2912

Outdoor clothing for country pursuits

Wearite manufacture the L'avenir range of well-made, practical outdoor clothing. Similar to Barbour in appearance but cheaper, the range includes waxed and quilted jackets and waistcoats suitable for country pursuits. An executive dry-waxed cotton jacket costs £39.50, a quilted casual jacket, £23.50; a hunter jacket, £60; and a wax fishing jacket, £26.

Catalogue A5, Catalogue, Colour, 15 pages, Free **Postal charges** Varies with item **Delivery** Parcelforce **Methods of Payment** Cheque, Postal Order, Credit Card

WELLERWEAR
(R G H LTD)
Flaska House
Troutbeck
Penrith
Cumbria
CA11 0ST
Telephone
017687 79012
Fax
017687 79014

Country clothing

Wellerwear, a Cumbrian company, offers a wide range of outer clothes suitable for wear in the wettest part of England. With the emphasis on comfort, the range of sizes is exceptional: the Lakelander waxed cotton jacket starts from a child's 24in, going up to a large adult's 60in. Prices: £22–£29.50. There's a nylon quilted riding jacket for £16.50 and a 'Countryman' waxed cotton waistcoat for £18.50. Chaps (waxed cotton and suede) cost £37.50.

Catalogue Third A4, Brochure, Colour, 12 pages, Free **Postal charges** Add £3.00 for adult sizes and £2.00 for children's sizes. Hats and caps are post free **Delivery** Parcelforce **Methods of Payment** Cheque, Credit Card

WEST CLOTHING
36–38 Station Street West
Coventry
West Midlands
CV6 5NB
Telephone
01203 638121

Clothes for larger men

Everything for the bigger man in one publication. Clothes and accessories to ensure that you are well-dressed for the office, party, weekend and even in bed. With suits up to 60in chest and trousers, including chinos, up to 60in waist, the range is both fashionable and practical. There is a generous choice of colours and many of the goods are very reasonably priced. Wool/polyester sports jacket, £72.95 to £96.95; classic check trousers, £21.95 to £32.95; polyester/cotton striped shirt, £18.95 to £21.95 (21in collar).

Catalogue Annually, A5, Catalogue, Colour, 28 pages, Free **Postal charges** £1.90 **Methods of Payment** Cheque, Credit Card

WETHERALL LTD
Dept MS19
Freepost CS1385
Love Lane
Denbigh
Clwyd
LL16 3LE
Telephone
01745 815592
Fax
01745 815147

Women's clothes

This company produces up-market, sophisticated co-ordinates for women. The idea is that by carefully choosing a limited number of items you can combine them in a huge number of ways. The clothes themselves are conservative in style, with plenty of skirts, jackets, trousers and tops, some reversible. Straight wool skirt, £59.95; reversible swing jacket, £149.95; mackintosh, £159.95.

Catalogue Quarterly, A4, Catalogue, Colour, 16 pages, Free **Postal charges** £3.75 **Delivery** Royal Mail, Parcelforce **Methods of Payment** Cheque, Credit Card

WIGGLETS
50 Stockwell Park Crescent
London
SW9 0DG
Telephone
0171 738 5124

Classic night clothes for children

The Wigglets range of quality classic children's nightclothes for babies to 12 year olds caters for every season. For winter, there is a range of pyjamas and dressing gowns in brushed cotton and for summer they have a selection of short-sleeved cotton pyjamas in Bermuda length and full length. Prices start at £19 for pyjamas and £34 for dressing gowns. They also offer Jermyn Street Junior shirts and Sally Membery dresses.

Catalogue Annually, A5, Catalogue, Colour, 11 pages, Free **Postal charges** Add £1.25 for first garment; 50p per garment thereafter, up to maximum of £3.50 **Delivery** Parcelforce **Methods of Payment** Cheque, Postal Order, Credit Card

WOODS OF MORECAMBE
42 Queen Street
Morecambe
Lancashire
LA4 5EL
Telephone
01524 412101
Fax
01524 832947

Women's underwear

Underwear and nightwear are Woods' speciality. With an emphasis on modesty, there's nothing here to give your grandmother a heart-attack or for that matter to make your lover break out in a heavy sweat. But if you're looking for something comfortable and feminine, Woods has it. Anti-static nylon underslip, £19; fancy knit wool long john, £13.50; Doreen firm control long-line bra, £22.50; cotton short bra, £16; Winceyette nightdress, £17.50. Woods also offers a selection of girdles and corsets.

Catalogue Bi-annually, A5, Catalogue, Colour, 35 pages, Free **Postal charges** Varies with item **Delivery** Royal Mail, Parcelforce **Methods of Payment** Cheque, Postal Order, Credit Card

ZIG ZAG DESIGNER KNITWEAR
Riverford Mill
Stewarton
Ayrshire
Scotland
KA3 5DH
Telephone
01560 485187
Fax
01560 485195

Knitwear

Zig Zag makes good-quality, well-designed knitwear for women and men at its mill in Scotland. The summer catalogue contains an attractive selection of cotton sweaters, cardigans and waistcoats, some in plains and neutrals and others a jamboree of colours and patterns. Pastel parfait cardigan, £39.50, and matching short-sleeved top, £22.50; waistcoat, £24.50; tunic, £33.50; fishermen's rib, £39.50; children's sweaters from £18.95.

Catalogue Bi-annually, A5, Catalogue, Colour, 20 pages, Free **Postal charges** Varies with item **Delivery** Royal Mail, Parcelforce **Methods of Payment** Cheque, Postal Order, Credit Card, Switch, American Express

Collectables

A B WOODWORKING
Unit J
Pentre Wern
Gobowen
Oswestry
Shropshire
SY10 7JZ
Telephone
01691 670425
Fax
01691 670235

Shaker boxes
The Shakers made their boxes by the thousand and used them for storing thread, buttons, tools, spices, medicines and paint ingredients. Today they are collector's items and change hands for large sums. A B Woodworking uses the same materials and lovingly hand craft every box. They make traditional oval boxes (from £8.40), boxes with swing handles (from £20), lined boxes (from £23), hat boxes (from £31) and trays (from £18) in a variety of finishes, or unfinished for your own decoration.
Catalogue Annually, A4, Catalogue, Colour and B/W, 12 pages, £2, refundable with order **Postal charges** Varies with item **Delivery** Royal Mail, Parcelforce **Methods of Payment** Cheque

A BUCKINGHAM LTD
Benham House
Folkestone
Kent
CT20 1SD
Telephone
01303 226777/850041
Fax
01303 221327

First-day covers
Buckingham advertise themselves as 'The First in First Day Covers'. One of their most prestigious products is their range of silk covers – a technique imported from America. Among this range are 'Railway Cover', a regular series since 1980; 'Royalty Covers', to cover all major royal events (though probably not infidelity, separation or divorce); 'Cricket Covers', all of them illustrating great players of today, some of them signed by the players themselves; and 'Signed Covers', which have been personally autographed by a person directly involved with the stamp issue.

Catalogue Monthly, A4, Newspaper, B/W, 20 pages, Free
Delivery Royal Mail Methods of Payment Cheque, Credit
Card, Postal Order, Diners Club, American Express, COD,
Switch

**ANCESTRAL
COLLECTIONS LTD**
The Old Corn Store
Burghley Courtyard
Stamford
Lincolnshire
PE9 3JY
Telephone
01780 482522
Fax
01780 65305

Replicated antique pieces

The concept behind Ancestral Collections is very simple. They make it possible for good design and historical information to come together in a collection of replicated pieces from the treasured collections contained within Britain's Historic Houses. These are heirlooms of the future.

There are unusual pieces from Blair Castle, Burghley House, Castle Howard, Elton Hall and Knebworth. Cherub wall-bracket from Blair Castle, £45; The Burghley 'Fly' Brooch from Burghley House, £65; 'Georgian Stool' from Castle Howard, £390; Tole Chestnut Urn from Elton Hall, £375; and Regency Planter from Knebworth, £132.

Ideal gifts to mark a birthday or retirement, Christmas or for a wedding present. These replicas make it feasible to furnish rooms to the highest order without astronomical insurance premiums.
Catalogue Annually, A4, Brochure, Colour, 14 pages, Free
Postal charges £5.50, with the exception of some postcode areas, where there is a surcharge **Delivery** Royal Mail **Methods of Payment** Cheque, Postal Order, Credit Card, Switch

ANDREW BOTTOMLEY
The Coach House
Huddersfield Road
Holmfirth
West Yorskhire
HD7 2TT
Telephone
01484 685234

Antique arms and armour

Andrew Bottomley's Antique Arms & Armour catalogue contains hundreds of antique weapons from all over the world, each fully described and generally accompanied by a photograph. There are pistols and revolvers (30-bore English full-stocked percussion holster pistol, £90; pair of 16-bore Flintlock carriage pistols c. 1765, £4,800), long

Fax
01484 681551

guns, swords and daggers, North American Indian artefacts, bayonets and powder flasks. All items are guaranteed original.

Catalogue Annually, A4, Catalogue, Colour and B/W, 144 pages, Free **Postal charges** Varies with item **Delivery** Royal Mail, Parcelforce, Courier **Methods of Payment** Cheque, Postal Order, Credit Card, American Express

BENHAM
Benham House
Folkestone
Kent
CT20 1SD
Telephone
01303 226777
Fax
01303 221327

First-day stamp covers

Benham first-day covers are hand-crafted works of art. Each has a full-colour illustration, printed onto a silken fabric and hand-mounted into a gold-blocked frame. The five Royal Mail stamps are then affixed and the covers sent off to the Royal Mail to be franked with the specially designed postmark which is available for one day only.

The National Trust Centenary first day covers in 1995 cost £12.50 for a set of 5. There are also special offers on older covers you may have missed. You can reserve your cover by telephoning and using your credit card (Cover Club members take preference).

Catalogue A4, Catalogue, Colour, 8 pages, Free **Delivery** Royal Mail **Methods of Payment** Cheque, Credit Card

BIRCHALL'S
The Pipe Shop
14 Talbot Road
Blackpool
Lancashire
FY1 1LF
Telephone
01253 24218
Fax
01253 291659

Pipes, tobacco and coffee

Birchall's was founded in 1834 and is one of the country's oldest tobacconists. Its attractive, sepia catalogue features specialist loose, chewing and wrapped tobaccos, each with a brief description of aroma and smoking qualities, plus cigars, coffees, and a video, *At Peace With Your Pipe*. There are pipes and accessories, and a repair and renovation service is offered. Loose tobaccos from £2.60/25g; Birchall's pipes, £19.99; Ferndown pipes, £79.95.

Catalogue Annually, A5, Catalogue, B/W, 16 pages, 25p **Postal charges** 10% of total **Delivery** Royal Mail **Methods of Payment** Cheque, Postal Order, Credit Card

COLLECTABLES

BUTTERFLIES GALORE
21 Westall Centre
Holberrow Green
Nr Redditch
Worcestershire
B96 6JY
Telephone
01386 793240
Fax
01386 793253

Decorative butterflies
These ornamental butterflies come in two sizes — 15in (£23.50) and 7½in (£12.80) across the wingspan and can be displayed on walls, fences or pictures. Special fixings are supplied and presentation gift boxes are available. The six most popular British butterflies are represented (Peacock, Swallowtail, Purple Emperor, Clouded Yellow, Red Admiral and Marbled White). The company also makes giant ladybirds (£12 each) and mushroom-shaped slug traps (from £10 each).
Catalogue A4, Leaflets, Colour, 4 pages, Free **Postal charges** £2.40 **Delivery** Parcelforce **Methods of Payment** Cheque, Postal Order

CHARLES EDE LTD
20 Brook Street
London
W1Y 1AD
Telephone
0171 493 4944
Fax
0171 491 2548

Roman glass
There is only a fraction of stock available by mail order in this brochure, but there is a constantly changing display of new material in the gallery at Brook Street. This particular catalogue contains Roman Glass with prices which reflect collectable items. A bottle in pale green of 2nd-3rd century is £225, whilst an Amphoriskos in cobalt blue with opaque handles, Sidon 1st century is £3500. Certainly an interesting brochure for the discerning collector.
Catalogue Annually, A5, Brochure, Colour, 12 pages, Free **Postal charges** 5% on orders less than £400, 2½% on orders over £400 **Delivery** In-house delivery **Methods of Payment** Cheque, Credit Card

COINCRAFT
45 Great Russell Street
London
WC1B 3LU
Telephone
0171 636 1188

Coins, bank notes, ancient coins, antiquities
Founded in 1955, Coincraft is a family firm which deals in coins, bank notes, ancient coins and antiquities. Their shop is just across the street from the British Museum. For mail-order customers, they issue a catalogue and monthly newspaper, 'The Phoenix'. This is a 24-page black and white

Fax
0171 323 2860

publication, A3 size, which is also free. They pride themselves in helping collectors and tell us they just might have the most interesting shop/catalogue in the country – and they may well be right! Certainly, the range is impressive. Charles II Silver Crowns issued in the 1600s sell from £50, ancient Roman oil lamps from the 3rd–4th century AD are from £29, while 100 different uncirculated world bank notes are just £28. They also stock all the supplies and books you need to start or advance a collection. A fascinating company.

Catalogue Bi-annually, A4, Catalogue, Colour and B/W, 52 pages, Free **Postal charges** £1 per order **Delivery** Royal Mail, Courier, Parcelforce **Methods of Payment** Cheque, Postal Order, Credit Card, American Express, Diners Club, Switch

CONNOSSIEUR COLLECTORS' CLUBS
Express Buildings
Howsell Road
Malvern Link
Worcestershire
WR14 1TF
Telephone
01684 567770
Fax
01684 892865

Exclusive collectables club

This company, staffed by a small team of enthusiasts, runs three Clubs for Collectors. These are The Connoisseur Thimble Collectors' Club, The Connoisseur Spoon Collectors' Club, and The Connoisseur Bell Collectors' Club. Membership, which is free, brings a quarterly newsletter featuring articles on collecting, collectors' correspondence and Club news. Members also have the opportunity to acquire a wide variety of thimbles, spoons, bells or plates, many designed and crafted exclusively at the company's studios in Worcestershire. The company was moving as we went to press but the phone number remains the same.

Catalogue By advertising, Free **Postal charges** Varies with item **Delivery** Royal Mail **Methods of Payment** Cheque

CORGI CLASSICS
Freepost SO4438
Southampton
Hampshire

Classic collectable cars

Corgi classic collectable cars range from Lovejoy's Morris Minor at £9.99 to the connoisseur collection which includes the Jaguar XK-120 at

SO14 0WD
Telephone
01703 336600

£30 which is accompanied by an individually numbered Certificate of Authenticity. Both collections contain cars from a bygone era.

Catalogue Annually, A4, Catalogue, Colour, 8 pages, Free **Postal charges** Add £2.95 **Delivery** In-house delivery **Methods of Payments** Cheque, Postal Order, Credit Card

CORGI CLASSICS
FREEPOST (SO4438)
Southampton
Hampshire
SO14 0WD
Telephone
01703 336600

Model cars

Available only by mail order, Corgi Cameo collections come with certificates of authenticity and are widely sought-after. The 6 collections of 10 vehicles are 'Classic Drinks', 'Grocery Store', 'Unilever', 'Whitbread', 'Christmas' and 'D-Day' and cost £24.95 each. Other Corgi Classics include the Morris J Van, the Ford Popular Van, the Leyland Tiger Coach and the Bedford OB Coach.

Catalogue Annually, A4, Leaflets, Colour, 6 pages, Free **Postal charges** £2.50 **Delivery** Parcelforce **Methods of Payment** Cheque, Postal Order, Credit Card

THE DOLLS' HOUSE EMPORIUM
Victoria Road
Ripley
Derbyshire
DE5 3YD
Telephone
01773 513773
Fax
01773 513772

Dolls' houses, furniture and accessories

The Dolls' House Emporium has an excellent reputation for quality and service to customers. The catalogue is a treasure trove of exquisite houses which can be purchased built, painted and wallpapered or as a kit. There are pages of accessories: lighting kits, wallpapers, room sets, individual pieces of furniture, food for the table, pots for the kitchen, families of dolls, nursery toys and pets. This catalogue will enchant you, whether a child or serious collector. Classical dolls' house kit, £109.90; built, painted and wallpapered, £379.90. Blossom Cottage flatpack, £49.90.

Catalogue Annually, A4, Catalogue, Colour, 48 pages, Free **Postal charges** Varies with item **Delivery** Royal Mail, Parcelforce **Methods of Payment** Cheque, Credit Card

ERIC HORNE COLLECTORS' TOYS
54 Majorfield Road
Topsham
Exeter
Devon
EX3 0QQ
Telephone
01392 877600
Fax
same

Wooden dolls

Eric Horne has been making classic wooden Dutch dolls since 1976 and he has since been joined by his son, Peter. The Dutch doll is a descendant of the *Grodnertal*, a wooden doll produced in the early 1800s in Austria and Bavaria and made famous in the late 1800s when Florence Upton wrote and illustrated story books about the adventures of two such dolls. Hand-turned from beechwood and individually painted, all the dolls are jointed, available as male or female, with a choice of hair and shoes. Prices from £9.15 to £83.25.

Catalogue Annually, A5, Brochure, B/W, 8 pages, Free **Postal charges** Varies with item **Delivery** Royal Mail, Parcelforce **Methods of Payment** Cheque

LAWLEYS BY POST
Minton House
London Road
Stoke on Trent
Staffordshire
ST4 7QD
Telephone
01782 744787
Fax
01782 416962

Collectors' pieces

Lawleys By Post offers a range of collectable porcelain figurines, commemorative tankards, plates, floral boxes and prints by renowned makers such as Minton, Royal Albert, Royal Crown Derby and Royal Doulton. The collection includes Royal Doulton's limited edition of Henry VIII and his Six Wives modelled by the sculptor Pauline Parsons (£195 for Catherine of Aragon; £295 for Henry himself). Commemorative war tankards, £49.95 each; Heroes of Arnhem print, £49.50.

Catalogue Annually, A5, Catalogue, Colour, 28 pages, Free **Postal charges** Free **Methods of Payment** Cheque, Postal Order, Stage Payments, Credit Card

MERCHANTMEN
664 Garratt Lane
London
SW17 0NP

China and cutlery

Merchantmen offers you the opportunity to build up a dinner service or set of cutlery month-by-month. Choose from Wild Pastures, a service featuring golden poppies from the Seltmann

COLLECTABLES

Telephone
0181 947 9733
Fax
0181 879 3940

factory in Bavaria; or Julia, a collector's service from the same factory. There are bone china chocolate beakers from Stoke-on Trent, decorated with British flowers (£19.95 each), and from Thailand you can collect solid bronze Royal Siam cutlery. Six dinner plates: Wild Pastures £48.08, Julia £55.95. Six dinner knives and forks, £27.95.
Catalogue Annually, A4, Leaflets, Colour and B/W, 7 pages, Free **Postal charges** Varies with item **Delivery** Royal Mail, Parcelforce **Methods of Payment** Cheque, Stage Payments, Credit Card

MILDRED PEARCE (MAIL ORDER) LTD
FREEPOST LON99
PO Box 4292
London
SW11 3YY
Telephone
0171 379 5128
Fax
0171 738 0053

Cups, clocks, bowls, scent bottles, mirrors, candlesticks

Full of original creations by talented young designers, everything is beautifully made and individually signed by the artist, but can be used everyday. This catalogue contains unusual, hand-crafted gifts for a special occasion. Kate Brett wall clocks, £89; Kate Byrne fish toothbrush holders, £18.50 each; Janice Wahnich scent bottles from £55 each.
Catalogue Annually, A5, Catalogue, Colour, 19 pages, Free **Postal charges** Up to £29.99, add £2.99; over £30.00, add £3.99 **Delivery** Royal Mail **Methods of Payment** Credit Card, Postal Order, Cheque

THE ORIGINAL BUTTERFLY MAN
Craft Workshop
Berwyn Lodge
Glyndyfrdwy Village
Corwen
Clwyd
North Wales
LL21 9HW
Telephone
01490 430300

Decorative metal butterflies for home decoration

The Original Butterfly Man produces beautiful replicas of some of Britain's best-loved butterflies. With rust-resistant aluminium wings and durable nylon bodies, these hand-painted, eye-catching models look stunning when attached to walls and surfaces. All butterflies have legs, proboscis and antennae and are fitted with a sprung-steel fixing bracket so they flutter in the breeze. Sizes range from 16 × 10in to 12 × 6in. A selection of 15 species are available, from the Peacock at £45 to the Large Garden White at £25.50.

Catalogue Annually, Third A4, Leaflets, Colour, 3 pages, Send SAE 14in × 6in, first-class stamp and £1 postal order payable to The Original Butterfly Man **Postal charges** Varies with item **Delivery** Royal Mail **Methods of Payment** Cheque, Postal Order

PETER JONES CHINA
PO Box 10
22 Little Westgate
Wakefield
West Yorkshire
WF1 1LB
Telephone
01924 362510
Fax
01924 290234

Fine bone china and glass

This is a well-illustrated, glossy catalogue of commemorative china, limited editions and gifts. There are plenty of household names such as Wedgwood and Royal Doulton and a multitude of figurines, mugs, vases and plates. Aynsley Queen Mother tribute plate, £29.95; Henry VIII mug, £19.95; Caithness Battle of Britain paperweight, £35; Beatrix Potter figurine, £99.

Catalogue Annually, A4, Catalogue, Colour, 16 pages, Free **Postal charges** Varies with item **Delivery** Royal Mail, Parcelforce **Methods of Payment** Cheque, Postal Order, Stage Payments, Credit Card

ROYAL MINT COIN CLUB
FREEPOST
PO Box 500
Cardiff
Caernarvon
CF1 1YY
Telephone
01433 223366

Coins

What better way to celebrate an important occasion than to give a present that will be treasured as a keepsake, a classic gift that you know someone special would like to receive? A gift of gold for that extra special someone, silver for a christening or perhaps an educational coin set for a youngster. The 1995 Wedding Collection and the 1995 Baby Gift set are two of the Royal Mint's most popular items at £14.95 each.

Catalogue Annually, A4, Brochure, Colour, 2 pages, Free **Postal charges** Free **Delivery** Royal Mail **Methods of Payment** Cheque, Credit Card

COLLECTABLES

SCOTLAND DIRECT
Thistle Mill
Station Road
Biggar
Scotland
ML12 6LP
Telephone
01899 21001
Fax
01899 20456

Thimbles and other collectables
Scotland Direct incorporates The Thimble Guild which sends out monthly programmes with selections of thimbles to members. Thimbles start at £3.95; a set of four porcelain thimbles depicting handpainted Chinese landscapes costs £29.88. The company also supplies small decorative items such as china boxes and models of country cottages, churches and post boxes. They also stock a range of novelty items, such as the animal and bird teapot collection.
Catalogue A5, Leaflets, Colour, Free **Delivery** Royal Mail **Methods of Payment** Cheque, Credit Card, Switch, American Express

STAFFORDSHIRE ENAMELS
Western Coyney Road
Stoke-on-Trent
Staffordshire
ST3 5JT
Telephone
0500 026209
Fax
01782 599397

Handpainted enamel gifts
Staffordshire Enamels are descendants of the 18th-century English Enamels now highly praised by collectors. Whether you are giving or collecting, these exquisite pieces could well become heirlooms. There are love tokens (boxes from £55), yearboxes (from £69.50), pillboxes (from £72.50) and egg-shaped boxes (from £47.50).
Catalogue Annually, A5, Catalogue, Colour, 29 pages, Free **Postal charges** £1.95 **Delivery** Royal Mail, Parcelforce **Methods of Payment** Cheque, Credit Card, Switch

TEDDY BEARS OF WITNEY
99 High Street
Witney
Oxford
Oxfordshire
OX8 6LY
Telephone
01993 702616
Fax
01993 702344

Teddy bears for collectors
Established as a shop in 1985, Teddy Bears have always aimed to offer collectors the best possible choice of old and new teddy bears. Their new annual catalogue is in full colour, containing more than 200 traditional bears over its 28 pages. Most of these bears are exclusive limited editions. Favourites include Barnaby by Merrythought, which sells for £58, Little Bertie by Deans, at £38, and Baby Alfonzo by Steiff at £145.
Catalogue Annually, A4, Catalogue, Colour, 28 pages, £5

Postal charges £3 per bear within UK; £5 overseas **Delivery** Parcelforce **Methods of Payment** Cheque, Postal Order, Credit Card

THE THIMBLE GUILD
Thistle Mill
Station Road
Biggar
Strathclyde
Scotland
ML12 6LP
Telephone
01899 21001
Fax
01899 20456

Thimbles
This is a long-established family-run society for collectors of thimbles, dedicated to offering members the finest hand-crafted thimbles from Britain and around the world. On joining you may choose any number of thimbles from a selection of 20 offered at half price. Thereafter you will receive a monthly magazine and it is hoped you will buy at least four thimbles during your first year. Prices from £4.96 (£2.46 to new members).
Catalogue Annually, A5, Brochure, Colour, 6 pages, Free **Postal charges** £1.65 **Delivery** Royal Mail **Methods of Payment** Cheque, Credit Card, Switch, American Express

VICTORIA DOLLS
White House
Orchard Rise
Pwllmeyric
Chepstow
Gwent
NP6 6JT
Telephone
01291 623573
Fax
same

Porcelain dolls
This selection of traditional and individual hand-crafted porcelain dolls from German, French and American moulds are all beautifully dressed in high-quality fabrics in the style of the Victorian period. 'Tiny Tantrums' (toddler size boy) is £185, while 18in 'Claire' is £69. Baby life-size 'Amy' is £195 and 12in Rufus is £59.
Catalogue A5, Leaflets, Colour, 7 pages, Free **Postal charges** Free **Delivery** Parcelforce **Methods of Payment** Cheque

WENTWORTH COLLECTION
10 Tennyson Road
Brentwood
Essex
CM13 2SJ

Model horses
Breyer model horses are made of tenite, a strong plastic, and are individually painted by hand. All models are gift boxed. The Traditional Series is the largest, the adult horse is about 9in (23cm) high to the ears and 12in (30cm) long with accessories (saddles, riders) to fit. There are three smaller

Telephone
01277 216285
Fax
same

series. Horses cost around £20, with a few at £9.95; rider, £9.95; saddle, £17.95; bridle and blanket, £9.95; stable, £49.95.

Catalogue Annually, A3, Leaflets, Colour and B/W, 8 pages, Free **Postal charges** £2.50 for orders up to £20; £3.50 for orders of more than £20 **Delivery** Royal Mail, Parcelforce **Methods of Payment** Cheque, Postal Order, Credit Card, Switch

WESTMINSTER COLLECTION LTD
Freepost
PO Box 100
Watford
Hertfordshire
WD2 5WD
Telephone
01923 212100
Fax
01923 249950

Coins and stamps

Westminster's coins are specially minted to commemorate certain events, such as Britain's new silver £2 coin (£26.50), to celebrate VE-Day, or the 1994 silver bullion coins depicting America's silver eagle, Canada's maple leaf, China's panda and Australia's kangaroo (£12.50 each).

The stamps also commemorate events or people, such as the Queen Mother, and there is a Disney classics collection (£9.95) which includes a special set of stamps issued for Mickey Mouse's 60th birthday. The World Cup coin costs £5.95 and the Olympic stamps £14.95.

Catalogue A5, Leaflets, Colour, 14 pages, Free **Postal charges** Varies with item **Delivery** Royal Mail **Methods of Payment** Cheque

Computers

ACI
82 Chaplin Road
London
NW2 5PR
Telephone
0181 830 1958
Fax
0181 830 1959

Notebook computers
This award-winning company is a direct vendor of notebook computers under the name ACI Performer. The range is fully upgradable. Prices from £999 for the AC486SX-33 mono to £2249 for the AC486DX4-100 with TFT active colour; car adaptor, £75; fax modem, from £149.
Catalogue Annually, A4, Brochure, Colour, 6 pages, Free **Postal charges** £15 **Delivery** Courier **Methods of Payment** Cheque, Credit Card

ACTION COMPUTER SUPPLIES
12 Windmill Lane
Southall
Middlesex
UB2 4QD
Telephone
0800 333 333
Fax
0800 10 20 30

Computers – hardware and software
Action Computers produce a fat A5 catalogue crammed with everything for the computer buff. They sell a good range of computers themselves, including models from Toshiba, Compaq, Canon, AST, IBM, NEC and Hewlett Packard. Then there is a huge range of accessories and hardware, including cards, modems, carrying cases, VDU filters and so on.

The software section covers DOS, Windows and Mac applications on floppies and CD-ROMS. Finally there are printer supplies, disks, cartridges and cassettes. In short, a one-stop catalogue for everything to do with computers.
Catalogue Bi-monthly, A5, Catalogue, Colour and B/W, 784 pages, Free **Postal charges** Varies with item **Delivery** Parcelforce, Securicor, minicabs same day **Methods of Payment** Cheque, Postal Order, Credit Card, American Express, Diners Club, Switch

COMPUTERS

AJP BUSINESS COMPUTERS
Units 6 & 7
The Edge Business Centre
Humber Road
London
NW2 6EN
Telephone
0181 452 9090
Fax
0181 450 6360

Notebook computers

AJP has received many accolades in the computer press. A favourite among the experts, it provides portable computers which are versatile and powerful at prices that won't break the bank. Prices start at £749; the AJP 3600 series Pentium Multimedia Notebook costs between £1,799 and £2,475. A number of options and upgrades are available.

Catalogue Annually, A4, Leaflets, Colour, 5 pages, Free **Postal charges** Varies with item **Delivery** Parcelforce **Methods of Payment** Cheque, Credit Card

BEST BUYS OFFICE EQUIPMENT DIRECT
533 High Road
Ilford
Essex
IG1 1TZ
Telephone
0181 514 7887
Fax
0181 553 3343

Office equipment and computers

Best Buys Computer Warehouse catalogue offers an extensive range of notebook machines, such as the Adler Walkstation from £739. It also features conventional PCs from major manufacturers, including Hewlett Packard, IBM and Olivetti. As for printers, there are bubblejet versions by Cannon (from £189), and models by Hewlett Packard, Epson, Olivetti and Brother. Best Buys also sells fax machines, copiers and an assortment of office equipment. Prices are competitive and exclude VAT.

Catalogue Annually, A4, Catalogue, Colour and B/W, 20 pages, Free **Postal charges** Varies with item **Delivery** Courier **Methods of Payment** Cheque, Credit Card, Switch

CLP COMPUTER SUPPLIES
Units 7 & 8
Holland Way
Blandford Forum
Dorset
DT11 7TA
Telephone
01258 459544

Computer supplies

CLP Computer Supplies have now installed a BT video telephone so if you also have one, you just give them a ring and see before you buy!

The catalogue lists every conceivable computer accessory such as paper and labels, ribbons and toners, cables and connectors, screen filters (from £10.95), copy holders (from £3.45) and even some computer furniture (the ECO Total PC

Fax
01258 459565

Table costs £119.95). They also have a competitive line in disks (from £2.95 per box of 10) and mice mats (from 95p).

Catalogue Bi-annually, A4, Catalogue, Colour, 47 pages, Free **Postal charges** Orders under £50.00, add £3.45; orders over £50.00, free **Delivery** Royal Mail, Courier **Methods of Payment** Cheque, Credit Card, American Express, Switch

COMPUSYS
58 Edison Road
Rabans Lane Industrial Estate
Aylesbury
Buckinghamshire
HP19 3TE
Telephone
01296 395531
Fax
01296 24165

Computers and computer systems

Whatever your needs, personal or corporate, Compusys can build a PC system to suit and will provide maintenance and support. It prides itself on personal service which is so important when trying to set up a new system. There are several choices under £2,000: a Business PCI Solution costs £1,399. Prices rise to £3,000 plus.

Catalogue Annually, A4, Leaflets, Colour, 8 pages, Free **Postal charges** Varies with item **Delivery** Parcelforce, Courier **Methods of Payment** Cheque, Credit Card

COMPUTER MANUALS
50 James Road
Birmingham
West Midlands
BA11 2BA
Telephone
0121 706 6000
Fax
0121 706 3301

Computer books

Subscription to this catalogue is free and it is updated three times a year. It lists an enormous range of computer books from highly technical programming languages and techniques titles to the user-friendly *Computers for Dummies* series. It even promises to try and find anything for you that is not in the catalogue.

Some products are liable to VAT, such as software, and are marked accordingly. *How the Internet Works Instructors' Kit*, £76.89; *MS-DOS 6.0 For Simpletons*, £9.95.

Catalogue Three times a year, A4, Catalogue, Colour and B/W, 32 pages, Free **Postal charges** Varies with item **Delivery** Royal Mail **Methods of Payment** Cheque, Credit Card

CONNECT SOFTWARE

3 Flanchford Road
London
W12 9ND
Telephone
0181 743 9792
Fax
0181 743 8073

Accounting software

Connect Software supplies a selection of software suitable for businesses. Office Manager (£58.69) combines database, word-processing, invoicing, contact management and document processing in one easy-to-use package. Money Manager is available in three editions (personal £39.95, standard £58.95, business £93.94) to help you to manage your finances, and Final Accounts is an add-on program for producing end-of-year reports with a tax calculations option (£58.69; with tax option £93.94).

Catalogue Annually, A4, Leaflets, Colour, 3 pages, Free **Postal charges** Free **Delivery** Royal Mail **Methods of Payment** Cheque, Credit Card, American Express

DN COMPUTER SERVICES PLC

Truedata House
Green Lane
Heywood
Manchester
Greater Manchester
OL10 2DY
Telephone
01706 367567
Fax
0800 367567

Computers, accessories and software

DNCS offer hardware that includes IBM, AST, Compaq, Canon and Toshiba computers as well as laptops from a number of other suppliers such as Hewlett Packard. They also sell data communications equipment, printer supplies, faxes, answering machines, disks and computer furniture. Delivery is overnight and you can also arrange to lease equipment at very competitive rates.

Catalogue Bi-annually, A4, Catalogue, Colour, 226 pages, Free **Postal charges** Free **Delivery** Courier, Royal Mail **Methods of Payment** Cheque, Credit Card, American Express, Switch

EASTERN SOFTWARE PUBLISHING LTD

Cowdray Centre House
Suite 2
Cowdray Avenue
Colchester
Essex
CO1 1GF

Spreadsheet software

A catalogue containing spreadsheet software for business users. You will find products for business planning, risk analysis, neural networks, business forecasting and spreadsheet organisation, plus many more products. There is 30 days free technical support where you simply pick up the phone and are in touch with the experts.

COMPUTERS

Telephone
01206 44456
Fax
01206 763313

Catalogue Quarterly, A4, Catalogue, Colour, 24 pages, Free **Postal charges** £10.50 **Methods of Payment** Cheque, Postal Order, Credit Card, American Express, Diners Club

GUILDSOFT
The Software Centre
Lee Mill Industrial Estate
Ivybridge
Nr Plymouth
Devon
PL21 9PE
Telephone
01752 895100
Fax
01752 894833

Computer software

GuildSoft deals in a variety of specialist, relatively unusual software for the home, business and 'edutainment' markets. Random House Kids Encyclopaedia, CD-ROM, £38.25; Magic Theatre, CD-ROM, £38.25; Bodyworks 3.0, diskette or CD-Rom, £49.95; Learn to Speak Spanish, CD-ROM, £139; 500 Fonts for Windows, CD-ROM, £14.99.

Catalogue Annually, A5, Catalogue, Colour, 34 pages, Free **Postal charges** £5 next-day delivery **Delivery** Courier **Methods of Payment** Cheque, Credit Card, Switch, American Express

THE JUMPING BEAN CO
Leen Gate
Lenton
Nottingham
Nottinghamshire
NG7 2LX
Telephone
0115 9792838
Fax
0115 9780963

Computer games

Noddy's Big Adventure, the sequel to Noddy's Playtime, is a graded creativity and entertainment package for three to seven-year-olds containing a Junior Word processor for developing story-telling skills. The Jumping Bean Co price is £24.99 (IBM PC and Amiga versions). For bigger kids, Cardmania, two games inspired by Blackjack and poker, is available for £24.99 (IBM PCs and compatibles).

Catalogue Annually, A5, Leaflets, Colour and B/W, 4 pages, Free **Postal charges** Free **Delivery** Royal Mail **Methods of Payment** Cheque, Postal Order

THE MAC ZONE
PO Box 34
Ripley
Woking
Surrey

Computers, accessories and software

The Mac Zone sells exclusively Apple Macintosh products. An alphabetical list gives brief product details, system requirements, restrictions and drawbacks. If you register with the Mac Zone,

GU23 6YR
Telephone
01483 211456
Fax
01483 211567

you receive a certain number of Air Miles every time you buy a product. All the most popular software seems competitively priced: Illustrator (£279.95); Photoshop (£399.95); and PageMaker (£449.95). Hardware includes the Nokia 15in Triniton monitor (£329.95) and Magneto optical drive (£549.95). A Mac User Best Buy is the CD-ROM drive (£179.95). Prices correct at time of going to press.

Catalogue A4, Catalogue, Colour, 47 pages, Free **Postal charges** Free for orders of £100 or more where payment accompanies the order. Otherwise, £5.00 per order (UK) **Delivery** Courier **Methods of Payment** Cheque, Postal Order, Credit Card, American Express, Switch

MACWAREHOUSE
Unit 6
Wolsey Business Park
Tolpits Lane
Watford
Hertfordshire
WD1 8QP
Telephone
0800 181 332
Fax
01923 234 122

Apple computers
MacWarehouse is a long-established American company with a base in this country selling everything for Apple computers, including the computers themselves. A thoroughly professional publication, it offers a huge range of products each of which is given a helpful description. Apple CD-ROM players are currently £149.95; Power-Book 150, £949; and Microsoft Word 6.0, £244.95. Note, all prices exclude VAT. An invaluable catalogue for any Apple user or user-to-be.

Catalogue Annually, A4, Catalogue, Colour, 100 pages, Free **Postal charges** £5 **Delivery** Courier **Methods of Payment** Cheque, Postal Order, Credit Card

MESH COMPUTERS PLC
Mesh House
3–4 Apsley Court
Apsley Way
London
NW2 7HF

Computers
MESH computers have been supplying to government, corporate and educational users since 1987 and they offer all types of computer systems, from notebooks to extremely powerful professional models. For example, the new MESH Universal Media complete with 4Mbyte Ram, lifetime

Telephone
0181 452 1111
Fax
0181 208 4493

warranty and Multi Media (double-speed CD-ROM, SoundBlaster 16 Pro, speakers, and 15-title CD bundle including Microsoft Encarta) can be yours for a mere £999 plus VAT (prices correct at time of going to press).

Catalogue A4, Catalogue, Colour, 7 pages, Free **Postal charges** £18.00 including insurance **Delivery** Courier **Methods of Payment** Cheque, COD, Credit Card

MISCO
Misco Computer Supplies Ltd
FREEPOST
Wellingborough
Northamptonshire
NN8 6BR
Telephone
01933 400400
Fax
01933 401520

Computer supplies and accessories

Misco offers an extensive range of supplies for the modern office. They deliver goods such as computers, filing cabinets, printers, and floppy disks, and the four-minute desk, which can be self assembled. Prices are reasonable with some reductions offered for customers buying two or more products.

Catalogue Monthly, A4, Catalogue, Colour, 120 pages

NIGHTHAWK ELECTRONICS LTD
PO Box 44
Saffron Walden
Essex
CB11 3ND
Telephone
01799 540881
Fax
01799 541713

Computer accessories

Nighthawk goods – a range of easy-to-install PC accessories which can save money and power – are British-made. The accessories include a Modem Mate to provide remote access to PCs (£199) and the Ecomonitor, a screen-saver that will help prevent screen-burn and cut down on radiation emissions (£49). There is an impressive range of printer switches and buffers. The APS and Jellybean range can increase the performance of your printer as well as the number of PCs that can be linked to it.

Catalogue A4, Leaflets, Colour and B/W, 26 pages, Free **Postal charges** Buffer switches, NDX & DXS-16, £8.50 per unit; all other products, £3.75 per unit **Delivery** Royal Mail, Parcelforce **Methods of Payment** Cheque

COMPUTERS

PORTABLE COMPUTERS LTD
Arden Court
Arden Road
Alcester
Warwickshire
B49 6HN
Telephone
01789 400067
Fax
01789 765493

Laptop computers
Portable Computers Ltd provide top-name laptops for government, educational and business establishments around the country from among brand names such as Toshiba, NEC and AST. Their 'Star Buy' at £1,299 (prices correct at time of going to press) is the AST NB 4/25 Bravo ColorPlus which comes with a trackball mouse and standard software including MS DOS Version 6.0 and Microsoft Windows Version 3.1.
Catalogue Annually, A4, Brochure, Colour, 6 pages, Free **Postal charges** Add £20.00 for computers; £8.00 for accessories **Delivery** Royal Mail **Methods of Payment** Cheque, Credit Card

PORTABLE OFFICE DIRECT
PO Box 808
Stapleford
Cambridge
Cambridgeshire
CB2 5NX
Telephone
01223 843448
Fax
01223 576859

Portable computers
Winner of the *Byte Magazine* 'Best of Computex' award, the Dual Group notebooks from Portable Office Direct are a step forward in portable computers, combining all the power of a desktop with the advantages of flexibility. Prices from £999. The catalogue includes accessories, multimedia equipment, docking stations and software to connect you to the Internet.
Catalogue Annually, A4, Catalogue, Colour, 16 pages, Free **Postal charges** Varies with item **Delivery** Royal Mail, Parcelforce **Methods of Payment** Cheque, Credit Card

THE PUBLIC DOMAIN & SHAREWARE LIBRARY
Winscombe House
Beacon Road
Crowborough
Sussex
TN6 1UL
Telephone
01892 663298

Computer software
This company stocks the widest range of Public Domain and Shareware in the UK, everything from business to astronomy. As the name implies, shareware can be used for a limited period on your PC without the threat of something dire when Big Brother finds out you've got unlicensed software up and running. By joining the library (from £23 a year) you can receive disks at members' rates. Public Domain also provides a

Fax
01892 667473

disk format translation service, from £10.50 a disk.

Catalogue Annually, A5, Catalogue, B/W, 144 pages, £2.50 **Postal charges** Varies with item **Delivery** Royal Mail **Methods of Payment** Cheque

RICKITT EDUCATIONAL MEDIA
Great Western House
Langport
Somerset
TA10 9YU
Telephone
01460 57152
Fax
01460 53176

Educational software

Rickitt's catalogue features the best educational programs from leading software houses. It supports all the important platforms, including Archimedes A3000 and A5000, IBM PC, Nimbus BBC, Amiga, Amstrad, Atari and Apple Mac. The catalogue is well-arranged with programs listed by subject (such as English Language, History or Music) and within that by age group and key stage. Each program is given a full description so you can make an informed choice. All About Me (age 3–5 years), £16.45; Structured Spelling (5–9 years), £25.95; Micro German (11–adult), £28.20.

Catalogue Annually, A4, Catalogue, Colour, 90 pages, £2 **Postal charges** Free **Delivery** Royal Mail, Parcelforce **Methods of Payment** Cheque, Postal Order, Credit Card

SELECTDIRECT
FREEPOST (NG5 132)
Nottingham
Nottinghamshire
NG7 1BR
Telephone
0115 986 5782

Apple computer software and hardware

SelectDIRECT is the mail order division of KRCS Group plc. Through it, they supply a comprehensive range of Macintosh and third-party hardware, plus all the latest Macintosh software from professional applications to games and leisure. Their continued aim is to provide quality products and value for money, with efficient and prompt shipment to their customers' desktop. They offer next-day delivery on items in stock and accept payment by cash, cheque, Switch, Visa and Access cards. Call their telesales department on 0115 986 5782 to discuss your specific requirements.

Catalogue Quarterly, A4, Catalogue, Colour, 68 pages, FOC **Postal charges** Varies with item **Delivery** Courier **Methods of Payment** Cheque, Credit Card, Postal Order, Switch

SHAREWARE PUBLISHING
Station Road
Colyton
Devon
EX13 6HA
Telephone
01297 552222
Fax
01297 553366

Shareware

Shareware's 'Software Source Reference Guide' takes you through the options for low-cost, high-quality software for the IBM PC and compatibles. The bulk of the catalogue consists of shareware disks, but there's also fully licensed shareware and non shareware. Shareware allows you to 'try before you buy'. The author receives nothing until you've decided whether you want to keep the program. All shareware disks in the catalogue incur a £3 handling charge.

Catalogue A4, Catalogue, Colour, 104 pages

TINY COMPUTERS
53 Ormside Way
Holmethorpe Industrial Estate
Redhill
Surrey
RH1 2LW
Telephone
01737 779511
Fax
01737 779541

Computers

Tiny Computers' Building Block range of IBM-compatible personal computers are well-priced and fully upgradable. There is something for everyone here and they can be custom-built to meet your needs. The 486SX-33MHz, 1MB RAM costs £249; colour monitors from £129; hard disk drives from £79. The 486DX2-33MHz system, 4MB RAM, costs £899 (prices excluding VAT).

Catalogue Annually, A4, Catalogue, Colour and B/W, 6 pages, Free **Postal charges** Varies with item **Delivery** Royal Mail, Parcelforce, Courier **Methods of Payment** Cheque, Credit Card

WHITE KNIGHT TECHNOLOGY
PO Box 38
Ware
Hertfordshire

Computer accessories

White Knight, an Amiga specialist, supplies a wide range of professional computer hardware and software, audio and video products and broadcast equipment. On offer are a range of

SG11 1TX
Telephone
01920 822321
Fax
01920 822302

A4000 accelerators including the Cyberstorm 50 MHz 68060 for £995; and hard drives from £159. **Catalogue** Annually, A4, Leaflets, B/W, 2 pages, Free **Postal charges** Varies with item **Delivery** Courier, Parcelforce, Royal Mail **Methods of Payment** Cheque, Credit Card, Switch

DIY Supplies

ARISTOCAST ORIGINALS LTD
Dept HB10
Bold Street
Sheffield
South Yorkshire
S9 2LR
Telephone
01742 561156
Fax
0114 2431835

Ornamental plaster mouldings
This brochure contains the complete range of plaster mouldings available. Centre-pieces from 12-inch, price £23 to 56-inch, price £130. The range has been assembled to meet most design requirements. Panel moulding, 1.5m length from £8, quadrant corners from £3.50. Pedestals, archways, corbels and fire-surrounds are also stocked. The designs are ornate and traditional.
Catalogue Annually, A4, Brochure, Colour, 16 pages, Free **Postal charges** £15 per complete order **Delivery** Courier **Methods of Payment** Cheque, Credit Card

CLAYTON MONROE
Kingston West Drive
Kingston
Staverton
Totnes
Devon
TQ9 6AR
Telephone
01803 762626
Fax
01803 762584

Architectural ironmongery
The catalogue for all DIY enthusiasts who are looking for something unique. A specialist company operating in the heart of South Devon with a specialist team making brass, natural steel/pewter colour door knockers, hinges, fingerplates, drawer or cupboard pulls to name but a few of the items available. Known as the Feron Collection, this catalogue is ideal for anyone who is renovating an old house or wants something of good quality which will last. Electrical fittings such as wall sockets and light switches are featured as well.
Catalogue Annually, A3, Brochure, Colour, 24 pages, Free **Postal charges** Varies with item **Delivery** Courier, Royal Mail **Methods of Payment** Cheque, Postal Order, Credit Card

CLAYTON-MUNROE

Kingston West Drive
Kingston
Staverton
Totnes
Devon
TQ9 6AR
Telephone
01803 762626
Fax
01803 762584

Architectural ironmongery

A major problem with restoring a period building is finding materials as close to the original style as possible. Clayton-Munroe has recreated a range of authentic door furniture called Rough at the Edges. Each item is handmade and no two pieces are identical. Staverton thumb latch, £25.36. In addition, the company produces a full range of Feron handles, hinges and cabinet fittings in classic and contemporary styles.

Catalogue Annually, A4, Catalogue, B/W, 17 pages, Free **Postal charges** Varies with item **Delivery** Royal Mail, Parcelforce **Methods of Payment** Cheque, Credit Card

DAVIES & CLIFFORD

Beta Works
Oxford Road
Tatling End
Gerrards Cross
Buckinghamshire
SL9 7BB
Telephone
01753 886254
Fax
01753 887319

Portable wooden buildings

Portable wooden buildings made by qualified craftsmen. The catalogue features a large range of buildings with their different sizes and specifications, including garden sheds, garages, workshops, chalets, dens, pavilions and greenhouses. A 2.1 × 1.5m garden shed in deal cladding will cost £292.50; 3 × 2.4m shed, £458.43. Erection by the company is a further 15%. The company will also quote for the construction of individual designs to the customer's own specification.

Catalogue Annually, A5, Brochure, B/W, 24 pages, Free **Postal charges** Free delivery except to Scotland and the Islands (price on application) **Delivery** In-house delivery **Methods of Payment** Cheque, Credit Card

DIY PLASTICS (UK) LTD

Regal Way
Faringdon
Oxfordshire
SN7 7XD
Telephone
01367 242932

Building materials

DIY Plastics offers plastics for most projects. This includes a wide variety of plastic glazing suitable for greenhouses, conservatories or extensions. The clearly designed catalogue contains not only measurement tables but also illustrations showing how to go about a number of typical DIY tasks – a useful addition. It also offers a range of tools and

Fax
01367 242200

accessories along with draught excluders, sealants and security equipment. Rigid plastic sheets, 2mm thick, 610 × 457mm (24 × 18in), £2.97; 4mm thick, 2440 × 1220mm (96 × 48in), £60.16.

Catalogue Annually, A4, Catalogue, Colour, 24 pages, Free **Postal charges** Varies with item **Delivery** Royal Mail, Parcelforce, Courier **Methods of Payment** Cheque, Postal Order, Credit Card

F. PARR
Merse Road
North Moons Moat
Heddltch
Worcestershire
B98 9PL
Telephone
01527 585777
Fax
01527 66430

Factory, warehouse, shop and office equipment

Parrs catalogue is mainly for factories, shops, offices, workshops and garages, but there is a good deal of interest to the general public as well. There is a marvellous range of porters' trolleys, called 'sack trucks', shelving, plastic storage containers, water pumps, staple guns, wrapping materials, filing cabinets, fire extinguishers, step ladders, safety mats and so on. Sack truck, from £49.99; steps from £35.20; hand tacker, £21.95 (prices excluding VAT).

Catalogue Annually, A4, Catalogue, Colour, 258 pages **Postal charges** Varies with item **Methods of Payment** Cheque, Credit Card

FIRED EARTH
Twyford Mill
Oxford Road
Adderbury
Oxfordshire
OX17 3HP
Telephone
01295 812088
Fax
01295 810832

Tiles, floorcoverings, rugs

Fired Earth made its name selling tiles from around the world and its catalogue displays an enticing array of tiles for every situation. There are marble, earthenware, stoneware and slate floor tiles, decorative ceramic wall tiles and borders, insets and mosaics, English craft tiles and French ateliers' tiles. Natural floor-coverings, tribal rugs and kelims also feature. Honey terracotta, £28.08/sq m; Tuscany stoneware, from £55.49/sq m or 58p each; rugs from £143.83; floor adhesive £10/20kg (all prices excluding VAT). Fixing service available.

Catalogue Annually, A4, Catalogue, Colour, 72 pages, Free **Postal charges** Varies with item **Delivery** In-house delivery **Methods of Payment** Cheque, Credit Card

HAND TOOLS LTD
Wreakes Lane
Dronfield
Sheffield
South Yorkshire
S18 6PN
Telephone
01246 413139
Fax
01246 415208

Hand tools

For a comprehensive selection of gardening, agricultural, carpentry and engineering tools, look no further than Hand Tools Ltd's brochure. It contains products from Sorby & Hutton, Green Acre, and Fedco and offers substantial savings on retail prices. Dutch hoe, £9.35; carpenter's vice, £16.85; hedging shears from £13.35.

Catalogue Annually, A4, Catalogue, Colour and B/W, 6 pages, Free **Postal charges** Varies with item **Delivery** Royal Mail, Parcelforce, Courier **Methods of Payment** Cheque, Credit Card

HARMONY
28 Butcher Row
Beverley
East Yorkshire
HU17 0AB
Telephone
01482 865092
Fax
same

Paint effects and stencil designs

Now you can achieve those decorative effects emblazoned on the pages of glossy homes and interiors magazines for yourself. Harmony offers a wide range of paint kits for lime-washing wood, spattering fire surrounds, antiquing furniture, crackling picture frames and colour-washing walls, and a selection of essential accessories such as dragging brushes and varnishes. It also produces 100 exclusive stencil designs – pre-cut, washable and reusable – to transform walls, furniture and floors. Verdigris kit, £14.99; colour-wash kit, £13.99; Scumbleglaze, £5.99/200ml.

Catalogue Annually, Third A4, Leaflets, Colour, 3 pages, Free **Postal charges** Varies with item **Delivery** Royal Mail, Parcelforce **Methods of Payment** Cheque, Postal Order, Credit Card

HOUSE OF BRASS
122 North Sherwood Street
Nottingham
Nottinghamshire
NG1 4EF
Telephone
0115 947 5430

Brass fittings for the home
House of Brass offers a large selection of quality classical period reproduction brassware hand-finished to high standards. The range includes door knockers; letter boxes; light, socket and bathroom fittings; locks and window furniture; fenders; and even bedsteads. Double Victorian period bedstead, £479; bath mixer set in brass, £240; brass fenders from £85; Georgian period lever latch, £7.50 pair.

Catalogue Annually, A4, Catalogue, Colour, 14 pages, Free **Postal charges** £3.50 **Delivery** Royal Mail, Parcelforce **Methods of Payment** Cheque, Credit Card

J SIMBLE & SONS
76 Queens Road
The Broadway
Watford
Hertfordshire
WD1 2LD
Telephone
01923 226052
Fax
01923 817526

Tools
Simble produce two catalogues, an extensive 250-page one which costs £2.50, and a shorter black-and-white supplement which is free. There is a terrific range of tools, from large power drills and saws to individual wrenches and chisels. Prices are competitive. Basin wrench, £5.95; Draper combi cordless drill, from £88; Draper bandsaw and disc grinder, £209.

Catalogue Annually, A5, Catalogue, B/W, 250-page catalogue, £2.50; 32-page supplement free **Postal charges** Varies with item **Delivery** Royal Mail, Parcelforce **Methods of Payment** Cheque, Postal Order, Credit Card, Switch, American Express

JALI
Apsley House
Chartham
Canterbury
Kent
CT4 7HT
Telephone
01227 831710

Decorative pelmets, brackets, radiator covers and corner units
Jali offers reasonably priced and well-designed self-assembly kits for decorative pelmets, brackets, radiator covers, shelves, corner units and edge trims, manufactured from MDF. Screws and plugs are supplied where necessary and all you need is a screwdriver and a little wood glue. Any paint applied by brush or spray can be used. Edge trim,

Fax
01227 831950

1220 × 45 × 6mm, from £3.99; pelmets, 1830 × 175 × 6mm, from £12.99; radiator trellis cover, 1830 × 600 × 6mm, £35.99; corner shelf unit, £65.99.

Catalogue Annually, A5, Catalogue, Colour, 20 pages **Postal charges** £4 standard; £12 overnight courier **Delivery** Royal Mail, Parcelforce, Courier **Methods of Payment** Cheque, Credit Card, Switch

PEELS OF LONDON LTD
PO Box 160
Richmond
Surrey
TW10 7XL
Telephone
0181 948 0689
Fax
same

Artificial stained glass

Peels enable you to obtain a stained-glass effect with the minimum of effort. You can transform your doors and windows in minutes using pre-made transfers which peel off and can then be pressed into place. A variety of designs are available, such as 'Art Deco' and 'Forget-me-not' (both £23.99 for a 37½ × 26½in section). 'Peels' come with fully illustrated instructions and a special smoothing tool.

Catalogue A5, Brochure, Colour, 8 pages, Free **Postal charges** £3.00 **Delivery** Parcelforce **Methods of Payment** Cheque, Postal Order

PERKINS
105 Ack Lane East
Bramhall
Cheshire
SK7 2AB
Telephone
0161 440 9860
Fax
0161 440 7624

Radiator covers

Perkins specialise in decorative radiator grilles and surrounds to suit traditional or modern interiors. Styles include trellis, club, mosaic and filigree. The covers are made from kiln-dried timber or MDF. The grille fronts are easily opened for valve adjustment and can be removed if you want to redecorate. There are clear instructions for measuring your radiators and a 3ft-wide grille cover starts at £179 (£119 for self-assembly). Radiator shelves are also available (from £35; add £10 for a built-in towel rail).

Catalogue A5, Brochure, Colour, 4 pages, Free **Postal charges** Carriage, packing and insurance, £20 for each cover **Delivery** Royal Mail **Methods of Payment** Cheque, Credit Card

THE RADIATOR COVER COMPANY
2 Stile Hall Parade
Chiswick
London
W4 3AG
Telephone
0181 995 2447

Radiator covers
The Radiator Cover Company produces 'Flexiform', a range of woven mesh covers that can be cut to your requirements. Prices are based on overall length and grille choice. There are three types of cover: brass-backed ('brass'), wire mesh-backed ('lattice') and hardboard-backed ('screenlite'). Then there is a choice of 16 grille designs from 'Regency' to 'Mosaic'. Prices start at £6.00 per sq ft for a screenlite cover finished in white satin paint to £25 per sq ft for a brass cover.
Catalogue A4, Leaflets, Colour, 6 pages, Free **Delivery** Parcelforce **Methods of Payment** Cheque, Credit Card

THE STAMPING GROUND
PO Box 1364
London
W5 5ZH
Telephone
0181 758 8629

Decorative stamps for household surfaces
As an alternative to stencilling, try stamping. The Stamping Ground supplies stamps, rollers and gold paint (although any water-soluble paint can be used) in a variety of gothic, country, marine and nursery motifs, with clear instructions. It's a simple way to create borders, patterns or decorative features on walls, ceilings, floors or fabrics. A 3in (75 × 75mm) stamp costs £8.95, a 5in (125 × 120mm) costs £10.95; roller £2.99; gold paint, £2.99.
Catalogue Annually, A5, Catalogue, Colour and B/W, 6 pages, Free **Postal charges** £1.99 **Delivery** Royal Mail **Methods of Payment** Cheque

STOP SHOP BY MAIL
Unit 1A
Fowler Street Industrial Estate
Wakefield Road
Bradford
West Yorkshire
BD4 7NE
Telephone
01274 738777

Security products
With the current crime figures escalating there is now an increasing demand for high-quality and low-cost security systems. Stop Shop claim to provide everything necessary to protect the home and the office. Ideal for homes, the Logic 4 DIY burglar alarm system starts at £63.95. Or you could invest in the Phillips Observation Kit, a complete closed-circuit TV system, for £385.

Fax
01274 743555

Car alarms include the Sparkrite SR 70, featuring a coded radio remote, current sensing and a high-output siren (£45). Reasonably priced security lighting is also available, plus a collection of dummy security boxes and cameras.

Catalogue Bi-annually, A4, Catalogue, Colour, 14 pages, Free **Postal charges** Free **Delivery** Royal Mail **Methods of Payment** Cheque, Credit Card

TURNSTYLE DESIGNS
1 Bridge Chambers
Barnstaple
Devon
EX31 1HB
Telephone
01271 25325
Fax
01271 328248

Door knobs, handles and back plates

Turnstyle produces a unique range of door knobs and cabinet handles in shell, fossil, bird, sun and moon, animal and fish designs. Colours include subtle ochre, verdigris, aqua blue and terracotta. Many of the knobs, such as the frog design, are suitable for use as pegs, too. Door furniture from £35 a pair; cabinet knobs, £6 each.

Catalogue Annually, A4, Leaflets, Colour and B/W, 9 pages, Free **Postal charges** Varies with item **Delivery** Royal Mail, Parcelforce **Methods of Payment** Cheque, Postal Order, Credit Card

WOOD FLOOR SALES
Unit 4 Tything Park
Arden Forest Trading Estate
Alcester
Warwickshire
B49 6ES
Telephone
01789 400050
Fax
01789 400049

Wood flooring

This company supplies glorious wooden flooring in a variety of different woods and hardnesses. In the first instance, you can obtain an estimate over the telephone and be sent samples. Prior to fitting, either by the company's craftsmen or your own builder, a surveyor will take exact measurements. The flooring is laid over a sub-floor and only the tongues require glue. It comes with five coats of durable lacquer and is therefore ready to walk on as soon as it has been laid. From £30.50/sq m excluding VAT.

Electrical Appliances

BRITISH TELECOM
In Touch
BT FREEPOST GW 7520
Glasgow
Strathclyde
G2 6BR
Telephone
0800 800 150

Telephones and accessories

In Touch magazine brings you the latest and best ideas from British Telecom. There is a vast range of telephones, answering machines and mobile phones, with helpful and flexible options on renting or buying ... but there is also much more.

The latest in video technology is now available for only a few pounds a month. For £399, Videophones can bring you face to face with family and friends, and for only £19.99 a month (plus installation) the Sky multi-channel package, including Sky Movies Gold and Sports Channel, can be delivered straight to your living room. The rental options also have the benefit of full maintenance protection by BT's trained staff. You can pay by Switch if you visit a BT shop personally.

Catalogue Bi-annually, A4, Magazine, Colour, 44 **Postal charges** Varies with item **Delivery** Royal Mail **Methods of Payment** Cheque, Postal Order, Credit Card

BUYERS & SELLERS LTD
120/122 Ladbroke Grove
North Kensington
London
W10 5NE
Telephone
0171 229 1947/8468

Domestic appliances

Buyers & Sellers supply almost every brand of cooker, fridge, freezer, oven, hob, vacuum cleaner, microwave, washing machine and tumble-drier currently available in the UK. They have an advice line for telephone shoppers as well as a large showroom/warehouse for personal callers. Although they do not have a catalogue as such, they

Fax
0171 221 4113

will send out a selection of makers' brochures to assist choice. They often have 'special purchases' on display or end-of-line models and are well-known for their competitive prices. Delivery is undertaken countrywide – and even throughout Europe.

Catalogue A5, Brochure, Colour and B/W, 2 pages, Free **Postal charges** Free **Delivery** In-house delivery **Methods of Payment** Cheque, Credit Card, American Express, Diners Club

Electronics

LORRAINE ELECTRONICS SURVEILLANCE
716 Lea Bridge Road
Leyton
London
E10 6AW
Telephone
0181 558 4226
Fax
0181 558 1338

Surveillance equipment
Lorraine Electronics manufacture an extensive range of professional audio surveillance equipment. Room conversations can be monitored by either portable or static systems, for example 'The Recording Briefcase with VHF transmitter' (£600). Telephone conversations can be monitored by telephone transmitters (from £200). These products are supplied for export only. Transmitting radio signals without a licence and connecting unapproved equipment to the public telephone network is an offence in the UK.

Catalogue A4, Catalogue, Colour, 20 pages, Free **Postal charges** Varies with item **Delivery** In-house delivery **Methods of Payment** Cheque, Credit Card, American Express, Diners Club, Switch

TANDY BY MAIL
Bilston Road
Wednesbury
West Midlands
WS10 7JN
Telephone
0121 556 0786
Fax
same

Electronics, hi-fi, computers, parts
The high street chain Tandy stocks a huge range of most types of electrical goods and accessories that are also available by mail order. Telephone answering machines start at £29.99, portable televisions at £69.99. Yamaha keyboards start at £59.99 and 35mm cameras at £19.99. Tandy also stocks computer games from SEGA, Amiga, Nintendo and Commodore and offers a selection of business and entertainment software for personal computers. CD-ROM software titles include Microsoft Encarta for £99.99.

ELECTRONICS

Catalogue Annually, A4, Catalogue, Colour, 131 pages, Free **Postal charges** £3.00; goods over £100.00 will be sent by courier at a charge of £10.00 **Delivery** Royal Mail, Courier **Methods of Payment** Cheque, Postal Order, Credit Card

Flowers

BLOOMS OF GUERNSEY
Portinfer Coast Road
Vale
Guernsey
Channel Islands
GY6 8LG
Telephone
01481 53085
Fax
01481 53840

Fresh flowers

Blooms of Guernsey grow, pick, select and pack all their own flowers and have won the British National Carnation Society silver medal three years in a row.

Prices start at £7.20 for 6 carnations. Freesias are from £7.85 for 15. Mixed bouquets of 10 carnations and 20 freesias cost £16.50. Prices include fern.

Bearlooms of Guernsey can provide bears with personalised messages on their sweaters instead of flowers. There's Emile for £15.00, Amos for £25.00 and Monty for £12.45.

Catalogue Annually, Third A4, Brochure, Colour, 6 pages, Free **Postal charges** Free **Delivery** Royal Mail **Methods of Payment** Cheque, Postal Order, Credit Card, American Express

BUNCHES
PO Box 20
Kirkby-in-Ashfield
Nottingham
Nottinghamshire
NG17 8ES
Telephone
01623 750343
Fax
01623 758704

Flowers

The Post Office now offers a flowers-by-post service. There are four bouquets to choose from, one of which is exclusively of roses (£15.99) and the others are of carnations in various colour schemes (from £9.99).

Optional extras are a 175g box of continental-style chocolates for £6.99, a 5in jointed teddy for £3, and gypsophila for £2. Orders should be placed at least three days in advance (five for special occasions such as Mother's Day).

Catalogue A4, Leaflets, Colour, 1 page, Free **Postal charges** Free **Delivery** Royal Mail **Methods of Payment** Cheque, Credit Card, American Express

CHARITY FLOWERS DIRECT
PO Box 555
Guernsey
GY1 6JA
Telephone
0990 300 600

Floral gifts

Wholly owned by charities with all the profits going to charity, Charity Flowers Direct is the new way to send postal flowers. The beautiful blooms are gift-packaged with ribbons and there are 18 arrangements from which to choose.

Catalogue Third A4, Leaflets, Colour, 6 pages, Free **Postal charges** Free **Delivery** Royal Mail **Methods of Payment** Cheque, Postal Order, Credit Card Switch

CHURCHTOWN FARM
St Martin's
Isles of Scilly
TR25 OQL
Telephone
01720 422169
Fax
same

Flower gifts by post

The Isles of Scilly have long been famous for growing flowers. Churchtown Farm specialises in scented narcissi and show pinks. Flowers are sent all year round although the varieties depend on the time of year. All flower gifts are sleeved and ribbon-wrapped with a card for a personal message. There are five sizes of gift packs: 12 flowers cost £6; 30 flowers are £9 (3 bunches); 40 flowers (4 bunches), £11; 50 flowers, £13; and 60 flowers for £16.

Catalogue Updated regularly, Third A4, Brochure, Colour, 6 pages, Free **Postal charges** Free **Delivery** Royal Mail **Methods of Payment** Cheque, Postal Order, Credit Card

THE CORNISH BULB COMPANY
Ashdown Nurseries
Ashton
Helston
Cornwall
TR13 9BR
Telephone
01736 762469

Fresh flowers and chocolates

This company sends out fresh flowers including freesias (£9.95 for 20), spray carnations (from £10.95 for 15), roses (from £12.95 for 10), daffodils (from £5.50 for 15), anemones (£9.50 for 40) and Cornish pinks (£7.45 for 30). They also offer luxury candies and chocolates such as Clotted Cream Fudge (£2.95 for 170g), Turkish Delight (£2.95 for 170g), and Chocolate Easter

Fax
01736 763662

Eggs decorated with sugar flowers (£3.35).
Catalogue Bi-annually, A5, Leaflets, B/W, 4 pages, Free
Postal charges For guaranteed next-day delivery add £2.70 to flower cost (UK), £4.00 (Europe) **Delivery** Royal Mail **Methods of Payment** Cheque, Credit Card, Postal Order

DE GARIS FLOWERS
PO Box 154
Macclesfield
Cheshire
SK10 5TR
Telephone
01625 500545
Fax
same

Flowers by post
An easy way to say thank you, or to send love, congratulations, or birthday wishes – simply send flowers. De Garis offers three selections: spray carnation and gypsophila bouquet, £9.95; a dozen carnations with gypsophila and fern, £11.95; and a mixed bouquet of alstroemeria, carnations and blooms of the season, £13.95. They are sent in a tissue-lined gift box with your personal message.
Catalogue Annually, A5, Brochure, Colour, 4 pages, Free
Postal charges Free **Delivery** Royal Mail **Methods of Payment** Cheque, Postal Order, Credit Card

DIAMOND FLOWERS
Les Arbres
Les Gigands
St Sampsons
Guernsey
Channel Islands
GY2 4YX
Telephone
01481 46375
Fax
01481 43462

Flowers
Diamond Flowers will post flowers from Guernsey to the UK by the first-class post Mondays to Thursdays. They will send carnations, spray carnations and freesias or a mixed bouquet in various sizes. As well as growing their own flowers, the company picks, packs and posts them too. Each selection contains the customer's selection, plus fern and a gift card containing the message from the sender. Diamond Flowers also include in the box a complimentary sachet of plant food together with hints on flower care. These helpful tips should ensure that the flowers remain fresh and in bloom for longer. Prices at time of going to press (which were valid until January 1996) are: 12 carnations, £8.65; 20 carnations, £11.60; 30 carnations, £14.75;

10 spray carnations, £7.55; 25 freesias, £9.75; 35 freesias, £11.75; mixed bouquets from £10–£20.
Catalogue Brochure, Colour, 1 page, Free **Postal charges** To Europe add £5.50 extra to cover express post (carnations only) **Delivery** Royal Mail **Methods of Payment** Cheque, Postal Order, Credit Card

FLORAL REVENGE
Flowerzone
370 Green Lanes
London
N13 5XL
Telephone
0181 447 8250

Flowers

Flower-arranging and delivery service which caters for divorcees and dumped lovers who want to express their feelings to their partners but can't quite find the words. Black roses, tulips and irises and headless thorn stems are available, including Fatal Attraction: The Last Bloom (a single black rose in a satin-lined box, £18.50) and A Prickly Parting (a black rose and thorn stems in a ceramic pot, £29.50).
Delivery Royal Mail **Methods of Payment** Cheque, Postal Order, Credit Card

FLOWERS BY POST
Bellefleur Nursery
PO Box 259
L' Islet
St Sampson's
Guernsey
Channel Islands
GY1 3QP
Telephone
01481 52528
Fax
01481 56522

Fresh flowers

All the flowers sent in this company's postal boxes are of the highest quality and treated with preservative before despatch to prolong their life. They specialise in carnations: 10 spray carnations cost £10.50; 10 spray carnations and 10 freesias cost £13.50. A presentation box of 15 carnations, 10 spray carnations and 20 freesias costs £17.15.
Catalogue Annually, Third A4, Brochure, Colour, 6 pages, Free **Postal charges** Free **Delivery** Royal Mail **Methods of Payment** Cheque, Credit Card

FLYING FLOWERS
PO Box 500
St Helier
Jersey

Fresh-flower bouquets

Flying Flowers, the UK's largest carnation grower and fresh-flower postal company, will send beautiful nursery-fresh bouquets direct from

Channel Islands
JE4 8XA
Telephone
01534 865665
Fax
01534 865554

Jersey to any UK address. Flowers are sent 'in-bud' with greenery and bouquet wrap in a protective gift box, together with flower food, care leaflet and a message card. A bouquet of 12 mixed carnations costs just £9.99; 18 assorted carnations, £13.99; and 30 assorted carnations and freesias, £17.99. (Prices include delivery.)
Catalogue A5, Leaflets, Colour, 1 page, Free **Delivery** Royal Mail **Methods of Payment** Cheque, Postal Order, Credit Card

FOREVER FLOWERING
Orchard House
Mortlake Road
Kew Gardens
Surrey
TW9 4AS
Telephone
0181 392 9929
Fax
0181 876 6166

Fresh flowers
Imagine the thrill of receiving a basket of white lilies, lilac freesias or red roses in the depths of winter, a hand-tied bouquet of tulips in spring, or a trug full of peonies in summer. These are just some of the items offered by Forever Flowering. Ring before noon for next-day delivery anywhere in the UK and discuss which blooms are freshest that morning and how you would like them presented. Prices from £20, plus delivery.
Catalogue Annually, Third A4, Brochure, Colour, 2 pages, Free **Postal charges** Varies with item **Delivery** Courier, Royal Mail **Methods of Payment** Cheque, Credit Card

GARLAND FLOWERS JERSEY
Le Pressoir
Rue de Bechet
St John
Jersey
Channel Islands
JE3 4FT
Telephone
01534 863621
Fax
01534 862439

Flowers
Fresh cut flowers, all year round, delivered by first-class post. A dozen long-stemmed carnations cost just £8.99 and there are also spray roses, single red roses, coloured roses, seasonal bouquets and freesias. Flowers are posted only on Mondays, Tuesdays and Wednesdays at noon to avoid weekend delays in the post.
Catalogue Annually, A5, Leaflets, B/W, 3 pages, Free **Postal charges** Free **Delivery** Royal Mail **Methods of Payment** Cheque, Postal Order, Credit Card

GROOM BROTHERS

Pecks Drove Nurseries
Spalding
Lincolnshire
PE12 6BR
Telephone
01775 722421
Fax
01775 712252

Flowers for Christmas

Flowers for Christmas make a refreshing alternative to the more usual gifts. Groom Bros offers 30 daffodils for £8.70, or 10 mixed carnations for £9.50. For a more lasting present, an amaryllis bulb which flowers in the spring costs £5.29, pot and saucer, £1.67. Alternative gifts include a port and stilton hamper, £21.50, and smoked salmon, £20.08/1.25lb sliced. (Daffodils and amaryllis available until March, carnations for Christmas and New Year.)

Catalogue Annually, A5, Catalogue, Colour, 6 pages, Free **Postal charges** Varies with item **Delivery** Royal Mail, Parcelforce **Methods of Payment** Cheque, Postal Order, Credit Card

GUERNSEY FLOWERS BY POST

La Fallaize Vineries
St Martin's
Guernsey
Channel Islands
GY4 6RA
Telephone
01481 35261
Fax
01481 37244

Fresh flowers

Guernsey Flowers offers a selection of bouquets that are available all year round, plus a range of seasonal bouquets. Prices include your choice of bouquet with decorative greenery, gift-box presentation, flower food and care instructions and your personal message.

A dozen orchids cost £15.95; a dozen red roses, £16.50; and Guernsey Glory seasonal bouquets come in shades of pink, red, gold or mixed shades and cost from £7.25 for 6 stems to £29.95 for 33 stems.

Catalogue Annually, A5, Catalogue, Colour, 17 pages, Free **Postal charges** Free **Delivery** Royal Mail **Methods of Payment** Cheque, Postal Order, Credit Card, American Express

GUERNSEY FRESH FLOWERS

La Couture Road
St Peter Port
Guernsey

Flowers

Guernsey Fresh Flowers sends bouquets of carnations, roses and freesias in a presentation box anywhere in the UK or Europe. Prices start at £10 for 12 carnations and rise to £20.25 for 20

FLOWERS

Channel Islands
GY1 2EA
Telephone
01481 722280
Fax
01481 714656

red, pink and yellow roses. Orders to Europe cost £4 more. For prices from £12.45 they will also send out fluffy teddybears!
Catalogue Brochure, Colour, 1 page, Free **Postal charges** Free **Delivery** Royal Mail **Methods of Payment** Cheque, Postal Order, Credit Card

INTERFLORA

Interflora House
Watergate
Sleaford
Lincs
NG34 7TR
Telephone
0500 434343 or 01529 304545
Fax
01529 414340

Floral arrangements and other gifts

Interflora offers a guaranteed personal flower-delivery service which operates in over 150 countries worldwide. The product range includes the 'Gift Collection' which includes flowers and helium balloons; hand-made chocolates; and soft toys. Orders placed for UK delivery before 1pm will arrive the same day and sometimes this applies to overseas orders, depending on time difference. Flower prices start from £7.50 for a single bloom in an attractive presentation box, £15 for a seasonal bouquet, £17.50 for a dainty hand-tied bouquet and £13.95 for handmade chocolates and flowers. There is a service and transmission charge of £2.95 for the UK. If you phone on the freephone 0500 number, the call is automatically directed to your nearest florist; if they are engaged, it goes back to the central operator who will take your order and then pass it on. The 01529 number goes direct to the central operator.

Catalogue Quarterly, Visiting card concertina, Leaflets, Colour, 4 pages, Free **Postal charges** £2.95 **Delivery** Local florist delivery **Methods of Payment** Cheque, Postal Order, Credit Card, Switch, American Express, Diners Club

PETER BEALES ROSES

London Road
Attleborough
Norfolk
NR17 1AY

Roses

Considered to be the most comprehensive commercial collection of classic roses in the world, Peter Beales Roses are grown on virgin soil around Attleborough producing hardy plants with good

Telephone
01953 454707
Fax
01953 456845

fibrous roots which will transplant into any type of soil anywhere. Their heritage collection of old roses includes the Georgian and Regency collection (£58.50) which consists of 10 roses including Hermosa and Bourbon Queen. Climbing roses average £6.35; hybrid tea roses, such as the beautiful orange Just Joey, cost around £4 each. Orders taken from 1st May onwards are despatched between November and March.

Catalogue Annually, A4, Catalogue, Colour, 57 pages, Send two 25p stamps **Postal charges** Varies with item **Delivery** Royal Mail **Methods of Payment** Cheque, Credit Card, Postal Order, COD

PINKS BY POST
320 London Road
Charlton Kings
Cheltenham
Gloucestershire
GL52 6YJ
Telephone
01242 234961
Fax
same

Fresh flowers

Chris and Tony Pickering run their own firm sending fresh, fragrant pinks by first-class post anywhere in the British Isles. They also grow anemones and freesias at their Devon nurseries. If you phone before 2pm your order will be in the post that day, packed in a rigid but elegant container, with personal message included. Standard Box of 20 blooms, £9; De Luxe Box of 30 blooms, £12; Special Box of 20 pinks and 10 freesias, £15; Winter Box of 15 pinks and 15 anemones, £12.

Catalogue Annually, A5, Leaflets, Colour and B/W, 2 pages, Free **Postal charges** Free **Delivery** Royal Mail **Methods of Payment** Cheque, Credit Card

PROFRUITION
63 Beulah Road
Tunbridge Wells
Kent
TN1 2NS
Telephone
01892 541332

Exotic dried fruits

Profruition dries and packages all variety of fruit and vegetables on the premises for use in decorative flower-arrangements for shops, functions, private houses, restaurants, etc. Packs are sold in 5, 10, 20 and 50. The range is endless and consists of fruits and vegetables of all varieties that are available in this country. Prices for 5

Aubergine slices, 65p; 10 Chestnut Funghi, £1.25. They will dry any other vegetable/fruit slices on request.
Catalogue Annually, A5, Leaflets, Colour and B/W, 12 pages, Free **Postal charges** Carriage: minimum order £10; orders up to £50, add 10%; orders up to £100, add 7.5%; orders over £100, carriage free **Delivery** In-house delivery **Methods of Payment** Cheque, Postal Order

SCENT DIRECT
PO Box 1042
Pulborough
West Sussex
RH20 2FF
Telephone
01798 812340
Fax
01798 815111

Flowers
Scent Direct delivers fresh flowers to the door for every occasion. Whether remembering an anniversary or birthday, offering congratulations or saying thank you, this is an easy way to send a floral gift. The flowers are delivered in pre-arranged bouquets ready to put straight into a vase. A mixed bouquet of 20 freesias with gypsophila, £10.99; 10 roses, £17.49; pastel pink or yellow mixed bouquet, £12.50 to £24.99; a stem of orchids, £22.49.
Catalogue Annually, Third A4, Catalogue, Colour, 2 pages, Free **Postal charges** Free **Delivery** In-house delivery, Courier **Methods of Payment** Cheque, Credit Card

TELEFLORIST
British Teleflower Service Ltd
Teleflower House
Unit 35
Romsey Industrial Estate
Greatbridge Road
Romsey
Hampshire
SO51 OHR
Telephone
01794 541116
Fax
01794 511199

Flowers
To send flowers by Teleflorist, you first have to find a florist displaying the Teleflorist 'dove' sign and order through the shop. The order is then telephoned to the Teleflorist nearest the recipient. The florist will have a design book from which you can select arrangements. Orders placed before midday can be delivered on the same day.
Delivery Courier, In-house delivery **Methods of Payment** Cheque, Credit Card

TESCO FLORAL EXPRESS
Tesco Stores Ltd
Cheshunt
Hertfordshire
EN8 9SL
Telephone
0800 226611

Flowers and chocolates
Brighten up someone's day with fresh flowers delivered to the door in a beautiful presentation box, complete with ribbon and greetings card. There are five bouquets to choose from including a cheerful Sunburst Bouquet, £17.99; an elegant Classic Bouquet £20.99; and a soft-coloured Luxury Bouquet, £24.99. For an additional £4 you can send a 200g box of handmade Belgian chocolates.
Catalogue Annually, A5, Catalogue, Colour, 10 pages, Free **Postal charges** Free **Delivery** Courier **Methods of Payment** Credit Card, Switch

TRESILLIAN FLOWER FARM
Truro
Cornwall
TR2 4AQ
Telephone
01872 520209
Fax
01872 520606

Cornish daffodils
Surprise someone on Mother's Day with a box of 60 Cornish daffodils (£11.50), or send a birthday, thank-you, or get-well-soon message. Tresillian Flower Farm is a family farm growing more than 100 acres of daffodils and narcissi which it sends to market all over Britain and exports to Holland. Its Bulb Shop is open from late July to October offering 50 varieties of daffodils as well as Cornish lilies and Dutch bulbs.
Catalogue Annually, A5, Leaflets, Colour and B/W, 4 pages, Free **Postal charges** Free **Delivery** Royal Mail **Methods of Payment** Cheque, Credit Card

WAITROSE DIRECT FRESH FLOWERS
Telephone
0800 592761

Floral and chocolate home-delivery
Two varieties of bouquets at £17.95; two at £19.95; a hand-tied posy at £22.95; a luxury bouquet at £24.95; basket arrangements in two different colours at £24.95. Also, with the bouquets, a 230g box of Belgian chocolates for £4.85 extra. This is a phone service only so you can pay only by credit card or Switch/Delta.
Catalogue Quarterly, A5, Leaflets, Colour, 8 pages, Free **Postal charges** Free **Delivery** Courier **Methods of Payment** Credit Card, Switch, American Express

WORLDWIDE FLOWERS
25 The Orchards
Haywards Heath
West Sussex
RH16 3FZ
Telephone
01444 451492/417651
Fax
01444 483777

Flowers and chocolates

Worldwide Flowers sends blooms from around the world, beautifully presented in a special gift box with a personal message card. But it doesn't stop at flowers: luxury Belgian chocolates and English hand-made truffles can be included, too, or sent on their own. Floral gift boxes from £13.95, chocolates from £5.50.

Catalogue Annually, Third A4, Catalogue, Colour, 6 pages, Free **Postal charges** Free **Delivery** Courier **Methods of Payment** Cheque, Postal Order, Credit Card

Food & Drink

ABERGAVENNY FINE FOODS
Pant-Ysgawn Farm
Unit 4
Castle Meadows Park
Abergavenny
Gwent
NP7 7RZ
Telephone
01873 850001
Fax
01873 850002

Welsh food
Abergavenny specialises in fine Welsh foods, mostly cheeses. They have an interesting selection of cheeses from their own dairy including Pantysgawn Farm, a soft goat's cheese; St Illtyd, a mature cheddar; Y-Fenni, a mature cheese with wholegrain mustard and brown ale; and St David's Welsh, a washed rind cheese.

They also sell Glamorgan sausages, a traditional Welsh vegetarian savoury product made from a mixture of farmhouse Cheddar and Caerphilly cheeses with leeks, herbs and spices. We also received leaflets from other cheese producers in Wales with the Abergavenny leaflet, namely Little Acorn Products which produces Skirried Welsh Ewe's Milk Cheese marinaded in Milk, and Pumpkin Produce which produces Merlin Cheddar goat's milk cheeses.

Catalogue Updated regularly, A4, Leaflets, Colour, 2 pages, Free **Postal charges** Varies with item

ADNAMS WINE MERCHANTS
The Crown
High Street
Southwold
Suffolk
IP18 6DP
Telephone
01502 724222

Fine wines
Three-times listed Wine Merchant of the Year, this Suffolk-based company has been selling wine through mail order for many years. It also has two retail outlets in Norwich and Southwold which are well worth a visit. The catalogue is splendidly laid out with a comprehensive and carefully chosen selection, and excellent and witty reviews of both the wines and regions. There is a best-buy

Fax
01502 724805

section for bottles under £5, £5–£8 and £8–£12, along with ranges of fortified wines and spirits. Other products include olive oil, vinegar and, for the enthusiast, Adnams ties at £19.50 and silk waistcoats at £65.

Catalogue Annually, A4, Catalogue, Colour, 100 pages, £2.50 **Postal charges** For single or part case orders, add £5; two cases or more, carriage free **Delivery** Courier **Methods of Payment** Credit Card, Cheque, Postal Order

ALGERIAN COFFEE STORES
52 Old Compton Street
London
W1V 6PB
Telephone
0171 437 2480
Fax
0171 437 5470

Coffees and teas

If you enjoy good coffee and tea, you'll welcome the opportunity to sample something from the Algerian Coffee Stores, whether by mail order or at the Soho shop. The comprehensive list includes full roast Café Torino, £2.30/½lb; pure Blue Mountain, £10.40/½lb; mocha berry flavoured coffee, £4.12/1¼lb. From the tea list: Assam Broken Orange Pekoe, £1.30/125g; Gunpowder Green, £1.15/125g. Herbal and fruit teas, teapots and coffee machines are also stocked.

Catalogue Annually, Third A4, Leaflets, B/W, 2 pages, Free **Postal charges** Varies with item **Methods of Payment** Cheque, Credit Card, American Express, Diners Club

BARLEYCORN NATURAL & ORGANIC FOODS
97–99 Lancaster Road
Enfield
Middlesex
EN2 0JN
Telephone
0181 363 2345
Fax
0181 364 4266

Natural and organic foods

Barleycorn are suppliers of a wide range of naturally produced foods, household goods and dietary supplements. There is a separate list for organically grown fruit and vegetables which is updated weekly. There is also a fresh fish list included. To their knowledge none of the products they stock contain artificial additives, colourings or flavourings. They will give assistance on special diets. Orders should be placed 24 hours before delivery or earlier. Everything is stocked from grains, sugar pasta, cereals to aromatherapy and medicines. Prices vary according to item.

Catalogue Annually, A4, Catalogue, B/W, 15 pages, Free **Postal charges** Varies with item **Delivery** In-house delivery **Methods of Payment** Cheque, Postal Order

THE BEER CELLAR & CO LTD
31 Norwich Road
Strumpshaw
Norwich
Norfolk
NR13 4AG
Telephone
01603 714884
Fax
01603 714624

Premium bottled beer

The Beer Cellar is Britain's leading specialist beer supplier. They have a huge a range of over 150 of the world's finest bottled beers from more than 30 countries. Their full-colour catalogue comes complete with tasting notes by Roger Protz, a world authority on beer. You can select your own case or choose from a range of pre-selected 12- or 24-bottle cases. Prices start at £17.90 for 12 different beers from as many countries. A new line is Golden Promise, Britain's first organic beer, brewed with selected hops and malted barley (£19.99 for 12).

Catalogue Annually, A5, Catalogue, Colour, 31 pages, Free **Postal charges** UK mainland and Isle of Wight only: add £3.50 for 1 case; £4.90 for 2 cases; £5.95 for 3 cases; £7.75 for 4 cases **Delivery** Parcelforce **Methods of Payment** Cheque, Postal Order, Credit Card, American Express, Diners Club

BEER PARADISE LTD
Unit 11, Riverside Place
South Accommodation Road
Leeds
Yorkshire
LS9 0RQ
Telephone
0113 2359082
Fax
0113 2359217

Beers

This membership-only club offers more than 300 beers at cash-and-carry prices direct to your door. Beer Paradise specialises in Belgian beers. The Belgian Chimay Grande Reserve costs £3.95 per bottle or £45.26 per case; the aptly named Delirium Tremens costs £1.75 per bottle or £35.91 per case. Among the few Dutch beers is the Grolsch Swingtop at £1.54 per bottle, £21.49 per case.

There is a deposit on each returnable bottle. They also do hampers, gift packs and glassware.

Catalogue Bi-annually, A4, Catalogue, B/W, 23 pages, Free **Postal charges** I case to 1 address, £4.50; 2 cases to 1 address, £7.00 **Delivery** In-house delivery **Methods of Payment** Cheque, Credit Card, Switch

BERKMANN WINE CELLARS LTD
12 Brewery Road
London
N7 9NH
Telephone
0171 609 4711
Fax
0171 607 0018

Wines

Berkmann has built up a reputation for supplying restaurant wines, with an accent on prompt and useful service extras like the possibility of reserving wine to ensure a continuous stock. Their minimum order for free delivery is three cases, but they're quite happy to supply mixed cases and single cases for a small extra charge. Their house wines start at £41.40 for a dozen bottles of Cuvé Duboeuf Blanc or Rouge.

Catalogue Bi-annually, A5, Catalogue, B/W, 46 pages, Free **Postal charges** Add £3.00 per case for 1–3 cases; over 3 cases, delivery is free **Delivery** Courier **Methods of Payment** Access/Mastercard, COD, Switch, Credit Card, Cheque

BERRY BROS & RUDD LTD
3 St James Street
London
SW1A 1EG
Telephone
0171 396 9600
Fax
0171 396 9611

Wines and spirits

Connoisseurs of wines, spirits, liqueurs and cigars will no doubt be familiar with Berry Bros & Rudd. Its packed catalogue is organised by country and region, giving maps and useful background information on each wine. A separate brochure explains its Clockwork service, a handy way of receiving a regular supply of imaginatively chosen wines. You pay £75, plus a monthly standing order of £25 for a case a quarter. A number of other services are available including laying down wine for children or god-children. Prices are by bottle from £3.15, half-bottle or magnum with discounts on larger orders. There is also a Christmas gift catalogue which offers champagne and cigars as other options.

Catalogue Annually, A5, Catalogue, B/W, 228 pages, Free **Postal charges** Free **Methods of Payment** Cheque, Credit Card, American Express, Diners Club

BERRYDALES
Berrydale House
5 Lawn Road
London
NW3 2XS
Telephone
0171 722 2866
Fax
0171 722 7685

Dairy-free, diabetic and carob chocolates

For children unable to indulge in 'normal' chocolate, Berrydales do gift packs of dairy-free plain Belgian chocolates which include children's books (*Berrydale Bear & the Cocoa Tree* and *Berrydale Bear meets Chocosaurus the Dinosaur*) suitable for the 3–6 year age group. The diabetic chocolate range includes 50g bunnies at £2.29 each and in the carob range you can buy a 70g bag of 7 animal shapes for £1.99. In addition there is a home-bake range of frozen vegetable ready-prepared meals including basmati and wild rice pilaff which is dairy-, gluten- and egg-free.

Catalogue A4, Leaflets, Colour and B/W, 5 pages, Free **Postal charges** Up to £7.50, add £1.50; £7.50-£15.00, add £2.25; £15.00-£20.00, add £3.25; £20.00-£30.00, add £4.50 **Delivery** Royal Mail **Methods of Payment** Cheque

BETTYS & TAYLORS BY POST
1 Parliament Street
Harrogate
North Yorkshire
HG1 2QU
Telephone
01423 886055
Fax
01423 881083

Tea, coffee and gift suppliers

Bettys & Taylors of Harrogate supply specialist teas and coffees along with presentation gifts. Traditional Easter specialities range from a luxury hamper, £139.84, including sparkling wine, Simnel cake, coffee, tea and chocolate goodies, to milk-chocolate eggs hand-decorated with sugarpaste primroses and bluebells, in two sizes, £11.30 or £13.40. The eggs are made from the finest quality Belgian chocolate and the company's team of Swiss-trained confectioners fill the moulds twice to give an extra luxurious coating of chocolate.

Catalogue Bi-monthly, Third A4, Catalogue, Colour, 17 pages, Free **Postal charges** £5.60 **Delivery** Courier, Parcelforce **Methods of Payment** Cheque, Credit Card

BEVERLY HILLS BAKERY
3 Edgerton Terrace
London
SW3 2BX
Telephone
0171 584 4401
Fax
0171 584 1106

Cakes
Deep in the heart of Knightsbridge, the Beverley Hills Bakery produces unusual hand-made mini-muffins, cookies and brownies. Made to order each day, the goods are baked on the premises using only the finest ingredients: Belgian chocolate, Georgia pecans, fresh lemon juice and buttermilk. Each order is carefully packaged to make an ideal gift. An 18-piece gift basket costs £16, prices rise to £75 for a 118-piece basket, just in case you're throwing a banquet. Gift tins are slightly more expensive, at £25 for 24 pieces and £35 for 38 pieces.

Catalogue Annually, A5, Brochure, Colour, 4 pages, Free **Postal charges** Free

BIBENDUM WINE
FREEPOST NW4811
London
NW1 1YR
Telephone
0171 916 7706
Fax
0171 916 7705

Wines
Bibendum buys its wines direct from growers around the world in order to keep costs as low as possible and to stay abreast of the latest developments. Regular tastings are held at 113 Regents Park Road, London (tel 0171 722 5577 for tickets), and it also produces a large, helpful catalogue. Vin de table from £35.88 a case; Muscadet from £57 a case; Chianti, from £59.88 a case; Vouvray, from £99 a case; Yarra Valley Chardonnay, £165 a case; Pommery Vintage, £237 a case.

Catalogue Annually, A4, Catalogue, Colour, 52 pages, Free **Postal charges** Mainland England (minimum one mixed case), free; Wales, Scotland and non-mainland England, one to four cases £10, five cases or more free **Delivery** By arrangement, Courier **Methods of Payment** Cheque, Credit Card, American Express, Stage Payments

BORDEAUX DIRECT
New Aquitaine House
Paddock Road
Reading

Wine
Bordeaux Direct is the UK's leading home-delivery wine company and has earned a reputation for pioneering superb wines from quality

Berkshire
RG4 0JY
Telephone
01734 481718
Fax
01734 461953

vineyards worldwide. Its enthusiasm for finding specially selected cuvées made by individuals with a passion for their craft spills over into its catalogue and newsletters with informative, entertaining descriptions of each wine. Alionza Italian 'designer' fizz, £44.99 for 12 bottles; French country wines, £59.99 for 12; Burgundy gold-medal winner, £96.98 for 12.

Catalogue Quarterly, A5, Catalogue, Colour, 16 pages, Free **Postal charges** £4.50; free for orders over £50 **Delivery** In-house delivery **Methods of Payment** Cheque, Credit Card, American Express, Diners Club, Stage Payments, Switch

BRADLEY GARDENS NURSERY
Sled Lane
Wylam
Northumberland
NE41 8JL
Telephone
01661 852176

Herb plants

This nursery, set in a restored walled garden and featured in the *Good Gardens Guide*, specialises in herbs. It offers a unique service for both chefs and home cooks: fresh cut herbs by post with guaranteed next-day delivery. More than 20 varieties are available in 100g (£2.55) or 50g (£1.90) packs. Edible flowers for garnish cost £2 for a punnet. Bedding plants, container and patio plants are also available in season.

Catalogue Annually, A4, Catalogue, B/W, 1 page, Free **Postal charges** Free **Delivery** Royal Mail **Methods of Payment** Cheque

CAPEL GARMON BAKERY AND POST OFFICE
Capel Garmon
Llanrwst
Gwynedd
Wales LL26 0RW
Telephone
01690 710223

Fresh bread

The Capel Garmon Bakery is famous for its breads which it posts to customers all over the country. A 2lb Barabrith costs £1.80; a 1lb Barabrith, £1.05. These loaves are ideal for freezing so it makes sense to buy in bulk.

Catalogue Annually, A4, Leaflets, B/W, 2 pages, Free **Postal charges** Varies with item **Delivery** Royal Mail, Parcelforce **Methods of Payment** Cheque

FOOD & DRINK

CAREW OYSTERS

Tything Barn
West Williamston
Carew
Kilgetty
Pembrokeshire
SA68 OTN
Telephone
01646 651452
Fax
01646 651307

Oysters

Carew Oysters are named after the River Carew. They are grown about two miles downstream from Carew Castle, in the upper reaches of Milford Haven within the Pembrokeshire Coast National Park. Mail-order prices range from £66 for 20 × 1 dozen (approx 27p each) to £12 for 1 × 1 dozen pack (£1 each). The commonest purchase is a group buy of 12 dozen at 32p each (£47). All prices include 24-hour delivery. Oyster knives are available at £2.50 each or £5 for a knife and rubber holding-block.

Catalogue Leaflets, Colour and B/W, 1 page, Free **Postal charges** Free **Delivery** Royal Mail **Methods of Payment** Cheque, COD, Credit Card

CARLUCCIO'S

28a Neal Street
London
WC2H 9PS
Telephone
0171 240 5710
Fax
0171 497 1361

Gourmet Italian food

Carluccio's Christmas catalogue offers a mouth-watering selection of Italian produce: baskets of dried mushrooms, cheeses from the hills of Piedmont, oils from Tuscany, pastas and antipasti from Puglia, fruity jams from Sicily and many other delicacies, all exquisitely packaged. Treat yourself, or send them specially gift-wrapped to foodie friends. Choose from a traditional panettone Veneziana cake (£12.49); the Piccolo Gourmet, £30, the perfect introduction to Italian cooking packed in a scarlet box tied with red and gold ribbon; La Dolce Stravaganza, £90, an indulgent and extravagant box of sweet things; or La Riserrva del Parroco, £92, a feast for a gourmand with little cheeses, Pugliese wild mushroom pasta, dried porcini sauce and salami and wine.

Catalogue Annually, A4, Catalogue, Colour, 18 pages, Free **Postal charges** Varies with item **Delivery** Royal Mail, Parcelforce **Methods of Payment** Cheque, Postal Order, Credit Card, American Express

CELLAR-SELECT LTD
Bath Brewery
Toll Bridge Road
Bath
Avon
BA1 7DE
Telephone
01225 852711
Fax
01225 858632

Wine
Every two months, Cellar-Select offers its customers a focused selection of around 100 wines in 'Winefinds'. Their specialist tasting panel evaluates around 1,000 each issue, less than one in 25 of which make it into 'Winefinds'. Their panel's tasting notes, quality ratings and value indexes help you to make your choices. Prices are reasonable: Château du Grand Vernay, Beaujolais-Villages 1993 is on offer at £5.19 (list price £6.49); Enate, Crianza 1992 is on offer at £5.59 (list price £6.99).

Catalogue A4, Brochure, Colour, 6 pages, Free **Postal charges** Free if ordering 24 bottles or more; £4.50 if ordering 12 or 18 bottles **Delivery** Parcelforce **Methods of Payment** Cheque, Credit Card, American Express, Switch

CHAMPION HAGGIS
Lindsay Grieve
29 High Street
Hawick
Scotland
Telephone
01450 372109

Haggis by post
This haggis is prepared by hand to a Grieve family recipe using traditional ingredients including Border mutton, wholesome oatmeal and a special blend of seasonings. There is also a vegetarian haggis, suitable for vegans, made of oatmeal, kidney beans, lentils, nuts, mushrooms, carrots, swede, onion, vegetable fat, vegetable stock, seasoning. The skin is plastic and both freeze well. The minimum amount for posting is 1½lb; for a main course, each person should have 6–8 oz. Parcels can be sent out first-class, standard parcel post, 12- or 24-hour or 48-hour service.

Catalogue Updated regularly, A5, Leaflets, B/W, 6 pages **Postal charges** Varies with item **Delivery** Royal Mail **Methods of Payment** Cheque, Postal Order, Credit Card

CHARBONNEL ET WALKER
One, The Royal Arcade

Chocolates
Charbonnel et Walker offers a series of tempting leaflets to take you through its range of high-

28 Old Bond Street
London
W1X 4BT
Telephone
0171 491 0939
Fax
0171 495 6279

quality confectionery. There is a sumptuous-looking plain-chocolate assortment (from £6/4oz to £61/4lb) with a choice of hard or soft centres, an after-dinner selection which includes chocolate bittermints (£5 to £15), and for children there are novelty animals in plain, milk or white chocolate (£8.30/8oz). You can even have a personal message spelled out in foil-covered chocolate letters (£34/1½lb).

Catalogue Annually, A5, Leaflets, Colour and B/W, 6 pages, Free **Postal charges** Varies with item **Delivery** Royal Mail, Parcelforce, Courier **Methods of Payment** Cheque, Credit Card, American Express, Diners Club

CHATSWORTH
31 Norwich Road
Strumpshaw
Norwich
Norfolk
NR13 4AG
Telephone
01603 716815
Fax
01603 715440

Catering supplies

Chatsworth is a 'purveyor of high-quality catering supplies' and its simple brochure lists quite a range. There are seven varieties of cling film alone, plus all sorts of bags, kitchen foils, bin-liners and cleaning supplies as well as a Cook's Corner offering herbs and spices, essences, coffees and chocolates. Pop-up foil sheets, £3.25 for 50; food bags, £5.75 for 500, 7 × 5in; baking parchment, from £7.25; mini-roll for lining the side walls of baking tins or for soufflé collars, £1.50.

Catalogue Annually, A4, Catalogue, Colour, 4 pages, Free **Postal charges** £2.95 for orders up to £29.99; free for orders of more than £30 **Delivery** Royal Mail, Parcelforce **Methods of Payment** Cheque, Credit Card, American Express, Diners Club

CHATSWORTH FARM SHOP
Stud Farm
Pilsley
Bakewell
Derbyshire

Fine foods and hampers

The Chatsworth Farm shop produces Olde English rustic fayre from one of Derbyshire's most famous stately homes. There is an enormous range of hampers crammed with delicious, traditional farm produce, or you can choose from the Farm

DE45 1UF
Telephone
01246 583392
Fax
01246 582514

Shop. Chatsworth was voted Best Hamper by *The Daily Telegraph* at Christmas 1994.
Catalogue Annually, A5, Brochure, Colour, 30 pages, Free
Postal charges Varies with item **Delivery** Royal Mail and overnight delivery for fresh food **Methods of Payment** Cheque, Postal Order, Credit Card, Switch, American Express

CHOC EXPRESS BY THORNTONS
Mint House
Newark Close
Royston
Hertfordshire
SG8 5HL
Telephone
01763 241444
Fax
01763 245460

Luxury chocolates by post
With Choc Express you can send luxury chocolate gifts including the Chocolate Hamper, Luxury Chocolate Hamper, and Luxury Chocolate and Champagne Hamper to any address in the UK and most countries overseas. You can also send Easter eggs by post, children's eggs or a Luxury Easter Hamper. If you're not sure when the recipient of your gift will be at home, send a ChocoGram, which is designed to fit into most letterboxes. Each ChocoGram contains a selection of luxury Thorntons milk, dark and white chocolates in a crush-proof outer box designed to fit through the letterbox. A full-size greetings card is included with your personal message up to 20 words. Standard, 200g, £12.95. Other selections are available and the ChocoGram Deluxe, £24.95, even includes a half-bottle of Champagne.
Catalogue Annually, A5, Brochure, Colour, 8 pages, Free
Postal charges Special delivery, £5 extra **Delivery** Royal Mail, Courier **Methods of Payment** Cheque, Credit Card

THE CHOCOLATE SOCIETY
Clay Pit Lane
Roecliffe
Boroughbridge
North Yorkshire
YO5 9LS

Chocolates
The Chocolate Society was formed five years ago by three dedicated chocolate enthusiasts who believe that fine chocolate is every bit as sophisticated as a great claret. A typical chocolate bar, they say, contains 20 per cent cocoa solids, a single square of their Guanaja Noire (made in France) contains 70 per cent. Each variety has its

Telephone
01423 322230
Fax
01423 322253

own distinctive character, aroma and flavour and to savour chocolate at its best you can order from their extensive list. Gift bar, 55 per cent cocoa, £3.17/85g; handmade truffles, £8/250g; Guanaja Noire, 70 per cent cocoa, £15.20/1kg. They also pack and deliver hampers of specialist foods and chocolate.

Catalogue Quarterly, A4, Catalogue, B/W, 10 pages, Free **Postal charges** £6.95 **Delivery** Royal Mail, Courier **Methods of Payment** Cheque, Switch, Credit Card

THE CLARK TRADING COMPANY
17 Southbrook Road
London
SE12 8LH
Telephone
0181 297 9937
Fax
0181 297 9993

Imported luxury foods

The Clark Trading Company imports exotic food items from France and Italy, such as truffles, foie gras, extra virgin olive oils and wild porcini mushrooms. The catalogue is full of ideas for recipes for pasta sauces, etc.

The French foie gras products (from £12.75 per tin) come from Auguste Cyprien, a company based in the Périgord region, while the red wine vinegar (£6.75 per bottle) comes from south of Modena, Italy, and is produced in the traditional method, using heated oak chippings.

Catalogue A4, Catalogue, B/W, 5 pages, Free **Postal charges** £2.95; free if order exceeds £50.00 **Delivery** Parcelforce, Royal Mail, Courier **Methods of Payment** Cheque

CLARKSONS OF DEVON
1–7 Alansway
Ottery St. Mary
Devon
EX11 1NR
Telephone
01404 813581
Fax
01404 815973

Meat, fish and organic produce

Clarksons is well-known for its hampers and offers quality packs of meat including bacon, gammon joints, sausages, beef steaks and barbecue packs. A 14lb fridge and freezer pack costs £42; 15lb of gammon joints, £36; 20lb chops and steaks, £56; cooked food Easter hamper, £38. From its range of fish you can purchase smoked salmon (£18/lb) and trout. It also sells produce from West Country Organic Foods (tel: 01647 24724; fax: 01647

24031): lean mince, £3.10/lb; whole chicken, £2.40/lb; guinea fowl, £3/lb; organic Cheddar cheese, £2.84 per pack.

Catalogue Annually, A5, Leaflets, Colour and B/W, 7 pages, Free **Postal charges** Free **Delivery** Royal Mail, Courier **Methods of Payment** Cheque, Credit Card, Postal Order

COOKIE CRAFT
Michaelmas
Common Platt
Purton
Wiltshire
SN5 9LB
Telephone
01793 770250

Cakes and cookies

This is a real cottage industry, with all the cakes being made in the home. They can be packed up in tins and sent anywhere, along with a card if you wish. There are 12 different varieties, which can be ordered in small or large sizes. There is an English wine cake, honey and mead cake, spiced apple cake and organic cider cake. They also sell truffles, marzipan fruits and Christmas puddings.

Catalogue Annually, Third A4, Brochure, B/W, 6 pages, Free **Postal charges** Varies with item **Delivery** Royal Mail **Methods of Payment** Cheque, Postal Order, Credit Card

CORNEY & BARROW
12 Helmet Row
London
EC1V 3QJ
Telephone
0171 251 4051
Fax
0171 608 1373

Wine

Corney started his wine merchants in 1780 and the company has since earned three Royal Warrants. Their aim is to supply high-class wines which are not only chosen with extreme care but are exclusive to them.

Their marvellous catalogue is packed with useful information: full-page descriptions of the wines and regions and pictures of the labels. There is also a service brochure which gives information on tastings, opening wine, storage, plus a drinking guide.

Catalogue Annually, Catalogue, Colour and B/W, 115 pages, Free **Postal charges** In the London area, free for two or more mixed cases; for the rest of mainland Britain, free for three or more mixed cases. All other deliveries

CRAIGROSSIE SMOKE HOUSE

Hall Farm
Auchterarder
Perthshire
Scotland
PH3 1HD
Telephone
01764 662596
Fax
01764 663172

charged at £7.00 plus VAT **Delivery** Courier **Methods of Payment** Cheque, Credit Card

Smoked foods

The Craigrossie Smoke House sells vacuum-packed smoked foods that come with a 'use by' date and a recommendation that fish be eaten within 3 weeks and meat within 5 weeks.

Their range includes salmon, trout, duck and chicken breast, wild venison and Scottish beef. Their Gourmet Special Offer Selection consists of 2 × 8oz sliced trout, 8oz duck breast and 8oz salmon pieces for £29. A 1lb pack of sliced salmon is £16.30; 8oz sliced venison, £11; and 8oz sliced duck breast, £11.80.

Catalogue Bi-annually, A5, Brochure, Colour and B/W, 6 pages, Free **Postal charges** Free **Delivery** Royal Mail **Methods of Payment** Cheque

DAVID FELCE, DAUGHTERS & SON

Waterlane Farm
Randwick
Stroud
Gloucestershire
GL6 6EW
Telephone
01453 750806

Organic farmed salmon

This small family business has been smoking fish for 17 years. Its supplies come from a UK farm which does not use chemicals or antibiotics, the pens are out at sea in strong tides which keep the site clean and give the fish plenty of exercise thus producing a healthy firm-fleshed product. The fish is salted for the minimum time, hung up to drain dry and smoked over oak and beech. It will stay good for two weeks after delivery under refrigeration. Smoked salmon, £8.65 for ½lb packet; side of smoked salmon on skin, sliced or unsliced, £23.50.

Catalogue Annually, A5, Leaflets, Colour and B/W, 4 pages, Free **Postal charges** Free **Delivery** Royal Mail, Parcelforce **Methods of Payment** Cheque

DENHAY FARMS LTD
Broadoak
Bridport
Dorset
DT6 5NP
Telephone
01308 422770
Fax
01308 424846

Cheeses and hams
Denhay Farms, a family business, has been breeding and maturing top-quality British pigs for 40 years. The pigs are fed on whey produced in Denhay's Cheesehouse where milk from their own cows is made into prize-winning Denhay Farmhouse Cheddar. Microbial rennet is used, making the cheese suitable for vegetarians. There are no artificial additives or preservatives. The prize-winning Denhay Air Dried Ham comes in vacuum packs and costs £4.95 for 115g (£8.50 for 230g). The 4½lb Dorset Cheese Drums cost £18.20 each.
Catalogue Leaflets, Colour and B/W, 4 pages, Free **Postal charges** Free **Delivery** Royal Mail, Parcelforce **Methods of Payment** Cheque, Credit Card

DUKESHILL HAM COMPANY
Deuxhill
Bridgnorth
Shropshire
WV16 6AF
Telephone
01746 789 519
Fax
01746 789 533

Hams
Dukeshill, based in Shropshire, specialises in finest-quality cooked and uncooked ham on the bone. Choose from either smoked or unsmoked Wiltshire or York cured. York ham, often called the smoked salmon of the meat world, is the traditional farmhouse ham. Half Wiltshire ham (8lb), uncooked, £23; whole dry-cured York ham (14lb), cooked, £59.
Catalogue Annually, A5, Catalogue, Colour, 4 pages, Free **Postal charges** Varies with item **Delivery** Parcelforce, Courier **Methods of Payment** Cheque, Credit Card, American Express

THE DRURY TEA AND COFFEE COMPANY
37 Drury Lane
London
WC2B 5RR
Telephone
0171 836 2607

Coffees and teas
Drury has been supplying tea and coffee lovers for half a century, blending the finest products to suit every taste. It offers light roast Brazilian blend at £3.76/lb; high roast Café de Paris, £4/lb; dark roast Costa Rican Tarrazu, £4.60/lb. Discounts are available on multi-packs. Teas include Ceylon

Fax
0171 633 0923

Orange Pekoe at £1.45/125g or £4.80/500g; Chun Mee green tea from China, £1.35/125g; Kenya Fine Leaf Fannings, £1/125g; and from India, Darjeeling Castleton, 2nd Flush, £2.95/125g.

Catalogue Annually, Third A4, Leaflets, B/W, 2 pages, Free **Postal charges** £2.50, for orders up to £10; £3, up to £25; free for orders of more than £25 **Delivery** Royal Mail **Methods of Payment** Cheque, Credit Card

EASTBROOK FARM
Bishopstone
Swindon
Wiltshire
SN6 8PW
Telephone
01793 790460
Fax
01793 791239

Organic meats

Eastbrook Farm supplies a full range of fresh, organically produced meats, all of which come up to Soil Association Standards. You can choose from pork, beef, lamb and poultry, plus 14 varieties of delicious meaty sausages, some of which are gluten-free. It also sells home-cured and oak-smoked hams, bacon, gammon and organic cheeses. Rolled topside, £3.82/lb; pork chops, £3.77/lb; smoked streaky bacon, £2.53/lb; whole free-range chicken, £1.96/lb; crown of lamb, £7.65/lb; beef and Guinness sausages, £2.12/lb; Pencarreg cheeses, £2.27 each.

Catalogue Annually, Third A4, Brochure, Colour, 6 pages, Free **Postal charges** Varies with item **Delivery** Courier **Methods of Payment** Cheque, Credit Card

EL VINO
47 Fleet Street
London
EC4Y 1BJ
Telephone
0171 353 5384
Fax
0171 936 2367

Wines

This famous Fleet Street wine bar, dating back to 1879, offers an attractive list of wines and spirits in its 'Armchair Wine Buyer's Guide'. There are interesting descriptions of each area and a short description about each wine. You might be tempted to buy a case of vintage champagne – Dom Perignon 1985/6, from the stable named after the monk who 'invented' the *méthode champenoise* – for £683.40; or a dozen bottles of Choisi de Boyier house wine for £45.

Catalogue Annually, A4, Catalogue, Colour, 16 pages, Free **Postal charges** Free carriage to mainland U.K. on orders to the same address of two dozen bottles or more **Delivery** Courier, In-house delivery **Methods of Payment** Cheque, Credit Card, American Express

FERRY FISH SMOKEHOUSE

Rock Cottage
Carsluith Creetown
Newton-Stewart
Dumfries and Galloway
Wigtownshire
Scotland
DG8 7DW
Telephone
01671 820630
Fax
same

Smoked fish

Ferry Fish Smokehouse is one of the last remaining smokeries to operate in south-west Scotland using the traditional smoking process. Oak-smoked salmon is available sliced in packs from 8oz (£10) to 1lb (£15). A whole side, trimmed and unsliced, costs £22 for 2lb. Oak-smoked Loch Fyne kippers, free from artificial colourings, £3.20/lb.

Catalogue Annually, A4, Leaflets, B/W, 2 pages, Free **Postal charges** Free **Delivery** Royal Mail, Parcelforce **Methods of Payment** Cheque

FINDLATER MACKIE TODD & CO LTD

BF1R 1026
Deer Park Road
Merton Abbey
London
SW19 3TU
Telephone
FREEPHONE 0800 413331
Fax
0181 543 2415

Wines, spirits and liqueurs

Through Waitrose, the supermarket chain of the John Lewis Partnership, Findlater Mackie Todd & Co Ltd/Waitrose Direct supplies fine wines from all over the world. It sells spirits, cigars and liqueurs, offers a gift-pack service, and will create personal labels, too. It also runs a wedding advisory service and will advise on the building and maintaining of a wine collection. Findlater's Club Claret, £52.68 a case; Pouilly Fumé AC 1993, £95.88 a case; one bottle of Duc de Marre, Special Cuvée Brut Champagne, packed in a wooden box, £23.85 including delivery. Findlater also accepts the John Lewis/Waitrose account card in payment. For enquiries, please phone 0181 543 0966.

Catalogue Monthly, A4, Catalogue, Colour, 44 pages, Free **Postal charges** Free for orders of two or more full cases;

FOOD & DRINK

£3.95 for a single case **Delivery** In-house delivery; Carrier **Methods of Payment** Cheque, Postal Order, Switch, Credit Card

FITZBILLIES BAKERS AND CONFECTIONERS
52 Trumpington Street
Cambridge
Cambridgeshire
CB2 1RG
Telephone
01223 352500

Chelsea buns, cakes and hampers

Fitzbillies was established in the 1920s by the Mason Brothers and soon became Cambridge's most popular bakery and favourite haunt of students, dons and townspeople alike. Today, its Chelsea buns and cakes are still much sought-after and for those with a yearning for the 'old country' they can be posted all over the world. Chelsea buns in a box, from £6.95 (from £10.50 overseas); Dundee cake in a tin, from £16.75; Cambridge Eight cake in a tin, from £20.50.

Catalogue Annually, A5, Leaflets, Colour, 4 pages, Free **Postal charges** Varies with item **Delivery** Royal Mail **Methods of Payment** Cheque, Credit Card

FORTNUM & MASON
181 Piccadilly
London
W1A 1ER
Telephone
0171 465 8666
Fax
0171 437 3278

Food and wine

From the prestigious Fortnum & Mason – purveyor of groceries for 300 years to the Royal Family – comes this tantalising catalogue of food and wine. It features teas and coffees, preserves, pickles and dressings. There is a good selection of biscuits, chocolates and fresh foods, including cheeses, smoked salmon and foie gras, plus wines and spirits. And, of course, there are the hampers for which Fortnum's is so justly famous. Hampers and baskets, from £20 (Fortnum's Classic Hamper, £250); Beluga caviar, from £76/50g tin; Fortnum's Cheese Selection Tray, £35; Aigier et Fils truffles from £20.50/12.5g jar; Stilton, from £10.95/7oz jar; Dijon mustard, £2.50/200g jar.

Catalogue Annually, A4, Catalogue, Colour, 24 pages, Free **Postal charges** Varies with item **Delivery** Royal Mail, Parcelforce, Courier, In-house delivery **Methods of Payment** Cheque, Postal Order, Credit Card

FOX'S SPICES

Units J & K
Mason's Road Industrial Estate
Stratford-Upon-Avon
Warwickshire
CV37 9NF
Telephone
01789 266420
Fax
01789 267737

Spices, herbs, seasonings and condiments

Fox's Spices is a 28-year-old family-owned company specialising in herbs, spices, seasonings and condiments. It offers exclusive products in 'no frills' economy packaging and maintains a regular turnover, thus ensuring freshness. Cumin seeds, £1.65/8oz; vanilla pods, £1.80 for two; fine herbs, £1.60/3oz; high roast Brazilian black peppercorns, £2.20/8oz. Fox's also produce Indonesian Bumbus, wet spice mixtures including lemon grass, galangal and lime leaves, £1.25/4oz sachet; fresh garlic purées, £1.95/150g jar; poppadoms and gift selections.

Catalogue Annually, A5, Catalogue, B/W, 24 pages, Free **Postal charges** Varies with item **Delivery** Royal Mail, Parcelforce **Methods of Payment** Cheque, Postal Order

THE FRESH FOOD CO

PO Box 5710
London
W10 5WB
Telephone
0181 969 0351
Fax
same

Fresh organic foods

The Fresh Food Co sends the very best fresh fish, meat and vegetables direct to the general public. Most of its suppliers are well-known in the kitchens of Britain's top hotels and restaurants and are recognised by the Soil Association and other organic organisations. The fish comes direct from a traditional Cornish fishery. A subscription scheme operates, so, for example, you could choose to receive a weekly or fortnightly 15lb box of organic produce for £21.95; a 10lb box of organic meat for £55; or 8–10lb catch of the day for £44.50.

Catalogue Annually, A4, Leaflets, B/W, 3 pages, Free **Postal charges** Free **Delivery** Royal Mail, Parcelforce **Methods of Payment** Cheque, Credit Card, Switch

FRUITFUL OCCASIONS
Highfield Drive
St Leonards on Sea
East Sussex
TN38 9PP
Telephone
01424 850950
Fax
01424 855000

Baskets of fruit
Fruitful Occasions fruit baskets make wonderful gifts for any occasion. Packed with healthy and delicious treats, the Traditional Basket is £24.99 and the Exotic Basket is £29.99. Prices include delivery anywhere in mainland UK and your own special message.
Catalogue By Advertising, Colour, 1 page, Free **Postal charges** Free **Delivery** Royal Mail **Methods of Payment** Cheque, Credit Card

FUDGE'S BAKERY
Leigh
Sherborne
Dorset
DT9 6HJ
Telephone
01935 872253
Fax
01935 873397

Handmade biscuits
Mouthwatering hand-made butter, cheese and savoury biscuits from a traditional Dorset bakery. Toasted almond, £12.35 for a case of 12 packs; garlic cheddar wafers, £13.90 for a case of 12 packs.
Catalogue Annually, A4, Leaflets, B/W, 2 pages, Free **Postal charges** Varies with item **Delivery** Royal Mail **Methods of Payment** Cheque

GLENDEVON SALMON
Crook of Devon
Kinross
Fife
Kinrossshire
KY13 7UL
Telephone
01577 840297
Fax
01577 840626

Smoked salmon
Glendevon Salmon is a well-established, family-run business selling finest-quality, oak-smoked Scottish salmon (oak shavings from old whisky barrels are used in the process). Presented in a scarlet box, it makes an ideal gift for all occasions. Sliced smoked salmon, 1lb, gift-packed, £17; on the skin, fully trimmed, no bones, 2lb, £25. Glendevon has considerable experience in sending smoked salmon overseas; prices in the brochure.
Catalogue Annually, Third A4, Leaflets, Colour, 2 pages, Free **Postal charges** Free **Delivery** Royal Mail, Courier **Methods of Payment** Cheque, Credit Card

GOODFELLOWS OF DUNDEE
81 Gray Street

Traditional Scottish cakes
Goodfellows produce the original Dundee cake, a once closely guarded secret of Mrs Keiller, who

Broughty Ferry
Dundee
Tayside
Scotland
DD5 2BQ
Telephone
01382 730181
Fax
01382 736041

together with her husband produced the famous Dundee Marmalade. Made with Scottish milled flour, sugar from the Indies, whole egg and vegetable fat, it is finished with the traditional split almonds, packaged in a hermetically sealed tin and costs £9.30 (airmail rates on application). There are other cakes, too: whisky cake, £9.80, and cherry and ginger, £9.50.

Catalogue Annually, Third A4, Brochure, Colour, 2 pages, Free **Postal charges** Free **Delivery** Royal Mail, Parcelforce **Methods of Payment** Cheque

GOODMAN'S GEESE
Goodmans Brothers
Walsgrove Farm
Great Witley
Worcester
Worcestershire
WR6 6JJ
Telephone
01299 896272
Fax
01299 896889

Free-range geese
Judy Goodman started rearing geese in 1982 as a hobby and now rears 2,000 a year in Walsgrove Farm's grass paddocks. She has won several awards and now gives talks and demonstrations on 'how to prepare, cook and serve your goose'. The geese are supplied to individuals, food halls or butchers from September until Christmas. Each goose comes with a recipe leaflet and prices are approx £1.40 per lb for long-legged and £2.35 per lb for oven-ready. Goodman's Geese also produce free-range bronze turkeys.

Catalogue Leaflets, Colour and B/W, pages, Free **Postal charges** Free **Delivery** Royal Mail **Methods of Payment** Cheque

GRAIG FARM
Dolau
Llandrindod Wells
Powys
Wales
LD1 5TL
Telephone
01597 851655
Fax
same

Organic and additive-free meat
Winner of the 1993 and 1994 National Organic Food Awards, Graig Farm is accredited by the Soil Association. The organically reared animals are fed on wholesome food, given no routine drugs and weaned naturally. Graig Farm produces Conservation Grade pork, lamb, mutton, beef and poultry. A whole organic chicken costs £1.98; organic topside of beef costs £9.01 per lb. Their wild game selection includes venison (steaks are

£4.73 per lb), rabbit and wild boar. They also offer additive-free fish, caught by dolphin-friendly hook and line, from the island of St. Helena.

Catalogue Annually, A5, Leaflets, B/W, 12 pages, Free **Postal charges** Free for weekdays, or a flat-rate charge of £6.00 for Saturday to mainland UK (except Highland Scotland) **Delivery** Royal Mail **Methods of Payment** Cheque

GREAT GLEN FINE FOODS
FREEPOST PO Box 10
North Ballachulish
Fort William
Scotland
PH33 6BR
Telephone
01855 821277
Fax
01855 821577

Scottish speciality foods

Great Glen Foods has a speciality food shop on the West Coast of Scotland stocking the best of Scottish produce. It now offers a selection by mail order of over 160 items of the best and most popular foods among more than 1,200 lines stocked in the shop. You can make your own choice of individual items or request any other foods in stock in the shop, including jam, honey, sauces, chutney, shortbread, cakes, haggis, smoked fish and meat, spirits, cheese and oatcakes, and its own home-made confectionery. There are also five Special Gift Selections ranging from £15 to £75, all of which are packed in plain boxes so that the value is all in the food and not in fancy packaging. Highland smoked salmon, £5.65/227g; Moniack horseradish sauce, £1.95; Walkers luxury Dundee cake, £2.40/400g; Great Glen chocolate malt-whisky truffles, £4.35/150g. Gift packs are available from £15.

Catalogue Annually, A5, Brochure, Colour and B/W, 14 pages, Free **Postal charges** £4.75 **Delivery** Parcelforce **Methods of Payment** Cheque, Postal Order, Credit Card

HAMPERS OF BROADWAY
Cotswold Court
The Green

Food hampers

Winners of the London Food Hamper Competition 1990, Hampers of Broadway make up all kinds of hampers, from fitted picnic willow

Broadway
Worcestershire
WR12 7AA
Telephone
01386 853040
Fax
01386 853548

hampers with bone china or earthenware for two to six people (£99–£600) to presentation food baskets, such as 'B1' which contains a bottle of red wine, oat cakes, pheasant pâté, dressed lobster, liqueur jams and hand-made cookies, all for a very reasonable £19.95.

Catalogue Bi-annually, A5, Catalogue, B/W, 8 pages, Free **Postal charges** Varies with order **Delivery** Royal Mail **Methods of Payment** Cheque, Postal Order, Credit Card, Diners Club

HARRODS HAMPER AND GIFT BOX SELECTION
Mail Order Department
Admail 1234
London
SW1A 2XX
Telephone
0800 730123
Fax
0171 225 5830

Seasonal hampers

Sumptuous catalogue, beautifully photographed with contents to match. Each hamper is given its own name and displayed separately. Harrods Hampers can be tailored to suit any occasion or to meet your specific requirements. All items are presented in traditional wicker baskets or Harrods boxes. For £40 a head, you could have The Ascot Hamper containing avocado prawn cocktail, slices of duckling fillet with salad, Stilton and Brie, exotic fruit pavlova and Harrods mints. This comes with complimentary cutlery, plates, glasses, mineral water, salt and pepper and a corkscrew. The children needn't feel left out: there's a Mini Hamper for them containing edible teddies as well as a real cuddly one wearing a baseball cap (price: £50).

Catalogue Annually, Catalogue, Colour, 19 pages, Free **Postal charges** Varies with item **Delivery** Royal Mail, In-house delivery **Methods of Payment** Cheque, Postal Order, Credit Card, American Express, Diners Club

HARRODS LTD
Mail Order Department
Admail 1234
London
SW1A 2XX

Wines, champagne and spirits

The Grapevine catalogue shows the best of Harrods wine department including more and more with the Harrods own label. It also includes Harrods Beer. There are special collection cases

Telephone
0800 730123
Fax
0171 225 5777

which are discounted such as the Harrods Collection Case, a mixed case of 12 bottles of white, red, sherry, port, claret, whisky, cognac and Champagne, reduced from £120.50 to £108. There are wines from Bordeaux, the Loire, Alsace, Burgundy, the Rhône, Italy, Sicily, Spain, Portugal, Germany, Austria, Hungary, England, Israel, Lebanon, Chile, Argentina, South Africa, Australia, America and New Zealand. There's also sherry, port, schnapps, vodka, Madeira, whisky, rum, armagnac, cognac, brandy, Calvados, liqueurs, ginger wine, vermouths and beer, cider and minerals. The back of the catalogue also features cigars.

Catalogue Annually, A4, Catalogue, Colour and B/W, 28 pages **Postal charges** £5; within M25, order over £50, free **Delivery** Royal Mail **Methods of Payment** Cheque, Postal Order, Credit Card, American Express

HAY HAMPERS
The Barn
Church Street
Corby Glen
Grantham
Lincolnshire
NG33 4NJ
Telephone
01476 550 420/476/548
Fax
01476 550 777

Food, wine and hampers

Hay Hampers is a friendly family-owned business which provides a wide range of gift packs and picnic hampers. The range includes Stilton Packs (from £13.62 for a bottle of claret and Stilton in a ceramic jar), Chocolate Packs (from £10.86 for a bottle of wine and truffles), Smoked Salmon Packs, Wine Gift Packs, and hampers from £55.15 to £211.81. Hampers can also be made up on request and both the gifts and hampers are beautifully presented in wooden boxes, wicker baskets or colourful cartons.

Catalogue Annually, A4, Catalogue, Colour, 8 pages, Free **Postal charges** Varies with item **Delivery** Royal Mail, Parcelforce, Courier **Methods of Payment** Cheque, Postal Order, Credit Card, American Express

HEAL FARM
Kings Nympton
Umberleigh
Devon
EX37 9TB
Telephone
01769 574341
Fax
01767 572839

Traditional meats

Heal Farm, a West Country Food Award Gold winner, produces meats naturally and is certified by the Rare Breeds Survival Trust. It specialises in traditional breeds of pigs and also produces its own beef and lamb. Sirloin on the bone, £7.88/lb; lamb casserole meat, £5.45/lb; farmhouse sausages, from £2.40/lb; cider-cooked smoked ham, £5.98/lb; Trelough ducks, £2.95/lb. You can also order delicious ready-cooked seasonal dishes (Roman Lamb, 6–8 servings, £19), or potted beef (£5.25/350ml jar); and from local farms, cheeses, clotted cream, honey and chocolates.

Catalogue Annually, A5, Catalogue, Colour and B/W, 8 pages, Free **Postal charges** £8.50 courier (minimum order £25-worth of produce for courier delivery) **Delivery** Courier **Methods of Payment** Cheque, Credit Card, Postal Order

HOLME FARMED VENISON
Thorpe Underwood
York
North Yorkshire
YO5 9SR
Telephone
0423 331212
Fax
0423 330855

Venison

This farm produces naturally reared venison which is specially packed and dispatched by overnight courier or first-class post. Venison is low in cholesterol, lean and easy to cook and the brochure provides appetisingly illustrated recipes. Venison haunch steaks, 2 × 6oz, £4.95 a pack; diced venison steak, £3.30/lb; smoked venison sausages, £4.30/lb; game pies, £1.35/8oz pie. Ready-prepared meals include roast pheasant chausseur in 12oz vacuum packs, £2.80 a pack.

Catalogue Annually, Third A4, Brochure, Colour, 6 pages, Free **Postal charges** £6 for orders up to £20; £4 for orders of more than £20 **Delivery** Courier, Royal Mail **Methods of Payment** Credit Card, Cheque, Postal Order

HOMEBREW MAIL ORDER
FREEPOST
67/69 Park Lane

Beer and wine kits

For those who prefer to make their own wine or beer, Homebrew is just the catalogue. It offers a good range of kits, ingredients and equipment for

Hornchurch
Essex
RM11 1BR
Telephone
01708 745943
Fax
01708 743699

beginners and experts alike. Dry white wine kit, £11.99; Winecraft Blend, £3.89/1kg, £15.45/5kg; Harris Mk 2 Filter Kit, £9.36; Caxton Bitter 40 Pint, £4.75; barrels from £13.91; beer yeast, 54p.

Catalogue Annually, A5, Catalogue, Colour and B/W, 12 pages, Free **Postal charges** £4.50 for orders up to £35; free for orders of more than £35 (UK mainland, Northern Ireland and Isle of Man) **Delivery** Royal Mail, Parcelforce **Methods of Payment** Cheque, Credit Card

HOUSE OF HAMILTON LTD
13 Brewster Square
Brucefield Industrial Park
Livingston
West Lothian
EH54 9BJ
Telephone
01506 418434
Fax
01506 418413

Oak-smoked Scottish salmon and gravadlax

House of Hamilton oak-smoked Scottish salmon and gravadlax (fresh Scottish salmon marinated in dill) are enjoyed by some of the finest and most prestigious hotels and premium retail outlets in the country. They are now also available direct from the 'house', by mail order.

The company recently won the *Connoisseurs Scotland* magazine taste test and all their smoked Scottish salmon has 'quality approved' status, a scheme run and enforced by independent inspectors. The fish have the benefit of clean, clear, tidal waters and their flesh is pink and translucent with the minimum of fat. No artificial colouring or preservatives are used at any time. The Company now also offer sliced smoked duck breast and smoked wild boar as well as a range of accessories from boards, aprons and knives to ladies' handbags and tartan men's washbags, scarves, luggage accessories and a shooting accessory range. A Hamilton's 15-year-old blended Scotch whisky and cigar range is a new addition to the catalogue.

All the food products are prepared fresh to order, then vacuum-packed and dispatched 'on ice'. They are ideal for home freezing for up to 3 months with no loss of flavour or texture.

Catalogue A4, Catalogue, Colour, 12 pages, Free **Postal charges** £6 **Delivery** Parcelforce, UPS, Courier **Methods of Payment** Cheque, Postal Order, Credit Card, American Express, Diners Club

HUMPHREY'S EXCLUSIVE CONFECTIONERY
16 Leeds Road
Ilkley
West Yorkshire
LS29 8DJ
Telephone
01943 609477

Handmade chocolates

The proprietor, a trained continental chocolatier, emphasises that Humphrey's chocolates are made with pure cocoa butter – no vegetable fats. The Belgique range includes Pralines and Marzipan; the English range includes Ginger, Apricot Parfait and Rose Creams, and there are more than 20 varieties of Swiss-style truffles. Humphrey's also make personalised moulds and boxes for hotels and restaurants. Their Gold Box, containing 15 chocolates, is £5.20 whilst a medium-sized presentation box, containing 30 chocolates, is £10.75.

Catalogue A5, Leaflets, Colour and B/W, 2 pages, Free **Postal charges** Varies with item **Delivery** Royal Mail **Methods of Payment** Cheque

IAIN MELLIS, CHEESEMONGER
30a Victoria Street
Edinburgh
Lothian
EH1 2JW
Telephone
0131 226 6215

Cheese

A wide range of cheeses from the Isle of Mull, including £6 for 1lb of small cheeses, which are waxed, cloth-bound and ripened in brand new cellars, a real Christmas treat. Wellington cheese, £14 for 2lb, is a creamy Cheddar-style cheese made from Guernsey milk and matured in state in the cellars of the Duke of Wellington's house at Stratfield Saye. All the cheeses supplied are cloth-bound and natural rinded, not vacuum-packed. The above are baby cheeses, but larger cheeses are also supplied. A taste of what cheese used to taste like!

Catalogue Annually, A4, Leaflets, B/W, 3 pages, Free **Postal charges** £9 for each parcel weighing up to 10 kilos for delivery anywhere in the UK. By Royal Mail Parcelforce

£5 for up to 30 kilos **Delivery** Royal Mail, Courier **Methods of Payment** Cheque, Credit Card, Postal Order

INVERAWE SMOKEHOUSES
Taynuilt
Argyll
Scotland
PA35 1HU
Telephone
01866 822446
Fax
01866 822274

Traditional smoked salmon

Inverawe has been associated with the fishing industry since medieval times and at one time had to render up salmon to the Crown. Robert and Rosie Campbell-Preston founded their family business in 1974 – he is in charge of the smoking, she runs the mail order. Their slow-but-sure smoking methods ensure a traditional result. Smoked Scottish salmon, £9.25/8oz sliced; smoked trout, whole side trimmed, £12.90/lb. Gravadlax, smoked halibut, eel fillets and trout caviar are among their many products. Specials are regularly available, such as smoked-trout mousse, £5.95/8oz jar.

Catalogue 3 times a year, A5, Catalogue, Colour, 16 pages, Free **Postal charges** Varies with item **Delivery** Royal Mail, Courier **Methods of Payment** Cheque, Credit Card, Switch

JAMES WHITE APPLE JUICES
Whites Fruit Farm
Main Road
Ashbocking
Ipswich
Suffolk
IP6 9JS
Telephone
01473 890111
Fax
01473 890001

Apple juices

James White is a small company which sells freshly pressed fruit juices. Bottled like fine wines, the range includes apple, pear and grape juices and Suffolk cider, made from a number of different apples. All are available by the case. Bramley apple juice is £23.00 per case, Pear juice £23.00, and Grape juice £25.00. Special Edition Suffolk Cider is £24.50. Mixed cases are available for £24.50.

Catalogue A4, Leaflets, Colour and B/W, 1 page, Free **Delivery** Parcelforce **Methods of Payment** Cheque

JEROBOAMS
6 Clarendon Road
London
W11 3AA
Telephone
0171 727 9792
Fax
0171 792 3672

Fine cheeses and wines
Jeroboams opened its first shop in South Kensington in 1984 and has built up its reputation to become one of London's finest purveyors of cheeses and wines. Its catalogue contains a tempting selection of British and French farmhouse cheeses, French and Italian charcuterie, olive oils and other delicatessen products, and an impressive range of wines and spirits. The products are sent attractively packaged and with gift cards. French farmhouse collection of cheeses, £35; Rectory ham, £62.50; luncheon hamper, £125.

Catalogue Annually, A4, Catalogue, Colour, 24 pages, Free **Postal charges** Free **Delivery** Royal Mail, Courier **Methods of Payment** Cheque, Credit Card, American Express

KEEPSAKES
41 Dyserth Road
Rhyl
Clwyd
Wales
LL18 4DR
Telephone
01745 354971
Fax
same

Drinks with personalised labels
Here's a great idea for celebrating a special occasion. Send a personalised bottle (or bottles) of Champagne, port or spirits. You supply a colour photograph and message and Keepsakes will produce a unique label. A bottle of personalised vintage Champagne (0.75 litre) costs £39.95; Glen Grant Highland Malt, £33.50.

Catalogue Annually, A4, Leaflets, Colour and B/W, 5 pages, Free **Postal charges** Varies with item **Delivery** Courier **Methods of Payment** Cheque, Credit Card

KENDRICKS
Ocean Parade
South Ferring
Worthing
West Sussex
BN12 5QQ
Telephone
01903 503244

Teas and coffees
Kendricks supplies teas and coffees from around the world and includes with its price list a helpful run-down of the different characteristics. It roasts its own coffees, generally 100 per cent Arabicas, which come in sealed 500g valved foil bags for freshness. Teas and teabags are selected from the originals to produce fine blends and packed in

Fax
01903 502610

125g foil bags. Orders are dispatched within 24 hours of receipt. Kenya-blend roasted coffee beans, £7.30/kg, ground £7.60/kg; Earl Grey 100 tagged tea bags, £2.50/250g.

Catalogue Annually, A4, Leaflets, B/W, 4 pages **Postal charges** Varies with item **Delivery** Royal Mail, Parcelforce **Methods of Payment** Cheque, Credit Card

L ROBSON & SONS
Craster
Alnwick
Northumberland
NE66 3TR
Telephone
01665 576223

Smoked kippers and salmon

L Robson & Sons of Northumberland produce a range of traditionally Oak Smoked Kippers and Oak Smoked Salmon as well as other fish. Kippers cost £3.90 for a ¼ box (approx 1lb), £6.75 for a ½ box (approx 2lb), £10.45 for a large box (approx 4½lbs) and £18.50 for an extra large box (approx 10lb).

Salmon is priced at £6.95 for ½lb, sliced and vacuum-packed; £10.95 for 1lb, sliced and vacuum-packed; and £6.50 per lb for sides of unsliced salmon, vacuum-packed, plus p&p. Prices are subject to change during the season.

Catalogue Updated regularly, A4, Leaflets, B/W, 2 pages **Postal charges** Free **Delivery** Royal Mail, Parcelforce **Methods of Payment** Cheque, Postal Order

LEWIS & COOPER
92 High Street
Northallerton
North Yorkshire
DL7 8PP
Telephone
01609 772880
Fax
01609 777933

Food hampers

Lewis & Cooper have been established for more than 100 years and are well-known to food lovers. In their Northallerton shop they have been making up gift packs and food hampers for business and personal customers for well over half a century. Special hampers can be assembled for any occasion – wedding, anniversary, prize or presentation – containing mouth-watering selections. Ginger Gift Pack, £15; Hambleton Box, £40.90; Fresh Hamper (in a wicker basket), £116.70.

Catalogue Annually, Third A4, Brochure, Colour, 8 pages, Free **Postal charges** Varies with item **Delivery** Royal Mail, In-house delivery **Methods of Payment** Cheque, Credit Card

LIQUID ID
Unit 30
Jaggard Way
London
SW12 8SG
Telephone
0181 675 9494
Fax
0181 675 9595

Personalised bottles of Champagne

Whether a corporate occasion, family celebration or birthday, Liquid ID can supply Champagne with an extra touch – a personalised label. The Single Bottle Service offers next-day delivery (not weekends) of a bottle of house Champagne with personalised label for £24.95. The Classic Service allows you to choose from a range of Champagnes, wines, ports and spirits and the Premier Service is available for customers ordering in excess of 120 bottles.

Catalogue Annually, A5, Catalogue, Colour, 6 pages, Free **Postal charges** Varies with item **Delivery** Royal Mail, Courier, Parcelforce **Methods of Payment** Cheque, Credit Card

LOCH FYNE OYSTERS
Clachan Farm
Ardkinglas
Cairndow
Argyll
PA26 8BH
Telephone
01499 600264
Fax
01499 600234

Oysters, smoked fish, gift boxes

This award-winning Scottish producer's catalogue lists a gourmet's selection of delicious smoked and cured fish, oysters, langoustines and herring marinades, with details of size, price and shelf-life. It even offers the all-essential oyster knife (£5.95). The items are produced fresh to order (please give 48 hours' notice prior to delivery), chilled and vacuum-packed. Whole side, semi-trimmed, unsliced smoked salmon, £19.25; whole smoked eel, £6.20 (minimum order, two eels); 12 Loch Fyne rock oysters, £9.60.

Catalogue Quarterly, A4, Brochure, B/W, 4 pages, Free **Postal charges** £5.95; non-food items, £2.95; free on orders over £100 **Delivery** Courier, Royal Mail **Methods of Payment** Cheque, Postal Order, Switch, Diners Club

LOCH FYNE WHISKIES

Inverary
Argyll
Scotland
PA32 8UD
Telephone
01499 302219
Fax
01499 302238

Whisky

Loch Fyne Whiskies stocks more than 400 malts. Its price list is user-friendly, with helpful tips for the novice buyer, including a taste score to help you to sort out the softer varieties, and a highlighted selection of what it regards as excellent examples of the distillers' craft. Miniatures are available, too, plus a number of books on the subject and a personalised label service. Dalwhinnie, £23.90/70cl; Lochnagar, £21.90/70cl; Whyte & Mackay, £11.90/70cl.

Catalogue Annually, Third A4, Catalogue, B/W, 8 pages, Free **Postal charges** Varies with item **Delivery** Royal Mail, Parcelforce **Methods of Payment** Cheque, Credit Card, Switch

MAJESTIC WINES MAIL ORDER

55 Victoria Street
St Albans
Hertfordshire
AL1 3UW
Telephone
01727 847912
Fax
01727 810884

Beers, wines and spirits

A comprehensive list of the best of the wines, beers and spirits on offer at Majestic's 44 warehouses and available via mail order. Divided into countries, it lists the best wines from the finest grape-growing areas in the world, as well as beers, spirits and soft drinks. Prices are very reasonable with French reds from as little as £2.89 a bottle and Australian white wines from £3.99. Lager prices are competitive with 24 bottles of Becks for only £19.92.

Catalogue Bi-annually, A3, Catalogue, Colour and B/W, 4 pages, Free **Postal charges** Varies with item **Delivery** Parcelforce **Methods of Payment** Postal Order, Cheque, Credit Card

THE MASTER OF MALT

The Corn Exchange
The Pantiles
Royal Tunbridge Wells
Kent
TN2 5TE

Malt whiskies

For the connoisseur who wants the best without leaving the comfort of an armchair, The Master of Malt's extensive list is the answer. With a comprehensive range of more than 200 whiskies from Scotland, America and Ireland, there is a

Telephone
01892 513295
Fax
01892 750487

wide selection to suit everyone's taste (10-year-old Laphroaig, £23.45; 28-year-old Clynelish, £57.95), and if you are unable to make up your mind, miniatures are available from £3.75. Join the Malt Whisky Association (£12.50 for one year) and take advantage of valuable discounts, both by mail order and at the Master of Malt shop in Tunbridge Wells, and exclusive bottlings.

Catalogue Annually, A5, Brochure, B/W, 14 pages, Free **Postal charges** £4.95 (free for orders over £60) **Delivery** Courier **Methods of Payment** Cheque, Credit Card, American Express, Diners Club

MEAT MATTERS
2 Blandy's Farm Cottages
Bassett Road
Letcombe Regis
Wantage
Oxfordshire
OX12 9LJ
Telephone
01235 762461

Organic meat, poultry and game

Mel and Diane Glass of Meat Matters sell a wide range of Soil Association Organically Produced meat, poultry, eggs and game as well as smoked salmon from Suffolk. All cuts are available in lamb, pork and beef as well as organic chickens and chicken pieces. In addition, you can choose from a variety of home-recipe organic sausages, children's sausages and beef burgers, including gluten-free products. They also offer dinner party marinaded dishes, barbecue products for the summer and Christmas organic turkeys. There is no minimum order. Best minced beef, £2.95/lb; sirloin steak, £8.99; whole chicken, £2.29/lb; traditionally cured back bacon, £5.25/lb; beef and Guinness sausages, £3.25/lb; children's sausages, £5.99/2lb.

Catalogue Annually, A5, Catalogue, B/W, 4 pages, Free **Postal charges** Free delivery to local towns and London; £2.50 elsewhere in UK **Delivery** In-house delivery, Courier, Parcelforce **Methods of Payment** Cheque, Credit Card, COD, Postal Order

MEG RIVERS
Middle Tysoe
Warwickshire
CV35 0SE
Telephone
01295 688101
Fax
01295 680799

Cakes and gifts
Order a cake on Monday and Meg Rivers will get it to you by the weekend. Her catalogue is full of enticingly illustrated goodies, hand-baked using organic flour, free-range eggs and English butter, and securely packed in special boxes for delivery. Ginger cake, £12.50/kg; iced children's birthday cake, £15.50/900g (6½in dia.); wedding cakes from £150. Gift boxes can be assembled to order from a selection of wines, preserves, dried fruits and the famous cakes.

Catalogue Annually, A5, Catalogue, Colour, 16 pages, Free **Postal charges** £2.95; express £7; Europe and Eire £6.95 **Delivery** Royal Mail, Parcelforce **Methods of Payment** Cheque, Postal Order, Credit Card, Switch

MELCHIOR CHOCOLATES
Tinto House
Station Road
South Molton
Devon
EX36 3LL
Telephone
01769 574442
Fax
01769 573301

Chocolates
This company produces several different boxes of chocolates, all of which come in white, milk, dark chocolate or a combination. An oval opera box of truffles (230g net weight) costs £14.95. A 500g clear bag of truffles and pralines costs £16.95 (£7.95 for 250g).

Catalogue A4, Leaflets, Colour and B/W, 2 pages, Free **Postal charges** Free **Delivery** Royal Mail **Methods of Payment** Cheque, Credit Card

THE MOFFAT FISHERY
Hammerlands
Moffat
Dumfriesshire
Scotland
DG10 9QL
Telephone
01683 21068
Fax
same

Superior fish and game produce
The Moffat Fishery's Glenmoffat smoked salmon is hand-produced using traditional recipes in a non-automated process. The fresh salmon is selected from its Scottish waters; then, using a small-batch technique, the Fishery believes it is able to impart flavour and texture unachievable by larger processors supplying the supermarkets. With low overheads it aims to pass on cost savings to customers. The price list includes a 2lb side of hand-sliced

smoked salmon, £26; 4oz pack long-sliced smoked salmon, £6; 1lb smoked trout fillets, £9; 1lb pack of sliced smoked salmon delivered by post once a month for 12 months, £14.50 a month; fresh salmon, £2.80/lb; venison rump steaks (4–8oz), £4.75; hare (whole in skin), £1.10; pheasant (oven-ready), £3.

Catalogue Annually, A4, Catalogue, B/W, 2 pages, Free **Postal charges** Free **Delivery** Royal Mail or Datapost for larger orders, Royal Mail, Parcelforce **Methods of Payment** Cheque, Credit Card

MONTGOMERY MOORE

17 Tunsgate
Guildford
Surrey
GU1 3QT
Telephone
01483 451620
Fax
same

Fine chocolates, fruit and nut delicacies

Montgomery Moore chocolates are a treat. Made from French chocolate with a high cocoa content, they are not 'too sweet' and make ideal presents. Gift-wrapping and a personalised card are included. Chocolate selection, £4.94/12 chocolates, £24.75/63 chocs; bittermint creams, £4.25/20 chocolates; truffle selection, £5.25/11 chocolates, £15.95/36 chocolates. Chocolate sauce, fruit coulis and vermicelli (32 per cent cocoa) are also available.

Catalogue Annually, A5, Brochure, Colour, 4 pages, Free **Postal charges** £4.95 **Delivery** Royal Mail **Methods of Payment** Cheque, Credit Card

MOORLANDS CHEESEMAKERS

Blackwood Hill
Rushton Spencer
Nr Macclesfield
Cheshire
SK11 0RU
Telephone
01260 226336
Fax
01260 226447

Cheese-making equipment

Moorlands sell everything you might need for cheese-making, from butter churns to draining racks. They also sell cheese-making kits, that include fermenting, for soft cheese (£16.50), hard cheese (£53.50) and combined cheeses (£59.50). Presses are available separately, from £32.45. All their equipment is suitable for all types of milk. There is no VAT on starters, rennet or books.

Catalogue A5, Catalogue, B/W, 6 pages, Free **Postal charges** Varies with item **Delivery** Parcelforce **Methods of Payment** Cheque, Credit Card

MOREL BROS, COBBETT & SON LTD

Unit 7
129 Coldharbour Lane
London
SE5 9NY
Telephone
0171 346 0046
Fax
0171 346 0033

Fine foods and groceries

Two Italian warehousemen, Lewis Morel and Arthur Cobbett, started selling fine foods and groceries in the late 18th century and today Morel Bros, Cobbett & Son Ltd continues to supply the best British and Continental products to your home. The catalogue itself is a work of art and one can only marvel at the variety of foods it contains. There are foods, syrups, sauces and spices from all over the world – olive oils from Italy, Spain, Portugal and the Peloponnese; vinegars from Modena; pâtés from Perigord; anchovies from Sardinia; wild white pepper from Cameroon; tapenade; Bizac truffles; mackerel fillets in Muscadet sauce; plus confits and cassoulets, caviar and chocolates, teas, coffees and more. All the foods are specially selected from companies that Morel Bros, Cobbett & Son believe provide the highest possible quality products.

Catalogue Annually, A4, Catalogue, Colour, 40 pages, Free **Postal charges** £3.95; free for orders of more than £75; £7.95 for fresh food **Delivery** Courier, Parcelforce **Methods of Payment** Cheque, Credit Card, American Express, Switch

MRS GILL'S COUNTRY CAKES

5 Link House
Leat Street
Tiverton
Devon
EX16 5LG
Telephone
01884 242744
Fax
01884 257440

Cakes

Winner of Best Cakes Rosette in Henrietta Green's *Food Lovers' Guide to Britain*, Mrs Gill's mouth-watering cakes include the Gourmet Devon Fruit Cake; the Almond Cake which can be eaten as a pudding with a fruit compote; the Dundee Cake containing a dash of English Sherry and Celebration Cakes which can be decorated to your specification. Dark green gift boxes are available.

Catalogue Annually, Third A4, Brochure, B/W, 6 pages, Free **Postal charges** Varies with item **Delivery** Parcelforce **Methods of Payment** Cheque

NATURAL CASING COMPANY
PO Box 133
Farnham
Surrey
GU10 5HT
Telephone
01252 850454
Fax
01252 851284

Materials for home sausage-making
For chefs, caterers or the enthusiastic cook, the Natural Casing Company supplies all you need bar the fillings to make sausages. It stocks sausage skins, including 25yd of hog casings to make 20lb of sausages (£5.80), beef runners for black pudding, beef middles for salami and beef bungs for haggis. It also supplies seasoning and nozzles and several books on the subject.

Catalogue Annually, A4, Leaflets, B/W, 2 pages, Free **Postal charges** Free **Delivery** Royal Mail **Methods of Payment** Cheque, Credit Card

NEAL'S YARD DAIRY
17 Shorts Gardens
London
WC2H 9AT
Telephone
0171 379 7646
Fax
0171 240 2442

Farm cheeses from the British Isles
Their leaflet describes a comprehensive range of British cheeses available for delivery to yourself or friends throughout the world. Also available are complementary products such as mustards and olive oils. A personal message card can be attached to gifts for your gourmet friends. The *Guardian* Big Cheese Club also offers a 20% discount for an annual fee of £15 bringing six offers a year containing a selection of cheeses.

Catalogue A4, Leaflets, B/W pages, Free **Postal charges** A basic rate of £6 applies anywhere in the UK **Delivery** Courier **Methods of Payment** Cheque, Postal Order, Credit Card

THE ORGANIC WINE COMPANY
PO Box 81
High Wycombe
Buckinghamshire
HP13 5QN
Telephone
01494 446557

Organic wine
Organic wine is produced using the most natural ingredients available. No herbicides, pesticides or artificial yeasts are used and traditional methods are employed to clarify the wine. The result, the company claims, is richer, more complex wines with more interesting tastes. Their Champagnes, such as 'Cuvée des Trois Cépages' cost around £16.99 a bottle. A 'Blanc de Blancs' *vin de table* costs around £3.50 a bottle (£40.50 per case) and

bottles of claret start at around £3 (£31.50 per case).
Catalogue Bi-annually, A5, Catalogue, B/W, 24 pages, Free **Postal charges** Within a 15-mile radius of High Wycombe, free. 1 case: £3.95 within 40-mile radius of High Wycombe, and all London postal districts; £5.00 elsewhere. 2–3 cases, £6.95; 4-5 cases, £9.50; more than 6 cases, free. **Delivery** Courier **Methods of Payment** Cheque, Postal Order, Credit Card

NORMAL R. HOLLAND
159 Gordon Road
Ilford
Essex
IG1 2XS
Telephone
0181 478 0192

Teas

A one-man business, Norman Holland combines quality with prompt, personal service. He stocks a small range of some of the best known teas, as well as decorative tins, infusers and linen tea-cloths. Finest Assam is priced at £2.20/500g, Finest Ceylon at £2.30/500g, Finest Earl Grey (scented with real oil of Bergamot) £3.70/500g, and Finest China Jasmine at £3.50/500g. Infusers are one-cup size and cost £1.80 each. Tea-cloths, with a design of teas and teapots, are £3 each.
Catalogue Annually, A4, Leaflets, B/W, 1 page, Please send sae for price list **Postal charges** Varies with item **Delivery** Royal Mail **Methods of Payment** Cheque

ORIENTALIS TRADING COMPANY
Tuborg House
Mandell Road
London
SW2 5DL
Telephone
0171 737 2883
Fax
0171 737 2838

Innovative Oriental snacks

Orientalis provides a wide range of exciting Oriental foodstuffs. Among those available are satay broad beans (£1/150g) and garlic and chilli flavoured peanut crackers (£1/200g). You can also buy satay marinade (55p/50g), Szechuan pepper beef mix (65p/25g), and vegetarian curry powder (65p/75g), as well as coconut cream (60p/200ml).
Catalogue Annually, A4, Leaflets, Colour and B/W, 3 pages, Free **Postal charges** Varies with item **Delivery** Royal Mail **Methods of Payment** Cheque, Credit Card

PAXTON & WHITFIELD
93 Jermyn Street
London
SW1Y 6JE
Telephone
0171 930 0259
Fax
0181 944 9311

Quality cheeses
Paxton & Whitfield have been cheesemongers since the 1700s. Their mail-order list offers a selection from their stock of postable cheeses, hams, smoked salmon and wines (baby Stilton £31.50/5lb; Cheddar truckle, £27.50/4lb). Hampers are also available. One way of learning more about cheese and sampling the pick of the world's finest is by joining their Cheese Society. For £19.95 a month you will receive a monthly cheeseboard selection and quarterly newsletter.

Catalogue Annually, A4, Catalogue, Colour, 12 pages, Free **Delivery** Royal Mail, Parcelforce **Methods of Payment** Cheque, Credit Card, Diners Club, American Express

R TWINING AND COMPANY
216 Strand
London
WC2R 1AP
Telephone
0171 353 3511

Teas and coffees
Twining, the world-famous tea and coffee merchant, offers a selection of its teas and coffees by mail order. Finest loose teas, 250g: Assam £3.85, Oolong £5.15; Earl Grey decaffeinated tea bags, £2.45 for 50. Coffee beans or ground, 250g: Pure Colombian £1.73, Old Brown Indonesian £1.93.

Catalogue Annually, A5, Leaflets, B/W, 4 pages, Free **Postal charges** Varies with item **Delivery** Royal Mail **Methods of Payment** Cheque, Credit Card

RANNOCH SMOKERY
Kinloch Rannoch
by Pitlochry
Perthshire
Scotland
PH16 5QD
Telephone
0800 319 319
Fax
01 882 633 319

Smoked foods
Rannoch Smokery supplies smoked venison, smoked venison pâté, smoked pheasant and other such delicacies. There is no tastier starter for a dinner party than smoked venison which can be eaten on its own or with salads. It is available either plain, or with oil and herbs from £5.80 per pack, packs of three at £15.99, packs of six £29.40. A whole smoked pheasant is £5, with p&p per pheasant £2.50. Pheasant breasts and drumsticks are also available.

Catalogue Annually, A4, Leaflets, Colour, 2 pages, Free **Postal charges** Varies with item **Delivery** Royal Mail **Methods of Payment** Cheque, Postal Order

THE REAL MEAT COMPANY
East Hill Farm
Heytesbury
Warminster
Wiltshire
BA12 0HR
Telephone
01985 840501
Fax
01985 840243

Additive-free, quality meat

The award-winning Real Meat Company offers a genuine alternative to factory farming. Beef, lamb, pork, bacon, ham, chickens, ducks, turkeys and geese are all produced free range on small family-run farms. No growth promoters or routine drug regimes are used. Next-day delivery is guaranteed and orders arrive chill-packed and vacuum-sealed in insulated boxes. Lean mince, £3.12/lb; silverside joint, £4.75/lb; pork spare rib chops, £2.69/lb; whole chicken, £2.09/lb; gammon joints, £3.69/lb.

Catalogue Annually, A4, Leaflets, Colour, 5 pages, Free **Postal charges** £3.95 **Delivery** Courier **Methods of Payment** Cheque, Credit Card

REID WINES (1992) Ltd
The Mill
Marsh Lane
Hallatrow
Bristol
Avon
BS18 5EB
Telephone
01761 452645
Fax
01761 453642

Fine wines and spirits

Reid pride themselves on their extensive list of fine wines, especially their Burgundy and Bordeaux. The helpful and honest commentaries on their stock are invaluable aids to the expert, and clear enough to guide even the novice. Their own favourites, the 'Selection', seem to be good value for money, with Chardonnay at £5.85 a bottle and House Champagne at £11.50 a bottle.

There is also an impressive range of sherries, ports, Madeiras, dessert wines, liqueurs, spirits and *eaux de vie*.

Catalogue Annually, A5, Catalogue, B/W, 39 pages, Free **Postal charges** Carriage is free in central London, for local deliveries and to hotels and restaurants for orders of more than two cases. Carriage may be charged on small orders. **Delivery** Most orders are delivered in their own vehicles. In any other event they send by carrier or Royal Mail Courier,

FOOD & DRINK

In-house delivery, Royal Mail **Methods of Payment** Cheque, Postal Order, Credit Card, American Express, Diners Club, Switch

RICHARD KIHL
Slaughden House
140/144 High Street
Aldeburgh
Suffolk
IP15 5AQ
Telephone
01728 454455
Fax
01728 454433

Fine and rare wines

Richard Kihl is no ordinary wine merchant. It specialises in the top end of the market, selling quality wines at good but nevertheless hefty prices. Its simple price list gives only the year, name and price and is clearly aimed at people who know their wines well. A case of 1928 Chateau Lafite costs £4,080 (ex VAT); 1988 Puligny-Montrachet, £185; Armagnac from £660.

Catalogue Bi-monthly, A4, Leaflets, B/W, 12 pages, Free **Postal charges** £2 a case, minimum £12 per consignment **Delivery** Courier **Methods of Payment** Cheque, Credit Card

RICHARD WOODALL
Lane End
Waberthwaite
Nr Millom
Cumbria
LA19 5YJ
Telephone
01229 717237
Fax
01229 717007

Cumberland hams and dry cured beef

The Woodall family has been producing finequality hams since 1828 on its farm in Cumbria. The Cumberland hams are about 11–17lb in weight (£3/lb or £3.95/lb cooked) and spend one month in a dry cure before hanging for a further two months to produce a true depth of flavour. Cumbria air-dried ham is a Parma style with herbs (on the bone, £4.65/lb). Other varieties are available including home-cured bacon and drycured beef.

Catalogue Annually, A5, Brochure, Colour and B/W, 6 pages **Postal charges** Varies with item **Delivery** Royal Mail, Parcelforce **Methods of Payment** Cheque

SANDRIDGE FARMHOUSE BACON
Sandridge Farm
Bromham
Chippenham

Sliced bacon, joints and cooked hams

Roger Keen's herd of 350 sows and progeny enjoy a natural diet free from artificial hormones, growth promoters or antibiotic feed additives. Sandridge Farm has revived the traditional methods of curing

FOOD & DRINK

Wiltshire
SN15 2JN
Telephone
01380 850304

pig meat and prides itself on its 'cured bacon that sizzles in the pan and traditional hams with texture and flavour'. Old local recipes are used to produce their Five Exclusive Hams, all individually selected and prepared, some taking eight months to mature.
Catalogue A4, Leaflets, Colour, 1 page, Free **Postal charges** Orders up to £7.00, add postage at £4.50; orders over £7.00, add carriage at £10.00 **Delivery** Royal Mail **Methods of Payment** Cheque

SARA JAYNE'S TRUFFLES
517 Old York Road
London
SW18 1TF
Telephone
0181 874 8500
Fax
0181 874 8575

Chocolate truffles

Sara Jayne produces chocolate truffles using the best French and English Couverture chocolate, double Devon cream and . . . love. Each one is made, piped and dipped by hand by people who adore chocolate. But beware, they are not for the faint-hearted! Choose from plain, Calvados, ivory Champagne, milk, ginger, Lapsang Souchong and many more. Prices £17/1lb, £10/½lb.
Catalogue Annually, A4, Leaflets, B/W, 1 page, Free **Postal charges** £4 **Delivery** Royal Mail, Parcelforce **Methods of Payment** Cheque, Postal Order

SARAH MEADE'S SPECIAL OCCASION CAKES
8 The Calvert Centre
Woodmancott
Winchester
Hampshire
SO21 3BN
Telephone
01256 397163
Fax
01256 397874

Handmade fruit cakes

Sarah Meade's luxury fruit cakes are all handmade using wholesome ingredients and baked in the traditional way. Packaged either in attractive oval-shaped wooden or presentation boxes, the cakes can be despatched for special occasions, with messages iced on at no extra charge. The Victorian Plum Fruit Cake contains plums, raisins, sultanas, currants and aromatic spices of mace, cinnamon and coriander, and costs £13.95 for a presentation-boxed family size (575g).
Catalogue A4, Leaflets, Colour, 3 page, Free **Postal charges** Free **Delivery** Royal Mail, Parcelforce **Methods of Payment** Cheque, Postal Order, Credit Card, Switch, Diners Club

THE SCOTTISH GOURMET
Thistle Mill
Station Road
Biggar
Strathclyde
Scotland
ML12 6LP
Telephone
01899 21001
Fax
01899 20456

Fresh Scottish produce

The Scottish Gourmet is Britain's leading home-dining club. It sends out a monthly menu featuring seasonal Scottish produce purchased from the country's small suppliers. Orders are chilled, packed in ice and delivered to the door within 24 hours of despatch. Membership costs £10 for one year. A monthly feature is a 'Dinner for Two' of, for example, summer vegetable soup, Highlander Parcels of ground pork, beef and bacon in cabbage leaves and lemony sauce with gourmet vegetables, and Raspberry Cranachan, all for £12.95.

Catalogue Annually, A5, Brochure, Colour, 12 pages, Free **Postal charges** Varies with item **Delivery** Royal Mail **Methods of Payment** Cheque, Credit Card, Switch, American Express

SCOTTISH TEA SELECTORS
The Home Farm
Brodick
Isle of Arran
Scotland
KA27 8DD
Telephone
01770 302595
Fax
01770 302599

Quality teas

Scottish Tea Selectors supply a large range of quality traditional teas, fruit teas and spices in attractive packs, ceramic pots and wooden chests. Earl Grey teabags in wooden chest, £1.50/50g; Assam loose tea in wooden chest, £1.50/125g; whisky toddy muslin sachets, £1.20 for six; Mexican chilli spice-blend box, £2.70/200g. Note: minimum order £75.

Catalogue Quarterly, A4, Leaflets, Colour and B/W, 6 pages, Free **Postal charges** Varies with item **Delivery** Royal Mail, Parcelforce **Methods of Payment** Cheque, Credit Card

SEDLESCOMBE VINEYARD
Robertsbridge
East Sussex
TN32 5SA

Organic wine

This English vineyard produces organic wines, ciders and fruit juices which are approved by the vegetarian society and suitable for vegans. Their 1994 Late Harvest Muscadet-style white wine (11% vol) is priced at £6.95 a bottle. Their

Telephone
01580 830715
Fax
01580 830122

organic Brut 1992 Méthode Champenoise bubbly (12% vol) has a heady bouquet of apples and limes and is priced at £11.95. They also produce an interesting range of fruit wines, such as the medium sweet blackcurrant (8% vol), a rosé, priced at £4.50 a bottle.

Catalogue A4, Leaflets, B/W, 1 page, Free **Postal charges Delivery** Free if order value exceeds £59.00; add £7.00 per case if total order value less than £59.00 **Delivery** Royal Mail **Methods of Payment** Cheque, Credit Card

SEVERN & WYE SMOKERY
Walmore Hill
Minsterworth
Gloucestershire
GL2 8LA
Telephone
01452 750777
Fax
01452 750776

Smoked fish and poultry

The Severn & Wye Smokery is situated on the edge of the Forest of Dean, between two of England's most celebrated salmon rivers. Here the art of smoking locally-caught fish and meats is still carried out by hand using traditional skills, and the Smokery lists Harrods among its customers. A 2lb pack of pre-sliced smoked salmon costs £19. Other smoked products include prawns, kippers, fillets of mackerel, trout and eel, as well as chicken and duck breasts.

Catalogue Annually, Third A4, Brochure, B/W, 2 pages, Free **Postal charges** £5.50 on orders below £60 **Delivery** Royal Mail **Methods of Payment** Cheque

SIMPLY SALMON
Severals Farm
Arkesden
Saffron Walden
Essex
CB11 4EY
Telephone
01799 550143
Fax
01799 550039

Salmon and food hampers

Simply Salmon's smoked salmon comes from lochs on the Isle of Skye and north-west coast of Scotland and is smoked in old-fashioned kilns over oak chippings (sliced pack, £8.55/8oz; fully trimmed side, £25.95/1¾–2lb). In 1995 it introduced honeyroast salmon, a cross between fresh and smoked with a smoky orange crust (£14.95/150–200g). Picnic boxes (Glyndebourne, £32.95), hampers (from £13.95) and gift boxes (from £10.95) are available, too.

Catalogue Annually, A4, Leaflets, B/W, 4 pages, Free **Postal charges** Free **Delivery** Royal Mail, Parcelforce **Methods of Payment** Cheque, Credit Card

ST JAMES'S TEAS LTD
Sir John Lyon House
Upper Thames Street
London
EC4V 3PA
Telephone
0171 236 0611
Fax
0171 454 0006

Quality teas
St James's Teas specialise in high-quality teas. There is a full description of each tea to help you to appreciate their different qualities and to guide you towards exciting blending possibilities. Teas on offer include Assam, Darjeeling, Ceylon and China Keemun. Prices start at £1.60 per 125g packet. St James's Decaffeinated Tea costs £3.50 for 250g. Teas can also be bought in the St James's range of caddies featuring historical and classical designs, from £3.50 for a 125g caddie.

Catalogue Leaflets, Colour and B/W, Free **Postal charges** Free **Delivery** Parcelforce **Methods of Payment** Cheque, Credit Card

STEAMBOAT FOOD & DRINK LTD
PO Box 452
Bradford
West Yorkshire
BD4 7TF
Telephone
01274 619826
Fax
same

Oriental foods
Steamboat sell foods from exotic places all around the world. You can choose from an enormous range of herbs and spices, including black onion seed at 69p for 50g, bouquet garni at 49p for 10 sachets, juniper berries at 69p for 50g and alfalfa seeds at 49p for 50g.

New additions to the catalogue include wines and beers, such as sake and sopporo, and an extensive range of hardware, from woks (starting at £6.99) to chopsticks (starting at 99p a pair). A wonderful resource for the adventurous cook.

Catalogue Bi-annually, A4, Catalogue, B/W, 19 pages, Free **Postal charges** Add £2.95 for orders up to £39.99. Orders over £39.99, free **Delivery** Royal Mail **Methods of Payment** Cheque, Postal Order, Credit Card

SWADDLES GREEN FARM
Hare Lane
Buckland St Mary
Chard
Somerset
TA20 3JR
Telephone
01460 234387
Fax
01460 234591

Organic meat

Bill and Charlotte Reynolds run an organic holding in the the Blackdown Hills specialising in fine-quality meat full of old-fashioned succulence and flavour which is also accredited organic by UKROFS. Their range includes pork, beef, lamb, chicken, bacon, gammon, offal, charcuterie, ham, pâté and a successful line of sausages and burgers for children. All the meat is farmed the old way from traditional English breeds ideally suited to the slower, gentler rearing methods. It is butchered at the farm in their refrigerated cutting rooms and delivered vacuum-packed and ready to cook. They also prepare freezer and dinner party meals. Everyday minced beef, £2.70/lb; shoulder of lamb, £2.25/lb; apple, cider and rosemary pork sausages, £4.05/lb; cassoulet, £4.20 or £6.05; children's pork and bean burgers, £5.50/2lb pack.
Catalogue Bi-monthly, A5, Catalogue, Colour and B/W, 10 pages, Free **Postal charges** Varies with item **Delivery** Courier, In-house delivery **Methods of Payment** Cheque, Credit Card

TANNERS WINES LTD
26 Wyle Cop
Shrewsbury
Shropshire
SY1 1XD
Telephone
01743 232007
Fax
01743 344401

Wines and spirits

Recently voted 'Central England Wine Merchant of 1995', Tanners Wines has been trading in Shropshire and the Welsh Marches since 1872 and is now firmly established as one of the leading mail-order wine merchants in the country. Excellent wines at all price levels are available from throughout the world with a particularly fine selection from France, Australia, New Zealand and Chile. Orders over £75 in value are delivered free of charge in mainland UK; smaller orders incur a £6 delivery charge; local orders of one case or more are delivered free of charge. Knowledgeable advice is always available, as is a wide range of other services including weddings and parties, *en primeur* and tastings. Tanners Claret is £4.99 a bottle, Tanners Champagne £12.60, Tanners Chardonnay £4.99 and Tanners White Bordeaux, £4.95.

Catalogue Bi-annually, A5, Catalogue, B/W, 127 pages, Free **Postal charges** Free in local delivery area for one case of wine or more **Delivery** Courier, In-house delivery **Methods of Payment** Cheque, Credit Card

TAVERNORS
Yew Tree House
Lucton
Leominster
Herefordshire
HR6 9PJ
Telephone
01568 780384
Fax
same

Traditional hampers

This Herefordshire company specialises in all things traditional with an emphasis on old-fashioned flavour. Incorporating a carefully chosen selection of British fare, these hampers make an ideal gift. The Abbeydore, for example, contains honey, plum chutney, mint and apple jelly, pheasant pâté, marmalade and strawberry conserve, all packed in a box (£15.33) or traditional willow hamper (£29.34); the Christmas Hamper No 3, full of festive goodies, costs £56.07.

Catalogue Annually, A5, Catalogue, Colour, 8 pages, Free **Postal charges** Varies with item **Delivery** Royal Mail, Parcelforce **Methods of Payment** Cheque, Credit Card

TAYLOR NASH
31 St Giles Street
Oxford
Oxfordshire
OX1 3LD
Telephone
01865 511700
Fax
same

Hampers, gift baskets and boxes

Taylor Nash produces delightful traditional hampers and gift boxes which it will deliver worldwide. These make perfect prizes or memorable presents and come beautifully presented in either standard versions or made up to your own specifications. Gift baskets containing wine, Stilton and relish, £25; hampers from £40; Christmas Box, £45. You can also pamper your guests with Taylor Nash picnics, from £5.95 for a Farmhouse selection.

Catalogue Annually, A5, Catalogue, Colour, 15 pages, Free **Postal charges** Free **Delivery** Royal Mail, Parcelforce **Methods of Payment** Cheque, Credit Card

THE TEA HOUSE
15 Neal Street
Covent Garden
London
WC2H 9PU
Telephone
0171 240 7539/836 6252
Fax
0171 836 4769

Quality teas
The Tea House specialises in fine teas, infusions, loose-leaf teas and tea-bags. It sells nearly 100 varieties of pure and blended tea from around the world, and tea-time accessories such as infusers and teapots. Favourites include Assam, Earl Grey and Darjeeling (from £1.25/125g). There are fruit-, flower- and spice-flavoured teas from £1.60/100g and herbal infusions from £1.50/100g. For those who enjoy a tipple, try a Tipsy Tea such as the vodka-flavoured Fire and Ice, £1.60.

Catalogue Annually, Third A4, Leaflets, B/W, 1 page, Free **Postal charges** £2.20/500g; £2.80/750g; £3.60/1500g; £4.80 for orders of more than 1500g; £3.95 for teapot **Delivery** Royal Mail **Methods of Payment** Cheque, Credit Card

TICKLEMORE CHEESE SHOP
1 Ticklemore Street
Totnes
Devon
TQ9 5EJ
Telephone
01803 865926

Cheeses
Ticklemore supplies an interesting range of British cheeses from its Totnes shop. The list indicates whether supplies are seasonal, suitable for vegetarians or made from unpasteurised milk. Ducketts' Caerphilly, £2.95/lb; smoked Cheddar, £4.15/lb; Devon Rustic, £3.35/lb; Harbourne blue goat's milk cheese, £4.55/lb; and Beenleigh Blue, which they make themselves from ewe's milk, £5.05/lb.

Catalogue Annually, A4, Leaflets, B/W, 1 page, Free **Postal charges** £2 per lb **Delivery** Royal Mail, Parcelforce **Methods of Payment** Cheque

A TOAST BY POST
829 Lisburn Road
Balmoral
Belfast
Northern Ireland
BT9 7GY

Named-brand gift bottles
What better way to celebrate a special occasion, a birthday or to say thank-you than by sending a Toast By Post? The company offers a choice of well-known drinks, including Martell VSOP Cognac, £33.95, Lambert Extra Dry NV Champagne, £24.95, and Lindemans Cabernet Sauvi-

FOOD & DRINK

Telephone
01232 661122
Fax
01232 666686

gnon Red Wine, £15.95, which it sends by first-class post, well-packaged in a gift box with a personal message card.

Catalogue Annually, Third A4, Leaflets, Colour, 4, pages, Free **Postal charges** Free **Delivery** Royal Mail **Methods of Payment** Cheque, Postal Order, Credit Card

THE TOFFEE SHOP
7 Brunswick Road
Penrith
Cumbria
CA11 7LU
Telephone
01768 862008
Fax
same

Toffee and fudge

The Toffee Shop is based in Cumbria and supplies a small range of handmade toffees and fudges by mail order. Assortments can be made up from the following: Butter Fudge, Chocolate Fudge, Butter Toffee and Treacle Toffee. Mint Fudge is also available but is not mixed with anything else. A variety of box sizes are available: ½lb at £3.25, 1lb at £5.95, 1½lb at £9.15, 2lb at £11.20, and 3lb at £15.50. Messages can be enclosed with your order.

Catalogue Annually, A5, Leaflets, B/W, 1 page, Free **Postal charges** Free **Delivery** Parcelforce **Methods of Payment** Cheque, Postal Order

UMMERA SMOKED PRODUCTS
Ummera House
Timoleague
Co Cork
Ireland
Telephone
00 353 23 46187
Fax
00 353 23 46419

Smoked salmon, eel and chicken

Ummera smokes only wild Irish salmon which has a firm yet tender flesh developed while swimming freely in the Atlantic Ocean without recourse to artificial feeds and antibiotics. The oak smoking and salt simply enhance the salmon's natural flavour. This much-praised product costs £27 for 1kg delivered to a UK address.

Catalogue Annually, Third A4, Catalogue, Colour and B/W, 6 pages, Free **Postal charges** Free **Delivery** Royal Mail **Methods of Payment** Cheque, Credit Card

VIGO VINEYARD SUPPLIES
Bollhayes Park
Clayhidon

Fruit presses and crushers

This is a wonderful catalogue for anyone with one or more fruit trees in their garden and too much fruit for their family and friends to eat. Vigo

Collumpton
Devon
EX15 3PN
Telephone
01823 680230
Fax
01823 680807

supplies fruit crushers and presses to make juices and cider, so you can put all those apples or whatever to good use. It also stocks accessories such as straining bags, funnels and yeast. Fruit presses from £75; crushers from £125.

Catalogue Annually, A5, Catalogue, Colour and B/W, 6 pages, Free **Postal charges** Varies with item **Delivery** Courier, Royal Mail **Methods of Payment** Cheque, Credit Card

THE VILLAGE BAKERY
Melmerby
Penrith
Cumbria
CA10 1HE
Telephone
01768 881515
Fax
01768 881848

Organic bakery goods
This traditional bakery produces organic bread and cakes from wood-fired brick ovens. The result is food you can trust, combining traditional craftsmanship with a modern concern for the environment. Specialities include a 900g 'Rich Fruit Cake' for £9.25; Borrowdale Teabread (£6.50 for 2 × 350g cakes); Flapjacks made without sugar (£6.75 for 3 packets) and Christmas hampers from £14.95.

Catalogue Annually, A5, Brochure, Colour and B/W, 6 pages, Free **Postal charges** Free **Delivery** Royal Mail, Parcelforce **Methods of Payment** Cheque, Credit Card, Diners Club

VILLAGE CAKES
Rosemullion
Zelah
Cornwall
TR4 9HH
Telephone
01872 540644
Fax
same

Home-baked cakes
Village Cakes makes luxury, home-baked cakes using natural ingredients, including Cornish butter, free-range eggs, organic flour and the finest quality dried fruits. The celebration cakes are decorated by hand. Each order is dealt with quickly to ensure a fast, fresh-baked delivery. Dundee Cake, £12.50 (7in); Surfers Cake, ideal for picnics, containing sultanas, orange and lemon peel pre-soaked in Cointreau, £13.50 (6in), £15.50 (7in); children's birthday cake, £15.50 (7in).

Catalogue Annually, A4, Catalogue, Colour, 6 pages, Free **Postal charges** £2.95 **Delivery** Royal Mail, Parcelforce **Methods of Payment** Cheque, Postal Order, Credit Card

VINCEREMOS
65 Raglan Road
Leeds
West Yorkshire
LS2 9DZ
Telephone
0113 2431693
Fax
0113 2431691

Organic and speciality wines, beers and spirits

Vinceremos distributes fine, organic and speciality wines. Organic wines are made from grapes grown without synthetic chemical fertilisers and pesticides. Many come from high-quality producers in the major regions of France, Italy, Germany, Hungary, Australia and New Zealand. Vinceremos also sells organic beers from Germany, organic ciders from Herefordshire, Russian vodkas and Cuban rums. An organic taster case of 12 different wines costs £49.95, while a bargain selection of two bottles each of six organic wines is just £45. A case of German organic lager (20 50cl bottles) is £26.

Catalogue Annually, A5, Catalogue, B/W, 16 pages, Free **Postal charges** £5.95; free delivery on orders of more than five cases **Delivery** Courier **Methods of Payment** Cheque, Credit Card

W T WARREN & SON
Boswedden Road
St Just
Penzance
Cornwall
TR19 7JU
Telephone
01736 788538
Fax
01736 788354

Cakes

Traditional bakers since 1860, W T Warren & Son make the legendary Cornish Saffron Cake said to date back to the time when Phoenician traders exchanged spices for Cornish tin. Saffron was added to give flavour and a warm, buttery appearance to bread and cakes. Saffron Cake is a rich, highly fruited dough cake, usually eaten cold or with butter. It can also be heated or lightly toasted. Only £4 per cake in the UK, prices for Europe and Rest of World are £5.60 and £8.50 respectively (prices correct at time of going to press).

Catalogue A4, Leaflets, Colour, 2 pages, Free **Postal charges** Free for second class; add 60p per cake for first class **Delivery** Royal Mail **Methods of Payment** Cheque, Postal Order, Credit Card

WAITROSE DIRECT WINES
Deer Park Road
Merton Abbey
London
SW19 3TU
Telephone
0800 413 331
Fax
0181 543 2415

Wines, spirits and Christmas hampers

Wider range of wines than in the shops, including Waitrose wines from around the world. Also spirits: A special Christmas brochure deals with hampers from £45 to £125.

Catalogue Bi-annually, A4, Catalogue, B/W, 36 pages
Postal charges Varies with item **Delivery** Royal Mail
Methods of Payment Credit Card, American Express, Switch, Cheque, Postal Order, Diners Club

WARDS OF ADISHAM
Little Bossington Farmhouse
Adisham
Canterbury
Kent
CT3 3LN
Telephone
01227 720596

Home-made farmhouse fudge

Sally and Ian Ward make mouth-watering fudge to their four-generation-old family recipe. They use pure and wholesome ingredients – sugar, butter, milk, golden syrup, vanilla essence and real flavourings – mixed in open pans. The finished product is packed in decorated boxes. Elizabeth David, doyenne of cookery writers, used to buy Wards fudge by post – for herself! Prices from £4.85/½lb (£6.30 to Europe) to £15.80/2lb (£18.50 to Europe).

Catalogue Annually, A5, Brochure, B/W, 4 pages, Free
Postal charges Free **Delivery** Royal Mail, Parcelforce
Methods of Payment Cheque

THE WATERMILL
Little Salkeld
Penrith
Cumbria
CA10 1NN
Telephone
01768 881523

Traditonal flours

The Watermill at Little Salkeld produces stoneground flour in the traditional manner and is one of the country's few millers of organic grains. Its 100 per cent wholemeal flour was a Soil Association Organic Product of the Year in 1993. The company also offers a range of organic dried fruits and nuts, pastas, teas and coffees, herbs and books, including *The Watermill*

Baking Book (£1.95). Wholewheat flour, £2.15/3kg; rye flour, £2.50/3kg; four-grain blend flour, £2.40/3kg; oatmeal, 80p/800g; Watermill muesli, £1.65/1kg.

Catalogue Annually, A5, Catalogue, Colour and B/W, 8 pages, Free **Postal charges** £6.75 **Delivery** Royal Mail, Parcelforce **Methods of Payment** Cheque, Postal Order, Credit Card

THE WEALD SMOKERY
Mount Farm
Flimwell
East Sussex
TN5 7QL
Telephone
01580 879601
Fax
01580 879564

Smoked foods

The Weald Smokery offers a wide range of smoked foods most of which can be served straight from the pack without the need for cooking. The brochure does, however, offer some recipes which enhance the smoked flavour of the produce. Choose from smoked salmon, trout, chicken, duck, eel, Toulouse sausage, haddock, ham, venison and mussels. Smoked Scottish salmon, sliced from £6.75/8oz, sides from £20/2lb; smoked Scottish trout, £4.10/1lb; smoked duck breasts, £5.50/breast/approx ½lb.

Catalogue Annually, Third A4, Catalogue, B/W, 6 pages, Free **Postal charges** Varies with item **Delivery** Royal Mail **Methods of Payment** Cheque, Credit Card

THE WHISKY CONNOISSEUR
Thistle Mill
Biggar
Scotland
ML12 6LP
Telephone
01899 221001
Fax
01899 220456

Whisky

This Scottish-based club sends out regular lists of specialist whiskies for the connoisseur. Many of the blends are old and rare and unavailable in the shops. They include outstanding cask-strength single malts from the Highlands, Islands, Lowlands and Speyside. The club also have their own bottlings and new presentations from the leading independent bottlers. Membership is £10 per year, £30 for 5 years, £50 for lifetime. Whiskies change with each programme.

A sister company is the Scottish Gourmet which provides gourmet food, predominantly the best of

Scottish fare, by mail order. This is a club concept with monthly mailings with ever-changing menus from which members select.

Catalogue By Advertising **Postal charges** Over 8 items, free **Delivery** Parcelforce **Methods of Payment** Cheque, Postal Order, Credit Card, American Express, Diners Club, Switch

THE WHITE HOUSE COFFEE ROASTERS (NOTTINGHAM)
104 Parliament Terrace
Upper Parliament Street
Nottingham
Nottinghamshire
NG1 5FX
Telephone
0115 9419033

Coffee and tea

The White House has a delightful shop in Nottingham selling all kinds of speciality teas and freshly roasted coffees, roasted daily in their own roastery. They offer a range of coffee-making equipment and are agents for Gaggia Espresso coffee makers. Recently they have expanded to offer a mail-order service, producing an attractive catalogue with informative background information on coffees and teas and an extensive price list. If you send for a free brochure, they will send you a free sample of their Swiss Blend No 1 coffee – at least they did with ours, which was much enjoyed. Postal charge is £4.56 per order (minimum order 5lb) but you can still order up to 30 kilos for that same postal charge.

Catalogue Annually, Third A4, Catalogue, Colour, 6 pages, Free **Postal charges** Varies with item **Delivery** Parcelforce **Methods of Payment** Cheque, Credit Card, Postal Order

WHITTARD OF CHELSEA
73 Northcote Road
London
SW11 6PJ
Telephone
0171 924 1888
Fax
0171 924 3085

Specialist teas and coffees

Since 1886 Whittard has imported pure estate teas. It is also famous for its blends such as Earl Grey (started in 1898) and Original (1904). Great attention is paid to flavour and quality, as you would expect of this reputable company. Its coffees are estate-grown Arabicas which give a delicious flavour and aroma and are available in various strengths, beans or ground. Darjeeling

Puttabong tea per 125g, loose £7, tin £7.99; Assam Hajua Broken Pekoe, loose £1.50, tin £2.49. China teas, jasmine and fruit infusions are also available. High-roast after-dinner coffee, £6.40/1lb.

Catalogue Annually, Third A4, Leaflets, B/W, 4 pages, Free **Postal charges** £3; overseas rates on application **Delivery** Royal Mail, Parcelforce, In-house delivery **Methods of Payment** Credit Card, Cheque

WICKER & BOX
St Leonards House
141 Moore Road
Mapperley
Nottingham
Nottinghamshire
NG3 6EL
Telephone
0115 960 3485

Champagne hampers
Wicker & Box will deliver Champagne gifts nationwide. These include pine boxes or wicker hampers containing just champagne or also port, Belgian chocolates, smoked salmon and Stilton cheese. A bottle of champagne in a gift box costs £30; a bottle of Champagne and smoked salmon, £40. Two bottles of champagne and Belgian chocolates in a hamper, £50; a bottle of port and a bottle of Champagne, £40.

Catalogue Third A4, Brochure, Colour, 6 pages, Free **Postal charges** Free **Delivery** Royal Mail, Parcelforce **Methods of Payment** Cheque, Postal Order

WILLIAM GRANT & SONS INTERNATIONAL LTD
The Glenfiddich Distillery
Dufftown
Banffshire
AB55 4DH
Telephone
01340 820373
Fax
01340 820805

Whisky and associated products
William Grant is a whisky distillery selling Glenfiddich malt whisky and accessories including waiter trays (£2.95), ancient reserve water jugs in green or blue (£12.95) and crystal whisky tumblers £24.95 each. The whisky starts at £20.49 for 70cl of BV Founder's Reserve through to £40 for 70cl of Classic Glenfiddich pure malt scotch whisky. A special gift presentation is also available for the Excellence, an 18-year-old Glenfiddich pure malt.

Catalogue None **Postal charges** Varies with item **Delivery** Parcelforce **Methods of Payment** Cheque, Credit Card, American Express

WINE FINDS

Cellar-Select Ltd
Freepost BS8471
Bath
Avon
BA1 7UZ
Telephone
0800 373052
Fax
01225 858632

Wines

Wine Finds takes a different approach in delivering the best value wines on the market today. If you are interested in the quality and personality of the wines you drink, an easy-to-understand and constantly changing selection of the best wines chosen after a continuous and exhaustive sampling programme is to be found in these brochures. All the wines are offered at discounted prices.

Catalogue Quarterly, A4, Leaflets, Colour, 5 pages, Free **Postal charges** £4.50 – free on orders over £90 **Delivery** Courier **Methods of Payment** Cheque, Postal Order, Credit Card, American Express, Switch

WOOTTON VINEYARD

North Wootton
Shepton Mallet
Somerset
BA4 4AG
Telephone
01749 890359

English wines and eau de vie

Wootton Vineyard of Somerset has been making fine wine since 1973. Schonburger is a medium dry wine costing £54.45 for a case of 12 bottles, excluding delivery. Single bottles can be sent through the post at £4.95 each, excluding p&p. This enterprising vineyard is the only producer of eau de vie in England. Made from one of its grape varieties, it comes in an attractive long, thin, dark bottle with a green outer tube, making it a very postable gift (£15.65/50cl excluding p&p).

Postal charges Varies with item **Delivery** Royal Mail, Courier **Methods of Payment** Cheque, Postal Order

Footwear

BUSINESS EMPHASYS LTD
22 Four Oaks Road
Four Oaks
Sutton Coldfield
West Midlands
B74 2TJ
Telephone
0121 308 4472
Fax
0121 308 2521

Slippers
Kiwi Slippers are made in New Zealand and are handcrafted in genuine sheepskin and hand-crocheted in durable pure new wool. When the slippers wear out, you can buy a Repair Kit (from £10.00) to extend their life, at one-third of the price of a replacement pair.

Available in children's sizes and adult sizes up to 11, they cost from £30 to £36. For babies under 18 months of age there are Kiwee slippers for £10.

Catalogue Annually, Third A4, Brochure, B/W, 6 pages, Free **Postal charges** Free **Delivery** Parcelforce **Methods of Payment** Cheque, Credit Card

CAPUT MAGNA LTD
The Chase
18 High Street
Moulton
Spalding
Lincolnshire
PE12 6QB
Telephone
01406 371370

Sandals
Handmade in masses of bright summer colours and natural shades, there's something different for sandal wearers from Sundaes. Hard-wearing and comfortable, Sundaes are created using the best quality materials with leather uppers and linings. There are 35 styles for all the family (some women's up to size 10), including a selection of award winning ECCO shoes and Hogl courts, plus the unique Sundaes sandals and belts.

Catalogue Bi-annually, A5, Catalogue, Colour, 20 pages
Postal charges £2.50 per pair **Delivery** Royal Mail
Methods of Payment Cheque, Postal Order, Credit Card, Switch

CARTMELL'S OF KESWICK
16 Lake Road
Keswick
Cumbria
CA12 5BX
Telephone
017687 72740
Fax
same

Shoes
Cartmell's offers a range of AA and B-fitting shoes and sandals in classic designs. It works closely with Crockett & Jones in Britain and Dexter in America and stocks other makes including Rieker anti-stress shoes for men and women. The brochure provides clear line drawings and descriptions. Prices start at £49.50.

Catalogue Annually, A4, Catalogue, B/W, 4 pages, Free
Postal charges Varies with item **Delivery** Royal Mail
Methods of Payment Cheque, Credit Card

COSYFEET
5 The Tanyard
Leigh Road
Street
Somserset
BA16 0HR
Telephone
01458 447275
Fax
01458 445988

Footwear
Cosyfeet produce an interesting range of products for people who suffer from foot problems. This could be because of swollen feet, arthritis, odema, diabetes and so on. Their slippers are soft and washable, while the shoes are lightweight with leather uppers. Some come with 'easy entry' Velcro fastenings which make getting them on and off painful feet much less of a business. Ladies' bootee washable slippers are £15.95, while the men's are £17.95. The lightweight leather shoes are £40 and £43 respectively.

Catalogue Annually, A5, Brochure, B/W, 28 pages, Free
Postal charges Varies with item **Delivery** Royal Mail
Methods of Payment Cheque, Postal Order, Credit Card, Switch

JAMES INGLIS
Eastwark House
Eastgate
Peebles
Borders
Scotland
EH45 8AD
Telephone
01721 720648

Women's shoes in narrow and specialist fittings
Marie-Rose and Richard Inglis have travelled throughout the world to build up their collection of comfortable and distinctive shoes for slim, narrow feet. In their catalogue you will find a selection of the large range of styles, colours and sizes available in their Peebles shop, with handbags to match. Shoes from £37.99 for linen lace-ups, to £99 for a low-heeled basket weave with soft calf.

FOOTWEAR

Fax
01721 723327

Catalogue Bi-annually, A5, Catalogue, Colour, 8 pages, Free **Postal charges** £3.50 a pair **Delivery** Royal Mail, Parcelforce **Methods of Payment** Cheque, Credit Card, American Express, Diners Club

MADE TO LAST
8 The Crescent
Hyde Park Corner
Leeds
West Yorkshire
LS6 2NW
Telephone
0113 2304983

Handmade shoes and boots

Made to Last is a workers' co-operative producing handmade casual boots, shoes and sandals for women, men and children. They use top-quality leathers in a stunning range of colours with a choice of soles, and offer a vegan range in flexible, breathable non-leather. By following simple instructions you are asked to make a drawing of your foot from which your order is individually sized. Allowances can be made for problem areas (ie enlarged joints). Child's buckle sandal, £25; adult strap shoe, £44.50; Oxford shoe (adult 10–14), £67.

Catalogue Annually, A5, Catalogue, Colour, 13 pages, Free **Postal charges** £4 **Delivery** Parcelforce, Royal Mail **Methods of Payment** Cheque

NEXT DIRECTORY
PO Box 299
Leicester
Leicestershire
LE5 5GH
Telephone
0345 100 500
Fax
0116 2738749

Men's, women's and children's clothes and shoes

The Next Directory was in the forefront of the transformation of British mail order and remains one of the most stylish ways to order clothes through the post. The catalogue itself is a well-designed hardback featuring ranges available in the high street shops. For women, a double-breasted blazer costs £99; pleated skirt, £49.99; low-heel court shoe, £29.99. For men, a suit costs £99.99 for a navy gabardine jacket and £49.99 for the matching trousers; American brogue shoe, £59.99. There is also a selection of children's wear: blue stone-washed denims for a six to nine-month-old baby, £8.99; lightweight jacket from £19.99; Nubuck lace-up shoe, £19.99. A must for any serious catalogue shopper.

Catalogue Bi-annually, A4, Catalogue, Colour, 387 pages, £3 **Postal charges** £2.50 **Delivery** Courier, Parcelforce, In-house delivery **Methods of Payment** Cheque, Stage Payments, Credit Card, American Express, Diners Club

THE NEW SHOE COMPANY
Dept CL
PO Box 170
Gloucester
Gloucestershire
GL4 7ZF
Telephone
01452 612446

Baby shoes

New shoes are simple and neat, handmade in England from top-quality 100% cotton drill and lined in soft, natural cotton. In ten single colours, with no pattern or frills, New Shoes match everything a baby might wear. They are machine-washable and maintain their colour and shape. Bigger sizes are ideal as slippers for toddlers in 'proper shoes'. All sizes are £4.95 per pair.

Catalogue Annually, A5, Leaflets, B/W, 2 pages, Free **Postal charges** Free **Delivery** Royal Mail **Methods of Payment** Cheque, Postal Order

OFFICE LONDON
26 Park Royal Road
London
NW10 7JW
Telephone
0181 838 4447
Fax
0181 961 7289

Shoes and accessories

Office London offer good quality footwear for men and women. The classic men's square-toed flat Italian leather-lined loafer in leather and patent or patent croc, sizes 6–11, costs £56.99. The 'Toledo' leather sandal with block heel and buckle, sizes 3–8, costs £29.99. The 'Red or Dead' high-heeled jelly sandal in a kaleidoscope of colours comes in sizes 3–7 and costs £14.99. Office's own Italian trainer comes in 11 colours, sizes 3–8, and costs £29. Accessories include sunglasses and T-shirts.

Catalogue Annually, A4, Catalogue, Colour, 27 pages, Free **Postal charges** UK: add £5.00 per total order; Eire: add £5.00 per pair; Europe: add £8.00 per pair **Delivery** Royal Mail **Methods of Payment** Cheque, Postal Order, Credit Card, Switch

PURPLE FISH

The Gate House
Chalford Industrial Estate
Chalford
Stroud
Gloucestershire
GL6 8NT
Telephone
01453 882820
Fax
01453 886606

Shoes for all the family

Purple Fish is a comprehensive catalogue of children's shoes, which now includes adult sizes. All the shoes have soft, padded arch supports and reinforced stitching. The insole is lined with an anti-bacteria sponge fabric which also prevents odour.

The back of the catalogue has an easy-order planner, but the really good point about this company is that they give you their FREEPOST number with your order so you can return shoes at their cost. Hopefully, this will not be because the shoes don't fit as they also include a clever fish chart for measuring your feet and plenty of sound advice on how to make sure your children's shoes fit. Trendy, up-to-the minute footwear from Velcro boots from £23.50 for children, £30 for adults, to clogs at £15 for children, £19 for adults. Colours range from navy to red, green, purple, black, pink, rust, white and tan.

Catalogue includes home fitting/conversion chart for metric sizes. Every pair of shoes is sent in a recycled box and the catalogue is printed on a paper obtained from the husks of sugar cane. 10 pence from every pair of shoes is donated to the Whale and Dolphin Conservation Society. There is also a cotton gym bag and free name tags supplied with every pair.

Catalogue Annually, A4, Catalogue, Colour, 24 pages, A small charge may be made in the future **Postal charges** £2.50 **Delivery** Royal Mail **Methods of Payment** Cheque, Postal Order, Credit Card

SALLY SMALL

71 York Street
London
W1H 2BJ

Women's shoes in small sizes

Sally Small produces quality ladies' shoes in the smallest sizes. Most are all-leather (uppers, linings and soles), some are available with resin or rubber

Telephone
0171 723 5321
Fax
same

soles. There are styles for all occasions in a range of colours. Shoe sizes range from Continental 31 to 34, English 13 to 2½. Prices from £45 to £75.
Catalogue Bi-annually, Third A4, Catalogue, Colour, 6 pages, Free **Postal charges** £1.75 **Delivery** Royal Mail, Parcelforce **Methods of Payment** Cheque, Postal Order, Credit Card

SHELLYS INTERNATIONAL
1–3 Edgware Road
London
NW2 6JZ
Telephone
0181 450 0066
Fax
0181 208 4340

Shoes

Shellys have several well-known and fashionable shops in London selling trendy footwear, but they also run a sophisticated mail-order operation which spans the world.

Their colourful catalogue comes in an impressive folder along with various money-off offers adding up to £18. It features a good range of men's and women's shoes, including many with Dr Martens soles. These are mostly for the fashion-conscious youth market. Prices are reasonable, at around £42 for a pair of Docs. An excellent source.

Catalogue Annually, A4, Catalogue, Colour, 32 pages pages, Free **Postal charges** £4 per pair **Delivery** TRAK-BAK **Methods of Payment** Cheque, Credit Card, American Express, Switch, Diners Club

SHIRLINA LTD
PO Box 498
London
W10 5QH
Telephone
0171 289 1145

Height-increasing shoes

A range of height-increasing shoes for men. A special manufacturing process is used so the elevation inside the shoe can be worked in natural cork which is so strong it will last for years. Glovesoft leather covers the natural cork, guaranteeing comfort and easy wear. The shoe itself looks like any other ordinary shoe without particularly high or clumsy-looking heavy heels. Each shoe is pictured with details of the height increase afforded – usually between 5 and 7 cm. There are many styles to suit most activities and fashions.

Catalogue Bi-monthly, A5, Catalogue, Colour, 40 pages, Free **Postal charges** Varies with item **Delivery** Parcelforce **Methods of Payment** Cheque, Postal Order, Credit Card

SOLED OUT
Unit 8, Saltash Business Park
Forge Lane
Moorlands Industrial Estate
Saltash
Cornwall
PL12 6LX
Telephone
01752 841080

Handmade boots and shoes
This small Cornish company makes leather and calf shoes and boots with crêpe soles to fit any size of foot. Their leaflet gives clear instructions on how to measure your feet so that the shoes will be a perfect fit. Styles include mules, open sandals, T-bar sandals (all from £26–£48) and walking boots (from £48–£68). Samples of the different coloured leathers they use are sent with the order form.

Catalogue Bi-annually, A4, Leaflets, B/W, 1 page, Free **Postal charges** Children's sizes 5–13$\frac{1}{2}$, no charge; sizes 1–6$\frac{1}{2}$, add £5.00; sizes 7–11$\frac{1}{2}$, add £6.00; sizes 12 and over, add £8.00 **Delivery** Parcelforce **Methods of Payment** Cheque, Credit Card

SUNDAES SANDALS
The Chase
18 High Street
Moulton
Spalding
Lincolnshire
PE12 6QB
Telephone
01406 371370
Fax
01406 371646

Sandals
Children's leather open-toed sandals (the 'Robby' range) come in sizes small 10 to big 4 and in a choice of colours: navy, delft-blue, white, brown and bright multi and are priced at £24.95. There are four men's open-toed styles, ranging in price from £37.95 to £42.95. For women the styles are more varied, ranging from flip-flop style slip-ons ('Lilly' comes in sizes 3–9, price £37.95) to the slingback ocean shoe with peep toe ('Monroe' comes in sizes 3–10 in calf or suede, prices £43.95 and £45.95 respectively).

Catalogue Bi-annually, A5, Catalogue, Colour, 19 pages, Free **Postal charges** UK only: add £2.50 per pair; add £4.00 for two or more pairs; belts are post-free **Delivery** Royal Mail **Methods of Payment** Cheque, Credit Card, Switch

Furniture

THE ANTIQUE BEDSTEAD COMPANY
Baddow Antique Centre
The Bringy
Great Baddow
Chelmsford
Essex
CM2 7JW
Telephone
01245 471137

Restored bedsteads
The Antique Bedstead Company has around 300 restored Victorian brass and iron bedsteads of every conceivable style and size. These wonderfully crafted beds are not only beautiful pieces of period furniture but also genuine investments. The company also supplies quality mattresses. A typical 4ft 6in cottage bedstead from 1865 costs £565. If customers are unable to visit the showroom at Great Baddow, the company will deliver anywhere in the country and payment will only be requested upon approval.
Catalogue Annually, A4, Brochure, B/W, 20 pages, Free **Postal charges** Varies with item **Delivery** Courier, In-house delivery **Methods of Payment** Cheque, Credit Card, COD

A BARN FULL OF SOFAS AND CHAIRS
Furnace Mill
Lamberhurst
Kent
TN3 8LH
Telephone
01892 890285
Fax
01892 890988

Furniture
All the sofas and chairs in the brochure are made with solid beechwood frames that are dowelled and screwed; the arms, backs and seats are all 'hand-tied' with copper coil springs, worked with horsehair, faced with hessian and topped with feather and down cushions. Sample prices: £1950 plus 14 metres of fabric to choice for the humpy backed two-seater sofa; £995 plus 6 metres of fabric to choice for the iron-framed chair.

The Old Mill offers a full upholstery and loose cover service for any of the old and original pieces they also keep on the premises.

FURNITURE

Catalogue A4, Catalogue, Colour, 19 pages, Free **Postal charges** A nominal charge will be made for delivery within the radius of the M25 **Delivery** Royal Mail **Methods of Payment** Cheque, COD, American Express, Credit Card

ARTISAN
Unit 4A
Union Court
20 Union Road
London
SW4 6JP
Telephone
0171 498 6974
Fax
0171 498 2989

Wrought-iron furniture and accessories

This company makes traditional wrought-iron bedsteads including an impressive four-poster; they also make iron curtain rail packs, stair handrails and stair rods, door and window furniture and accessories such as heart door knockers and toilet roll holders.

Catalogue Annually, A4, Catalogue, Colour, 15 pages, Free **Postal charges** Under £20, £3.75; under £100, £6.85; over £100, £11.75; beds £35 each **Delivery** Royal Mail, Parcelforce **Methods of Payment** Cheque, Postal Order, Credit Card

BENTLEY & HILLMER
PO Box 7
Stow-on-the-Wold
Cheltenham
Gloucestershire
GL54 1YE
Telephone
01451 870074
Fax
01367 253621

English country furniture

Five useful and decorative pieces make up the English Country Range from Bentley & Hillmer. An apron table, price £175; boarded shelves, price £160; gabled shelves, £170; box table, £175; and a simple trunk, £150. All are based on 18th- and 19th-century originals. Unpainted items will be supplied with a base spray coat of cream paint inside and out. If painting is required a choice of five historic colours is available for the exterior with contrasting interiors. Five contemporary colours are also available all with black interiors.

Catalogue Annually, A5, Brochure, Colour and B/W, 4 pages, Free **Postal charges** £17.50 on each item **Delivery** In-house delivery **Methods of Payment** Cheque, Credit Card

CANE COMFORT
Pandora's Box
48 High Street

Cane furniture

Many of Cane Comfort's suites use leather binding for added durability and have Pirelli webbing

Nairn
Invernesshire
Scotland
IV12 4AU
Telephone
01667 452060
Fax
same

bases for extra support and comfort. Most have zipped removable covers for easy cleaning and all glass is toughened safety glass.

The 'Cambridge' three-piece suite costs £1,165 and matching long table, £235. The 'Ultra' honey or rosewood three-piece suite is cheaper at £399 and the matching round table costs only £79. There is a choice of upholstery fabrics and samples are available on request.

Catalogue A4, Brochure, Colour, 9 pages, Free **Postal charges** Free **Delivery** Parcelforce **Methods of Payment** Cheque, Credit Card

CLASSIC CHOICE FURNISHINGS LTD
Unit 1
Brynmenyn Industrial Estate
Bridgend
Mid Glamorgan
CF32 9TD
Telephone
01656 725111
Fax
01656 725404

Quality upholstered furniture

Classic Choice has been making quality upholstered furniture for more than 10 years. Besides the attractive prices, which are kept down by being direct from the manufacturer, the main advantage is the ease of ordering. There is a wide choice of fabrics – over 50 – and these can be interchanged between the models. In addition, there are matching fabrics for curtains and cushions to give a completely co-ordinated look. A full-colour catalogue of their leather range shows modern and traditional furniture in a range of real leather colours. For those anxious about ordering furniture by mail, there is a reassuring 21-day money back and 2-year construction guarantee. They also believe that they are the first British mail-order furniture company to offer loose covers in a washable velour fabric.

Catalogue Bi-annually, A4, Catalogue, Colour, 28 pages, Free **Postal charges** £30 **Delivery** In-house delivery **Methods of Payment,** Cheque, COD, Credit Card

COUNTRY DESKS
78 High Street
Berkhamsted

Traditional desks

Have you ever dreamed of writing your letters at a Georgian bureau, or swivelling in a director's

Hertfordshire
HP4 2BW
Telephone
01442 866446
Fax
01422 872306

deep-buttoned chair at a leather-topped city desk lit by a green glass shaded banker's lamp? These products are just some of the range available from Country Desks. A Traditional Country Desk with three drawers across the top, three further drawers on one side and two on the other, in yew, mahogany or oak with an antiqued leather top, costs from £335 (3ft × 1ft 9in) to £975 for a partners' desk. Director's swivel chair, £560; banker's lamp, £55.

Catalogue Annually, A5, Catalogue, Colour, 12 pages, Free **Postal charges** Varies with item **Delivery** Courier, In-house delivery **Methods of Payment** Cheque, Credit Card

ELEPHANT INDUSTRIES
Unit 14
Lansdowne Workshops
London
SE7 8AZ
Telephone
0181 858 1945
Fax
same

Fun furniture for children

Elephant Industries' handmade painted children's furniture, which arrives fully assembled, has achieved distinction for its inspired blend of fun and function.

The 'Elephant' (£60) functions both as a step-up and a seat. The 'Bookshell' (£199) is a free-standing, snail-shaped double-sided bookcase with a secret compartment for cassettes or drawing materials and a convenient seat too. The 'Hangaroo' (£139) is a child-size valet for a week's worth of outfits plus a detachable pouch for sports kit or laundry.

Catalogue A4, Leaflets, Colour, 1 page, Free **Postal charges** Free **Delivery** Parcelforce **Methods of Payment** Cheque, Credit Card

ELMLEY HERITAGE
Stone House
Elmley Lovett
Droitwich
Worcestershire
WR9 0PS

Pine furniture

An attractive range of practical, well-made pine furniture. Colour leaflets describe each item in detail and clearly state dimensions. For the kitchen there are traditional wall-mounted plate and wine racks (from £50), clothes airers (from £19); for the bedroom a bedstead (from £90) and mattress

Telephone
01299 851447
Fax
01299 851520

range; plus a selection of coffee-tables and a storage box.
Catalogue Annually, A5, Leaflets, Colour, 6 pages, Free **Postal charges** Varies with item **Delivery** Royal Mail, Courier, Parcelforce **Methods of Payment** COD

ESSENTIAL ITEMS
Church House
Plungar
Nottingham
Nottinghamshire
NG13 0JA
Telephone
0115 9456252
Fax
0115 9843254

Upholstered stools and ottomans
Essential Items are one of the country's most established companies manufacturing and designing 'made to order' upholstered stools, ottomans, window seats and bed-end stools. The most interesting ottoman is the single or double filing cabinet. Different styles and sizes can be made to suit every room in your home. Essential Items have built up an enviable reputation for personal attention to customers' needs and can help with advice on customers' own fabrics and tapestries. Stools (76 × 36 × 26cm) start from £125 covered in customers' own fabric. Ottomans (56 × 48 × 50cm) from £195 plus £15 p&p.
Catalogue Annually, A4, Catalogue, Colour and B/W, 6 pages, Free **Postal charges** £15 for every item within the UK **Delivery** Parcelforce **Methods of Payment** Postal Order, Cheque, Credit Card

FOAMPLAN (RUBBER & PLASTICS) LTD
350 Holloway Road
London
N7 6PA
Telephone
0171 609 2700/8569
Fax
0171 700 0275

Foam for mattresses, seating and cushions
Foamplan is one of the leading mail-order, made-to-measure bedding and upholstery companies in the UK. Its quality foams, in several grades and thicknesses, can be cut to any shape or size from round beds to simple cushions. Covers are available in a choice of fire-retardant cottons and vinyls. The catalogue is helpful and informative and explains how to make a template for an awkwardly shaped item. Cushion 17 × 16in, in economy foam, £1.42/1in thick, £8.50/6in thick. Single mattress, economy foam, £33.60/4in thick; latex, £143.40/4in thick.

FURNITURE

Catalogue Annually, A5, Catalogue, Colour, 16 pages, Free **Postal charges** £8, Varies with item **Methods of Payment** Cheque, Postal Order, Credit Card

FUTON EXPRESS
23/27 Pancras Road
London
NW1 2QB
Telephone
0171 833 3945
Fax
0171 833 8199

Futons

The futon is a firm yet comfortable mattress made from several layers of cotton fibres. Used in conjunction with a slatted wooden base, it converts easily from a bed to provide extra seating. The mattress is available in a choice of thicknesses and colours with co-ordinated accessories. The self-assembly bases come either unfinished or finished and varnished, with tables and boxes as optional extras. Prices from £5 for a cushion to £565 for a designer-print double sofabed.

Catalogue Annually, A5, Catalogue, Colour and B/W, 14 pages, Free **Postal charges** Varies with item **Delivery** In-house delivery **Methods of Payment** Cheque, Credit Card

GLOBAL VILLAGE
17 St James Street
South Petherton
Somerset
TA12 5BS
Telephone
01460 241166
Fax
01935 242282

Craft gifts

Global Village promotes craftsmanship from around the world and the mail-order catalogue is full of interesting artefacts and furniture. There's an antiqued colonial rattan chair for £175, an Indian wooden cupboard for £995, hand-blown Mexican glass paperweights for £3.95 and a large selection of African masks from £75.

Catalogue A4, Catalogue, Colour, 12 pages, Free **Postal charges** Orders under £100.00, add £4.50; orders over £100.00, free **Delivery** Parcelforce **Methods of Payment** Cheque, Postal Order, Credit Card

GRANGE MEUBLES UK
PO Box 18
Stamford
Lincolnshire
PE9 2FY

Furniture

This catalogue is more like an exquisite French interiors magazine than a product directory, and is an inspiration to any home decorator. Leafing through page after page of photographs of

Telephone
01780 54721
Fax
01780 54718

glorious French rooms, some sumptuous, others simple and uncluttered, with atmospheric captions in both French and English, you come to shots of the individual items, with their history and measurements (but no prices). The style is classic French country house, elegantly designed and superbly finished in the tradition of Joseph Grange, the cabinet-maker who founded the company in 1905.

Catalogue Annually, A4, Catalogue, Colour, 118 pages, £4 **Postal charges** Varies with item **Delivery** In-house delivery **Methods of Payment** Cheque, Credit Card

GROVEWOOD CANE PARADISE
1 Taverners Square
Silver Road
Norwich
Norfolk
NR3 4SY
Telephone
01603 219310
Fax
01603 219315

Cane and rattan furniture

Smart catalogue featuring the furniture, many in room settings. Grovewood cane furniture is produced to a high standard which means that every joint is screwed and dowelled to provide a sturdy framework and all fabrics are top quality, satin-finished, fire-retardant and treated against sunlight. Cushion covers are removable for cleaning purposes on the top range of suites. Each item has a name, a code number for easy ordering and the dimensions. A separate list gives the up-to-date prices. Swatches can be sent on request. The range includes sofas, coffee tables, footstools, plant tubs, magazine racks, rockers, chairs, dining tables, dining chairs, scatter cushions, and side tables. The company is a member of Safe-Buy which, according to a quote in the catalogue from TV personality Judith Chalmers, means 'you can place your order with complete confidence, knowing you're dealing with a company you can trust to do an excellent job at a fair price.'

Catalogue Annually, A4, Catalogue, Colour, 24 pages, Free **Methods of Payment** Cheque, Postal Order, Credit Card

FURNITURE

HAMLET FURNITURE
The Furniture Factory
McMullen Road
Darlington
Co Durham
DL1 1XY
Telephone
01325 381811

Solid wood furniture

Every item of furniture in the Hamlet range is made from solid oak or pine, including the carcasses, backs of units and drawer components. Most pieces, other than beds and tables, arrive assembled and ready for use. The range includes chairs (ladderback, £149), tables (refectory, £548), dressers (from £375), wardrobes (£957), bookcases (£360), and beds (from £521). Fitted kitchens are also made to order and chairs and stools can be upholstered in your own choice of fabric.

Catalogue Annually, A4, Catalogue, Colour, 24 pages, Free **Postal charges** Varies with item **Delivery** Courier, In-house delivery **Methods of Payment** Cheque, Postal Order, Credit Card, Stage Payments

HAMPTONS LEISURE
The Pin Mill
New Street
Charfield
Wotton-under-Edge,
Gloucestershire
GL12 8ES
Telephone
01453 842889
Fax
01453 843938

Garden furniture

Windsor Designs make attractive, good-quality outdoor furniture in teak, cast aluminium and hardwood for Hamptons Leisure. The stately Dolphin grand table with cast top will set you back £750 and the Dolphin armchairs are £171 each. There's a wonderful 8ft Lutyens shorea bench at £859, and in teak the 54in Narberth round table is priced at £495; chairs £166 each. (All prices include VAT and carriage anywhere on the UK mainland.)

Hamptons Leisure also stock a colourful range of indoor and outdoor hammocks (prices from £21 for a 1.9m baby hammock in interwoven cotton yarn to £41.50 for a 3.1m one).

Catalogue Annually, A4, Brochure, Colour, 31 pages, Free **Postal charges** Free **Delivery** Courier **Methods of Payment** Cheque, Credit Card

FURNITURE

THE HEVENINGHAM COLLECTION
Peacock Cottage
Church Hill
Nether Wallop
Stockbridge
Hampshire
SO20 8EY
Telephone
01264 781124
Fax
same

Iron furniture

The Heveningham Collection by Annie Eadie is a range of very elegant old Italian-style wrought-iron furniture for interior or exterior use. All items are supplied in black or dark green metal paint finish with cream natural canvas or, for external use, showerproof fabric cushions. Alternative fabrics are available at extra cost.

The range includes a chaise longue (£725), dining tables (£325), chairs (from £365), Versailles tubs (£150) and candlesticks (£135). Prices include VAT and carriage to mainland UK.

Catalogue A4, Catalogue, Colour, 8 pages, Free **Postal charges** If only one item ordered, add £35.00 for carriage in mainland UK **Delivery** Royal Mail **Methods of Payment** Cheque, Credit Card

HOLLOWAYS
Lower Court
Suckley
Worcestershire
WR6 5DE
Telephone
01886 884754/884665
Fax
01886 884665

Conservatory furniture and garden ornaments

Holloways is a family-run business specialising in conservatory furnishings and garden ornaments. The catalogue features a wide variety of designs from rattan or green iron-framed suites to Cretan terracotta pots and lead ornaments. A smaller catalogue features decorative accessories including wall fountains, barometers, trellising and blinds. Wirework jardinières, from £82; bronze reclining cat, £59; cherub fountain, £195; willow two-seater, £295.

Catalogue Annually, A4, Catalogue, Colour, 16 pages, Free **Postal charges** Varies with item **Delivery** Royal Mail, Parcelforce, Courier **Methods of Payment** Cheque, Credit Card

INDIAN OCEAN TRADING COMPANY
28 Ravenswood Road
Clapham South
London

Garden furniture

Indian Ocean Trading Company's catalogue contains a wide range of outdoor and conservatory teak furniture. The famous York Steamer with three reclining positions costs £350. There are

SW12 9PJ
Telephone
0181 675 4808
Fax
0181 675 4652

tables and benches, folding chairs and deck chairs, and wooden parasols with cotton covers. Bude deck chair, £119; Hamilton armchair, £230; Sunningdale table, 48in/1.2m × 28in/70cm, £265; scatter cushion, £15.

Catalogue Annually, A4, Catalogue, Colour, 32 pages, Free **Postal charges** £15 for orders up to £400; free for orders of more than £400 **Delivery** Courier **Methods of Payment** Cheque, Credit Card

JARABOSKY
PO Box 112
Halifax
West Yorkshire
HX5 0SZ
Telephone
01422 311922
Fax
01422 374053

Original railway-sleeper furniture

Jarabosky's exclusive range of furniture is made out of hardwood timbers that have been retrieved from Colonial African railways. A conscious effort to help preserve the environment, this recycling also produces wonderful furniture. As well as its standard range, the company will make items to the customer's specification. Each piece is completely heat, water and alcohol proof.

A 25in-square 'half wafer' coffee table in Rhodesian teak costs £295; an 8-seater Chateau dining table, £1,675; and a 36in-long telephone stand, £425.

Catalogue A4, Catalogue, Colour, 14 pages, Free **Postal charges** The maximum delivery charge is £30.00 **Delivery** In-house delivery **Methods of Payment** Other, Cheque

K RESTORATIONS
2A Ferdinand Place
London
NW1 8EE
Telephone
0171 482 4021
Fax
0171 284 2806

Furniture restoration

All you have to do is measure the leather that needs replacing and choose the new colour and gold tooling. K Restorations will then supply the leather and paste and simple instructions for you to re-leather your desk. Their leaflets include copies of many satisfied customers' letters and favourable reviews from magazines and newspapers. Prices start at £27 for a section 12 × 12in and increase to £52 for a piece 36 × 18in.

Catalogue A5, Brochure, Colour, 2 pages, Free **Postal**

FURNITURE

charges £3.00 **Delivery** Royal Mail **Methods of Payment** Cheque, Credit Card

LEEDS FUTONS
13 Hyde Park Corner
Leeds
West Yorkshire
LS6 1AF
Telephone
0113 2743753

Futons

Leeds Futons manufacture and sell three types of futons, five different pine bases, covers, cushions, tables, chests and screens. Non-standard sizes can be produced to suit your needs. Futons are Japanese-style mattresses containing 1in-thick layers of cotton or cotton mix (six layers are recommended for general use). Six-layer futon, £79 single, £117 double; bases from £85 single, £105 double; covers from £28.

Catalogue Annually, A4, Catalogue, Colour, 8 pages, Free **Postal charges** Varies with item **Delivery** Courier **Methods of Payment** Cheque

LLOYD LOOM DIRECT
PO Box 75
Spalding
Lincolnshire
PE12 6NB
Telephone
01775 725876
Fax
01775 761255

British-made woven-fibre furniture

Made in the UK in a way which is faithful to the originals of American inventor Marshall B. Lloyd, Lloyd Loom furniture is manufactured neither from cane, nor wicker, nor rattan, but from a specially woven fabric which is wrapped around wire and is thus immune to splitting, cracking or woodworm. It is finished with three coats of water-borne lacquer in a choice of eight colours. Cushions and seat pads are available in a range of fabrics. Dressing table, £397; Burghley armchair, £189; round coffee table, £153; stool, £86.

Catalogue Annually, A5, Catalogue, Colour, 16 pages, Free **Postal charges** £15 **Delivery** Courier **Methods of Payment** Cheque, Postal Order, Credit Card

THE MANCHESTER FUTON COMPANY
33 Blossom Street
Ancoats
Manchester

Futons and bases

From a workshop in the heart of Manchester comes a little bit of the East. The Futon Company can provide everything you need for a good night's sleep and turn it into an attractive piece of

Greater Manchester
M4 6AJ
Telephone
0161 236 8196

furniture by day. Choose the finish of your base from the catalogue and the colour of your cover from the swatches enclosed. Six-layer pure cotton futon, £85 single, £110 double; loose covers from £28; bases, from £40 single, £55 double.
Catalogue Annually, A5, Leaflets, Colour and B/W, 14 pages, Free **Postal charges** Varies with item **Delivery** Courier, In-house delivery **Methods of Payment** Cheque, Credit Card

M C REPRODUCTIONS
16 Queens Road
Petersfield
Hampshire
GU32 3BD
Telephone
01730 823278
Fax
01428 607005

Oak furniture
M C Reproductions makes a range of solid English oak tables using traditional methods of carpentry. The tables are antiqued, distressed and hand-polished to a high standard. Coffee table, £225; coffee table with shelf, £315; end table, £165.
Catalogue Annually, Third A4, Leaflets, Colour, 2 pages, Free **Postal charges** Packaging, transport and insurance included in price **Delivery** Courier **Methods of Payment** Cheque, Credit Card

MARSHCOUCH
14 Robinsfield
Hemel Hempstead
Hertfordshire
HP1 1RW
Telephone
01442 63199/257 832
Fax
01442 866 786

Portable couches for physical therapy
Designed to meet the demands of the physical therapist, Marshcouch's portable treatment couches are custom-built using sustainable materials. Just specify your choice of height, width and upholstery. Sheets, pillows and covers are also stocked. Prices start from £164.50 for a standard hardwood leg-folding couch and rise to £340.75 for a multi-height lifting backrest couch. A refurbishment service is available.
Catalogue Annually, A4, Catalogue, Colour, 4 pages **Postal charges** Varies with item **Delivery** Royal Mail, Courier **Methods of Payment** Cheque, Credit Card

THE ODD CHAIR COMPANY
66 Derby Road

Restored chairs and sofas
The Odd Chair Company specialises in the restoration and re-upholstery of Victorian chairs

FURNITURE

Longridge
Preston
Lancashire
PR3 3FE
Telephone
01772 786262
Fax
01772 784290

and sofas of the 1850–1900 period. You make your choice from photographs with dimensions, prices and fabric samples, and you can ask for advice on selecting fabrics that are in keeping with the piece. Viewing can also be arranged on the premises at Longridge.

Catalogue Annually, A4, Brochure, Colour, 4 pages, Free **Postal charges** Varies with item **Delivery** Courier, In-house delivery **Methods of Payment** Cheque, Credit Card

OMEGA FURNITURE
FREEPOST
Delamare Road
Cheshunt
Hertfordshire
EN8 9TF
Telephone
01992 626686
Fax
01992 631287

Made-to-measure sofas and armchairs

Omega is a family-run company specialising in the manufacture of sofas, chairs, sofabeds and corner units to suit individual requirements. It will even deepen seats, enlarge backs or change the arms at no extra cost, and there is a choice of 18,000 fabrics. Two-seater sofa from £795. Off-the-peg designs are also available (sofabed, £900).

Catalogue Annually, A4, Catalogue, Colour, 12 pages, Free **Postal charges** Varies with item **Delivery** Courier, In-house delivery **Methods of Payment** Cheque, Credit Card, Stage Payments

PAST PRESENTS
47–49 The Street
Ashtead
Surrey
KT21 1AA
Telephone
01372 279047

Dumb waiters

Until Victorian times humanoid 'dumb waiters' would be stood in a hallway as a receptacle for calling cards. Then, usually in the form of butlers, blackamoors or bears, they were used to wait upon their master. Now Past Presents have created a whimsical new range of dumb waiters which can be used as occasional tables, telephone tables, potted-plant holders or even loo-roll holders! Priced at £79.95 each, designs range from 'Winnie the Pooh' to 'Mermaid'.

Catalogue A4, Leaflets, Colour, 2 pages, Free **Postal charges** Free **Delivery** Royal Mail **Methods of Payment** Cheque, Postal Order, Credit Card

PINE CANDLE BOX
Watkin Roberts
Felin Isaf
Llwyngwril
Gwynedd
LL37 2JA
Telephone
01341 250567

Pine furniture
Watkin Roberts are woodworkers who make attractive small-furnishing items including pine candleboxes complete with eight 6-inch classic ivory church candles (£24 + £3 p&p), pine stools (£32 + £5 p&p) and pine cabinets suitable for the bathroom or kitchen (£35 + £6 p&p). All have wax finishes.

Catalogue Third A4, Leaflets, Brown tint, 1 page, Free **Postal charges** Varies with item **Delivery** Royal Mail **Methods of Payment** Cheque

PLUMBS
Brookhouse Mill
Old Lancaster Lane
Preston
Lancashire
PR1 7PZ
Telephone
01772 250811
Fax
01772 561328

Loose furniture covers
Plumbs has everything you need to give your three-piece suite a new lease of life. It claims it can provide covers for any shape or size of furniture, made from the latest machine-washable fabrics. A Queen Anne two-seater sofa cover in Tiger Lily or Diana designs costs £80.46, with a further £12.79 for a frilled valance.

Plumbs also offers co-ordinating made-to-measure curtains, pelmets, tie-backs and scatter cushions.

Catalogue Annually, A4, Catalogue, Colour, 32 pages, Free **Postal charges** Varies with item **Delivery** Royal Mail, Parcelforce **Methods of Payment** Cheque, Credit Card

ROCKINGHAM FENDER SEATS
Grange Farm
Thorney
Peterborough
Cambridgeshire
PE6 OPJ
Telephone
01733 270233
Fax
01733 270512

Fender seats
Rockingham makes decorative fender seats for the fireplace in a variety of styles and materials. These include traditional club fenders, custom-made to your requirements; standard-size Manor House club fenders; low-level fenders; fire curtains, fire guards and fireside accessories. Prices start at £590 for a fender seat.

Catalogue Annually, A5, Leaflets, Colour and B/W, 12 pages, Free **Postal charges** £30 **Delivery** Courier **Methods of Payment** Cheque, Credit Card

SAXON LEATHER UPHOLSTERY
Eldon Street
Bolton
Lancashire
BL2 2HX
Telephone
01204 365377
Fax
01204 387554

Traditional leather furniture
This family business prides itself in upholding standards of craftsmanship while reducing costs, to bring its range of leather settees and chairs within reach of as many people as possible. Items are made to order in a choice of 20 styles and 50 colours. Chesterfield chair, £529; three-seater settee, £799; three-seater bed-settee, £1150.

Catalogue Annually, A4, Catalogue, Colour, 16 pages, Free **Postal charges** £39 **Delivery** In-house delivery **Methods of Payment** Cheque, Stage Payments, Credit Card, American Express, Diners Club

SEVENTH HEAVEN
Chirk Mill
Chirk
Clwyd
Wales
LL14 5BU
Telephone
01691 777622/773563
Fax
01691 777313

Antique bedsteads and quality bedding
Seventh Heaven aims to recapture the romance of the bed with its extensive collection of antique beds, most dating from between 1800 and 1920. Specialising in Victorian cast-iron and brass bedsteads, the company also restores and sells antique wooden beds, and produces quality mattresses in virtually any size. It offers a range of fine, lace-trimmed bed linen, samples of which are provided. Standard double Victorian cast-iron bedstead, from £395; Renaissance-style four-poster, £8950.

Catalogue Annually, A4, Catalogue, Colour and B/W, 16 pages, Free **Postal charges** Varies with item **Delivery** In-house delivery **Methods of Payment** Cheque, Credit Card

SOFAS AND SOFA-BEDS
219 Tottenham Court Road
London
W1P 9AF
Telephone
0171 636 6001

Sofas and sofa-beds
This well-known high street chain offers a wide range of armchairs, sofas and sofa-beds. The catalogue shows 33 different styles such as the 'Hertford' two-seat sofa which costs £886 exclusive of fabric and the Knole compact three-seat sofa-bed which costs £1,171. The covering service allows customers to choose from a wide range of fabrics or to provide their own. Delivery

time on items made to order is 6–8 weeks and is free within 10 miles of any of their shops, a full list of which is given in the catalogue.
Catalogue Bi-annually, Third A4, Catalogue, Colour, 33 pages, Free **Postal charges** Free within a 10-mile radius of the nearest shop **Delivery** In-house delivery **Methods of Payment** Cheque, Credit Card

TRESKE
Station Works
Thirsk
North Yorkshire
YO7 4NY
Telephone
01845 522770
Fax
01845 522692

Solid wood furniture

Treske produce the widest range of furniture of any UK manufacturer and pride themselves in retaining complete control over the woods used in their products, buying, sawing and curing everything they use. Individual items of furniture range from rush-seated chairs (£95) and beds (from £339 for a single) to dining tables (from £336 for a cottage table) and desks (£360 for a computer desk). Treske also make fitted kitchens in two styles: an attractive Sycamore version and a more traditional Painted Kitchen.
Catalogue A4, Catalogue, Colour and B/W, 40 pages, £1.00 **Delivery** Royal Mail, Courier **Methods of Payment** Cheque, Credit Card

TULLEYS OF CHELSEA
289–297 Fulham Road
London
SW10 9PZ
Telephone
0171 352 1078
Fax
0171 352 5677

Furniture

Tulleys' smart colour catalogues display a comprehensive range of sofas and armchairs, beds and reproduction furniture. Quality materials are guaranteed, including hardwood frames and natural curled feather cushion fillings. Two-seater sofa, uncovered from £975, covered from £1185 plus 14.5m fabric; oval coffee table, from £350.
Catalogue Annually, A4, Catalogue, Colour, 24 pages, Free **Postal charges** Varies with item **Delivery** Courier, In-house delivery **Methods of Payment** Cheque, Credit Card, American Express

WOODEN TOPS
4 Holbein Gardens
Northampton
Northamptonshire
NN4 9XT
Telephone
01604 705056

Furniture and fabrics
Wooden Tops offer a range of flexible options with their furniture: supplying the uncovered furniture and leaving the furnishings to you; supplying the furniture and all the drapes from their range of plain and patterned fabrics in any combination; or making up your own fabric for you. Their kidney dressing tables start at £42.50; occasional tables start at £13; and cabinet tables start at £22.50. They also make cushions (from £14), toy/blanket boxes (from £55), and mirrors – both vanity (from £49), and cheval (from £85).
Catalogue Catalogue, Colour, 20 pages, Free **Postal charges** Varies with item **Delivery** Royal Mail **Methods of Payment** Cheque, Postal Order, Credit Card

Gadgets

BETTERWARE UK LTD
Stanley House
Park Lane
Castle Vale
Birmingham
West Midlands
B35 6LJ
Telephone
0121 693 1111
Fax
0121 693 1137

Household goods
Betterware is a home-shopping system whereby goods are ordered from a locally appointed co-ordinator. The catalogue contains every household gadget you can imagine. Sample prices: £9.99 for a combi-grater; £10.99 for a post and milk delivery box; £3.99 for a bucket and spade playset.

Betterware cares about the environment and works towards improvements in the conservation of energy and natural resources and the minimisation of waste.

Catalogue Catalogue, Colour, 143 pages, £1.50 **Postal charges** Free **Delivery** Local distributor **Methods of Payment** COD, Cheque

C C PRODUCTS
152 Markham Road
Charminster
Bournemouth
Dorset
BH9 1JE
Telephone
01202 522260

Portable car loos
The emergency portable loo is a unique polythene product designed to allow urination quickly and discreetly. Two separate hand-held reusable applicators are available, one male and one female. A family pack contains 2 applicators and 1 reservoir and costs £25.

Catalogue Third A4, Leaflets, Colour and B/W, 4 pages, Free **Postal charges** £2.00 **Delivery** Parcelforce **Methods of Payment** Cheque, Postal Order, COD

CROW'S NEST FARM PRODUCTS
28 Frogge Street

All-in-one bellows, poker and toasting fork
The Blow-Poke is practical, elegant and efficient. Made from polished steel with removable brass

Ickleton
Saffron Walden
Essex
CB10 1SH
Telephone
01799 531009

mouthpiece and hanging ring, it measures 83cm and acts as a bellows, poker and toasting fork. Simplicity itself, the Blow-Poke is perfect for barbecues and the fireplace – you just 'put your lips together and blow'. It costs £19.50 plus £2 p&p.
Catalogue 8"× 4", Leaflets, Colour, 2 pages, Free **Postal charges** Add £2 **Delivery** Royal Mail **Methods of Payment** Cheque, Postal Order

DIRECT CHOICE
Euroway Business Park
Swindon
Wiltshire
SN5 8SN
Telephone
01793 480000
Fax
01793 487002

Innovative gadgets
The weird and wonderful items in this catalogue include a table-top plate warmer for £29.95; a parachute luggage set which weighs next to nothing for £19.95; and a personal speaking clock for £14.95.
Catalogue Bi-annually, A5, Catalogue, Colour, 62 pages, Free **Postal charges** Free **Delivery** Parcelforce **Methods of Payment** Cheque, Postal Order, Credit Card

HOME SHOPPING SELECTIONS
118 West Street
Faversham
Kent
ME13 7JB
Telephone
01227 771555

Gadgets
This interesting selection of gadgets includes fleecy joint warmers for £4.95, a Greenair purifier for £14.95, a Whisper XL hearing aid for £19.95, and a pet grooming glove for £7.95.
Catalogue Bi-annually, A5, Catalogue, Colour, 23 pages, Free **Postal charges** Add £2.95 for 1 item; £3.95 for 2 items; £4.95 for 3 or more items **Delivery** Parcelforce **Methods of Payment** Cheque, Postal Order, Credit Card

INNOVATIONS (MAIL ORDER) LTD
Euroway Business Park
Swindon
Wiltshire
SN5 8SN
Telephone
01793 431441
Fax
01793 487002

Innovative gadgets
'Tomorrow's products today' include a 24-hour flea trap (£19.95), a 'Snorebuster' for £19.95, an instant desk-top organiser for £15.48, and a stress-free 'natural daylight' bulb (£13.95 for 3).
Catalogue Bi-annually, A5, Catalogue, Colour, 47 pages, Free **Postal charges** £3.90; £2.95 for orders over £20.00 **Delivery** Parcelforce **Methods of Payment** Cheque, Postal Order, Credit Card, American Express, Diners Club

LAKELAND PLASTICS

Alexandra Buildings
Windermere
Cumbria
LA23 1BQ
Telephone
015394 88100
Fax
015394 88300

Creative kitchenware

Lakeland Plastics is a family-run business supplying all you'll ever need for the kitchen and home. The catalogue contains hundreds of intriguing ideas to save time and money from foil, clingfilm and baking parchment through preserving, microwave and freezer accessories to specialist items for food preparation, cooking, serving and storing. The bright, interesting catalogue, coupled with a genuinely friendly service makes this an ideal source for kitchen products. There are 50 cake-tin liners for £3.75; a lattice pastry cutter for £4.95; pure vanilla extract for £4.95; and lemon tap for just 99p. Lakeland also offers other specialist catalogues such as the Christmas, gifts, Summer Special and Storage Solutions.

Catalogue Quarterly, A5, Catalogue, Colour, 80 pages, Free **Postal charges** Varies according to value **Delivery** Parcelforce **Methods of Payment** Cheque, Credit Card, Switch, Postal Order

MAGIC SHOWCASE

Forge Court
Reading Road
Yateley
Camberley
Surrey
GU17 7RX

Innovative products for the home

A host of gadgets for the home such as the microwavable egg cups which cook your eggs in 20 seconds; plastic dish cover which stops food from drying up; apple microvate gadget; pastry rolling bag; colourful covers for your dishes; special chestnut-roasting pan; roll dispenser with 2 drawers and a compartment; non-stick bun tin; madeleine moulds; shower-head attachments; hotplate cleaning cloths; mobile vegetable rack; ornamental water pump; auxiliary coat rail; remote control case; compact disc storage unit; mouth organ; teddy piggy bank; and tiny doll's house furniture.

Catalogue A5, Catalogue, Colour, 40 pages, Free **Postal charges** £2.95 over £7; £3.45 under £7 **Delivery** Royal Mail **Methods of Payment** Credit Card, Cheque, Postal Order

GADGETS

MICHAEL LAZARUS ASSOCIATES
242-244 St John Street
London
EC1V 4PH
Telephone
0171 250 3988
Fax
0171 608 0370

Kites and dog coats

MLA make two kinds of kites: the Ferrari Sky Ram Kite, made from Ripstop Nylon, a translucent material which has no sticks or spars and can be folded into your pocket (from £18.95); and the Ferrari Sky Blade Stunt Kite, a new revolutionary 'swinging' kite designed to fly in any wind, from the lightest breeze to gale force strength (from £39).

MLA also make lightweight, weatherproof dog coats which fasten with Velcro and fold into your pocket. Prices start at £12.95.

Catalogue A5, Leaflets, Colour, 7 pages, Free **Postal charges** Free **Delivery** Parcelforce **Methods of Payment** Cheque, Postal Order, Credit Card

MULTI-SHARP TOOLS
Dept C94, Buyer's Choice
88 Station Road
Burton Latimer
Northamptonshire
NN15 5JW
Telephone
0181 200 7551
Fax
0181 200 3420

Labour-saving gadgets

This range of labour-saving household and gardening items includes 'The Silver Solution' (£16.95) and a 'High Reach Pruner and Saw Outfit', an ingenious device for cutting high branches without a step ladder (£34.95). The company offers a no-quibble, no-questions-asked guarantee that if the product does not meet with the customer's approval, then it can be returned and money refunded.

Catalogue A5, Brochure, B/W, 8 pages, Free **Postal charges** Varies with item **Delivery** Parcelforce **Methods of Payment** Cheque, Postal Order, Credit Card

STRUCTURED WHOLESALING LTD
287 Finchley Road
London NW3 6ND
Telephone
0171 431 5423
Fax
0171 431 5420

Magnascreens for TVs and VDUs

The Magnascreen fits any TV or monitor from 12in to 33in. Its purpose is to enlarge the screen by up to 50% to relieve eye strain. Easy to fit, it costs from £42.99 to £149.99 depending on the size.

Catalogue A4, Leaflets, Colour, 2 pages, Free **Postal charges** Varies with item **Delivery** Parcelforce **Methods of Payment** Cheque

TENSOR MARKETING LTD
Yarm Road Industrial Estate
Darlington
Co Durham
DL1 4XX
Telephone
01325 469 181
Fax
01325 381 386

Gadgets and electrical goods for home, garden and office

Whether you want to be your own weather forecaster, give a chipped glass a second chance, vacuum your pet or make your own rubber stamp, Tensor Marketing has the product for you. A catalogue full of innovative ideas and clever gifts. Pet Vac, from £14.95; Shower Radio, £10.95; Drain Buster, £10.99; Talking Watch, £12.99; Spellchecker/Ruler, £24.99.

Catalogue Annually, A4, Catalogue, Colour, 12 pages, Free **Postal charges** Varies with item **Delivery** Royal Mail, Parcelforce **Methods of Payment** Cheque, Credit Card

Gardening

AGRIFRAMES
Charlwoods Road
East Grinstead
West Sussex
RH19 2HG
Telephone
01342 328644
Fax
01342 327233

Gardening products
Agriframes is one of the biggest and best of the gardening catalogues. It offers an extensive range of specialist gardening products and equipment and a wide selection of decorative framework for training plants, from arches to obelisks. Personal callers are welcome at its East Grinstead offices. Floral arches from £69.95; obelisks from £59.95; link stakes from £8.45 for 24.
Catalogue Annually, A5, Catalogue, Colour, 48 pages, Free **Postal charges** Varies with item **Delivery** Royal Mail, Parcelforce **Methods of Payment** Cheque, Credit Card, Switch

ALLWOOD BROTHERS
Mill Nursery
London Road
Hassocks
West Sussex
BN6 9NB
Telephone
01273 844229

Plant and flower suppliers
Allwood's Carnations and Pinks catalogue gives a range of gardening aids, as well as every imaginable type of carnation and pink to purchase by mail order. The company exhibits at all the leading flower shows: Chelsea, Harrogate Spring Show, Malvern, The Royal, South of England, Southport, etc. The Ariel Collection of 10 modern AllwoodII Pinks is £12 (including p&p), and the Gold Medal Collection of 16 perpetual flowering carnations is £25 (including p&p).
Catalogue Annually, A5, Catalogue, B/W, 14 pages, 30p
Postal charges Varies with item **Delivery** Royal Mail
Methods of Payment Cheque

GARDENING

ARCADIA NURSERIES
FREEPOST (M1699)
Middlesborough
Cleveland
TS8 9BR
Telephone
01642 310782
Fax
01642 300817

Fuchsias and other flowers and plants

Arcadia specialise in fuchsias and their colourful catalogue features just about every variety imaginable. Other flowers include geraniums, primroses, roses, begonias and petunias.

There is also a good range of accessories such as baskets and patio plant holders, and even earrings and greetings cards. Prices are competitive and on certain items postage is free.

Catalogue Annually, A5, Catalogue, Colour, 31 pages, 50p **Postal charges** 1–10 plants, £3.45; 11–20 plants, £4.45; 21–30 plants, £4.95; 31–40 plants, £5.45; 41–49 plants, £5.95; over 50 plants, £6.45 **Delivery** Royal Mail, Parcelforce **Methods of Payment** Cheque, Postal Order, Credit Card

BANANA BARN
Street Farm
Stinchcombe
Dursley
Gloucestershire
GL11 6AW
Telephone
01453 544276
Fax
same

Wildlife products

Norman and Linda Sellers developed this business from their own interest in creating a wildlife garden. Their catalogue is packed with information. Did you know that hedgehogs are a natural controller of slugs? A Hedgehog House from Banana Barn costs £34.50. They sell bird-feeders and badger mix, bat boxes and dormouse boxes, wildflower seeds and flowering lawn mix. Through their fascination with fossils and crystals another part of the business grew up. They also sell Navajo and Zuni jewellery hand-crafted from turquoise and silver.

Catalogue Annually, A5, Catalogue, B/W, 28 pages, Free **Postal charges** £2.50 for orders up to £15 **Delivery** Royal Mail, Parcelforce **Methods of Payment** Cheque, Credit Card

THE BAY TREE TRADING CO LTD
La Plata Works
Holme Lane

Quality kitchen and garden products

Bay Tree offer unusual, attractive products that are made to last. Burgon & Ball classic garden shears and pruning knife are priced at £13.95

GARDENING

Sheffield
South Yorkshire
S6 4JY
Telephone
0114 285 4525
Fax
0114 285 2518

each. The Haws water-cart with galvanised steel body and cast-iron wheels for collecting rainwater weighs in at £550 while the Haws traditional steel watering-can costs £24.95. Other unusual items include the edible flower garden kit (£9.95), armillary sundial (£129) and *trompe-l'oeil* orange tree (£49.95). For the kitchen, the wooden-slatted suspended pot-rack costs £29.95, as does the bootjack and scraper.

Catalogue Bi-annually, A4, Catalogue, Colour, 10 pages, Free **Postal charges** Add £3.95 for orders up to £150.00 (weight supplement of £4.95 for lead planters). Orders over £150, free **Delivery** Royal Mail **Methods of Payment** Cheque, Credit Card

BLACK DOG OF WELLS
18 Tor Street
Wells
Somerset
BA5 2US
Telephone
01749 672548

Decorative terracotta

This small family business has been making decorative terracotta (literally 'fired earth') for over 20 years. Their small brochure illustrates a range of miniature relief plaques, such as house and garden blessings and inscribed cartouches, designed by Philippa Threlfall. Each piece is hand-finished and fired at 1100 degrees which means it can be displayed outside.

The terracottas are mounted on 5in-square dark blue card and come in special plastic bags. A 4.5in piece is £10.50; 3.5in, £8.50.

Catalogue A4, Brochure, B/W, 1 page, Free **Postal charges** Free **Delivery** Parcelforce **Methods of Payment** Cheque

BRADLEY GARDENS NURSERY
Sled Lane
Wylam
Northumberland
NE41 8JL

Herb plants

This nursery, set in a restored walled garden and featured in the *Good Gardens Guide*, specialises in herbs. It offers a unique service for both chefs and home cooks: fresh cut herbs by post with guaranteed next-day delivery. More than 20 varieties are available in 100g (£2.55) or 50g

Telephone
01661 852176

(£1.90) packs. Edible flowers for garnish cost £2 for a punnet. Bedding plants, container and patio plants are also available in season.

Catalogue Annually, A4, Leaflets, B/W, 1 page, Free **Postal charges** Free **Delivery** Royal Mail **Methods of Payment** Cheque

BRESSINGHAM GARDENS
Diss
Norfolk
IP22 2AB
Telephone
01379 687464
Fax
01379 688034

Garden plants

A wonderfully informative and colourful catalogue for all garden lovers. Choice, new and exciting plants plus rare species. Perennials, alpines, shrubs and trees, climbers, conifers, heathers are all here. Bressingham Reserves List for true plant-hunters features 515 species and varieties ranging from the rare to the classic. Collections Corner features collections of plants at special prices. Great gift ideas such as Dainty Daylilies, 4 plants £11.95 saving £3.85.

Catalogue Quarterly, A4, Catalogue, Colour, 102 pages, £2 **Postal charges** £3.95, orders over £50 free **Delivery** Courier **Methods of Payment** Cheque, Postal Order, Credit Card

THE BRITISH MUSEUM COMPANY LTD
46 Bloomsbury Street
London
WC1B 3QQ
Telephone
0171 323 1234
Fax
0171 636 7186

Garden statuary

The British Museum's garden statuary range has been selected from some of the most spectacular pieces in the Museum and from moulds in the Museum's collection. Each replica has been carefully moulded in resin/marble powder composite from moulds of the original sculpture and then hand-finished. If you would like to view the range, the statuary can be seen in their show garden beside the British Museum, telephone for an appointment. Prices start from £50 for an owl statuette to £995 for a 117cm Statue of Pan. A 66cm British Museum Lion is £140. Most are suitable for conservatory, interior or garden and would enhance any home.

Catalogue Annually, A4, Brochure, Colour, 3 pages, Free **Postal charges** Please obtain a carriage quote from their office **Delivery** In-house delivery **Methods of Payment** Cheque, Credit Card, American Express, Diners Club, Stage Payments

CANNOCK GATES
Martindale
Hawks Green
Cannock
Staffordshire
WS11 1BR
Telephone
0800 462500
Fax
01543 506237

Steel and timber gates

Cannock Gates manufacture and sell both steel and timber gates in a huge variety of sizes and styles, as well as accessories such as railings and letter boxes. They will also make a made-to-measure gate. Garden products are available, too, including wooden arbours, wrought-iron arches, planters, hoses and a portable pathway. Single 4ft-high and up to 3ft 3in-wide wrought-iron garden gate, £29.95; Swedish redwood County Gate, from £58.04 (3ft) to £144.76 (12ft); Nelson pointed-top arbour, £119; carry cart, £29.99.

Catalogue Annually, A5, Catalogue, Colour, 32 pages, Free **Postal charges** Varies with item **Delivery** United Carriers, Royal Mail, Parcelforce, Courier **Methods of Payment** Cheque, Postal Order, Credit Card, Switch, American Express

CLASSIC GARDEN
Lower Puncheston
Pembrokeshire
SA62 5TG
Telephone
01348 881451
Fax
same

Plant containers and supports

Classic Garden made its name with the elegant Versailles box, which can be seen adorning many a stately home and hotel, and has gone on to develop a range of equally attractive planters and wall panels. Posts and rails are manufactured from British hardwoods, panels from exterior grade ply, liners from rigid polypropylene. Planters can be supplied finished or simply sanded and flat-packed. Versailles, from £52; trough from £43; wall panel from £32; room divider from £125. Discounts on pairs.

Catalogue Annually, Third A4, Catalogue, Colour and B/W, 7 pages, Free **Postal charges** Delivery included to mainland UK; £5 supplement to Highlands and Islands of Scotland, Northern Ireland, Isle of Man and Channel Islands **Delivery** Parcelforce **Methods of Payment** Cheque, Credit Card

DAVID AUSTIN ROSES
Bowling Green Lane
Albrighton
Wolverhampton
West Midlands
WV7 3HB
Telephone
01902 373931
Fax
01902 372142

Roses
The David Austin handbook is not simply a mail-order catalogue, but an essential reference source for everyone with an interest in rose-growing. Every rose offered warrants a description with cultivation tips, too. David Austin is a renowned rose-breeder and the nursery's extensive gardens at Albrighton are open to visitors (old roses are at their best in June and July; English roses and repeat-flowering shrub roses can be seen all summer). Eglantyne, £10.95; Rosa Mundi, £6.45; Elizabeth Harkness, £3.95.

Catalogue Annually, A5, Catalogue, Colour, 85 pages, £1.95 **Postal charges** Varies with item **Delivery** Royal Mail **Methods of Payment** Cheque, Postal Order, Credit Card

DEACONS NURSERY
Moor View
Godshill
Isle of Wight
PO38 3HW
Telephone
01983 840750/522243

Fruit trees and soft-fruit bushes
Deacons Nursery specialise in the production of over 250 varieties of apple trees; also Peach, Plum, Pear, Medlar, Raspberry, Strawberry, Redcurrant and Kiwi Fruit. They have a wide range of family trees (trees with more than one variety of fruit grafted on). Trees like Bramleys sell at £16.25; simple Apple trees go for £7.95. Also Wine Fruits, Hops, Grapes, Japanese Wineberry's.

Catalogue Annually, A5, Catalogue, B/W, 50 pages, Free **Postal charges** Varies, but orders over £200 are free **Delivery** Royal Mail, Courier, Parcelforce **Methods of Payment** Cheque, Postal Order, Credit Card

E W KING & CO. LTD
Monks Farm
Kelvedon

Vegetable and flower seeds
Kings have been supplying seed to commercial growers of flowers and vegetables, wholesale to

GARDENING

Colchester
Essex
C05 9PG
Telephone
01376 570000
Fax
01376 571189

large users of seed, and to the home gardener for over a hundred years. Dotted throughout the catalogue are recipes for vegetables, handy tips, historic pieces and suggestions for hanging baskets and bedding displays.

Packets of seed start at 55p. For £1.39 you can buy a packet of azalea seeds; tomatoes range from 55p to £1.75 per packet; even rhubarb can be bought from seed for 85p.

Catalogue Annually, Catalogue, B/W, 72 pages, Free **Postal charges** Add £1.20 for orders under £15.00; orders over £15.00, free **Delivery** Royal Mail **Methods of Payment** Cheque, Postal Order, Credit Card

ELIZABETH MACGREGOR
Ellenbank
Tongland Road
Kirkudbright
Dumfries and Galloway
Scotland
DG6 4UU
Telephone
01557 330620
Fax
same

Violas, violettas, violets and cottage-garden plants
Violas and violettas make excellent garden plants, many flowering from spring until autumn, and Elizabeth Macgregor's catalogue lists numerous varieties, priced £1.70 each. This useful handbook describes each plant in detail and offers a wide selection of cottage-garden plants: campanula from £2.10, clematis from £5, hardy geraniums from £2.30, phlox, salvia, veronica and many, many more. Customers are welcome to visit Ellenbank, too.

Catalogue Annually, A5, Catalogue, Colour and B/W, 32 pages, £1 **Postal charges** Varies with item **Delivery** Parcelforce **Methods of Payment** Cheque

ENGLISH BASKET AND HURDLE CENTRE
Curload
Stoke St Gregory
Taunton
Somerset
TA3 6JD
Telephone
01823 698418

Willow fencing, trellis and furniture
Willow-ware is one of the most ancient environmentally friendly products around and here on the Somerset Levels withies are still fashioned by hand, as they have been for centuries, into hurdles and baskets. Conical plant climber, from £12; garden gate, from £45; hurdles for fencing from £18/6ft × 2ft to £33/6ft × 6ft; rose arch, £94; bower seat, £290.

Fax
01823 698859

Catalogue Annually, Third A4, Leaflets, Colour and B/W, 3 pages, Free **Postal charges** Varies with item **Delivery** Courier **Methods of Payment** Cheque, Credit Card

EXMOUTH GARDEN PRODUCTS
Units 7–8 Salterton Workshops
Budleigh Salterton
Devon
EX9 6RJ
Telephone
01395 442796
Fax
01395 442851

Greenhouse accessories

This catalogue focuses on products for the greenhouse. The range includes shrub and tree ties, automatic vent-openers, open-mesh shelving, glazing clips and hanging-basket chains. They also sell bubble insulation film and shade-netting in packs or by the metre.

A new and unique product is the Ex-Fit Support System which makes the best use of space in your greenhouse. It will hold seed and drip trays, troughs, shelves, plant pots and spigots and is easy to fit (starter pack costs £49.50).

Catalogue A5, Leaflets, Colour and B/W, 8 pages, Free **Postal charges** Add £1.00 for orders up to £10.00; add £2.50 for orders between £10.00 and £20.00; add £3.50 for orders between £20.00 and £40.00; orders over £40.00, free **Delivery** Royal Mail **Methods of Payment** Cheque, Postal Order, Credit Card

GARDEN TRADING COMPANY
The Old Brewery
Priory Lane
Burford
Oxfordshire
OX18 4SG
Telephone
01993 823595
Fax
01993 822710

Traditional gardening equipment

If you're after a galvanised watering-can or an outdoor Gothic plant trellis, this little catalogue is for you. It features some of those bygone products gardeners of old would not have been without. There are wooden wheelbarrows, galvanised incinerators and florists' buckets, beechwood planting dibbers, wooden hay forks, and conservatory chests to stow it all away.

Catalogue Annually, A5, Brochure, Colour, 4 pages, Free **Postal charges** Varies with item **Delivery** Royal Mail, Parcelforce **Methods of Payment** Cheque, Credit Card

GLOBAL ORANGE GROVES
PO Box 644
Poole
Dorset
BH17 9XB
Telephone
01202 691699

Fertilisers for citrus trees

Global Orange Groves UK is a specialist citrus nursery supplying citrus trees of every variety which are guaranteed for 6 months. A help-line is available for any problems which may arise. They supply fertilizers specifically for the requirements of citrus trees. Summer food for citrus trees aims to boost bushiness and growth, helps to prevent fruit drop and premature ripening of fruits, £3.75 per pot including postage. Also stocked is winter food for citrus trees which is a balanced formula for the same price. A comprehensive list is available with a full description of each type of tree. The price for each tree is £30 unless otherwise stated. A 4–6ft Olive Aragonesa is £40; a 4–7ft Apricot Canino, £15–£20. A suitable pot can be supplied with the trees at a cost of £12.

Catalogue Annually, A4, Leaflets, B/W, 8 pages, Free **Postal charges** £15 for the first tree and £4 for every other tree sent at the same time **Delivery** In-house delivery **Methods of Payment** Cheque

GROOM BROS LTD
Pecks Drove Nurseries
Spalding
Lincolnshire
PE12 6BJ
Telephone
01775 722421

Bulbs for autumn and spring planting

Included are all the popular and well-known varieties of tulips and daffodils. More exotic hyacinths together with crocuses and rockery-type bulbs are contained in this packed publication. A complete selection for the spring garden. A 5% discount is available on purchases over £40 and terms can be discussed for orders over £100. Large trumpet daffodils, 50 for £13.60; patio pack of dwarf spring flowers, 70 bulbs for £13.99; and colourful lilies from £3.25 for 3. A final section is dedicated to dahlias, border plants and gladioli.

Catalogue Annually, A5, Catalogue, Colour, 43 pages, Free **Postal charges** Orders under £20, £1.50 **Delivery** Royal Mail **Methods of Payment** Credit Card, Cheque, Postal Order

HADDONSTONE
The Forge House
Church Lane
East Haddon
Northamptonshire
NN6 8DB
Telephone
01604 770711
Fax
01604 770027

Decorative stonework
This magnificent catalogue displays the Haddonstone collection of decorative stonework for architects, landscape designers, contractors and individuals in all its glory. Here you can choose an urn (from £63) as a focal point for your garden, an Italian jardinière (£133.50), Doric pedestal (£210), pool surround (from £65.43 for a kerb section), or a dovecote (£991). The skilled craftsmen also produce balustrading, copings and gate piers.

Catalogue Annually, A4, Catalogue, Colour, 96 pages, Free **Postal charges** Varies with item **Delivery** In-house delivery **Methods of Payment** Cheque, Credit Card

HAND TOOLS LTD
Wreakes Lane
Dronfield
Sheffield
South Yorkshire
S18 6PN
Telephone
01246 413139
Fax
01246 415208

Hand tools
For a comprehensive selection of gardening, agricultural, carpentry and engineering tools, look no further than Hand Tools Ltd's brochure. It contains products from Sorby & Hutton, Green Acre, and Fedco and offers substantial savings on retail prices. Dutch hoe, £9.35; carpenter's vice, £16.85; hedging shears from £13.35.

Catalogue Annually, A4, Catalogue, Colour and B/W, 6 pages, Free **Postal charges** Varies with item **Delivery** Royal Mail, Parcelforce, Courier **Methods of Payment** Cheque, Credit Card

JACQUES AMAND BULB SPECIALISTS LTD
The Nurseries
Clamp Hill
Stanmore
Middlesex
HA7 3JS
Telephone
0181 954 8138

Bulbs
Gardening specialists Jacques Amand stock a wide range of seasonal flowering bulbs, including all the usual plants, from begonias (starting at £2.75 for three) to geraniums (starting at £1.95 each). But in their spring catalogue, they also introduce a number of new, unusual plants.

Orchid-growers may like to investigate the striking outdoor orchid Cypripedium reginae (£11.95 each; three for £34.95). Laboratory

GARDENING

Fax
0181 954 6784

grown, it takes two years to flower – but the wait looks worth it. For indoor planting, they present Eucrosia (telephone for prices), a bulbous plant originally from Ecuador and Peru. You can also visit the Jacques Amand nurseries in March and April when the spring-flowering bulbs for their autumn collection are in full bloom.

Catalogue Quarterly, A4, Catalogue, Colour, 55 pages, £1.00 per catalogue **Postal charges** Orders of £45.00 and over have carriage paid to any destination in Great Britain. Orders under this amount carry a charge of £3.25 **Delivery** In-house delivery **Methods of Payment** Cheque, Credit Card, American Express, Postal Order

JOHN CHAMBERS'
WILD FLOWER SEEDS
15 Westleigh Road
Barton Seagrave
Kettering
Northamptonshire
NN15 5AJ
Telephone
01933 652562
Fax
01933 652576

Wildflower species, mixes and herbs

Enliven your garden with John Chamber's Wild Flower Seeds. This is the most comprehensive range of seeds in the country for native British flowers; there are also ornamental and cultivated grass species and mixtures, everlasting flowers and agricultural crops. For 90p you can choose wild angelica, wild basil or colt's foot. Recreate a meadow on your own back lawn. Wonderful flowers like Scottish primrose, Michaelmas daisy and parsley are all here. You can even order nettles – common, small or stinging.

Catalogue Annually, A5, Catalogue, Colour and B/W, 54 pages, Free **Postal charges** 50p for orders under £5; otherwise free

JOHNSONS SEEDS
London Road
Boston
Lincolnshire
PE21 8AD
Telephone
FREEPHONE 0800 614323

A wide variety of flower and vegetable seeds

This catalogue is divided into various sections, beginning with flower seeds, detailed alphabetically and coded to denote their variety, and vegetables, beans, peas and lawn seed. This is followed by Johnsons spring selection of summer-flowering bulbs, onion sets, perennial plants, roses and young plants. Prices are given beside each

Fax
01205 310148

entry and there are up to 14 colour photographs of the grown items on each double-page spread. Descriptions include planting time, colour, height and habit. Order by freephone, credit card or prepaid post, by cheque or by postal order.

Catalogue Annually, A4, Catalogue, Colour, 80 pages, Free **Postal charges** Free **Delivery** Royal Mail **Methods of Payment** Cheque, Postal Order, Credit Card, Switch

LES AMIS DU JARDIN
187 Sussex Gardens
London
W2 2RH
Telephone
0171 262 9141
Fax
same

Self-watering plant containers

These self-watering classical wooden plant containers are '18th-century in design, made with 19th-century craftsmanship using 20th-century technology'. There is a built-in 7-litre reservoir, providing a self-sufficient interval between watering that can last for several weeks. The St James window box comes in green, black or white and costs from £126.95. The Villandry planter (458mm × 470mm) costs £139.95.

Catalogue A5, Brochure, Colour, 4 pages, Free **Postal charges** Add £14.95 per individual planter or window box; 2 items, add £16.50; 4 items, add £32.50 **Delivery** Parcelforce **Methods of Payment** Cheque, Credit Card

LINK-STAKES LTD
30 Warwick Road
Upper Boddington
Daventry
Northamptonshire
NN11 6DH
Telephone
01327 260329
Fax
01327 262428

Plant supports

This company sells ingenious plant supports. Made of strong galvanised wire coated with dark green plastic, they are durable, unobtrusive, and safe. Link-Stakes, suitable for clumps, are available in 5 sizes ranging from 12in high (£8.45 for 2 dozen) to 40in high (£17 per dozen). Loop-Stakes are for specimen plant stems and come in 3 sizes from 24in (£7.40 per dozen) to 48in (£11.25 per dozen). Other useful gardening aids include the cloister cloche (£19.90) and the micro-cage (£24.90).

Catalogue A5, Leaflets, Colour, 3 pages, Free **Postal charges** £2.90 for orders up to £40.00; over £40.00, free. **Delivery** Royal Mail **Methods of Payment** Cheque, Credit Card

MARSHALLS
Fen Bred Seeds
FREEPOST
Wisbech
Cambridgeshire
PE13 2BR
Telephone
01945 583407
Fax
01945 588235

Vegetable seed specialists

All Marshalls seeds are carefully selected to meet the special requirements of the amateur gardener. This company, which has been in business for 40 years, sells seeds for vegetables, potatoes and onion sets as well as fruit and flowers. Vegetables include swede, spinach, potatoes, beetroot, asparagus, celery, cabbage, Brussel sprouts, broccoli, Jerusalem artichokes, French beans – and each category has several sub-categories. The back of the catalogue features a wide range of starter plants and flowers, all set out in alphabetical order. The catalogue also offers organic manure, cold frames, seed-sowers and other useful gadgets for the keen gardener. There is a money-back guarantee on all products. A first-class paid envelope is included.

Catalogue Bi-annually, A5, Catalogue, Colour, 62 pages, Free **Postal charges** Under £14, 75p; otherwise free **Delivery** Royal Mail **Methods of Payment** Cheque, Postal Order, Credit Card

NEWBROOK PRODUCTS LTD
Hillside Mill
Swaffham Bulbeck
Cambridge
Cambridgeshire
CB5 0LU
Telephone
01223 811215
Fax
01223 812725

Gardening products

This company sells a number of interesting products including the outdoor housefly trap (£6.45), the pit slug and snail trap (£3.96), and the adhesive bug belt which protects trees from caterpillars and other pests (£4.27). 'Bugchasers' are wristbands incorporating a slow release insecticide-free mosquito repellent (£2.50). The 'Portapath' is an award-winning lightweight but extremely strong system of interlocking treads and connectors which simply clip together to form instant pathways, patios or floors (£19.95 for 10sq ft).

Catalogue A4, Leaflets, Colour, 2 pages, Free **Postal charges** Orders under £5.00, add 75p; orders between £5.00 and £15.00, add £1.30; orders over £15.00, free **Delivery** Royal Mail **Methods of Payment** Cheque, Credit Card

NORFOLK GREENHOUSES LTD
PO Box 22
Watton
Norfolk
IP25 6PA
Telephone
01638 510568

Garden structures

As well as greenhouses, Norfolk Greenhouses make carports, garden rooms, conservatories and sheds. They are the originators of PVC greenhouses, and all their products have a galvanised steel frame, shatterproof PVC sheeting that is as clear as glass, and need no foundations. 'Suffolk' sheds and 'Rotunda' greenhouses both cost from £89. A standard carport costs £179, and a Victorian conservatory with tubular aluminium frame and finished in epoxy white coating costs £999.

Catalogue Brochure, Colour, Free **Postal charges** Free **Delivery** Parcelforce **Methods of Payment** Cheque, Credit Card

THE ORGANIC GARDENING CATALOGUE
Coombelands
Addlestone
Surrey
KT15 1HY
Telephone
01932 820958
Fax
01932 829322

Organic gardening stock

The Organic Gardening Catalogue provides everything for the environmentally friendly gardener. Whether you are after vegetable or wild-flower seeds, strawberry plants or fertilisers, liquid feeds or a wormery, you'll find it here. Seeds from 66p a packet; cornflower plants, £7.75 for 10; wormery kit, £48.50. There is also a range of organic food: untreated honeycomb, £3.99; dried vegetable couscous with lentils, £1.35; baby meals from 75p.

Catalogue Annually, A4, Catalogue, Colour, 48 pages, Free **Postal charges** Free **Delivery** Royal Mail, Parcelforce **Methods of Payment** Cheque, Credit Card

PELCO FERTILIZERS LTD
251 London Road East
Batheaston
Bath
Avon
BA1 7RL
Telephone
01225 859962
Fax
01225 859006

Fertiliser
Pelco Fertilizers produce Super-dug, a concentrated organic dung which enriches all soil types, improving texture by breaking down clay and adding body to light soils. At the same time it slowly releases vital plant foods and trace elements. It is weed-free, environmentally friendly, economical (you use handfuls, not barrow-loads) and can be used all year round. Super-dug is available in Giant Economy 25kg sacks at £13.25 for 1 sack, £11.75 each for 2, £10 each for 3 to 5 sacks and £9.50 each for 6 or more sacks.
Catalogue Annually, A4, Leaflets, B/W, 2 pages, Free **Postal charges** Free **Delivery** Parcelforce **Methods of Payment** Cheque, Postal Order, COD, Credit Card

PETER BEALES ROSES
London Road
Attleborough
Norfolk
NR17 1AY
Telephone
01953 454707
Fax
01953 456845

Roses
Considered to be the most comprehensive commercial collection of classic roses in the world, Peter Beales Roses are grown on virgin soil around Attleborough producing hardy plants with good fibrous roots which will transplant into any type of soil anywhere. Their heritage collection of old roses includes the Georgian and Regency collection (£58.50) which consists of 10 roses including Hermosa and Bourbon Queen. Climbing roses average at £6.35; hybrid tea roses, such as the beautiful orange Just Joey, cost around £4 each.
Catalogue Bi-annually, A4, Catalogue, Colour, 52 pages, £2.00 **Postal charges** All orders below £25.00, add £3.95; all orders over £25.00, add £4.95; all orders over £300.00, free (UK only). All orders which include standard roses irrespective of value, add £7.00. **Delivery** Royal Mail **Methods of Payment** Cheque, Credit Card

PLANTIFLOR

PO Box 111
Spalding
Lincolnshire
PE12 6EL
Telephone
01775 711411
Fax
01775 711381

Plants and garden equipment

Plantiflor offers a wealth of plants and gardening equipment to transform your plot of land in its three catalogues, Bakker, Hortico and Spalding Bulb. From Bakker you can order patio dahlias at £6.95 for five; a dwarf peach tree, £13.95; or a pair of garden shoes, £1.95. Hortico sells Marguerites at £4.95 for three; bonsais from £16.75; Caucasian scabious, £5.75 for five. Spalding Bulb offers convolvulus at £9.95 for three; scented lilies from £3.95 for five; and a rhododendron hedge collection, £15.95 for three.

Catalogue Bi-annually, A4, Catalogue, Colour, 84 pages, Bakker and Hortico, free; Spalding Bulb, £1 **Postal charges** £1.95 **Delivery** Royal Mail **Methods of Payment** Cheque, Postal Order, Credit Card

POSH POTS

Elkstone Manor
Elkstone
Cheltenham
Gloucestershire
GL53 9PB
Telephone
01242 870525
Fax
01242 870530

Flowerpots

These bright, elegant flowerpots come in two colour ranges: 'Bright and Beautiful' and 'Country Cousins'. The former are in strong, vibrant colours; the latter, soft shades to blend with antiqued pine and rustic wickerwork. The pots come in 12, 16, 20, 24 and 34 centimetre sizes with saucers and cost from £5.99 to £25.99 each.

Catalogue A4, Brochure, Colour, 2 pages, £2.00 refundable against order **Postal charges** £5.15 **Delivery** Parcelforce **Methods of Payment** Cheque, Postal Order, Credit Card

R HARKNESS & CO

The Rose Gardens
Hitchin
Hertfordshire
SG4 0JT
Telephone
01462 420402

Plants and flowers

If it's roses you want, Harkness is the catalogue for you. It comes complete with full descriptions of the many varieties on offer and suggested collections for edging paths and borders, ground cover, or to train as climbers (from £11.50). Prices are reasonable: hybrid tea bush roses from £3.75; climbing from £5.45; miniatures from

£3.45; ground-cover from £4.45; and patio half-standards from £14.85.

Catalogue Bi-annually, A4, Catalogue, Colour, 31 pages, Free **Postal charges** £4.75; express, £9.95 **Delivery** Courier, Royal Mail, Parcelforce **Methods of Payment** Cheque, Postal Order, Credit Card, American Express

THE ROMANTIC GARDEN NURSERY
Swannington
Norwich
Norfolk
NR9 5NW
Telephone
01603 261488
Fax
01603 871668

Garden products
Situated in the heart of Norfolk, the Romantic Garden Nursery is a specialist supplier of box topiary and ornamental standards. For £124 you can order a box tree in the shape of a swan, peacock or triple crown; a cone-shaped box costs just £29.99. Plants for hedging, knots and parterres are stocked alongside pot-grown camellia japonica, citrus limon (lemon), gooseberry, jasminium, and wisteria, to name but a few. If you are in the area, the nursery is open three days a week.

Catalogue Annually, A5, Catalogue, B/W, 14 pages, Free **Postal charges** Varies with item **Delivery** Courier **Methods of Payment** Cheque

SAMUEL DOBIE & SON LTD
Broomhill Way
Torquay
Devon
TQ2 7QW
Telephone
01803 616888
Fax
01803 615150

Seeds, bulbs, young plants, garden equipment
Dobie's are a long-established supplier of over 1,000 varieties of flower and vegetable seeds. They also stock bulbs and a selection of garden equipment. None of the products are sold through retail outlets so they can only be ordered by mail. In recent years Dobie's have developed an extensive range of young bedding and patio plant packs which offer excellent value.

Flower and vegetable seeds start at 47p a packet while a pack of 100 petunia mini plants is £9.75. Thirty-five impatiens (busy lizzie) easiplants are £7.85 and a pair of self-watering hanging baskets £15.95.

Fax
01462 422170

SOUTH DOWN TRUGS & CRAFTS LTD

Thomas Smith's Trug Shop
Hailsham Road
Herstmonceux
East Sussex
BN27 4LH
Telephone
01323 832137
Fax
01323 833801

Catalogue Annually, A4, Catalogue, Colour, 129 pages, Free **Postal charges** Orders of £5 or over, free; for orders below £5, add 50p **Delivery** Royal Mail **Methods of Payment** Cheque, Postal Order, Credit Card

Garden trugs

Trugs have been handmade in Sussex since Anglo-Saxon times. The name is believed to come from the Anglo-Saxon word 'trog' meaning 'boat-shaped'.

Used for carrying flowers, seeds, fruit, plants, tools or logs, their shapes vary accordingly. Made from plywood, they are available with natural or coloured rims and handles in any of 12 colours, and in 6 different sizes. Prices range from £21 to £61.20 for a stripped Royal Sussex trug with sweet-chestnut handle and rim and cricket-bat willow boards.

Catalogue A4, Leaflets, Colour and B/W, 2 pages, Free **Postal charges** Free **Delivery** Royal Mail **Methods of Payment** Cheque, Postal Order

SUFFOLK HERBS

Monks Farm
Pantlings Lane
Kelvedon
Essex
CO5 9PG
Telephone
01376 572456
Fax
01376 571189

Organic seeds, gardening tools, dried herbs and spices, essential oils

A comprehensive organic seed catalogue annotated with helpful descriptions, tips and even recipes. Seeds for growing herbs, garden and wild flowers, vegetables and for sprouting are listed alongside gardening equipment, organic products, dried herbs and spices, pot pourri, herb teas and tisanes, health products, essential oils, books and gifts. You can even order a Bean Feast Box containing 12 packs of dried beans (£23.95). Seeds from 65p; cloches from £19.75; lavender essential oil, £4.65/10ml.

Catalogue Annually, A4, Catalogue, Colour and B/W, 70 pages, £1 **Postal charges** Free **Delivery** Royal Mail **Methods of Payment** Cheque, Postal Order, Credit Card

SUTTONS SEEDS LTD
Hele Road
Torquay
Devon
TQ2 7QJ
Telephone
01803 614455
Fax
01803 615747

Seeds
Suttons Seeds' mail-order catalogue features seeds for flowers, shrubs, fruit and vegetables with a brief description of each plant plus its growing habit. Sample prices: 85p a packet for sunflower seeds and 69p for spinach seeds. Seedlings, plantlets, pot-ready plants and vegetables, soft-fruit plants, bulbs, corms and tubers are also available plus a small range of useful, unusual garden equipment such as the rocket log splitter (£12.95).

Catalogue Annually, A4, Catalogue, Colour, 97 pages, Free **Postal charges** Free **Delivery** Royal Mail **Methods of Payment** Cheque, Credit Card, Postal Order

TERRACE & GARDEN
Orchard House
Patmore End
Ugley
Bishop's Stortford
Cambridgeshire
CM22 6JA
Telephone
01799 543289
Fax
01799 543586

Garden ornaments
Terrace & Garden, as the name implies, supply unusual ornaments for your terrace and garden, from wind chimes to weather-vanes. These products are something different for the discerning gardener.

Catalogue Annually, A4, Brochure, Colour, 4 pages, Free **Postal charges** £2 for orders below £20; £4 for orders between £20 and £75; free on orders over £75 **Delivery** Royal Mail **Methods of Payment** Credit Card, Cheque, Postal Order

THE THAI HOUSE CO
11 The Paddock
Maidenhead
Berkshire
SL6 6SD
Telephone
01628 75091
Fax
same

Thai-style garden houses
The Thai house is based on a traditional design found in rural Thailand. It is made of softwood and stands raised from the ground on eight circular posts. Five steps lead up to the door and there are window shutters on each side. The roof is covered with waterproof felt. It would certainly add interest to any garden and would make an ideal children's play-house. From £604, prefabricated, for the Rayong, to £1195, assembled, for the Bangkok.

GARDENING

THOMPSON & MORGAN
Poplar Lane
Ipswich
Suffolk
IP8 3BU
Telephone
01473 690869
Fax
01473 680199

Catalogue Annually, A4, Leaflets, Colour and B/W, 2 pages, Free **Postal charges** Varies with item **Methods of Payment** Cheque

Garden seeds

Thompson & Morgan first published a catalogue in 1855 and now, 140 years on, the seedsmen are still finding new varieties to include. This is a most comprehensive handbook featuring annuals, perennials, houseplants, bulbs and orchids, and containing an A–Z of both flower seeds and vegetables, complete with full descriptions and even chef's tips. Nicotiana, £1.89 for 100 seeds; pansies, from £1.29 for 50 seeds; runner beans, from £1.79 for 25 beans.

Catalogue Annually, A5, Catalogue, Colour, 208 pages, Free **Postal charges** 70p for orders up to £6 **Delivery** Royal Mail **Methods of Payment** Cheque, Postal Order, Credit Card, Switch

THE TRADITIONAL GARDEN SUPPLY COMPANY
Unit 12
Hewitts Industrial Estate
Elmbridge Road
Cranleigh
Surrey
GU6 8LW
Telephone
01483 273366
Fax
01483 273388

Gardening equipment

The Traditional Garden Supply Company offers everything you'll ever need to complete your garden. You can even inspect the items first hand at its Elmbridge Road shop. Some of its beautifully made furniture has been inspired by the American Shaker ideal of simplicity and functionality. For example, the Shaker-style boot bench (from £139.95), made from cedar, is a practical and attractive box seat to keep near the back door to store wellies and other odds and ends. The catalogue contains greenhouses, cold frames, tools, a whisky-barrel water garden (£199.99), rugged tip bags (from £9.99), and many more ideas.

Catalogue Annually, A4, Catalogue, Colour, 40 pages, Free **Postal charges** Over £20, free; under £20, £2.95 **Delivery** Royal Mail, Parcelforce **Methods of Payment** Cheque, Postal Order, Credit Card, Switch

GARDENING

THE TRUGGERY
Coopers Croft
Herstmonceux
Hailsham
East Sussex
BN27 1QL
Telephone
01323 832314

Trugs
These Sussex trugs are still primarily handmade. The word 'trug' is derived from the Anglo-Saxon word 'trog' meaning wooden vessel or boat-shaped article. The smaller sizes are ideal for displaying flowers, eggs and fruit, and the larger ones for harvesting garden produce and carrying logs. An 8in × 5in oval trug costs £12.50 and a 26in × 14in is £35. A round or square 10in-diameter trug costs £19.50 and a 'Large Log' (23in × 16in) is £34.

Catalogue A6, Leaflets, B/W, 4 pages, Free **Postal charges** Add £3.00 for sizes 0–3 and £4.50 for all other sizes **Delivery** Parcelforce **Methods of Payment** Cheque

TWO WESTS & ELLIOT
Unit 4
Carrwood Road
Sheepbridge Industrial Estate
Chesterfield
Staffordshire
S41 9RH
Telephone
01246 451077
Fax
01246 260115

Equipment for greenhouse and conservatory
The Two Wests (Josephine and Christopher) and Elliott offer a wealth of gardening information, encouragement and tips as page-by-page they describe products specially developed for the greenhouse and conservatory, from watertight gravel trays (£6.50 each) to a Dewpoint Propagation Cabinet (£369.50).

Catalogue Annually, A5, Catalogue, Colour, 56 pages, Free **Postal charges** Varies with item **Delivery** Royal Mail, Parcelforce **Methods of Payment** Cheque, Postal Order, Credit Card, Switch

UNWINS SEEDS LTD
Mail Order Department
Histon
Cambridgeshire
CB4 4ZZ
Telephone
01945 588522
Fax
01945 475 255

Garden seed, bulbs and young plants
Unwins offer hundreds of high-quality seed varieties of flowers and vegetables that have all been tried and tested to make sure that they will thrive in typical British conditions. Sweet Peas are Unwins' speciality and their catalogue lists over 50 premium-quality varieties giving customers the opportunity to grow superior plants and blooms. They also sell bulbs for all seasons, young plants

and soft fruit. All products are backed by a no-quibble guarantee.

Catalogue Quarterly, A5, Catalogue, Colour, 32 pages, Free **Postal charges** Free **Delivery** In-house delivery **Methods of Payment** Cheque, Postal Order, Credit Card

THE VALLEY CLEMATIS NURSERY
Willingham Road
Hainton
Lincoln
Lincolnshire
LN3 6LN
Telephone
01507 313398
Fax
01507 313705

Clematis plants

The Valley Clematis Nursery stocks more than 350 varieties, most of which are available through the catalogue. Each plant is described in terms of colour, height, planting aspect, pruning details and flowering months. The majority of plants are priced between £5 and £7. For autumn delivery you are advised to order in March or April.

Catalogue Annually, A5, Catalogue, Colour, 38 pages, £1 **Postal charges** Varies with item **Delivery** Royal Mail, Parcelforce **Methods of Payment** Cheque, Credit Card, Switch

VAN MEUWEN
Wardentree Lane
Spalding
Lincolnshire
PE11 3UU
Telephone
01775 712345
Fax
01775 760019

Plant and garden accessories

You will find page after page of superb gardening values in the latest edition of this catalogue. The colourfully presented displays will tempt any armchair gardener into his garden to bring a vivid splash of colour to his life. Their trailing petunia at £7.99 must be seen to be believed, 20 ground-cover plants provide a carpet of colour for £14.99 or a pack of 40 for £26.99 with 5 additional shrubs free. From acalypha to zinnias the whole alphabet of flowers is covered.

Catalogue Quarterly, A4, Catalogue, Colour, 32 pages, Free **Postal charges** £2.99 **Delivery** Royal Mail **Methods of Payment** Cheque, Postal Order, Credit Card

THE VERNON GERANIUM NURSERY
Cuddington Way
Cheam

Geraniums and fuchsias

Vernon grows a vast array of geraniums and fuchsias and its well-presented catalogue will appeal to all – from the beginner to the expert. It

GARDENING

Sutton
Surrey
SM2 7JB
Telephone
0181 393 7616
Fax
0181 786 7437

pictures many of the 1,000 varieties available and is packed with helpful information and growing tips, making it almost a reference book in itself. Prices for geranium cuttings start at £1.20; fuchsias from 80p. The nursery sales area is open to the public from February to August.

Catalogue Annually, A4, Catalogue, Colour, 42 pages, £1.50 **Postal charges** Varies with item **Delivery** Royal Mail **Methods of Payment** Cheque, Postal Order, Credit Card

W W JOHNSON & SON LTD
London Road
Boston
Lincolnshire
PE21 8AD
Telephone
01205 365051
Fax
01205 310148

Flowers, vegetables and herbs

Now celebrating their 175th anniversary as seed producers, Johnson's Seed Line catalogue is packed with colourful pictures and information about all kinds of plants and vegetables. Their award-winning seed packets give full cultural instructions plus a coloured bedding label so you can see what you have sown where. Dahlias are £1.95 a packet, pansies from 95p and scotch moss £1.55. Cauliflowers are from 79p, sweet corn from 85p, strawberries from £1.69 and tarragon, 85p.

Catalogue A5, Catalogue, Colour, 103 pages, Free **Postal charges** Add 50p; orders over £5.00, free **Delivery** Royal Mail **Methods of Payment** Cheque, Postal Order, Credit Card, Switch

WALLACE & BARR LTD
Staplehurst Road
Marden
Kent
TN12 9BP
Telephone
01622 831235
Fax
01622 832416

Plants and bulbs

Flower-bulb specialists and nurserymen since 1870, Wallace & Barr offer more than 500 varieties of bulbs and plants, including the largest selection of lilies in Europe. The catalogue gives lots of useful information about each plant. Begonias are from £2.95 per 3 (tuber size 6–7cm); irises from £1.95 each, and paeonies from £3.95 each. Their special lily collections include the 'Conservatory' which consists of six different types of lily for

£7.50 or for £20.50 you can have 3 each of the 6 varieties.

Catalogue Bi-annually, A5, Catalogue, Colour, 95 pages, Free **Postal charges** £3.50 for orders under £50.00; orders over £50.00, free **Delivery** Parcelforce **Methods of Payment** Cheque, Postal Order, Credit Card

WINDRUSH MILL
Witney
Oxfordshire
OX8 6BH
Telephone
01993 779555
Fax
01993 700749

Gardening products

This appealing catalogue contains items ranging from decorative pots and display stands to practical tools, furniture and unusual plant collections. There's a telescopic grass rake for £8.95, garden shoes for £9.95, a wall-mounted hurricane lamp for £16.95, and a wooden bat box for £24.95. Plants include yarrow, achillea and delphinium (all in pots at £3.95 each). Also rattan tables and chairs, watering-cans, citrus trees, plant supports, picket-fence pot holders, peasant boy fountain, rustic six-pot holder, versatile plant stands, slug and snail traps, rootmasters, log splitter maul, diamond sharpener, grenade log splitter, saw, cat bird-scarer and bark mulch.

Catalogue Bi-annually, A4, Catalogue, Colour, 32 pages, Free **Postal charges** £2.95 **Delivery** Royal Mail **Methods of Payment** Cheque, Postal Order, Credit Card, American Express, Switch

General Catalogues

ARGOS DISTRIBUTORS LTD
489–499 Avebury Boulevard
Central Milton Keynes
Hertfordshire
MK9 2NW
Telephone
01908 690333

Huge range of goods
Argos is the innovative high street store where you order by catalogue within the shop itself. But to make shopping even easier, Argos have set up a free home-delivery service called Argos Direct. This is available on selected large items such as 3-piece suites from £499.99, multi-gyms from £195.00, and mountain bikes from £129.00.

To order is easy: look through the Argos catalogue, check that the item is available for free home-delivery, and call 01345 427467, quoting your order and credit card details. They will then deliver to your door within 14 days. NOTE: catalogues themselves are only available through Argos stores, as are mail-order booklets.

Catalogue Bi-annually, A4, Catalogue, Colour, 679 pages, Free **Postal charges** Free **Delivery** Royal Mail **Methods of Payment** Cheque, Credit Card, Postal Order

BOMBAY DUCK
16 Malton Road
London
W10 5UP
Telephone
0181 964 8882
Fax
0181 964 8883

Exclusive ranges of gifts, textiles, jewellery, stationery, wrought-iron furniture and home accessories
Bombay Duck not only supply by mail order but have a warehouse from where they sell direct to the public on Sundays only from 11am to 5pm. Their range includes gifts, textiles, jewellery, stationery, wrought-iron furniture and home accessories, which are handmade in India and Indonesia. A small tin lantern £5.95, a traditional

towel rail in wrought-iron £160. Some unusual and tempting gifts too numerous to mention.
Catalogue Annually, A4, Catalogue, Colour and B/W, 4 pages, Free **Postal charges** £5, orders over £50 free **Delivery** Royal Mail **Methods of Payment** Cheque, Postal Order

BRAITRIM
Braitrim House
98 Victoria Road
London
NW10 6NB
Telephone
0500 225588
Fax
0181 723 3003

Fashion and retail supplies
Although this catalogue is aimed at the fashion and retail industry, many of the useful items in it can be bought singly. For needlework enthusiasts, there are tape measures, tailors' chalk, tailors' wax, tailors' dummies, and textile staplers. For those at home, there are garment bags, hangers, rails, suit hangers, suit covers, skirt hangers, scissors, first-aid kits, plastic gloves, wall mirrors. There is plenty of office equipment, racking systems which could be used in a home office, Sellotape, batteries, pens. An interesting catalogue, even for those not in business. The company offers next-day delivery.
Catalogue Bi annually, A4, Catalogue, Colour, 190 pages, Free **Methods of Payment** Cheque, Postal Order, Credit Card, Switch

CHESTER-CARE
Sidings Road
Low Moor Estate
Kirkby in Ashfield
Nottinghamshire
NG17 7JZ
Telephone
01623 722337
Fax
01623 755585

Accessories and gadgets to help the elderly or disabled in the home
This catalogue has been designed to make daily living easier for the elderly and the disabled. It features more than 750 items including walking frames from £39.99; lap desk, £17.75; kettle tipper, from £12.25; incontinence pads, £4.29 for 40; tap turner, £4.29; non-slip placemats, from £4.09; needle threaders, £2.29; and the Arran riser chair which costs £438.
Catalogue Annually, A4, Catalogue, Colour, 44 pages, 50p **Postal charges** Varies with item **Delivery** Royal Mail, Parcelforce, Courier **Methods of Payment** Cheque, Postal Order, Credit Card

GENERAL CATALOGUES

THE COMPLETE COLLECTION
You magazine special offers
Admail 11
London
EC4Y 0DP
Telephone
01274 571611

Clothes and household goods
The Mail on Sunday's *You* magazine has collected all its special offers into this catalogue. Clothes include a fabulous sandwashed silk pewter jacket for only £49.99 and a jersey pantsuit for £24.99. Items for the home include a Toyota sewing machine (£149.99), an Electrolux vacuum cleaner (£59.99), garden gazebo (£59.99) and Praktica camera (£29.99) with free binoculars.
Catalogue Bi-annually, A4, Catalogue, Colour, 207 pages, £2.00 **Postal charges** £2.99 **Delivery** Royal Mail **Methods of Payment** Cheque, Credit Card

COUNTRYWIDE WORKSHOPS CHARITABLE TRUST
47 Fisherton Street
Salisbury
Wiltshire
SP2 7SU
Telephone
01722 326886
Fax
01722 411092

Clothes, gifts, furniture and toys
Countrywide Workshops is a charitable trust whose aim is to create work for disabled people by selling the goods they make and encouraging their abilities. This catalogue contains a selection of beautifully made products from both home-workers and sheltered workshops. Made-to-measure skirts in Welsh wool, from £45; leather handbag, £41.25; hand-engraved glasses, from £22.50 for a set of six liqueur tumblers; hand-shaped nursery ark with 18 animals, £69.50; shoebag with ballet or trainer motif, £4.70; teddy clock, £16.50; bunkbeds, £305; and for the garden, a wooden slatted composter, £35.75.
Catalogue Annually, A5, Catalogue, Colour, 40 pages, Free **Postal charges** Free **Delivery** Royal Mail, Parcelforce **Methods of Payment** Cheque, Postal Order, Credit Card, Switch, Diners Club

F PARR
Merse Road
North Moons Moat
Redditch
Worcestershire

Factory, warehouse, shop and office equipment
Parrs catalogue is mainly for factories, shops, offices, workshops and garages, but there is a good deal of interest to the general public as well. There is a marvellous range of porters' trolleys, called

B98 9PL
Telephone
01527 585777
Fax
01527 66430

'sack trucks', shelving, plastic storage containers, water pumps, staple guns, wrapping materials, filing cabinets, fire extinguishers, step ladders, safety mats and so on. Sack truck, from £49.99; steps from £35.20; hand tacker, £21.95 (prices excluding VAT).

Catalogue Annually, A4, Catalogue, Colour, 258 pages **Postal charges** Varies with item **Methods of Payment** Cheque, Credit Card

FAMILY ALBUM
Home Shopping Department
London Road
Preston
Lancashire
PR1 4BU
Telephone
0171 707 1022

Clothes and general household items

This weighty catalogue carries a number of inspiring fashion items such as the Ultra Fine Microfibre Blouson for £59.99 and Kickers 'Caterpillar' boots for £94.99. There is also an elegant stone-coloured suit with longline semi-fitted jacket and long half-lined skirt with front vent for £79.99.

Household items include a rocking chair for £59.99, a Kodak Cameo camera for £37.99, and bath sets from £9.99. A Black & Decker Hovermaster costs from £149.99.

Catalogue Bi-annually, A4, Catalogue, Colour, 1062 pages, Free **Postal charges** Free **Delivery** In-house delivery **Methods of Payment** Cheque, Stage Payments, Credit Card

FREEMANS
139 Clapham Road
London
SW99 OHR
Telephone
0345 900 100
Fax
0171 587 1059

General goods

Virtually synonymous with mail order, Freemans offers everything from lingerie to motor insurance. From computer games to garden ponds, its range is as thorough as it is diverse. A greater proportion of this gigantic catalogue is devoted to clothes at very reasonable prices, although you won't find exclusive designer labels here. Look out for special discounts. Women's long-lined single-breasted jacket, £54.99; pack of three T-shirts, £17.99; classic loafers, £19.99; men's wool/

polyester suit jacket, £85, and matching trousers, £44.99; babies' pack of three sleepsuits, £15.99; girls' top and leggings from £13.99; Chesterfield three-piece suite, £699.85; Flymo hover mower, £54.99.

Catalogue Bi-annually, A4, Catalogue, Colour, 1096 pages, Free **Postal charges** Free **Delivery** Courier **Methods of Payment** Cheque, Postal Order, Stage Payments, Credit Card

GRATTAN PLC
Anchor House
Ingleby Road
Bradford
West Yorkshire
BD99 2XG
Telephone
01274 575511
Fax
01274 625588

Everything!

Providing one of the widest range of goods through mail order in the country, Gratton's giant catalogues are classics. Each of the many sections is easy to follow and filled with great-value items as well as some luxury goods. Everything is here from new shoes to a new bedroom, with plenty of brand names in electronics, appliances and clothes, including designer labels. Like other similar operations they offer discounts on your first order as well as the option to pay in instalments.

Customers order the goods and pay after receiving a statement. You can send payment with a cheque, take it to the post office (which makes a small charge) or take it to a bank. You can pay over 20, 40 or 50 weeks by interest-free credit or over 100 weeks with interest. You can only pay by credit card if you pay the full amount in one go.

Grattan also produce Look Again for younger consumers, *TV Times*, *You* and *Sunday* magazine direct-response catalogues, Kaleidoscope, Scotcade, and Rainbow.

Catalogue Bi-annually, A4, Catalogue, Colour, 1,095 pages, Free **Postal charges** Free **Delivery** In-house delivery **Methods of Payment** Cheque, Postal Order, Credit Card

GREAT UNIVERSAL STORES
Home Shopping Department
London Road
Preston
Lancashire
PR1 4BU
Telephone
0800 269396

General
Great Universal stock a broad range of products, from men's and women's clothing to soft furniture and bathroom fittings. Catering for the mass market, here's where you'll find an astonishing variety of floral furniture covers, extensively veneered reproduction furniture and assorted keep-fit equipment. Of the clothing, a woman's 'Essential Nightdress', available in a choice of two lengths and three colours, costs just £9.99. You can pick up a pack of two nightdresses for £16.99. Children's hooded tops in two colours cost only £6.99 and men's twill shirts start at £14.99.

THE GREEN STORE
Admail 641
Bath
Avon
BA1 1AD
Telephone
01672 542266
Fax
01672 542234

Environmentally oriented products
None of the products featured in this catalogue are tested on animals and all are vegan except the beeswax-based products, the natural bristle toothbrushes and the Ecover washing-up liquid. They sell the biggest range of organic cotton clothing in the UK. There is glassware made from reused bottles in South Africa and hampers of organic food and drink. Recycled pillows and duvets that use converted bottles, such as Coca Cola, and a range of natural unbleached bedlinen. A wonderful catalogue for the environmentally aware.
Catalogue Annually, A4, Catalogue, Colour, 35 pages, Free **Postal charges** Add £1.25 for orders up to £5 and £3.50 for orders between £5 and £100. Orders over £100 are free. **Delivery** Royal Mail **Methods of Payment** Cheque, Credit Card

GREENPEACE CATALOGUE
PO Box 10
Gateshead

Gifts
Profits from this catalogue go towards helping Greenpeace to fund its campaigning activities. As one might expect, it is full of environmentally

GENERAL CATALOGUES

friendly products. These include well-designed clothes, mugs, badges, bowls, cards and a children's Eco Kit for tracking acid rain and water pollution. Elephant T-shirt, £8.50 children, £12.50 adult; whale mug, £2.99; 3-D wooden farm puzzle, £8.95; solar garden light, £79.99.

Catalogue Bi-annually, A5, Catalogue, Colour, 19 pages **Postal charges** £2.99 for orders up to £15; £3.99 for orders of more than £15 **Delivery** Royal Mail, Parcelforce **Methods of Payment** Credit Card, Cheque

HEATHER VALLEY (WOOLLENS) LTD
16 Comely Bank Avenue
Edinburgh
Scotland
EH4 1EL
Telephone
0161 236 9911
Fax
0161 238 2626

General catalogue

A good comprehensive catalogue containing everything from women's clothing to kitchen appliances. Sizes for women from 12 to 30, with standard and shorter sizes catered for. A footwear guide is available free with shoe widths available up to Ultra Wide EEE.

The home-furnishing section comprises lounge furniture and bedroom furniture and there is even a section for the garden.

Catalogue Bi-annually, A4, Catalogue, Colour, 129 pages, Free **Postal charges** Free **Delivery** Courier **Methods of Payment** Cheque, Postal Order, Stage Payments, Credit Card, Switch

IAN ALLAN REGALIA
Coombelands House
Coombelands Lane
Addlestone
Surrey
KT15 1HY
Telephone
01932 820560
Fax
01932 821 258

Masonic regalia and books

Ian Allan Regalia aims to satisfy the needs of all freemasons. The catalogue features a vast array of Masonic regalia including full-dress aprons and collars, breast jewels, swords and scabbards. For those curious as to what freemasons actually do, there are books, including *Masonic Ritual – A Commentary on the Freemasonic Ritual*, by Dr E H Cartwright (£12.95), which might provide enlightenment. Provincial district breast jewel, £6.95; Supreme Grand Chapter apron and sash, £172.95.

Catalogue Annually, A5, Catalogue, Colour, 36 pages, Free **Postal charges** Varies with item **Delivery** Royal Mail, Parcelforce **Methods of Payment** Cheque, Credit Card, Postal Order

IDEAL HOME MAIL ORDER
9 Flag Business Exchange
Peterborough
Cambridgeshire
PE1 5TX
Telephone
01733 890155
Fax
01733 344977

General household, car, gardening and DIY

The Ideal Home Mail Order offers a range of gadgets and goods for all age groups. There is something useful for everyone here, whether it's for the kitchen, garden or car. There are also personal aids, DIY equipment, computers and gifts. Compaq Presario with CD drive and 4MB RAM, £1499; aquarium kit, £45; pet's vacuum, £14.99; backache support belt, £10.99; Nanette dust and polish brush, £9.95; anti-slide tape, £5.99; all-weather covers from £4.99.

Catalogue Quarterly, A5, Catalogue, Colour, 38 pages, Free **Postal charges** £2.95 for one item; free for more than one item **Delivery** Royal Mail, Parcelforce **Methods of Payment** Cheque, Postal Order, Credit Card

KALEIDOSCOPE
Wembley Road
Leicester
Leicestershire
LE3 1XX
Telephone
01274 571611

General goods

The Kaleidoscope range extends from clothing and swimwear to barbecues and garden furniture. Its fashion section will appeal to career women unable to splash out in Covent Garden boutiques but wanting to steer clear of the high street stores. Pure cotton tops are available for £9.99; floral print trousers for £16.99. Kaleidoscope also supplies the *You* Magazine Special Offers, tel: 01274 571611. Moving to the bedroom, a sun-and-moon double duvet set costs £19.99. For the green-fingered, six dazzling petunias cost £7.99.

Catalogue Quarterly, A4, Catalogue, Colour, 200 pages, Free **Postal charges** Varies with item **Delivery** Royal Mail, Parcelforce **Methods of Payment** Cheque, Postal Order, Credit Card, American Express, Diners Club, Stage Payments

KAY & COMPANY LTD
23 The Tything
St Oswald's Road
Worcester
Worcestershire
WR99 2BR
Telephone
0171 707 1000

General
Kay & Company is one of Britain's largest mail-order companies. They offer an introductory 20% discount for first orders and interest-free credit.

Goods include the latest fashions for men, women and children, sports equipment, electrical goods, jewellery, furniture and general household items. A basic portable Yamaha keyboard costs £129.99; a bouncing cradle, £14.99; denim jeans for 8–15 year olds start at £13.99; and a home-assembly three-drawer chest costs only £19.99.

Catalogue Bi-annually, A4, Catalogue, Colour, 1046 pages, Free **Postal charges** Free **Delivery** Royal Mail **Methods of Payment** Cheque, Postal Order, Credit Card

LITTLEWOODS HOME SHOPPING GROUP LTD
Kershaw Avenue
Crosby
Merseyside
L72 OLG
Telephone
0800 616611

Wide range of clothes, accessories, and household products
Littlewoods Home Shopping Group is one of the most established general home-shopping companies, with over 60 years experience in the sector. The Littlewoods Home Shopping catalogue is published twice a year and comprises over 1,000 pages featuring fashion clothing, childrenswear, top sportswear brands, a full range of household goods, furniture, electrical equipment, and toys. The Littlewoods catalogue is also noted for its production of exclusive top-name designer ranges by Workers for Freedom and Vivienne Westwood.

Catalogues published by Littlewoods Home Shopping Group also include Littlewoods, John Moores, Peter Craig, Janet Frazer, Burlington and Brian Mills.

Littlewoods works on a credit system whereby you pay in instalments and they check each application against their own credit-scoring system. If you want to order and pay the total at the same time, ask for Direct Sales when ordering.

Catalogue A4, Catalogue, Colour, Free **Postal charges**
Varies with item **Delivery** Royal Mail **Methods of Payment**
Cheque, Postal Order, Stage Payments

MARKS AND SPENCER HOME CHOICE
FREEPOST
PO Box 288
Warrington
Cheshire
WA1 4SS
Telephone
01925 851100

General household items

Marks & Spencer Home Choice handles flowers, home furnishings, furniture, gift vouchers, wine, horticulture, seasonal hampers, gifts, wedding lists and business clothing by mail order. Their 'Floral Basket' (£25 plus £3.50 next-day delivery charge) comes with a selection of yellow and blue flowers or cerise and pink. Their Wine Cellar offers cases of 'Critics' Choice' wines for £59.95 and 'Star Buys' for £39.95. Or you could have a bottle of champagne for just £22.50 (including gift box and delivery).

Catalogue Quarterly, Leaflets, Colour, Free **Postal charges** Varies with item **Delivery** Parcelforce, Royal Mail **Methods of Payment** Cheque, Switch, Postal Order

McCORD
Blagrove
Swindon
Wiltshire
SN5 8SN
Telephone
01793 433499
Fax
01793 487002

General household goods

This is a brand-new home-shopping catalogue combining traditional products with new design in a way that is original, practical and affordable. You will also find craft products with a timeless design heritage like the Portugese Cazelas and the Hunza Hanging Lamp from India. Larger items include the McCord Chesterfield settee for £499 plus £25 delivery & packing, or 4 payments of £131. A corduroy rocking horse 25" high, for £49. For the garden, a Verdigris Heron for £199 or 4 payments of £50.50, incl. p&p.

Catalogue Bi-annually, A4, Catalogue, Colour, 51 pages, Free **Postal charges** $3.50 for orders up to £250 value **Delivery** Royal Mail **Methods of Payment** Cheque, Credit Card, American Express, Diners Club

THE MEMORIAL FIRMS
Masonry Works
Priors Haw Road
North Weldon Industrial Estate
Corby
Northamptonshire
NN17 5JG
Telephone
01536 260781
Fax
01563 204265

Funerals
The Memorial Firms carry out a comprehensive service in supplying, engraving and installing headstones and monuments crafted from stone, marble or granite. Granite lawn design memorial, from £331; white marble kerb design, from £475; vases from £46.

Catalogue Annually, A4, Catalogue, Colour and B/W, 20 pages, Free **Postal charges** Varies with item **Delivery** Courier, In-house delivery **Methods of Payment** Cheque, Stage Payments, Credit Card

THE NATURAL HISTORY MUSEUM CATALOGUE
Euroway Business Park
Swindon
Wiltshire
SN5 8SN
Telephone
01793 431900
Fax
01793 487002

General gifts
This catalogue has been designed to provide a wealth of ideas for gifts and also to raise valuable funds for educational and research work at the Museum. There are over 200 items on offer, all inspired by the natural world from a Dinosaur Hunter's Kit, £17.50, to a Didgeridoo, £49.95. There are some wonderful and unusual gifts in this catalogue to support a worthwhile cause.

Catalogue Annually, A5, Catalogue, Colour, 31 pages, Free **Postal charges** £3.25 **Delivery** Royal Mail **Methods of Payment** Cheque, Postal Order, Credit Card, American Express, Diners Club

RSPCA TRADING LTD
FREEPOST
PO Box 38
Burton on Trent
Staffordshire
DE14 1BR
Telephone
01283 506125

Gifts
A comprehensive catalogue of quality gifts, household items, cards and clothes which supports a well-known charity. Choose from a colourful bone china cafetière, £49.95, with mugs to match, set of three £14.99, to a set of wildlife selection birthday cards, 2 packs for £3.75.

Catalogue Bi-annually, A4, Catalogue, Colour, 40 pages, Free **Postal charges** Up to £69.99, £3.35; £70 and over, free **Methods of Payment** Cheque, Postal Order

TRAIDCRAFT PLC
Kingsway North
Gateshead
Tyne & Wear
NE11 0NE
Telephone
0191 491 0855
Fax
0191 487 0133

Clothes, household items, stationery

Traidcraft challenges the economic exploitation of the poor by demonstrating that trade with the Third World can and should be based on justice, concern for people and care for the environment. Traidcraft presents a variety of original products: you could choose, for example, a beautifully embroidered waistcoat from Thailand (£35), a handwoven dhurrie from India (£39), or stationery from Nepal (£5.95 for a wallet with 20 sheets of natural A5 writing paper and 10 blue envelopes).

Catalogue Bi-annually, A4, Catalogue, Colour, 47 pages, 95p **Postal charges** Orders up to £75.00, add £3.50; orders over £75.00, free. **Delivery** Royal Mail **Methods of Payment** Cheque, Credit Card

Gifts

A TOAST BY POST
829 Lisburn Road
Balmoral
Belfast
Northern Ireland
BT9 7GY
Telephone
01232 661122
Fax
01232 666686

Named-brands gift bottles
What better way to celebrate a special occasion, a birthday or to say thank-you than by sending a Toast By Post? The company offers a choice of well-known drinks, including Martell VSOP Cognac, £33.95, Lambert Extra Dry NV Champagne, £24.95, and Lindemans Cabernet Sauvignon Red Wine, £15.95, which it sends by first-class post, well-packaged in a gift box with a personal message card.
Catalogue Annually, Third A4, Leaflets, Colour, 4, pages, Free **Postal charges** Free **Delivery** Royal Mail **Methods of Payment** Cheque, Postal Order, Credit Card

ACTIONAID TRADING PROMOTIONS
Nancegollan
Helston
Cornwall
TR13 OTT
Telephone
01209 831456

Stationery and gifts
Actionaid is a registered charity working in 20 countries with some of the world's poorest children, families and communities to make lasting improvements in health and education to their standard of living. Its well-produced catalogue features an attractive selection of cards, wrapping paper and gifts, including a Nefertiti silk scarf, £35.95; aromatherapy bath oil set, £8.95; silver filigree brooch, £17.99; Hasseena rug, £10.95; and T-shirts from £9.95.
Catalogue Annually, A5, Catalogue, Colour, 20 pages, Free **Postal charges** Varies with item **Delivery** Royal Mail, Parcelforce **Methods of Payment** Cheque, Credit Card, Switch

ALEXANDERS THE JEWELLERS
Alexander House
3 Castle Street
Farnham
Surrey
GU9 7HR
Telephone
01252 737373
Fax
01252 733721

Classic gifts
Alexanders offers a selection of classic gifts suitable for weddings, christenings, birthdays or to treat yourself. There are leather and silver books (Bible, £32.50; photograph album, £52.50), silver and reed picture frames (from £25.95), decanter labels (£12.50) and hand-painted enamel boxes (from £21).

Catalogue Annually, Third A4, Brochure, Colour, 6 pages, Free **Postal charges** £2.50 **Delivery** Royal Mail **Methods of Payment** Cheque, Credit Card, American Express, Diners Club

ALISON PERRYMAN
Contemporary Pewter
102 Stondon Park
London
SE23 1JS
Telephone
0181 291 2609

Pewter gifts
Alison Perryman sells unusual pewter items such as cocktail stirrers in flame, cone, shell or Aztec designs in a pewter or black finish for £5; letter-openers in snake, shell or sea-horse design for £14.95; and candlesticks from £10. There are also cuff-links, tie-clips, key-rings, pendants, cork screws and mirrors.

Catalogue A4, Leaflets, Colour and B/W, 1 page, Free **Postal charges** Varies with item **Delivery** Parcelforce **Methods of Payment** Cheque, Credit Card

THE ALPACA COLLECTION
16 Warstone Parade East
Hockley
Birmingham
West Midlands
B18 6NR
Telephone
0121 212 2550
Fax
0121 212 1948

Latin American handicrafts, textiles and clothing
The Alpaca Collection's folder of photographs features colourful woven bags and backpacks; adults' and children's clothing; wood and ceramic handicrafts; mobiles; textiles, jewellery and accessories from Latin American countries. Aimed more at the retail trade than individuals, there is a minimum order of £150 for account customers and £100 for customers at the warehouse. Trio Alpaca cardigan, £31.90; Peruvian chess set, £10.60; Bolivian backpack, £10.60; alpaca knitted hats, £12.75 for three; Pappallacta bells

mobile, £7.25; bread-dough earrings, £5 for 10; Ecuadorian shawl, £2.75; ceramic toucan, £1.75.

Catalogue Annually, A4, Leaflets, Colour and B/W, 14 pages, Free **Postal charges** £7 for orders up to £200 **Delivery** Royal Mail, Parcelforce, Courier **Methods of Payment** Cheque, Credit Card

THE ANIMAL WELFARE TRUST
Tylers Way
Watford by-Pass
Watford
Hertfordshire
WD2 8HQ
Telephone
0181 950 8215
Fax
0181 420 4454

Gifts

The Animal Welfare Trust is a registered charity founded in 1971 to care for and re-home dogs, cats and other animals which would otherwise be abandoned, left to stray or put to sleep. The catalogue offers a range of gifts, the proceeds of which are used to assist in the upkeep of the Trust's Animal Rescue Centre. Pack of 10 Christmas cards with envelopes, £2.50; soft toys, £2.50; PVC apron, £5.50; duck door wedge, £6.25; sweatshirt with logo, £16.99.

Catalogue Annually, A4, Brochure, Colour, 6 pages, Free **Postal charges** Varies with item **Delivery** Royal Mail, Parcelforce **Methods of Payment** Cheque, Postal Order, Credit Card

APPALACHIA: THE FOLK ART SHOP
14a George Street
St Albans
Hertfordshire
AL3 4ER
Telephone
01727 836796
Fax
01992 467560

Traditional American-made arts, crafts and soft furnishings

A spin-off from the successful shop of the same name in St Albans, this small brochure features the most popular items from the retail outlet. The range includes a set of five decorated Shaker boxes, £47.99; Tillie, the herb lady doll, £39.99; attractive blanket throws from the US, from £39.99; Kentucky clocks, from £24.99; and wooden hearts with homespun tie, £3.99.

Catalogue Annually, A4, Leaflets, Colour, 1 page, Free **Postal charges** Varies with item **Delivery** Royal Mail **Methods of Payment** Cheque, Credit Card

GIFTS

BALLOON CITY
65/66 Woodrow
London
SE18 5DH
Telephone
0181 856 5222
Fax
0181 317 0394

Balloons, chocolates and gifts
Delight and surprise your friends and relations with a helium-filled balloon, Godiva chocolates, Champagne, a teddy bear, or another gift. The 14in-diameter balloon, pre-printed with a message of your choice, is posted in a candy-striped box filled with tissue paper. It has lots of ribbon attached and a personal card and will stay inflated for about 10 days, price £15.95. Balloon plus 4oz Godiva chocolates, £21; balloon plus one bottle of French Champagne, £37.
Catalogue Annually, A4, Leaflets, Colour and B/W, 4 pages, Free **Postal charges** Free **Delivery** Royal Mail, Courier **Methods of Payment** Cheque, Credit Card

BARCLAY & BODIE
7–9 Blenheim Terrace
London
NW8 0EH
Telephone
0171 372 5705
Fax
0171 328 4266

Gifts
The Barclay & Bodie catalogue contains a superior selection of gifts. Ruth Barclay and Sherrie Bodie have chosen their favourites from their London shop and offer a gift-wrapping and personal message service, too. Hand-painted tooth fairy on a wooden box, £8.50; linen hand-towels, £12.50; hand-thrown pottery cat and dog bowls with bone, mouse or paw motif, £19.95, and plastic mats, £5.95; brocade sewing roll, £30; Parisian check cotton hanging photograph frame, £36; Harold Lloyd clock for silent movie fans, £45.50.
Catalogue Annually, A5, Catalogue, Colour, 28 pages, Free **Postal charges** £4.50 **Delivery** Royal Mail, Parcelforce **Methods of Payment** Cheque, Credit Card, American Express

BECKETT AND GRAHAM
3 Langton Street
London
SW10 0JL

Gifts
Beckett and Graham's philosophy is to stock original and unusual items which are unlikely to be found elsewhere – in fact many are exclusive to the company. Their stock is sourced from Italy,

Telephone
0171 376 3855
Fax
0171 376 3856

France, Belgium, the UK and the USA and includes stylish telephone-directory covers from America, and L'Artisan Parfumeur collection of scented candles, room sprays and burning oils. Gifts include rose-ended pencils £2.99; Scottie dog candle, box of three £9.95; toiletries; Christmas-tree decorations and gifts for golfers; urn-shaped lampbase; rectangular table mats; leopardskin perspex letter rack or book holder; silver-plated pens with silver horse, duck or fox; wired cherub ribbon in red in rolls of 20m; men's drawstring shoe bag in burgundy/white stripe; Trumpres extract of lime soap; Scrabble pure silk braces, boxed with both clip and button ends; and Tempus Fugit box clock by Matthew Rice. There is also a Beckett and Graham shop.

Catalogue Annually, A4, Brochure, Colour, 19 pages, £1.70 **Postal charges** Varies with item **Delivery** In-house delivery **Methods of Payment** Cheque, Postal Order, Credit Card

BETTYS & TAYLORS BY POST
1 Parliament Street
Harrogate
North Yorkshire
HG1 2QU
Telephone
01423 886055
Fax
01423 881083

Tea, coffee and gifts

Bettys & Taylors of Harrogate supply specialist teas and coffees along with presentation gifts. Traditional Easter specialities range from a luxury hamper, £139.84, including sparkling wine, Simnel cake, coffee, tea and chocolate goodies, to milk-chocolate eggs hand-decorated with sugarpaste primroses and bluebells, in two sizes, £11.30 or £13.40. The eggs are made from the finest quality Belgian chocolate and the company's team of Swiss-trained confectioners fill the moulds twice to give an extra luxurious coating of chocolate.

Catalogue Bi-monthly, Third A4, Catalogue, Colour, 17 pages, Free **Postal charges** £5.60 **Delivery** Courier, Parcelforce **Methods of Payment** Cheque, Credit Card

BEVERLY HILLS BAKERY
3 Egerton Terrace
London
SW3 2BX
Telephone
0171 584 4401
Fax
0171 584 1106

Muffins, cookies and brownies
Freshly baked in their Knightsbridge bakery every day, these cakes are free from preservatives and made with the best ingredients including Belgian Chocolate and Georgia Pecans.

Gift Baskets containing mini-muffins, cookies and brownies are delivered throughout London and cost from £21 per basket. Gift Tins containing mini-muffins and brownies are delivered nationwide and cost £35.

Catalogue Annually, A5, Brochure, Colour, 4 pages, Free
Postal charges Free **Delivery** Parcelforce, Royal Mail
Methods of Payment Credit Card

BIRCHALL'S
The Pipe Shop
14 Talbot Road
Blackpool
Lancashire
FY1 1LF
Telephone
01253 24218
Fax
01253 291659

Pipes, tobacco and coffee
Birchall's was founded in 1834 and is one of the country's oldest tobacconists. Its attractive, sepia catalogue features specialist loose, chewing and wrapped tobaccos, each with a brief description of aroma and smoking qualities, plus cigars, coffees, and a video, 'At Peace With Your Pipe'. There are pipes and accessories, and a repair and renovation service is offered. Loose tobaccos from £2.60/25g; Birchall's pipes, £19.99; Ferndown pipes, £79.95.

Catalogue Annually, A5, Catalogue, B/W, 16 pages, 25p
Postal charges 10 percent of total **Delivery** Royal Mail
Methods of Payment Cheque, Postal Order, Credit Card

BITS & PIECES (UK) LTD
Harrington Dock
Liverpool
Merseyside
L70 1AX
Telephone
0151 702 8858
Fax
0151 708 8803

Gifts and puzzles
Bits & Pieces catalogue contains the very best quality puzzles, models, games, books and gifts, from a build-your-own Russian cathedral (St Basil's) to The Kamei Secret Box Collection, including the Bow Gift Box where the bow is the secret to the lock with its intricate movements; savings bank slot-machine, great for kids, and the Eiffel Tower in a 3-D jigsaw. Wonderfully different presents for everyone.

Catalogue Annually, A4, Catalogue, Colour, 31 pages, Free **Postal charges** £2.95 **Delivery** Royal Mail **Methods of Payment** Cheque, Credit Card

BLOOMS OF GUERNSEY
Portinfer Coast Road
Vale
Guernsey
Channel Islands
Telephone
01481 53085
Fax
01481 53840

Flowers and dolls
Blooms of Guernsey have won several awards for their exhibits and they offer a mail service sending pinks, gypsy, chincherinchees, lilies, carnations, Miss Dianas and freesias. To the UK, there is no charge for postage and packing, and complimentary fern is added. For the rest of Europe there is a £5 charge, and flowers sent to Europe are done so at the purchaser's risk. Blooms also sell teddy bears and rabbits which can have a personal message on a red or blue sweater and a Guernsey Lily doll with a porcelain face and soft body, but which cannot have a message.

BOW ART (PRINTS BY POST)
PO Box 6471
London
E3 5UB
Telephone
01225 892009
Fax
01225 892009

Pictures
Bow Art specialises in reproductions of fine art. Their new series of works by Modern British Painters includes two prints by Eric Ravilious: 'Tea at Furlongs' and 'Interior at Furlongs', painted in 1939 while Ravilious was staying with friends near Lewes in Sussex. These two editions are printed on acid-free paper with light-fast inks. Price: £34.50 each. All prints are supplied unframed.

Catalogue A5, Leaflets, Colour, 1 page, Free **Postal charges** £2.00 (UK); £6.00 (Europe and Eire); £9.00 (rest of world) for up to 4 prints **Delivery** Parcelforce **Methods of Payment** Cheque, Postal Order

BRITISH MUSEUM PUBLICATIONS
British Museum Connection
(Mail Order)

Books and gifts
The catalogue is designed to give a unique flavour of the Museum's varied collections from remote antiquity to the present. There is everything from hand-crafted replicas to gifts inspired by

Unit A
Chettisham Business Park
Ely
Cambridgeshire
CB6 1RY
Telephone
01353 668400

the exhibits. For example, Egyptian cat with earrings, £85; pharaoh scarves, £39.95; Egyptian blue earthenware and tea towels; hieroglyph bags, £11.95; a Roman copy of Socrates, £85. There are also pretty Christmas cards with pheasants, robins, doves, the Madonna and the Lamb of God designs. If you want to send as a gift, you can include a gift message and the item will be sent direct to the recipient at a charge of £1 extra.

Catalogue Annually, A6, Catalogue, Colour, 24 pages, Free **Postal charges** Up to £40, £3.95; up to £100, £5.95; over £100, £6.95 within UK. 48-hr express delivery, £3.50 extra **Delivery** Royal Mail **Methods of Payment** Cheque, Postal Order, Credit Card

BRITISH RED CROSS
FREEPOST
PO Box 38
Burton-on-Trent
Staffordshire
DE14 1BR
Telephone
01283 510111

Gifts and clothes

This is a charity catalogue, with the usual diverse range of goods, many of which are of ethnic origin. You can buy an entire set of tableware for four, including cutlery, napkins and place mats for £29.99 or a pack of assorted birthday cards for £3.99. Products are clearly illustrated and range from stationery and office accessories, which can be personalised, to sweatshirts and T-shirts with flora or fauna motifs. Some worthwhile bargains are to be found.

BRUFORD & HEMING LTD
28 Conduit Street
New Bond Street
London
W1R 9TA
Telephone
0171 629 4289
Fax
0171 493 5879

Silverware

While they are renowned for their fine antique silver and jewellery, Bruford & Heming produce a catalogue that features only newly produced silver items, all fully hallmarked. Gift items include photograph frames (from £20), small perfume bottles (from £43), silver bookmarks (from £11) and cutlery sets (from £1,200).

New and antique jewellery is displayed in an additional colour brochure, arranged according to price. An antique five-stone rhodolite garnet half-hoop ring (Chester 1878) will set you back £320, or for £1,530 you could buy a ruby, diamond and rock crystal Art Deco-style brooch.

Catalogue A5, Catalogue, Colour, 36 pages, Free **Postal charges** Free **Delivery** Royal Mail **Methods of Payment** Cheque, Credit Card, American Express

BURBERRY'S
18–22 Haymarket
London
SW1Y 4DQ
Telephone
0171 930 7803
Fax
0171 839 2418

Clothes, accessories, food and gifts

Burberrys of London provide a wide range of tailored clothes for both adults and children. All the merchandise in the catalogue is available from their stores in the United Kingdom or direct through mail order. Other goods on offer are toys (£25.00 for a teddy bear), knitwear, raincoats (£405.00), umbrellas, luggage, fragrances and watches (£325.00). There are also food hampers on offer containing jams, whisky, biscuits, chocolate, etc.

If you order clothes, the Burberrys visiting-tailor service will see that you have them made to measure and cut to your size and style. All gifts are gift-wrapped on request with no extra charge and you can even have your raincoat monogrammed with your own initials.

Catalogue Bi-annually, A4, Catalogue, Colour and B/W, 20 pages pages, £2.00 **Postal charges** For UK orders £3.50 **Delivery** In-house delivery **Methods of Payment** Cheque, Postal Order, Credit Card, American Express, Diners Club, Switch

BYGONE NEWS
56 Hill Road
Weston-super-Mare
Somerset
BS23 2RZ
Telephone
01934 412844

Birthday, anniversary and historical newspapers

Bygone News hold vast stocks of original newspapers for the years 1890–1995, providing an unusual and authentic gift for birthdays, anniversaries and retirements. Each newspaper is supplied in an attractive printed presentation folder,

Fax
01934 412844

together with a matching gift card, and these are despatched in a strong postal carton. For really special occasions, there is an attractive black leather folder with golden motif on the front cover (£11 each). These can be personalised with the recipient's initials for £3.50. Gifts can be sent direct to the recipient, enclosing a personal message. Delivery is normally 10–14 days and a small surcharge is made for the 24-hour service. Newspapers can be sent worldwide, the only additional cost being the overseas postage. Newspaper gifts start at £18. Also available are Pathé newsreel videos from 1930.

Catalogue A4 and A5, Leaflets, B/W, 3 pages, Free **Delivery** Royal Mail **Methods of Payment** Cheque, Postal Order, Credit Card, Switch

CANCER RESEARCH CAMPAIGN
6–10 Cambridge Terrace
Regents Park
London
NW1 4JL
Telephone
01283 506444

Gifts and cards

Each purchase from this catalogue makes a direct contribution to the Campaign's work. There is a diverse range of gifts including a 'Floating Whale Plug' and a 'Fish Design Waistcoat', T-shirts, and holdalls. The easy tick-off order form makes sure you waste no time choosing between those gift-card sets or the wealth of personalised pens, pencils and even luggage straps.

Catalogue Annually, A4, Catalogue, Colour, 32 pages, Free **Postal charges** Varies with item **Delivery** Royal Mail **Methods of Payment** Cheque, Postal Order, Credit Card

CHANTAL DEVENPORT
28 The Avenue
London
W4 1HT
Telephone
0181 995 6564

Hand-painted gifts for children

For an individual, personalised present which will be treasured for years to come, Chantal Devenport's collection of personalised hand-painted gifts for children are exquisite. Colouring boxes with a pirate design for boys and with a floral design for girls contain 12 coloured pencils, 3 lead pencils, a sharpener, eraser and ruler. Also featured is a wooden skipping rope with initials on the handles; a glass pen with a glass stand and a tiny pot of Indian ink – all hand-painted with pink rosebuds. The Baby Boxes are the ultimate gift for a baby. For boys, there's the Dancing Teddy Design and for girls the Baby Mouse Design. Each box contains a face-cloth trimmed and embroidered, hand-painted nappy pins, hand-painted nail scissors, a set of soaps and other wonderful treats.

Catalogue Annually, A5, Brochure, Colour, 8 pages, Free **Postal charges** Varies with item **Delivery** Royal Mail **Methods of Payment** Cheque, Postal Order

CHERWELL DIRECT LIMITED
Hawkins House
14 Black Bourton Road
Carterton
Oxfordshire
OX18 3DJ
Telephone
01993 843700
Fax
01993 840168

Gifts for men

Cherwell describe their catalogue as 'a unique medley of inspired ideas to delight the most discerning man'. These gifts include the Oxford library quartz alarm clock, bookend storage files, a traditional huntin' desk clock, genuine coach hide hip wallet and credit-card case, the traveller pocket alarm clock, a golf scorer, gold address book or bag tag, solid brass paperweights, a spirit flask, personal pewter motifs, personal sports flannel and matching hand-towels, and some old-fashioned games. Prices range from £5 to £70.

Catalogue A5, Catalogue, Colour, 8 pages, Free **Postal charges** £1.95; £5 in Europe; £7 elsewhere **Delivery** Royal Mail **Methods of Payment** Cheque, Postal Order, Credit Card, Switch

CHOC EXPRESS BY THORNTONS
Mint House
Newark Close
Royston
Hertfordshire
SG8 5HL

Luxury chocolates by post

With Choc Express you can send a ChocoGram direct to any UK address (overseas service also available). Each ChocoGram contains a selection of luxury Thorntons milk, dark and white chocolates in a crush-proof outer box designed to fit through the letterbox. A full-size greetings card

Telephone
01763 241444
Fax
01763 245460

is included with your personal message up to 20 words. Standard, 200g, £12.95. Other selections are available and the ChocoGram Deluxe, £24.95, even includes a half-bottle of Champagne.

Catalogue Annually, A5, Brochure, Colour, 8 pages, Free **Postal charges** Special delivery, £5 extra **Delivery** Royal Mail, Courier **Methods of Payment** Cheque, Credit Card

COMPASSION IN WORLD FARMING
Charles House
5A Charles Street
Petersfield
Hampshire
GU32 3EH
Telephone
01730 264208
Fax
01730 260791

Gifts
Profits from the Compassion in World Farming catalogue go directly towards funding its campaigns for farm animals. The products offered are well-designed and good quality. Free-range T-shirt, £11.99; A World of Difference for Farm Animals mug, £3.99; campaign window stickers, £1.50; recycled pens, 99p.

Catalogue Annually, A5, Catalogue, Colour, 8 pages, Free **Postal charges** £2.50 for orders up to £50; free for orders of more than £50 **Delivery** Royal Mail, Parcelforce **Methods of Payment** Cheque, Postal Order, Credit Card

THE CORNISH BULB COMPANY
Ashdown Nurseries
Ashton
Helston
Cornwall
TR13 9BR
Telephone
01736 762469
Fax
01736 763662

Fresh flowers and chocolates
This company sends out fresh flowers including freesias (£9.95 for 20 boxed freesias), spray carnations (from £10.95 for 15), roses (from £12.95 for 10), daffodils (from £5.50 for 15), anemones (£9.50 for 40) and Cornish pinks (£7.45 for 30). They also offer luxury candies and chocolates such as Clotted Cream Fudge (£2.95 for 170g), Turkish Delight (£2.95 for 170g), and Chocolate Easter Eggs decorated with sugar flowers (£3.35).

Catalogue Bi-annually, A5, Leaflets, B/W, 4 pages, Free **Postal charges** For guaranteed next-day delivery add £2.70 to flower cost (UK), £4.00 (Europe) **Delivery** Royal Mail **Methods of Payment** Cheque, Credit Card, Postal Order

COUNTRYWIDE WORKSHOPS CHARITABLE TRUST

47 Fisherton Street
Salisbury
Wiltshire
SP2 7SU
Telephone
01722 326886
Fax
01722 411092

Clothes, gifts, furniture and toys

Countrywide Workshops is a charitable trust whose aim is to create work for disabled people by selling the goods they make and encouraging their abilities. This catalogue contains a selection of beautifully made products from both home-workers and sheltered workshops. Made-to-measure skirts in Welsh wool, from £45; leather handbag, £41.25; hand-engraved glasses, from £22.50 for a set of six liqueur tumblers; hand-shaped nursery ark with 18 animals, £69.50; shoebag with ballet or trainer motif, £4.70; teddy clock, £16.50; bunkbeds, £305; and for the garden, a wooden slatted composter, £35.75.

Catalogue Quarterly, A5, Catalogue, Colour, 40 pages, Free **Postal charges** Free **Delivery** Royal Mail, Parcelforce **Methods of Payment** Cheque, Postal Order, Credit Card

CURIOUS CATERPILLAR BY POST

Ravensden Farm
Bedford Road
Rushden
Northamptonshire
NN10 0SQ
Telephone
01933 410650
Fax
01933 410108

Toys and gifts

Curious Caterpillar supplies party presents, toys and gifts suitable for any time of year. It has a particularly good range of small toys for Christmas stocking fillers. Impressively, most orders are dispatched within two days and prices are very reasonable. Mini animals, 20p; dolphin eraser, 23p; animal mug, 50p; troll-top pencil, 70p; bendable dinosaurs, £1.50; Friendship Bracelets kit, £2.95; Potato Clock, £12.95. A bulk price list is available for schools and fund raisers.

Catalogue Annually, A5, Catalogue, Colour, 32 pages, Free **Postal charges** £2.95 for orders up to £60; free for orders of more than £60 **Delivery** Royal Mail, Parcelforce **Methods of Payment** Cheque, Postal Order, Credit Card

CYNOSURE LTD
351 Fulham Palace Road
London
SW6 6TB
Telephone
0171 610 9395
Fax
0171 610 9394

Modern and antique silver and silver plate

Established in 1985, Cynosure has always aimed at offering the best possible choice of the highest quality hallmarked modern silver and silver plate, from sporting-related decorative items to presentation cups or salvers, from tableware and flatware to cuff-links, creamers and photograph frames. No special commission, engraving, replating or repair is beyond Cynosure's silversmiths' reputation for excellence in materials, quality, style and handicraft. No gift suggestion is beyond their imagination. Cynosure is now expanding to include fine antique silver and silver plate to complete the full silver range. With a small team of expert silver and jewellery valuers, Cynosure can offer insurance valuations, as well as reliable antique-silver collecting, purchasing and reparation services. The silver and silver plate are clearly illustrated in Cynosure's annual catalogue and are included in their mail-order services. Alternatively, you can visit their new premises where their silver experts will be pleased to show you around and answer any queries. Modern silver prices start from £7 for a charm and antique silver prices start from £10 for teaspoons. Cynosure have two other catalogues: a 56-page colour A4 catalogue which costs £8, refundable against any purchase, and a 6-page colour cutlery catalogue which is free.

Catalogue Annually, A4, Catalogue, Colour and B/W, 8 pages, Free **Postal charges** Varies with item **Delivery** Royal Mail, Parcelforce, Carriers **Methods of Payment** Cheque, Postal Order, Credit Card, Switch, Diners Club

DECORATIVE STAINED GLASS KENMORE LTD
Queensberry Street
Annan

Decorative stained glass

The Decorative Stained Glass range includes roundels, mirror boxes and photograph frames for trade or retail. You can choose from a variety of

Dumfriesshire
Scotland
DG12 5BL
Telephone
01461 204051
Fax
01461 203718

co-ordinated designs such as 'Harvest Mice and Poppies'.

Small Flower Fairies or Beatrix Potter boxes start at £11.50; photograph frames cost £15.50; and large brass window roundels cost £13.95.

Catalogue A4, Leaflets, Colour, 5 pages, Free **Postal charges** Free **Delivery** Royal Mail **Methods of Payment** Cheque

DIVINE INSPIRATION (DIRECT) LTD
PO Box 1110
Windsor
Berkshire
SL4 2SX
Telephone
01753 620777
Fax
01753 832799

Craft gifts

Divine Inspiration acts as an outlet for Christian artists and craftsmen to offer their products to the public. Items range from jewellery with an 'angel' or 'cross' theme (prices from £9.95 for an angel brass charm or cross of nails); to framed prints (from £19.95); afghan rugs (£39.95); and handmade mirrors (from £29.95); and clocks (£49.95) with a textured plaster finish.

Catalogue Catalogue, Colour, 15 pages, Free **Postal charges** Varies with item **Delivery** Royal Mail **Methods of Payment** Cheque, Credit Card

EDRADOUR DISTILLERY
Pitlochry
Perthshire
PH16 5JP
Telephone
01796 472095
Fax
01796 472002

Distillery gifts

Edradour, founded in 1825, is the smallest whisky distillery in Scotland. Set in the hills above Pitlochry, it is a fine example of traditional Scotch Whisky distilling. The colour brochure provides a clear presentation of the distillery's labelled gifts, including the Edradour decanter, £69; presentation flagon of Edradour Single Malt Whisky, £31; sweatshirt with logo £13.95; and Edradour whisky fudge, £2.

Catalogue Annually, A5, Brochure, Colour, 6 pages, Free **Postal charges** Varies with item **Delivery** Royal Mail **Methods of Payment** Cheque, Credit Card, American Express, Switch

ESSCENTS

Downs Court Business Centre
29 The Downs
Altrincham
Cheshire
WA14 2QD
Telephone
0161 929 6654
Fax
0161 428 5439

Gifts inspired by nature

The Esscents Collection is packed full of attractive gifts, 90 per cent of which are made in Great Britain. Many of the items are refreshingly different from those offered in other catalogues. There is a seascene mirror, signed by the artist (£29.99); Jacob wool cushion (£45); banana paper pot pourri (£5.85); and a unique collapsible sycamore wood basket (£49.99).

Catalogue Annually, A5, Catalogue, Colour, 30 pages, Free **Postal charges** £2.95 **Delivery** Royal Mail, Parcelforce **Methods of Payment** Cheque, Credit Card, Switch

EXIMIOUS LTD

10 West Halkin Street
Belgravia
London
SW1R 8JL
Telephone
0171 235 7828
Fax
0171 259 5542

Luxury gifts

Eximious takes pride in providing a unique and personal service to all customers. The majority of products are designed by and manufactured exclusively for them and many may be monogrammed or inscribed.

A ladybird trunk box in French Limoges porcelain, hand-painted, for £87; a personalized nappy-pin cup with the handle in the shape of a nappy pin made in pewter, can be personalized for £36. Monogrammed shoe bags for £23 would make an ideal present for Christmas, as would the personalized silver-plated bottle stopper for £26.50, and for the golfer a pair of golfer cuff-links in sterling silver and enamelwork for £37.50.

Catalogue Quarterly, A4, Brochure, Colour, 23 pages, Free **Postal charges** £5.50 per order **Delivery** Royal Mail **Methods of Payment** Cheque, Credit Card, American Express

FAVOURITE THINGS

1 Carrigshaun
Old Avenue
Weybridge
Surrey

Nursery accessories

Favourite Things is a delightful collection of hand-made gifts for babies and children using colourful fabrics, quilting and appliqué. There is an ingenious crayoning apron with little pockets

GIFTS

KT13 0PG
Telephone
01932 843720
Fax
01932 846044

along the bottom to hold crayons (£8.95); a sailor teddy playmat/quilt (£42); a soft carrying house containing six stuffed zoo animals (£14.99); enchanting pyjama cases (from £18.99); and fun swimming bags with plastic linings (£8.95).

Catalogue Annually, A4, Leaflets, Colour and B/W, 5 pages, Free **Postal charges** Varies with item **Delivery** Royal Mail **Methods of Payment** Cheque, Postal Order

THE FINISHING TOUCH
197 New King's Road
London
SW6 4SR
Telephone
0171 736 0410
Fax
0171 371 9102

Quality affordable gifts
With a shop also at New King's Road, this catalogue gives a taste of the much larger range of items in stock. Many of the items shown here are under £5 and thus make affordable gifts. There are nickel-plated multi-ring key holders, coloured stone cuff-links, travelling CD cases, Italian travelling accessories, silver-plated sewing kit, gentleman's desk tidy, the initialled hedgehog, silver-plated disc bottle stopper, leather initialled box, gift-wrapped clock, labrador key-rings, set of three cachepots on a tray, a range of costume jewellery, enamelled handbag atomiser, printed leather glasses case, square leather sticky-note holder, silver-plated double-faced mirror and leather credit-card case.

Catalogue Annually, A5, Catalogue, Colour, 12 pages, Free **Postal charges** £2.99 **Delivery** Royal Mail **Methods of Payment** Cheque, Postal Order, Switch, Credit Card

FIRST IMPRESSIONS
Lewes Road
Forest Row
East Sussex
RH18 5AX
Telephone
01342 824246
Fax
01342 822289

Jewellery and gifts
'First Impressions' describes the metalwork this company makes. Everything is a first copy of the antique, or it is stamped in the original French steel dies. All their jewellery is stamped first in brass then finished and silver-plated.

Their 'Roses' catalogue contains attractive and inexpensive gift items such as a Dartington crystal pot-pourri jar (£18.50) and a silver Clary brooch (£16.50). There are also buckles, perfume flasks,

GIFTS

blotters, pomanders, dinner table decorations and photograph frames.

Catalogue A6, Catalogue, Colour, 23 pages, Free **Postal charges** Free **Delivery** Royal Mail **Methods of Payment** Credit Card, Cheque

THE FLYING DUCK COMPANY
47 Castelnau
London
SW13 9RT

Unusual gifts and stocking fillers

Small catalogue with unusual gifts such as the Gary Larson Desk Calendar, a set of flying ducks, a car coffee-maker, a bridge cloth, key finder, duck clothes brush, frog candlesticks, disco specs, radio hats, talking teddy bear, braid-your-hair kit and friendship-bracelet kit. Useful for adults who have everything, including a sense of humour, and older children. Prices range from £3.99 to £15.99. The catalogue does not contain a telephone-ordering number.

Catalogue Bi-annually, A5, Catalogue, Colour, 8 pages, Free **Postal charges** £2.95 **Delivery** Royal Mail **Methods of Payment** Credit Card, Postal Order, Cheque

FRUITFUL OCCASIONS
Highfield Drive
St Leonards On Sea
East Sussex
TN38 9PP
Telephone
01424 850950
Fax
01424 855000

Baskets of fruit

These fruit baskets contain a selection of either Traditional or Exotic Fruits which are hand-picked and carefully packaged to arrive at your door in perfect condition. The Traditional Basket costs £24.99 and the Exotic Basket £29.99. Prices include mid-week delivery anywhere in mainland UK and your own special message.

Catalogue By Advertising, Colour, 1 page, Free **Postal charges** Free **Delivery** Royal Mail **Methods of Payment** Cheque, Credit Card

THE GENERAL TRADING COMPANY LTD
144 Sloane Square
London
SW1X 9BL

Furniture, kitchenware, accessories, gifts

The General Trading Company has been selling superior household goods for the last 120 years. Their shop, in Sloane Square, London, boasts no less than four Royal Warrants and includes a floor of antiques.

Telephone
0171 730 0411
Fax
0171 823 4624

The catalogue, while just scraping the surface of the vast range in the shop, nevertheless has an excellent selection of items for all parts of the house. There are chairs, lamps, picture frames, candlesticks, garden furniture, cutlery, plates, glassware and some toys. All the goods are beautifully made and the sort of the thing you might not find elsewhere.

Catalogue Annually, A5, Catalogue, Colour, 31 pages **Postal charges** £5.50 for orders sent within the UK **Delivery** Royal Mail **Methods of Payment** Cheque, Postal Order, Credit Card, American Express, Diners Club

THE GRANARY
Church Road
Bacton
Norfolk
NR12 OJP
Telephone
01692 651086
Fax
same

Danish pottery, candles and mobiles

This small Danish company based in Norfolk offers attractive flower pots and bowls in interesting colours. A plain lime-green bowl 17cm in diameter and 5cm in height costs £6; a blue pot (height 12cm, diameter 13cm) with an angel on one side and a saucer costs £25. Their candles come in many colours and include a cinnamon-scented candle ball in oxblood red for £3. The paper mobiles are in the form of pandas, bassett hounds and dolphins and there are special Christmas and Easter designs. Prices from £2.50.

Catalogue A4, Leaflets, Colour, 8 pages, Free **Postal charges** Orders up to £50.00, add £3.25; up to £100.00, £4.50; up to £150.00, £5.00; up to £200.00, £7.00; over £200.00, free **Delivery** Parcelforce **Methods of Payment** Cheque, COD

GRANTS OF DALVEY
FREEPOST 1032
Alness
Ross-shire
Scotland
IV17 0BR

Scottish gifts, whisky

The Grants of Dalvey range of gentlemen's personal accessories includes a Pocket Flask made from polished stainless steel (£28.95) which can hold the equivalent of five measures of your favourite tipple; an elegant Voyager travel clock

GIFTS

Telephone
01349 884111
Fax
01349 884100

(£49.95); and an invaluable Notebook Case (£29.95). All the items can be engraved and would make ideal gifts or presentations.

Catalogue Annually, A5, Leaflets, Colour, 6 pages, Free **Postal charges** £2.95 **Delivery** Royal Mail **Methods of Payment** Cheque, Credit Card, American Express

GREENPEACE CATALOGUE
PO Box 10
Gateshead
Tyne & Wear
NE8 1LL
Telephone
0191 491 0034
Fax
0191 487 0133

Gifts

Profits from this catalogue go towards helping Greenpeace to fund its campaigning activities. As one might expect, it is full of environmentally friendly products. These include well-designed clothes, mugs, badges, bowls, cards and a children's Eco Kit for tracking acid rain and water pollution. Elephant T-shirt, £8.50 children, £12.50 adult; whale mug, £2.99; 3-D wooden farm puzzle, £8.95; solar garden light, £79.99.

Catalogue Bi-annually, A5, Catalogue, Colour, 8 pages **Postal charges** £2.99 for orders up to £15; £3.99 for orders of more than £15 **Delivery** Royal Mail, Parcelforce **Methods of Payment** Credit Card, Cheque

GREY GOOSE CRACKERS
Unit 16
Blake House Centre
Rayne
Braintree
Essex
CM7 8SH
Telephone
01376 550354
Fax
01376 341444

Exclusive Christmas crackers

Grey Goose crackers stand out among the range of crackers offered in department stores and high street shops with unusual designs and even more unusual gifts inside.

Catalogue A4, Leaflets, Colour, Free **Delivery** Royal Mail **Methods of Payment** Cheque, Postal Order

HAWKIN & CO
St Margaret
Harleston

Toys, puzzles, scientific wonders

Hawkin's catalogue contains things you thought had gone for ever and things you never knew

GIFTS

Norfolk
IP20 0PJ
Telephone
01986 782458
Fax
01986 782468

existed, from toys that teach to curiosities and oddities. Revolving Bicycle Bell, £2.90, is larger than the usual and much louder. Butterfly Garden contains a 14in clear plastic and card butterfly house together with a feeding kit; with this comes a 'caterpillar voucher' which you free-post to the caterpillar farm and within a week you receive by post a container of special nutrient and five active caterpilllars, which within a short time hatch into Painted Lady Butterflies. The complete process takes about one month, price £19.95. There is a section of gifts suitable for stocking fillers all under £1. Hair-growing cat soap which comes in a sealed bag; when exposed to the air it begins to grow hair which after a few days becomes long and silky until the soap is used for washing when it reverts for ever to its hairless form.

There is also a wonderful selection of tin toys for collectors, which are not suitable for children, but are reminiscent of a bygone age, with a running dog at £8.90

Catalogue Annually, A4, Catalogue, Colour, 47 pages, Free **Postal charges** £2.95 on orders under £25 **Delivery** Royal Mail, Parcelforce **Methods of Payment** Cheque, Postal Order, Credit Card

INITIAL IDEAS
Ford House
48 Brownston Street
Modbury
Ivybridge
Devon
PL21 ORQ
Telephone
01548 831070
Fax
01548 831074

Gifts
The Initial Ideas catalogue contains a range of unusual and attractive gifts, many of which can be personalised with names or initials at no extra cost. Set of coloured pencils with name, £4.50; quilted initial hot-water bottle cover, £27.50; wooden perpetual calendar with hand-painted blocks, £52; child's rush-seated wooden chair with name, £89; découpage lamp, £135.

Catalogue Annually, A4, Catalogue, Colour, 16 pages, Free **Postal charges** £3.50 for each address regardless of how much you order **Delivery** Royal Mail, Parcelforce **Methods of Payment** Cheque, Credit Card, Switch

J G S METALWORK
Broomstick Estate
High Street
Edlesborough
Nr Dunstable
Bedfordshire
LU6 2HS
Telephone
01525 220360
Fax
01525 222786

Traditional weathervanes

'Imagine a cold grey day when unexpectedly a shaft of sunlight emerges from behind a cloud and plays upon your Golden Cockerel, he glistens and gleams and lightens your heart while pointing proudly into the wind.' So runs the inspirational description of one of this company's many hand-made weather-vanes. Commissions are taken, hand-painting is an option, and other items, including curtain rods and boot-scrapers, are offered. Small weathervane, £51.50; large, from £162.75.

Catalogue Annually, A5, Catalogue, B/W, 16 pages, Free **Postal charges** Varies with item **Delivery** Royal Mail, Parcelforce **Methods of Payment** Cheque, Postal Order, Credit Card

J & J CASH LTD
Torrington Avenue
Coventry
Warwickshire
West Midlands
CV4 9UZ
Telephone
01203 466466
Fax
01203 462525

Woven labels, gifts and greetings cards

Established since 1846, Cash's is synonymous with woven name tapes for school uniforms. This catalogue, however, shows that its range is much wider. They also offer framed woven pictures (including limited-edition woven silk ones), bookmarks, hand-crafted boxes and stationery.

Cash's recycled executive stationery and their luxury linen stationery cost £21.95 and £29.95 respectively for 100 printed sheets and envelopes. Personalised address labels in a choice of two typestyles cost £5.99 for 250.

Catalogue A4, Catalogue, Colour, 23 pages, Free **Postal charges** £2.95 **Delivery** Royal Mail **Methods of Payment** Cheque, Postal Order, Credit Card

JOHN HAMILTON STUDIO
The Parade
St Mary's
Isles of Scilly
TR21 0LP
Telephone
01720 422856
Fax
01720 422421

Tablemats, chopping boards, etc
John Hamilton's Scilly Island scenes are now reproduced on high-quality melamine laminate to make table-mats, coasters, trays, chopping boards, key racks and servers. A set of 6 table-mats, each with a different scene, costs £26.50 and the chopping boards are £10.50 each. The Studio also offers packs of notelets depicting John Hamilton's scenes of St Martins, Tresco, St Agnes and Bryher.

Catalogue A5, Leaflets, Colour, 4 pages, Free **Postal charges** Free **Delivery** Parcelforce **Methods of Payment** Cheque, Credit Card

KEEPSAKES
41 Dyserth Road
Rhyl
Clwyd
Wales
LL18 4DR
Telephone
01745 354971
Fax
same

Drinks with personalised labels
Here's a great idea for celebrating a special occasion. Send a personalised bottle (or bottles) of Champagne, port or spirits. You supply a colour photograph and message and Keepsakes will produce a unique label. A bottle of personalised vintage Champagne (0.75 litre) costs £39.95; Glen Grant Highland Malt, £33.50.

Catalogue Annually, A4, Leaflets, Colour and B/W, 5 pages, Free **Postal charges** Varies with item **Delivery** Courier **Methods of Payment** Cheque, Credit Card

LEUKAEMIA RESEARCH FUND/LRF TRADING
Yorke Road
Croxley Green
Rickmansworth
Hertfordshire
WD3 3TP
Telephone
01923 779181
Fax
01923 896745

Gifts and stationery
Profits from the sale of goods in this catalogue are covenanted entirely to the Leukaemia Research Fund, a registered charity. It offers an attractive range of Christmas cards, some with Welsh greetings, from £2.40 for a pack of 10; wrapping paper; stocking fillers; and gifts (book light, £3.45; games set, £2.95).

Catalogue Annually, A5, Catalogue, Colour, 32 pages, Free **Postal charges** Varies with item **Delivery** Royal Mail, Parcelforce **Methods of Payment** Cheque, Postal Order, Credit Card

LINDSAY OLINS
20 Upper Wimpole Street
London
W1M 7TA
Fax
0171 289 4771

General gifts
Lindsay Olins offers a range of gifts including silver cuff-links, silver-plated alphabet pots and fluted dishes, sterling silver circular key-rings, all individually boxed; leather-bound photograph albums, memo pads, looseleaf address books and entertaining books in bottle green, navy or burgundy as well as a range of pens; hand-painted wooden toys in four different themes: Zippo the Clown, Toytown, Mr and Mrs Teddy and Guardsman; washbags and newborn brush-and-comb sets made up in blue gingham; plus candles and pot pourri in various sizes, water carafes with hand-painted designs, notice boards in two sizes with various fabrics, notice boards for children in gingham check material. The items are all shown on individual postcards within an envelope with a separate price list.

Catalogue A6, Cards, Colour, Free **Postal charges** Varies with item **Delivery** Royal Mail **Methods of Payment** Cheque, Postal Order

LOCH FYNE OYSTERS
Clachan Farm
Ardkinglas
Cairndow
Argyll
PA26 8BH
Telephone
01499 600264
Fax
01499 600234

Oysters, smoked fish, gift boxes
This award-winning Scottish producer's catalogue lists a gourmet's selection of delicious smoked and cured fish, oysters, langoustines and herring marinades. It even offers the all-essential oyster knife (£5.95). The items are produced fresh to order (please give 48 hours' notice prior to delivery), chilled and vacuum-packed. Whole side, semi-trimmed, unsliced smoked salmon, £19.25; 12 Loch Fine oysters, £9.60. For a special occasion you can order a gift box containing 24 Loch Fine rock oysters and two half bottles of Champagne, £35.

Catalogue Quarterly, A4, Brochure, B/W, 4 pages, Free **Postal charges** £5.95; non-food items, £2.95; free on orders over £100 **Delivery** Courier, Royal Mail **Methods of Payment** Cheque, Postal Order, Switch, Diners Club

LORNA DE GALLEGOS
49 Perrymead Street
London
SW6 3SN
Telephone
0171 371 0751

China for children
The artist Lorna de Gallegos paints china for children. Her charming designs of alphabets, teddies or dots, complete with the child's name, make unique gifts. Each piece costs £15 including p&p. A set of three pieces (plate, bowl, mug) costs £40.50. A Teaching Plate with name, birth date, painting of the child and information such as 'My hair is black ... my socks are blue' costs £25.

Catalogue Annually, A6, Leaflets, Colour and B/W, 2 pages, Free **Postal charges** Free **Delivery** Royal Mail, Parcelforce **Methods of Payment** Cheque

MAGNIFICENT MOUCHOIRS
Quayside Lodge
William Morris Way
London
SW6 2SY
Telephone
0171 371 0017
Fax
0171 371 7115

Handkerchiefs
Magnificent Mouchoirs don't just make handkerchiefs. In addition to a range that includes handkerchiefs (all at £6.95) decorated with chess boards, balloons, a monopoly board or even a section of the Bayeux tapestry, they produce ties, braces and boxer shorts.

Ties (all £19.95) are covered in various designs, including classic cars, a chess set and a musical score. There are also ready-tied silk bow ties (£14.95) in the same designs. Boxer shorts (£12.95) are made from these patterns and a selection of tartans.

There is also a range of Monopoly T-shirts (£14.95), featuring the traditional designs including 'Mayfair', 'Go To Jail' and 'Pay £10 fine or take a Chance'.

Catalogue Annually, A5, Catalogue, Colour, 5 pages, Free **Postal charges** Varies with item **Delivery** In-house delivery **Methods of Payment** American Express, Credit Card, Cheque, Postal Order

MAP MARKETING
92–104 Carnwath Road
London
SW6 3HW

Maps
Map Marketing offers a range of 500 laminated wall maps and charts from around the world. If you need a reference source or a permanent

GIFTS

Telephone
0171 736 0297
Fax
0171 371 0473

reminder of where you are or where you're going, you couldn't ask for more. It will also create composite maps, overprint and frame. The meticulous among us will no doubt be pleased to own the *Postcode Areas Map* (from £7.50), and for businesses the *Bartholomew Postcode Atlas* (£35) would be invaluable. Those who just want to see the world in all its glory will enjoy the *Earth From Space* map (from £9.99), created from images recorded by satellites.

Catalogue Annually, A5, Leaflets, Colour and B/W, 10 pages, Free **Postal charges** £3.95 **Delivery** Royal Mail **Methods of Payment** Cheque, Postal Order, Credit Card, American Express, Diners Club

THE MARITIME COMPANY
Witney
Oxfordshire
OX8 6BH
Telephone
01993 770450
Fax
01993 700749

Nautical gifts and practical presents

For anyone with a nautical bent, this is the gift catalogue for you. You could make any genuine or even armchair sailor happy with a gift from this collection. From the pocket mechanic multi-tool that beats the Swiss army knife for usefulness, to Titanic the video! Ship's bells (£24.95), Russian submarine clocks (£69.50), and ship's cat magnets (£5.95) make this a fascinating read for landlubbers and sea-dogs alike.

Catalogue Bi-annually, A4, Catalogue, Colour, 32 pages, Free **Postal charges** P&P £2.95; express delivery available at £4.95 extra **Methods of Payment** Cheque, Postal Order, Switch, Credit Card, American Express

MARVAL PRODUCTS
67 Headley Chase
Brentwood
Essex
CM14 5DH
Telephone
01277 225839

Clocks

Marval produces decorative wall clocks, with or without pendulums. They are silk-screen printed on to rigid PVC in a variety of designs and colours and are supplied with battery-powered quartz movements and a one-year guarantee. For car enthusiasts, choose from a

Morgan, Porsche or VW Beetle among the many designs. There are dinosaurs and ballerinas, too. From £14.95.

Catalogue Annually, Third A4, Leaflets, Colour, 10 pages, Free **Postal charges** £1.50 per item **Delivery** Royal Mail **Methods of Payment** Cheque, Postal Order

MATCHRITE
167 Winchester Road
Bristol
Avon
BS4 3NJ
Telephone
0117 9774334
Fax
same

Saucy jokes
Matchrite's 'Saucy Jokes By Post' catalogue is for adults only and includes such macho material as 'The willy grow kit' (£4.99) and 'Chocolate after-dinner nipples' – irresistible at £5.99. If you are holding a party, how about breaking the ice with 'Striptease snakes and ladders', a snip at £5.99? Saucy Jokes such as the 'dick lighter' (£2.99) and 'coughing ashtray' (£12) might even cure a few bad habits!

Catalogue A5, Catalogue, B/W, 32 pages, Free **Postal charges** Varies with item **Delivery** Royal Mail **Methods of Payment** Cheque, Postal Order, Credit Card

MEG RIVERS
Middle Tysoe
Warwickshire
CV35 OSE
Telephone
01295 688101
Fax
01295 680799

Cakes and gifts
Order a cake on Monday and Meg Rivers will get it to you by the weekend. Her catalogue is full of enticingly illustrated goodies, hand-baked using organic flour, free-range eggs and English butter, and securely packed in special boxes for delivery. Ginger cake, £12.50/kg; iced children's birthday cake, £15.50/900g (6½in diameter); wedding cakes from £150. Gift boxes can be assembled to order from a selection of wines, preserves, dried fruits and the famous cakes.

Catalogue Annually, A5, Catalogue, Colour, 16 pages, Free **Postal charges** £2.95; express £7; Europe and Eire £6.95 **Delivery** Royal Mail, Parcelforce **Methods of Payment** Cheque, Postal Order, Credit Card, Switch

MILLS & MILLS
Squash Court
Home Farm
Nr Burford
Oxfordshire
OX18 4TQ
Telephone
01451 844 744
Fax
01451 844 471

General Gifts

All the products in this catalogue are of the highest quality and come with a guarantee that if you are not satisfied with your purchase, or if any items arrive damaged, then you will be fully refunded on receipt of goods. They have a display room to see any of the goods, but please telephone to make an appointment. Faux Books handcrafted in the Cotswolds from resin and then hand-painted to look like authentic antique books, from £8.10. Cool bags and bottle wraps from £4.95; candles and candlesticks in different designs and prices. Sterling silver stirrup cups from £245. Miscellaneous items such as Harley Davidson pens from £18.95.
Catalogue Annually, A5, Brochure, Colour, 10 pages, Free **Postal charges** Free **Delivery** Royal Mail **Methods of Payment** Cheque, Postal Order, Credit Card

MIN & DELL LTD
51 St George's Drive
London
SW1V 4DE
Telephone
0171 976 6645

Traditional handmade gifts

This small business markets the crafts of older people with traditional skills including jewellery and fine metalwork, handknits for children and children's aprons, hand-crafted toys, wooden trinket boxes and needlecraft and textiles. Their policy is to develop exclusive designs and to market high-standard, reasonably priced goods which are not available elsewhere, and to use only natural materials.
Catalogue A5, Leaflets, Colour, 16 pages, £2.50 **Postal charges** £1.50 for orders under £15.00; £3.50 for orders between £15.00 and £75; over £75.00, free **Delivery** Royal Mail, Parcelforce **Methods of Payment** Cheque, Postal Order, Credit Card

NATIONAL CANINE DEFENCE LEAGUE
17 Wakley Street
London
EC1V 7LT

Gifts, stationery and pet products

This registered charity's catalogue is devoted to products for dog and animal lovers alike. You can buy a Scotty door mat for £23.95, a neat carry loo for £4.50, a furry cat's cradle to hook over a

GIFTS

Telephone
0171 837 0006
Fax
0171 833 2701

radiator for £15.95, doggy Christmas cards for £1.95 for a pack of 10, ear wipes for £1.75, grooming products for your pet and sweatshirts for you, as well as books and animal bedding.

Catalogue Annually, A4, Catalogue, Colour, 8 pages, Free **Postal charges** Varies with item **Delivery** Royal Mail, Parcelforce **Methods of Payment** Cheque, Postal Order, Credit Card

NATIONAL PORTRAIT GALLERY
Publications (Mail Order)
FREEPOST (LON 5125)
London
WC2H 0BR
Telephone
0171 306 0055 EXT 280
Fax
0171 306 0092

Gifts

An attractively presented catalogue offering a selection of unusual and exclusive items usually available only in the National Portrait Gallery shop. Proceeds from the sales go towards funding the gallery's exhibitions, lectures and running costs. Guy Fawkes mug, £4.95; the wives of Henry VIII teaspoon set, £21; Shakespeare T-shirt, £9.99; Zandra Rhodes bow by Andrew Logan, £115.

Catalogue Annually, A4, Catalogue, Colour, 20 pages, Free **Postal charges** Varies with item **Delivery** Royal Mail, Parcelforce **Methods of Payment** Cheque, Credit Card, American Express

THE NATIONAL TRUST (Enterprises) LTD
PO Box 101
Melksham
Wiltshire
SN12 8EA
Telephone
01225 706209

Gifts

The National Trust catalogue contains over 350 gift ideas for every taste and occasion. Gifts range from the Spode Calke Abbey Loving Cup to silk ties featuring a design from the floor tiles at Belfast's Crown Saloon Bar and the fireplace in the Owl Suite in Cragside, Norrrthumberland. There is a Wedgwood collection, and much more to please the discerning buyer. The Calke Abbey Loving Cup sells for £45.95; the Wedgwood collection prices start from £19.95.

Catalogue Annually, A5, Catalogue, Colour, 45 pages, Free **Postal charges** £15 and under, £1.95; £15.01 or over, £3.95 **Delivery** Royal Mail **Methods of Payment** Cheque, Credit Card, American Express, Diners Club, Switch, Postal Order

NAUTICALIA
Ferry Lane
Shepperton-on-Thames
Middlesex
TW17 9LQ
Telephone
01932 253333
Fax
01932 241679

Maritime novelties and clothes
Nauticalia publishes the Greenwich Zero catalogue and donates a proportion of its income to The Maritime Trust for the conservation and upkeep of historic British vessels such as Sir Francis Chichester's single-handed round-the-world ketch Gipsy Moth IV. With the support of HRH Prince Philip, the catalogue contains a vast array of products and clothes connected with the water. Lightweight telescope, £12.95; sailor's dice box, £29.95; Breton cotton jersey, £34; fisherman's knife, £44.50; naval duffel coat, £169; Admiral Fitzroy's mercury barometer, £195.

Catalogue Annually, A4, Catalogue, Colour, 32 pages, Free **Postal charges** £2.95 **Delivery** Royal Mail, Parcelforce **Methods of Payment** Cheque, Postal Order, Credit Card

NORFOLK LAVENDER
England's Lavender Farm
FREEPOST 196
Kings Lynn
Norfolk
PE31 7BR
Telephone
01485 572383
Fax
01485 571176

Lavender and related gift items
This lavender farm extends to 100 acres at Heacham, and is open to the public during the summer months. As well as predictable ranges of lavender-based toiletries, fragrances, soaps, sachets and gifts, the company also supplies the plants themselves (minimum order: six plants at £2.50 each). The fragrances include 'Rose with English Lavender Cologne', £8.45, and 'Men of England', £9.95. A set of six coasters featuring pictures of lavender costs £7.95, as does a botanical print PVC apron and tea-towel set.

Catalogue Annually, A5, Catalogue, Colour, 31 pages, Free **Postal charges** £3.00; free for orders over £35.00 **Delivery** Royal Mail, Parcelforce **Methods of Payment** Cheque, Postal Order, Credit Card, Switch

NOTTING HILL HOUSING TRUST
Aspen House
1 Gayford Road

Gifts
The Notting Hill Housing Trust provides homes for people in desperate need, such as families who live in bed-and-breakfast accommodation. Its

London
W12 9BY
Telephone
0181 563 4888
Fax
0181 563 4899

Christmas catalogue helps to raise funds for its work and contains a sophisticated selection of gifts and items for the home. There are colourful check tablecloths (£12.99) and chenille throws (£29.99), a metal Christmas-tree candle-holder (£12.99), opaque glass vases (£14.99), a verdigris coat rack, £14.99, and ivory pyramid candles, 99p.

Catalogue Annually, A2, Catalogue, Colour, 16 pages, Free **Postal charges** £3.50 **Methods of Payment** Cheque, Postal Order, Credit Card

OCCASIONS
30 Barn Owl Way
Woodland View
Burghfield Common
Reading
Berkshire
RG7 3XX
Telephone
01734 834078

Pottery portraits

Pamela Stannard glazes personal photographs on to pieces of china, such as shields (eg to record a prizegiving), tankards (eg to record a christening) and plates. She can also supply hangers or stands for the plates. The 10½in 'Porcelain Lace' round plate takes a 6in photograph and costs £19.50; the 'Jumbo Pink Tray' takes a 7in × 5in photo and costs £18.50; and the 'Medium Shield' takes a 2½in photo and costs £9.00.

Catalogue Annually, A5, Catalogue, Colour, 8 pages, Free **Postal charges** Free **Delivery** Parcelforce **Methods of Payment** Cheque, Postal Order

ORIEL INTERNATIONAL
The Priory
Newport
Essex
CB11 3TH
Telephone
01799 540995
Fax
01799 541966

Harvest boxes

This small company produces imaginative boxed pictures made from collections of dried flowers, beans, seeds and seashells set behind glass in wooden frames. The result is a very attractive wall decoration. They are available in eight sizes and nine frame colours. Each picture is handmade in England using wood from a sustainable source. Prices from £10 to £38.

Catalogue Annually, A4, Brochure, Colour, 4 pages, Free **Postal charges** £2 **Delivery** Royal Mail, Parcelforce **Methods of Payment** Cheque, Credit Card

THE ORIGINAL BUTTERFLY MAN
Craft Workshop
Berwyn Lodge
Glyndyfrdwy Village
Corwen
Clwyd
North Wales
LL21 9HW
Telephone
01490 430300

Decorative metal butterflies for home decoration

The Original Butterfly Man produces beautiful replicas of some of Britain's best-loved butterflies. With rust-resistant aluminium wings and durable nylon bodies, these hand-painted, eye-catching models look stunning when attached to walls and surfaces. All butterflies have legs, proboscis and antennae and are fitted with a sprung-steel fixing bracket so they flutter in the breeze. Sizes range from 16 × 10in to 12 × 6in. A selection of 15 species are available, from the Peacock at £45 to the Large Garden White at £25.50.

Catalogue Annually, Third A4, Leaflets, Colour, 3 pages, Send SAE 14in × 6in, first-class stamp and £1 postal order payable to The Original Butterfly Man **Postal charges** Varies with item **Delivery** Royal Mail **Methods of Payment** Cheque, Postal Order

OXFAM TRADING
PO Box 72
Bicester
Oxfordshire
OX6 7LT
Telephone
01869 245 011
Fax
01869 247 348

Gifts from around the world

A colourful publication containing hand-crafted products from around the world. Oxfam has done much to encourage and promote the skills of third-world producers, ensuring they are paid properly for their work and giving grants to strengthen their businesses. The catalogue contains an attractive selection of exotic homeware, clothes, jewellery, stationery and foods with descriptions of the craft skills and countries of origin. Embroidered bedcover from Bangladesh, £75; Mexican rug, £125; Thai shirt, £6.95; child's white dress from El Salvador, £12.95.

Catalogue Bi-annually, A4, Catalogue, Colour, 32 pages, Free **Postal charges** £2.95 **Delivery** Royal Mail, Parcelforce **Methods of Payment** Cheque, Postal Order, Credit Card

GIFTS

PAST TIMES
Witney
Oxfordshire
OX8 6BH
Telephone
01993 779444
Fax
01993 700749

Historical gifts and decorative accessories

Past Times is Britain's leading historic gifts retailer with a worldwide mail-order service and 60 shops throughout the country. The catalogue offers a unique range of fine and unusual gifts and decorative accessories, all with an authentic feel of the past. Arranged in chronological order from Celtic times to the Twentieth Century, the catalogue includes fine silk scarves, jewellery, games, toys, stationery, books, food, toiletries, and household and garden items. *Winnie Ille Pu* is a Latin translation of *Winnie the Pooh* with E.H. Shepard's original illustrations (£7.95), from the Medieval period there is Hazard, a game from the *Canterbury Tales*, £14.95; and from the Victorian era there are some unusual folding fan cards (£10.95 for 3) and beautifully finished pure cotton Victorian nightdresses, £24.50. Past Times accepts Eurocard, Delta and JCB, as well as Access/Mastercard and Visa.

Catalogue Bi-monthly, 265mm×200mm, Catalogue, Colour, 64 pages, Free **Postal charges** £2.95 per order **Delivery** Royal Mail, Courier, Parcelforce **Methods of Payment** Other, Cheque, Postal Order, Credit Card, American Express, Switch, Diners Club

PATRICIA LUKE
Chapel Cottage
Lutener Road
Midhurst
West Sussex
GU29 9AT
Telephone
01730 812728

Gifts and cards

This small mail-order company sells limited-edition prints in the form of cards, mounted prints, coasters, table-mats, trays, chopping boards, even Post-it pad boards! Most feature farm animals and are also available on fine china mugs. Prices are very reasonable: cards 75p, table-mats £3, coasters £1.50, and mugs £4.

Catalogue A5, Brochure, Colour, 4 pages, Free **Postal charges** Up to £3.00, add 50p; £3.01-£14.99, add £2.50; £15.00-£49.99, add £3.50; over £50.00, free **Delivery** Royal Mail **Methods of Payment** Cheque

GIFTS

PENHALIGON'S
FREEPOST WC4189
London
N4 1NH
Telephone
0800 317 332
Fax
0181 800 5789

Fine-quality beauty products and toiletries
A catalogue with a difference. Brush your finger across the pictures and you will be able to smell each perfume. Penhaligon's offers the most luxurious collection of beauty products and toiletries for men and women – eau de toilette, soap, oil, bath essence, aftershave and talc – all exquisitely packaged and using William Henry Penhaligon's century-old formulae. There are silver hairbrushes, mock-ivory hand mirrors, shaving equipment and cuff-links, too. Soap, box of three, £16; eau de toilette, from £22; aftershave, £29; shaving stand with bowl, £110.
Catalogue Annually, A4, Catalogue, Colour, 24 pages, Free **Postal charges** £2.50 standard service; £5 priority **Delivery** Royal Mail **Methods of Payment** Credit Card, Cheque, Switch, American Express, Diners Club

PETER RABBIT AND FRIENDS
FREEPOST (LA 12 44)
Burrow
Lancashire
LA6 2BR
Telephone
015242 74344
Fax
015242 74252

Gifts for babies and children
Peter Rabbit never fails to charm young children. In this catalogue he and his friends can be found as cuddly toys (from £14.99); climbing over pencils (39p), rubbers, rulers; printed on pyjamas, sweatshirts and T-shirts (from £9.99); painted on china (mug £6.75); pictured on nursery furnishings; etched on silverware (photograph frame £9.99); and written about in Beatrix Potter's classic books.
Catalogue Annually, A4, Catalogue, Colour, 8 pages, Free **Postal charges** £2.95 **Delivery** Royal Mail, Parcelforce **Methods of Payment** Cheque, Postal Order, Credit Card, Switch

POPPY
44 High Street
Yarm
Cleveland
TS15 9AE

Children's clothes, bedding and gifts
This delightful catalogue contains a selection of cotton printed clothes for babies and children, with co-ordinated caps (£13.99), floppy hats, headbands, bows and duffel bags. There is

GIFTS

Telephone
01642 790000
Fax
01642 788235

something for every occasion and children will delight in choosing which way round to wear the reversible jacket (from £33.99) and whether to wear the smock over the petticoat (from £53.99 a set), or just the petticoat as a sun-dress. Poppy also stocks an enchanting range of co-ordinated wallpapers (£11.95/roll), fabrics (£11.95/metre), bedding (cot quilt, £33.95) and gifts (bookends, clocks, lamps) for children's nurseries, in pastels and primaries.

Catalogue Annually, A4, Catalogue, Colour, 8 pages, Free **Postal charges** Varies with item **Delivery** Royal Mail **Methods of Payment** Cheque, Credit Card

PRESENTS FOR MEN
PO Box 16
Banbury
Oxford
Oxfordshire
OX17 1TF
Telephone
01295 750100
Fax
01295 750800

Gifts for men

Men are notoriously difficult to buy for, so to make things easy Presents for Men has assembled a catalogue of stylish, practical and affordable gift ideas. Treat him to a Champagne sealer, £3.50; Rapid Ice wine-cooler jacket, £6.95; madcap party game, £4.95; bicycle tool kit, £5.95; Horny Old Devil boxer shorts, £9.95; stainless steel vacuum flask, £25.95; and to store all his presents, a Trojan bag made from heavy-duty canvas with six exterior and two interior pockets, and big enough to hold a two-gallon bucket, DIY tools or an enormous picnic, £14.95.

Catalogue Annually, A4, Catalogue, Colour, 20 pages, Free **Postal charges** Varies with item **Delivery** Royal Mail, Parcelforce **Methods of Payment** Cheque, Postal Order, Credit Card

PULL THE OTHER ONE
Church Farm House
Herstmonceux
East Sussex
BN27 1QJ

Adult crackers

These handmade adult crackers present a novel way to break the ice at parties, stag and hen nights, sports dinners, birthday and office celebrations. Each one contains a raunchy gift, naughty

Telephone
01323 833138

limerick, sexy picture on the outside (if you want), party popper or Alka-Seltzer and costs £2.50. They are available in several colours and can be tailor-made to your own requirements.

Catalogue Annually, A5, Leaflets, Colour, 1 page, Free **Postal charges** Varies with item **Delivery** Royal Mail **Methods of Payment** Cheque

RED LETTER DAYS
Melville House
8–12 Woodhouse Road
North Finchley
London
N12 ORG
Telephone
0181 343 8822
Fax
0181 343 9030

Experience activities and gifts

This is where you can make dreams come true. Red Letter Days' catalogue offers an amazing range of 'experience activities' from motor racing (from £99) to tank driving (£225), breaking the sound barrier in a Russian fighter-plane to hot-air ballooning, land yachting to white-water rafting. There are sports experiences at famous venues and luxury trips on the QE2, Concorde or the Orient-Express. You can book a Champagne weekend for two, hire a stretch limo for the day or have an aromatherapy massage. There is something for everyone here and certainly a 'day to remember'. Prices from £25 to well over £1,000.

Catalogue Annually, A4, Catalogue, Colour, 52 pages, Free **Postal charges** Varies with item **Delivery** Royal Mail, Courier **Methods of Payment** Cheque, Postal Order, Credit Card, Switch, American Express

REID & WATERERS LTD
FREEPOST TK1621
Hounslow
Middlesex
TW4 5BR
Telephone
01345 626268
Fax
0181 572 5623

Home and gardening gifts

There are lots of imaginative gift ideas in this catalogue, from a lightweight wooden wastepaper basket with stencilled design (£19.95) to a decorative wooden egg cupboard (£29.95). For the keen gardener there's a gardener's holdall with lots of pockets (£29.95), a traditional trug (£37.50), and traditional watering-can (£21.95).

Catalogue Bi-annually, A4, Catalogue, Colour, 23 pages, Free **Postal charges** Add £2.95. For orders over £100.00, free **Delivery** Royal Mail **Methods of Payment** Cheque, Credit Card

GIFTS

REMEMBER WHEN
The Tithe Barn
520 Purley Way
Croydon
Surrey
CR0 4RE
Telephone
0181 688 6323
Fax
0181 781 1227

Original newspapers

Remember When provides original issues of historical newspapers, but since it stocks up to two million copies it cannot supply a catalogue. If you want to celebrate a birthday, anniversary or other memorable event, just phone and specify your desired date and newspaper – some go back as far as 1642. Each newspaper costs £17, folded in four and sent in a card wrap; £19, rolled and sent in a presentation tube; or £32.50 in a personalised portfolio.

Catalogue Annually, A5, Leaflets, Colour and B/W, 1 page, Free **Postal charges** Free **Delivery** Royal Mail **Methods of Payment** Cheque, Postal Order, Credit Card, Switch

THE ROYAL ACADAMY OF ARTS
Harrington Dock
Liverpool
L70 1AX
Telephone
0151 708 0555
Fax
0151 708 8803

Gifts for discerning givers

By purchasing your gifts from this catalogue you help support the activities of The Royal Academy. The carefully chosen range of goods reflects a variety of influences from Venetian to Modigliani and Elizabeth Blackadder to playschool painting. Prices range from £5.95 for a tiny trinket box to £260 for a replica of the ancient bronze statue known as the Spinario. No one could fail to find something to their liking in this collection.

Catalogue Annually, A5, Catalogue, Colour, 35 pages, £1 **Postal charges** £3.95, with express delivery available for an extra £3 **Methods of Payment** Cheque, Credit Card, American Express, Postal Order

RSPCA TRADING LTD
FREEPOST
PO Box 38
Burton on Trent
Staffordshire
DE14 1BR

Gifts

A comprehensive catalogue of quality gifts, household items, cards and clothes which supports a well-known charity. Choose from a colourful bone china cafetière, £49.95, with mugs to match, set of three £14.99, to a set of

Telephone
01283 506125

wildlife selection birthday cards, two packs for £3.75.
Catalogue Bi-annually, A4, Catalogue, Colour, 40 pages, Free **Postal charges** Up to £69.99, £3.35; £70 and over, free **Methods of Payment** Cheque, Postal Order

RURAL CRAFTS DIRECT
The Ridge House
Duns Tew
Oxfordshire
OX6 4JL
Telephone
01869 340002
Fax
01869 340670

Products made by members of the Rural Crafts Association
The Rural Crafts Association has 600 craft members whose work can be seen at the Association's shows around the country. This is its first mail-order catalogue representing the work of a selected few. All the items are hand-crafted and include tapestries, jewellery, baskets, carpet-bags, weather-vanes, wooden toys, printed cushions and many more. Claire Valentine's country jacket, £189; Ma Scott's folk-art bread-box, £32.95; David and Judy Hodgson's weather-vane, £49.
Catalogue Annually, A4, Catalogue, Colour; 27 pages, Free **Postal charges** £3 **Delivery** Royal Mail, Parcelforce **Methods of Payment** Cheque, Postal Order, Credit Card, Switch

SAY IT WITH HOURS
Long Cottage
Fountains Row
Market Overton
Leicestershire
LE15 7PJ
Telephone
0171 289 7001

Personalised clocks
Clock up the Brownie points! Mark all kinds of occasions (weddings, christenings, retirements, etc), and have someone think of you whenever they check the time by giving a clock with your own special message on the face. These 24cm-diameter handmade clocks, fitted with fully guaranteed quartz movements, are available in black, dark red or dark green and the clock faces come with a choice of Roman or Arabic numerals printed in black on a white background. Your message, also in black, can be printed in Gentry, Nonchalant or Coronet.
Catalogue A4, Leaflets, B/W, 1 page, Free **Postal charges** Free **Delivery** Royal Mail **Methods of Payment** Cheque, Postal Order

GIFTS

SCOPE CENTRAL TRADING LIMITED
FREEPOST
PO Box 66
Burton upon Trent
Staffordshire
DE14 1BR
Telephone
01283 506506

Cards and gifts for Christmas
A selection of Christmas cards, gift-wrapping paper, printed Christmas tapes, gift label dispenser, curling ribbons, calendars, gifts and stocking fillers from £2.99 such as a Noah's Ark rug, magnet building set, activity ring, soft blocks, name jigsaws, child's single duvet set, personalised pencil box, personalised pen watch, golfer's caddy kit, CD cleaning systems, cricket-ball clock, golf-bag towel, gorilla T-shirt, poppy peg-bag, turtle shoe brush, chopping board, mini-cake gift pack, kittens sandwich tray, hot toddy glasses, natural wood fruit bowl, Victorian Santa tins, bath mats, whale shower curtain, cosmetics bag, towel bales, crackers, candles, and Zodiac signs tea-towel. Scope is the charity for people with cerebral palsy.

Catalogue Annually, A5, Catalogue, Colour, 36 pages, Free **Postal charges** Up to £70, £3.35; £70 and over, free **Methods of Payment** Switch, Credit Card, Cheque, Postal Order

SCROLL NAMES
PO Box 82
Blackpool
Lancashire
FY2 0GA
Telephone
01253 595454

Surname histories and heraldry scrolls
The 'Hall of Names' has researched the histories of more than 100,000 English, Irish, Scottish, Welsh and Continental surnames from about AD 1100 which it offers individually, beautifully reproduced on a printed scroll with heraldic border. They make an ideal gift for birthdays or any other special occasion and cost £5.99 unframed, or £15.99 framed. Also available are Coats of Arms from £13.99, chivalry models, first-name pictures and blazer badges.

Catalogue Annually, A5, Leaflets, B/W, 4 pages, Free **Postal charges** Varies with item **Delivery** Royal Mail **Methods of Payment** Cheque, Postal Order, Credit Card

SILVER DIRECT
PO Box 925
Shaftesbury
Dorset
SP7 9RA
Telephone
01747 828977
Fax
01747 828961

Silver and silver-plated goods
Silver Direct say they can deliver Bond Street silver at affordable prices. Their top-quality, solid, hallmarked silver and silver-plated items include everything from photograph frames, bottle stoppers, polo dishes, paperknives and candlesticks and from clocks and pocket peppermills, teddy honey bowls and Paloma ice jugs to candle snuffers. Many of the designs are classic and traditional in style, making ideal presents for anniversaries, christenings, weddings and birthdays. Prices start at a very reasonable £10 rising to £500 for the more elaborate items.

Catalogue Annually, A5, Brochure, Colour, 20 pages, Free **Postal charges** Free **Delivery** Royal Mail **Methods of Payment** Cheque, Postal Order, Credit Card, Switch

SILVER EDITIONS
PO Box 16
Chalfont St Giles
Buckinghamshire
HP8 4AU
Telephone
01494 876206
Fax
01494 876227

Fine sterling silver and silver plate
Silver Editions offers a fine selection of sterling silver, silver-plated and pewter gifts. All are clearly photographed with a code number next to them and the price in a black and white column beside the photograph. But the best thing about Silver Editions is the prices. The company is committed to providing quality merchandise at genuine value for money. Thus, there are two prices given for each item: the normal retail price and the Silver Editions price, which is always considerably lower. For example, a pewter hip flask with a cricket-bat design would normally cost £39.95 in the high street; here it costs £27.95. There are also silver-plated and sterling silver wine coasters, drinks mats, drinks labels, decorative bottle corks, vases, candlesticks, desk items, letter openers, pen and inkwell sets, sweet bowls, grape scissors, card holders, napkin rings, owls, condiments, pill boxes, cufflinks, child's cutlery set, child's cup, birth-record frame, tooth-fairy box, trinket boxes,

photograph frames, fruit servers, and canteens. Perfect for christening, birthday, anniversary and Christmas gifts.
Catalogue A4, Catalogue, Colour and B/W, 16 pages pages, Free **Postal charges** £2.95; £12 Europe and USA **Delivery** Royal Mail **Methods of Payment** Cheque, Postal Order, Credit Card

SOUTH KENSINGTON MUSEUMS CATALOGUE
Euroway Business Park
Swindon
Wiltshire
SN5 8SN
Telephone
01793 514141
Fax
01793 487002

A variety of products from around the world
The Natural History Museum, Science Museum and the Victoria & Albert Museum have joined forces to publish a catalogue of enterprising ideas, original gifts, clothes, jewellery, gadgets and toys. If you are looking for a present with a difference, this is the catalogue. From the Victoria & Albert: cultured pearl necklace, £46.50; old teak book-rest, £24.95; cherub garden fountain, £199. From the Natural History Museum: rainbow hammock, £30; bird feeder, £19.95; botanical sofa throw, £65. From the Science Museum: loony lenses, £7.95; Pockite kite, £15.95; skeleton pyjamas, £14.95.
Catalogue Annually, A5, Catalogue, Colour, 30 pages, Free **Postal charges** £3.25 **Delivery** Royal Mail, Parcelforce **Methods of Payment** Cheque, Postal Order, Credit Card, American Express, Diners Club

SPECIAL EFX LTD
3 Ettington Park
Stratford upon Avon
Warwickshire
CV37 8BT
Telephone
01789 450915
Fax
01789 450916

Contemporary designed products
Special EFX is a company specialising in contemporary designed products. Awarded *Homes & Gardens* best gift 1995 for their Horn Shaped Bottle Opener retailing for under £10. Their catalogue comprises a wide choice of gifts in unusual designs from Quadro pens (from £11.95) to a variety of key-rings (from £3.95). Practical luggage tags in black or nickel from £7.50. Abstract and arty is the influence here.
Catalogue Quarterly, A4, Catalogue, Colour, 21 pages, Free **Postal charges** Free **Methods of Payment** Cheque, Credit Card, American Express

STAFFORDSHIRE ENAMELS
Western Coyney Road
Stoke-on-Trent
Staffordshire
ST3 5JT
Telephone
0500 026209
Fax
01782 599397

Hand-painted enamel gifts
Staffordshire Enamels are descendants of the 18th-century English enamels now highly prized by collectors. Whether you are giving or collecting, these exquisite pieces could well become heirlooms. There are love tokens (boxes from £55), yearboxes (from £69.50), pillboxes (from £72.50) and egg-shaped boxes (from £47.50).

Catalogue Annually, A5, Catalogue, Colour, 29 pages, Free **Postal charges** £1.95 **Delivery** Royal Mail, Parcelforce **Methods of Payment** Cheque, Credit Card, Switch

STEAMERS
Tregidden Mill
St Martin
Helston
Cornwall
TR12 6DS
Telephone
01326 231419

Decorative half-model wall plaques of steamships
Ian Dunlop makes decorative half-model wall plaques of steamships that can be hung like a picture. He uses driftwood and salvaged timber to capture the romance of the coasters, freighters and ocean liners that once plied the seas. A Falmouth tug, c.1910 and approximately 16in long, costs £20; a Cunard ocean liner, c.1915, 36in, £45. Perfect presents for sea-lovers.

Catalogue Annually, A4, Catalogue, Colour and B/W, 3 pages, Free **Postal charges** £3; £4.75 for larger orders **Delivery** Royal Mail, Parcelforce **Methods of Payment** Cheque

SWEET PEA
6 Cundell Drive
Cottenham
Cambridge
Cambridgeshire
CB4 4RU
Telephone
01954 252039
Fax
01954 252543

Novel baby and children's gifts
Large brochure unfolds to reveal colour photographs with long explanations and prices of items from the Skwish, a baby's first toy which moves and rattles and always bounces back into shape, £9.99; the Bye Bye Lullaby Playbook, £18.50; the ABC animal playbag; the Seatneat, which protects car seats, etc from muddy feet.

Catalogue A3, Brochure, Colour, 4 pages, Free **Postal charges** £1.95

TAYLOR NASH
31 St Giles Street
Oxford
Oxfordshire
OX1 3LD
Telephone
01865 511700
Fax
same

Hampers, gift baskets and boxes
Taylor Nash produces delightful traditional hampers and gift boxes which it will deliver worldwide. These make perfect prizes or memorable presents and come beautifully presented in either standard versions or made up to your own specifications. Gift baskets containing wine, Stilton and relish, £25; hampers from £40; Christmas Box, £45.
Catalogue Annually, A5, Catalogue, Colour, 15 pages, Free **Postal charges** Free **Delivery** Royal Mail, Parcelforce **Methods of Payment** Cheque, Credit Card

TENSOR MARKETING LTD
Yarm Road Industrial Estate
Darlington
Co Durham
DL1 4XX
Telephone
01325 469 181
Fax
01325 381 386

Gadgets and electrical goods
Whether you want to be your own weather forecaster, give a chipped glass a second chance, vacuum your pet or make your own rubber stamp, Tensor Marketing has the product for you. A catalogue full of innovative ideas and clever gifts. Pet Vac, from £14.95; Shower Radio, £10.95; Drain Buster, £10.99; Talking Watch, £12.99; Spellchecker/Ruler, £24.99.
Catalogue Annually, A4, Catalogue, Colour, 12 pages, Free **Postal charges** Varies with item **Delivery** Royal Mail, Parcelforce **Methods of Payment** Cheque, Credit Card

UNIVERSITIES FEDERATION FOR ANIMAL WELFARE (UFAW)
8 Hamilton Close
South Mimms
Potters Bar
Hertfordshire
EN6 3QD
Telephone
01707 658202
Fax
01707 649279

Animal welfare publications, Christmas cards and gifts
UFAW is an organisation working to improve the welfare of animals in zoos, laboratories, on farms, as pets and in the wild. It provides funds for education, brings together experts to offer advice internationally and produces a wide range of books, leaflets and videos on the subject. Prices from 50p to £50. It also offers a selection of low-cost Christmas cards and gifts from 75p to £12.50.
Catalogue Annually, A5, Catalogue, Colour and B/W, 12 pages, Free **Postal charges** Free **Delivery** Royal Mail **Methods of Payment** Cheque, Postal Order

Health & Beauty

AROMATHERAPY ASSOCIATES LTD
68 Maltings Place
Bagleys Lane
London
SW6 2BY
Telephone
0171 371 9878
Fax
0171 371 9894

Aromatherapy products
A unique range of genuine aromatherapy products carefully created by professional therapists. Tried and tested within the tranquillity of their London Treatment Centre, the Aromatherapy Associates range is known and loved by their many discerning clients. Previously available only through selected clinics, spas and health clubs, these blends – renowned for their quality – offer an opportunity for experiencing the pleasures of aromatherapy within the home.

Aromatherapy Associates' brochure features the complete range, grouped for Body, Mind, Spirit or Skin, with fragrance notes to help selection. Choose from Bath, Body or Facial Oils, Body Creams or Essences.

Catalogue Quarter A4, Catalogue, Colour, 8 pages, Free
Postal charges £2.00 for one to two items; £3.00 for three to four items; £4.00 for five to six items; £6.00 for more than six items up to the value of £100.00; no charge for items worth more than £100.00 **Delivery** Royal Mail, Parcelforce
Methods of Payment Cheque, Postal Order, Visa, Access/Mastercard

ARRAN AROMATICS LTD
The Home Farm
Brodick
Isle of Arran
Scotland
KA27 8DD

Soaps, bath and body preparations and teas
Arran Aromatics Ltd produces a range of environmentally friendly body preparations produced without cruelty to animals. The four ranges include 'The Aromatherapy Range' (including Mandarin & Lime Bath Foam, £4.99 for 250ml)

Telephone
01770 302595
Fax
01770 302599

and 'The Country Range' (including Avocado & Almond Massage Soap, £2.49 for 200g). They also sell teas, including Fruit Tea Gift Packs: £4.99 for 12 × 15g fruit tea cubes in a tray; Scottish Breakfast Teas: a 15g mini chest of loose tea in the 'checked' range costs 99p; and Gourmet and Mulling Spices.

Catalogue Annually, Third A4, Leaflets, B/W, 3 pages, Free **Postal charges** £3.50 **Delivery** Parcelforce **Methods of Payment** Cheque, Credit Card

AVEDA COSMETICS LTD
75-77 Margaret Street
London
W1N 7HB
Telephone
0171 636 7911
Fax
0171 636 6914

Beauty products

Aveda does not conduct or endorse animal testing and the ingredients in their products are grown in plants all over the world. They make plant-derived formulations for every skin type and condition, shampoos, 'purefumes', and natural-colour cosmetics. A 150ml cream cleanser costs £16; a 50ml Black Malva herbal shampoo is £2; 'Avia Heart of Africa' Purefume Absolute costs £60; and 'Rubia' Fresh Essence Lip Colour costs £10.

Catalogue A4, Catalogue, Colour, 41 pages, £2 **Postal charges** Varies with item **Delivery** Royal Mail, Parcelforce **Methods of Payment** Cheque, Credit Card

AVON COSMETICS LTD
Earlstrees Road
Industrial Estate
Corby
Northamptonshire
NN17 4AZ
Telephone
0800 663664

Cosmetic and gifts

Established in the UK in 1959, Avon is probably best known for its direct-selling methods and distinctive dingdong trademark. Now available through mail order, it has also considerably expanded its range. You can now buy jewellery, haircare products, CDs and videos, giftware, lingerie and handbags in addition to its original cosmetics and skincare products.

Although all products exclusively carry the Avon label, much of the packaging is reminiscent of high street competitors. Prices remain reasonable with lipstick from £2.99 and there are often added incentives to purchase, with free extras or reduced-price jewellery.

Catalogue Catalogue, Colour, 127 pages, Free **Postal charges** £1.95 **Delivery** Royal Mail **Methods of Payment** Cheque, Postal Order, Credit Card, Switch

BAY HOUSE AROMATICS
88 St George's Road
Brighton
East Sussex
BN2 1EE
Telephone
01273 601109
Fax
01273 601174

Aromatherapy products

The motto of Bay House Aromatics is 'pure oils in plain bottles'. And they seem to live up to this, with no fancy packaging or fancy prices, just the purest quality oils by return. As well as essential oils, they sell massage blends, vegan skin creams and lotions, aromatic oil vaporisers, gift baskets and aromatherapy starter kits. In short, they stock everything for aromatherapy, whether you're a complete beginner or qualified practitioner. Sample prices: 9ml lavender oil for £2.05, vaporisers from £3.95, 100ml sweet almond oil for £2, 120ml lemon and rose hand and body lotion for £3.80.

Catalogue Bi-annually, A5, Leaflets, Colour and B/W, 20 pages, Free **Postal charges** Up to 4 items, add £1; over 4 items, £2; over £50, free **Delivery** Royal Mail, Parcelforce **Methods of Payment** Cheque, Credit Card

BIOCEUTICALS
Nutri House
26 Zennor Road
London
SW12 0PS
Telephone
0181 675 5664
Fax
0181 675 2257

Natural vitamins, minerals and herbal supplements

Bioceuticals offer complete natural high-potency supplements, hypo-allergenic formulas, digestive aids, sustained-release vegetarian and vegan products, Biopathy, colon-cleansing programmes and Ayurvedic natural supplements. Vitamin supplements from £32.18; multi-mineral supplements from £2.75; Ayurvedic supplements from £9.50; Korean Ginseng extract, £21.10. They also supply organic aromatherapy oils, from £3.20.

Catalogue Annually, A4, Brochure, Colour and B/W, 6 pages, Free **Postal charges** Varies with item **Delivery** Royal Mail **Methods of Payment** Cheque, Postal Order

HEALTH & BEAUTY

THE BODY SHOP BY MAIL
Hawthorn Road
Wick
Littlehampton
West Sussex
BN17 7LR
Telephone
01903 733888
Fax
01903 734949

Naturally based health and beauty products
Founded by Anita Roddick in 1976, The Body Shop uses only natural ingredients to make exclusive products to their own original recipes. This catalogue covers hair products such as Brazil Nut Conditioner, for dry or chemically treated hair, that comes direct from the Kayapo Indians in the Amazonian rainforest (60ml for £1.10); face cleansers such as Cucumber Cleansing Milk (60ml for £1); naturally based cosmetics which involve no animal testing, and a range of perfumes, bath and shower products.
Catalogue A4, Catalogue, Colour, 21 pages, 25p **Postal charges** 1 item, 80p; 2–3 items, £1.75; 4 or more items, £3.00 **Delivery** Royal Mail **Methods of Payment** Cheque, Postal Order, Credit Card, American Express, Switch

BUTTERBUR AND SAGE LTD
101 Highgrove Street
Reading
Berkshire
RG1 5EJ
Telephone
01734 314484
Fax
01734 314504

Essential oils
Butterbur and Sage provide a range of beauty products, including Essential Oils, which are obtained from organic compounds found in plants and used in the bath or as massage oils in aromatherapy. The prices reflect the yield of oil in the plants. Fragrant roses produce very little oil (Rose Absolute costs £34.58 for 10ml), whereas Eucalyptus gives a high yield and is relatively cheap (£1.55 for 10ml). All prices are exclusive of VAT. The oils can be bought by the litre.
Catalogue Leaflets, Free **Postal charges** Add £2.50 to orders under £50.00; orders over £50.00, free **Delivery** Royal Mail, Courier **Methods of Payment** Cheque, Postal Order, Credit Card

CAMEO CARDS
Linken House
48 Spa Road
Melksham
Wiltshire

Foot massagers
The name of this company belies its single product, a foot massager. The brochure gives plenty of technical information about the history of foot massage and reflexology, as well as its

SN12 7NY
Telephone
01225 709795
Fax
01225 791341

applications today. There are also detailed diagrams of the areas of the feet which respond to reflexology and their corresponding body zones. The massage device itself resembles a flattened abacus and seems easy to use. It retails at £19.90.

Catalogue By Advertising **Postal charges** Free **Delivery** Parcelforce **Methods of Payment** Cheque, Postal Order

CEDAR HEALTH
Pepper Road
Hazel Grove
Cheshire
SK7 5BW
Telephone
0161 483 1235
Fax
0161 456 4321

Natural health products
Cedar Health provides a range of products from Biostrath pick-me-ups to sugar-free Swiss herb lozenges, and a wide selection of leaflets explaining each item. Aromatherapy products also feature prominently. Tegarome costs £8.49 for a 30ml bottle; Babibad, £6.49 for a 125ml bottle; and Flexarome, £9.49 for the same amount.

Catalogue Annually, A5, Leaflets, Colour, 38 pages, Free **Postal charges** Varies with item **Delivery** Royal Mail **Methods of Payment** Cheque, Credit Card

THE CLAY COMPANY
Clay House
Penny Lane
Liverpool
Merseyside
L18 1DG
Telephone
0151 733 6900

Body and skincare products
The Clay Company produces a range of products using only natural French clays which are non-animal tested, contain no added colouring and are suitable for all skin types. The high mineral content of the clays are said to enrich the body system, improve circulation and stimulate cellular rejuvenation. Tissue-improving face mask, £3.95; tissue-toning body mask, £7.95; Body Contour Wrap to aid inch loss, from £15.95.

Catalogue Annually, A5, Leaflets, Colour and B/W, 10 pages, Free **Postal charges** £2 **Delivery** Royal Mail **Methods of Payment** Cheque, Postal Order, Credit Card

CRABTREE & EVELYN OVERSEAS LTD
FREEPOST
36 Milton Park

Toiletries and home fragrances
Crabtree & Evelyn is well-known for its distinguished, high-quality and exquisitely packaged toiletries and fragrances. Everything is made to

Abingdon
Oxfordshire
OX14 4BR
Telephone
01235 862244
Fax
0171 602 4959

Crabtree's specifications and rigorously tested, but not on animals. The brochure describes each of the different ranges and is illustrated with sketches of the products. Avocado body cream, £10/200ml; Jojoba After Bath Refresher, £7.95/250ml; Lavender Bath Oil, £5.25/60ml; Savannah Soap/100g, £2.15; pot pourri in glass jar, £8.95.

Catalogue Annually, A4, Catalogue, B/W, 10 pages, Free **Postal charges** £3.50 **Delivery** Royal Mail **Methods of Payment** Cheque, Credit Card, American Express

D R HARRIS & CO
29 St James's Street
London
SW1A 1HB
Telephone
0171 930 3915
Fax
0171 925 2691

Toiletries

D R Harris, Royal Warrant holder, has been making fine-quality perfumes, toiletries and soaps for more than 200 years. Shaving preparations are a speciality: almond, cologne and lavender shaving soap in a wooden bowl, £10.90; badger shaving brushes, from £35.80. Skincare preparations contain natural ingredients: almond oil skinfood, £7.95. For Mondays (or the morning after the night before) you could try Harris's world-famous Crystal Eye Drops (£5.65) and Pick-Me-Up (£5.10).

Catalogue Annually, Third A4, Leaflets, B/W, 6 pages, Free **Postal charges** Varies with item **Delivery** Royal Mail, Parcelforce **Methods of Payment** Cheque, Credit Card, American Express

DENISE BROWN ESSENTIAL OILS
16 Dittons Road
Eastbourne
East Sussex
BN21 1DW
Telephone
01323 724855
Fax
01323 641676

Essential oils

Denise Brown is the author of *Aromatherapy Lifeguide*, plus two further books on aromatherapy and massage. Her brochure contains Aromacare for mother and baby, oils for professional aromatherapists and a bath and haircare range (vegan approved). There are pre-mixed organic skin creams for a variety of conditions as well as Bach Flower Remedies. Relaxation tapes are also on offer.

Catalogue Bi-annually, A4, Brochure, Colour, 4 pages, Free **Postal charges** Under £25, £4; otherwise free **Delivery** Royal Mail, Parcelforce **Methods of Payment** Cheque, Postal Order, Credit Card

DIRECT COSMETICS LTD
Long Row
Oakham
Rutland
Leicestershire
LE15 6LN
Telephone
01572 724477
Fax
01572 756948

Beauty products, toiletries and jewellery

Direct Cosmetics sell a wide range of perfume and cosmetic products from leading houses such as Vichy, Cacherel, Potter & Moore, Nina Ricci and Max Factor at discounted prices. The RRP for Anais Anais body lotion is £18, for example, but Direct Cosmetics sell it for £5.95; the RRP for Ricci Club After Shave Lotion is £22 but Direct Cosmetics sell it for £11.95. Stock changes constantly according to supply; monthly full-colour newsletters keep customers up-to-date with what's available.

Catalogue Annually, A4, Brochure, Colour and B/W, 4 pages, Free **Postal charges** £2.50 **Delivery** Parcelforce **Methods of Payment** Cheque, Credit Card

DOLMA
19 Royce Avenue
Hucknall
Nottinghamshire
NG15 6FU
Telephone
0115 9634237
Fax
same

Vegan perfumes and toiletries

This tiny but neat catalogue features a range of beauty products free from animal substances which vegans and vegetarians can use with confidence. Testing is on human volunteers not animals, including the partners in the business! Products include vegan perfumes, aromatic body shampoos, hair care, soap, men's shaving lotions, skin care and facial oils. Perfumes, from £7.75/6ml; massage oil, £3.35/50ml; moisturiser, £3.95/50g; deluxe aftershave balm, £2.95/15ml.

Catalogue Annually, A6, Catalogue, Colour, 14 pages, Free **Postal charges** Varies with item **Delivery** Royal Mail, Parcelforce **Methods of Payment** Cheque, Postal Order

ESPA
22 London Road
Guildford
Surrey
GU1 2AF
Telephone
01483 454444
Fax
01483 62355

Aromatherapy, hydrotherapy and spa products
ESPA's products include deeply relaxing and anti-stressing oils, revitalising seaweeds and cleansing masks to help hydrate, purify, firm and protect the body and soothe the mind. You can choose individual items such as soothing bath and body massage oils, £16.50/100ml, or a selection of ESPA products such as the Calming Package (£56.95).
Catalogue Annually, Third A4, Catalogue, B/W, 6 pages, Free **Postal charges** Varies with item **Delivery** Royal Mail, Parcelforce **Methods of Payment** Cheque, Postal Order, Credit Card

ESSENTIAL THERAPEUTICS
25 Buckley Road
Kilburn
London
NW6 7LY
Telephone
0171 624 1022
Fax
same

Aromatherapy preparations
The aromatherapist Michelle Roques-O'Neil has developed a system of aromatherapy preparations using essential oils. She offers a range of bath, body, face, hair and scalp oils, concentrates, environmental preparations and kits such as the Essential Starter. Prices from £7.50 to £39.50.
Catalogue Annually, A5, Catalogue, B/W, 14 pages, Free **Postal charges** £2.50 **Delivery** Royal Mail, Courier **Methods of Payment** Cheque, Credit Card

ESSENTIAL WELL BEING
PO Box 160
Wokingham
Berkshire
RG40 3YX
Telephone
01734 791737

Aromatherapy products for mothers and babies
Essential Well Being specialises in high-quality aromatherapy products for mothers and babies. Their range has been specially formulated by one of the world's leading aromatherapists and uses only oils known to be safe for use on mothers-to-be and babies. For mums, the range covers pregnancy through labour to motherhood. Most popular products include a Tummy Rub (£5.50 for 50ml) for stretch marks, Tummy Tightener (£7.25 for 100ml), Labour Day Back Rub (£3.95 for 50ml) and Pick Me Up Lotion (£7.25 for 100ml). There is also a baby range, including a massage lotion, nappy gel, fretfulness lotion and

gentle shampoo. Everything in the range is made from natural ingredients, and is hypo-allergenic, lanolin- and colour-free. None of the products are tested on animals. Products can be sold individually or gift-wrapped. Gift pack prices range from £6.50 to £14.99.

Catalogue Annually, Third A4, Brochure, B/W, 6 pages, Free **Postal charges** £1.75 **Delivery** Royal Mail, Parcelforce, Parceline **Methods of Payment** Cheque, Postal Order

FLORIS OF LONDON
89 Jermyn Street
London
SW1Y 6JH
Telephone
0171 930 2885
Fax
0171 930 1402

English perfumes and toiletries

Floris has been making and selling perfumes and toiletries since 1730 and can boast two royal warrants. It has a delightful shop in London and operates a worldwide mail-order service. The products are very English, subtle, understated and beautifully packaged. Toilet waters from £14.50/50ml, perfumes from £19.95/7.5ml. There is a wonderful range of bathroom luxuries and shaving products for men. Cologne, £24.25/100ml; aftershave £16.95/100ml.

Catalogue Annually, A5, Catalogue, Colour, 16 pages pages, Free **Postal charges** £3 for orders under £50; free for orders over £50 **Delivery** Royal Mail, Parcelforce **Methods of Payment** American Express, Diners Club, Cheque, Credit Card

G BALDWIN & CO
171–173 Walworth Road
London
SE17 1RW
Telephone
0171 703 5550
Fax
0171 252 6264

Herbs, essential oils, dried flowers

G Baldwin & Co were established as medical herbalists in 1844. They supply a mind-boggling range of oils, herbal powders, culinary herbs, roots and barks, along with books, homeopathic medicines, incense sticks, oil burners and charcoal. Their 100% pure essential oils include Camphor (£1.25 for 10ml), and Myrrh (£5.55 for 10ml). Herbal fluid extracts include Bayberry (£2.78 for 25ml) and Gentian Root (£1.80 for 25ml).

GEO F TRUMPER
166 Fairbridge Road
London
N19 3HT
Telephone
0171 272 1765
Fax
0171 281 9337

Catalogue Bi-annually, A5, Catalogue, B/W, 23 pages, Free Postal charges Varies with item Delivery Royal Mail, Parcelforce Methods of Payment Cheque, Credit Card, American Express, Switch, Postal Order

Gentlemen's toileteries
Geo F Trumper's tasteful catalogue exudes quality and tradition. Trumper's has been a barber and perfumer since 1875, and the history of Trumper and his products is given both here and in a small poetic booklet, *The Art of Shaving*. The delightful range of luxury and everyday toiletries are beautifully packaged. Aftershaves, from £13.25/100cc glass; hairdressings, from £6/100cc travel pack; shampoos, from £6.50/200cc; colognes, from £15/100cc glass; soaps, £5. Shaving accessories, brushes, hampers and gifts are also available.

Catalogue Annually, A5, Catalogue, Colour, 28 pages, Free Postal charges Varies with item Delivery Royal Mail Methods of Payment Cheque, Credit Card, American Express, Diners Club

GOLDSHIELD NATURAL CARE
Bensham House
324 Bensham Lane
Thornton Heath
Surrey
CR7 7EQ
Telephone
0181 665 9670
Fax
0181 665 6433

Healthcare
Goldshield Natural Care is one of the premier vitamin, mineral and food supplement companies in the UK. Specialising in mail order, it provides consumers with a range of high-quality products. Evening Primrose Oil with Cod Liver Oil, £9.95/180 capsules; Chewable Vitamin C, 300mg, £6.45/100 tablets; Multi-Fem Daily Pack, £14.95/30 days; Calcium, 46g, £5.95/54 tablets. The body care range includes hair formula, body wash, baby cream and elderflower eye gel.

Catalogue Annually, A5, Catalogue, Colour, 24 pages, £2 Postal charges £1.95 Delivery Royal Mail Methods of Payment Cheque, Postal Order, Credit Card

HEALTH & BEAUTY

THE GREEN BOOK OF BEAUTY
Yves Rocher
664 Victoria Road
South Ruislip
Middlesex
HA4 ONY
Telephone
0181 845 1222
Fax
0181 845 1023

Natural beauty products

The Green Book of Beauty upholds Yves Rocher's strong belief in protecting the environment. The face, body and hair care products, perfumes, make-up and the preparations for men listed here are all plant-based. None is tested on animals. Sprays are propelled by pure air, and refills are available. Photo Reflet shampoo with camomile, £3.50/250ml; Muscle Relaxing Oil with essential oil of rosemary, £7.95/150ml; shaving foam for sensitive skin, £4.95/150ml.

Catalogue Annually, A4, Catalogue, Colour, 90 pages, Free **Postal charges** £1.95 for orders up to £15; free for orders of more than £15 **Delivery** Royal Mail, Parcelforce **Methods of Payment** Cheque, Postal Order, Stage Payments, Credit Card

GREEN THINGS
PO Box 59
Tunbridge Wells
Kent
TN3 9PT
Telephone
01892 861132
Fax
01892 863558

Naturally based beauty care products

Green Things was established in 1980 to manufacture an extensive range of beauty products using natural ingredients which are not tested on animals. It buys essential oils, plant extracts and other materials from around the world, incorporating them for their therapeutic, cleansing, toning and moisturising properties. Marigold and elderflower cleanser, £3.25/120g; Neroli eye cream, £3.45/15g; juniper and sandalwood aftershave toner, £12.75/1000ml.

Catalogue Annually, Third A4, Brochure, Colour, 12 pages, Free **Postal charges** Varies with item **Delivery** Royal Mail, Parcelforce **Methods of Payment** Cheque

HARTWOOD AROMATICS
Coronet House
Upper Well Street
Coventry
West Midlands
CV1 4AG

Aromatherapy products

Hartwood Aromatics is a friendly, long-established family business specialising in high-quality, pure essential oils, aromatherapy products and books. All the products are natural and vegan-safe with no animal testing. There are health-enhanc-

Telephone
01203 634931
Fax
01203 555422

ing aromatherapy goods for the whole family, from babycare teething creams to luxurious facial care and exotic perfumes for adults. Aromatherapy Beginner's Kit, £12.95; essential oils, from £2.50/10ml; Lotus facial cream, £9.60/50g.
Catalogue Annually, A5, Leaflets, Colour and B/W, 15 pages, Free **Postal charges** £1.75 **Delivery** Royal Mail **Methods of Payment** Cheque, Credit Card

HELIOS HOMEOPATHIC PHARMACY
97 Camden Road
Tunbridge Wells
Kent
TN1 2QR
Telephone
01892 536393
Fax
01892 546850

Homeopathic remedies

Helios Pharmacy was formed in 1986 and 70 per cent of their fully potent homeopathic remedies are created by strictly Hahnemannian methods using the original substance, plant, or mother tincture as the starting point. Mother tinctures cost £2 for 5ml; medicating potencies (in 90% alcohol) cost £3.10 for 3.5ml drops; tablets and pillules cost £2 for 4g. There are also vitamin, mineral and herbal supplements, ointments and other items, plus an extensive booklist.
Catalogue Bi-annually, A5, Leaflets, B/W, 4 pages, Free **Postal charges** Varies with item **Delivery** Royal Mail **Methods of Payment** Cheque, Credit Card

THE HOMEOPATHIC SUPPLY CO
Fairview
4 Nelson Road
Sheringham
Norfolk
NR26 8BU
Telephone
01263 824683
Fax
01263 821507

Storage containers and books

This company supplies storage containers for homeopathic remedies. Cardboard storage boxes covered in black leatherette material cost from £2 (empty) to £4.99 (with 10 brown-glass screw-cap bottles of 8g-tablet size). Dropper bottles cost from £24.75 for 30ml and amber soda glass jars cost from £12.60. Books include *A Guide to Homeopathic First Aid* (£2.50) and *Homeopathy for Common Ailments* (£7.99).
Catalogue Bi-annually, A4, Catalogue, Colour and B/W, 11 pages, Free **Postal charges** Free **Delivery** Royal Mail, Parcelforce **Methods of Payment** Cheque, Credit Card, American Express

JERSEY LAVENDER

Rue du Pont Marquet
St Brelade
Jersey
Channel Islands
JE3 8DS
Telephone
01534 42933
Fax
01534 45613

Lavender beauty products

This small but attractive brochure features toiletries, fragrances, pot-pourri and tasteful gifts from the family-run lavender farm of David and Elizabeth Christie in Jersey. First planted in 1983 the lavender now extends to seven acres and is open to the public during the summer. There are essential oils at £4.15/10ml, soaps at £1.95, and bath foams at £3.50/225ml. Gifts include a lavender bag, £1.75; coat-hanger, £4.99; tea-towel, £2.95; cards and books.

Catalogue Annually, A5, Catalogue, Colour, 6 pages, Free
Postal charges Varies with item **Delivery** Royal Mail
Methods of Payment Cheque

LARKHALL GREEN FARM

225 Putney Bridge Road
London
SW15 2PY
Telephone
0181 874 1130
Fax
0181 871 0066

Natural health products

Larkhall Green Farm offers a full range of health products, from multi-vitamins, fish oils and evening primrose oil to ocean supplements, digestive enzymes and skincare. Its catalogue, almost a complete reference book in itself, lists an Executive Life Complex, a One-a-Day Osteo Formula and multi-vitamins for animals, too. Golden Years multi-vitamins, £14.95/180 tablets; Clear Skin Formula, £4.20/30 tablets; Jojoba Energiser Shampoo, £11.95.

Catalogue Annually, A4, Catalogue, Colour, 120 pages
Postal charges Varies with item **Delivery** Royal Mail
Methods of Payment Cheque, Postal Order, Credit Card

MARTHA HILL

FREEPOST
Corby
Northamptonshire
NN17 3BR
Telephone
01780 450259

Natural beauty products for women and men

Martha Hill launched her first skincare preparations in the 1960s and became one of the early pioneers of cruelty-free, environmentally friendly products. Her comprehensive catalogue lists the items with full descriptions, beauty care routines and entertaining and informative Did You

HEALTH & BEAUTY

Fax
01780 450398

Knows? Herbal cleanser, £2.60/50ml, £14.95/500ml; elderflower eye gel, £2.75/15ml; essence of rose body and hair shampoo, £4/150ml. David Hill has developed a range of natural grooming products for men: herbal shaving cream, £2.75/50ml; all-weather skin shield, factor 10, £4.85/50ml. The company offers a free gift-wrapping service.

Catalogue Annually, A5, Catalogue, B/W, 32 pages, Free **Postal charges** £1, first-class **Delivery** Royal Mail **Methods of Payment** Cheque, Credit Card, Switch, American Express, Credit Card

MASON PEARSON BROS LTD
37 Old Bond Street
London
W1X 3AE
Telephone
0171 491 2613
Fax
0171 499 6235

Hairbrushes
The distinctive Mason Pearson hairbrush is not mass-produced. Most of the work is carried out by hand, using techniques pioneered and patented by the founder – Mason Pearson – over a hundred years ago. There are three types of tuft: boar bristle, for fine to normal hair; boar bristle and nylon for normal to thick hair; and nylon for thick hair. For men there's the 'Military' style with no handle from £17.50; for women, the 'Handy' size costs from £12.75; and for young children, the pocket-size 'Child' costs £13.50.

Catalogue A4, Brochure, Colour, 3 pages, Free **Postal charges** £1.50 per brush **Delivery** Royal Mail **Methods of Payment** Cheque

MEADOWS
Unit 7
Stour Valley Business Park
Chartham
Canterbury
Kent
CT4 7HS
Telephone
01227 731489

Natural creams and oils
Meadows sell a very large range of essential oils for aromatherapy and other uses (prices from around £1.20 for 5g). Everything is made from totally natural ingredients and not tested on animals. They also stock 14 different 'natural creams' for skincare. These include 'Tea Tree and Lavender' (£1.30 for 30ml) and 'Peppermint and Honey Foot Cream' (£1.50 for 30ml). They also sell

HEALTH & BEAUTY

Fax
01227 731810

toners, pot pourri, containers, vaporisers, candles and incense sticks.

Catalogue Leaflets, B/W, Free **Postal charges** Up to £20.00, add £1.50; up to £50.00, add £2.50; over £50.00, free **Delivery** Parcelforce **Methods of Payment** Cheque

MEDIVAC
FREEPOST
Wilmslow
Cheshire
SK9 5YE
Telephone
01625 539401
Fax
01625 539507

Anti-allergy vacuum cleaner and bedding

Medivac produces a range of products which provide relief from asthma, rhinitis, eczema and dust mite allergy. The Medivac vacuum cleaner incorporates a microfiltration system not found in any conventional cleaner and comes with a range of accessories such as extension hoses, mattress nozzle and crevice nozzle. It costs £425 excluding VAT (as an acknowledged medical aid it is VAT-free when supplied to eligible persons). The Banamite range of anti-allergy bedding includes mattress covers, duvets and pillows. Prices from £29.50 (exc VAT) for a pillow.

Catalogue Annually, A4, Catalogue, Colour, 12 pages, Free **Postal charges** £3.95 **Delivery** Royal Mail, Parcelforce, Courier **Methods of Payment** Stage Payments, Cheque, Switch, Credit Card, American Express

MEGAFOOD
PO Box 5
South Kirkby
Pontefract
West Yorkshire
WF9 3XQ
Telephone
0800 252 207
Fax
01977 646797

Vitamin supplements

MegaFood Vitamin and Mineral Supplements are made from plant-food concentrates. Research by world-renowned scientists indicates that MegaFood's nutrients are better absorbed and more effective than the refined nutrients used in other supplements. MegaFood's Full spectrum Bone Formula (£11.49 for 90 tablets) provides minerals, trace minerals and vitamins to maintain healthy bones and joints. MegaFood's Blood Builder (£3.99 for 30 tablets) consists of easily absorbable GrowForm iron, folic acid and Vitamin B12.

Catalogue Third A4, Brochure, Colour, 16 pages, Free **Delivery** Royal Mail **Methods of Payment** Cheque, Postal Order, Credit Card

MICHELINE ARCIER AROMATHERAPY
7 William Street
Knightsbridge
London
SW1X 9HL
Telephone
0171 235 3545

Aromatherapy products
Madame Micheline Arcier is a leading aromatherapy practitioner and teacher. Her products are blended on the premises in Knightsbridge from pure plant extracts, essential oils and vegetable oils. They are not tested on animals. Pure essential oils, citronella £4/5ml, myrrh £13/5ml; body oils, £15.50/75ml; bath oils, from £19/75ml; hand and nail oil, £8.50/30ml; children's products from £12.50. Trial sizes are available, from £4/15ml and aromatherapy kits from £14.95.

Catalogue Annually, A4, Catalogue, B/W, 8 pages, Free **Postal charges** Varies with item **Delivery** Royal Mail **Methods of Payment** Cheque, Postal Order, Credit Card

MOLTON BROWN BY MAIL
PO Box 2514
London
NW6 1SR
Telephone
0171 625 6550
Fax
0171 624 0737

Healthcare and beauty products
Molton Brown beauty products are created with herbal extracts and pure essential oils and for over 20 years these preparations have been made without animal testing. There are beauty products for both men and women and all of them are packaged colourfully but simply.

For men, there is a Sea Moss body range (bath salts, firming lotion, soap and shower gel) and for women, the skin sense range (cleansers, washing gel and toners). They also offer make-up products with a shade chart allowing you to choose from a variety of colours (fawn, red gold, mango, ink).

Catalogue A5, Catalogue, Colour, 23 pages

NATURAL HEALTH PRODUCTS
PO Box 102
Lytham St Annes
Lancashire
FY8 1EG
Telephone
01253 795505

Beauty products
This company offers silica tablets for healthy hair and nails (£9.95 for 1 month's supply), multi-vitamins (£4.95 for 3 months' supply), hormone precursor supplement tablets (£9.95 for 1 month's supply), slimming aids, hair stimulants and a new dental formula that purports to attack plaque. There are also herbal remedies for sleeplessness,

bladder discomfort and muscular aches and pains.
Catalogue A5, Catalogue, Colour, 32 pages, Free **Postal charges** Free **Delivery** Parcelforce **Methods of Payment** Cheque, Postal Order, Credit Card

NECTAR BEAUTY SHOPS
95a Belfast Road
Carrickfergus
Northern Ireland
BT38 8XX
Telephone
01960 351580
Fax
01960 351740

Beauty and skincare products

A comprehensive range of cruelty-free beauty products which includes face, hair and eyecare products, hand and body lotions, bath and shower gels, massage and aromatherapy oils, men's toiletries, perfumes and cosmetics and items for babies. There is a fragrance-free range, too. Rose and glycerine toner, £1.50/100ml; witch hazel blemish gel, £2.95/50ml; jojoba and melon shampoo, £2.95/250ml; fragrance-free camomile and lindenflower body lotion, £1.85/100ml; aromatherapy oils from £2.85.
Catalogue Annually, Third A4, Leaflets, Colour and B/W, 18 pages, Free **Postal charges** Varies with item **Delivery** Royal Mail, Parcelforce **Methods of Payment** Cheque, Credit Card, Postal Order

NEWTONS TRADITIONAL REMEDIES LTD
5 High Street
Solihull Lodge
Shirley
West Midlands
B90 1HA
Telephone
0121 430 7847

Unusual remedies

This catalogue comes from a small, but long-established family firm of medical herbalists who market alternative medicines and health supplements. There are slimming pills, hypertension remedies, internal cleansing systems, anti-rheumatics, laxatives, muscle-builders, energy-givers, beauty products, sleeping pills and aphrodisiacs.
Catalogue Annually, A4, Catalogue, Colour, 27 pages, Free **Postal charges** £1.50 **Delivery** Parcelforce **Methods of Payment** Cheque, Postal Order, Credit Card

PENHALIGON'S
FREEPOST WC4189
London
N4 1NH

Fine-quality beauty products and toiletries

Simply brush your finger across the pictures and you will be able to smell each perfume for yourself. Penhaligon's offers the most luxurious collection

Telephone
0800 317 332
Fax
0181 800 5789

of beauty products and toiletries for men and women, all exquisitely packaged and using William Henry Penhaligon's century-old formulae. There are silver hairbrushes, mock-ivory hand mirrors, shaving equipment and cuff-links, too. Soap, box of three, £16; eau de toilette, from £22; aftershave, £29; shaving stand with bowl, £110.

Catalogue Annually, A4, Catalogue, Colour, 24 pages, Free **Postal charges** £2.50 standard service; £5 priority **Delivery** Royal Mail **Methods of Payment** Credit Card, Cheque, Switch, American Express, Diners Club

PETWORTH HOUSE
Polesdon Lane
Ripley
Woking
Surrey
GU23 6LR
Telephone
01483 225222/223188
Fax
01483 223141

Keep-fit equipment

Petworth House provides a broad and exclusive range of sporting, leisure and fitness equipment. The Smooth-Air 2 dual-action exercise cycle and the ISS 150 stair climber are available for £99.99 each; the Compact Home Gym costs £199.99; and you can purchase snooker tables, pool tables and table-tennis tables, as well as motorised treadmills and cross-country ski exercisers.

Catalogue Annually, A4, Catalogue, Colour, 16 pages, Free **Postal charges** Varies with item **Delivery** Courier **Methods of Payment** Cheque, Credit Card, American Express, Diners Club

PIA INTERNATIONAL LTD
Pia House
7 Whittlesea Terrace
Woodford
Kettering
Northamptonshire
NN14 4JA
Telephone
01832 734301

Cosmetics

Beautician Pia St Luce has created her own range of colour cosmetics and beauty preparations which are not tested on animals. Although she uses only the finest ingredients, her prices are very reasonable. Duo lipsticks with two-toning colours are priced at £4.35; blusher duos at £4.85. Eyeshadow compacts with nine colours cost £5.25; mascaras, £4.35. There are also skincare and haircare products, such as passion fruit and melon cleanser (£4.85), and limeflower and rosemary shampoo which tackles dandruff in greasy hair (£2.95). Discounts are available for members.

Catalogue A5, Catalogue, Colour, 15 pages, Free **Postal charges** £2.00 **Delivery** Royal Mail **Methods of Payment** Cheque, Credit Card, Postal Order

PURPLE FLAME AROMATICS
61 Clinton Lane
Kenilworth
Warwickshire
CV8 1AS
Telephone
01926 55980
Fax
01926 512001

Aromatherapy supplies and training

Purple Flame supplies pure essential oils, lotions, creams, burners, books, charts, videos, a computer programme and a free telephone consultancy service. Their aromatherapy massage sequence video (£23) is a useful teaching aid introducing the various techniques involved. Or, for £420, you could enrol on one of their six-day training courses.

Catalogue A4, Leaflets, B/W, 4 pages, Free **Postal charges** £3.30 or less for small orders **Delivery** Royal Mail, Parcelforce **Methods of Payment** Cheque, Credit Card

QUINESSENCE
1 Birch Avenue
Whitwick
Leicestershire
LE67 5GB
Telephone
01530 838358
Fax
same

Aromatherapy products

The Quinessence aromatherapy collection includes essential oils, remedies and carriers, massage oils and lotions, enhancers and fragrances. Leaflets provide helpful information on each product and its uses, and a range of aromatherapy books is available. Pure essential oils, from £1.80/5ml, or from £2.75/10ml. Massage oils, arranged according to use, can be used to treat numerous complaints from cellulite to stretch marks and cost £3.50/50 ml, £5.99/100 ml.

Catalogue Annually, A5, Leaflets, Colour and B/W, 20 pages, Free **Postal charges** Varies with item **Delivery** Royal Mail **Methods of Payment** Cheque, Credit Card

RENAHALL LTD
61 Lime Tree Avenue
Rugby

Vitamins and oils

Renahall offer a basic range of vitamins and oils with regular new introductions. They have been

HEALTH & BEAUTY

Northamptonshire
Warkwickshire
CV22 7QT
Telephone
01788 811454

in business for 12 years and avoid glossy advertising and coloured brochures. Many of their customers are elderly and appreciate the basic range and prices. Vitamin C ascorbic acid costs £6.25 for 240 grams; 150 Vitamin E capsules cost £4.95. Fish oil (1,000mg capsules) costs £4.40 for 60 capsules and Evening Primrose oil (500mg capsules) costs £5 for 90.

Catalogue A5, Leaflets, B/W, 1 page, Free **Postal charges** Free **Delivery** Royal Mail **Methods of Payment** Cheque

SCENT TO YOU
Trading House
Penn Street
Nr Amersham
Buckinghamshire
HP7 0PX
Telephone
01494 712855

Perfumes

Although printed on glossy paper with colour photographs, the emphasis in this catalogue is definitely on price. The brochure is backed up by more regular leaflets, with up-to-date and new product offers. The products are mainly discounted perfumes. All the top names are here including YSL, Dior, Chanel and Givenchy. There is also a small range of cosmetics, skincare goods and accessories. Savings vary. On Chanel No.19 at £32, for example, discounted to £29.99, you are only saving £2.01, whereas a Miss Dior spray at £47 discounted to £25 saves you a hefty £22. Stock changes constantly.

Catalogue Regular leaflets, A4, Brochure, Colour, 8-16 pages, Free **Postal charges** £1.99 **Delivery** Royal Mail, Parcelforce **Methods of Payment** Cheque, Postal Order, Credit Card, American Express, Diners Club, Switch

SHIRLEY PRICE
AROMATHERAPY
Essentia House
Upper Bond Street
Hinckley
Leicestershire
LE10 1RS

Aromatherapy products

This is an aromatherapy catalogue offering a full range of essential oils, skin, hair and body care products, books and videos, with clear descriptions and tips. Shirley Price also runs training courses for anyone interested in aromatherapy, from beginners to the professional who wishes to

Telephone
01455 615466
Fax
01455 615054

advance his or her skills. Prices for essential oils range between £2.80 for 12ml of cedarwood and £43 for 3ml of the much rarer Jasmin Absolute. A starter kit is available for £33.95.

Catalogue Annually, A5, Catalogue, Colour, 15 pages, Free **Postal charges** Varies with item **Delivery** Royal Mail **Methods of Payment** Cheque, Credit Card

SLENDERTONE
36 George Street
London
W1H 5RE
Telephone
0171 935 0631

Bodyshaping products

Ultratone from Slendertone simulates the natural impulses causing muscles to contract and relax at a controlled and comfortable rate in a regular pattern. In this way it tones the muscles and is said to promote inch loss. The brochure contains detailed illustrations and comprehensive information. For those who just want to concentrate on toning up their face, there's the Ultratone Facial. Prices range from £115 for Ultratone Facial to £642 for Salon 10 Plus and Facial Accessory.

Catalogue Annually, A4, Catalogue, Colour, 12 pages, Free **Postal charges** Free **Delivery** Royal Mail, Parcelforce **Methods of Payment** Cheque, Credit Card, American Express, Diners Club

SUMMERBEE PRODUCTS
Windsor House
Lime Avenue
Torquay
Devon
TQ2 5JL
Telephone
01803 212965
Fax
same

Natural health products

Summerbee specialise in natural health products. As their name suggests, many of the products are made with honey. Examples include Honey Pollen Body Lotion, at £4.80 for 125ml, and finest quality Golden Pollen Capsules, at £6.95 for two bottles. Royal Jelly, for feeling vital and healthy, comes in 'mega strength' doses, in Acacia honey (£23), or merely 'double strength' (£16). Essential oils, moisturisers, cleansers and tonics are also on offer; and there's a good selection of minerals and food supplements to help you feel on top of the world.

Catalogue Annually, A4, Leaflets, B/W, 4 pages, Free

HEALTH & BEAUTY

Postal charges All prices include second-class postage (UK only) and VAT. Add £1.00 for first-class delivery **Delivery** Royal Mail **Methods of Payment** Cheque, Postal Order, Credit Card

VITAL FOODS LTD
FREEPOST BD 257
PO Box 13
Bingley
West Yorkshire
BD16 1BR
Telephone
01274 589026
Fax
01274 581515

Health food and supplements

This catalogue is like a small health food shop. On one side you have a range of vitamin and mineral supplements and on the other skin care and beauty products made from herbs and plants. There is plenty of dietary information to help you choose and discounts up to £12 are available for orders over £100.

The beauty and body care products are made by Creighton's and there are also aromatherapy oils, healthcare books, water filters and ionisers. A pack of 30 Ginseng tablets is £4.25 and 30 Evening Primrose Oil capsules £5.25.

Catalogue Annually, A5, Brochure, Colour, 22 pages, Free **Postal charges** £1 for orders under £10; orders over £10, no charge **Delivery** Royal Mail **Methods of Payment** Cheque, Postal Order, Credit Card, Switch

WELEDA (UK)
Heanor Road
Ilkeston
Derbyshire
DE7 8DR
Telephone
0115 930 9319
Fax
0115 944 0349

Homeopathic medicines, oils and remedies

Weleda has maintained its principles concerning the balance of the body and health with nature since 1923. Founded in Switzerland, this company offers a homoeopathic remedy for most ailments. Included with the catalogue are brochures outlining Weleda's many other products, from essential oils to herbal deodorant, almond face packs, rosemary shampoo, toothpastes and baby toiletries. Essential oils, £3.40/10ml, or a starter pack of 16 oils, £47.29; Calendula baby moisturiser, £3.95/75ml; Gelsemium, £2.99; plant gel toothpaste, £1.75/75ml.

Catalogue Annually, A5, Brochure, B/W, 16 pages, Free **Delivery** Royal Mail **Methods of Payment** Cheque

WHOLISTIC RESEARCH COMPANY
Dept GMO
Bright Haven
Robin's Lane
Lolworth
Cambridge
Cambridgeshire
CB3 8HH
Telephone
01954 781074

Holistic lifestyle products, devices and books
This interesting company sells a range of devices for 'healthy living in a modern world', including water purifiers, ionisers, natural light bulbs, juicers and a selected range of books. It takes the trouble to test every model on the market and presents an unbiased view of which it has found to be the best and most efficient. The catalogue goes to considerable lengths, for example, to discuss the merits of various water purification systems, finally coming down in favour of distillation, which removes virtually all impurities. The best juicer comes out at some £348, but there are cheaper models. A water distiller is £199 and ionisers are from around £20. There is also a range of other, often more unusual products.
Catalogue On request, Book, B/W, 72 pages, Free **Postal charges** Varies with item **Delivery** Royal Mail, Parcelforce **Methods of Payment** Cheque, Postal Order

WOODS OF WINDSOR
Unit 3
Lakeside Industrial Estate
Colnbrook
Berkshire
SL3 OED
Telephone
01753 684241
Fax
01753 680881

Perfumery and toiletry products
Woods of Windsor began in a pharmacy in the shadow of Windsor Castle in 1770. Two centuries later Roger and Kathleen Knowles acquired the run-down premises and while cleaning out the attic discovered a treasure trove of old recipe and prescription books. Using the original formulae for inspiration they now produce attractively presented perfumery and toiletry products from their factory at Colnbrook. The shop in Windsor, built in 1699, is devoted solely to the sale of Woods of Windsor products. Prices range from £45 for a shaving brush to £7.95 for Nourishing Massage Lotion and £1.35 for a Perfumed Paper Drawer Sachet.
Catalogue Annually, A4, Brochure, Colour, 26 pages, Free **Postal charges** Varies with item **Delivery** Royal Mail **Methods of Payment** Credit Card, American Express, Diners Club, Cheque

HEALTH & BEAUTY

ZENA COSMETICS (UK) LTD
5 The Woolmarket
Cirencester
Gloucestershire
GL7 2PR
Telephone
01285 640159
Fax
01285 642898

Beauty products

Zena Cosmetics are skincare consultants promoting Ella Baché products. Rather than testing her products on animals, Madame Baché tests them on her own skin. Her skincare products include cleansers (from £12.95 for 55g), fast-acting treatments to eradicate acne and other spots and blemishes (from £12.75 for 60ml), and special anti-ageing creams (from £21.50 for 100ml) as well as soaps (from £5.95 per cake), masks (from £15.50 for 60ml) and cosmetics (from £13.25 per 30ml for treatment foundation for blemished skin).

Catalogue A5, Catalogue, Colour and B/W, 15 pages, Free
Postal charges £2.50 post, packing and insurance
Delivery Royal Mail **Methods of Payment** Cheque, Postal Order, Credit Card, American Express

Hobbies & Crafts

ALEC TIRANTI
70 High Street
Theale
Reading
Berkshire
RG7 5AR
Telephone
01734 302775
Fax
01734 323487

Materials for sculpture
Alec Tiranti sells an extensive range of tools, materials and equipment for modelling, wood-carving and sculpture and stocks a variety of books and technical booklets on the various techniques. Extra-fine stainless steel modelling tool, £6.52; carvers' A punch, £2.47; high-speed cutter, £6.94.
Catalogue Annually, A5, Catalogue, B/W, 104 pages, Free **Postal charges** Varies with item **Delivery** Royal Mail, Parcelforce, Courier **Methods of Payment** Cheque, Postal Order, Credit Card

THE ART VENEERS COMPANY
Industrial Estate
Mildenhall
Suffolk
IP28 7AY
Telephone
01638 712550
Fax
01638 712330

Veneers and marquetry supplies
The Art Veneers Company publish a fully illustrated combined manual/catalogue with a price list. The catalogue comprises a series of informative articles on various aspects of veneering and the techniques used in marquetry. It contains full details of the company's selections of veneers, tools, polishes, and has colour pages illustrating a range of veneers, motifs and bandings. The company also produce a range of Collectors sets which comprise veneer samples which can be used for restoration. For sizes 18×6in, cabinet veneers such as Elm cost 90p, Plum £1.80 and Rosewood, Santos £2.00.
Catalogue Catalogue, Colour **Methods of Payment** Cheque, Postal Order, Credit Card

ARTS ENCAUSTIC

Glogue
Dyfed
Wales
SA36 OED
Telephone
01239 831401
Fax
01239 831767

Heat-applied art

Encaustic art means to burn in. It is the use of heat as a solvent for pigmented wax. The Ancients used this medium for many portraits before oil paints were developed. But you don't need to light a fire nowadays – just plug in your low-heat tools and get started. Encaustic art involves smoothing – spreading wax with a light ironing motion; lifting and dabbing – intricate effects created by suction; edge work – creating fine lines and broad sweeps; and point work – the finest details and the start of graphic work. Tools include coloured wax, a stylus with a constant low temperature and interchangeable tips, wax blocks, scribing tool, brushes and painting cards. The company's leaflet also includes details of the Encaustic Art Teaching Video, a 57-minute video which costs £19.75.

Catalogue As required, A5, Leaflets, B/W, 4 pages, Free **Postal charges** Under £15, add £1; under £30, £2; under £50, £3; over £50, free **Delivery** Royal Mail **Methods of Payment** Cheque, Postal Order, Credit Card

BARNYARNS

PO Box 28
Thirsk
North Yorkshire
YO7 3YN
Telephone
01845 524344
Fax
01845 525046

Embroidery kits and samplers

Madeira Threads (UK) Ltd is part of Europe's leading manufacturing group of high-quality embroidery threads. They produce a wide range of embroidery kits in cross-stitch, both charted and printed. The Oriental Collection OR1-OR6 costs £9.95 each. They also produce Samplers (Scottish 17th-Century Sampler, £18.25); Surface Stitchery (Keepsakes, £9.75); Raised (Floral Fantasy, £16.00); Ribbon, which costs between £6.95 and £7.50; Crewel embroidery (Cushion HCEC 07, £23.30); Jacobean designs; plus seasonal, greeting and anniversary card embroidery designs.

Madeira manufactures wooden embroidery hand frames and offers various ranges of their threads suitably packed in gift boxes for the embroiderer, lacemaker, quilter or fisherman. A handling charge of £1.00 per order, plus postage at cost, is made.

Catalogue Annually, A4, Catalogue, Colour, 40 pages

BECKFOOT MILL
Clock Mill
Denholme
Bradford
West Yorkshire
BD13 4DN
Telephone
01274 830063
Fax
01274 834430

Soft toy patterns, filling fibres and wadding

Beckfoot Mill is a specialist supplier of soft toy kits, quilting, wadding and sewing supplies. The irresistible furry animals are simple and easy to make, especially as the kits include everything you need – fabric, eyes, nose, washable filling, pattern and instructions (from £2.35 for Tiny Ted to £8.75 for Bertie, the Old-Fashioned Bear). Toy-filling is available by the metre, from £6.75; nylon-backed wadding £2.99/m; fur fabrics, from £4.30/m. Accessories include quilting threads, felt, toy components (eyes, noses, etc), sequined motifs and ribbons.

Catalogue Annually, A5, Brochure, Colour and B/W, 16 pages, Free **Postal charges** £1 for orders up to £17; free for orders of more than £17 **Delivery** Royal Mail, Parcelforce **Methods of Payment** Cheque, Postal Order, Credit Card

BRAITRIM
Braitrim House
98 Victoria Road
London
NW10 6NB
Telephone
0500 225588
Fax
0181 723 3003

Fashion and retail supplies

Although this catalogue is aimed at the fashion and retail industry, many of the useful items in it can be bought singly. For needlework enthusiasts, there are tape measures, tailors' chalk, tailors' wax, tailors' dummies, and textile staplers. For those at home, there are garment bags, hangers, rails, suit hangers, suit covers, skirt hangers, scissors, first-aid kits, plastic gloves, wall mirrors. There is plenty of office equipment, racking systems which could be used in a home office, Sellotape, batteries, pens. An interesting catalogue, even for those not in business. The company offers next-day delivery.

HOBBIES & CRAFTS

Catalogue Bi-annually, A4, Catalogue, Colour, 190 pages, Free **Methods of Payment** Cheque, Postal Order, Credit Card, Switch

CLASSIC SILKS, SCREENS & INTERIORS
140 Watlington Road
Runcton Holme
Kings Lynn
Norfolk
PE33 0EJ
Telephone
01553 810604
Fax
same

Silk screens and fabrics

Thinking about making a wedding dress, but wondering where to go to find all the materials? Classic Silks has the answer. It offers by the metre a wide range of pure silk dupion, taffeta, damask, brocade, chiffon, organza, crêpe de chine and seersucker. And to top it all, silk tulle veiling. For interior decoration, furnishing silks, linings and interlinings are available, and Classic Screens make attractive silk-covered free-standing screens to complement your décor. Pure silk Indian dupion dress fabric (ivory), £7.95/m; silk dupion tartans and stripes for furnishing, £17.95/m; screens from £270.

Catalogue Annually, Third A4, Leaflets, Colour and B/W, 5 pages, Free **Postal charges** Varies with item **Delivery** Royal Mail, Parcelforce, Courier **Methods of Payment** Cheque, Credit Card

CRAFT DEPOT
1 Canvin Court
Somerton Business Park
Somerton
Somerset
TA11 6SB
Telephone
01458 274727
Fax
01458 272932

Arts and crafts supplies

This catalogue features an enormous range of materials for the craftsperson. There are dolls to dress, chairs to seat, animals to make, clocks to assemble and jewellery to fashion, plus needlecraft supplies, items for woodcraft and a large selection of craft books. Safety cat eyes, £1.32 for six pairs; brooch pins, 72p for 12; three wooden trays for stencilling, £19.95.

Catalogue Annually, A4, Catalogue, B/W, 72 pages, £3 **Postal charges** Varies with item **Delivery** Royal Mail, Parcelforce **Methods of Payment** Cheque, Credit Card

CROFT MILL
Lowther Lane
Foulridge
Colne
Lancashire
BB8 7NG
Telephone
01282 869625
Fax
01282 870038

Sheeting, furnishing and clothing fabrics
Home of one of the best selections of sheeting and furnishing fabrics, Croft Mill is situated in Lancashire and welcomes visitors to its mill shop. The catalogue lists a vast range of fabrics and haberdashery items with entertaining descriptions. Plain dyed poly/cotton sheeting, 94in wide, £3.50/m; white cotton jersey T-shirting with train print, 64in wide, £2.50/m; 33m reel of ½in-wide cotton bias binding, £2.

Catalogue Quarterly, A4, Catalogue, Colour, 16 pages, Free **Postal charges** £2.95 **Delivery** Parcelforce, Royal Mail **Methods of Payment** Cheque, Credit Card, Switch

ELIZABETH BRADLEY DESIGNS
1 West End
Beaumaris
Anglesey
North Wales
LL58 8BD
Telephone
01248 811055
Fax
01248 811118

Needlework kits and designs
Elizabeth Bradley's catalogue features a collection of traditional needlework designs, many based on Victorian patterns and pieces. They can be made up as cushions, pictures, chair or stool covers or joined together to create a needlework carpet. The majority of kits cost £50 or £55 and contain interlock canvas with printed design and wool code, chart, wool and wool card, history and instruction leaflets and two needles. Accessories and finishing packs are available.

Catalogue Annually, A3, Brochure, Colour, 4 pages, Free **Postal charges** Free **Delivery** Royal Mail **Methods of Payment** Cheque, Credit Card

FABERDASHERY
Midhurst Walk
West Street
Midhurst
West Sussex
GU29 9NF
Telephone
01730 817889

Patchwork and quilting materials and supplies
The shelves of this South Downs' shop are packed with everything you need to make perfect patchwork or colourful quilts, from needles and pins to inspirational books. Faberdashery's mail-order catalogue contains a number of leaflets outlining its wares and a colour palette for choosing materials. Stencils and templates, £4.95; wadding (2oz Terylene), £1.45/yd; material from

HOBBIES & CRAFTS

£5.50/yd; octettes from £5.95 for eight pieces.
Catalogue Annually, A5, Leaflets, Colour, 6 pages, £1
Postal charges Varies with item **Delivery** Royal Mail
Methods of Payment Cheque, Credit Card

FRED ALDOUS LTD
PO Box 135
37 Lever Street
Manchester 1
Greater Manchester
M60 1UX
Telephone
0161 236 2477
Fax
0161 236 6075

Craft materials

Fred Aldous Ltd was founded in 1886, selling rattans and willows for making hampers and skips used in the cotton mills. Now corporate members of the Guild of Master Craftsmen, they pride themselves on their carefully manufactured quality products and customer service. They supply materials as diverse as soldering irons for glasswork and wax dyes and perfumes for candlemaking.
Catalogue A5, Catalogue, Colour and B/W, 78 pages, Free
Postal charges Up to 500g, add £1.00; up to 1kg, add £3.00; up to 3kg, add £4.00; up to 24kg, add £6.00; over 24kg, add £9.00. Discounts: £1.00 off orders from £20.00 to £39.99; £3.00 off orders from £60.00-£99.99; £12.00 off orders of £100.00 and over **Delivery** Royal Mail
Methods of Payment Postal Order, Cheque, Switch, Credit Card

GREEN & STONE
259 King's Road
London
SW3 5EL
Telephone
0171 352 0837
Fax
0171 351 1098

China restoration

A catalogue containing everything for china restoration. Also supplies books on china restoration for beginners to antique care and repair. Books from £4.50. Ancillary materials, such as brush pots and pencils to water-colour papers, varnishes, glues and cleaning agents, are all available.
Catalogue Annually, A5, Catalogue, B/W, 15 pages, Free
Postal charges Varies with item **Delivery** Royal Mail
Methods of Payment Cheque, Credit Card, American Express

HOBBIES & CRAFTS

GUILD OF MASTER CRAFTSMEN PUBLICATIONS LTD
Castle Place
166 High Street
Lewes
East Sussex
BN7 1XU
Telephone
01273 477374
Fax
01273 478606

Books, magazines and videos

This catalogue features a wide range of woodworking and craft books and videos. Books include *Making Wooden Toys and Games* (£14.95) and *Making Collector Plates on Your Scroll Saw* (£9.95). Videos include *Traditional Upholstery Workshop*, a set of two videos by David James for £23.45. There are also magazines on wood-turning and wood-carving.

Catalogue Annually, A4, Catalogue, Colour, 14 pages, Free **Postal charges** Add £2.50 for the first book or video and an additional £1.00 per book thereafter or 50p per video **Delivery** Parcelforce **Methods of Payment** Cheque, Credit Card, American Express, Diners Club

JACKSONS OF HEBDEN BRIDGE
Croft Mill
Hebden Bridge
West Yorkshire
HX7 8AP
Telephone
01422 842964
Fax
01422 842385

Needlework and tapestry kits

Jacksons of Hebden Bridge is a fourth-generation family business. Their general collection of complete kits for needlework and tapestry contains a wide range of items both decorative and practical, from pictures to cushions, door stops, bell-pulls and rugs. Sample prices: easy-to-work cottage or rooster teacosy kits, £29.95 each; spectacles case kits, £15.95; children's stitch-a-card kits, £5.95; and cuddly toy kits from £10.95. Their specialist products include complete tapestry kits for items of church furnishings in which they are world leaders. The range includes kneelers (from £25.95 per kit) and pew cushion fronts (from £19.95 per kit).

Catalogue A4, Catalogue, Colour, 21 pages, £1.00 **Postal charges** £2.10; for orders over £50, free **Delivery** Royal Mail **Methods of Payment** Cheque, Postal Order, Credit Card

JANET COLES BEADS LTD
1 Shire Business Park

Loose beads, necklaces, earrings, jewellery kits

Rich-looking colour catalogue which introduces you to the world of beads. The catalogue is

HOBBIES & CRAFTS

Worcester
Worcestershire
WR3 8QA
Telephone
01905 756018
Fax
01905 756641

divided into sections according to materials and is suitable for newcomers, who are looking for kits to make up their own necklaces and earrings, to practised beaders. All the jewellery is supplied in both kit and made-up form. Each kit contains everything you will need to make it up (except a needle) and includes ear-fittings for pierced ears. If you want clip-on ear-fittings, these have to be ordered separately as an extra. All the beads are pictured 'same size' so you can see exactly what they will look like. They are also used in many of the made-up necklaces so you can get a clear idea of what they will look like strung up. The business is run by the Cole family and the catalogue is written in a very personal and at the same time, educational, way. Prices range from jewel colour beads, 10 for 18p and desert earrings, £1.50 for a kit, £3.00 made-up, to Meteorite two-strand necklace, £27.95 made-up, £23.95 in kit form.
Catalogue Annually, A4, Catalogue, Colour, 112 pages pages, £3.50 (inc postage) **Postal charges** Under £10, add £1; over £10, add £1.40; over £50, add £2.25 **Delivery** Royal Mail **Methods of Payment** Cheque, Postal Order, Credit Card, Switch

JANIK ENTERPRISES LTD
Brickfield Lane
Denbigh Road, Ruthin
Ruthin
Clwyd
LL15 2TN
Telephone
01824 702096
Fax
01824 707383

Wood crafts

Suppliers of high-quality wooden products for pyrography (pokerwork, which involves burning any chosen design on to wood, leather or bone), and folk painting, Janik's sales are entirely by catalogue or recommendation. Their pyrography starter kit costs £56.75 and includes the Janik Pyrograph G4 and a book entitled *An Introduction to Pyrography* by Stuart Grainger. Other good-value, stylish products include kitchenware (salt and pepper set, £2.55; hornbeam corkscrew, £2.45), toys (skipping ropes, £2.75; tops and whips, £2) and fireside bellows self-assembly kits (£25.12).

Catalogue A5, Catalogue, Colour, 34 pages, Free **Postal charges** To cover administration, postage, packing and insurance. For pyrography points, wire for G4HW and brands only, 75p. All other goods up to £25, £2.50. All other goods over £25 and up to £75, £4. All other goods over £75, free **Delivery** Royal Mail, Courier **Methods of Payment** Cheque, Postal Order, Credit Card, Switch

JOLLY RED TAPESTRY KITS
FREEPOST
Langport
Somerset
TA10 0BR
Telephone
01460 281809
Fax
01460 281810

Tapestry kits

Each tapestry kit can be worked from Jolly Red's enlarged charts and many of them can also be worked from a full-colour printed canvas. Each kit comes complete with its own free, handmade yarn bag. Printed canvas kits include 'Animal Magic', 'Sealife' and 'Jamboree' (£36.95 each) and charted kits include 'Carnival', 'Seashore' and 'Tree of Life' (£26.95 each). A 24in frame is also available for £7.50 including postage.

Catalogue A5, Brochure, Colour, 6 pages, Free **Postal charges** £2.00 for all kits except 'Alphabet' (£1.50). Any additional kits ordered at the same time, no charge **Delivery** Parcelforce **Methods of Payment** Cheque, Postal Order

KERNOWCRAFT ROCKS & GEMS LTD
Bolingey
Perranporth
Cornwall
TR6 0DH
Telephone
01872 573888
Fax
01872 573704

Jewellery-making equipment

Kernowcraft is a leading supplier of semi-precious stones and jewellery components, providing a prompt and efficient mail-order service to silversmiths, jewellers, craftworkers and students. The catalogue includes an unrivalled range of semi-precious stones – beads, cabochons, faceted stones, tumbled stones, etc; a comprehensive range of jewellery findings and mounts in sterling silver, 9car gold and plated metal; as well as tools, books and much more. A range of crystals and minerals, gemstone spheres, eggs and slabs and the more unusual and difficult to obtain cabochons and

HOBBIES & CRAFTS

faceted stones are listed separately. Regularly updated lists are available free on request.

Catalogue Annually, A5, Catalogue, Colour, 56 pages, Free **Postal charges** £1.20 **Delivery** Royal Mail **Methods of Payment** Cheque, Credit Card, Switch, Postal Order

LIBERTY FABRICS DIRECT
Fabric Mail Order Department
210–220 Regent Street
London
W1H 6AH
Telephone
0171 734 1234
Fax
0171 734 8323

Fabrics

Liberty has been producing textile collections since 1878. The classic Liberty collections are made either in Tana Lawn (100% cotton) or Varuna wool (100% wool). The catalogue reproduces a wide range of Liberty's patterns in their true colours and actual sizes to aid reference.

The Tana Lawn collection includes the famous paisley pattern 'Peacock Feather' and the equally well-known range of flower prints inspired by Japanese art. Tana Lawn is generally available in 90cm widths at £11 per metre and Varuna wool in 140cm widths. All Varuna wool fabrics cost £22 per metre.

Three free swatches are sent out on request, but Liberty make the point that they cannot guarantee colour matching. Most of the fabrics are shown on the roll and made up, whether into decorative accessories such as cushions or waistcoats.

Catalogue Annually, A4, Catalogue, Colour, 40 pages, £3.50 **Postal charges** Varies with item **Delivery** In-house delivery **Methods of Payment** Diners Club, American Express, Credit Card, Cheque

MULBERRY SILKS
2 Old Rectory Cottage
Easton Grey
Malmesbury
Wiltshire
SN16 0PE
Telephone
01666 840881

Embroidery silks

Patricia Wood of Mulberry Silks offers a wide range of hand-wound pure silk twist for embroiderers in medium or fine thickness. Her Silk Topics, each consisting of 12 spools of pure silk twist in a selected colour scheme, cost £12 per pack. Colour schemes include buttercups and daisies, coffee and cream, early morning mist and sapphire and steel. Mulberry Silk 'tri-tones' are three 30m spools of fine silk thread in tones of one colour priced at £5.75. She can also supply 50m spools in medium thickness for £8 each.

Catalogue Bi-annually, A5, Leaflets, B/W, 1 page, Free **Postal charges** Group orders valued up to £100.00, add £2.00; individual orders, add £1.00. Orders over £100.00, no charge, but please allow £3.00 for insurance if first-class post is required **Delivery** Royal Mail **Methods of Payment** Cheque

OAKLEY FABRICS LTD
8 May Street
Luton
Bedfordshire
LU1 3QY
Telephone
01582 424828
Fax
01582 455274

Materials for making stuffed toys

Oakley's brochure is aimed at home toymakers, and includes a clear explanation of the latest safety standards. The materials include everything from fillers of mohair, duckdown or velour to complete kits of 'luv-a ducks', 'hug-a-bunnies', 'flop-a-dogs', 'adorable donkeys', and 'floppy cats' costing from £18 per kit. Acessories such as cats' eyes cost from 60p for 5 pairs.

Catalogue Bi-annually, A4, Catalogue, B/W, 10 pages, Free **Postal charges** £3.80 **Delivery** Parcelforce **Methods of Payment** Cheque, Credit Card, Switch

PANDURO HOBBY
Westway House
Transport Avenue
Brentford
Middlesex
TW8 9HF
Telephone
0181 847 6161
Fax
0181 847 5073

Craft and hobby supplies

A large colour catalogue containing every conceivable hobby and craft material from paints and brushes to textiles, baskets and dried plants, beads, stones and jewellery accessories. There is also a separate catalogue of Christmas assortments available. Whole rolls of fabric can be purchased in 10-metre rolls. There are also sewing threads, ribbons, lampshade kits, silk painting kits, dolls' heads and hands, boxes and bowls. The catalogue contains 11,000 items, a must for every hobby and craft enthusiast.

Catalogue Annually, A4, Catalogue, Colour, 394 pages, £3.95; sold at W H Smith **Postal charges** Under £50, £2.95

plus £1.50 handling charge, minimum order, £20 **Delivery** Parcelforce **Methods of Payment** American Express, Switch, Credit Card, Cheque, Postal Order

PRIMAVERA
FREEPOST
PO Box 141
Cardiff
South Glamorgan
Wales
CF4 1ZZ
Telephone
0800 243400
Fax
01222 521800

Needlepoint kits and accessories

Primavera offers needlepoint kits featuring fresh, colourful floral and fruit designs. Thirty-four designs are available for cushion covers, as well as a set of curtain tie-backs and three smaller items on one canvas to create treasured gifts. Cushion kits from £39, canvas only from £19.20; 20in frame, £15.95; stool, £39.95. A making-up service is available.

Catalogue Annually, A4, Catalogue, Colour, 16 pages, £1.50 **Postal charges** Free **Delivery** Royal Mail, Parcelforce **Methods of Payment** Cheque, Credit Card, Switch, Postal Order

PRINCESS PLEATERS
Checkley Fields
Checkley
Hereford
Hereford & Worcester
HR1 4ND
Telephone
01432 850140
Fax
01432 851180

Pleating machines

The Princess Pleater is an all-British, 24-needle machine that will gather fabrics for smocking or elasticating, saving dressmakers vast amounts of time. It comes complete with full instructions and is suitable for amateur and professional use, and in schools. Price £89.95; extra needles available.

Catalogue Annually, A4, Leaflets, Colour, 2 pages, Free **Postal charges** Free **Delivery** Parcelforce **Methods of Payment** Cheque, Credit Card

READICUT RIDINGS CRAFT
Terry Mills
Ossett
West Yorkshire
WF5 9SA
Telephone
01924 810810

Doll-making kits

Readicut Ridings brings you an extensive range of doll-making and doll-dressing kits for the enthusiastic doll collector. There are porcelain dolls, vinyl dolls and wax-look dolls, male and female, and a vast array of outfits, accessories and patterns. A porcelain doll kit costs £33.99 and her seaside promenade outfit, £25.99 (pattern only, £2.75); vinyl strap shoes, 59p.

Fax
01924 810813

Catalogue Annually, A4, Catalogue, Colour, 24 pages, £1.95 **Postal charges** £2.25 **Delivery** Royal Mail, Parcelforce **Methods of Payment** Cheque, Stage Payments, Credit Card, Switch

READICUT WOOL
Terry Mills
Ossett
West Yorkshire
WF5 9SA
Telephone
01924 810810
Fax
01924 810813

Needlecraft kits

Readicut is one of the largest needlecraft mail-order companies in Britain and its catalogue is packed with projects from tapestry-making kits and samplers to cushion covers and cards. Books, accessories and a framing service are offered, and there are kits for kids, too. Cat by the Garden Gate kit, £8.99; Wedding Sampler kit, £13.99; Winter Trellis cushion cover kit, £23.99. You can even send a photograph and Readicut will reproduce it on canvas for you to produce your own piece of needlework (from £16.99).

Catalogue Annually, A5, Catalogue, Colour, 78 pages, £1.95 **Postal charges** £1.95; orders of more than £25, free **Delivery** Royal Mail, Parcelforce **Methods of Payment** Cheque, Stage Payments, Credit Card, Switch

ROWAN YARNS
Green Lane Mill
Holmfirth
West Yorkshire
Telephone
01223 66841
Fax
same

Knitting

Rowan Yarns publish a brochure of knitting kits with shade cards and prices of yarns by the ball, buttons, needles and magazines of knitting. All the kits are the latest in knitting fashion and colours. Those people who would like to buy by mail order will receive a special pack containing newsletter, broadsheet, price list and order form plus a free shade card. Pattern and product updates will be sent regularly. Knitting kits for autumn/winter start at approximately £50. Yarn by the ball starts at £1.45 for a 25g ball of lightweight double knitting wool. An interesting brochure for the knitting enthusiast.

Catalogue Annually, A4, Brochure, Colour and B/W, 7 pages, Free **Postal charges** Varies with item **Delivery**

RUSSELL HOUSE TAPESTRIES
PO Box 12
Wiveliscombe
Taunton
Somerset
TA4 2YZ
Telephone
01984 624135

Royal Mail **Methods of Payment** Cheque, Postal Order, Credit Card, Switch

Needlepoint kits
Russell House Tapestries produce kits for the needleworker. The brochure is accompanied by colour photographs showing a range of designs inspired by the patterns and rich colour combinations found in oriental rugs. Both printed and charted versions are available. Prices range from £23.99 to £43.95. To complete your work, finishing kits are offered at £12.99 in 31 colours. Components come ready cut and marked for easy assembly with the zip inserted and piping cord covered.

Catalogue Annually, A5, Brochure, Colour and B/W, 12 pages, Free **Postal charges** £2.50 refundable with first order **Delivery** Royal Mail **Methods of Payment** Cheque

SARA DAVENPORT TAPESTRIES
PO Box 21
Newbury
Berkshire
Telephone
0171 225 2223/4
Fax
0171 581 3629

Tapestry kits
Sara Davenport Fine Paintings is the only gallery in the UK to specialise in antique dog paintings. It now also features cats and horses. Tapestry kits taken from these paintings are available from the gallery as well as from their mail-order outlet in Berkshire. The 16 × 16in printed canvas kits cost £45 and are suitable for cushion covers, footstools, fire screens or wall tapestries. The larger size kits (32 × 42in) are suitable for rugs or coffee-table stools and cost £100.

Catalogue A5, Brochure, Colour, 6 pages, Free **Delivery** Parcelforce **Methods of Payment** Cheque

SILK SHADES
12 Market Place
Lavenham
Suffolk
CO10 9QZ

Silk material for interiors and dressmaking
Silk Shades offer an extensive range of silks for dressmaking, upholstery and curtains. There are more than 20 different silks including embroidered silks and classics such as dupion, organza and

Telephone
01787 247029
Fax
same

taffeta. Accessories include ribbon, beaded and chantilly lace, hats, shoes and headdresses. For a small charge, they can provide large swatches of their fabrics and there's a 10% discount on orders over £250.

Catalogue Catalogue, Colour, 14 pages, Free **Postal charges** 24hr, £8.50; 48hr, £6.00; 3–5 days, £3.75 **Delivery** Royal Mail, Parcelforce **Methods of Payment** Cheque, Postal Order, Credit Card

SMITCRAFT
Unit 1
Eastern Road
Aldershot
Hampshire
GU12 4TE
Telephone
01252 342626
Fax
01252 311700

Arts and crafts materials

This must be one of the most comprehensive handicraft catalogues. Whether a professional or amateur, you will find this catalogue brimming over with materials and kits at competitive prices. There is everything you need for cane seating and basket making, picture framing, marquetry, creative jewellery, leatherwork, Christmas decorations, floral work, toy making, rug making, sewing, knitting, needlework, model making, plus brushes and paints and more. You can buy a dolls' house kit for £43.95, a fort kit for £33.95. Traced embroidery kit with threads and frame, £3.70. Prices exclude VAT.

Catalogue Annually, A4, Catalogue, Colour, 158 pages, Free **Postal charges** £4.50 plus VAT for orders up to £50; free to mainland UK for orders of more than £50 **Delivery** Royal Mail, Parcelforce, Courier **Methods of Payment** Cheque, Credit Card

THE SORCERER'S APPRENTICE
6–8 Burley Lodge Road
Leeds
West Yorkshire
LS6 1QP

Books, curiosities and essences

The Sorcerer's Apprentice offers 'supernatural substances' such as aromatics, roots and philtres as well as relics and artifacts such as a 2,000-year-old copper talisman used by priests in Benares (£4.97), 'ideal for time-travel exercises'. Books include *Aspects of Occultism* (£7.50), *Celtic Myth*

HOBBIES & CRAFTS

Telephone
0113 2451309
Fax
same

and *Legend* (£12.99) and *Herbs in Magic and Alchemy* (£8.95).
Catalogue Leaflets, Colour and B/W, Free **Postal charges** Add £1.00 to orders totalling £7.00 or less **Delivery** Royal Mail **Methods of Payment** Cheque, Postal Order, Credit Card

STAMPING HEAVEN
4 South Parade
Headingley
Leeds
West Yorkshire
L56 3LF
Telephone
01532 740440

Art stamps

Art stamping originated in America and uses rubber stamps to produce an image using an ink pad or by colouring directly on to the rubber itself using colour brusher pens. You will be amazed at the decorative effects you can create. Stamping Heaven has helpfully put together a selection of starter kits from £8.50 and stocks a range of accessories including a set of 10 brusher pens, £3.25, and colourbox pads from £4.99.
Catalogue Annually, A4, Leaflets, B/W, 13 pages, Free **Postal charges** £1.50 **Delivery** Royal Mail **Methods of Payment** Cheque, Postal Order

STANLEY GIBBONS
5 Parkside
Christchurch Road
Ringwood
Hampshire
BH24 3SH
Telephone
01425 472363
Fax
01425 470247

Stamp-collecting products

Stanley Gibbons Publications have been serving the needs of stamp-collectors since 1865 and still offer the most comprehensive range of philatelic products. They have a wide range of catalogues, from 'Railways on Stamps' (£9.50) to 'Chess on Stamps' (£5). Luxury hingeless, one country, blank and thematic albums are available – at a price. More down-to-earth examples, such as the Universal stamp album, with 40 white unfaced leaves, are more reasonably priced (£22.50). Lighthouse stamp mounts are from 75p per packet of 35 and watermark detectors are £14.75.
Catalogue Annually, A5, Catalogue, Colour, 31 pages, Free **Postal charges** Add £3.00 (UK) or £6.00 (overseas) to all orders **Delivery** Royal Mail **Methods of Payment** Cheque, Postal Order, Credit Card

HOBBIES & CRAFTS

THE STENCIL STORE COMPANY
20/21 Herongate Road
Chorleywood
Hertfordshire
WD3 5LG
Telephone
01923 285577
Fax
01923 285136

Stencils, paint effects and accessories
This is the world's largest distributor of retail stencils. The Stencil Store's attractive catalogue will fill you with inspiration. Here you will find all you need to start stencilling from ready-cut designs, paints and brushes to the tools necessary for cutting your own. Rose Peony Border, £9.99; Bluebell Posy, £7.99; stencil brushes from £2.50; paints from £2.45. Fabric paints and materials to create paint effects are also stocked.
Catalogue Annually, A4, Catalogue, Colour, 28 pages, £1.50 **Postal charges** Varies with item **Delivery** Royal Mail, Parcelforce **Methods of Payment** Cheque, Credit Card

TREFRIW WOOLLEN MILLS
Trefriw
Gwynedd
Wales
LL27 0NQ
Telephone
01492 640462
Fax
01492 641262

Woollen tweed by the length
The Trefriw Woollen Mills produce a range of traditional woollen clothing, knitting wools, tableware, rugs and bedspreads. As one might expect there is a strong Welsh flavour to everything here and visitors are welcome. Pure new wool tweed by the yard is available by mail order and samples are supplied. The fabric is approx. 60in (150cm) wide and costs £11.95 per yard.
Catalogue Annually, A4, Leaflets, Colour and B/W, 4 pages, £1 for tweed samples **Postal charges** Varies with item **Delivery** Royal Mail, Parcelforce **Methods of Payment** Cheque, Credit Card

WILLOW FABRICS
27 Willow Green
Knutsford
Cheshire
WA16 6AX
Telephone
01565 621098
Fax
01565 653233/phone/day

Needlework materials
Willow Fabrics is a mail-order house specialising in embroidery fabrics and accessories (one page alone is devoted to scissors). It stocks linens, tapestry canvases, ribbons, threads, wools, place mats, cross-stitch rugs, lace edgings and many more items including books and leaflets. Willow is very popular with its customers for its personal service and has many repeat orders. Embroidery hoops from 50p; Aida 8 count fabric, £6.70/m;

Bantry Cashel linen, £18.10/m; white tapestry canvas, £13.80m (fabrics are available in half-width half-metre sizes).

Catalogue Quarterly, A4, Leaflets, B/W, 24 pages, Please send three first-class stamps for a price-list **Postal charges** £1.50 **Delivery** Royal Mail **Methods of Payment** Cheque, Credit Card, American Express

---

WRANGLE POINT KITES
Belle Vue
Bude
Cornwall
EX23 8JY
Telephone
01288 353905
Fax
same

Kites

Kites vary from the fairly conventional stunt and sport kites capable of doing loops, swoops and dives in a variety of wind speeds to the Flexifoil Power Kites capable of performing aerobatic stunts at over 100mph. Prices start at £12.99 for a Highflyer and rise to £329 for the Flexifoil Hyper-12.

The company has another outlet for jewellery inspired by surfing: the hallmarked sterling silver 'surfer' and 'bodyboarder' are available as charms, earrings, necklaces and key-rings (prices start at £13.00).

Catalogue Annually, A5, Catalogue, B/W, 6 pages, Free **Postal charges** Add £2.75 on all orders below £100.00; orders over £100.00, free **Delivery** Royal Mail, Parcelforce **Methods of Payment** Cheque, Postal Order, Credit Card

---

YATELEY INDUSTRIES FOR THE DISABLED LTD
Mill Lane
Yateley
Camberley
Surrey
GU17 7TF
Telephone
01252 872337
Fax
01252 860620

Hand-printed textiles

This sheltered workshop, providing employment for people with disabilities, produces good-quality fabrics and craft items. Using block and screen printing they can produce several thousand designs in over 30 different colours. After designing and carving the pattern blocks in their workshops, the Yateley team use high-quality natural fabric to produce items such as aprons (from £6), silk cravats (£12), oven gloves (£3.20) and screen-printed sweatshirts (from £9+VAT).

Catalogue A5, Catalogue, B/W, 12 pages, Free **Postal**

charges Up to £5.00, add 95p; up to £15, add £1.20; up to £50, add £2.50; up to £100, add £5.00; over £100, free **Delivery** Royal Mail **Methods of Payment** Cheque, Postal Order, Credit Card, American Express

Home

A B WOODWORKING
Unit J
Pentre Wern
Gobowen
Oswestry
Shropshire
SY10 7JZ
Telephone
01691 670425
Fax
01691 670235

Shaker boxes
The Shakers made their boxes by the thousand and used them for storing thread, buttons, tools, spices, medicines and paint ingredients. Today they are collector's items and change hands for large sums. A B Woodworking uses the same materials and lovingly hand crafts every box. It makes traditional oval boxes (from £8.40), boxes with swing handles (from £20), lined boxes (from £23), hat boxes (from £31) and trays (from £18) in a variety of finishes, or unfinished for your own decoration.
Catalogue Annually, A4, Catalogue, Colour and B/W, 12 pages, £2, refundable with order **Postal charges** Varies with item **Delivery** Royal Mail, Parcelforce **Methods of Payment** Cheque

ABBEY QUILTING LTD
Selinas Lane
Dagenham
Essex
RM8 1ES
Telephone
0181 592 2233
Fax
0181 593 3787

Mattress protectors
Abbey Quilting's Cumulus mattress protectors are synthetic, non-allergenic and stain-resistant and are available in both flame-retardant and waterproof versions. Machine-washable and easy to fit, the Cumulus protector retails at £17.99 (£20.99 for waterproof version) for a standard 2'6" single bed and £24.99 for a standard double. The company will also make special sizes to order and offers waterproof ones.

Abbey Quilting also produce duvets (from £18.49 for a 13.5 tog single duvet), hollowfibre pillows (£11.49), and quilting materials.

Catalogue A5, Leaflets, Colour, 1 page, Free **Postal charges** Free **Delivery** Royal Mail **Methods of Payment** Cheque

ALAN FOXLEY CERAMICS
26 Shepherds Way
Saffron Walden
Essex
CB10 2AH
Telephone
01799 522631

Ceramics

Designer and craftsman Alan Foxley specialises in handmade stoneware house name plaques and numbers. All signs are individually made to order and are frostproof and maintenance free. Each piece of work comes complete with screwholes, solid brass screws and small discs to fit over the screwheads. Number plaques start at £16.95 for 7in diameter; name plaques start at £55.10 for 11in diameter. Photographs (eg of your house) can be copied and other sketches prepared at a cost of £7.

Catalogue A5, Leaflets, Colour and B/W, 4 pages, Free **Postal charges** Free **Delivery** Parcelforce **Methods of Payment** Cheque

APPALACHIA: THE FOLK ART SHOP
14a George Street
St Albans
Hertfordshire
AL3 4ER
Telephone
01727 836796
Fax
01992 467560

Traditional American-made arts, crafts and soft furnishings

A spin-off from the successful shop of the same name in St Albans, this small brochure features the most popular items from the retail outlet. The range includes a set of five decorated Shaker boxes, £47.99; Tillie, the herb lady doll, £39.99; attractive blanket throws from the US, from £39.99; Kentucky clocks, from £24.99; and wooden hearts with homespun tie, £3.99.

Catalogue Annually, A4, Leaflets, Colour, 1 page, Free **Postal charges** Varies with item **Delivery** Royal Mail **Methods of Payment** Cheque, Credit Card

ARISTOCAST ORIGINALS LTD
Dept HB10
Bold Street

Ornamental plaster mouldings

This brochure contains the complete range of plaster mouldings available. Centre-pieces from 12-inch, price £23, to 56-inch, price £130. The

Sheffield
South Yorkshire
S9 2LR
Telephone
01742 561156
Fax
0114 2431835

range has been assembled to meet most design requirements. Panel moulding, 1.5m length from £8, quadrant corners from £3.50. Pedestals, archways, corbels and fire-surrounds are also stocked. The designs are ornate and traditional.

Catalogue Annually, A4, Brochure, Colour, 16 pages, Free **Postal charges** £15 per complete order **Delivery** Courier **Methods of Payment** Cheque, Credit Card

ARTISAN
Unit 4A
Union Court
20 Union Road
London
SW4 6JP
Telephone
0171 498 6974
Fax
0171 498 2989

Wrought-iron furniture and accessories

This company makes traditional wrought-iron bedsteads including an impressive four-poster; they also make iron curtain rail packs, stair handrails and stair rods, door and window furniture and accessories such as heart door knockers and toilet-roll holders.

Catalogue Annually, A4, Catalogue, Colour, 15 pages, Free **Postal charges** Under £20, £3.75; under £100, £6.85; over £100, £11.75; beds £35 each **Delivery** Royal Mail, Parcelforce **Methods of Payment** Cheque, Postal Order, Credit Card

BEAMERS
Well Cottage
Westhope
Herefordshire
HR4 8BT
Telephone
01432 830466

Handmade animal clocks, earrings, badges and magnets

Beamers makes a charming collection of affordable animal clocks in 17 endearing designs. All come with brass hands, black or white numbers, quartz movement and a two-year guarantee, for £12.95 each. Other products on the animal theme include picture frames, £8.95; drop earrings, £2.50; magnets, £1.40; and clever wellie pegs to keep your boots together, £1.40.

Catalogue Annually, A4, Leaflets, Colour, 2 pages, Free **Postal charges** Varies with item **Delivery** Royal Mail, Parcelforce **Methods of Payment** Cheque

BLACK DOG OF WELLS
18 Tor Street
Wells
Somerset
BA5 2US
Telephone
01749 672548

Decorative terracotta
This small family business has been making decorative terracotta (literally 'fired earth') for over 20 years. Their small brochure illustrates a range of miniature relief plaques, such as house and garden blessings and inscribed cartouches, designed by Philippa Threlfall. Each piece is hand-finished and fired at 1100 degrees which means it can be displayed outside. The terracottas are mounted on 5in-square dark blue card and come in special plastic bags. A 4.5in piece is £10.50; 3.5in, £8.50.
Catalogue A4, Brochure, B/W, 1 page, Free **Postal charges** Free **Delivery** Parcelforce **Methods of Payment** Cheque

BOMBAY DUCK
16 Malton Road
London
W10 5UP
Telephone
0181 964 8882
Fax
0181 964 8883

Exclusive ranges of gifts, textiles, jewellery, wrought-iron furniture and home accessories
Bombay Duck not only supply by mail order but have a warehouse from where they sell direct to the public on Sundays only from 11am to 5pm. Their range includes gifts, textiles, jewellery, stationery, wrought-iron furniture and home accessories, which are handmade in India and Indonesia. A small tin lantern £5.95, a traditional towel rail in wrought-iron £160. Some unusual and tempting gifts too numerous to mention.
Catalogue Annually, A4, Catalogue, Colour and B/W, 4 pages, Free **Postal charges** £5, orders over £50 free **Delivery** Royal Mail **Methods of Payment** Cheque, Postal Order

THE BRADLEY COLLECTION LTD
The Granary
Flowton Brook
Flowton
Suffolk

Curtain poles
Bradley products can be purchased from Harrods, Heals, John Lewis, Liberty and Sanderson as well as by mail order. The collections are steel, wood or decorative. The latter are cast in resin and individually finished and decorated by hand. The

IP8 4LJ
Telephone
01473 652651
Fax
01473 652657

decorative finial styles are gothic and baroque (eg 'Acanthus on Scroll') and cost from £60 each. There are also co-ordinating brackets (from £32) and tie-backs (from £65).

Catalogue A4, Leaflets, Colour, 8 pages, Free **Postal charges** Free **Delivery** Royal Mail, Parcelforce **Methods of Payment** Cheque, Credit Card

THE BRUSH FACTORY
Lord Roberts Workshops
6 Western Corner
Edinburgh
Scotland
EH12 5PY
Telephone
0131 337 6951
Fax
same

Brushes
Lord Roberts Workshops produce an astonishing variety of brushes. The brochure, entitled 'The Brush Factory' features a range of hand-crafted boot scrapers (from £24) and a special set of brushes for a golfer (£9.40). There are also novelty brushes such as the Bobby Badger, hand-made to keep boots and shoes from soiling your best carpets, and household items such as a vegetable brush (£2.50) and a lavatory brush, (£2.96). Lord Roberts is a registered charity.

Catalogue Annually, A5, Leaflets, Colour, 4 pages, Free **Postal charges** Free **Methods of Payment** Cheque, Credit Card

BUYERS & SELLERS LTD
120/122 Ladbroke Grove
North Kensington
London
W10 5NE
Telephone
0171 229 1947/8468
Fax
0171 221 4113

Domestic appliances
Buyers & Sellers supply almost every brand of cooker, fridge, freezer, oven, hob, vacuum cleaner, microwave, washing machine and tumble-drier currently available in the UK. They have an advice line for telephone shoppers as well as a large showroom/warehouse for personal callers. Although they do not have a catalogue as such, they will send out a selection of makers' brochures to assist choice. They often have 'special purchases' on display or end-of-line models and are well-known for their competitive prices. Delivery is undertaken countrywide – and even throughout Europe.

Catalogue A5, Brochure, Colour and B/W, 2 pages, Free **Postal charges** Free **Delivery** In-house delivery **Methods**

of Payment Cheque, Credit Card, American Express, Diners Club

BYRON & BYRON LTD
4 Hanover Yard
Noel Road
London
N1 8BE
Telephone
0171 704 9290
Fax
0171 226 7351

Curtain poles

Byron & Byron offer a range of distinctive decorative curtain poles, finials, and holdbacks in ironwork and wood. A gilt-finished ball finial ('Cronkhill'), in the 'Découpage' collection and a painted wooden holdback (90mm diameter) are both priced at £34.40. Some of the more ornate examples of finials and holdbacks are in the 'Animantia' collection, which features starfish, clams and scallops. Then there is the aluminium 'Ottoman' collection whose 20mm-diameter poles and brackets are rust-proof. They offer a choice of six finials and three lengths of pole pre-arranged in sets. Prices start at £81.90 for a set.

Catalogue A4, Leaflets, Colour, 11 pages, Free **Postal charges** £10.00 **Delivery** Royal Mail **Methods of Payment** Cheque

CELEBRATION CRYSTAL CO LTD
FREEPOST
Montford Bridge
Shrewsbury
Shropshire
SY4 1BR
Telephone
01743 850851
Fax
01743 850146

Cut-glass crystal

A family-run business, Celebration Crystal has been producing decorative glassware for more than 15 years. There are three ranges, one of which is machine-made, the other two hand-cut from lead crystal. The products can be etched, giving a frosted effect, coloured, with up to three enamel colours, or silvered, or a combination of all three.

A full range of glassware is available from tankards to decanters, jugs, glasses, trophy cups, rose bowls and plaques. Prices are individually determined according to requirements.

Catalogue A4, Brochure, Colour and B/W, 1 page, Free **Postal charges** For all orders below £100.00, add £10.00; orders over £100.00, free. For express overnight delivery, add an extra £6.00 **Delivery** Royal Mail, Parcelforce **Methods of Payment** Cheque

HOME

CHAMBERS FINE FURNITURE
7 Enterprise House
Thomlinson Road
Hartlepool
Co Durham
TS25 1NS
Telephone
01429 863523

Beds
All Chambers beds are handmade from solid wood and each bed is made to personal order. The majority of woods used are oak, maple, sycamore, douglas fir or cherry and painted beds are in Tulip Wood. Single painted beds from £526, double beds made from oak £831. These are all with two moveable head and foot sprung slatted bases for a double and one for a single.

Catalogue Annually, A5, Brochure, Colour, 4 pages, Free
Postal charges Double beds – £35, single beds – £27
Delivery In-house delivery **Methods of Payment** Cheque

CHANGE WEAR OFFICE FURNITURE
17–20 High Street
Wootton Bassett
Swindon
Wiltshire
SN4 7AA
Telephone
01793 853887
Fax
01793 848551

Linen sheets and pillowcases
Change Wear do not produce a catalogue for the sheets and pillowcases as there is only a limited stock. The sheets were made for the government 41 years ago for officers' issue and then put into storage. They are new and still in their packing from various spinning mills in Ireland. The company bought them from the Ministry, which is why they are able to offer them at such reasonable prices. Single sheets, 108 × 70in, cost £16; double sheets cost £30; pillowcases, 17½ × 29in, cost £3; and napkins, 22 × 22in, cost £3.50.

Catalogue Annually, A4, Leaflets, B/W, 1 page, Free
Delivery Parcelforce **Methods of Payment** Cheque, Credit Card

CHELSEA TRADING COMPANY
Bemco Building
Wandsworth Bridge South
London
SW18 1TN
Telephone
0181 877 9635

Traditional household equipment
A basic leaflet with simple drawings illustrates the Chelsea Trading Company's traditional and practical items for the home. These include a wooden towel rail (30in high by 27in wide) in either a natural or mahogany, £25, and a valet stand, £28. The Traditional Clothes Airer (from £30) comes complete with detailed assembly instructions and

Fax
0181 877 9645

a variety of helpful hints on what else you can hang from it.

Catalogue Annually, Third A4, Leaflets, Colour, 2 pages, Free **Postal charges** Free **Delivery** Royal Mail, Parcelforce **Methods of Payment** Cheque, Credit Card, Postal Order

THE CHINA BOX
2 Penarth Place
St Thomas Street
Winchester
Hampshire
SO23 9HR
Telephone
01962 851250

English-made earthenware and china

The China Box is a family business run from a small shop near Winchester Cathedral. They sell quality English-made earthenware and china, hand-crafted in well-established potteries in Staffordshire and other unusual potteries around the country. They specialise in a large range of blue and white patterns still produced by underglaze engravings. They are stockists of Calico, Arden, Davenport, FRB, Matilda's Kitchens, Asiatic Pheasant and many others. They also hold several patterns of spongeware and a farmyard range which is delicately hand-stencilled. They can provide beautiful plates for a dresser, a breakfast set or an animal jug, delivered to your door.

Catalogue Bi-annually, Colour postcards, 13 pages, 75p refundable against order **Postal charges** UK: add £3.25 on orders up to £15.00; add £5.75 on orders over £15.00 **Delivery** Parcelforce, Royal Mail **Methods of Payment** Cheque, Postal Order, Credit Card

CIEL DECOR
187 New King's Road
London
SW6 4SW
Telephone
0171 731 0444
Fax
0171 731 0788

Provençal furnishing fabrics and gifts

This family-run business has its origins in the Vaison-la-Romaine region of Provence where its products are made. The attractive cotton furnishing fabrics are woven in traditional rich colourways and would add a flavour of Southern France to any home. Prices start at £5.95/m (150mm width) and rise to £24.95/m (280mm width). Gifts are from £4.95 for a printed cotton purse to £50 for a quilted beach bag.

THE CLASSIC MAIL ORDER CO
Branksome
Hilton Road
Cowes
Isle of Wight
Hampshire
PO31 8JB
Telephone
01983 281086

Fine items for the home
Decorative and functional, these 'fine items' include a traditionally crafted solid pine coat rack with five brass hooks from £49.95; book-ends for £14.95 a pair; kitchen shelf without back, £145; plate rack without back, £150. Traditional cast kitchenware includes food warmers from £16.95 and recipe-book holders (£24.95). Wrought-iron curtain tie-backs range from £14.95 to £17.95, and hand-painted flowerpots are priced at £12.95.

Catalogue Annually, A4, Brochure, Colour and B/W, 5 pages, Free **Postal charges** £5 for most items; material from £3.12/2m to £8.50/32m; gift-wrapping £1 extra **Delivery** Royal Mail, Parcelforce **Methods of Payment** Cheque

Catalogue A5, Brochure, Colour, 1 page, Free **Postal charges** £3.00 in the UK **Delivery** Royal Mail **Methods of Payment** Cheque, Postal Order

CLASSIC SILKS, SCREENS & INTERIORS
140 Watlington Road
Runcton Holme
Kings Lynn
Norfolk
PE33 0EJ
Telephone
01553 810604
Fax
same

Silk screens and fabrics
Thinking about making a wedding dress, but wondering where to go to find all the materials? Classic Silks has the answer. It offers by the metre a wide range of pure silk dupion, taffeta, damask, brocade, chiffon, organza, crêpe de chine and seersucker. And to top it all, silk tulle veiling. For interior decoration, furnishing silks, linings and interlinings are available, and Classic Screens make attractive silk-covered free-standing screens to complement your decor. Pure silk Indian dupion dress fabric (ivory), £7.95/m; silk dupion tartans and stripes for furnishing, £17.95/m; screens from £270.

Catalogue Annually, Third A4, Leaflets, Colour and B/W, 5 pages, Free **Postal charges** Varies with item **Delivery** Royal Mail, Parcelforce, Courier **Methods of Payment** Cheque, Credit Card

CLOAKROOMS
Dodbrooke House
Kingsbridge
Devon
TQ7 1NW
Telephone
01548 853583

Traditional wooden cloakroom furnishings
John and Jenny Crellin established Cloakrooms in 1992. Working from their Victorian rectory in Kingsbridge, their range has gradually extended to incorporate a number of hand-crafted innovative designs from coat stands and racquet holders to boot jacks and shoe-cleaning boxes in a choice of finishes. Coat and hat rack, £18.50; roller towel-rail, £9.95; shoe-cleaning box, £42.50.

Catalogue Annually, Third A4, Brochure, B/W, 2 pages, Free **Postal charges** £3.50 **Delivery** Royal Mail, Parcelforce **Methods of Payment** Cheque, Credit Card

CLOCK HOUSE FURNITURE
The Old Stables
Overhailes
Haddington
East Lothian
Scotland
EH41 3SB
Telephone
01620 860 968
Fax
01620 860 984

Footstools
The complete range of footstools in a beautifully illustrated brochure, from bedroom footstools to Victorian fender stools. The variety is endless. They can be made in any size and with any fabric, which includes a needlepoint collection and woven tapestry collection. You can supply your own fabric but this must comply with current fire regulations' cigarette and match tests.

Catalogue Annually, A4, Brochure, Colour, 8 pages, Free **Delivery** Parcelforce **Methods of Payment** Cheque

COLOGNE & COTTON
74 Regent Street
Leamington Spa
Warwickshire
CV32 4NS
Telephone
01926 332573
Fax
01926 332575

Cotton bed and table linen, and eau de cologne
Cologne & Cotton was established in 1989 by Victoria Shepherd and Jenny Deeming to reintroduce the pleasures of pure cotton bed and table linen, and eau de cologne based on original 18th-century formulae. Their catalogue pictures inviting beds made up with crisp white sheets and Welsh woollen check blankets, baskets full of fresh candy-striped pillows, tables with embroidered cloths and neat piles of waffle towels. Candy-striped double duvet cover, £45; double

HOME

flat sheet, £22.50; pillowcase, £8.95. Colognes from £9.95.

Catalogue Annually, A4, Catalogue, Colour, 16 pages, Free **Postal charges** Varies with item **Delivery** Royal Mail, Parcelforce **Methods of Payment** Cheque, Credit Card, American Express

---

THE COMPLEAT STENCILLER
The Saddle Room
Capesthorne Hall
Macclesfield
Cheshire
SK11 9JY
Telephone
01625 860970
Fax
same

Stencils

American Traditional Stencils are the largest manufacturer of solid brass and laser cut stencils in the world. They also supply paints, crayons, brushes, tools and instructions for embossing; electric heat pens and cutting knives; marbling, colourwash and liming kits; and dolls' house stencils. On receipt of £1, they will send their mail-order list of craft books and products. Their full-colour catalogue which shows multi-layer stencils, some 5ft long, is available on receipt of £6.

Catalogue Annually, A4, Catalogue, Colour, 30 pages, Free **Postal charges** £2.00 **Delivery** Parcelforce, Royal Mail **Methods of Payment** Cheque, Credit Card, Postal Order

---

COPPELIA DECORATIVE STENCILS
Newton Villa
Ashfield Crescent
Ross-on-Wye
Herefordshire
HR9 5PH
Telephone
01989 566838
Fax
01989 768345

Stencils

Coppelia's attractive stencils and stencil borders include an 'Oriental' collection with ginger jar (£18.95, pre-cut), fan dish (£8.95) and willow-pattern plate (£8.95). The 'Conservatory' collection includes a climbing clematis (life-size), an arranged urn and a delphinium (£15.95 each). The borders include 'Deco sunray' and 'Alpine strawberries' (£11.95 each). Stencil brushes are also available in sizes 4, 6 and 8 from £2.50.

Catalogue A4, Catalogue, Colour, 7 pages, Free **Postal charges** UK: £1.50; overseas: £5.00 **Delivery** Royal Mail, Parcelforce **Methods of Payment** Cheque

CROFT MILL
Lowther Lane
Foulridge
Colne
Lancashire
BB8 7NG
Telephone
01282 869625
Fax
01282 870038

Sheeting, furnishing and clothing fabrics

Home of one of the best selections of sheeting and furnishing fabrics, Croft Mill is situated in Lancashire and welcomes visitors to its mill shop. The catalogue lists a vast range of fabrics and haberdashery items with entertaining descriptions. Plain dyed poly/cotton sheeting, 94in wide, £3.50/m; white cotton jersey T-shirting with train print, 64in wide, £2.50/m; 33m reel of ½in-wide cotton bias binding, £2.

Catalogue Quarterly, A4, Catalogue, Colour, 16 pages, Free **Postal charges** £2.95 **Delivery** Parcelforce, Royal Mail **Methods of Payment** Cheque, Credit Card, Switch

CRUCIAL TRADING LTD
The Market Hall
Craven Arms
Shropshire
SY7 9NY
Telephone
01588 673666
Fax
01588 673623

Natural-fibre floor covering

Crucial Trading, the natural alternative to carpet, offers the largest collection of natural-fibre floor-coverings in Europe. Fibres woven into really practical floor-coverings suitable for virtually any room in the house include seagrass, sisal, coir, jute, cotton (perfect for bedrooms and bathrooms) and fabulous wool floor-coverings. Free catalogue and samples are available on request, and fitting can be arranged throughout mainland Britain. Crucial Trading also offer an enormous range of natural rugs (made from their floor-coverings and edged with cotton, tapestry or even leather borders). Full details are contained in the Rugs & Mats catalogue which will also be sent without charge.

Catalogue Annually, A4, Catalogue, Colour, 32 pages, Free **Postal charges** Varies with item **Delivery** Courier, In-house delivery **Methods of Payment** Cheque, Credit Card, American Express, Diners Club, Switch

CUBESTORE
38 Grosvenor Road
Chiswick
London

Modular furniture

CubeStore has specialised in shelving and storage systems for home and work for more than 25 years. It produces cubes, oblongs, drawers, record units,

HOME

W4 4EG
Telephone
0181 994 6016

cupboards and wardrobes as well as special units, trestles and table-tops, modules to create a bed or provide inexpensive base units for a kitchen. The super-slim aluminium wall shelving comes with neat brackets and made-to-measure shelves. There are also free-standing, stacking shelf units. Finishes include white, grey and real beech veneer. White cubes start from £14.70, beech cubes from £26.65.

Catalogue Annually, A5, Catalogue, Colour, 32 pages, Free **Postal charges** Varies with item **Delivery** Courier **Methods of Payment** Cheque, Credit Card

CUSHIONS
No 8 Impress House
Vale Grove
London
W3 7QP
Telephone
0181 932 8788
Fax
0181 932 8790

Cushions

Cushions are *the* cushion specialists. Their off-the-peg range features classic fabrics with a contemporary feel. These include raw silks, denim, chambray, gingham, ticking and towelling. They also offer a cushion couture service, where they will design, make-up and trim to any specification. An example of their product is the Beach Buddy, a small and convenient towelling cushion with a waterproof inner liner. Ideal for travelling, for use on the beach or by the pool they come in 9 colours and include the pad. Their cotton ticking, gingham, denim and chambray cushions start from £12.95 while silk tartans are from £18.50. The couture service starts at £9.50, excluding fabric.

Catalogue Bi-annually, A4, Brochure, Colour, 4 pages, Free **Postal charges** £7 **Delivery** Omega Securicor **Methods of Payments** Cheque, Postal Order

DAMASK
3/4 Broxholme House
New King's Road
Junction with Harwood Road
London
SW6 4AA

Bedlinen, tablecloths, etc

Damask has pages of elegant embroidered bedlinen, hand-quilted floral patchwork bedspreads, all in beautiful designs. Cotton table-linen, finely embroidered, 170 × 260cm, from £69; embroidered cushion covers in pure cotton from £21.

Telephone
0171 731 3470
Fax
0171 384 2358

Napkins sold in sets of six for £4 each. They also sell pure cotton nightwear and nursery bedding.
Catalogue Annually, Loose leaf, Catalogue, Colour and B/W, 44 pages, Free **Postal charges** For orders up to £100, add £3; orders over £100, add £6 **Delivery** In-house delivery **Methods of Payment** Cheque, Postal Order, Credit Card,

DIRECT IMPORT OF CHIPPING CAMPDEN
Chipping Campden
Gloucestershire
GL55 6PP
Telephone
01386 841923
Fax
01386 841937

Porcelain accessories

An interesting collection of imported porcelain accessories which will brighten your kitchen, bathroom or lounge. With a range of storage jars from £4.95 to £10.95, Limogès boxes for the collector from £49 to £56. The Limogès frog at £96 is particularly appealing. Or the cast-iron door-stop frog for £8.95. Other products include pizza cutter and spaghetti spoon for the gourmet!
Catalogue Quarterly, A5, Catalogue, Colour, 20 pages, Free **Postal charges** £3.95 **Delivery** Royal Mail **Methods of Payment** Cheque, Postal Order

THE DOMESTIC PARAPHERNALIA COMPANY
Unit 15
Marine Business Centre
Dock Road
Lytham
Lancashire
FY8 5AJ
Telephone
01253 736334
Fax
01253 795191

Clothes airers and plant stands

The Domestic Paraphernalia Company offers the Sheila Maid, a traditional pine and cast-iron clothes-airer on a pulley to suspend from your ceiling (from £33). Use it to air clothes or hang dried flowers, bunches of herbs or pots and pans. The cast-iron components are available in red, blue, green, black or white. Another useful piece of paraphernalia is the Chelsea Plant Stand – slatted, tiered shelving to display pots in the conservatory, greenhouse, garden or patio (£42).
Catalogue Annually, A5, Leaflets, Colour and B/W, 3 pages, Free **Postal charges** £3 **Delivery** Royal Mail, Parcelforce **Methods of Payment** Cheque, Postal Order, Credit Card

THE EASIRIDER COMPANY
60 Main road
Hackleton
Northamptonshire
NN7 2AB
Telephone
01604 870713
Fax
01604 870430

Sheepskin car-seat covers, footwear and other items for the home

Add a touch of comfort and luxury to your car with these tailored lambswool rugs, and headrest, steering-wheel, safety-belt and seat-covers. The Easirider company has been handcrafting these products from fine-quality sheepskins for more than 20 years. Its extensive range also includes sheepskin moccasins, underblankets, heel pads and toys. You need never feel cold again. Car-seat cover, £49.95; steering-wheel cover, £6; children's moccasins, £9.95; single underblanket, £39.95.

Catalogue Annually, A5, Brochure, Colour and B/W, 8 pages, Free **Postal charges** Varies with item **Delivery** Royal Mail, Courier **Methods of Payment** Cheque, Credit Card

EDWARD HARPLEY
'Crownings'
Buxhall Road
Brettenham
Ipswich
Suffolk
IP7 7PA
Telephone
01449 737999
Fax
01449 736111

Curtain poles, finials and pelmets

Most of Edward Harpley's finials are authentic copies of 19th-century originals and are hand-turned and hand-carved. The poles are made in four diameters in any available timber and can be made to fit bay windows on receipt of an accurate plan. A limed oak pole 1.5in in diameter costs £13.33 per foot. A pair of 'Faux Gilt' finials to fit that diameter would cost £63.05. Curtain tidies cost from £35.49 per pair. Pelmets start at £435.50 for a 5ft lath with 6in returns, with a painted or decorated finish.

Catalogue A4, Catalogue, Colour, 15 pages, Free **Postal charges** All carriage up to 20kg is charged at £16.00. Consignments over this weight are charged pro rata **Delivery** Courier **Methods of Payment** Cheque, Credit Card

ELEPHANT INDUSTRIES

Unit 14
Lansdowne Workshops
London
SE7 8AZ
Telephone
0181 858 1945
Fax
same

Fun furniture for children

Elephant Industries' handmade painted children's furniture, which arrives fully assembled, has achieved distinction for its inspired blend of fun and function. The 'Elephant' (£60) functions both as a step-up and a seat. The 'Bookshell' (£199) is a free-standing, snail-shaped double-sided bookcase with a secret compartment for cassettes or drawing materials and a convenient seat too. The 'Hangaroo' (£139) is a child-size valet for a week's worth of outfits plus a detachable pouch for sports kit or laundry.

Catalogue A4, Leaflets, Colour, 1 page, Free **Postal charges** Free **Delivery** Parcelforce **Methods of Payment** Cheque, Credit Card

EMBROIDERED CUSHIONS

The Bungalow
Gogerddan
Tanygroes
Cardigan
Dyfed
Wales
SA43 2HP
Telephone
01239 811216

Embroidered cushions

Order an embroidered cushion as a gift or for your home. Mrs Morgan-James offers a choice of three designs – signs of the zodiac, flowers or initials – on a chintz or satin background. The cushions come in three sizes and a selection of colours. A 12in chintz square cushion, piped or frilled, costs £10.

Catalogue Annually, A4, Leaflets, B/W, 3 pages, Free **Postal charges** £2 per cushion **Delivery** Royal Mail, Parcelforce **Methods of Payment** Cheque, Postal Order

THE EMPTY BOX COMPANY

Coomb Farm Buildings
Balchins Lane
Westcott
Nr Dorking
Surrey
RH4 3LE

Decorative boxes

This enterprising catalogue offers a range of Edwardian-style hat boxes, personalised wedding-dress boxes, shoe boxes, photograph boxes and miniature boxes. They can be covered from the company's selection of decorative fabrics or papers, or in your own fabric, and are pretty enough to grace any room. The hat boxes come

Telephone
01306 740193
Fax
01306 875430

with either ribbon or a carrying cord, tissue paper, lace trim and a sprinkling of rosebud pot-pourri. Hat box from £27.50; wedding-dress box, £39.90 or £55; shoe box £12.50.
Catalogue Annually, A5, Catalogue, Colour, 4 pages, Free **Postal charges** £4.20 for one item; £1 for each additional item **Delivery** Royal Mail, Parcelforce **Methods of Payment** Cheque, Postal Order, Credit Card

THE ENGLISH STAMP COMPANY
Sunnydown
Worth Matravers
Dorset
BH19 3JP
Telephone
01929 439117
Fax
01929 439150

Decorating with stamps

Another unusual and interesting catalogue. This one only sells devices to 'decorate with stamps'. This does not mean covering your wall with 25p stamps, but rather using specially made devices to make impressions on any surface. The stamps come in all kinds of patterns and are said to be easy to apply. You can scatter a wall with little stars, cherubs or roses for example. The catalogue will supply everything you need, which is simply a stamp, an applicator and stamp paint. A stamp of a moon is £5.95, fleur de lys £11.95. Paint is £2.95 and a roller £2.95. Complete kits are £22.95.
Catalogue Annually, A5, Catalogue, Colour and B/W, 16 pages, Free **Delivery** Royal Mail **Methods of Payment** Cheque

ESSENTIAL ITEMS
Church House
Plungar
Nottingham
Nottinghamshire
NG13 0JA
Telephone
01949 861172
Fax
0115 9843254

Upholstered stools and ottomans

Essential Items is one of the country's most established companies manufacturing and designing 'made to order' upholstered stools, ottomans, window seats and bed-end stools. The most interesting ottoman is the single or double filing cabinet. Different styles and sizes can be made to suit every room in your home. Essential Items have built up an enviable reputation for personal attention to customers' needs and can help with advice on customers' own fabrics and tapestries. Stools (76 × 36 × 26cm) start from £125 covered in customer's own fabric. Ottomans (56 × 48 × 50cm) from £195 plus £15 p&p.

Catalogue Annually, A4, Catalogue, Colour and B/W, 6 pages, Free **Postal charges** £15 for every item within the UK **Delivery** Parcelforce **Methods of Payment** Postal Order, Cheque, Credit Card

EXMOOR QUILTS
1 Traceys Cottage
Knowstone
South Moulton
North Devon
EX36 4RY
Telephone
01398 341527

Patchwork quilts

For her quilts, Jackie Harley uses only 100% cotton fabric, mainly from Laura Ashley. They contain flame-resistant wadding and are backed in co-ordinating fabric. The colours reflect the changing seasons of Exmoor: blues and buttercup yellow for the springtime quilt; browns, golds, reds and greens for the winter quilt. A single (84 × 66in) quilt in squares costs £70; kingsize (102 × 102in) £110.

The company also produces children's patchwork sweatshirts and sleeveless jackets. Prices from £14.95.

Catalogue A6, Leaflets, Colour and B/W, 2 pages, Free **Postal charges** £5.00 **Delivery** Royal Mail **Methods of Payment** Cheque

THE FAIRCHILD COMPANY
Yarford Orchards
Kingston St Mary
Taunton
Somerset
TA2 8AW
Telephone
01823 451881

Handmade mattresses

Handwoven from the purest, finest, new wool, the Fairchild mattress distributes the weight of the body evenly, supporting the back and spine. The filling construction means the mattress is firm and flat with no pressure points, buttons, tufts or lumps, never before available with pure wool. It has a fully removable cotton ticking cover, of which samples are attached to the booking form. Because the sanitized wool they use is resistant to mould, fungi, and bacteria which act as predigestors of fatty scales for dust mites, the profileration of dust mites is effectively hindered. The company also offer mattress overlays, pillows, duvets, and crib, cot and children's beds mattresses. Cot mattresses cost from £95, junior beds from £135, single beds, £210.

Catalogue Updated regularly, Third A4, Leaflet, Colour & b/w, 6 pages, Varies according to item **Postal charges** 48-hour service **Methods of Payment** Cheque, postal order, credit card

A FEAST OF FRAMES
17 Manchuria Road
London
SW11 6AF
Telephone
0171 738 9632
Fax
same

Photograph frames

No longer will you have to traipse around the shops looking for that perfect frame. The Feast of Frames brochure contains about 100 designs to suit both formal and informal photographs. There are frames for sporting fans, gardening experts, cat and dog owners, opera-goers and foodies, as well as leather travel frames, wooden frames, bevelled-glass frames, enamel frames, personalised children's name frames and self-adhesive montage frames as well as many more. They make perfect presents for all occasions and all ages.

Catalogue Annually, A5, Brochure, Colour, 12 pages, £1 refundable against order **Postal charges** Varies with item **Delivery** Royal Mail **Methods of Payment** Cheque, Credit Card, Postal Order

FILANTE PRODUCTS
2 Watership Drive
Hightown
Ringwood
Hampshire
BH24 1QY
Telephone
01425 479409

House numbers and names

Filante Products offer durable, individually made high-quality metal plaques for house names and numbers, from the ornate Art Deco to the simple English Classical. Available in your choice of colour, they are designed for clarity of vision and with a high night-time profile.

There is also a range of 'Francophilia' or signs with warnings in French, such as 'Défense de fumer'. Prices start at £12.75 for number plaques, £27.50 for name plaques and £13.00 for Francophilia plaques.

FIRED EARTH
Twyford Mill
Oxford Road
Adderbury
Oxfordshire
OX17 3HP
Telephone
01295 812088
Fax
01295 810832

Catalogue A4, Leaflets, Colour, 1 page, Free **Postal charges** Varies with item **Delivery** Parcelforce **Methods of Payment** Cheque

Tiles, floorcoverings, rugs
Fired Earth made its name selling tiles from around the world and its catalogue displays an enticing array of tiles for every situation. There are marble, earthenware, stoneware and slate floor tiles, decorative ceramic wall tiles and borders, insets and mosaics, English craft tiles and French ateliers' tiles. Natural floor-coverings, tribal rugs and kelims also feature. Honey terracotta, £28.08/sq m; Tuscany stoneware, from £55.49/sq m or 58p each; rugs from £143.83; floor adhesive £10/20kg (all prices exclude VAT). Fixing service available.
Catalogue Annually, A4, Catalogue, Colour, 72 pages, £2 **Postal charges** Varies with item **Delivery** In-house delivery **Methods of Payment** Cheque, Credit Card

GIVANS IRISH LINEN STORES LTD
207 Kings Road
Chelsea
London
SW3 5BR
Telephone
0171 352 6352
Fax
0171 351 5645

Linens for table, bed and bathroom
Girvans policy is to stock only the finest household textiles from around the world, but nothing can surpass the traditional quality and luxury of pure Irish linen. Whether it's crisp linen sheets or double damask table-cloths, this catalogue offers an unrivalled selection. Luxurious combed cotton towels in a superb collection of colours are offered at discount prices. A hand-towel £6.70, bath sheet £21.50, both showing a 50% saving on their normal price. Fancy bedspreads provide a brighter bedroom with their 'Arts & Crafts' embroidered cotton from £101 to £166 dependant upon size.
Catalogue Quarterly, A4, Catalogue, Colour, 27 pages, Free **Postal charges** Order value under £300, £5; over £300, free **Delivery** Royal Mail **Methods of Payment** Cheque, Postal Order, Credit Card, American Express, Diners Club

HOME

GLAZEBROOK & CO
PO Box 1563
London
SW6 3XD
Telephone
0171 371 7135
Fax
0171 371 5434

Sterling silver and silver-plate cutlery
Glazebrook & Co offers outstanding British cutlery in terms of quality and craftsmanship at competitive prices, with storage cloths and delivery included. A 44-piece sterling silver set costs from £1,130; silver plate from £415. Choose from time-honoured patterns such as Rattail and Old English Thread, or the classics such as Kings. Stainless steel cutlery in matt or mirror finish is also available: knife from £8.55, fork £5.50, dessert spoon £4.95.
Catalogue Annually, A4, Catalogue, Colour, 6 pages, Free **Postal charges** Free **Delivery** Parcelforce **Methods of Payment** Cheque, Credit Card

GLOBAL VILLAGE
17 St James Street
South Petherton
Somerset
TA12 5BS
Telephone
01460 241166
Fax
01935 242282

Craft gifts
Global Village promotes craftsmanship from around the world and the mail-order catalogue is full of interesting artefacts and furniture. There's an antiqued colonial rattan chair for £175, an Indian wooden cupboard for £995, hand-blown Mexican glass paperweights for £3.95 and a large selection of African masks from £75.
Catalogue A4, Catalogue, Colour, 12 pages, Free **Postal charges** Orders under £100.00, add £4.50; orders over £100.00, free **Delivery** Parcelforce **Methods of Payment** Cheque, Postal Order, Credit Card

GRAHAM & GREEN
4, 7 and 10 Elgin Crescent
London
W11 2JA
Telephone
0171 727 4594
Fax
0171 229 9717

Home accessories and gifts
Graham & Green offers unique and original accessories for the home, chosen from around the world. Four-poster bed, £785; appliqué bedspread, £225; steel lamp with orange shade, £53.50; brightly coloured glass goblet, £39.50; Moroccan slippers, £22.50; sponge bags, £8.95; leafy garlands, £7.95; check napkin, £2.50.
Catalogue Annually, A4, Catalogue, Colour, 6 pages, Free **Postal charges** Varies with item **Delivery** Royal Mail, Parcelforce **Methods of Payment** Cheque, Credit Card

GRAND ILLUSIONS

2–4 Crown Road
St Margarets
Twickenham
Middlesex
TW1 3EE
Telephone
0181 744 1046
Fax
0181 744 2017

Gift and home ideas

Grand Illusions covers a wide range of household items including furniture and gifts, photographed in room settings and displayed in a homes magazine style. It is a unique collection incorporating cushions, throws, decorative curtain poles to a 'Meuble à Farine' wardrobe with six drawers for £550. Neal's Yard Remedies are also available, as are soaps from France.

Catalogue Annually, A4, Catalogue, Colour, 32 pages, Free **Postal charges** £2.95; £20 for furniture unless far-flung **Delivery** In-house delivery **Methods of Payment** Cheque, Postal Order, Credit Card

GRANGE MEUBLES UK

PO Box 18
Stamford
Lincolnshire
PE9 2FY
Telephone
01780 54721
Fax
01780 54718

Furniture

This catalogue is more like an exquisite French interiors magazine than a product directory, and is an inspiration to any home decorator. Leafing through page after page of photographs of glorious French rooms, some sumptuous, others simple and uncluttered, with atmospheric captions in both French and English, you come to shots of the individual items, with their history and measurements (but no prices). The style is classic French country house, elegantly designed and superbly finished in the tradition of Joseph Grange, the cabinet-maker who founded the company in 1905.

Catalogue Annually, A4, Catalogue, Colour, 118 pages, £4 **Postal charges** Varies with item **Delivery** In-house delivery **Methods of Payment** Cheque, Credit Card

THE HEATED MIRROR CO LTD

Sherston
Wiltshire
SN16 0LW
Telephone
01666 840003

Heated mirrors

Designed to solve the age-old problem of steaming-up in the bathroom, these mirrors work off the lighting circuit, in the same way as a strip-light over a washbasin, and have been tested to a European safety standard. Quick and easy to install, the four attractive designs (pine frame, gold

Fax
01666 840856

frame, tiled frames, and with shaver light) measure from 500 × 420mm and prices start at £146.88.

Catalogue A4, Leaflets, Colour, 1 page, Free **Postal charges** Free **Delivery** Royal Mail **Methods of Payment** Cheque, Credit Card

HEIRLOOM PATCHWORK
Rose Hall
Sydenham Damerel
Tavistock
Devon
PL19 8PU
Telephone
01822 870256

Patchwork quilts

Christine Pattison makes her beautiful quilts from quality cottons and polycotton backing. They come with either 2oz or 4oz wadding. Machine and hand quilting are combined to make extremely durable, machine-washable quilts to a number of simple, elegant designs. Names and dates can be added to the quilts which can also be made from the customer's own materials. The range is augmented by pillows and cushions.

Catalogue A5, Brochure, Colour, 4 pages, Free **Postal charges** Free **Delivery** Royal Mail or Securicor if very valuable **Methods of Payments** Cheque, Postal Order

HELP THE AGED (MAIL ORDER)
PO Box 28
London
N18 3HG
Telephone
0181 803 6861
Fax
0181 884 0148

Gifts and cards

Help the Aged's catalogue is quite eclectic in its choice of practical and well-priced goods. Profits go towards improving the quality of life of elderly people, for instance by buying minibuses to give the housebound the opportunity of going out, and funding hospices and day centres. From the catalogue, you can buy a wall trellis, £7.99; extending garden loppers, £16.99; easy kneeler, £33.99; Nature's Best supplements, from £3.50; personal aids such as a pair of colour-coded tap turners, £5.50; and an extendible travel bag, £12.99.

Catalogue Bi-annually, A4, Catalogue, Colour, 24 pages, Free **Postal charges** Free **Delivery** Royal Mail, Parcelforce **Methods of Payment** Cheque, Credit Card

HINES OF OXFORD
Ancient Tapestry
Reproductions
Weavers Barn
Windmill Road
Headington
Oxford
Oxfordshire
OX3 7DE
Telephone
01865 741144

Wall hanging tapestries

A family-owned business importing fine-quality Woven Art Tapestries. The reproductions cover the period from medieval times to the 19th century, including some William Morris designs, and are woven in various attractive textures, such as wool, cotton and artificial silk. The tapestries are lined and ready for hanging. Information can be supplied relating to the historical background of the tapestries, if available. The tapestries can be viewed at Weavers Barn, preferably by prior appointment. Open Monday to Friday, 8.30am to 5pm.

Catalogue A4, Catalogue, Colour, 108 pages, £5 **Postal charges** Free **Delivery** UPS **Methods of Payment** Cheque, Postal Order

H L LINEN BAZAARS
Dept MS95 Churchbridge
Oldbury
Warley
West Midlands
B69 2AS
Telephone
0121 541 1918

Household linen

A comprehensive catalogue featuring bedlinen, towels, table linen, tea-towels and rugs, plus other items. Three-in-one duvet, single £28; duvet cover and pillowcase set, single £12.99, double £19.99; fine Egyptian cotton sheet, single £13.99, or three pairs for £39.99; cot duvet cover, £7; five-piece plain dye towel bale, £8. Substantial discounts are available on bulk orders.

Catalogue Annually, A4, Catalogue, Colour, 32 pages, Free **Postal charges** £2.85 **Delivery** Royal Mail, Parcelforce **Methods of Payment** Cheque, Postal Order, Credit Card, Switch

HOUSEHOLD ARTICLES LTD
Sanderstead Station Approach
South Croydon
Surrey
CR2 0YY
Telephone
0181 651 6321

Cafetières

Household Articles are makers and suppliers of La Cafetière plunge-filter coffee makers. The range starts with the 'Café Royale', available in 3-cup (£15.15), 6-cup (£17.55) and 8-cup (£18.40) sizes in cream, black, green, red, white or smoke. There are slight variations in price for each colour. Top of the range is a chrome, gold or copper finish

Fax
0181 651 4095

'La Cafetière'. They also supply replacement parts, such as the glass beakers, and accessories, such as coffee-pot covers and swizzle sticks.

Catalogue A4, Leaflets, B/W, 2 pages, Free **Postal charges** Varies with item **Delivery** Royal Mail, Parcelforce **Methods of Payment** Cheque

HYBURY CHINA
Higher Farm Barn
Milborne Wick
Sherborne
Dorset
DT9 4PW
Telephone
01963 250500
Fax
01963 250335

China seconds

Hybury China supplies white bone china seconds from famous English manufacturers. It offers two collections: Classic, with its plain, contemporary style, and Elegance, which has a delicate wave in the rim, giving a more traditional look. The Classic collection prices range from £3.25 for a 10½in plate and £1.80 for a 6¼in plate to £29.50 for a soup tureen. The Elegance collection includes a 10½in plate for £4.50, a 6½in plate for £1.95 and a covered vegetable dish for £26.

Catalogue Annually, A4, Leaflets, B/W, 5 pages, Free **Postal charges** £4.25 **Delivery** Royal Mail, Parcelforce **Methods of Payment** Cheque, Credit Card

THE INDIA SHOP
5 Hilliers Yard
Marlborough
Wiltshire
SN8 1NB
Telephone
01672 515585
Fax
01380 728118

Handicrafts made in India

The India Shop imports a selection of the best of the many handicrafts made in India. They buy only from India by travelling there personally two or three times a year, thereby ensuring quality products. The catalogue features an attractive range of bedspreads and throws, tablecloths, cushion covers and quilts, jewellery and table linen, block-printed and woven textiles at reasonable prices, as well as an increasing range of furniture, old and new. Designs vary from the simple Kutch cream and burgundy or navy range (single bedspread/throw, £29.95, cushion cover, £7.50) to vibrant Jaipur block prints (single bedspread/throw, £24.95, cushion cover, £4.50). The romantic China Rose quilt costs £57.50

single; £69.95 double. Rajasthan coffee-tables are available from £95. They have shops in Edinburgh, St Andrews and Marlborough as well as an expanding mail-order service.

Catalogue Annually, A5, Catalogue, Colour, 12 pages, Free **Postal charges** Free **Delivery** Royal Mail, Courier, Parceline **Methods of Payment** Cheque, Credit Card, Postal Order, Switch

THE IRON DESIGN COMPANY
Summer Carr Farm
Thornton-le-Moor
Northallerton
North Yorkshire
DL6 3SG
Telephone
01609 778143
Fax
01609 778846

Iron furniture

This attractive, glossy brochure features a selection of unusual yet classically designed metal furniture and accessories. Hand-crafted in a variety of paint finishes, such as smithy black and verdigris, the products are designed for both indoor and outdoor use. All are very attractive and fashionable. The company will also undertake bespoke commissions and adaptations to its standard range, which includes weather-vanes, gates, fencing, lamps, firegrates, curtain rails and finials as well as tables and mirrors.

Catalogue Annually, A4, Brochure, Colour, 18 pages, Free **Postal charges** Varies with item **Delivery** Courier **Methods of Payment** Cheque, Postal Order, Credit Card

THE IRONWORKS
Chiltern House
Leys Road
Brockmoor
Brierley Hill
West Midlands
DY5 3UT
Telephone
01384 484200
Fax
01384 484202

Curtain poles and accessories

Here is an original way to dress your windows with hand-crafted, high-quality forged or cast curtain poles with decorative finials. The Ironworks offers a distinctive collection in a range of styles and colours (matt black, cabinet-makers' blue, wild bayberry, antique yellow and antique pewter). Finials come in a choice of 12 designs including grapes, ram's head, scroll and collar and ball with matching tie-backs, rings and draw rods. Simple fitting instructions are included. Half-inch tulip-finial pole, up to 5ft long, £52; tie-backs, £15 each; curtain ring, 60p.

Catalogue Annually, A5, Catalogue, B/W, 6 pages, Free **Postal charges** £10 carriage **Delivery** Courier, Parcelforce **Methods of Payment** Cheque, Postal Order

J G S METALWORK
Broomstick Estate
High Street
Edlesborough
Nr Dunstable
Bedfordshire
LU6 2HS
Telephone
01525 220360
Fax
01525 222786

Traditional weathervanes
'Imagine a cold grey day when unexpectedly a shaft of sunlight emerges from behind a cloud and plays upon your Golden Cockerel, he glistens and gleams and lightens your heart while pointing proudly into the wind.' So runs the inspirational description of one of this company's many hand-made weather-vanes. Commissions are taken, hand-painting is an option, and other items, including curtain rods and boot-scrapers, are offered. Small weather-vane, £51.50; large, from £162.75.

Catalogue Annually, A5, Catalogue, B/W, 16 pages, Free **Postal charges** Varies with item **Delivery** Royal Mail, Parcelforce **Methods of Payment** Cheque, Postal Order, Credit Card

J & M DAVIDSON
62 Ledbury Road
London
W11 2AJ
Telephone
0171 243 2089
Fax
0171 243 2092

French design bedlinen
The tradition of European fabrics, weaves and patterns are inspirational for J & M Davidson's Linge de Maison – crisp cottons and cool lines work with strong blues, reds and whites – whilst the delicate tracery of Toile de Jouy is borrowed from 18th-century France. White linen cotton woven sheet with drawn threadwork, single £57, double £73. Rectangular classic pillowcase in blue cotton chambray, cuffed and fastened with plain white buttons, £20.

Catalogue Annually, A3, Brochure, Colour, 4 pages, Free **Postal charges** Free **Delivery** Royal Mail **Methods of Payment** Cheque, Postal Order, Credit Card, American Express

JALI

Apsley House
Chartham
Canterbury
Kent
CT4 7HT
Telephone
01227 831710
Fax
01227 831950

Decorative pelmets, brackets, radiator covers and corner units

Jali offers reasonably priced and well-designed self-assembly kits for decorative pelmets, brackets, radiator covers, shelves, corner units and edge trims, manufactured from MDF. Screws and plugs are supplied where necessary and all you need are a screwdriver and a little wood glue. Any paint applied by brush or spray can be used. Edge trim, 1220 × 45 × 6mm, from £3.99; pelmets, 1830 × 175 × 6mm, from £12.99; radiator trellis cover, 1830 × 600 × 6mm, £35.99; corner shelf unit, £65.99.

Catalogue Annually, A5, Catalogue, Colour, 20 pages
Postal charges £4 standard; £12 overnight courier
Delivery Royal Mail, Parcelforce, Courier **Methods of Payment** Cheque, Credit Card, Switch

KENNETH CLARK CERAMICS

The North Wing
Southover Grange
Southover Road
Lewes
East Sussex
BN7 1TP
Telephone
01273 476761
Fax
01273 479565

Tiles

This ceramic-tile company has been in operation for over 40 years. Their clients have included HRH The Queen Mother, John Cleese and Arthur Andersen Accountants. Styles range from 'Trellis' to 'Victorian reproduction' and there are some stunning murals such as the 'Tree of Life' and 'High Summer'. The tiles vary considerably in price, from 95p each to as much as £25 each. The company can produce a design to complement the customer's furnishings if required. To save on cost, many of the designs can be used in conjunction with H&R Johnson's plain opal white tiles.

Catalogue Third A4, Catalogue, Colour, 33 pages, Free
Postal charges Varies with item **Delivery** Royal Mail, Courier **Methods of Payment** Cheque, Postal Order

HOME

KNIGHTINGALES CATALOGUE
PO Box 555
South Shore
Blackpool
Lancashire
FY4 4QP
Telephone
01253 699633
Fax
01253 699698

Home furnishings

This catalogue offers duvet covers, patchwork bedspreads, pillow cases, sheets and a variety of bedroom and bathroom accessories. The duvet range extends from children's (Disney, Postman Pat, etc) to adults'; they also sell plain dyed towels at very reasonable prices, bath sheet £6.99. Beds complete with drapes for a four-poster for £249.99 for a 4' 6", to a single bed from £48.99. Other headboards stocked are brass effect or brass/white effect. They also stock coloured metal headboards from £17.99 for a single. Most items are illustrated.

As well as offering a mail-order service there are over 30 shops around Great Britain, although predominantly in the North of England, with a few in Scotland and a handful in and around Greater London. There is a warning that pricing in the shops may vary from mail order.

Catalogue Annually, A4, Catalogue, Colour, 23 pages, Free **Postal charges** Handling and delivery charge, £2.95; extra bed delivery charge, £7.05 **Methods of Payment** Cheque, Postal Order, Credit Card

L & L OBJETS FAUX
The Art Works
Market Harborough
Leicestershire
LE16 9EG
Telephone
01858 468448
Fax
01858 468186

Decorative plinths and plant boxes

The *objets* featured in this catalogue are contemporary interpretations of classic styles. Plant boxes, troughs and plinths are handmade from solid sustainable materials, hand-painted and antiqued. The Claude Plantbox (£79.50) features a Faux Claude of Lorraine circular landscape with Adam decorations and is finished in a crackle glaze. The Log Box (£99) could just as easily be filled with plants as logs, and the Opus Plinth (from £343) opens to reveal storage for 120 CDs or 40 videos.

Catalogue Annually, A4, Catalogue, Colour, 12 pages **Postal charges** Varies with item **Delivery** Courier **Methods of Payment** Cheque, Credit Card, Postal Order

LAND OF OZ STENCILS

Nightingale Farmhouse
London Road
Southborough
Tunbridge Wells
Kent
TN4 0UL
Telephone
01892 516414

Stencils

By dealing directly through mail order, Land of Oz can offer original hand-cut stencil designs at prices comparable to mass-produced stencils. Their designs include animals, such as the 5 × 7in stag (£4.95), flowers, such as the 12 × 7in wisteria border (£8.95), and other items, such as the 9 × 8in angels (£7.95). Orders are dealt with directly by the cutter so, for a small extra charge, it is possible to increase or decrease the size of the pattern to scale. A free tips and information sheet is included with every order.

Catalogue A4, Catalogue, B/W, 5 pages, £1.00 **Postal charges** Free **Delivery** Royal Mail **Methods of Payment** Cheque

LETTERBOX COMPANY (TEBWORTH) LTD

Wingfield Road
Tebworth
Leighton Buzzard
Bedfordshire
LU7 9QG
Telephone
01525 874599
Fax
01525 875746

Exterior letterboxes

Practical and elegant, these letterboxes and newspaper holders are made from high-quality zinc-plated steel, specially chosen for extra protection from all weather conditions. Each box is supplied with two keys and can easily be mounted on posts or walls. The boxes come in a range of colours and sizes with prices from £22 to £65. The newspaper holder has a left- or right-hand use flexibility and is priced at £15.00.

Catalogue A5, Brochure, Colour, 2 pages, Free **Postal charges** Free **Delivery** Royal Mail **Methods of Payment** Other, Cheque, Credit Card, American Express

THE LIGHT BRIGADE

20 Rodney Road
Cheltenham
Gloucestershire
GL50 1JJ
Telephone
01242 226777

Lights

The Light Brigade produces a range of handmade wall lights, candle sconces, shades and chandeliers in a wide variety of colours and finishes. The lights and shades can also be colour-matched to suit your décor or left unpainted for you to paint yourself. Double wall lights start at £39.50 unpainted and go up to £72.50 in antiqued or Florentine gold,

Fax same

pewter, or colour-matched. Single wall lights range from £29.50 to £89.50. Shades range from £5.50 to £15.95.
Catalogue Annually, A4, Catalogue, Colour and B/W, 11 pages, Free **Postal charges** £5 on orders up to £250; free on orders above **Delivery** Royal Mail, Parcelforce **Methods of Payment** Credit Card, Cheque, American Express

LIGHTS ON BROADWAY
17 Jerdan Place
Fulham Broadway
London
SW6 1BE
Telephone
0171 6100100

Lighting
Lights on Broadway is widely known for authentic period lighting. Designs are of the Art Nouveau period, being from later Victorian to the mid-1920s. From table lamps to wall lights and chandelier-type lights, prices £9.50 to £149.
Catalogue Annually, A4, Brochure, Colour, 15 pages, £1 **Postal charges** Varies with item **Delivery** Royal Mail **Methods of Payment** Cheque, Postal Order, Diners Club, Credit Card

LIMERICKS LINENS LTD
PO Box 20
Tanners Lane
Barkingside
Ilford
Essex
IG6 1QQ
Telephone
01268 284405

Linens
This traditional household linen company sells not only bedding and bedlinen but also table linen, cushions, rugs, towels and patchwork quilts. The patchwork cushions come in three attractive designs: 'Country Cottage', 'Country Cat' and 'Country Goose' and are priced at £12.99 each, while the pure cotton 'Manhattan' single patchwork quilt costs £97.75.
Catalogue Annually, A5, Catalogue, Colour, 23 pages, Free **Postal charges** Up to £24,99, add £2.95; £25.00 and over, add £3.49 **Delivery** Parcelforce **Methods of Payments** Cheque, Credit Card

THE LONDON SHUTTER COMPANY
St Martin's Stables
Windsor Road

High-quality wooden shutters
The London Shutter Company supplies crafted window and door shutters from Ohline, one of the largest shutter manufacturers in the USA. Made of

Ascot
Berkshire
SL5 7AF
Telephone
01344 28385
Fax
01344 27575

Incense Cedar from California and Oregon, these beautiful shutters are custom-made and can be supplied with either movable or fixed louvres, vertical or horizontal, in a wide choice of finishes. Samples are available, along with free advice, measuring and fitting services. Prices from £55.68 for a Brentwood shutter 18 × 6in, rising to £730 for a Bel Air shutter 102–108in × 36in.

Catalogue Annually, A4, Catalogue, Colour, 24 pages, Free **Postal charges** Varies with item **Delivery** In-house delivery **Methods of Payment** Cheque, Credit Card

THE MANOR BINDERY
Fawley
Southampton
Hampshire
SO4 1BB
Telephone
01703 894488
Fax
01703 899418

False books and replica book panels

Create the atmosphere of an 18th-century library in you own home without buying a book. How? The Manor Bindery casts replica book panels from original books, individually colouring, gilding and waxing each leather panel to create authentic-looking volumes. They can be used for decoration, or to disguise such 20th-century equipment as televisions and hi-fi systems. A panel of Scott's novels, approx 11 × 7in (300 × 180mm) costs £35; a video storage box for four tapes, £17.95. Note: prices exclude VAT.

Catalogue Annually, A4, Leaflets, Colour and B/W, 6 pages, Free **Postal charges** £7.50 for orders of less than £100; free for orders of more than £100 **Delivery** Royal Mail, Parcelforce **Methods of Payment** Credit Card, Cheque

MARION HAND-PAINTED HOUSE PLAQUES
39 St Matthews Road
Cosham
Portsmouth
Hampshire
PO6 2DL

Ceramic house plaques

Marion have been producing their delightful hand-painted ceramic house plaques for the last 12 years. Each plaque is fired in a kiln several times and as a result will not crack in frost or fade in the sun. Each one is unique, custom-painted and can feature any design you wish. Customers in the past have used house names, pets, the house itself,

HOME

Telephone
01705 384856

wildlife and flowers. Prices start from £22 for 6× 8in oval and rise to £41.25 for 11 × 13in oval.
Catalogue Leaflets, Colour, Free

MARKS AND SPENCER MAIL ORDER
Marks & Spencer Home Choice
FREEPOST
PO Box 288
Warrington
Cheshire
WA1 2DN
Telephone
01925 851100
Fax
01925 812485

Home Furnishings
Marks & Spencer Home Choice offers everything from glasses to furniture, at exceedingly high quality with delivery anywhere in the UK. The choice is wide and varied with a full range of prices to suit all pockets. There is a wedding list available at most stores and details of how to pay, with credit terms available.
Catalogue Bi-annually, A3, Catalogue, Colour, 153 pages, £1.50 **Postal charges** Delivery free if order is £200 or more; orders under £200 (excluding furniture), £3.50 **Delivery** In-house delivery **Methods of Payment** Cheque, Postal Order, Stage Payments, Credit Card, Switch

MARLBOROUGH FINE ENGLISH TILES
Elcot Lane
Marlborough
Wiltshire
SN8 2AY
Telephone
01672 512422
Fax
01672 515791

Tiles
Marlborough Tiles offer an interesting range of glazed terracotta, hand-painted and sculpted tiles, borders and insets. There are sculpted shell motifs, farmyard scenes, vegetables and flowers, with co-ordinating plain and delicately patterned tiles. Gardening panel of 35 tiles, £195.34; art glazes, £2.59 a tile; sculpted borders from £2.47 a tile.
Catalogue Annually, A4, Catalogue, Colour, 8 pages, Free **Postal charges** Varies with item **Delivery** Courier **Methods of Payment** Cheque, Credit Card

MELIN TREGWYNT
Tregwynt Mill
Castle Morris
Haverfordwest
Dyfed
Wales
SA62 5UX

Blankets, bedspreads and throws
Based in Wales, Melin Tregwynt produces high-quality woollen blankets and spreads in sizes to suit every bed, even a baby's cot, and large fringed throws – ideal for sofas, picnics and children's rooms. The designs are simple checks with strong, attractive colours. Single blanket, £88, king-size

Telephone
01348 891644
Fax
01348 891694

£122; single bedspread, £100; throw, £75; baby blanket, £27. It also produces the Designers' Guild range of new wool blankets in large-scale multi-checks and colourful plaids. Single, £115; king-size, £165.

Catalogue Annually, A5, Brochure, Colour, 8 pages, Free **Postal charges** Varies with item **Delivery** Royal Mail, Parcelforce, Next-day delivery service **Methods of Payment** Cheque, Postal Order, Credit Card, American Express

MERCHANTMEN
664 Garratt Lane
London
SW17 0NP
Telephone
0181 947 9733
Fax
0181 879 3940

China and cutlery

Merchantmen offers you the opportunity to build up a dinner service or set of cutlery month-by-month. Choose from Wild Pastures, a service featuring golden poppies from the Seltmann factory in Bavaria; or Julia, a collector's service from the same factory. There are bone china chocolate beakers from Stoke-on-Trent, decorated with British flowers (19.95 each), and from Thailand you can collect solid bronze Royal Siam cutlery. Six dinner plates: Wild Pastures £48.08, Julia £55.95. Six dinner knives and forks, £27.95.

Catalogue Annually, A4, Leaflets, Colour and B/W, 7 pages, Free **Postal charges** Varies with item **Delivery** Royal Mail, Parcelforce **Methods of Payment** Cheque, Stage Payments, Credit Card

MILLCRAFT
Maitlands
Faygate Lane
Faygate
Horsham
West Sussex
RH12 4SJ
Telephone
01293 851482

Toilet seats

This company crafts toilet seats from solid hardwood. Choose from two designs and seven woods, including cherry and sycamore. Each seat is highly polished, splinter-free and water-resistant, with adjustable chrome or brass hinges enabling it to be fitted without the use of specialist tools. Both models cost £79.95 each. Matching hardwood bath panels are available in standard sizes.

HOME

Fax
01293 851731

Catalogue Annually, A4, Brochure, Colour, 4 pages, Free **Postal charges** £5 **Delivery** Royal Mail, Parcelforce **Methods of Payment** Cheque, Credit Card

MUJI
26 Great Marlborough Street
London
W1V 1HL
Telephone
0171 494 1197
Fax
0171 494 1193

Stationery, clothes and accessories

For the minimalist look, Muji's catalogue of simply and effectively designed products is the one. Muji opened in Tokyo in 1983 and now has four shops in the UK selling a range of functional, uncluttered stationery, household goods, furniture, clothes, belts, bags and watches. Clever cardboard storage drawers, from £7.95; acrylic magazine holder, £10.95; plastic cosmetic bottle, 95p; zinc box, £22.50; cotton T-shirt, £9.50; nylon bucket bag, from £14.95; sofa, £475.

Catalogue Annually, A3, Catalogue, Colour, 8 pages, Free **Postal charges** Varies with item **Delivery** Royal Mail, Parcelforce **Methods of Payment** Cheque, Credit Card, American Express, Diners Club

MULBERRY HALL
Stonegate
York
North Yorkshire
YO1 2AW
Telephone
01904 620736
Fax
01904 620251

Fine china and crystal

Mulberry Hall, one of the finest medieval buildings in the ancient city of York, is also one of the world's leading fine china and crystal specialists. Its beautifully preserved building contains fifteen showrooms given over to an unsurpassed display of the finest porcelain and crystal which Britain and Europe have to offer, supported by stock in depth.

Mulberry Hall also specialises in dealing with orders by post, fax and telephone, both within the United Kingdom and overseas. Its beautiful colour mail-order catalogue, available on request, illustrates a selection from its magnificent collection, and its expert packers ensure trouble-free delivery to any part of the world.

Catalogue Annually, A4, Catalogue, Colour, 40 pages, Free **Postal charges** Varies with item **Delivery** Parcelforce **Methods of Payment** Cheque, Credit Card, American Express

NEWTON FORGE
Stalbridge Lane
Sturminster Newton
Dorset
DT10 2JQ
Telephone
01258 472407
Fax
01258 471111

Hand-forged ironwork
Ian Ring, the blacksmith at Newton Forge, specialises in ironwork curtain poles with a wide choice of styles and finishes. He also makes flower pedestals, coat racks, boot-scrapers, gates, railings, weather-vanes, garden furniture, lanterns, fire tools, canopies and screens: in fact, more or less anything that can be made out of iron.
Catalogue A4, Brochure, B/W, 3 pages, Free **Postal charges** Add 10%, 100 miles mainland UK **Delivery** Royal Mail **Methods of Payment** Cheque

NEXT DIRECTORY
PO Box 299
Leicester
Leicestershire
LE5 5GH
Telephone
0345 100 500
Fax
0116 2738749

Home furnishings, bedding and lighting
The Next Directory is a well-designed hardback featuring ranges available in the high street shops. Its Interiors section offers a far-reaching choice of well-priced, attractively designed wallcoverings, curtains, curtain accessories, cushions, towels, bedding, futons and lighting. Wallpaper, £7.99 a roll; ready-made curtains from £39.99; double duvet cover £29.99; lamp base, £17.99. A must for any home decorator.
Catalogue Bi-annually, A4, Catalogue, Colour, 387 pages, £3 **Postal charges** £2.50 **Delivery** Courier, Parcelforce, In-house delivery **Methods of Payment** Cheque, Stage Payments, Credit Card, American Express, Diners Club

NICK MUNRO LTD
The Canal Warehouse
Workshops
Whipcord Lane
Chester
CH1 4DE

Steel decorative accessories for the home
Winner of the Shell Young Entrepreneur of the Year Award, Nick Munro uses the best traditions of British engineering and craftsmanship to produce unique designs for the home. These include a fan-shaped toast rack in silver-plated steel wire, £15; spring silver-plated steel wire egg cups, £19.50 set of four; pewter triangular top and

rounded rocking base salt and pepper shakers, £37.50 pair; pewter vacuum flask with straight sides and a domed top and base; Venturi shaped pewter coffee grinder with curved crank handle; spherical glass light with pewter base, handblown and crackled in England; tall, slim lemonade jug, with pewter foot, handle and spout; curved goblet, handblown and featuring hand-appliquéd sterling silver fish pattern. The 'catalogue' is a sheaf of light blue A4 paper with line drawings of the products accompanied by a tiny concertina brochure showing some of the designs in colour. Prices include VAT and p&p.

Catalogue A4, Leaflets, B/W, Free **Postal charges** Free

OCEAN HOME SHOPPING LTD
PO Box 7837
London
SW15 1ZA
Telephone
0800 132985
Fax
0181 780 5505

Designer household goods
This catalogue is full of beautifully designed products. Each one is distinctive, unique and available for delivery within 24 hours. Ocean offers a range of colourful contemporary chinaware, wrought iron, glassware and soft furnishings to make your home a more attractive and welcoming place to live in. Handmade glass decanters £89, a tall wrought-iron stand with amphora vase in sand-blasted glass £139, and distinctive hand-made solid cherrywood coffee-table, £545, form part of this collection.

Catalogue Quarterly, A4, Catalogue, Colour, 32 pages, £2 **Postal charges** £2.95, free on orders over £100; gift-wrap £1.50 per selection **Delivery** Courier **Methods of Payment** Cheque, Credit Card, American Express, Diners Club

OLD PARK FURNISHINGS
Burley Lawn
Burley
Ringwood

Mowbray Stool
The Mowbray Stool is not only a decorative piece of furniture for the home, but a practical and versatile means of storing unsightly CDs and video cassettes. Each stool holds approximately 60 video

Hampshire
BH24 4DL
Telephone
01425 403505
Fax
01425 403678

cassettes and 230 CDs, or a combination of both. The stool comes painted and varnished in a choice of five colours or in solid mahogany. It comes with a fire-retardant upholstered cushion in calico ready for customers' own material. Alternatively, supply your own fabric and they will upholster your new stool for an additional charge. The stool requires 1.5 metres of fabric and 6 metres of gimp. Dimensions: 36in long × 18in wide × 14in high. Price £299 inc. VAT (includes upholstering), delivery extra.

Catalogue Annually, A4, Leaflets, Colour, 1 page, Free **Postal charges** Varies with item **Methods of Payment** Cheque, Postal Order

OLIVERS LIGHTING COMPANY
6 The Broadway
Crockenhill
Swanley
Kent
BR8 8JH
Telephone
01322 614224
Fax
same

Reproduction light switches

Olivers' classic reproduction light switches offer quality, authenticity and craftsmanship. Traditionally styled they still adhere to the most stringent modern safety standards. The switches are made from lacquered brass set into wooden backplates of mahogany or oak. Olivers also produces a range of matching sockets and accessories. Single switches from £24; quadruple switches from £60.

Catalogue Annually, A5, Brochure, Colour, 6 pages, Free **Postal charges** £5 **Delivery** Royal Mail **Methods of Payment** Cheque, Postal Order, Credit Card

THE ORIGINAL KEEPSAKE COMPANY
5 Station Road
Haxby
York
North Yorkshire
YO3 3LR
Telephone
01904 635 775
Fax
01904 766 193

Trinket boxes and chests

Having failed to find a special box to keep her baby's precious treasures in (hospital name tags, tiny clothes, first shoes, etc), Helen Robinson decided to make her own. Her chest has a rag-roll finish with bear motifs hand painted-on as well as the child's name and date of birth. Inside the lid is a picture frame and the chest contains a keepsake tray which lifts out to reveal a large storage area designed to hold a life-time's treasures. Size: 1ft 6in long × 1ft wide × 1ft deep. Price: £74.50 at time of going to press. Among other items, the company now also produces a wedding chest.

Catalogue A4, Leaflets, Colour, 1 page, Free **Postal charges** £10.00. Free delivery in York area **Delivery** Royal Mail **Methods of Payment** Cheque, Postal Order

PAINT MAGIC
79 Shepperton Road
Islington
London
N1 3DF
Telephone
0171 354 9696
Fax
0171 226 7760

Paints, washes and stencil paints for the home

The Paint Magic brochure is full of new products and ideas designed to put more excitement into your decorating projects. Jocasta Innes, who founded Paint Magic, believes that the right paint finish can transform quite ordinary rooms without exceptional furniture or expensive fabrics or accessories. Paint Magic sells new colours, old-fashioned as well as high-tech paints, a comprehensive range of pigments, varnishes, brushes, stencils, books and videos. New products are added constantly.

Catalogue A4, Brochure, Colour, 16 pages, Free **Postal charges** £3.10 **Delivery** Parcelforce **Methods of Payment** Cheque, Postal Order, Credit Card, Switch, American Express, Diners Club

PATCHWORK QUILTS
Top House Farm
Burn
Selby
North Yorkshire
YO8 8LR
Telephone
01757 270343

Patchwork quilts

Teresa Bell uses only 100% cotton traditional chintz fabrics, made by Sanderson, Jane Churchill, Osborne & Little among others, for her quilts, each of which is totally unique. The three designs, the 'Victoria', the 'Charlotte' and the 'Sophie-Louise', can be made up in a choice of colour schemes. Or, if you send in a wallpaper or curtain sample, a suitable colour scheme can be created to match.

Catalogue A4, Leaflets, Colour, 1 page, Free **Postal charges** £5.00 **Delivery** Parcelforce **Methods of Payment** Cheque, Credit Card

440 HOME

PHILIP BRADBURY GLASS
83 Blackstock Road
London
N4 2JW
Telephone
0171 2262919
Fax
0171 3596303

Decorative glass
Philip Bradbury makes patterned glass for door panels, windows, etc. He has a number of standard patterns and can match original Victorian pieces using both the conventional silkscreen method and his own patent process. He also custom-makes glass to any design for house numbers and names. Door panels start at £70 while transoms are from £60–£80. He will send sample paper patterns and a small square of sample glass free of charge.
Catalogue A4, Leaflets, B/W, 4 pages, Free **Delivery** Royal Mail **Methods of Payment** Cheque, Credit Card

POZZANI PURE WATER
Phoenix House
Newmarket
Louth
Lincolnshire
LN11 9EJ
Telephone
01507 608100
Fax
01507 608090

Domestic water purifiers
Tap water can frequently be unappetising, with unpleasant tastes, colours and smells from chemical treatment processes or other sources. The Pozzani IX230 system removes impurities and restores drinking water to its natural, refreshing taste using a three-stage filtration process. The system fits neatly under a sink unit and connects easily to the cold-water supply. Costing £78.95, it comes complete with a choice of taps, and is guaranteed for three years. Filter cartridges, priced £12.25, have a life-span of six months.
Catalogue Annually, A5, Leaflets, Colour and B/W, 4 pages, Free **Postal charges** £3 **Delivery** Royal Mail **Methods of Payment** Cheque, Credit Card

PRESENT PERFECT
18 Deane Croft Road
Eastcote
Pinner
Middlesex
HA5 1SR
Telephone
0181 866 3354

Cushions
Present Perfect offers a small range of cushions, the most popular of which is the antique white cushion trimmed with a border of Leavers lace (£27). The other designs, made with ribbon and with piped edges, are: 'perfect squares', 'zigger-zagger' and 'tumbling blocks' (from £20). Their brochure comes with generous samples of ribbon and backing fabrics. All pads are finest-quality

feather. The cushion sizes are either 12in- or 18in-square but other sizes can be accommodated.
Catalogue A5, Leaflets, Colour, 4 pages, Free **Postal charges** £1.25 per cushion **Delivery** Royal Mail **Methods of Payment** Cheque

PURVES & PURVES
80–81 & 83 Tottenham
Court Road
London
W1P 9HD
Telephone
0171 436 8860
Fax
0171 580 8244

Household
Purves & Purves' brochure contains unusual clocks, lights, mirrors, household, office and kitchen gadgets and equipment. Time-zone clocks in a set of 3 for £50. Clocks shaped like televisions and lollipops from £37. Sun mirrors handmade in mild steel from £30. A variety of kitchen aids from garlic slicer to espresso coffee makers.
Catalogue Annually, A4, Brochure, Colour, 7 pages, Free **Postal charges** UK mainland: for orders up to £84.99, add £4.50 for p&p; orders over £85, p&p is free. **Delivery** In-house delivery **Methods of Payment** Cheque, Postal Order, Credit Card, American Express, Switch

RAINBOW FAIRWEATHER DECORATIVE FURNITURE
Unit 14
The Talina Centre
Bagleys Lane
Fulham
London
SW6 2BW
Telephone
0171 736 1258
Fax
0171 384 2040

Domestic radiator cabinets
Rainbow's Cover Charm radiator cabinets do not simply 'disguise' a domestic radiator, they actually transform it into an elegant piece of furniture. Designed with ease of assembly and installation in mind, the fronts are easily removable for valve adjustments. The cabinets come with a choice of brass or wooden grilles and the hard-wearing finish is available in white or magnolia. Prices range from £91 for a 24in cabinet to £290 for a 38in cabinet with solid brass grille. They can also be custom-made.
Catalogue A4, Catalogue, Colour, 4 pages, Free **Postal charges** Add £15.00 per cabinet; 4 or more cabinets, carriage free **Delivery** Parcelforce **Methods of Payment** Cheque, Postal Order, Credit Card

RAINFORD HOUSE OF ELEGANCE
Wentworth Street
Birdwell
Barnsley
South Yorkshire
S70 5UN
Telephone
01226 350360
Fax
01226 350279

Decorative mouldings
Rainford specialises in the manufacture of period plasterwork and fittings which are recreated using traditional techniques and craft skills. It boasts an impressive range of fire-surrounds in plaster, cultured marble, cast-iron or wood. Prices from £99 to £1299. Also available are back panels and hearths, cornices, niches, domes, dado rails, wall friezes, plaques, overdoors, and more. Panel moulding is available in 5ft lengths and starts at £2.50. Corbels range from £22.50 to £29.50 a pair, centre-pieces from £9.95.

Catalogue Annually, A4, Catalogue, Colour, 35 pages, Free **Postal charges** Varies with item **Delivery** Courier **Methods of Payment** Cheque, Credit Card

READY-MADE CENTRE LTD
54 Stamford New Road
Altrincham
Cheshire
WA14 1EE
Telephone
0161 941 1714
Fax
0161 926 8408

Bedlinens, nightwear, home furnishings
Ready-Made Centre is a specialist company supplying top-quality traditional bedlinen and nightwear at very reasonable prices. Many items are exclusive to Ready-Made Centre and all are manufactured in the UK. Some bestsellers in the range include cotton chenille robes from just £29.99 and satin wraps from £19.95. Velour curtains are from £19.99 and easy-care cotton sheets from just £9.99. All goods are supplied with a full money-back guarantee.

Catalogue Annually, A5, Catalogue, Colour, 39 pages, Free **Postal charges** Up to £25.00, add £2.50; £26.00–£75.00, add £2.95; over £75.00, add £3.95 **Delivery** Royal Mail **Methods of Payment** Cheque, Postal Order, Credit Card

REJECT CHINA SHOP
1 Beauchamp Place
London
SW3 1NU
Telephone
0171 225 1696

Giftware, tableware and crystal
An independent family business, Chinacraft was established nearly 50 years ago and it is the largest British privately-owned tableware, gift and crystal specialist. They don't produce a catalogue but as long as you know what you want, you can order it

Fax
0171 225 2283

from them by letter or fax. They stock such major brand names as Wedgwood, Royal Doulton, Royal Crown Derby, Aynsley, Spode, Royal Worcester, Swarowski, Border Fine Arts, Country Artists and others too numerous to mention.
Delivery In-house delivery, Courier **Methods of Payment** Credit Card, Cheque, Postal Order

SAFE PRODUCTS GROUP
2A Ferdinand Place
London
NW1 8EE
Telephone
0171 267 5688/482 4021
Fax
0171 284 2806

Protective covers for furniture

The Safe Products Group produces protective covers for household objects. Chief among these is Tablesafe, a durable covering for tables that resists heat and water and prevents delicate surfaces from being scratched or dented. Tablesafe can be custom-made to fit any shape and costs £1.50/sq ft. The company also produces Bedsafe, a machine-washable, dry-cleanable mattress cover that prevents soiling and reduces dust-mite levels. Single-bed covers, £16.99; double-bed covers, £22.99.
Catalogue Annually, A4, Leaflets, Colour and B/W, 5 pages, Free **Postal charges** Varies with item **Delivery** Royal Mail, Parcelforce **Methods of Payment** Cheque, Credit Card

SCOTTS OF STOW
The Square
Stow-on-the-Wold
Gloucestershire
GL54 1AF
Telephone
01249 449111

Kitchenware and tableware from around the world

This catalogue is full of a splendid array of high-quality, value-for-money products for the kitchen and home. From patchwork quilts to sheepskin UGG slippers, stay-warm microwave bread-baskets to fine table linen, table-top steam grills to casserole sets, there is something for everyone. Insulated 4-cup cafetière, £19.95; juice extractor and pulper, £29.95; 30-piece dinner service, £39.95; hard-anodised cookware from £29.95; Dualit toasters from £104.95.
Catalogue Annually, A5, Catalogue, Colour, 36 pages,

Free **Postal charges** £2.95 on orders up to £29.99; £3.95 on orders of more than £30 **Delivery** Royal Mail, Parcelforce **Methods of Payment** Cheque, Credit Card, Postal Order

SHAKER KITCHENS
Acacia House
High Street
Mistley
Manningtree
Essex
CO11 1HD
Telephone
01206 392030
Fax
same

Kitchen furniture

Since 1988, Shaker Ltd has been selling products from the remaining Shaker communities and from specialist Shaker craftsmen. They are the only outlet for pure classic Shaker, plus many new items. The catalogue shows a selection of products available by mail order. Beautiful boxes, furniture and household accessories, bedding, tinware, kitchenware and books. It offers the perfect solution for the home and for gifts. There is also a booklet on The Shakers which gives further information on the fascinating background to these remarkable people.

Shaker kitchens are designed with care and special attention paid to the original Shaker designs. Each kitchen is tailor-made with a range of finishes from natural woods to handpainted, including the traditional Shaker colours. A Cherry Rocker chair £339, Maple Trestle Table £890. They also stock milk paint which is now gaining wider usage because it contains only ingredients that are non-toxic and are not harmful to the environment. It is packaged as a powder and water is added, so it can be made as thick or thin as required. A 6oz packet makes 1 pint of paint at £8.88. A 48oz packet makes 1 gallon for £60.64. Basic colours are beautiful earthy colours and when mixed with white become paler.

Catalogue Annually, A5, Leaflets, Colour and B/W, 13 pages, Free **Postal charges** Varies with item **Delivery** In-house delivery **Methods of Payment** Cheque

SIGNS OF THE TIMES

Tebworth
Leighton Buzzard
Bedfordshire
LU7 9QG
Telephone
01525 874185
Fax
01525 875746

House signs and letterboxes

Signs of the Times designs and produces hand-painted signs with raised lettering on a matt black background. They are cast in polymer or bronze, and varnished with a matt lacquer. Choose from a standard range of attractive rural scenes in a variety of shapes and sizes, or commission your own design. Prices from £21. The Letterbox Company, at the same address, makes elegant painted steel boxes and newspaper holders, from £22 for a US box.

Catalogue Annually, A5, Leaflets, Colour, 8 pages, Free **Postal charges** Varies with item **Delivery** Royal Mail, Parcelforce **Methods of Payment** Cheque, Postal Order, Credit Card, American Express

THE STAMPING GROUND

PO Box 1364
London
W5 5ZH
Telephone
0181 758 8629

Decorative stamps for household surfaces

As an alternative to stencilling, try stamping. The Stamping Ground supplies stamps, rollers and gold paint (although any water-soluble paint can be used) in a variety of gothic, country, marine and nursery motifs, with clear instructions. It's a simple way to create borders, patterns or decorative features on walls, ceilings, floors or fabrics. A 3in (75 × 75mm) stamp costs £8.95, a 5in (125 × 120mm) costs £10.95; roller £2.99; gold paint, £2.99.

Catalogue Annually, A5, Catalogue, Colour and B/W, 6 pages, Free **Postal charges** £1.99 **Delivery** Royal Mail **Methods of Payment** Cheque

STENCIL ESSENTIALS

Madhatters Emporium
26 High Street
Otford
Kent
TN14 5PQ
Telephone
01959 525578

Stencils and paints

Stencil Essentials supply original stencils either cut from clear acetate or as designs for you to cut. They can be used as borders, or individual motifs, on walls, curtains, furniture, trays, bins or boxes. Prices from £5 to £8. Stencils can also be designed and cut for you, and a heat pen for use on acetate is available (£19.95). The company also stocks two

Fax
01959 522778

ranges of paints, Jo Sonjas' acrylics and old-fashioned milk paint.
Catalogue Annually, A4, Catalogue, Colour and B/W, 8 pages, Free **Postal charges** Free **Delivery** Royal Mail, Parcelforce **Methods of Payment** Cheque

THE STENCIL FACTORY
105 Upgate
Louth
Lincolnshire
LN11 9HF
Telephone
01507 600948
Fax
same

Stencils
This brochure contains a range of hand-cut stencils for decorating walls and furniture. Most of the stencils are laser-cut from Mylar which can be used over and over again, and are coded according to difficulty of use. There are stencils for borders, eg 'Toadstools' (11 × 3in, £7.50) and 'Eight Pointed Stars' (9 × 3in, £5). There are corner stencils, 'Fishy' stencils ideal for bathrooms, 'In the Country' stencils and a range of children's stencils (eg 'Steam Train', 13 × 3in, £8.50).
Catalogue Bi-annually, A4, Brochure, B/W, 17 pages, Free **Postal charges** Free **Delivery** Royal Mail **Methods of Payment** Cheque

THE STENCIL STORE COMPANY
20/21 Herongate Road
Chorleywood
Hertfordshire
WD3 5LG
Telephone
01923 285577
Fax
01923 285136

Stencils, paint effects and accessories
This is the world's largest distributor of retail stencils. The Stencil Store's attractive catalogue will fill you with inspiration. Here you will find all you need to start stencilling from ready-cut designs, paints and brushes to the tools necessary for cutting your own. Rose Peony Border, £9.99; Bluebell Posy, £7.99; stencil brushes from £2.50; paints from £2.45. Fabric paints and materials to create paint effects are also stocked.
Catalogue Annually, A4, Catalogue, Colour, 28 pages, £1.50 **Postal charges** Varies with item **Delivery** Royal Mail, Parcelforce **Methods of Payment** Cheque, Credit Card

STEVENSONS OF NORWICH
Roundtree Way
Norwich
Norfolk
NR7 8SQ
Telephone
01603 400824
Fax
01603 405113

Plaster and GRP mouldings
Stevensons supply fibrous plaster, GRG and GRP mouldings worldwide to architects and individuals, bespoke or 'off-the-peg'. All the mouldings are produced in-house by highly trained craftsmen. From panel mouldings and corbels to classic columns and ceiling roses, Stevensons can produce virtually anything, even complete ceilings. Cornices from £15.35/3m; ceiling centre-pieces from £15.95; porticos from £1250.

Catalogue Annually, A4, Catalogue, Colour, 36 pages, Free **Postal charges** Varies with item **Delivery** Courier, Parcelforce **Methods of Payment** Cheque, Credit Card

SUE FOSTER FABRICS
57 High Street
Emsworth
Hampshire
PO10 7YA
Telephone
01243 378831
Fax
01243 373734

Furnishing fabrics
Established in 1978, Sue Foster Fabrics is a small company providing an efficient service in offering top-quality furnishing fabrics for curtains, loose covers and upholstery by most well-known manufacturers at discounted prices. Although the fabrics are discounted, none of them are seconds, and they guarantee to exchange any fabric with a flaw, as long as it hasn't been cut. They can only make an exact colour match if you write requesting a stock cutting or fill in their sample search questionnaire.

Catalogue A4, Leaflets, B/W, 3 pages, Free **Postal charges** Free **Delivery** Courier **Methods of Payment** Cheque, Credit Card, American Express

TILES OF NEWPORT AND LONDON
Unit 3, The Talina Centre
23A Bagleys Lane
Off The King's Road
London
SW6 2BW

Tiles
The inspirational floor and wall tiles displayed in this catalogue include designs from Italy, China, Spain and Mexico. For kitchen floors the traditional 8in Mexican Saltillo terracotta tiles are available at £28 per square yard. The patterned insets are 45p each. For bathroom walls, the

Telephone
0171 736 9323
Fax
0171 371 0809

distressed Fresco range from Tuscany is ideal, while for the kitchen there's a hand-painted mural depicting farm animals (£213). Prices do not include VAT.

Catalogue A4, Catalogue, Colour, 19 pages, Free **Postal charges** Varies with item **Delivery** Royal Mail, Parcelforce **Methods of Payment** Cheque, Postal Order, Credit Card

TIMNEY FOWLER
388 Kings Road
London
SW3 5UZ
Telephone
0171 352 2263
Fax
0171 352 0351

Furnishing fabrics, wallpapers and borders

Sue Timney and Grahame Fowler draw on the history of European art and images from Greek, Roman and Florentine objects to create their sophisticated ranges of wallpapers, friezes, borders and fabrics, some in vibrant colours, others in cool black and white. Fabrics from £18.90/m; wallpapers from £24.50/roll (prices excluding VAT).

Catalogue Annually, A4, Leaflets, Colour, 16 pages, Free **Postal charges** Varies with item **Delivery** Royal Mail, Parcelforce **Methods of Payment** Cheque, Credit Card

TOUCH DESIGN
PO Box 60
Andover
Hampshire
SP11 6SS
Telephone
01264 738060
Fax
01264 738067

Decorative items for home and garden

Erica Wolfe-Murray set out to find small workshops and individual craftspeople who would make up a range of items for the home and garden by hand. The result is Touch Design's appealing range of simple, carefully chosen items. The oak planters (£39.50) can be filled with fruit or blooms, while the square wicker shelf (£9.95) is ideal for small corners. To serve on plain white china is a refreshing relief (dinner plate, £9.95). For the garden there are withy flowerbed edgings and a conical planter. Children will delight in the canvas teepee on which they can paint their own designs, £25.

Catalogue Annually, A4, Catalogue, Colour, 16 pages, Free **Postal charges** Varies with item **Delivery** Courier **Methods of Payment** Cheque, Credit Card

TURNSTYLE DESIGNS
1 Bridge Chambers
Barnstaple
Devon
EX31 1HB
Telephone
01271 25325
Fax
01271 328248

Door knobs, handles and back plates
Turnstyle produces a unique range of door knobs and cabinet handles in shell, fossil, bird, sun and moon, animal and fish designs. Colours include subtle ochre, verdigris, aqua blue and terracotta. Many of the knobs, such as the frog design, are suitable for use as pegs, too. Door furniture from £35 a pair; cabinet knobs, £6 each.

Catalogue Annually, A4, Leaflets, Colour and B/W, 9 pages, Free **Postal charges** Varies with item **Delivery** Royal Mail, Parcelforce **Methods of Payment** Cheque, Postal Order, Credit Card

TURQUAZ LTD
The Coach house
Bakery Place
199 Abtenberg Gardens
London
SW11 1IQ
Telephone
0171 924 6894
Fax
0171 978 5854

Pure cotton bedlinen and table linen
Turquaz's pure cotton bedlinen and table linen is handwoven. Duvet covers cost from £48 to £68, depending on size. Oxford pillowcases are £12 each and square ones are £13.50. Fitted sheets are from £22 to £32.00. Table-cloths range from £13 to £24 depending on size, and napkins are £2.00 each. Silk throws are £75.

Co-ordinating fabrics can be obtained from The Malabar Cotton Company at leading interior designers nationwide.

Catalogue Annually, A4, Leaflets, B/W, 1 page, Free **Postal charges** £2.50 **Delivery** Courier **Methods of Payment** Cheque, Credit Card

UNITED CUTLERS OF SHEFFIELD
Petre Street
Sheffield
South Yorkshire
S4 8LL
Telephone
0114 243 3984
Fax
0114 243 7128

Cutlery
United Cutlers of Sheffield specialise in fine hallmarked sterling silver, silver plate and stainless steel, and boast an impressive pedigree of awards to back-up their successful sales history. The range includes 20 different patterns, all dishwasher-proof with the exception of the white-handled knives. Table knife: sterling silver, £35; silver-plated, £17.50; stainless steel, £12.50. Seven-piece place set: £282.50/£94.50/£62.

Cabinets, from £85; cutlery rolls, from £10.

Catalogue Annually, A5, Catalogue, Colour and B/W, 8 pages, Free **Postal charges** £5 **Delivery** Royal Mail, Parcelforce **Methods of Payment** Cheque, Postal Order, Credit Card, American Express, Diners Club

THE WHITE COMPANY
298–300 Munster Road
London
SW6 6BH
Telephone
0171 385 7988
Fax
0171 385 2685

Quality goods for the home

As its name suggests, this company offers a range of household items in fresh, crisp, uncluttered white. The catalogue includes an enticing collection of bedlinen with cushions and laundry bags, luxurious towels, bath robes and damask napkins. The white theme extends to bone china and honeycomb drying-up cloths, but there are concessions to colour in tartan rugs, rose-patterned quilts and blue gingham bedlinen. Double-row cord single flat sheet, £17.95; ribbon lace cushion cover, £12.50; single wool blanket, £38.95; set of three drying-up cloths, £8.95.

Catalogue Bi-annually, A5, Catalogue, Colour, 16 pages, Free **Postal charges** Varies with item **Delivery** Parcelforce **Methods of Payment** Cheque, Credit Card

WHOLESALE KITCHEN APPLIANCES
144 Buxton Road
Stockport
Cheshire
SK2 6PL
Telephone
0161 456 1187
Fax
0161 483 3500

Discounted kitchens and appliances

Steve Pickstock set up Wholesale Kitchen Appliances in the early 1990s to give the best possible advice on kitchen appliances and the quality of the product. He stocks a number of well-known names and guarantees to beat any quoted retail price by at least £10 (subject to verification). If you require an item not featured in the brochure, call him. Bosch gas hob, £149 (RRP £210); Bosch double oven, £499 (RRP £723).

Catalogue Annually, A4, Catalogue, Colour, 4 pages, Free **Postal charges** £20 for the first item; £12 for each additional item **Delivery** In-house delivery **Methods of Payment** Cheque, Credit Card, Switch

WHOLISTIC RESEARCH COMPANY
Dept GMO
Bright Haven
Robin's Lane
Lolworth
Cambridge
Cambridgeshire
CB3 8HH
Telephone
01954 781074

Holistic lifestyle products, devices and books

This interesting company sells a range of devices for 'healthy living in a modern world', including water purifiers, ionisers, natural light bulbs, juicers and a selected range of books. It takes the trouble to test every model on the market and presents an unbiased view of which it has found to be the best and most efficient. The catalogue goes to considerable lengths, for example, to discuss the merits of various water purification systems, finally coming down in favour of distillation, which removes virtually all impurities. The best juicer comes out at some £348, but there are cheaper models. A water distiller is £199 and ionisers are from around £20. There is also a range of other, often more unusual products.

Catalogue On request, A5, Book, B/W, 72 pages, Free **Postal charges** Varies with item **Delivery** Royal Mail, Parcelforce **Methods of Payment** Cheque, Postal Order

WOOLPIT INTERIORS
The Street
Bury St Edmunds
Suffolk
IP30 9SA
Telephone
01359 240895
Fax
01359 242282

Furniture accessories

Woolpit is one of the leading designers and manufacturers of decorative lighting and accessories. It offers a large selection of lamp bases in painted finishes and will colour-match to customer's specifications. A limed-oak square base from the Classic Column collection costs £98. Hand-painted shades start from £11. Steel chandeliers, wall sconces and painted bedside tables are also available.

Catalogue Annually, A4, Leaflets, Colour, 14 pages, Free **Postal charges** Varies with item **Delivery** Royal Mail, Parcelforce **Methods of Payment** Cheque, Credit Card

Kitchenware

ARGOS DISTRIBUTORS LTD
489–499 Avebury Boulevard
Central Milton Keynes
Hertfordshire
MK9 2NW
Telephone
01908 690333/01908 692301

Huge range of goods
Argos is the innovative high street store where you order by catalogue within the shop itself. But to make shopping even easier, Argos have set up a free home-delivery service called Argos Direct. This is available on selected large items such as 3-piece suites from £499.99, multi-gyms from £195.00, and mountain bikes from £129.00.

To order is easy: look through the Argos catalogue, check that the item is available for free home-delivery, and call 01345 427467, quoting your order and credit card details. They will then deliver to your door within 14 days. NOTE: catalogues themselves are only available through Argos stores, as are mail-order booklets.
Catalogue Bi-annually, A4, Catalogue, Colour, 679 pages, Free **Postal charges** Free **Delivery** Royal Mail **Methods of Payment** Cheque, Credit Card, Postal Order

BRIXTON POTTERY LTD
Hatton Gardens
Kington
Herefordshire
HR5 3RB
Telephone
01544 230700
Fax
01544 231600

Pottery
Brixton Pottery specialise in mugs (from £9.38) with animal motifs. Their attractive new designs include 'Oystercatcher', 'Labradors and puppies' and 'Swallows migrating'. Apart from mugs they make teapots (from £21.53), jugs, bowls, plates, soap dishes (from £11.05) and vases (from £16.22). Their warehouse is in Stoke-on-Trent.
Catalogue A4, Leaflets, Colour and B/W, 2 pages, Free **Postal charges** Add 10% (max £12.00, UK) **Delivery** Parcelforce **Methods of Payment** Cheque

CHURCHILL TABLEWARE

Churchill Factory Shop
Crane Street
Hanley
Stoke-on-Trent
Staffordshire
ST1 5RB
Telephone
01782 268870
Fax
01782 260051

China tableware

Churchill Tableware is a long-established family potter with a history in the business dating back to 1795. It offers a wide range of tea, lunch and dinner services. Priding itself on producing interesting designs, its selection includes traditional English blue and white prints (including the famous Blue Willow) through to modern designs. All products are crafted from English earthenware in the heart of Stoke-on-Trent. Seconds are available to the public through mail order from the Churchill Factory Shop. Prices for 17/18cm plate: Bramble Fayre, £1.22; Chelsea White, 94p; Chelsea Willow, £1.05; Stars, £1.05.

Catalogue Annually, A4, Catalogue, Colour, 23 pages, Free **Postal charges** Varies with item **Delivery** Royal Mail, Parcelforce **Methods of Payment** Cheque, Credit Card

DAVID MELLOR

4 Sloane Square
London
SW1W 8EE
Telephone
0171 730 4259
Fax
0171 730 7240

Kitchen equipment

David Mellor himself is a silversmith and when he opened his first shop in London in 1969, he brought to retailing his craftsman's knowledge of materials and his designer's eagle eye. This catalogue is an essential source of kitchen equipment for any cook, offering everything from wooden spoons to Mellor-designed cutlery. The items are carefully selected and beautifully designed, well-made and timeless. Sabatier knives from £6.30; slatted bread board, £23.85; nutmeg grinder, £18.75; Le Pentole stainless steel pans from £35; professional egg whisk, £7.20; cake pan, £4.90.

Catalogue Annually, A4, Catalogue, Colour, 33 pages, Free **Postal charges** £3.50 **Delivery** Royal Mail, Parcelforce **Methods of Payment** Cheque, Credit Card

DIVERTIMENTI (MAIL ORDER) LTD
FREEPOST G12881
London
SW6 6XU
Telephone
0171 386 9911
Fax
0171 386 9393

Kitchenware
Divertimenti offer a wide range of marvellous kitchenware, from the high-tech Magimix (£179.95) to the simple pestle and mortar (£12.95). There's a metal storage rack comprising wall rack, storage basket and six hooks for £29.95, a chrome-plated vegetable basket for £14.95, and a pasta drying stand for £11.95. Mail-order customers can also order a 24-page guide on caring for cooking utensils.

Catalogue Bi-annually, A4, Catalogue, Colour, 39 pages, Free **Postal charges** £3.50 **Delivery** Royal Mail, Parcelforce **Methods of Payment** Cheque, Postal Order, Credit Card

THE HANGING KITCHEN CO
Wyndham Farm
Station Road
Ningwood
Yarmouth
Isle of Wight
PO30 4NJ
Telephone
01983 760842
Fax
same

Cast iron and pine kitchenware
The Hanging Kitchen Company designs and produces practical, high-quality, traditional, kitchenware. All the items are handmade in cast-iron and pine and are available in a variety of colours and finishes to fit every style of kitchen. Best selling designs include the 'Original Kitchen Maid', a traditional clothes airer (4ft, £25); ceiling rack 'batterie de cuisine' (3ft, £30); and hand-painted pots (£6.95).

Catalogue Annually, Third A4, Brochure, Colour, 2 pages, Free **Postal charges** £2.95 **Delivery** Parcelforce **Methods of Payment** Cheque, Credit Card

LAKELAND PLASTICS
Alexandra Buildings
Windermere
Cumbria
LA23 1BQ
Telephone
015394 88100
Fax
015394 88300

Creative kitchenware
Lakeland Plastics is a family-run business supplying all you'll ever need for the kitchen and home. The catalogue contains hundreds of intriguing ideas to save time and money from foil, clingfilm and baking parchment through preserving, microwave and freezer accessories to specialist items for food preparation, cooking, serving and storing. The bright, interesting catalogue, coupled with a

KITCHENWARE

genuinely friendly service, makes this an ideal source for kitchen products. There are 50 cake-tin liners for £3.75; a lattice pastry cutter for £4.95; pure vanilla extract for £4.95; and a lemon tap for just 99p. Lakeland also offers other specialist catalogues such as the Christmas, Gifts, Summer Special and Storage Solutions.

Catalogue Quarterly, A5, Catalogue, Colour, 80 pages, Free **Postal charges** Varies according to value **Delivery** Parcelforce **Methods of Payment** Cheque, Credit Card, Switch, Postal Order

MILL POTTERY
Bridge Mill Workshops
St George's Square
Hebden Bridge
West Yorkshire
HX7 8ET
Telephone
01422 844559

Handthrown domestic stoneware

Bridge Mill pots are designed for tough everyday use: completely non-porous, they are microwave- and dishwasher-proof and the shapes are simple and functional. The butter/cheese bell costs £14, large jug £19, colander/pasta server with matching plate £30, and cutlery drainer £10. These reasonable prices include postage and packing.

Catalogue A5, Brochure, Colour and B/W, 4 pages, Free **Postal charges** Free **Delivery** Parcelforce **Methods of Payments** Cheque

PURVES & PURVES
80–81 & 83 Tottenham
Court Road
London
W1P 9HD
Telephone
0171 436 8860
Fax
0171 580 8244

Household

Purves & Purves' brochure contains unusual clocks, lights, mirrors, household, office and kitchen gadgets and equipment. Time-zone clocks in a set of 3 for £50. Clocks shaped like televisions and lollipops from £37. Sun mirrors handmade in mild steel from £30. A variety of kitchen aids from garlic slicer to espresso coffee makers.

Catalogue Annually, A4, Brochure, Colour, 7 pages, Free **Postal charges** UK mainland – for orders up to £84.99 add £4.50 for p&p. Orders over £85 p&p is free. **Delivery** In-house delivery **Methods of Payment** Cheque, Postal Order, Credit Card, American Express, Switch

KITCHENWARE

SCOTTS OF STOW
The Square
Stow on the Wold
Gloucestershire
GL54 1AF
Telephone
01249 449111

Kitchenware and tableware from around the world

This catalogue is full of a splendid array of high-quality, value-for-money products for the kitchen and home. From patchwork quilts to sheepskin UGG slippers, stay-warm microwave bread-baskets to fine table linen, table-top steam grills to casserole sets, there is something for everyone. Insulated 4-cup cafetière, £19.95; juice extractor and pulper, £29.95; 30-piece dinner service, £39.95; hard-anodised cookware from £29.95; Dualit toasters from £104.95.

Catalogue Annually, A5, Catalogue, Colour, 36 pages, Free **Postal charges** £2.95 on orders up to £29.99; £3.95 on orders of more than £30 **Delivery** Royal Mail, Parcelforce **Methods of Payment** Cheque, Postal Order, Credit Card

TUPPERWARE
Chapelin House
Widewater Place
Moorhall Road
Harefield, Uxbridge
Middlesex
UB9 6NF
Telephone
0800 500216
Fax
0895 826458

Food storage containers

The famous durable Tupperware containers are a must for any cook. These ingenious products come in a variety of shapes, sizes and colours and are guaranteed against chipping, cracking, breaking or peeling under normal domestic use. Choose from air-tight fridge boxes, microwave dishes, picnic ware, children's stencil sets and many more. Hand-grater with container and airtight seal, £11.50; three shallow stackable containers, £14.95; microwave oval container (1.5 litres), £27.95. Contact Tupperware for details of your local distributor.

Catalogue Bi-annually, A5, Catalogue, Colour, 32 pages, Free **Postal charges** Varies with item **Delivery** In-house delivery **Methods of Payment** Cheque, Postal Order, Credit Card

UNITED CUTLERS OF SHEFFIELD
Petre Street

Cutlery

United Cutlers of Sheffield specialise in fine hallmarked sterling silver, silver plate and

Sheffield
South Yorkshire
S4 8LL
Telephone
0114 243 3984
Fax
0114 243 7128

stainless steel, and boast an impressive pedigree of awards to back-up their successful sales history. The range includes 20 different patterns, all dishwasher-proof with the exception of the white-handled knives. Table knife: sterling silver, £35; silver-plated, £17.50; stainless steel, £12.50. Seven-piece place set: £282.50/£94.50/£62. Cabinets, from £85; cutlery rolls, from £10.
Catalogue Annually, A5, Catalogue, Colour and B/W, 8 pages, Free **Postal charges** £5 **Delivery** Royal Mail, Parcelforce **Methods of Payment** Cheque, Postal Order, Credit Card, American Express, Diners Club

Luggage

SNOWCHAINS EUROPRODUCTS
Bourne Enterprise Centre
Borough Green
Sevenoaks
Kent
TN15 8DG
Telephone
01732 884408
Fax
01732 884564

Snowchains and roof boxes
Snowchains Europroducts stock a wide range of snow chains, car-roof boxes and roof bars for passenger cars, light commercial vehicles and off-road vehicles. The range of snow chains is produced by Weissenfels and will fit most cars and sizes of tyre (from £38.26 per pair). Roof bars are available in different styles to take bicycles, sailboards, skis and luggage. Flight Deck roof boxes are available for as little as £99.95 and can easily be dismantled when not in use.
Catalogue A4, Catalogue, Colour, 6 pages, Free **Postal charges** Standard postal service, £4.50; 2-3 day carrier service (including insurance), £8.00; 24hr carrier service (including insurance), £10.00. **Delivery** Royal Mail, Courier **Methods of Payment** Cheque, Credit Card, Diners Club, American Express

THE STOCKBAG COMPANY
140 Battersea Park Road
London
SW11 4NB
Telephone
0171 498 8811
Fax
0171 498 0990

Travel bags
The Stockbag Company supplies distinctive canvas and leather luggage. Made from double-layered pure cotton canvas with a layer of rubber hidden in between, the bags are tough and waterproof and beautifully finished with leather straps and brass buckles and zips. The range includes shoulder bags (from £34.95), rucksacks (£46.95), traveller and overnight bags, sports carriers, suit carriers and briefcases (from £64.50), all in olive green, dessert tan and French navy.
Catalogue Annually, A5, Catalogue, Colour, 8 pages, Free **Postal charges** £3 **Delivery** Royal Mail, Parcelforce **Methods of Payment** Cheque, Credit Card

Medical & Scientific

COCHRANES OF OXFORD
Leafield
Witney
Oxfordshire
OX8 5NY
Telephone
01993 878641
Fax
01993 878416

Scientific equipment for schools
Cochranes of Oxford supply equipment for teaching science and astronomy to all age groups. Of the many items available, from Construct-o-Straws (£4.04) to crystals and molecular models, there is a Helios Planetarium working model of the planetary system combined with a star dome (£317.25). Cochranes also supply kites: Mini Fun Kite, £1.99; Dunford Flying Machine 1000, £17.95.
Catalogue Annually, A4, Leaflets, Colour and B/W, 20 pages, Free **Postal charges** £5 **Delivery** Royal Mail, Parcelforce **Methods of Payment** Cheque

COMFORT CARE
Unit 8a
Abbey Estates
Mount Pleasant
Alperton
Wembley
Middlesex
HA0 1QU
Telephone
0181 248 1743
Fax
0181 903 7162

Special needs
Comfort Care supplies special aids to those suffering from backache, bunions, claw and hammer toes and incontinence problems. They specialise in boots and slippers with accommodating fittings. For example, sufferers from swollen feet, raised or curled toes will find relief in the specially designed slippers or boots. These have been recommended or used by hospitals, nursing homes, chiropodists, social services and physiotherapists. They also offer a well-balanced range of health supplements including 'colon clean plus', for clean healthy bowels, 'feverfew' and 'valerian' capsules and balm for painful backs and joints. Their medi-patch is designed for external relief from aches and pains: it claims to go direct to the

MEDICAL & SCIENTIFIC

pain with no pills or side effects. They also supply a number of personal security products.
Catalogue Updated regularly, A5, Catalogue, B/W, Free **Postal charges** Varies with item **Delivery** Royal Mail, Courier, Parcelforce **Methods of Payment** Cheque, Postal Order, Credit Card

CONDOMANIA
Unit 5
Rivermead
Pipers Way
Thatcham
Berkshire
RG19 4EP
Telephone
01635 874393
Fax
01635 877622

Condoms
Condomania is, as you would imagine, a company selling condoms by mail order at discounted prices (about 25% off). Also novelty condoms, which are not recommended for contraceptive use, and international condoms such as American ones for larger sizes. A leaflet is also enclosed on product information and another on the history of the condom.
Catalogue Annually, A3, Catalogue, Colour, 16 pages, Free **Postal charges** Varies with item **Delivery** Royal Mail, Securicor **Methods of Payment** Cheque, Postal Order, Credit Card

INGRAMS MAIL ORDER
Amplivox House
Stanneylands Road
Wilmslow
Cheshire
SK9 4HH
Telephone
01625 530959
Fax
01625 530693

Hearing device assisters
This range of devices, which are designed to help when sight and hearing begin to fail, will be a great relief to the many people in this country who find day-to-day tasks more difficult as they get older. There are practical gadgets to let you watch television, carry on normal conversations in crowds and read small print more easily.

Many of the quality products provide simple solutions to the problems of getting older, such as the alarm clock with a vibrating plate which can be placed under a pillow to wake you, £11.95, and the portable door chime which can be carried around the house to ensure that you don't miss any important visitors.
Catalogue Annually, A5, Catalogue, Colour, 11 pages, Free **Postal charges** Varies with item **Delivery** Royal Mail,

Parcelforce, Courier **Methods of Payment** Cheque, Postal Order, Credit Card, Switch

LEISURETEC
815 London Road
Westcliff-on-Sea
Essex
SS0 9SY
Telephone
01702 470056
Fax
same

Binoculars, telescopes and microscopes
Leisuretec specialises in the sale of binoculars, telescopes and microscopes. Its catalogue offers an extensive array of equipment from many well-known manufacturers, including Ross-London, Zeiss and Bausch & Lomb. Hunter ZCF 8x30 binoculars, £43.95; Swift Audubon binoculars, from £289; Zenith YM-301 educational microscope, £82.25.

Catalogue Annually, A4, Catalogue, B/W, 66 pages, Free **Postal charges** Varies with item **Delivery** Royal Mail, Parcelforce **Methods of Payment** Cheque, Postal Order, Credit Card

NEW CONCEPT
Cox Hall Lane
Tattingstone
Ipswich
Suffolk
IP9 2NS
Telephone
01473 328006
Fax
same

Treatment couches
New Concept is a company of designer craftsmen who specialise in the production of portable treatment couches and accessories for therapists. The timber used for the couches comes from renewable sources and the upholstery is fire-retardant. The range includes the Professional, which has an adjustable leg-height system (from £272.31), and the Companion, a fully portable massage chair, £299.24.

Catalogue Annually, A4, Catalogue, Colour, 8 pages, Free **Postal charges** £17.33 **Delivery** Courier **Methods of Payment** Cheque, Credit Card

TFH
76 Barracks Road
Sandy Lane Industrial Estate
Stourport-on-Severn
Worcestershire
DY13 9QB

Toys for children with special needs
For the last 13 years, TFH has been supplying special schools, hospitals, social education centres and parents with quality special-needs equipment. By working together with their customers, work force and design engineers, they have developed the world's largest range of unique pastime, play

Telephone
01299 827820
Fax
01299 827035

and activity products for people of all ages and abilities. TFH is joined to and works closely with one of Britain's most established and respected toy companies, TP Activity Toys, so you can be confident TFH stands for quality. TFH produce three catalogues: Toys for Fun and Achievement, Age Appropriate Resources and Special Needs Books. The first catalogue, a 72-page full-colour publication which is aimed at children and teenagers with special needs, features over 1,000 toys and fun play ideas ideal for Christmas and birthdays. The second, a 40-page full-colour publication, is aimed at adults with special needs and features over 450 pastime, executive toys and recreational products. The third catalogue, a 12-page publication, is aimed at people of all ages and abilities as well as their parents and carers, and features 140 titles written about specific needs such as Cerebral Palsy, Down's Syndrome and Autism, as well as educational material. Service is fast and friendly.

Catalogue Annually, A4, Catalogue, Colour, 72 pages, Free **Postal charges** Varies with item **Delivery** Courier, Parcelforce **Methods of Payment** Cheque, Postal Order, Credit Card

Museums

BRITISH MUSEUM PUBLICATIONS
British Museum Connection (Mail Order)
Unit A
Chettisham Business Park
Ely
Cambridgeshire
CB6 1RY
Telephone
01353 668400

Books and gifts
The catalogue is designed to give a unique flavour of the Museum's varied collections from remote antiquity to the present. There is everything from hand-crafted replicas to gifts inspired by the exhibits. For example, Egyptian cat with earrings, £85; pharaoh scarves, £39.95; Egyptian blue earthenware and tea towels; hieroglyph bags, £11.95; a Roman copy of Socrates, £85. There are also pretty Christmas cards with pheasants, robins, doves, the Madonna and the Lamb of God designs. If you want to send as a gift, you can include a gift message and the item will be sent direct to the recipient at a charge of £1 extra.
Catalogue Annually, A6, Catalogue, Colour, 24 pages, Free **Postal charges** Up to £40, £3.95; up to £100, £5.95; over £100, £6.95 within UK. 48-hr express delivery, £3.50 extra **Delivery** Royal Mail **Methods of Payment** Cheque, Postal Order, Credit Card

NATIONAL PORTRAIT GALLERY
Publications (Mail Order)
FREEPOST (LON 5125)
London
WC2H 0BR
Telephone
0171 306 0055 EXT 280
Fax
0171 306 0092

Gifts
An attractively presented catalogue offering a selection of unusual and exclusive items usually available only in the National Portrait Gallery shop. Proceeds from the sales go towards funding the gallery's exhibitions, lectures and running costs. Guy Fawkes mug, £4.95; the wives of Henry VIII teaspoon set, £21; Shakespeare T-shirt, £9.99; Zandra Rhodes bow by Andrew Logan, £115.

SCIENCE MUSEUM

Euroway Business Park
Swindon
Wiltshire
SN5 8SN
Telephone
01793 480666
Fax
01793 485636

Catalogue Annually, A4, Catalogue, Colour, 20 pages, Free **Postal charges** Varies with item **Delivery** Royal Mail, Parcelforce **Methods of Payment** Cheque, Credit Card, American Express

Science-based goods

The Science Museum's catalogue is aimed at the younger generation with many of the products science-based, some useful, and others just great fun. The gifts on offer range from clothes and games to food processors (eg ice-cream makers) and household gadgets. The catalogue is brought out once a year, including new and fun ideas for the developing scientist.

Catalogue Annually, A3, Catalogue, Colour, 32 pages pagoo

SOUTH KENSINGTON MUSEUMS CATALOGUE

Euroway Business Park
Swindon
Wiltshire
SN5 8SN
Telephone
01793 514141
Fax
01793 487002

A variety of products from around the world

The Natural History Museum, Science Museum and the Victoria & Albert Museum have joined forces to publish a catalogue of enterprising ideas, original gifts, clothes, jewellery, gadgets and toys. If you are looking for a present with a difference, this is the catalogue. From the Victoria & Albert: cultured pearl necklace, £46.50; old teak bookrest, £24.95; cherub garden fountain, £199. From the Natural History Museum: rainbow hammock, £30; bird feeder, £19.95; botanical sofa throw, £65. From the Science Museum: loony lenses, £7.95; Pockite kite, £15.95; skeleton pyjamas, £14.95.

Catalogue Annually, A5, Catalogue, Colour, 30 pages, Free **Postal charges** £3.25 **Delivery** Royal Mail, Parcelforce **Methods of Payment** Cheque, Postal Order, Credit Card, American Express, Diners Club

Musical Instruments

ABORIGINALIA
3 Cotswold Court
The Green
Broadway
Worcestershire
WR12 7AA
Telephone
01386 853770
Fax
01386 40202

Ethnic musical instruments and artifacts
Aboriginalia's hand-crafted products enable you to 'experience the traditional myths of ancient Australia' without the heat, flies or Australians. There's a good range of products, from the inevitable boomerangs, (£3.65 for a 6" model) up to larger pieces such as a 3'6" painted didgeridoo. This will set back aspiring Rolf Harisses some £115 and an extra £2.95 for a cassette on how to play it.

There are a variety of wooden carvings from £15, along with clay pottery emus, koalas and kangeroos, each at £22.25. More obscure is the woomera, a spear-throwing aid or fighting stick costing £30 – though quite what one does with this is not clear. Although the company accepts credit cards, they cannot do so yet over the phone. Visit the shop at the address above.

Catalogue updated frequently, A5, Catalogue, B/W, 4 pages, Free **Postal charges** Varies with item **Delivery** Parcelforce **Methods of Payment** Cheque, Postal Order, Credit Card, American Express, Switch, Diners Club

Office Equipment

BT BUSINESS CATALOGUE
FREEPOST (BS7632)
Bristol
Avon
BS1 2QX
Telephone
0800 800968

Telephone systems and accesories

No expense seems to have been spared with this glossy publication aimed at the business user. Equipment is compared and analysed in detail and the various services of BT, such as 0891 and Lo-call 0345 numbers are explained. You can order fax machines, phone systems, answering machines, video conferencing equipment, pagers and payphones, and for £550 a quarter you can have access to all 17 million telephone listings on CD-ROM. For those leading simpler lives there is a good range of telephones to buy or rent.

Catalogue Quarterly, A4, Catalogue, Colour, 85 pages, Free **Postal charges** Varies with item **Delivery** In-house delivery **Methods of Payment** Cheque, Credit Card

CHARLES WHITE (OFFICE SUPPLIES) LTD
Unit C4–C18 Poplar
Business Park
10 Prestons Road
London
E14 9RL
Telephone
0171 515 2500
Fax
0171 515 3575

Office supplies

Charles White offer a range of quality products at affordable prices. There are computer workstations for only £61.87 and four-drawer steel filing cabinets for £81. A ream of A4-size Conqueror paper costs only £12.63 and clipboards are 98p each.

One of Charles White's specialities is conference planning, with complete presentation systems, conference furniture and stationery – everything except the refreshments in fact.

Catalogue A4, Catalogue, Colour, 31 pages, Free **Postal charges** £2.75; free if goods value £50.00 or more **Delivery** Royal Mail, Parcelforce **Methods of Payment** Cheque, Credit Card

MUJI
26 Great Marlborough Street
London
W1V 1HL
Telephone
0171 494 1197
Fax
0171 494 1193

Stationery, clothes and accessories

For the minimalist look, Muji's catalogue of simply and effectively designed products is the one. Muji opened in Tokyo in 1983 and now has four shops in the UK selling a range of functional, uncluttered stationery, household goods, furniture, clothes, belts, bags and watches. Clever cardboard storage drawers, from £7.95; acrylic magazine holder, £10.95; plastic cosmetic bottle, 95p; zinc box, £22.50; cotton T-shirt, £9.50; nylon bucket bag, from £14.95; sofa, £475.

Catalogue Annually, A3, Catalogue, Colour, 8 pages, Free **Postal charges** Varies with item **Delivery** Royal Mail, Parcelforce **Methods of Payment** Cheque, Credit Card, American Express, Diners Club

RAYDEK SAFETY PRODUCTS LTD
Raydek House
Saltley Business Park
Birmingham
West Midlands
B8 1BL
Telephone
0121 326 8800
Fax
0121 327 6281

Industrial safety equipment

By law companies are required to use safety signs to alert and inform employees of potential risks and dangers in the workplace. Raydek produce a comprehensive series of safety products, from 'Danger: wet floor' signs to ladder stoppers (£31.50) and chemical-resistant coveralls (from £27.25). Aluminium signs start at £9.94 for 300 × 450mm; all you have to do is describe the type of sign you want and they'll do the rest. All Raydek's products comply with the latest standards, regulations and legislation, and they guarantee to refund the difference of any product purchased from them if it could have been bought for less. (This price pledge relates only to mail-order purchases corresponding to list prices featured in similar 1996 publications.)

Catalogue Annually, A4, Catalogue, Colour, 99 pages, £1.50 **Postal charges** Any orders under £30 will incur a £5 handling charge. Carriage and VAT will be added to all orders **Delivery** Royal Mail **Methods of Payment** American Express, Credit Card

OFFICE EQUIPMENT

THANET BUSINESS SUPPLY SHOPS
2/3 Orange Street
Canterbury
Kent
CT1 2JA
Telephone
01227 450055
Fax
01227 760548

Globes and posture seating

Thanet offers a full range of antique-looking globes to compliment any office suite, library, study or living room. They come on desk stands, floor stands, set in curvilinear wrought iron, on a cube of weather instruments, or complete with miniature putting green for the avid golfer. From £315 to £7,900. The company also sells Balans correct posture seating, including the Stokke range, from £102 (ex VAT).

Catalogue Annually, A4, Catalogue, Colour and B/W, 16 pages, Free **Postal charges** Varies with item **Delivery** Courier, Royal Mail, Parcelforce **Methods of Payment** Cheque, Credit Card

Optical

C & T EYEWEAR LTD
PO Box 41
Teddington
Middlesex
TW11 05X
Telephone
0181 943 4815
Fax
0181 977 1717

Ray-Ban sunglasses
C&T offer 40% off the retail price for genuine Bausch & Lomb Ray-Ban sunglasses. Recently these have once again become fashion items, usually with prices to match. The leaflet pictorially displays their extensive range of glasses, ranging from the Wayfarer Black G-15 to The General II Gold RB-50. Every pair of Ray-Ban glasses sold has a one-year guarantee and prices include a soft or hard case, depending on model. All frames are adjustable.
Catalogue A4, Leaflets, Colour, 4 pages, Free

Outdoor (including Camping)

THE CANVAS & NYLON COMPANY
'Our Way'
North Street
Winkfield
Berkshire
SL4 4TF
Telephone
01344 882539
Fax
same

Portable garages and marquees
The Canvas & Nylon Company manufacture and repair all canvas and nylon goods. The portable garages have a strong galvanised pre-assembled frame, and operate on a perambulator system so they can be raised or lowered easily. They are covered with nylon (medium or heavy) or canvas (samples are attached to their catalogue). Prices start at £99 for a 9 × 4ft medium nylon garage. One-piece marquees start at £550 for 12 × 12ft. Frame marquees start at £2,500 for a 20 × 20ft. Or a cheaper option is an ex-hire marquee (£400 for a 12 × 12ft). Prices are exclusive of VAT.
Catalogue A4, Leaflets, Colour, 2 pages, Free **Postal charges** Add £20.00 (UK) **Delivery** Royal Mail, Courier **Methods of Payment** Cheque

FARLOW'S OF PALL MALL
5 Pall Mall
London
SW1
Telephone
0171 839 2423
Fax
01285 643743

Fishing tackle, shooting accessories and clothes
With a business that has been in operation since 1840 and a Royal Warrant holder since 1982, this mail-order side of the central London retail operation brings together products from the company's three shops. The catalogue features fishing rods, reels, fly boxes, flies, canvas bags, pouches, wading staffs, cool bags, men's shooting and fishing clothing: Fedoras, tweed caps, breeks, plus-fours, quilted jackets, boots, stockings, waterproof jackets, fishing waistcoats, waders — and country clothing for ladies, such as tweed shooting

suits, wax jackets, breeks and plus-twos. There's also a selection of shooting and fishing gifts such as the fish and bar cuff-links and sporting cartoon clocks. All the items are clearly shown with lengthy descriptions where necessary.

Catalogue Bi-annually, A4, Catalogue, Colour, 68 pages, free to UK customers. **Postal charges** Varies with item **Delivery** Royal Mail, Parcelforce, Courier **Methods of Payment** Cheque, Credit Card, American Express, Diners Club

TALL SHIPS PLAYFRAMES
Aveton Gifford
Kingsbridge
South Devon
TQ7 4JP
Telephone
01548 550131

Playframes

These imaginative climbing frames and accessories will delight any adventurous child. Made from oak, chestnut and preserved redwood, the basic pyramid-and-rungs shape can become a covered 'Tepee'; 'Deathslide', £135, with rope, tyre and pulley; 'Jungle Bridge', £220, with climbing rope and slides; 'Pirate Swingboat', £199, with sail and mast; 'Aerial Ropeway', £100, with swing and rope ladder; or a simple 'Swing Frame' with toddler slide, £199 (this fits easily on a lawn 4m square).

Catalogue Annually, A5, Leaflets, Colour and B/W, 6 pages, Free **Postal charges** Varies with item **Delivery** Courier **Methods of Payment** Cheque, Credit Card

Pets

ANIMAL HEALTH TRUST
PO Box 5
Newmarket
Suffolk
CB8 7DW
Telephone
01638 661111
Fax
01638 665789

Christmas cards and gifts
The Animal Health Trust produces a one-sheet leaflet featuring on one side its range of Christmas cards. These come in just three designs – all with animals of course – and cost from £1.85 for 5 or £4 for a pack of 10, depending on the design. The other side has colour photographs of promotional clothes. These include T-shirts, rugby sweatshirts and silk ties. All are printed with the Trust's logo and, of course, proceeds go toward their work. There are also some other items such as mugs, teddy bears, yo-yos and bottle stoppers.
Catalogue Leaflets, Colour, 2 pages, Free **Delivery** Royal Mail **Methods of Payment** Cheque, Postal Order, Credit Card

CATAWARE
Victoria Mill
Bakewell
Derbyshire
DE45 1DA
Telephone
01629 813993
Fax
01629 814419

Cat theme items
The Cataware *Mewsletter* is packed with more than 200 themed items for cat lovers and their furry friends. You can treat your cat to the ultimate indulgence, a Radiator Bed, £15.95, while you can snuggle up with a fur-fabric cushion with kitten motif, from £11.99. There are ceramic cats and draught-excluder cats, catty cards and catty clocks, stickers and T-shirts, stools and shelves.
Catalogue Quarterly, A5, Catalogue, Colour, 16 pages, £2.50 a year **Postal charges** £2.80 **Delivery** Royal Mail **Methods of Payment** Cheque, Credit Card, Switch

THE CATS PROTECTION LEAGUE
17 Kings Road
Horsham
West Sussex
RH13 5PN
Telephone
01403 261947
Fax
01403 218414

Gifts

If you're a feline fan, there's something here for you! 'Catty' items include leather bookmarks in various colours (40p), dustpics (special adhesive brushes that pick up fur (£2), and balloons with the Cats' Protection League logo (£1 per dozen). Sweatshirts and T-shirts also bearing the logo range in price from £4.50 (T-shirts) to £9.50 (sweatshirts).

Catalogue A5, Catalogue, Colour, 8 pages, Free **Postal charges** Total value up to £1, add 30p; total value up to £5, add 80p; total value over £5, add £1.30 **Delivery** Royal Mail **Methods of Payment** Cheque

THE DOG DIRECTORY
206 Walton Street
London
SW3 2JL
Telephone
0171 225 2223
Fax
0171 581 3629

Gifts for dog-minded people

The Dog Directory includes tapestry kits, made-up cushions, spill vases, cachepots, framed limited edition prints, porcelain and bronze sculptures, rag rugs and antiqued boxes, featuring over 40 different breeds of dogs from the cheeky-faced West Highland terrier to the graceful whippet and adorable pug. Prices start at £45 for the tapestry kits, prints and spill vases up to £80 for the porcelain dogs and £175 for the elegant bronze deerhound.

Catalogue A5, Leaflets, Colour, 2 pages, Free **Delivery** Royal Mail **Methods of Payment** Cheque, Postal Order, Credit Card

FELINE ADVISORY BUREAU (FAB)
C/o Mrs D W Savage
Middle Coombe Farm
Huish Champflower
Taunton
Somerset
TA4 2HG

Gifts, clothing and stationery

The Feline Advisory Bureau is a registered charity for the benefit of these furry animals. Its small selection of products will delight any cat-lover: kitten-covered drinks tray, £7; notepaper, £1.50 a pack; T-shirt with cat logo, £6.75. You can also brush up your knowledge of *Feline Behaviour Therapy* or learn *How to Talk to Your Cat* from its range of books and videos.

Telephone
01984 624683
Fax
same

THE INTERNATIONAL PRIMATE PROTECTION LEAGUE
116 Judd Street
London
WC1H 9NS
Telephone
0171 837 7227
Fax
0171 278 3317

Catalogue Annually, A5, Catalogue, Colour, 8 pages, Free **Postal charges** Varies with item **Methods of Payment** Cheque

Hampers for pets
IPPL was founded as a registered charity in 1974 to foil animal smugglers and has succeeded in the prosecution of many traffickers. It also contributes towards the care in sanctuaries of confiscated and abandoned primates which cannot be returned to the wild. Show your pets how much you love them by buying a gift hamper full of treats (from £12 for a dog, rabbit/hamster, cat, or budgie/canary hamper). Profits go towards primate welfare.

Catalogue Annually, Third A4, Brochure, Colour, 2 pages, Free **Postal charges** Varies with item **Delivery** Royal Mail, Parcelforce **Methods of Payment** Cheque, Postal Order, Credit Card

MICHAEL LAZARUS ASSOCIATES
242-244 St John Street
London
EC1V 4PH
Telephone
0171 250 3988
Fax
0171 608 0370

Kites and dog coats
As well as making kites, MLA also make lightweight, weatherproof dog coats which fasten with Velcro and fold into your pocket. Prices start at £12.95.

Catalogue A5, Leaflets, Colour, 7 pages, Free **Postal charges** Free **Delivery** Parcelforce **Methods of Payment** Cheque, Postal Order, Credit Card

NATIONAL CANINE DEFENCE LEAGUE
17 Wakley Street
London
EC1V 7LT
Telephone
0171 837 0006

Gifts, stationery and pet products
This registered charity's catalogue is devoted to products for dog and animal lovers alike. You can buy a Scotty door mat for £23.95, a neat carry loo for £4.50, a furry cat's cradle to hook over a radiator for £15.95, doggy Christmas cards for £1.95 for a pack of 10, ear wipes for £1.75,

PETS 475

Fax
0171 833 2701

grooming products for your pet and sweatshirts for yourself, as well as books and animal bedding.
Catalogue Annually, A4, Catalogue, Colour, 8 pages, Free **Postal charges** Varies with item **Delivery** Royal Mail, Parcelforce **Methods of Payment** Cheque, Postal Order, Credit Card

Photographic

CALENDAR MEMORIES
Bravequest
PO Box 7
Brentford
Middlesex
TW8 9BU
Telephone
0181 958 7194
Fax
0181 958 2962

Personalised calendars
This innovative company will take any photographs you send them and make them into a calendar. So you could have different photos of your family and pets each month – an ideal gift for someone living abroad. A 12-month calendar, requiring 12 photographs, costs £17.95 inclusive, while a quarterly version needing just 4 photos is £9.95. Originals can be in colour or black and white but must be prints, not slides or negatives.
Catalogue By Advertising **Postal charges** Free **Delivery** Royal Mail **Methods of Payment** Cheque, Postal Order, Credit Card

THE CPL GROUP
Duchess House
18–19 Warren Street
London
W1P 5DB
Telephone
0171 388 7836
Fax
0171 383 4629

Photographic laboratory services
The CPL Group offers a wide range of services for the development of photographs ranging from film processing, black and white printing, computer graphics and machine printing to print mounting, illuminated display boxes and reversal printing. Prices depend on the size of the photographs and the service needed. All of the handmade colour prints are of a high quality and the photographic services are carried out by trained, professional technicians.
Catalogue 29.8 × 16 mm, Catalogue, Colour, 39 pages **Delivery** Royal Mail **Methods of Payment** Cheque, Postal Order

FLASH FOTO LTD
4 Parkmead
Flower Lane
London
NW7 2JW
Telephone
0181 959 4513
Fax
0181 959 1388

Photographic equipment
Flash Foto market the Arrowfile photographic storage system that allows you to store prints, slides and negatives of varying sizes in their one-size 13 × 11in loose-leaf albums with locking bars to keep pages flat. The ring-binder albums start at £3.95. There is also an ingenious device for storing slides by suspending them in a standard filing cabinet. Arrowfile suspension pages cost from £15.99 for 15 or 24 slides.
Catalogue Bi-annually, Catalogue, Colour, 12 pages, Free **Postal charges** £3.25; £6.00 where credit is given on official orders. **Delivery** Royal Mail **Methods of Payment** Cheque, Postal Order, Credit Card

JESSOP GROUP LTD
Jessop House
98 Scudamore Road
Leicester
Leicestershire
LE3 1TZ
Telephone
0116 2320033
Fax
0116 2320060

Photographic accessories
Jessops have a great number of photographic shops up and down the country and they also operate a mail-order service. Along with camera accessories such as films (from £2.50), batteries (from £1.99), bags (from £9.99), filters (£19.99 for an 'effect filter starter kit') and tripods (from £11.99), their catalogue features darkroom chemicals and equipment; frames, mounts and storage systems; binoculars, telescopes, video accessories, projectors and screens.
Catalogue A4, Catalogue, Colour, 12 pages, Free **Postal charges** £2.50 per order for UK (allow 7 working days); £7.00 for next-day delivery **Delivery** Parcelforce **Methods of Payment** Switch, Credit Card, Cheque

OCCASIONS
30 Barn Owl Way
Woodland View
Burghfield Common
Reading
Berkshire
RG7 3XX

Pottery portraits
Pamela Stannard glazes personal photographs on to pieces of china such as plates, trays, tankards (eg to record a christening) and shields (eg to record a prizegiving). She can also provide wire or adhesive hangers or stands for the plates. A Jumbo Tray will take a 7 × 5in photo and costs £17.00; a Large

Telephone
01734 834078

Shield will take a 3in photo and costs £10.00; and a Tankard will take a 2¼in photo and costs £11.00.

Catalogue A5, Catalogue, Colour, 7 pages, Free **Postal charges** Free **Delivery** Parcelforce **Methods of Payment** Cheque, Postal Order

TECNO RETAIL LTD
Unit 9
Hampton Farm
Industrial Estate
Hampton Road West
Feltham
Middlesex
TW13 6DB
Telephone
0181 898 9934/0181 898 2772
Fax
0181 894 4652

Photographic, video and personal electronics

Tecno is a leading specialist retailer of imaging equipment, from conventional cameras starting at £29.99 right up to a Contax G-1 at £1,149.99. It also sells camcorders, editing equipment, video recorders and photographic and video accessories. Prices are always competitive, with frequent exclusive offers and discounts on bulk orders (eg Kodak Gold 200 135–36, single film £4.49, 12-pack £39.95, save £13.93). It also sells films and tapes at low prices, with a 10% discount on batches of 10, which can be mixed.

Catalogue Quarterly, A4, Catalogue, Colour, 68 pages, Free **Postal charges** £2.50; 48hr service, £6.50 **Delivery** Royal Mail, Parcelforce **Methods of Payment** Cheque, Postal Order, Credit Card, Switch, American Express, Diners Club, Stage Payments

TRUPRINT
Stafford Park 18
Telford
Shropshire
TL1 1TP
Telephone
01952 292162

Photoprocessing

Truprint is Europe's largest mail-order photo-processor. They return a free film with every order. All films are returned within 7 days or your money is refunded – guaranteed. Truprint also offer a full range of photo-related products, from reprints and enlargements through to photo transfer items such as photo-shirts, jigsaws, canvas texture prints and photo posters. Their competitive pricing includes 24 compact prints for £2.99, reprints from only 35p, photo-shirts from £7.50, and Truprint single-use cameras from £3.49.

Catalogue Bi-monthly, A5, Catalogue, Colour, Varies

pages, Free **Postal charges** Varies with item **Delivery** Royal Mail **Methods of Payments** Cheque, Postal Order

WRIGHT & LOGAN
20 Queen Street
Portsea
Portsmouth
Hampshire
PO1 3HL
Telephone
01705 829555

Photographs of warships

The Wright & Logan collection consists of over 50,000 different negatives of naval warships and support vessels, of different nationalities and types, from the 1920s onwards. Each photograph is dry mounted on to quality board and sealed into a bevelled cut matt overlay with a two-line caption consisting of the ship's name and any dates or names you may wish to provide. Prices from £38.95 to £40.95, depending on frame.

Catalogue Annually, A5, Brochure, B/W, 6 pages, Free **Postal charges** Free **Delivery** Royal Mail **Methods of Payment** Cheque, Credit Card

YORK EXCEL
FREEPOST
PO Box 101
Exeter
EX1 1XL
Telephone
0345 125653

York Excel is designed to meet the needs of the keen amateur photographer. Drawing on many years of photoprocessing experience, York Excel offers developing and printing for C41, Black & White, E6 (slide) and 120 roll of film. A full range of reprints and enlargements are also available. Additional services include: free printing of negative numbers on the back of prints and free titling for mounted slides.

Catalogue Catalogue, Colour, 12 pages, Free **Delivery** Royal Mail **Methods of Payment** Cheque, Postal Order, Credit Card

YORK PHOTO
Brunel Road
Newton Abbot
Devon
TQ12 4XL
Telephone
01626 67373

Mail-order photoprocessing

York Photo is the world's largest mail-order photoprocessing laboratory. Its no-frills, value-for-money approach means York supplies its customers with a high-quality product at the best price. Along with this basic service, York Photo offers reprints, enlargements, posters, photo-shirts, jigsaws, canvas texture prints, coasters, selective

enlargements, copy prints and photo-aprons, all made from customer photographs. Also single-use cameras, cameras, York and Kodak Gold film at special prices. Up to 27 compact prints cost just £1.90 while York film is available from £1.15.
Catalogue Bi-monthly, A5, Brochure, Colour **Postal charges** Varies with item **Delivery** Royal Mail **Methods of Payment** Other, Cheque, Postal Order

Recordings

ACCELERATED LEARNING SYSTEMS
50 Aylesbury Road
Aston Clinton
Aylesbury
Buckinghamshire
HP22 5AH
Telephone
01296 631177
Fax
01296 631074

Learning equipment, tapes and kits
Accelerated Learning courses are founded on extensive research into how people learn best through seeing, hearing and doing. These programmes use a combination of audio cassettes, videos, books and games to enable the student to learn in the most suitable way for them. There are a number of different courses: languages, drawing, music, diet control and even a 'Learning to Learn' programme. Each language course costs £125, with a choice of French, Spanish, German and Italian, and comes with a 15-day trial period.
Catalogue Annually, A5, Leaflets, Colour and B/W, 16 pages, Free **Postal charges** Varies with item **Delivery** Royal Mail, Courier **Methods of Payment** Cheque, Postal Order, Credit Card

ACORN MUSIC
PO Box 17
Sidmouth
Devon
EX10 9EH
Telephone
01395 578145
Fax
01395 578080

Music
Established since 1959, Acorn Music is one of Britain's oldest specialists for jazz, dance and big bands, Latin-American, vocalists and nostalgia. They hold large stocks of LPs, CDs, and small stocks of cassettes, videos and books. They import regular consignments from the USA, and can often help with unusual, scarce and out-of-print items (but not pop or classical).
Catalogue Annually, A5, Brochure, B/W, 100 pages, £2.50 **Postal charges** Varies with item **Delivery** Royal Mail, Parcelforce **Methods of Payment** Cheque, Postal Order, Credit Card

BRITANNIA MUSIC CO
60–70 Roden Street
Ilford
Essex
IG1 2AE
Telephone
0181 910 6666
Fax
0181 910 6655

CDs and cassettes
Join the Britannia Music Club and you can buy an album at a bonus price every time you buy one at a regular price. So, for instance, Bjork's *Debut* on CD is £13.49 regular, or £6.75 bonus. The club's *Music News* magazine offers a range of pop, rock, Motown, film soundtracks, compilations, country and dance music. On joining you will receive an introductory parcel of CDs and cassettes and the free monthly magazine. You will be asked to buy a further six regular-priced recordings during your membership.

Catalogue Monthly, A5, Catalogue, Colour, 32 pages, Free **Postal charges** Varies with item **Delivery** Royal Mail **Methods of Payment** Cheque, Postal Order, Credit Card

CAP & GOWN SERIES
PO Box 14
Penkridge
Stafford
Staffordshire
ST19 5SQ
Telephone
01785 713560

Maths videos
Cap & Gown Series have specialised in the making of maths videos for the last eight years and are the UK market leaders in this field. Situated in rural Staffordshire, they are able to keep costs down to a minimum and yet provide a fast delivery service to all parts of the UK.

The maths videos are extremely useful for students to catch up on work lost at school and means they can study in the privacy of their own home, saving the expense of a private tutor. The tapes are prepared by a Chartered Mathematician, Dr A K Hannaby. Prices range from £52.50 for National Curriculum Mathematics – Key stage 3 (a set of 3 tapes) to A-Level Maths – The Agreed Common Core (7 tapes) for £135.00.

Catalogue A5, Brochure, Colour, 8 pages, Free **Postal charges** £4 per order **Delivery** Parcelforce **Methods of Payment** Cheque, Postal Order, Credit Card, Switch

CASSETTES DIRECT
Hedgemoor Farm
Bridford
Exeter
Devon
EX6 7LW
Telephone
01647 52358
Fax
same

Fiction and non-fiction cassettes
Now you can catch up on Shakespeare's plays, pioneering voyages of discovery, short stories, famous trials, or composers and their music, whether you're travelling, ironing or lying in bed. Cassettes Direct's catalogue contains an extensive range of recorded fiction and non-fiction, with tapes for children, too. Adult cassettes, £4.99; children's, £3.49.
Catalogue Annually, A4, Brochure, B/W, 12 pages, Free **Postal charges** £1.90 **Delivery** Royal Mail, Parcelforce **Methods of Payment** Cheque, Postal Order

CD SELECTIONS
Dorchester
Dorset
DT2 7YG
Telephone
01305 848725
Fax
01305 848516

CDs, videos
CD Selections publish their main 60-page 'Buyers Guide to Bargain CDs' twice a year, with supplementary publications at intervals between. This full-colour guide offers a remarkable range of classical, opera, jazz, easy listening and popular CDs with prices starting at £1.99. Overstocks, deletions and ongoing titles are selected for value for money and all sales are backed by a full refund guarantee. CD Selections also sell cassettes, audio books, bargain books and ballet and opera videos.
Catalogue Bi-annually, A4, Catalogue, Colour, 60 pages, Free **Postal charges** £2.35; overseas postage at cost **Delivery** Parcelforce, Royal Mail **Methods of Payment** Cheque, Postal Order, Credit Card

CHATER & SCOTT
8 South Street
Isleworth
Middlesex
TW7 7BG
Telephone
0181 568 9750
Fax
0181 569 8273

Books and video on motoring
Chaters claims to be 'Europe's No 1 Choice for Motoring Books and Videos' and certainly they have an impressive range. Their tightly printed catalogue is really more of a price list, with each entry given just a brief description and price. There are sections on general interest as well as technical, motorsport, manufacturers, American cars and motorcycles. Clearly for the enthusiast

who knows what he or she wants, this is about as comprehensive as you can get.

Catalogue Bi-annually, A5, Catalogue, B/W, 40 pages, Free **Postal charges** £3; free over £45 **Delivery** Courier, Royal Mail **Methods of Payments** Cheque, Postal Order, Credit Card, Switch, American Express

THE CLASSIC PICTURES COLLECTION
Studio 50
Shepperton Film Studios
Studios Road
Shepperton
Middx
TW17 0QD
Telephone
01932 572017

Classic films

Small, well-produced catalogue which features classic and more modern films. The catalogue is divided into various sections: War (*Colditz*, £9.99; *On A Wing and A Prayer*, £9.99; and *The Memoirs of Women Who Went to War*, £9.99); A Year to Remember (60 Pathé News films from 1930–1993 at £10.99 each); Classic Comedy (*The Golden Years of British Comedy 1940s*, £10.99; *Peter Sellers – Very Best Of*, £10.99; *W C Fields – Uncensored*, £9.99); Laurel & Hardy (60 different films); War File (*Vietnam, The Chopper War*, £10.99; *Fighter Aces*, £10.99); Children (Paul McCartney's *Rupert and the Frog Song*, £4.99); Modern Music (Genesis Videos, £9.99; *James Brown – Live in London*, £9.99); Ballet and Opera (*Death in Venice*, £14.99); Stand Up Comedy (*Victoria Wood – Sold Out Live*, £12.99; *Billy Connolly – An Audience With*, £10.99); Special Interest (*Kama Sutra*, £12.99); and Sport and Fitness (*Cindy Crawford – The Next Challenge Workout*, £12.99; *The World's Greatest Goals*, £9.99).

Catalogue Quarterly, A5, Catalogue, Colour and B/W, 20 pages

DISCOUNT VIDEO SELECTIONS
Dorchester
Dorset
DT2 7YG

Less expensive videos, CDs and tapes

Discount Video Selections publish a 32-page catalogue specialising in less expensive videos, compact discs and tapes. Topics featured include films, westerns, military, comedy, adult and

Telephone
01305 848725
Fax
01305 848516

children's. Prices start at £2.99 for videos and CDs, while popular tapes are just £1.99. This remarkable catalogue is available free of charge. Orders are usually despatched immediately and all sales are backed by a no-quibble refund guarantee.
Catalogue Bi-annually, A5, Catalogue, Colour, 32 pages, Free **Postal charges** £2.35; overseas postage at cost **Delivery** Parcelforce, Royal Mail **Methods of Payment** Cheque, Postal Order, Credit Card

DRAKE EDUCATIONAL ASSOCIATES
St Fagans Road
Fairwater
Cardiff
South Glamorgan
Wales
CF5 3AE
Telephone
01222 560333
Fax
01222 554909

Educational aids for primary and middle schools
Drake specialises in multi-media resources for primary and middle schools. Its catalogue contains a wide range of educational aids including books, photocopy masters, wallcharts, 35mm slides, audio cassettes, videos, computer software, audio-card programmes and the Language Master System. Photoposters, from £1.75; Word Picture Matching by Geoff Drake, £16.50; Oxford Reading Tree Master Cards, £65.
Catalogue Annually, A4, Catalogue, Colour, 36 pages, Free **Postal charges** Varies with item **Delivery** Royal Mail, Parcelforce **Methods of Payment** Cheque, Credit Card

INTEGRITY MUSIC
PO Box 101
Eastbourne
East Sussex
BN21 3UX
Telephone
01323 430033
Fax
01323 411981

Christian cassettes, CDs, videos and tapes
Integrity Music is one of the leading suppliers of Christian music in the UK. It covers all tastes, from classical music to workout videos, from children's tapes to black gospel – and everything in-between, including song books and sheets. The company has earned a reputation for its range of family-orientated products. Cassettes £6.49–£7.99, videos £5.99–£9.99, compact discs £10.99, and kid's videos £7.99.
Catalogue Annually, A5, Brochure, Colour, 19 pages, Free **Postal charges** Varies with item **Delivery** Royal Mail **Methods of Payment** Cheque, Postal Order, Credit Card

LE CLUB TRICOLORE

10 Ballingdon Road
London
SW11 6AJ
Telephone
0171 924 4649
Fax
0171 978 5312

French language materials for children

Teresa Scibor, a linguist with experience of teaching at all levels, has developed a range of books and cassettes to help children learn French. In one, ZoZo, an amusing French clown, descends on an unsuspecting housewife from an out-of-control balloon and the result is an entertaining story by the end of which primary school-age children should have accumulated around 100 French words. An effortless and fun way to learn. Price £9.99.

Catalogue Annually, A4, Leaflets, B/W, 3 pages, Free **Postal charges** 10 per cent of total **Delivery** Royal Mail **Methods of Payment** Cheque

MAGPIE DIRECT MAIL ORDER

PO Box 25
Ashford
Middlesex
TW15 1XL
Telephone
01784 242224
Fax
01784 241168

Cassettes, CDs and records

Magpie have over 10 years experience of selling music by post. They stock *all* the British labels, both major and minor, which have released music from the 50s, 60s and 70s by the original artists. As well as offering a full search facility to customers for those hard-to-find CDs, LPs and cassettes, Magpie publish an informative monthly music magazine. CDs, such as 10CC's *Rock and Pop Legends*, start at £4.99, or you could buy Fleetwood Mac's *Greatest Hits* on cassette for £5.99.

Catalogue Annually, A4, Catalogue, B/W, 32 pages, Free **Postal charges** Free for UK orders over £5.00. Add £0.50 per item in the EC, or if UK order is under £5.00. Add £1.00 per item if overseas; add £2.00 per item for overseas airmail **Delivery** Royal Mail **Methods of Payment** Cheque, Credit Card

MDT CLASSICS

6 Old Blacksmiths Yard
Saddler Gate
Derby

Compact discs

MDT Classics offer big savings on small orders, with discounts of up to 15 per cent off bulk orders on stock supplied direct from the UK distribution

Derbyshire
DE1 3PD
Telephone
01332 368251
Fax
01332 383594

network. For example, three standard full-price titles from Chandos at £12.50 each would cost £37.50, less 10 per cent discount, making £33.75. The latest offer list is available by sending a stamped addressed envelope.

Catalogue Annually, A5, Leaflets, B/W, 4 pages, Free **Postal charges** Varies with item **Delivery** Royal Mail **Methods of Payment** Cheque, Postal Order, Credit Card

MEMORIES ON VIDEO
24 York Gardens
Winterbourne
Bristol
Avon
BS17 1QT
Telephone
01454 772857

Copying cine film on to video

A small family business, Memories on Video has become Britain's leading house for the transfer of cine film on to video tape. They can also transfer slides, photographs and negatives on to video. For just £17 they will transfer up to 100ft of film. For £30 they will copy 75 slides or photographs onto video. They can also convert any foreign video to play in Britain and vice versa. Other services include video tape duplication, video and audio tape repair and copying old reel-to-reel sound recordings on to modern cassettes. For any of these services the basic cost is £15.

Catalogue A4, Leaflets, B/W, 1 page, Free **Postal charges** £3.00 **Delivery** Royal Mail **Methods of Payment** Cheque, Postal Order, Credit Card

MR BENSON'S VIDEO COLLECTION
375 Harrow Road
London
W9 3BR
Telephone
0181 960 4868
Fax
0181 969 7211

Videos

Mr Benson's Video Collection contains many discounted video titles, as well as special offers on latest titles. Sample prices include the *Remains of the Day* (£12.99), *The Aristocats* (£15.99) and *The Tin Drum* (£15.99). Each new customer is automatically given a free Portfolio ring-binder and will receive a monthly newsletter to store in it, with the aim of building up a valuable home video reference catalogue. Searching for a title? 'If it exists on a VHS video, we can get it for you,' says Ron Benson.

Catalogue Leaflets, Colour, 1 page, Free **Postal charges** £2.25 **Delivery** Royal Mail **Methods of Payment** Cheque, Postal Order, Credit Card

NEW WORLD CASSETTES
Paradise Farm
Westhall
Halesworth
Suffolk
IP19 8RH
Telephone
01986 781682
Fax
01986 781645

Music for relaxation

Produced by New World, this exclusive collection of recordings aims to 'relax, inspire and uplift you'. Many titles are available on both chrome cassette and CD. Popular titles include 'Keeper of Dreams' (piano and strings) by Philip Chapman. Other titles include 'Cascade' (flute and pan pipes) and 'Resonance' (pan pipes) by Terry Oldfield (brother of Mike). One series of recordings ('The Sounds of Nature') combines three-dimensional environmental sounds with subliminals.

Catalogue A5, Catalogue, Colour, 31 pages, Free **Postal charges** £1.95 **Delivery** Royal Mail **Methods of Payment** Cheque, Postal Order, Credit Card

NEW WORLD MUSIC
FREEPOST
Paradise Farm
Westhall
Halesworth
Suffolk
IP19 8RH
Telephone
01986 781682

Music

New World Music remains the pioneer in producing and promoting restful music. It was founded in 1982 to introduce others to a range of outstanding recordings for well-being and enjoyment. From *Out of the Depths* by Terry Oldfield, voted Album of the Year, to the *Whale to Winter Harp* which is a serene collection of classical melodies inspired by the season of winter and performed on the harp by Patricia Spero – just some of the wonderful recordings in this catalogue. There is music for children and music for healing among many others to choose from. All cassettes are £6.95, compact discs are £10.95.

Catalogue Annually, A4, Catalogue, Colour, 16 pages, Free **Postal charges** £1.95 **Delivery** Royal Mail **Methods of Payment** Credit Card, Cheque

PILGRIM BY POST
48 Culver Street
Newent
Gloucestershire
GL18 1DA
Telephone
01531 821075

New world music and books

Pilgrim produce the kind of material that graces every New Ager's home. Tapes to inspire meditation and relaxation range from 'Spirit of the Rainforest' by Terry Oldfield: flute and pan pipes (£7.50), to 'Earth Healer' by Medwyn Goodall (£7.50). Pilgrim also produce books dealing with all the obvious subjects, from holistic health and healing to relaxation, meditation and astrology. Jessica Macbeth's *Moon Over Water* (£7.20) describes meditation techniques; *The Birth Chart Book* (£2.95) by Bill and Eileen Anderton shows you how to get the best from your birth chart.

Catalogue A5, Catalogue, Colour, 11 pages, Free **Postal charges** Free **Delivery** Royal Mail **Methods of Payment** Cheque, Postal Order, Credit Card

RECORD CORNER
27 Bedford Hill
Balham
London
SW12 9EX
Telephone
0181 673 9192
Fax
0181 675 6665

Country music

Record Corner offers a choice of almost 400 hits, from the all-time greats to the current bestsellers. CDs and singles of some of the best names are available at competitive prices, with Marvin Gaye's *A Tribute to the Great Nat King Cole* at £9.99 on CD and James Brown's *Roots of a Revolution* (2 CDs) for £29.99. Among the best-selling country albums are Doug Stone's *Greatest Hits* and Dolly Parton's *Heartsongs*.

Catalogue Monthly, A4, Catalogue, B/W, 30 pages, Free **Postal charges** Varies with item **Delivery** Royal Mail, Parcelforce **Methods of Payment** Cheque, Postal Order, Credit Card

SQUIRES GATE CD
Squires Gate Music Centre
Squires Gate Station Approach
Squires Gate Lane
Blackpool

Classical CD loan and purchase service

Squires Gate offers a loan service for collectors of classical music, giving you the opportunity to listen to recordings before purchase. You are under no obligation to buy, although each CD will show its generously discounted price, up to 20 per cent off list price. To join, you pay an annual subscription of £7.50 (renewable at £5.75). Your first package of three CDs and an extensive catalogue is included with initial payment. After this you will be charged 60p for each CD sent on a weekly basis (plus p&p).

Catalogue Annually, A5, Catalogue, B/W, 55 pages, Free **Postal charges** Varies with item **Delivery** Royal Mail **Methods of Payment** Cheque, Credit Card

STORYLINE
20 Carrbrook Crescent
Stalybridge
Cheshire
SK15 3LP
Telephone
01457 834406

Cassette lending library

Storyline is a 'books on tape' lending library – a brilliant idea for anyone who travels a lot by car. You can listen to Ben Kingsley read *A Passage to India* or Sir John Gielgud reading from *Brideshead Revisited*. Membership costs £9 for a year or £25 for life. After that, tapes cost just 80p per week. The catalogue gives colour-coded categories for easy reference and a brief description of the contents of each tape. The stock isn't limited to fiction. There are travel tapes and autobiographicial tapes too.

Catalogue A5, Catalogue, Colour and B/W, 118 pages, Free **Postal charges** Free **Delivery** Royal Mail **Methods of Payment** Cheque

THE TALKING BOOK CLUB
PO Box 993
London
SW6 4UW
Telephone
0171 731 6262
Fax
same

Books on cassette

The Talking Book Club offers a comprehensive range of books on tape including fiction, non-fiction, classics, biography, humour, thrillers, romance travel and children's books. Ideal for those with impaired sight, and just the thing to listen to on long journeys, or while ironing or decorating. Both full-length and abridged versions are available. It costs £7.50 to enrol, plus from £1.25 for a fortnight's hire per title. With 2000 books to choose from and 400 titles being

added every year, you won't have time to get bored.
Catalogue Bi-monthly, A4, Catalogue, Colour and B/W, 100 pages, Free **Postal charges** Free **Delivery** Royal Mail **Methods of Payment** Cheque, Credit Card

TAPEWORM
10 Barley Mow Passage
London
W4 4PH
Telephone
0181 508 9222

Cassettes for children

Tapeworm is the brainchild of two sisters-in-law: a company specialising in children's stories on cassette. There are over 160 titles to choose from, a boon for long car journeys, the sick room or any parent who finally tires of retelling little Johnnie's favourite story!

The selection includes fairy stories, stories for the very young, short stories for the 4 to 7 group and classics of children's literature along with some music and Christmas specials. They also stock a smaller selection of videos. Prices range from £3.50 to £11.
Delivery Royal Mail **Methods of Payments** Cheque, Postal Order

TRAVELLERS' TALES
Great Weddington
Ash
Canterbury
Kent
CT3 2AR
Telephone
01304 812531
Fax
same

Books on tape

Travellers Tales produce spoken-word versions of more than 2,000 book titles, the majority of which are unabridged. Among its distinguished narrators are Timothy West, Prunella Scales and Nigel Havers. The service is similar that of a library and membership costs £20 for a year, or £100 for life. Once a member, you can select fiction or non-fiction titles, history, plays and poetry, language courses, war stories and numerous biographies and autobiographies. Hire charges are £6.40 for four tapes for one week with a daily rate thereafter.
Catalogue Annually, A5, Catalogue, B/W, 94 pages, Free **Postal charges** Free **Delivery** Royal Mail **Methods of Payment** Cheque, Stage Payments, Credit Card

VIDEO PLUS DIRECT

PO Box 190
Peterborough
Cambridgeshire
PE2 6UW
Telephone
01733 232800
Fax
01733 238966

Videos and cassettes

As well as the BBC video catalogue featuring comedy (*Absolutely Fabulous*, £12.99), sport (*The Best of Wimbledon 1993*, £10.99) and children's collections (*Captain Pugwash – seafaring tales*, £6.99), Video Plus Direct handles the BBC's Radio Collection for mail order. Available on single, double and boxed-set audiotapes and, in some cases on compact disc, categories include classic comedy, such as *The Navy Lark*, and the best of BBC Radio and Television's readings and dramatisations including Alan Bennett's *Diaries* and *Around the World in 80 Days* read by Michael Palin.

Catalogue Bi-annually, A5, Catalogue, Colour, 33 pages, Free **Postal charges** Add £2.50 for up to 8 cassettes (UK). Add £3.50 for 1 cassette plus £3.00 for each additional cassette up to 5 (Europe). Add £5.50 for 1 cassette, £3.50 for each additional cassette up to 5 (Rest of World) **Delivery** Royal Mail **Methods of Payment** Cheque, Credit Card, Postal Order, American Express, Diners Club

WILDSOUNDS

Cross Street
Salthouse
Norfolk
NR25 7XH
Telephone
01263 741100
Fax
same

Wildlife recordings

With more than 60 titles to choose from, WildSounds is a leading supplier of wildlife sound recordings, the perfect gift for birdwatchers, naturalists and gardeners. The four-volume pack *All the Bird Songs of Britain and Europe* features 420 species on cassette, all of which are announced beforehand in English, for £29.95. The CD set is unannounced but indexed by track number for £49.95. Other titles include *Frogs and Toads*, the calls of 20 European species and *Forests of the Amazon*. Cassettes, £6.95, CDs £10.99.

Catalogue Annually, A4, Catalogue, B/W, 10 pages **Postal charges** Varies with item **Delivery** Royal Mail **Methods of Payment** Cheque, Postal Order, Credit Card

WINDOWS MAIL ORDER
1–7 Central Arcade
Newcastle upon Tyne
Tyne and Wear
NE1 5BP
Telephone
0191 232 8765

Classical records, tapes, CDs and sheet music
With one of the most extensive collections of classical recordings and sheet music in the country, Windows can provide any recording for musicians or enthusiasts and offer a '4 for the price of 3' special. CDs, records and tapes from names such as Decca, Philips and Deutsche Grammophon are available from £12.99. Windows also provide a selection of folk music, including traditional Northumbrian music and a range of musical instruments, sheet music and video tapes dealing with all aspects of music.

Catalogue Quarterly, A4, Brochures, B/W, 7 pages

WORLD OF LEARNING
Springfield House
West Street
Bedminster
Bristol
Avon
BS3 3YY
Telephone
0117 9639159
Fax
01272 639709

Language courses
Whether you want to learn a language for a holiday or a business trip, the World of Learning's PILL (Programmed Instruction Language Learning) is for you. The complete PILL package includes a set of easy-listening cassette tapes, programmed instruction books, fast word-finder and a letter-writing guide. Developed through computer analysis coupled to language learning and behavioural science, the method claims to overcome the two great barriers to language learning: time and effort. The languages covered are French, German, Spanish, Italian and Russian. You progress at your own rate (45 minutes per day is recommended) and will learn from day one to speak with the correct accent, and to understand and be able to speak at a normal conversational speed. The whole package costs £123.50.

Catalogue A6, Leaflets, Colour, Free **Postal charges** £4 to include post, package and insurance **Delivery** Royal Mail **Methods of Payment** Cheque, Postal Order, Credit Card, Diners Club, American Express

Software

AVP SOFTWARE
School Hill Centre
Chepstow
Gwent
NP6 5PH
Telephone
01291 625439
Fax
01291 629671

Educational software

AVP is the leading supplier of software for UK schools. They have catalogues for primary and secondary level and special needs, as well as for educational CD-ROMs and videos that can also be bought for use at home. *The Hutchinson Multimedia Encyclopedia 1995* costs £49.95 (IBM). Dorling Kindersley's *Eyewitness Encyclopedia of Science* for juniors costs £84.22 (IBM). In the special needs catalogue, 'First Steps to Reading' (£17.60) is a series of programs using nursery rhymes to help children who are beginning to read (age range 2–7), on Acorn, IBM, BBC and Nimbus formats.

Catalogue Annually, A4, Catalogue, Colour, 100 pages, Free **Postal charges** Postage and packing charged at cost except for prepaid orders (UK only) when there is no charge **Delivery** Royal Mail **Methods of Payment** Cheque, Credit Card

IANSYST LTD
United House
North Road
London
N7 9DP
Telephone
0171 607 5844
Fax
0171 607 0187

Computer training

As well as its comprehensive list of video, disk and audio-based training products for computers and software, Iansyst now offers a range of products for those with special educational needs, such as dyslexia. 'Dyslectech' includes hardware and software to make your computer speak, and the new 'TextHelp', a cunning drop-in tool for practically any Windows application that gives speech, word prediction, spellcheck and zoom

add-on for dyslexics and others who have difficulty getting correct English into print.
Catalogue Bi-annually, A4, Leaflets, Colour and B/W, 3 pages, Free **Postal charges** £3.40 **Delivery** Royal Mail, Parcelforce **Methods of Payment** Cheque, Credit Card

THE SOFTWARE SOURCE
The Shareware Village
Colyton
Devon
EX13 6HA
Telephone
01297 552222
Fax
01297 553366

Shareware disks

Shareware is a 'try-before-you-buy' marketing method for the IBM PC and compatibles. They charge a modest handling fee (around £4) per disk to supply the customer with a copy of the software. After a given evaluation period (21 to 90 days) the customer is required either to cease using the software or pay the registration fee. Minimum order value is £35 of goods excluding delivery and VAT. The catalogue gives helpful ratings on disks and programs and welcomes feedback from customers.

Catalogue A5, Catalogue, Colour, 130 pages, Free **Postal charges** £4.70 **Delivery** Courier **Methods of Payment** Cheque, Credit Card, American Express, Diners Club

Sports Equipment

AIR CIRCUS
20 Wansdyke Business Centre
Oldfield Lane
Bath
Avon
BA1 5AR
Telephone
01225 466333
Fax
01225 464188

Kites
Kite flying was invented by the Chinese thousands of years ago and is now a fast growing, popular outdoor sport. This colourful catalogue carries a full range of kites for beginners and experts alike. Starting at £4.99 for a traditional, one-line, cutter kite, prices go up to £200–300 for an advanced sports kite.

The catalogue gives helpful technical information, such as the wind power needed for various models, making it easy to choose the right kite for your needs. Line accessories are also supplied and an assortment of games such as juggling balls and frisbees.

ALLEGRO BAGS
19 Triangle
Halifax
West Yorkshire
HX6 3NE
Telephone
01422 834668
Fax
01422 834669

Customised sports bags
Allegro Bags manufacture promotional merchandise. The range is considerable and includes sports bags, holdalls, duffel bags and wrist bags. There is a large capacity holdall with handles set on to the shoulder of the bag specifically to allow an advertising slogan or company name to be seen uninterrupted. Prices on application.
Catalogue Annually, A4, Catalogue, Colour, 4 pages, Free
Postal charges Varies with item **Delivery** Royal Mail, Parcelforce **Methods of Payment** Cheque, Credit Card

ANDREW BOTTOMLEY
The Coach House
Huddersfield Road

Antique arms and armour
Andrew Bottomley's Antique Arms & Armour catalogue contains hundreds of antique weapons

SPORTS EQUIPMENT

Holmfirth
West Yorskhire
HD7 2TT
Telephone
01484 685234
Fax
01484 681551

from all over the world, each fully described and generally accompanied by a photograph. There are pistols and revolvers (30-bore English full-stocked percussion holster pistol, £90; pair of 16-bore Flintlock carriage pistols c.1765, £4,800), long guns, swords and daggers, North American Indian artefacts, bayonets and powder flasks. All items are guaranteed original.

Catalogue Annually, A4, Catalogue, Colour and B/W, 144 pages, Free **Postal charges** Varies with item **Delivery** Royal Mail, Parcelforce, Courier **Methods of Payment** Cheque, Postal Order, Credit Card, American Express

BIKE CITY LTD
Tranquility House
1 Tranquility
Crossgates
Leeds
West Yorkshire
LS15 8QU
Telephone
0113 232 6336

Cycles & accessories

Bike City sell a good selection of bicycles for gents, ladies and children. Adult cycles, such as the gents' Topeka with a 12-speed Shimano gearset, cantilever brakes and alloy rims start at £119.94. A ladies' model, the Masquerade with 5-speed Shimano indexed gearset and, again, alloy wheel rims is £99.99. Boys' and Girls' cycles start at £99.99. Bike City also offer their own 14-day discount prices off their retail prices.

The company also sells a range of accessories including racks. Their intro pack consists of a helmet, lights and lock and sells for £34.99.

Catalogue Annually, A5, Catalogue, Colour, 17 pages, Free **Postal charges** Free **Delivery** In-house delivery **Methods of Payment** Cheque, Postal Order, Credit Card, Stage Payments

CAPTAIN O M WATTS
7 Dover Street
London
W1X 3PJ
Telephone
0171 493 4633

Yachting goods

A catalogue for yachtsmen and women containing a selection of nautical products from the company's comprehensive stock on sale in its London store. You can kit yourself out in a waterproof suit, £99.95; yachting boots, £27.65; Arctic socks, £8.95; pack your possessions in a crew bag,

Fax
0171 495 0755

£39.95; check the weather with a digital barometer, £89.95; and ring the ship's brass bell, from £45.50. In addition, there are books, charts, and videos.

Catalogue Annually, A4, Catalogue, Colour, 18 pages, £2.50 **Postal charges** Varies with item **Delivery** Royal Mail, Parcelforce **Methods of Payment** Cheque, Credit Card, Switch, American Express

EVANS CYCLES
5 London Road
Croydon
Surrey
CR0 2RE
Telephone
0181 667 1423
Fax
0181 649 7798

Bicycle and accessories

Bikes & Bits from Evans Cycles is a catalogue with a difference. The glossy pages are laid out like a magazine, with editorial features, superb photography and detailed descriptions of a multitude of products. Everything a biking enthusiast could want from mountain bikes, cross bikes, touring bikes, frames and accessories to eye-protection shades with prescription lenses. Hardrock Ultra GX mountain bike, £349.95; Peugeot Performance 200, £292.95; Profile Logo Grip, £5.99.

Catalogue Quarterly, A4, Catalogue, Colour, 130 pages, £2.20 **Postal charges** £2.50 **Delivery** Royal Mail, Parcelforce **Methods of Payment** Cheque, Postal Order, Credit Card

FARLOW'S OF PALL MALL
5 Pall Mall
London
SW1
Telephone
0171 839 2423
Fax
01285 652446

Fishing tackle, shooting accessories and clothes

A Royal Warrant holder since 1982, Farlow's of Pall Mall has a large, thriving mail-order service. The catalogue features fishing rods, reels, cool bags, men's shooting clothing: Fedoras, tweed caps, breeks, plus-fours, quilted jackets, boots, stockings – and country clothing for ladies, such as tweed shooting suits, wax jackets, breeks and plus-twos. There's also a selection of shooting and fishing gifts such as the fish and bar cuff-links and sporting cartoon clocks. All the items are clearly shown with lengthy descriptions where necessary.

Catalogue A4, Catalogue, Colour, 11 pages, free to UK customers **Postal charges** UK: packets, £1.50; parcels, £3.00 **Delivery** Royal Mail, Parcelforce, Courier **Methods of Payment** Cheque, Credit Card, American Express, Diners Club

THE FRIENDLY FISHERMAN
25 Camden Road
Tunbridge Wells
Kent
TN1 ?PS
Telephone
01892 528677

Angling equipment

The Friendly Fisherman's 'Predator' catalogue for lure fishing and specialist pike tackle includes boat equipment, Plano tackle boxes, clothing, cookers and flasks, books and videos. Informative descriptions help you to select lures and describe various fishing methods. Apparently the last two record British pike were both caught on lures. All new equipment is field-tested before inclusion. Vortex electronic lures, £8.35; Hart spinnerbait, £3.95; 10ft Sportex High Modulus Carbon rod, £151.99.

Catalogue A4, Leaflets, B/W, 10 pages, Free **Postal charges** Varies with item **Delivery** Royal Mail, Parcelforce **Methods of Payment** Cheque, Credit Card

GOOD DESIGNS
60 Gwel Eryri
Llandegfan
Menai Bridge
Gwynedd
LL59 5RD
Telephone
01248 713624

Bicycle stabilisers

These new stabiliser wheels are adjustable inwards, which makes them the easiest way ever to learn to ride a bicycle as riders can practise and improve their balance in easy stages. They fit almost any bicycle (including geared bikes) and are durable, well designed, easily adjusted and very strong, taking riders weighing up to 11 stones. The junior version costs £18.75–£24.75 and fits 12" to 20"-diameter wheeled bikes. The senior version costs from £68–£70 including p&p and fits from 16" to 28"-diameter wheeled bikes.

Catalogue As necessary, A4, Brochure, Colour, 4 pages **Delivery** Parcelforce **Methods of Payment** Cheque

HAMILTON BILLIARDS & GAMES CO
Park Lane
Knebworth
Hertfordshire
SG3 6PJ
Telephone
01438 811995
Fax
01438 814939

Billiard tables and other games equipment
This interesting company sells reproduction Victorian and Edwardian billiard tables. Beautifully hand-crafted from oak, mahogany and walnut, there are a great many models to choose from, including 'convertibles' which can double up as dining tables. There is an excellent range of accessories such as marker boards, cues and cue racks. Other games equipment includes table-tennis tables, croquet sets, quoits, boule, dartboards, dominoes, chess and backgammon.

Catalogue A4, Catalogue, Colour and B/W, 20 pages, Free
Postal charges Varies with item **Delivery** Parcelforce
Methods of Payment Cheque, Postal Order, Credit Card

MULLARKEY & SONS
184–185 Waterloo Street
Burton-on-Trent
Staffordshire
DE14 2NH
Telephone
01283 538375/566777
Fax
01283 511001

Fishing tackle
Mullarkey & Sons produce a vast range of fishing tackle and accessories for the angler: poles, whips, match rods, coarse rods, carp rods, specimen rods, feeder rods, fly rods and more, plus reels, multipliers, fly lines, spinners, nets and tackle boxes. The Shakespeare luggage collection includes holdalls, carryalls, net bags and reel cases. Recently introduced is the Shakespeare Premier Surfer Holdall (£37.50) which, at 8' 5½" in length, will accommodate most beachcasters plus umbrella, rod rest, etc.

Catalogue Annually, A4, Catalogue, B/W, 76 pages, £1.00
Postal charges Orders over £125.00, free. Orders weighing up to 1kg, add £1.50; orders weighing over 1kg, add £4.75 **Delivery** Royal Mail **Methods of Payment** Cheque, Postal Order, Credit Card, COD, American Express

THE ORVIS COMPANY INC
The Mill
Nether Wallop
Stockbridge

Fly fishing, clothing and gifts
Although most of this catalogue is devoted to fishing tackle, there is a substantial section featuring casual country clothes for men and women and a gift section which includes luggage,

SPORTS EQUIPMENT

Hampshire
SO20 8ES
Telephone
01264 783283
Fax
01264 783277

watches and dog beds. Established in 1856, Orvis offer quality goods. Their salmon rods start at £295; kit bags from £79; disc drag reels from £23.00. Twenty flies for unknown waters cost £9.50; fly boxes from £6. Waders with integrated boot design start at £110. There are also fleece neck cushions, alarm clocks, waterproof rugs, log carriers, pewter hair brushes, cartridge cuff-links, folding magnifiers, travellers' watches, brass thermometers, loo-roll holders, pewter wine stoppers, wine racks, bellows, wall egg racks, giraffe alphabet puzzles, dog and cat angels, bear in a bag, Advent tree calendar, fleece dog toys, peanut feeders, stereo electronic earmuffs, cracker throwers, binoculars, plus a wide range of clothing for men and women.

Catalogue Bi-annually, A4, Catalogue, Colour, 67 pages, Free **Postal charges** Flies, leaders and toppets, add £2.00; all other goods, add £3.75 **Delivery** Royal Mail **Methods of Payment** Cheque, Postal Order, Credit Card, American Express

PEDOMETERS INTERNATIONAL
1 Whittle Close
Drayton Fields
Daventry
Northamptonshire
NN11 5RQ
Telephone
01327 706030
Fax
01327 71633

Pedometers, map measurers and compasses

Pedometers International has an extensive range of instruments for walkers, ramblers, runners and joggers. Pedometers are, as the name implies, the company's speciality, but compasses (for both walkers and drivers) and map measurers are also available. Pedometer prices vary from around £29.95 to £129.50.

Catalogue Annually, A5, Catalogue, Colour, 14 pages, Free **Postal charges** £1.95 **Delivery** Royal Mail **Methods of Payment** Cheque, Credit Card

PENDLE ENGINEERING
Unit 6
Pendle Industrial Estate
Southfield Street

Bicycle carriers

Pendle Engineering offers a comprehensive range of cycle carriers and accessories. The range accommodates most vehicles from small hatch-

Nelson
Lancashire
BB9 0LD
Telephone
01282 699555
Fax
01282 612904

backs to four-wheel drives. Choose from tow-bar racks (from £69), wheel-support racks (from £117), strap-on boot racks (£59.99) and roof-mounted tandem carriers (£140). As a safety feature Pendle recommends the use of a lighting unit if the cycles being carried obscure the rear lights, price £30.

Catalogue Annually, A4, Catalogue, Colour, 8 pages, Free **Postal charges** £7.50 **Delivery** Royal Mail, Parcelforce **Methods of Payment** Cheque, Credit Card

PETWORTH HOUSE
Polesdon Lane
Ripley
Woking
Surrey
GU23 6LR
Telephone
01483 225222/223188
Fax
01483 223141

Keep-fit equipment
Petworth House provides a broad and exclusive range of sporting, leisure and fitness equipment. The Smooth-Air 2 dual-action exercise cycle and the ISS 150 stair climber are available for £99.99 each; the Compact Home Gym costs £199.99; and you can purchase snooker tables, pool tables and table-tennis tables, as well as motorised treadmills and cross-country ski exercisers.

Catalogue Annually, A4, Catalogue, Colour, 16 pages, Free **Postal charges** Varies with item **Delivery** Courier **Methods of Payment** Cheque, Credit Card, American Express, Diners Club

PORTSMOUTH GOLF CENTRE
Great Salterns Golf Course
Burrfields Road
Portsmouth
Hampshire
PO3 5HH
Telephone
01705 699519
Fax
01705 650525

Golfing accessories
The Golf Centre stocks all major brands of clubs, balls and bags to improve your game and the smartest shirts and shoes to improve your look, for example, Hi-Tec golf shoes at £55. Many of the prices found here are competitive, with a Macgregor Wentworth golf bag for £34.99 and a dozen Dunlop balls for £7.99.

Catalogue Leaflets, Colour, 1 page, Free **Postal charges** Varies with item **Delivery** Parcelforce **Methods of Payment** Cheque, Credit Card

SCOTTS OF NORTHWICH
185–187 Witton Street
Northwich
Cheshire
CW9 5LP
Telephone
01606 46543

Fishing tackle

Scotts of Northwich is a supplier of angling equipment and accessories. Their catalogue features an impressive range of fishing poles and rods including designs by Daiwa and Shimano. At the top end of the range are Shakespeare poles available in their new modulus carbon Put-Over, starting at £450. Leger rods in all brands start at under £50 while reels start at under £20.

Accessories include the essential brolley boxes, bank sticks, tackle items, nets, feeders and floats. There are of course a large range of hooks by such makers as Tubertin and Kamasan.

Catalogue Every two years, A4, Catalogue, Colour, 70 pages, Free **Postal charges** Varies with item **Delivery** Royal Mail **Methods of Payment** Cheque, Postal Order, Credit Card, Switch, Diners Club, American Express

SNOWBEE UK
Unit 2A
Parkway Industrial Estate
St. Modwen Road
Plymouth
Devon
PL6 8LH
Telephone
01752 672226
Fax
01752 667070

Fishing tackle

Snowbee specialise in top-quality, practical fishing tackle and accessories, at value-for-money prices. The Snowbee brand was designed not to satisfy short-term trends, but to catch fish! It includes rods, reels, bags, nets, fly boxes, lines, waders, lure and spinner kits, tackle boxes, waistcoats and fishing accessories. Prices on application.

Catalogue Annually, A4, Catalogue, Colour, 16 pages pages, Free **Postal charges** Varies with item **Delivery** Royal Mail, Parcelforce **Methods of Payment** Cheque, Credit Card

SUPERNOVA CYCLES
Yarm Road Industrial Estate
Darlington
Co Durham
DL1 4XX
Telephone
01325 469181

Bicycles

Supernova Cycles sells bicycles for all the family at hugely reduced prices. The bicycles carry a 25-year guarantee and are delivered to your door needing only adjustments to the front wheel, saddle and pedals (instructions and free tool kit are included), so that within 15 minutes you should be

Fax
01325 381386

able to watch heads turn as you cruise through the streets. There is a bicycle to suit every pocket from the ladies' 5-speed Matrix at £119.99 to the 21-speed Matrix Hybrid at £199. With helmets at £19.99 and gel saddles at £14.99, discount prices extend to accessories, too.

Catalogue Annually, A4, Catalogue, Colour, 16 pages, Free **Postal charges** £6.95; free delivery for two or more bicycles; accessories, £1.95, free if ordered with a bicycle **Delivery** Royal Mail, Parcelforce, Courier **Methods of Payment** Cheque, Postal Order, Credit Card

3-D CRICKET
PO Box 300
The Runnings
Kingsditch Trading Estate
Cheltenham
Gloucestershire
GL51 9NJ
Telephone
01242 241819
Fax
01242 222994

Cricket clothes and equipment

This is one of the leading names in mail-order cricket supplies at discounted prices from major manufacturers. The extensive catalogue is pleasantly designed and packed with information such as how to prolong the life of your cricket bat. Bat repairs are, however, one of the services offered. Cricket bags, from £16; balls from £4; pads from £31; junior bats from £18, adult bats from £38 to £144; trousers from £14; shirts from £10.

Catalogue Annually, A4, Catalogue, Colour and B/W, 44 pages **Postal charges** Free **Delivery** Parcelforce, Courier **Methods of Payment** Cheque, Credit Card, Switch

W R PASHLEY
Masons Road
Stratford-upon-Avon
Warwickshire
CV37 9NL
Telephone
01789 292263
Fax
01789 414201

Bicycles

Pashley's bicycles might look as if they belong to a bygone age, but they are as up-to-the minute as any 1990s design. These bikes are handmade and expertly crafted. Here you will find the Pashley Princess Original, with upright handlebars, three gears, leather saddle and wicker basket (£269.95). If you prefer to cycle in company, the Prestige Tandem costs £649.95. You might be forgiven for thinking that the children's tricycle has vanished without trace, but the red Pickle is here in all its glory, £194.95; and for the school run,

the Picabac adult tricycle is fitted with two rear child seats, from £549.95.
Catalogue Annually, A4, Catalogue, Colour, 14 pages, Free **Postal charges** Free **Delivery** Courier **Methods of Payment** Cheque, Credit Card

Sportswear

BODY AWARE
Erskine House
Union Street
Trowbridge
Wiltshire
BA14 8RY
Telephone
01225 774164
Fax
01225 774452

Men's underwear and swimwear

The Body Aware range of underwear for men is the most up-to-date catalogue of its type. It features underwear and swimwear by European designers in styles that enhance the male anatomy yet feel good to wear, in sizes from S to XXL. Zip boxer, £18.50; form-fitting unitard, £16; leather short, £17; chamois leather thong, £15.50; swim trunk, £15.50; silk satin boxer, £15; swim bikini, £13.95; rubber brief, £11.50.

Catalogue Annually, A5, Catalogue, Colour, 24 pages, Free **Postal charges** £1.20 **Methods of Payment** Cheque, Postal Order, Credit Card

CAPTAIN O M WATTS
7 Dover Street
London
W1X 3PJ
Telephone
0171 493 4633
Fax
0171 495 0755

Yachting goods

A catalogue for yachtsmen and women containing a selection of nautical products from the company's comprehensive stock on sale in its London store. You can kit yourself out in a waterproof suit, £99.95; yachting boots, £27.65; Arctic socks, £8.95; pack your possessions in a crew bag, £39.95; check the weather with a digital barometer, £89.95; and ring the ship's brass bell, from £45.50. In addition, there are books, charts, and videos.

Catalogue Annually, A4, Catalogue, Colour, 18 pages, £2.50 **Postal charges** Varies with item **Delivery** Royal Mail, Parcelforce **Methods of Payment** Cheque, Credit Card, Switch, American Express

COLORADO MAIL ORDER LTD
The Ski Warehouse
Longtown
Carlisle
Cumbria
CA6 5TJ
Telephone
01228 792006
Fax
01228 792009

Skiwear and equipment specialists

Colorado sells big-name skiwear and equipment for men, women and children at what they claim are very special low prices. Brand names include Trespass, Descente, Hard Corps, Goretex and SOS. The ski outfits were photographed at Nevis Range, Fort William, and are clearly shown with full descriptions, colours, size availability and prices next to them. Each outfit has a recommended retail price and a Colorado price, which is always lower. For example, Ylenia microfibre suit for ladies, RRP £239.99, Colorado price £125.99. There are also skis such as the TWG 3 ski for beginners and intermediates, £89.99, usual price £249; the Dynamic, and ski bindings. A table gives you details of what the correct size of ski is in relation to your height. The back of the catalogue features gloves, visors, hats, ski bags, the children's range from tiny tots to teenagers, ski wallets, chapsticks and sun protection.

Catalogue Annually, A4, Catalogue, Colour, 16 pages, Free **Postal charges** £3.99; for skis, add another £3 **Delivery** Royal Mail **Methods of Payment** Cheque, Postal Order, Credit Card, Switch, American Express

FREETIME SPORTS
Fletcher's Yard
Wellowgate
Grimsby
South Humberside
DN32 0RG
Telephone
01472 357357
Fax
01472 242333

Training shoes, sportswear and equipment

Freetime Sports' colourful catalogue is packed with cut-price trainers and boots, football shirts, T-shirts, shorts and baggies, leotards and unitards, plus ankle supports, exercise bicycles and Reebok steps. Adidas leather cross trainer, £29.99 (RRP £49.99); Head exploration boot, £39.99 (RRP £69.99); England football shirt, £19.99 (RRP £34.99); jog pants, £12.99.

Catalogue Quarterly, A4, Catalogue, Colour, 31 pages, Free **Postal charges** £3.75 **Delivery** Royal Mail, Parcelforce **Methods of Payment** Cheque, Postal Order, Credit Card, Switch, American Express

SPORTSWEAR

M AND M SPORTS
Clinton Road
Leominster
Herefordshire
HR6 ORJ
Telephone
01568 616161
Fax
01568 612222

Sports goods

M and M Sports are the UK's largest sports mail-order company. Their vibrant catalogue is packed with bargains with Nike, Reebok, Adidas and all the other top brand names on offer, often at half price or below. The catalogue features a large range of footwear, clothing and equipment. It is a must for anyone interested in sport or who simply enjoys wearing the best leisurewear available at unbeatable prices. The company prides itself on its first-class service, friendly staff and state-of-the-art computer systems.

Catalogue Quarterly, A4, Catalogue, Colour, 32 pages, Free **Postal charges** Free on orders over £100 **Delivery** Parcelforce **Methods of Payment** Cheque, Postal Order, Credit Card

MAYBURY SPORTS LTD
139 Northwood Road
Thornton Heath
Surrey
CR7 8HX
Telephone
0181 653 5440
Fax
0181 771 3497

Netball equipment

This catalogue focuses on a sport traditionally played by women only – netball. Maybury supplies everything that is needed for the sport from clothes through nets to balls. Netball skirts, including tartan kilts, are available in a variety of styles and lengths. Colour choice is vast and sizing flexible. Prices range between £8.45 and £20.50. Other products include sweatshirts (from £8.95), polo shirts (£8.00), knickers (from £2.75), socks, waterproof jackets, windsuits, netball shoes (£29.95), and a referee's whistle (£2.50).

Catalogue A4, Brochure, Colour, 4 pages, Free **Postal charges** Orders up to £25.00, add £2.65; orders over £25.00, add £5.00; add £1.50 for single sweat top or T-shirt or kilt **Delivery** Royal Mail **Methods of Payment** Cheque, Postal Order, Credit Card

ONE UP GOLF LTD
61 The Warren
East Goscote Industrial Estate

Ladies' golf and leisurewear

Range of golf wear and leisurewear for ladies only. Cardigans, knickerbockers, trousers, skirts, waist-

East Goscote
Leicester
Leicestershire
LE7 3XJ
Telephone
0116 2696166
Fax
0116 2696155

coats, hats, windproof lined sweaters, cord trousers and golf shoes. All in lovely colours and very fashionable. Golf shoes from £55.99, socks £6.99, polar fleece pork-pie hat £12.50. Polar fleece jerkin, £35; sweaters vary in price. Just the brochure for the lady golfer.

Catalogue Quarterly, A4, Brochure, Colour, 11 pages, Free **Postal charges** Varies with item **Delivery** Royal Mail **Methods of Payment** Cheque, Postal Order, Credit Card, American Express

SHANKARA LIMITED
1 Jefferson Way
Thame
Oxfordshire
OX9 3SZ
Telephone
01844 218219
Fax
01844 218522

Swimwear
Shankara's glossy, well-produced catalogue features up-market women's swimwear from Paris. A St Tropez swimsuit, available from sizes 10 to 16, costs £95. More daring, the Yacht Club bikini costs £66. Many of these swimsuits and bikinis are quite stunning and unavailable elsewhere.

There is also a selection of summer shoes and some wraps and skirts as well as blouses and tops for warm weather. A thoroughly attractive catalogue. The company also produce a lingerie catalogue.

Catalogue Varies, A5, Catalogue, Colour, 24 pages, Free **Postal charges** £1.90; 24-hour delivery £5 extra **Delivery** Royal Mail **Methods of Payment** Cheque, Postal Order, Credit Card, American Express

SHORE THING
Halamana Cottage
Gillan
Manaccan
Helston
Cornwall
TR12 6HL
Telephone
01326 231652

Swimwear
This catalogue contains collections from France and America as well as Australia. The Rasurel range from France includes soft fabrics and co-ordinating beachwear. From America there is a range of Jantzen swimwear. The Australian range includes some vibrant and individual designs. Sarongs are designed in Cornwall and each one is hand-dyed on silk. Prices from £19.50 for a girl's swimsuit to £65 for a lady's swimsuit.

Fax
same

Catalogue Annually, A5, Catalogue, Colour, 7 pages, Free **Postal charges** £3 **Delivery** Royal Mail **Methods of Payment** Cheque, Postal Order, Credit Card

SWIMSHOP
Unit 3
Dencora Way
Luton
Bedfordshire
LU3 3HP
Telephone
01582 562111
Fax
01582 561199

Swimwear and swimming accessories

Swimshop sells a large range of swimwear in a variety of styles for men, women and children, including such names as Speedo, Maru, Arena and Kiefer. It also stocks lots of pool and beach equipment. There is a vast range of floats and inflatables from dolphins to alligators. There are paddles, kickboards, fins and snorkels, stopwatches and life-saving equipment – in short, anything and everything you could want at a beach or poolside. Their ranges are sourced from all over the world – their swim fins are in four different types from the UK and the USA and range from £8/£9 to £72 a pair.

Catalogue Annually, A5, Catalogue, Colour, 80 pages, Free **Postal charges** 95p on orders up to £75; free on orders of more than £75 **Delivery** Royal Mail, Parcelforce, Courier **Methods of Payment** Cheque, Credit Card, Switch, Postal Order

Stationery

AA COMPUTER PRINT
42 Priestlands
Romsey
Hampshire
SO51 8FL
Telephone
01794 512953
Fax
01794 830805

Computer stationery
This is a mail-order computer stationery catalogue for use in the home or office. It sells continuous word-processing paper, letterheads, cheques, listing paper and labels. They also have a range of fax rolls, invoice forms and envelopes. The catalogue even states which software is most compatible with what range and there is also a service for bespoke forms, where printing is in black on white or tinted NCR paper.
Catalogue Updated frequently, A4, Catalogue, B/W, 4 pages, Free **Postal charges** Varies with item **Delivery** Royal Mail **Methods of Payment** Cheque, Postal Order

CARE CARDS by JONES WILLIAMS
PO Box 170
Spartan Road
Bradford
Yorkshire
BD12 0RX
Telephone
01274 531834
Fax
01274 531829

Christmas cards & calendars
By purchasing Care Cards you will help to support 20 major British charities, from the British Diabetic Association to the Stroke Association, all very worthwhile causes. Cards range from Christmas classics such as Father Christmas, £40.30 for 25 cards, to Westminster Abbey, £35.10 for 25 cards. Some beautiful cards and calendars to choose from, catering for all tastes. You can order and then pay on invoice.
Catalogue Annually, A3, Brochure, Colour, 22 pages, Free **Postal charges** £4.95 **Delivery** Royal Mail **Methods of Payment** Cheque, Credit Card, Switch, Postal Order

CLD STATIONERY LTD
7 Imperial Studios
Imperial Road
London
SW6 2AG
Telephone
0171 610 9292
Fax
0171 610 9222

Stationery
Personalised stationery and gifts for all are found in this catalogue. A percentage of everything spent with this company will be donated to Feed the Children in Bosnia. Luxury Linen Fax Folder with personal fax index and 50 sheets of your design A4 fax paper, £16. Personalised stationery in various coloured paper, 50 sheets with matching envelopes £10, 100 sheets of same £17. Use your own photograph on a border card with a red or green border for Christmas. CLD can print, thermograph and engrave all the stationery you need using the highest quality paper from the USA.

Catalogue Annually, A5, Brochure, Colour, 11 pages, Free **Postal charges** Varies with item **Delivery** Royal Mail **Methods of Payment** Cheque, Postal Order

FARRER FINE BINDING
17 St Albans Hill
Hemel Hempstead
Hertfordshire
HP3 9NG
Telephone
01442 212426

Fine bound photograph albums and scrapbooks
Farrer Fine Binding produces a variety of books which combine modern materials with traditional methods of binding. Its photograph albums are produced in three sizes with a choice of six marbled papers or three plain bindings. Each one contains 15 sheets of thick black or cream paper for mounting on both sides. Scrapbooks are bound in hard-wearing black cloth and contain 40 sheets of black paper. Both use post bindings and refill packs are available. Albums, from £16; scrapbooks, from £9.95. Personalised names or logos can be added at extra cost.

Catalogue Annually, A4, Leaflets, Colour, 2 pages, Free **Postal charges** Varies with item **Delivery** Royal Mail, Parcelforce **Methods of Payment** Cheque

THE HOME FARM TRUST
Merchant's House
Wapping Road

Christmas cards and gifts
The Home Farm Trust is a charity which provides residential care for hundreds of people with learning disabilities, helping them to lead full

STATIONERY

Bristol
Avon
BS1 4RW
Telephone
0117 927 3746
Fax
0117 922 5938

lives, attend college courses and take employment. Its catalogue contains attractive and well-designed Christmas cards (from £2.20 for a pack of 10), a Build Yourself Advent Stable (£3.95), calendars, tea-towels and wrapping paper.
Catalogue Annually, A5, Catalogue, Colour, 12 pages, Free **Postal charges** £1.65 for orders up to £6; £3.10 for orders of more than £6 **Delivery** Royal Mail **Methods of Payment** Cheque, Postal Order, Credit Card

J & J CASH LTD
Torrington Avenue
Coventry
West Midlands
CV4 9UZ
Telephone
01203 466466
Fax
01203 462525

Woven labels, gifts and stationery

Established since 1846, Cash's is synonymous with woven labels for school uniforms. This catalogue, however, shows that its range is much wider. They also offer framed woven pictures (including limited-edition woven silk ones), bookmarks, hand-crafted boxes and stationery.

The Recycled Executive Stationery and Luxury Linen stationery cost £21.95 and £29.95 respectively for 100 printed sheets and envelopes. Personalised address labels in a choice of two typestyles cost £5.99 (including p&p) for 250.
Catalogue A4, Catalogue, Colour, 23 pages, Free **Postal charges** £2.95, Varies with item **Delivery** Royal Mail **Methods of Payment** Cheque, Credit Card

JUSTFAX
43 Broadwick Street
London
W1V 1FT
Telephone
0800 716909
Fax
0171 437 5281

Filofaxes, 'Swiss Army' knives and torches

As well as its large selection of plastic and leather Filofax organisers and accessories, Justfax sells the 'Mag-Lite', a rechargeable mini torch (with over 1,000 hours of battery life and high-intensity halogen lamp), and Victorinox, the original 'Swiss Army' knives. Filofax pocket organisers start at £18.95 (filled) and the standard personal organisers start at £19.95 (filled). The leather Deskfaxes have business/credit card pockets, a zip pocket, a flap pocket suitable for carrying vital loose papers, and a notepad. Price: from £59.95 (filled).

LUCY ADAM CARDS
11 Freelands Road
Cobham
Surrey
KT11 2NA
Telephone
01932 863145

Greetings cards
Lucy Adams produce a range of blank greetings cards that are suitable for almost any occasion. There are nine different packs, including a pack of 30 Turkish carpet designs, 20 ancient and modern embroideries, and 25 marbling designs, each available at £15 per pack. In addition to the pre-packed cards, you can select individual ones at prices ranging from 30p to 75p each.

Catalogue Annually, Catalogue, Colour, 27 pages, Free **Postal charges** At cost **Delivery** Royal Mail **Methods of Payment** Cheque, Credit Card, Switch

Catalogue A5, Leaflets, Colour, 8 pages, Free **Postal charges** Add 50p for orders less than 15 cards; free for larger orders **Delivery** Royal Mail, Parcelforce **Methods of Payment** Cheque

THE MEDICI GALLERY
7 Grafton Street
London
W1X 3LA
Telephone
0171 629 5675
Fax
0171 495 2997

Cards, calendars and wrapping paper
Medici produce fine art and modern cards for all occasions, with or without simple messages. Proceeds from the sale of certain cards are donated to selected charities. It also offers a personalised Christmas card service. Prices for cards without greetings start from £44 for 50 cards of the cheapest design and rise to £680 for 1000 of the most expensive. Overprinting charges start from £65 for 50 cards.

Catalogue Quarterly, A4, Catalogue, Colour, 39 pages, Free **Postal charges** Varies with item **Delivery** Royal Mail **Methods of Payment** Cheque, Postal Order, Credit Card

MINILABEL
Oak Hall Manor
Sheffield Park Gardens
Sheffield Park
Sussex
TN22 3QY

Labels – addresses, business cards, woven name tags
As you might guess from its name, this company produces every type of label you can imagine and they can be personalised in a wide range of colours and typefaces. In addition, there are many pre-

Telephone
01825 790889
Fax
01825 790461

printed labels, both humorous and useful and the company is a distributor of Cash's woven tapes. Several samples are included with the catalogue. Minilabel with six lines of text, £7.25 for 250, rising to £52.50 for 10,000.

Catalogue Annually, A5, Leaflets, Colour and B/W, 10 pages, Free **Postal charges** Varies with item **Delivery** Royal Mail **Methods of Payment** Cheque, Postal Order

NEAT IDEAS
Sandall Stones Road
Kirk Sandall Industrial Estate
Doncastor
South Yorkshire
DN3 1QU
Telephone
0800 500 192
Fax
0800 600 192

Stationery and office equipment

As its name suggests, Neat Ideas stocks a vast range of storage devices that should keep any home or office free from clutter. The well-designed catalogue features just about everything you need from adhesive tape, £1.99, to a Philips mini cassette transcriber, £309. There are pens and drawing boards, scissors and shelving systems, files and fax machines, labelmakers and word processors. Prices exclude VAT.

Catalogue Annually, A4, Catalogue, Colour, 258 pages, Free **Postal charges** £3.45 for orders up to £30; free thereafter **Delivery** Royal Mail, Parcelforce, Courier **Methods of Payment** Cheque, Credit Card, Switch, American Express

PAPER DIRECT BY DELUXE
FREEPOST (LE296)
Hinckley
Leicestershire
LE10 0BR
Telephone
0800 616244
Fax
0800 716563

Paper and office stationery

Paper Direct sells ingenious pre-printed paper which you can use in your laser printer or copier to produce full-colour brochures, letterheads, mailers, forms, business cards, invitations, presentation documents, labels and many other items. It offers a large selection of papers, formats and designs and can also supply software for most word-processing programs and DTP packages which will help with templates. Stationery accessories, including jazzy paper clips, shaped paper punches and creative cutters, are available, too. A 100-sheet box of A4 Desktop Design Papers for letterheads costs £15.95; 50 matching printed DL envelopes, £10.95 (prices exclude VAT).

Catalogue Annually, A5, Catalogue, Colour, 31 pages, Free **Postal charges** Varies with item **Delivery** Royal Mail, Parcelforce **Methods of Payment** Cheque, Postal Order, Credit Card, American Express, Switch

PAPIER MARCHE
8 Gabriels Wharf
56 Upper Ground
London
SE1 9PP
Telephone
0171 401 2310

Designer stationery

Trisha has worked as a designer in New York and London. Her range of attractive stationery printed on recycled paper and card is available only from her shop in London or by mail order. Choose from 16 designs of greetings cards with matching giftwraps. Select writing papers with borders of bright poppies and anemones or trailing pastel convolvulus. All supplied with toning colours of envelopes and matching notepads. There are also hand-painted cards, clip photo frames with hand-painted mounts, mirrors with hand-painted frames, and lots of gifts and household items, all of which are brightly coloured with unusual designs.

Catalogue Annually, A5, Leaflets, Colour and B/W, 8 pages, Free **Postal charges** £3.50 **Delivery** Royal Mail **Methods of Payment** Cheque, Postal Order, Credit Card

THE PARKER PEN COMPANY
Parker House
Newhaven
East Sussex
BN9 0AU
Telephone
01273 513233
Fax
01273 514773

Pens, pencils and accessories

From the name synonymous with writing utensils comes a range of luxury products. The Duofold collection consists of 8 designs, each of which is available as a set comprising two types of fountain pen (from £175), a roller-ball pen (from £125), ball pen (from £115), and propelling pencil (from £115). Top of the range is the 18K Gold Presidential fountain pen (£5,500) and ball pen (£3,500). More affordable is the stainless-steel Parker 25 range: fountain pen, £20, and ball pen and propelling pencil, £11.99 each.

Catalogue A5, Catalogue, Colour, 20 pages, Free **Postal charges** Add £8.00 for orders up to £100.00; orders over £100.00, free **Delivery** Royal Mail **Methods of Payment** Cheque

RIANCRAFT STATIONERY
24 Derby Road
Cheam
Sutton
Surrey
SM1 2BL
Telephone
0181 642 2315

Birth announcements and christening cards

Riancraft Stationery hand produce birth announcements and christening cards. All prices include envelopes and recorded delivery to you. Cards can be ribboned or bowed at an extra cost of £5 per 25 cards. There is a choice of typefaces and this is shown in the brochure. Cards from £24.90 for 25 cards, £42.70 for 50 cards and every 25 thereafter are £15. With every order to Riancraft Birth Announcement cards, 15 thank-you notelets and envelopes (pre-printed included) are sent free. If you want to design your own card this can be arranged.

Catalogue Annually, A4, Brochure, Colour, 2 pages, Free **Postal charges** Free **Delivery** Royal Mail **Methods of Payment** Cheque, Postal Order

STONE MARKETING
4 Ashby's Yard
Medway Wharf Road
Tonbridge
Kent
TN9 1RE
Telephone
01732 771771
Fax
01732 771767

Writing instruments, stationery and gifts

Stone Marketing, winner of the W H Smith Stationery Award, manufactures and distributes writing instruments, stationery and gifts. Its catalogues contain page after page of beautifully designed photograph albums, picture frames, journals, stationery sets, calligraphy kits, boxes and blotters. Each item is finished in plain or decorative cloth or paper. The Tombow writing instruments are equally attractive and ergonomically designed. Photograph album, 360 × 305mm, £22; boxed stationery, from £12; Tombow aluminium fountain pen, £19.99.

Catalogue Annually, A4, Catalogue, Colour, 20 pages, Free **Postal charges** £4 **Delivery** Royal Mail, Parcelforce **Methods of Payment** Cheque, Postal Order, Credit Card

Toys

A P E S ROCKING HORSES
Ty Gwyn
Llanefydd
Denbigh
Clwyd
LL16 5HB
Telephone
0174 579 365

Rocking horses
Members of the British Toymakers' Guild, Pam and Stuart MacPherson produce limited editions of their very lifelike 'Natural Pony' range (from around £1,600). Made of fibreglass, these horses are mounted on to wooden rockers, have horsehair manes and tails and authentic removable leather harnesses.

Their 'Gipsy Bridge' range of traditional wooden horses includes 'Daisy', for children up to eight years old (£850), and 'Albert' for any size rider (£1,850). The MacPhersons also restore old rocking horses.

Catalogue Annually, A5, Brochure, Colour, 5 pages, Free **Postal charges** Varies with item **Delivery** Royal Mail **Methods of Payment** Cheque

BABY BASICS LIMITED
PO Box 246
Southampton
Hampshire
SO14 0ZL
Telephone
01703 234949
Fax
01703 331805

Learning through play toys
Baby Basics features safe, quality toys, books, puzzles and games that claim to encourage creativity in your children, helping to promote physical and intellectual development. They are very selective in choosing each item so you won't find any poorly-made toys or toys based on TV characters or toys that encourage violence. The catalogue is divided into three sections: from birth, from age 3, and from age 5, each colour photo and description being accompanied by one or more of 10 symbols which helps you to work out which skills your child will be using with this toy:

learning and thinking, imagination and creativity, auditory skills, tactile skills, visual skills, co-ordination and control, balance and movement, language and communication, sharing and caring, and life skills. Toys include Ring-O-Links, Rolling Mirror, Roly Poly Penguin, Stringing Beads, Supermarket, Clay Creatures, and Paddle Drum. An envelope is included for your order, but you have to stamp it yourself.

Catalogue Annually, A4, Catalogue, Colour, 40 pages, Free **Postal charges** £2.95 **Delivery** Royal Mail **Methods of Payment** Cheque, Postal Order, Credit Card, American Express

THE DOLLS' HOUSE EMPORIUM
Victoria Road
Ripley
Derbyshire
DE5 3YD
Telephone
01773 513773
Fax
01773 513772

Dolls' houses, furniture and accessories
The Dolls' House Emporium has an excellent reputation for quality and service to customers. The catalogue is a treasure trove of exquisite houses which can be purchased built, painted and wall-papered or as a kit. There are pages of accessories: lighting kits, wallpapers, room sets, individual pieces of furniture, food for the table, pots for the kitchen, families of dolls, nursery toys and pets. This catalogue will enchant you, whether a child or serious collector. Classical dolls' house kit, £109.90; built, painted and wallpapered, £379.90. Blossom Cottage flatpack, £49.90.

Catalogue Annually, A4, Catalogue, Colour, 48 pages, Free **Postal charges** Varies with item **Delivery** Royal Mail, Parcelforce **Methods of Payment** Cheque, Credit Card

THE DOWNUNDER TRADING COMPANY
3 Camberwell Commercial Centre
99 Lomond Grove
London
SE5 7HN

Australian boomerangs
A range of boomerangs from Australia, each photographed in colour. An accompanying black and white leaflet describes the properties of each boomerang, suiting each to its prospective owner. Thus, the Albatross is a stunt model; the Rangemaster a long-range contest model with

Telephone
0171 277 2200
Fax
0171 277 2877

weighted tips; the Flexifly is a backyard starter for kids; and the Hornet is a easy, fine flier for beginners. They come in a range of finishes from natural and jarrah to decorated and timbercolour. Prices range from £2.54 up to £26.

Catalogue Third A4, Leaflets, Colour, 6 pages, Free **Postal charges** £2.50 **Delivery** Royal Mail **Methods of Payment** Postal Order, Cheque

EARLY LEARNING CENTRE
South Marston Park
Swindon
Wiltshire
SN3 4TJ
Telephone
01793 832832
Fax
01793 823491

Toys for young children
Early Learning Centres provide a wide range of durable and very reasonably priced toys for young children (70% of their toys cost less than £5). Their philosophy is to instruct small children through play so they only sell toys that are educational in some way. They don't sell toy weapons or dolls and avoid items that rely on fashion and TV fads. They have recently branched out into nursery furniture and equipment which is also available by mail order from a separate catalogue.

Catalogue Bi-annually, A4, Catalogue, Colour, 88 pages, Free **Postal charges** £3.95 **Delivery** Parcelforce **Methods of Payment** Cheque, Postal Order, Credit Card

FROG HOLLOW
21 High Street
Pewsey
Wiltshire
SN9 5AF
Telephone
01672 564222
Fax
01672 562462

Gifts and toys
The company offers a range of personalised gifts (pencils, door plaques, swimming bags, etc) as well the more usual toys, games and books. Among the more whimsical gift items are the 'Frog Loo Roll Holder' (£19.99), and 'Butt Head' (£9.99), a silly Velcro cap for catching soft balls. They also do children's party bags. Telephone 0171 581 5493 for details.

Catalogue Annually, A5, Catalogue, Colour, 14 pages pages, Free **Postal charges** UK: £2.95; orders over £50.00, free **Delivery** Parcelforce **Methods of Payment** Cheque, Postal Order, Credit Card

GALT EDUCATIONAL

Culver Street
Waterhead
Oldham
Lancashire
OL4 2ST
Telephone
0161 428 1211

Toys and educational products

Galt sell a huge range of educational toys and teaching materials, mostly to schools themselves but they will also supply individuals through the Play and Learn catalogue. Their well-produced, colour catalogue is about the size of a telephone directory and includes just about everything for the nursery and junior school. Sections cover Sand & Water, Furniture & Storage, Imaginative Play (puppets, dolls, models, etc), Art, Jigsaws & Games, Energetic Play (climbing frames, PE equipment), Nursery, Infant & Toddler, Language, Maths, Construction, Technology, Science, Music, Electronic Learning and Geography & History. In short, a comprehensive catalogue.

Catalogue Annually, A4, Catalogue, Colour, 68 pages, Free **Postal charges** £3.25; £4.25 for next-day delivery **Delivery** Royal Mail and Securicor **Methods of Payment** Cheque, Postal Order, Credit Card, Switch, Diners Club, American Express

HAMLEYS LTD

188/196 Regent Street
London
W1R 6BT
Telephone
0171 734 3161

Toys

Hamleys are, of course, one of the most famous toy shops in the world and their huge Regent Street store stocks every toy, doll and game available. They used to issue a catalogue but stopped doing so some years ago. However, they still have a mail-order department and will despatch goods anywhere in the country. The problem is you have to know what you want in the first place, but in these days of endless TV ads for toys children are usually amazingly well-informed on just what it is they do want, in which case all is needed is a call to Hamleys – and a bullet-proof credit card!

Postal charges £5; £10 within 48 hours; over £150, free **Delivery** Parcelforce **Methods of Payment** Cheque, Postal Order, Credit Card, American Express, Diners Club, Switch

THE HILL TOY COMPANY
PO Box 100
Ripon
North Yorkshire
HG4 4XZ
Telephone
01765 689955
Fax
01765 689111

Toys

The Hill Toy Company produces attractive hand-made wooden and traditional toys for children of all ages. There's a fort (27 × 17in) with a working drawbridge for £49.95; a working crane and trailer (£49.95); a puppet theatre (£34.95) as well as a range of beautiful dolls' houses made exclusively for The Hill Toy Company (from £49.95), plus dolls' house furniture and a dolls' house family (black or white) of four. Items under £10 include a self-assembly mobile; a guardsman and sentry box; an 18in-high rag doll; a construction kit; various babies' rattles; and a miniature coffee set. The items are ranged according to age from babies and the very young through small girls and boys to older children, with games and activities, dolls' houses, farms and trains, and items under £10 each on separate spreads.

Catalogue Annually, A5, Catalogue, Colour, 16 pages, £1
Postal charges Up to £20, £2; up to £40, £3.50; up to £125, £5.50; giftwrap, £1 **Delivery** Royal Mail **Methods of Payment** Credit Card, Cheque, Postal Order

IT'S CHILD'S PLAY
Treworthal Barn
Treworthal
Crantock
Newquay
Cornwall
TR8 5PJ
Telephone
01637 830896
Fax
same

Traditional wooden toys and furniture

This company manufactures traditional wooden toys as well as children's furniture and display shelving. The simple, pull-along toys are made from hardwood and finished in non-toxic paints. The hippo, elephant, dog and duck are all priced at £5.40. The push-alongs include a fire engine for £7.55. The whip and top is £1.60, the cart with bricks, £18.50. Indoor play equipment includes a climbing frame for £198.95, and a desk costs £49.60. (All these prices are exclusive of VAT.)

Catalogue A4, Catalogue, Colour and B/W, 8 pages, Free
Postal charges Orders over £265.00, free. Shelf orders

under £265.00, add £5.50; mixed orders (toys etc and shelves) under £265.00, P&P charged at cost **Delivery** Royal Mail **Methods of Payment** Cheque

J & M TOYS
46 Finsbury Drive
Wrose
Bradford
West Yorkshire
BD2 1QA
Telephone
01274 599314

Dressing-up costumes for children
In this catalogue there are lots of ideas for encouraging role play and discussions for many situations, whether in playgroup, nursery, schools or just for filling the home dressing-up box. There are different sections of dressing-up clothes, streetlife which includes traffic police, airline pilot and many others, medical team, knights at arms, castle and cavaliers, multicultural, playtime and wedding. A nurses outfit costs from £7.75, Robin Hood outfit from £9.00, depending upon age. Even archery sets and swords and shields can be purchased. Wonderful catalogue for imaginary play.
Catalogue Annually, A5, Catalogue, Colour, 12 pages, Free **Postal charges** P&P on hats etc, £1.35 on orders up to £13; over £13, add 10% **Delivery** Royal Mail **Methods of Payment** Cheque, Postal Order

KANTARA
Bishopswood Leigh
Ross on Wye
Hereford
Herefordshire
HR9 5QX
Telephone
01594 860328

Children's furniture and toys
Francis Suttill's quality wooden toys include a rocking horse for only £85.00. His fun shelves come in the form of biplanes, triplanes or Palladian dolls' houses and are available in a flat pack, painted or unpainted and with three or two shelves. All have battens under the top and bottom shelves for wall fixing. Prices: from £47 unpainted. The desk and stool are priced at £35 and the toy box at £27.
Catalogue A4, Leaflets, Colour, 1 page, Free **Delivery** Parcelforce **Methods of Payment** Cheque

**KATELLA LTD
(KIDDIEWISE)**
PO Box 433
Leek
Staffordshire
ST13 7TZ
Telephone
01538 304235
Fax
01538 304575

Children's garden play equipment
Kiddiewise is a tradename of Katella Ltd, a family-run company with many years experience in the supply and installation of heavy-duty play equipment which is manufactured in Belgium. From standard swings with add-on elements such as a treehouse, monkey ladder, slide and climbing wall. They also make sandboxes, see-saws and garden furniture for children. Accessories include a wigwam, fireman's pole and a swing ring to mention but a few. Prices are £138 for a standard swing to complete items for £1240 which include slide, swing, treehouse, etc. A child's dream is contained in this brochure.
Catalogue Annually, A5, Brochure, Colour, 18 pages, Free **Postal charges** Free **Delivery** Royal Mail **Methods of Payment** Cheque, Postal Order, Credit Card

KRUCIAL KIDS
56A Woodford Avenue
Ilford
Essex
1G2 6XF
Telephone
0181 550 4933
Fax
0181 551 4927

Toys and maternity lingerie
Krucial Kids distributes innovative play-stations and activity centres made by the award-winning Canadian firm Educo International. Called Supermaze, these mazes of rigid coloured wires bent into intriguing shapes, threaded with coloured balls and set into smooth wooden bases offer hours of entertainment. Price from £45. Krucial Kids sells Wimmer-Ferguson toys from America, too, and distributes the Bellybra, designed to relieve weight strain on the lower back and abdomen during pregnancy, from £34.99.
Catalogue Annually, A4, Catalogue, Colour, 8 pages, Free **Postal charges** Free **Delivery** Royal Mail, Parcelforce **Methods of Payment** Cheque, Postal Order

LETTERBOX
PO Box 114
Truro
Cornwall

Imaginative toys and personalised presents
This is a wonderful source of imaginative and traditional toys and personalised presents for children. The attractive catalogue features a

TR1 1FZ
Telephone
01872 580885
Fax
01872 580866

multitude of personalised gifts including hats, bags, clocks, stamps, mugs and necklaces. There are enchanting painted wooden toys such as a nursery rhyme maypole, £15.99; mechanical dancing frogs, £9.25; and a Noah's Ark with 18 animals, £19.99. A Georgian doll's house costs £99.99; a knight's castle, £44.99. Presents for older children include Shut the Box, £12.99. Parents will also be delighted to discover selections of presents under £5 and £3.

Catalogue Annually, A4, Catalogue, Colour, 24 pages, Free **Postal charges** Up to £19.99, £2; £20 to £99.99, £3.50; over £100, free **Delivery** Royal Mail, Parcelforce **Methods of Payment** Cheque, Postal Order, Credit Card, Switch

MICHAEL STOKES
The Old Rectory
Kelston
Bath
Avon
BA1 9AG
Telephone
01225 317318

Climbing frames

Michael Stokes's Campaign Climbing Frame has been sold by mail order for over 10 years. With its tactile wooden construction and unique design it stimulates the child's imagination and encourages physical confidence. Constructed from weatherproofed redwood timber with hardwood rungs and handrails, it is free-standing and measures 4ft (120cm) square and 6ft (180cm) high with projecting ladders and slide. Adaptations are possible. The price for the frame is £435; a three-ladder extension costs £125.

Catalogue Annually, Third A4, Leaflets, Colour and B/W, 5 pages, Free **Postal charges** Delivery included within 200 miles **Delivery** Courier **Methods of Payment** Cheque

THE ODDBALL JUGGLING COMPANY
323 Upper Street
Islington
London
N1 2XQ

Juggling supplies

Susi and Max, the owners of Oddball, were the first people in the UK to open retail juggling shops. They now also run a mail-order service with a catalogue that tells you what to buy for your level of skill as well as detailing the history of the art. Beanbags start at £3.25 a set. These are ideal

Telephone
0171 354 5660
Fax
0171 704 2577

for beginners since they're easier to catch than balls and won't roll away if you drop them. For the accomplished juggler, there are juggling torches from £7.90, clubs from £2.50 and fire devilsticks from £15.95.

Catalogue Bi-annually, A4, Catalogue, B/W, 29 pages, Free **Postal charges** UK: add 10% to your order (minimum: £2.75) **Delivery** Royal Mail, Parcelforce **Methods of Payment** Cheque, Credit Card, Switch

ORANGE TREE
22 Grosvenor Street
Cheltenham
Gloucestershire
GL52 2SG
Telephone
01242 251189
Fax
same

Childrens toys

Soft toys with a difference, brightly coloured and extremely appealing to youngsters. Dollys, mice, tortoises, dogs, snakes, clowns and teddy bears are all in the range and very reasonably priced. You have to buy in quantities of 2 or more but share the cost and save money. Polly Doll 12" £3.40 each for 6. Clowns, large soft clown 24" £5.50 each for 2. Small dolly rucksack £3.83 each for 6.

Catalogue Annually, A4, Leaflets, Colour, 3 pages, Free **Postal charges** Free **Delivery** Royal Mail **Methods of Payment** Cheque, Postal Order

PADDINGTON AND FRIENDS
1 Abbey Street
Bath
Avon
BA1 1NN
Telephone
01225 463598

Paddington bear products

The Original Paddington stands 20in tall with labels signed by his creator, Michael Bond, making him a real collectors' item. Numerous other Paddington products include books, stationery and jigsaws. Paddington's friends include Spot the dog, Winnie the Pooh, Thomas the Tank Engine, Noddy, and Postman Pat. You can buy a battery-operated Noddy car with flashing lights and 'bump and go' action or a round metal wall clock showing Christopher Robin dragging Pooh downstairs.

Catalogue Annually, A5, Catalogue, B/W, 16 pages, Free **Postal charges** £3.00 **Delivery** Royal Mail **Methods of Payment** Cheque, Postal Order, Credit Card, American Express

PARTY PIECES
FREEPOST (RG910)
Childs Court Farm
Ashampstead
Berkshire
RG8 7BR
Telephone
01635 201844
Fax
01635 201911

Toys for parties
A godsend for parents having to stage-manage ever more competitive children's birthday parties, this colourful catalogue has everything you could possibly need bar an entertainer and infinite patience. There is a good selection of party bags, plus items with which to fill them along with food boxes, party tableware, balloons, hats, games, books and themed partyware. A clown plate setting, which includes plate, bowl and cup/lid/straw is 40p while jungle and dinosaur masks are just 25p each.
Catalogue Catalogue, Colour, 23 pages, Free **Postal charges** £2.95; for overnight delivery, add £3.50 to normal P&P **Delivery** Royal Mail **Methods of Payment** Cheque, Credit Card

THE PINE CUPBOARD
Brookside Barn
Agars Lane
Hordle
Lymington
Hampshire
SO41 0FL
Telephone
01590 683666
Fax
same

Wooden toys and children's furniture
The Pine Cupboard shop in Lymington has an even wider range of items – most of which can be delivered nationwide – than those featured in the mail-order catalogue. Wooden toys include handmade Jack in the Boxes (from £15.99); 'Guardsman' coathangers (£3.99); and hobby horses (£34). Games include cribbage (£4.99) and solitaire (£18.99). Furniture items include a single 'Richmond' pine bed (£290 plus £30 delivery) and the 'Henry Hedgehog' boot-scraper (£29.99).
Catalogue A5, Catalogue, Colour, 14 pages, Free **Postal charges** Up to £20.00, add £2.50; £20.00–£50.00, add £3.95; over £50.00, add £5.00 **Delivery** Parcelforce **Methods of Payment** Cheque, Postal Order, Credit Card, Switch

PLAYRING LTD
53 Westbere Road
West Hampstead
London
NW2 3SP

Award-winning toys
Designers and child therapists have worked together to provide toys and equipment which really appeal to babies and children and enhance their development through multi-sensory

Telephone
0171 794 9497
Fax
same

stimulation. The Playring is an award-winning play system incorporating pockets, loops, zips, and squeakers that is especially enjoyed by children with special needs. The Playring system 1, incorporating one playring, half, quarter, matrix, wedge and playcushion is priced at £364.25. A whole range of accessories such as the 'hole doll' (£5.60) can then be added.

Catalogue A4, Catalogue, Colour, 31 pages, Free **Postal charges** Add £4.65 for orders below £60.00. For a book or small order, add £1.50 **Delivery** Royal Mail **Methods of Payment** Cheque, Credit Card

PRANKS UNLIMITED
Simple Logic
PO Box 101
Nottingham
Nottinghamshire
NG2 7NN
Telephone
0115 945 5250
Fax
0115 945 5305

Jokes
The ultimate source of jokes. Pranks Unlimited sells all the classic nasties from clockwork creepy crawlies to itching powder, dehydrated worms to exploding staplers. There are rude jokes for adults and things that go bang in boxes. Imitation chocolates, £1.95 for five; stink bombs, 75p for three; sneezing powder, 29p.

Catalogue Annually, A4, Leaflets, B/W, 2 pages, Free **Postal charges** £1.25 **Delivery** Royal Mail **Methods of Payment** Cheque, Postal Order

REAL LIFE TOYS
Holbrook Industrial Estate
Halfway
Sheffield
South Yorkshire
S19 5GH
Telephone
0114 2510300
Fax
0114 2510810

Electrical cars and life-size toys
Real Life make self-assembly electric cars for children which look and perform like the real thing and have all the features you'd expect of a full-size car. There are three models: the Jeep, the Mayfair (which looks like a Model T Ford), and the Scout. All are powered by 12-volt motors and cost around £550–£600 each. Real Life also produce a self-assembly rocking horse with real fur which is about the size of a small pony and is priced at £50 for a limited period (normal price: around £250). All the toys can be bought either as patterns, or as partial or complete kits.

Catalogue A4, Leaflets, Colour, 5 pages, Free **Postal charges** A standard carriage charge is added to the order. **Delivery** Royal Mail **Methods of Payment** Cheque, Credit Card

ROBERT MULLIS ROCKING HORSE MAKER
55 Berkeley Road
Wroughton
Swindon
Wiltshire
SN4 9BN
Telephone
01793 813583
Fax
same

Rocking horses

Robert Mullis is a maker of fine wooden rocking horses in the traditional manner. He selects the timber — pine, ash, beech, oak, walnut or mahogany — from carefully managed areas of reforestation and each horse takes six to eight weeks to hand-craft. These fine animals are designed to withstand the rigours of children's play and will survive to befriend grandchildren and great-grandchildren. Rocking horse prices from £750 to £1575. Rocking animals, £350.

Catalogue Annually, A4, Brochure, Colour, 6 pages, Free **Postal charges** Varies with item **Delivery** Courier, In-house delivery **Methods of Payment** Cheque, Credit Card, COD

THE ROCKING HORSE SHOP
Fangfoss
York
North Yorkshire
YO4 5QH
Telephone
01759 368737
Fax
01759 368194

Accessories for rocking-horse makers

Anthony Dew provides books, plans, videos, timber packs, tools and an extensive range of specialist accessories for making rocking horses. Complete rocking horses are made to commission and restorations are also undertaken. Horse timber packs start at £108.34. Manes and tails in real horsehair start at £26.15. Glass eyes start at 90p a pair and stirrups start at £6.50 a pair. There is also a choice of two dolls' houses: the accessory set for the Victorian one costs £19.95 and the plans cost £5.99.

Catalogue A5, Catalogue, Colour, 24 pages, Free **Postal charges** Minimum carriage charge, £3.00; maximum £10.00 **Delivery** Royal Mail **Methods of Payment** Cheque, Postal Order, Credit Card, Switch

SKILLS FOR KIDS
618 Lakeside Pavilion
Lakeside Shopping Centre
West Thurrock
Essex
RM16 1WT
Telephone
01708 860251

Educational wall-hangings and soft toys
Not only do they make attractive room decorations, these delightful and colourful cotton wall-hangings also help to develop children's mental and creative abilities. There are two types of ABCs, one with pockets and one with removable letters, 'My calendar', and 'Teddy's I can count' (all priced at £19.99); a colours bus with finger puppets (£18.99); and nursery rhymes (£2.99 each). The extremely versatile puzzle mats can be used to play hopscotch, build houses, make words or what you will. Weather-resistant, they come in packs of 4 to 26 tiles.

Catalogue A4, Catalogue, Colour, 8 pages, Free **Postal charges** £2.25 **Delivery** Royal Mail **Methods of Payment** Cheque, Credit Card, Postal Order

SKIPPER YACHTS
Granary Yacht Harbour
Docklane
Melton
Suffolk
IP12 1PE
Telephone
01394 380703
Fax
01394 380936

Wooden yachts and toys
Skipper produces the sort of wooden toy yacht that everyone imagines they had in their childhood. The loose-leaf brochure has colour photographs of nine different models, from a simple 6in Thames Barge up to a 32in Ocean Racer. All are handmade in wood and use child-safe paint and genuine sail cloth. They look splendid and are priced from £3.45 to £85. There are also kits to make your own. Other wooden toys are available.

Catalogue Annually, A4, Leaflets, Colour and B/W, 3 pages, Free **Postal charges** £5 **Delivery** Royal Mail, Parcelforce **Methods of Payment** Cheque, Postal Order

STEVENSON BROTHERS
The Workshop
Ashford Road
Bethersden
Ashford
Kent

Hand-crafted toys and rocking horses
Did you know that wooden horses have been in use since the Middle Ages when they were used by knights for jousting practice? Today they carry children into fantasy land, and these creatures from Stevenson Brothers are no exception. Each horse takes six weeks to carve and comes mounted

TN26 3AP
Telephone
01233 820363
Fax
01233 820580

on a bow rocker or safety stand. To date, 1500 of their fine steeds have made their way around the world, and nearly as many have been restored in their horse hospital. Prices from £750 for a medium-sized Stevenson Horse to £3,035 for a Carousel House. They also stock dolls, teddies and rocking animal toys.

Catalogue Annually, A4, Catalogue, Colour, 15 pages, Free **Postal charges** Varies with item **Delivery** Royal Mail, Courier **Methods of Payment** Cheque, Credit Card

STOCKINGFILLAS
Euroway Business Park
Swindon
Wiltshire
SN5 8SN
Telephone
01793 480330
Fax
01793 485636

Stocking-filler toys and novelties

The Stockingfillas catalogue is bursting at the seams with all those little toys and novelties that are so much part of Christmas, but always hard to find. Many items are under a £1. Choose from an alphabet bracelet, 99p; magic finger chopper, £1.25; bath basketball, £1.99; cracker kit, £2.99; Bubblemania, £3.50; musical socks, £3.99 a pair; and hundreds more items including many personalised gifts.

Catalogue Annually, A5, Catalogue, Colour, 56 pages, Free **Postal charges** £1.99 **Delivery** Royal Mail, Parcelforce **Methods of Payment** Cheque, Postal Order, Credit Card

TALL SHIPS
PLAYFRAMES
Aveton Gifford
Kingsbridge
TQ7 4JP
Telephone
01548 550 131

Garden play equipment

Featured among this company's play equipment for the garden are the crow's nest, deathslides, nets, rope ladders, teepees, boats, swings, climbing frames, slides, and rope bridges. The crow's nest is a complete play system ideal for climbing, bouncing and all sorts of action games. There are two versions, each with a canvas roof with roll-up windows, a flagpole and flags, a cabin for about 6 with two trapdoors and a nylon playnet halfway down the ladders. A canvas dodger can be supplied for the slatted cabin. Prices were due to change as

we went to press, but prices are about £700.
Catalogue Updated regularly, Postcard, Colour and B/W, 1 page **Methods of Payment** Cheque, Postal order, Credit card

TFH
76 Barracks Road
Sandy Lane Industrial Estate
Stourport-on-Severn
Worcestershire
DY13 9QB
Telephone
01299 827820
Fax
01299 827035

Toys for children with special needs

For the last 13 years, TFH has been supplying special schools, hospitals, social education centres and parents with quality special needs equipment. By working together with their customers, work force and design engineers, they have developed the world's largest range of unique pastime, play and activity products for people of all ages and abilities. TFH is joined to and works closely with one of Britain's most established and respected toy companies, TP Activity Toys, so you can be confident TFH stands for quality. TFH produce three catalogues: Toys for Fun and Achievement, Age Appropriate Resources and Special Needs Books. The first catalogue, a 72-page full-colour publication which is aimed at children and teenagers with special needs, features over 1,000 toys and fun play ideas ideal for Christmas and birthdays. The second, a 40-page full-colour publication, is aimed at adults with special needs and features over 450 pastime, executive toys and recreational products. The third catalogue, a 12-page publication, is aimed at people of all ages and abilities as well as their parents and carers, and features 140 titles written about specific needs such as Cerebral Palsy, Down's Syndrome and Autism, as well as educational material. Service is fast and friendly.

Catalogue Annually, A4, Catalogue, Colour, 72 pages, Free **Postal charges** Varies with item **Delivery** Courier, Parcelforce **Methods of Payment** Cheque, Postal Order, Credit Card

TODDLER TOYS
4 Harriet Street
London
SW1X 9QT
Telephone
0171 245 6316
Fax
0171 245 6310

Children's toys
A wide-ranging catalogue containing toys, books, games and puzzles for children as young as newborn to 12 years. It is helpfully divided into sections variously entitled Early Years, Pretend Play, Construction, and Arts and Crafts. The Science and Learning section offers a Crystal Radio Kit (£11.95) and Map Maker Kit (£8.95). A price list is included that also states which toys require batteries. Toddler Toys also offers giftwrapping, free local delivery and an overseas airmail delivery service.

Catalogue Annually, A4, Catalogue, Colour, 35 pages pages, £2 **Postal charges** Varies with item **Delivery** Royal Mail, Parcelforce, Courier **Methods of Payment** Cheque, Credit Card, American Express

TREASURE CHEST
1 Mill View Close
Bulkeley
Nr Malpas
Cheshire
SY14 8DB
Telephone
01829 720507
Fax
01829 720565

Children's toys
A charming selection of traditional toys and games for the nursery, playroom or classroom. Pirate skipping rope, £5.99; Treasure Island game, £7.50; Russian dolls, from £7.99; hand-painted wooden Noah's Ark with 10 animals, £25. In addition, the catalogue offers delightful fabric wall-hangings with Velcro-backed accessories featuring Clown ABC, My Calendar, two advent calendars, Teddy's I Can Count and a colour bus with finger puppets.

Catalogue Annually, A5, Catalogue, Colour, 16 pages, Free **Postal charges** Free **Delivery** Royal Mail, Parcelforce **Methods of Payment** Cheque, Credit Card

TREASURES & HEIRLOOMS
Glasallt Fawr
Llangadog
Dyfed
SA19 9AS

Wooden gifts and toys
Durable and sturdy, these hand-crafted toys and gifts are often used by educational establishments to stimulate imagination and creative play. The Classic Train Set costs £87.50; Trawler £27.25; Bubble Whale £5.95; Beech Tree £11.75; and

Telephone
01550 777809

Squirrel £6.25. Noah's Ark, which comes complete with Mr and Mrs Noah, nine pairs of animals and a gangplank, costs £69.75, and there's a farm set for £42.75.

Catalogue A5, Brochure, Colour, 8 pages, Free **Postal charges** Free **Delivery** Parcelforce, Royal Mail **Methods of Payment** Cheque, Postal Order, Credit Card

TRIDIAS
124 Walcot Street
Bath
Avon
BA1 5BG
Telephone
01225 469455
Fax
01225 448592

Toys
Tridias, with four shops and a mail-order department, is one of the largest independent toy retailers in the UK. Its selection is based on the strict criteria of quality, value for money and design, with an interesting or educational element. It ranges from cheap pocket money/stocking fillers (glow dinosaur, 39p) to exclusive wooden toys (puppet theatre £19.95, fort £34.95, rocking horses £575), with dressing-up clothes, craft materials, toys, games and scientific kits in between.

Catalogue Annually, A5, Catalogue, Colour, 48 pages, Free **Postal charges** £2.95 **Delivery** Royal Mail, Parcelforce, Courier **Methods of Payment** Cheque, Postal Order, Credit Card

VICTORIA DOLLS
White House
Orchard Rise
Pwllmeyric
Chepstow
Gwent
NP6 6JT
Telephone
01291 623573
Fax
same

Porcelain dolls
This selection of traditional and individual handcrafted porcelain dolls from German, French and American moulds are all beautifully dressed in high-quality fabrics in the style of the Victorian period. 'Tiny Tantrums' (toddler-size boy) is £185, while 18in 'Claire' is £69. Baby life-size 'Amy' is £195 and 12in Rufus is £59.

Catalogue A5, Leaflets, Colour, 7 pages, Free **Postal charges** Free **Delivery** Parcelforce **Methods of Payment** Cheque

WANSBECK DOLLS' HOUSES
Cherry Lodge
Outwood Lane
Bletchingley
Surrey
RH1 4LR
Telephone
01883 744728
Fax
same

Dolls' houses, furniture and kits
Wansbeck sell quality wooden dolls' houses, dolls' house furniture and kits. The range of furniture includes handmade items for serious collectors, as well as more sturdy designs for children. They also stock porcelain dolls and kits, rugs and rug kits, shop furniture and 12-volt light fittings and kits and all kinds of DIY materials, including wallpapers, mouldings, sheet and stripwood, doors and windows.

Catalogue A4, Catalogue, Colour and B/W, 28 pages, £2.75 **Postal charges** Up to £2.00, add 85p; £2.01–£4.00, add £1.25; £4.01–£10.00, add £2.10; £10.01–£20.00, add £2.30; over £20.00, add £2.95 **Delivery** Royal Mail **Methods of Payment** Cheque, Postal Order, Credit Card

WENTWORTH COLLECTION
10 Tennyson Road
Brentwood
Essex
CM13 2SJ
Telephone
01277 216285
Fax
same

Model horses
Breyer model horses are made of tenite, a strong plastic, and are individually painted by hand. All models are gift-boxed. The Traditional Series is the largest, the adult horse is about 9in (23cm) high to the ears and 12in (30cm) long with accessories (saddles, riders) to fit. There are three smaller series. Horses cost around £20, with a few at £9.95; rider, £9.95; saddle, £17.95; bridle and blanket, £9.95; stable, £49.95.

Catalogue Annually, A3, Leaflets, Colour and B/W, 8 pages, Free **Postal charges** £2.50 for orders up to £20; £3.50 for orders of more than £20 **Delivery** Royal Mail, Parcelforce **Methods of Payment** Cheque, Postal Order, Credit Card, Switch

WHITE HORSES
The Old Exchange
19 Mill Lane
Welwyn
Hertfordshire
AL6 9EU

Rocking horses
These rocking horses are traditionally hand-carved using hardwoods such as ash, beech and mahogany. Tropical timbers are obtained only from countries where an established reafforestation policy is in force. Each horse is unique. Saddles and

Telephone
01438 715819

bridles are made from leather, fittings are of brass, and manes and tails are of genuine horsehair. For a small extra charge, a brass plate with an inscription can be supplied. Prices range from £265 for a small horse (42in long and 33in high) to £1,095 for a large horse (60in long and 48in high).

Catalogue A5, Brochure, Colour, 2 pages, Free **Postal charges** If customers are unable to collect, delivery can be arranged for a small charge **Delivery** In-house delivery **Methods of Payment** Cheque

WOODEN HORSE STABLES
Llandeilo Lodge
Llanfynydd Road
Dryslwyn
Carmarthen
Dyfed
Wales
SA32 7BY
Telephone
01558 668232
Fax
same

Rocking horses

Wooden Horse Stables produce rocking horses from the broadleaved trees of its native Welsh woodlands. Before it is eventually honed to make a rocking horse, each plank will have been air-dried, then passed through a kiln to reduce the moisture content for crafting. The Court Henry collection is available in elm, ash, oak, sweet chestnut, sycamore and cherry. Leather saddles and tack, along with horsehair manes and tails, give each horse the perfect finish. A small Court Henry Elm will set you back £692.

Catalogue Annually, A5, Catalogue, Colour and B/W, 12 pages, Free **Postal charges** Varies with item **Delivery** Courier **Methods of Payment** Cheque, Credit Card

WOODPECKER GIFTS
Sophia Ltd
Unit 7/8
Capel Hendre Industrial Estate
Ammanford
Dyfed
SA18 3SJ
Telephone
01269 845277

Hand-crafted wooden toys and gifts

Woodpecker Gifts, shown in catalogue form as Treasures and Heirlooms, make good-quality toys and gifts using many different European hardwoods with non-toxic finishes. The masts of the fishing boats double as fishing rods for catching the magnetised fish. The fishing rod and three fish costs £4.95 and the cargo boat with tackel and cargo is priced at £29.95. The desk tidy (£24.95), with a selection of five trees in a copse that will

Fax
01269 845358

hold your vital paperwork, also has two pen-holders and wells for large and small Post-It notes.
Catalogue A4, Leaflets, Colour, 29 pages, Free **Postal charges** Free **Delivery** Royal Mail **Methods of Payment** Cheque

Travel

THE EASIRIDER COMPANY
60 Main road
Hackleton
Northamptonshire
NN7 2AB
Telephone
01604 870713
Fax
01604 870430

Sheepskin car-seat covers, footwear and other items for the home
Add a touch of comfort and luxury to your car with these tailored lambswool rugs, and headrest, steering-wheel, safety-belt and seat covers. The Easirider company has been hand-crafting these products from fine-quality sheepskins for more than 20 years. Its extensive range also includes sheepskin moccasins, underblankets, heel pads and toys. You need never feel cold again. Car-seat cover, £49.95; steering-wheel cover, £6; children's moccasins, £9.95; single underblanket, £39.95.
Catalogue Annually, A5, Brochure, Colour and B/W, 8 pages, Free **Postal charges** Varies with item **Delivery** Royal Mail, Courier **Methods of Payments** Cheque, Credit Card

INTERNATIONAL VIDEO NETWORK LTD
FREEPOST
Snowdon Drive
Winterhill
Milton Keynes
Buckinghamshire
MK6 1BR
Telephone
0800 227722
Fax
0181 995 7871

Travel videos
Authoritative names such as Fodor's and Reader's Digest are featured in this catalogue. Fodor's travel videos give useful hints on language, currency, accommodation, transport and customs and each one comes with a Traveller's Handbook. The Reader's Digest titles emphasise the world's scenic beauty, such as the Great National Parks, and the 'Video Visits' titles are aimed at the adventurous traveller, covering more than 70 exotic destinations from Alaska to Zimbabwe. There is also a SuperCities series, priced at £8.99.

Catalogue Bi-annually, A5, Catalogue, Colour, 31 pages, Free **Postal charges** UK: £1.95 for 1–2 tapes, £2.50 for 3 tapes, £3.00 for 4 or more tapes. Europe: £2.50 per tape. Rest of world: £3.00 per tape surface mail **Delivery** Royal Mail **Methods of Payment** Cheque, Credit Card, American Express

SNOWCHAINS EUROPRODUCTS
Bourne Enterprise Centre
Borough Green
Sevenoaks
Kent
TN15 8DG
Telephone
01732 884408
Fax
01732 884564

Snowchains and roof boxes

Snowchains Europroducts stock a wide range of snow chains, car roof boxes and roof bars for passenger cars, light commercial vehicles and off-road vehicles. The range of snow chains is produced by Weissenfels and will fit most cars and sizes of tyre (from £38.26 per pair). Roof bars are available in different styles to take bicycles, sailboards, skis and luggage. Flight Deck roof boxes are available for as little as £99.95 and can easily be dismantled when not in use.

Catalogue A4, Catalogue, Colour, 6 pages, Free **Postal charges** Standard postal service, £4.50; 2–3 day carrier service (including insurance), £8.00; 24-hr carrier service (including insurance), £10.00. **Delivery** Royal Mail, Courier **Methods of Payment** Cheque, Credit Card, Diners Club, American Express

Watches & Clocks

BEAMERS
Well Cottage
Westhope
Herefordshire
HR4 8BT
Telephone
01432 830466

Handmade animal clocks, earrings, badges and magnets

Beamers makes a charming collection of affordable animal clocks in 17 endearing designs. All come with brass hands, black or white numbers, quartz movement and a two-year guarantee, for £12.95 each. Other products on the animal theme include picture frames, £8.95; drop earrings, £2.50; magnets, £1.40; and clever wellie pegs to keep your boots together, £1.40.

Catalogue Annually, A4, Leaflets, Colour, 2 pages, Free **Postal charges** Varies with item **Delivery** Royal Mail, Parcelforce **Methods of Payment** Cheque

CLOCKWORK & STEAM
The Old Bakery
24 Brackley Road
Towcester
Northamptonshire
NN12 6DJ
Telephone
01327 358080
Fax
01327 358388

Mechanical and quartz movement watches

Clockwork & Steam specialise in collectible watches. The expanding range from around the world will appeal to anyone who loves timepieces made with traditional engineering skills. One striking feature (though not literally) is the number of watches commemorating Russia's past, including the Red Guard Full Hunter and the KGB Full Hunter (£37.95 each). There is a Red Star wristwatch for £24.95 and a French Railways Half Hunter for £79.95. And for the left-handed, there is a backward running quartz watch, £49.95.

Catalogue Annually, A5, Catalogue, Colour, 16 pages, Free **Postal charges** £2.95 **Delivery** Royal Mail **Methods of Payment** Cheque, Credit Card

CRAZY CLOCKS

Unit C3
Hays Bridge Business Centre
South Godstone
Surrey
RH9 8JW
Telephone
01342 842129
Fax
01342 844027

Clocks

Crazy Clocks, also known as Accutec, have been manufacturing clocks in the UK for over fifteen years, alongside distributing some of the best clocks from overseas. All clocks are manufactured to the highest standards and range from reproduction pine clocks to humorous pendulum and alarm clocks and commercial clocks. There's the Octagonal Drop Dial Clock; the Backward Clock; the Black Cat Washing Clock; and the Football Clock, among others.

Catalogue Annually, A5, Catalogue, Colour, 16 pages, Free **Postal charges** Free **Delivery** Royal Mail **Methods of Payments** Cheque, Postal Order, Credit Card

MARVAL PRODUCTS

67 Headley Chase
Brentwood
Essex
CM14 5DH
Telephone
01277 225839
Fax
same

Clocks

Marval produces decorative wall clocks, with or without pendulums. They are silk-screen printed on to rigid PVC in a variety of designs and colours and are supplied with battery-powered quartz movements and a one-year guarantee. For car enthusiasts, choose from a Morgan, Porsche or VW Beetle among the many designs. There are dinosaurs and ballerinas, too. From £14.95.

Catalogue Annually, Third A4, Leaflets, Colour, 10 pages, Free **Postal charges** £1.50 per item **Delivery** Royal Mail **Methods of Payment** Cheque, Postal Order

MIKE FITZ DESIGNS

37 Meadway
Harpenden
Hertfordshire
AL5 1JN
Telephone
01582 762231
Fax
same

Pocket watch stands

Pocket watch stands were first used in the 18th century when a man's watch was placed on a stand at night near a candle so that it could be seen. Later they were used on the mantelpiece to make more of a feature. Mike Fitz has made a range of stands to complement any watch or heirloom. He uses rosewood, yew and walnut (from sustainable sources) and a French polish and wax finish. Prices from £20 to £76.

WATCHES & CLOCKS

Catalogue Annually, A4, Leaflets, Colour and B/W, 3 pages, Free **Postal charges** Free **Delivery** Parcelforce, Royal Mail **Methods of Payment** Cheque, Credit Card

NEXT DIRECTORY
PO Box 299
Leicester
Leicestershire
LE5 5GH
Telephone
0345 100 500
Fax
0116 2738749

Men's, women's and children's clothes and accessories

The Next Directory was in the forefront of the transformation of British mail order and remains one of the most stylish ways to order clothes and accessories through the post. The catalogue itself is a well-designed hardback featuring ranges available in the high street shops. It offers a small selection of watches from £29.99 for a women's quartz analogue bracelet watch to £49.99 for a men's two-tone sports watch.

Catalogue Bi-annually, A4, Catalogue, Colour, 387 pages, £3 **Postal charges** £2.50 **Delivery** Courier, Parcelforce, In-house delivery **Methods of Payment** Cheque, Stage Payments, Credit Card, American Express, Diners Club

OGDEN OF HARROGATE LTD
38 James Street
Harrogate
North Yorkshire
HG1 1RQ
Telephone
01423 504123
Fax
01423 522283

Jewellery, watches, silverware and gifts

Ogden of Harrogate is a well-established family business offering an extensive selection of jewellery and silverware, watches and clocks. Its range includes antique and secondhand items in addition to traditional and modern designs. Prices from £65 to £23,500. The company's craftsmen offer a design, re-design, alteration and repair service. A valuation service is also available.

Catalogue Annually, A5, Brochure, Colour, 31 pages, Free **Postal charges** £5 approx. **Methods of Payment** Cheque, Credit Card, American Express, Diners Club

SMALLCOMBE CLOCKS
Towers Road Industrial Estate
Rectory Road
Grays

Clocks

Smallcombe Clocks is renowned for its superior handmade timepieces. Its brochure offers floor-standing longcase clocks (£395–£2,550) available in mahogany or oak finish, with pendulum or

Essex
RM17 6ST
Telephone
01375 377181
Fax
01375 390286

concealed battery-operated quartz movement. Every longcase is personally delivered and installed by the clockmakers. Mantel clocks are available from £49.95.

Catalogue Annually, A4, Catalogue, Colour, 10 pages, Free **Postal charges** Delivery included for mainland UK **Delivery** Courier, In-house delivery **Methods of Payment** Cheque, Credit Card

INDEX

3-D Cricket 504
A B Woodworking 148, 401
A Buckingham Ltd 148
AA Computer Print 511
Abbey Quilting Ltd 401
Abergavenny Fine Foods 194
Aboriginalia 465
Accelerated Learning Systems 481
ACI 160
Acorn 76
Acorn Music 481
Actionaid Trading Promotions 62, 315
Action Computer Supplies 160
Admiralty Charts 42
Adnams Wine Merchants 194
Agriframes 279
Air Circus 496
AJP Business Computers 161
Alafoss of Iceland 77
Alan Foxley Ceramics 402
Alec Tiranti 19, 382
Alexanders the Jewellers 316
Algerian Coffee Stores 195
Alison Perryman 316
Allegro Bags 496
Allen Gray 77
Allwood Brothers 279
Alpaca Collection, The 316
Ancestral Collections Ltd 149
Andrew Bottomley 149, 496
Animal Health Trust 62, 472
Animal Welfare Trust, The 63, 317
Ankaret Cresswell 77
Annabel Lee 78
Antiquarian Cookery Books 42
Antique Bedstead Company 257
Apes Rocking Horses 518
Appalachia: The Folk Art Shop 317, 402
Applause Theatre Books 43
Arcadia Nurseries 280
Argos Distributors Ltd 303, 452
Aristocast Originals Ltd 172, 403

Aromatherapy Associates Ltd 358
Arran Aromatics Ltd 358
Art Room 19
Art Veneer Company, The 20, 382
Artagraph Reproduction Technology Ltd 20
Artigiano 78
Artisan 258, 403
Artista Studio Publications 20
Arts Encaustic 383
Atlas Kingsize 78
Aveda Cosmetics Ltd 359
Avon Cosmetics Ltd 11, 359
AVP Software 494

Baby Basics Limited 518
Bags of Books 43
Baldwin & Co, G 366
Balloon City 318
Banana Barn 11, 280
Barclay & Bodie 318
Barleycorn Natural & Organic Foods 195
Barn Full of Sofas and Chairs, A 257
Barnyarns 383
Bay House Aromatics 360
Bay Tree Trading Co Ltd, The 280
BCA 44
Beamers 403, 540
Beckett and Graham 318
Beckfoot Mill 384
Bed-Side-Bed Company, The 30
Beer Cellar & Co Ltd, The 196
Beer Paradise Ltd 196
Beetlebug 79
Benetton Direct 79
Benham 150
Bentley & Hillmer 258
Berkmann Wine Cellars Ltd 197
Berrydales 198
Bery Bros & Rudd Ltd 197
Best Buys Office Equipment Direct 161

Better Baby Sling Company, The 30
Betterware UK Ltd 274
Bettys & Taylors by Post 198, 319
Beverly Hills Bakery 199, 320
Bibendum Wine 199
Bibliophile Books 45
Bike City Ltd 497
Bioceuticals 360
Birchall's 150, 320
Birkett & Phillips 80
Bits & Pieces (UK) Ltd 320
Black Dog of Wells 281, 404
Blackwell's Extra 45
Blooming Marvellous Ltd 80
Blooms of Guernsey 183, 321
Boden 81
Body Aware 81, 506
Body Shop by Mail, The 361
Bombay Duck 303, 404
Books for Children 46
Bookworm Club, The 46
Bordeaux Direct 199
Bow Art (Prints by Post) 21, 321
Bradley Collection Ltd, The 404
Bradley Gardens Nursery 200, 281
Braitrim 304, 384
Bravissimo 82
Bressingham Gardens 282
Breton Shirt Company, The 82
Britannia Music Co 482
British Museum Company Ltd, The 282
British Museum Publications 321, 463
British Red Cross 63, 322
British Telecom 179
Brixton Pottery Ltd 452
Brora 83
Bruford & Heming Ltd 12, 322
Brush Factory, The 405
Bruton Street Gallery, The 21
BT Business Catalogue 466
Bubbles Children's Clothes 83
Bumps N Babes 83
Bunches 183

INDEX

Burberry's 84, 323
Business Emphasys Ltd 250
Butterbuy and Sage Ltd 361
Butterflies Galore 151
Buyers & Sellers Ltd 179, 405
Bygone News 323
Byron & Byron Ltd 406

C & T Eyewear Ltd 12, 469
C C Products 274
Caboodle Bags 31
Cairncross of Perth 13
Calendar Memories 476
Californian Kids 84
Cameo Cards 361
Cancer Research Campaign 63, 324
Cane Comfort 258
Cannock Gates 283
Canvas & Nylon Company, The 470
Cap & Gown Series 482
Capel Garmon Bakery and Post Office 200
Captain O M Watts 497, 506
Caput Magna Ltd 250
Caradoc 85
Care Cards by Jones Williams 64, 511
Carell Leather 13
Carew Oysters 201
Carlsen 85
Carluccio's 201
Carrson Artistic Products 21
Cartmell's of Keswick 251
Cashmere Store Ltd, The 86
Cassettes Direct 483
Cataware 472
Cats Protection League, The 64, 473
Cavenagh Ltd 86
CCC Galleries 22
CD Selections 483
Cedar Health 362
Celebration Crystal Co Ltd 406
Cellar-Select Ltd 202
Celtia 13
Chambers Fine Furniture 407
Champion Haggis 202
Change Wear Office Furniture 407
Chantal Devenport 324
Charbonnel et Walker 202
Charity Flowers Direct 184
Charles Ede Ltd 151
Charles Tyrwhitt Shirts 87
Charles White (Office Supplies) Ltd 466
Charlotte 31
Chater & Scott 483

Chatsworth 203
Chatsworth Farm Shop 203
Chauson Company 31
Chelsea Trading Company 407
Cherwell Direct Limited 325
Chester-Care 304
China Box, The 408
Choc Express by Thorntons 204, 325
Chocolate Society, The 204
Chromacolour International 22
Churchill Tableware 453
Churchtown Farm 184
Ciel Decor 408
Claire (Int) Ltd 87
Clark Trading Company, The 205
Clarksons of Devon 205
Classic Choice Furnishings Ltd 259
Classic Garden 283
Classic Mail Order Co, The 409
Classic Pictures Collection, The 484
Classic Silks, Screen & Interiors 385, 409
Clay Company, The 362
Clayton Monroe 172
CLD Stationery Ltd 512
Clifford James 88
Clivedon Collection, The 14
Cloakrooms 410
Clock House Furniture 410
Clockwork & Steam 540
CLP Computer Supplies 161
Coach Store, The 14
Cochranes of Oxford 459
Cocoon Coats 88
Coincraft 151
Collar Company, The 89
Cologne & Cotton 410
Colorado Mail Order 507
Comfort Care 459
Comics by Post 47
Compassion in World Farming 65, 326
Compleat Stenciller, The 23, 411
Complete Collection, The 305
Compusys 162
Computer Manuals 162
Condomania 460
Connaught Heritage, The 23
Connect Software 163
Connoisseur Collectors' Club 152
Cookie Craft 206
Coppelia Decorative Stencils 24, 411
Cordings by Mail 89
Corgi Classics 152

Corney & Barrow 206
Cornish Bulb Company, The 184, 326
Corrymoor Mohair 15
Cosyfeet 251
Cotswold Collections 90
Cotton Moon 90
Cotton Traders Direct 90
Cottontail 91
Country Desks 259
Country Shop, The 91
Countrywide Workshops Charitable Trust 65, 305, 327
CPL Group, The 476
Crabtree & Evelyn Overseas Ltd 362
Craft Depot 24, 385
Craigrossie Smoke House 207
Crazy Clocks 541
Croft Mill 386, 412
Crofters Traditional Knitwear 92
Crow's Nest Farm Products 274
Crucial Trading Ltd 412
Cubestore 413
Curious Caterpillar by Post 327
Cushions 413
Cynosure Ltd 328

D R Harris & Co 363
Daisy Diapers 32
Dale Street Mail Order Holiday Shop 92
Damart 93
Damask 414
David Austin Roses 284
David Felce, Daughters & Son 207
David Mellor 453
David Nieper 93
Davies & Clifford 172
Daxon 93
De Garis Flowers 185
Deacons Nursery 284
Deanes 94
Decorative Stained Glass Kenmore Ltd 328
Delia Marketing 94
Denhay Farms Ltd 208
Denise Brown Essential Oils 363
Denny Andrews 95
Designer Discount Club 95
Diamond Flowers 185
Dillons Direct 47
Direct Choice 275
Direct Cosmetics Ltd 364
Direct Import of Chipping Campden 414
Discount Video Selections 484
Disney Book Club 48

INDEX

Divertimenti (Mail Order) Ltd 454
Divine Inspiration (Direct) Ltd 329
DIY Plastics (UK) Ltd 172
DN Computer Services plc 163
Dog Directory, The 473
Dolls' House Emporium, The 153, 519
Dolma 364
Domestic Paraphernalia Company, The 414
Donaldson's of Crieff 96
Downunder Trading Company, The 519
Drake Educational Associates 485
Drury Tea and Coffee Company, The 208
Duffelcoat Company, The 96
Dukeshill Ham Company 208
Dunn & Co 96

E W King & Co Ltd 284
Early Learning Centre 520
Easirider Company, The 415, 538
Eastbrook Farm 209
Eastern Software Publishing Ltd 163
Eddington Hook Ltd 48
Edradour Distillery 329
Edward Harpley 415
El Vino 209
Eleanor House 97
Elephant Industries 260, 416
Elgar Shirts 97
Elizabeth Bradley Designs 386
Elizabeth MacGregor 285
Elmley Heritage 260
Embroidered Cushions 416
Emporio Armani 98
Empty Box Company, The 416
English Basket and Hurdle Centre 285
English Naturals 98
English Stamp Company, The 24, 417
Environmental investigation Agency 65
Eric Hill 99
Eric Horne Collectors' Toys 154
Espa 365
Esscents 330
Essential Items 261, 417
Essential Therapeutics 365
Essential Well Being 32, 365
Evans Cycles 498
Eximious Ltd 330
Exmoor Quilts 418

Exmouth Garden Products 286

F Frith & Co 25
F Parr 173, 305
Faberdashery 386
Fairchild Company, The 418
Family Album 306
Farlow's of Pall Mall 470, 498
Farrer Fine Binding 512
Fashion World 99
Favourite Things 330
Feast of Frames, A 419
Feline Advisory Bureau (FAB) 66, 473
Ferry Fish Smokehouse 210
Filante Products 419
Findlater Mackie Todd & Co Ltd 210
Fine Figures 99
Finishing Touch, The 331
Fired Earth 173, 420
First Impressions 331
Firstborn 32
Fitzbillies Bakers and Confectioners 211
Flamborough Marine 100
Flash Foto Ltd 477
Floral Revenge 186
Floris of London 366
Flowers by Post 186
Flying Duck Company, The 332
Flying Flowers 186
Foamplan (Rubber & Plastics) Ltd 261
Foley & Foley 100
Forever Flowering 187
Fortnum & Mason 211
Fox's Spices 212
Fred Aldous Ltd 387
Free Association Books 48
Freemans 306
Freetime Sports 507
Fresh Food Co, The 212
Friendly Fisherman, The 499
Frog Hollow 520
Fruitful Occasions 213, 332
Fudge's Bakers 213
Fun-Garees 101
Futon Express 262

Gale Classic Clothes 101
Galt Educational 521
Garden Trading Company 286
Garland Flowers Jersey 187
Garstang & Co, A. 76
General Trading Company Ltd, The 332
Geo F Trumper 367
Givans Irish Linen Stores Ltd 420

Glazebrook & Co 421
Glendevon Salmon 213
Global Orange Groves 287
Global Village 262, 421
Goldshield Natural Care 367
Golly Gosh Designs Ltd 102
Good Book Guide, The 49
Good Designs 499
Goodfellows of Dundee 213
Goodman's Geese 214
Graham & Green 421
Graig Farm 214
Granary, The 333
Grand Illusions 422
Grandfather Shirt Company, The 102
Grange Meubles UK 262, 422
Grants of Dalvey 333
Grattan plc 102, 307
Great Glen Fine Foods 215
Great Little Trading Company, The 33
Great Ormond Street Ltd 66
Great Universal Stores 308
Green & Stone 387
Green Book of Beauty, The 368
Green Store, The 308
Green Things 368
Greenpeace Catalogue 308, 334
Grey Goose Crackers 334
Grizzly Bear Kiddies Wear 103
Groom Bros Ltd 188, 287
Grovewood Cane Paradise 263
Guernsey Flowers by Post 188
Guernsey Fresh Flowers 188
Guild of Master Craftsmen Publications Ltd 49, 388
Guildsoft 164

H L Linen Bazaars 424
Haddonstone 288
Hamilton Billiards & Games Co 500
Hamlet Furniture 264
Hamleys Ltd 521
Hampers of Broadway 215
Hamptons Leisure 264
Hand Tools Ltd 174, 288
Hanging Kitchen Co, The 454
Hanro Direct 103
Harkness & Co, R 294
Harmony 174
Harrods Hamper and Gift Box Selection 216
Harrods Ltd 216
Hartwood Aromatics 368
Hawk Books 50
Hawkin & Co 334
Hawkshead Countrywear 104

INDEX

Hay Hampers 217
Heal Farm 218
Heated Mirror Co Ltd, The 423
Heather Valley (Woollens) Ltd 309
Heirloom Patchwork 423
Helios Homeopathic Pharmacy 369
Help The Aged (Mail Order) Ltd 67, 423
Herbert Johnson 104
Heritage Cashmere Ltd 104
Heveningham Collection, The 265
Higginbotham 105
High and Mighty 105
Hill Toy Company, The 522
Hines of Oxford 424
I lit The Sac 106
Holloways 265
Hollywood Scripts 50
Holme Farmed Venison 218
Home Farm Trust, The 67, 512
Home Shopping Direct 106
Home Shopping Selections 275
Homebrew Mail Order 218
Homeopathic Supply Co, The 369
House of Brass 175
House of Hamilton Ltd 219
Household Articles Ltd 425
Humphrey's Exclusive Confectionery 220
Hybury China 425

Iain Mellis Cheesemonger 220
Ian Allan Regalia 309
Iansyst Ltd 494
Ideal Home Mail Order 310
India Shop, The 425
Indian Ocean Trading Company 265
Indisposables 33
Infant Isle Products 33
Ingrams Mail Order 460
Initial Ideas 335
Innovations (Mail Order) Ltd 275
Integrity Music 485
Interflora 189
International Primate Protection League, The 67, 474
International Video Network Ltd 51, 538
Inverawe Smokehouses 221
Iron Design Company, The 426
Ironworks, The 427
It's Child's Play 522

J & J Cash Ltd 336, 513
J & M Davidson 427

J & M Toys 523
J G S Metalwork 336, 427
J R Productions 34
Jacamanda 106
Jacksons of Hebden Bridge 388
Jacques Amand Bulb Specialists Ltd 288
Jake 107
Jali 175, 428
James Inglis 251
James Meade 107
James Smith & Sons 15
James White Apple Juices 221
Janet Coles Beads Ltd 388
Janet Reger 108
Janik Enterprises Ltd 389
Jarabosky 266
Jean Jerrard 108
Jeroboams 222
Jersey Lavender 370
Jessop Group Ltd 477
John Brocklehurst 108
John Chambers' Wild Flower Seeds 289
John Hamilton Studio 336
Johnson & Son Ltd, W W 301
Johnsons Seeds 289
Johnstons of Elgin 109
JoJo 34, 109
Joli Jolie 109
Jolliman 110
Jolly Red Tapestry Kits 390
Juidth Glue 110
Jumping Bean Co, The 164
Justfax 513

K Restorations 266
Kaleidoscope 310
Kantara 523
Katella Ltd (Kiddiewise) 524
Kay & Company Ltd 311
Keepsakes 222, 337
Kendricks 222
Kenneth Clark Ceramics 428
Kent & Carey 111
Kernowcraft Rocks & Gems Ltd 390
Kiddycare 34
Kids'Stuff 111
Kings of Maidenhead 112
Kingshill Collection Ltd, The 112
Kinloch Anderson 113
Knightingales Catalogue 429
Kooshies 35
Krucial Kids 35, 114, 524

L & L Objets Faux 429
La Redoute 114
Laetitia Allen Ltd 115
Lakeland Plastics 276, 454

Land of Stencils 430
Lands' End Direct Merchants 115
Larkhall Green Farm 370
Laura Ashley by Post 116
Lawleys by Post 154
Lawrence & Turner 25
Le Club Tricolore 486
Leeds Futon 267
Leisuretec 461
Les Amis Du Jardin 290
Letterbox 524
Letterbox Company (Tebworth) Ltd 430
Letterbox Library 51
Leukaemia Research Fund/LRF Trading 68, 337
Lewin & Sons, T.M. 140
Lewis & Cooper 223
Liberty Fabrics Direct 391
Light Brigade, The 431
Lights on Broadway 431
Limericks Linens Ltd 431
Lindsay Olins 337
Link-Stakes Ltd 290
Liquid I D 224
Listening Post 52
Little Elefant Kiri 116
Little Treasures 117
Littlewoods Home Shopping Group Ltd 311
Lloyd Loom Direct 267
Loch Fyne Oysters 224, 338
Loch Fyne Whiskies 225
Locketts 26
London Shutter Company, The 432
Long Tall Sally 117
Lorna de Gallegos 339
Lorraine Electronics Surveillance 181
Lucy Adam Cards 514

M and M Sports 508
M C Reproductions 268
Mac Zone, The 164
MacCulloch & Wallis 118
Mac Warehouse 165
Made in America 118
Made to Last 252
Magic Showcase 276
Magnificent Mouchoirs 339
Magpie Direct Mail Order 486
Majestic Wine Mail Order 225
Manchester Futon Company, The 267
Manor Bindery, The 432
Map Marketing 339
Marion Hand Painte House Plaques 433

INDEX

Maritime Company, The 340
Marks & Spencer Mail Order 433
Marks & Spencer Home Choice 312
Marlborough Fine English Tiles 433
Marshalls 291
Marshcouch 268
Martha Hill 370
Marval Products 340, 541
Mason Pearson Bros Ltd 371
Master of Malt, The 225
Matchrite 341
Maverick Mail Order 119
Maybury Sports Ltd 508
McCord 312
MDT Classics 486
Meadows 371
Meat Matters 226
Medici Gallery, The 514
Medivac 372
Meg Rivers 227, 341
Megafood 372
Melchior Chocolates 227
Melin Tregwynt 434
Memorial Firms, The 313
Memories on Video 487
Mencap Ltd 68
Merchantmen 154, 434
Merle's Studio 26
Mesh Computers plc 165
Michael Lazarus Associates 277, 474
Michael Stokes 525
Micheline Arcier Aromatherapy 373
Midnight Lady 119
Mike Fitz Designs 541
Milberry Silks 391
Mildred Pearce (Mail Order) Ltd 155
Mill Pottery 455
Millcraft 434
Mills & Mills 342
Min & Dell Ltd 342
Minilabel 514
Misco 166
Moffat Fishery, The 227
Molton Brown by Mail 373
Monckton Ltd 119
Montgomery Moore 228
Moorlands Cheesemakers 228
Morel Bros, Cobbett & Son Ltd 229
Mothercare Home Shopping 36
Mr Benson's Video Collection 487
Mrs Gill's Country Cakes 229
Muji 120, 435, 467

Mulberry Hall 435
Mullarkey & Sons 500
Multi-Sharp Tools 277
Mums2Be 120
Music Sales Limited 52
My Adventure Books 52
Myerscough-Jones of Leigh 120

National Anti-Vivisection Society 69
National Association of Nappy Services 36
National Canine Defence League 69, 342, 474
National Gallery Publications 26
National Maritime Museum 53
National Portrait Gallery 343, 463
National Trust (Enterprises) Ltd, The 343
Natural Casing Company 230
Natural Fact Ltd 121
Natural Health Products 373
Natural History Museum Catalogue, The 313
Nature's Baby 36
Nature's Nappies 37
Nauticalia 344
NCT Maternity Sales 37, 122
Neal's Yard Dairy 230
Neat Ideas 515
Nectar Beauty Shops 374
New Concept 461
New Shoe Company, The 253
New World Cassettes 488
New World Music 488
Newbold, R 131
Newbrook Products Ltd 291
Newton Forge 436
Newtons Traditional Remedies Ltd 374
Next Directory 122, 252, 436, 542
Nick Hern Books 53
Nick Munro Ltd 437
Nicola Jane 123
Nighthawk 166
Nightingales 123
Norfolk Greenhouses Ltd 292
Norfolk Headwear 124
Norfolk Lavender 344
Norman R Holland 231
Northampton Footwear Distributors 124
Notting Hill Housing Trust 69, 344
NSPCC Trading Company Ltd 70
Numero Verde 16

Oakley Fabrics Ltd 392
Occasions 345, 477
Ocean Home Shopping Ltd 437
Odd Chair Company, The 268
Oddball Juggling Company, The 525
Office London 253
Ogden of Harrogate Ltd 16, 542
Old Park Furnishings 438
Olivers Lighting Company 438
Omega Furniture 269
One Up Golf Ltd 508
Orange Tree 526
Organic Gardening Catalogue, The 292
Organic Wine Company, The 230
Oriel International 345
Orientalis Trading Company 231
Original Butterfly Man, The 155, 346
Original Keepsake Company, The 439
Orkney Angora 124
Orvis Company Inc, The 125, 500
Osborne's Big Man's shop 125
Ottakar's 54
Oxfam Trading 70, 346
Oxford Hat Company, The 126

Paddington and Friends 526
Paint Magic 439
Pakeman Catto & Carter 126
Paloma Designs 127
Pamandra 127
Panduro Hobby 392
Paper Direct by Deluxe 515
Papier Mache 516
Parker Pen Company, The 516
Party Pieces 527
Pashley, W R 504
Past Presents 269
Past Times 347
Patchwork Quilts 439
Patra Selections 128
Patricia Luke 347
Paxton & Whitfield 232
Peal, N 121
Pedometers International 501
Peels of London Ltd 176
Pelco Fertiliziers Ltd 293
Pendle Engineering 501
Penhaligon's 348, 374
Penny Plain 128
Perkins 176
Peruvian Connection 128
Peter Beales Roses 189, 293
Peter Jones China 156
Peter Rabbit and Friends 348

INDEX

Petworth House 375, 502
Profruition 190
Philip Bradbury Glass 440
PIA International Ltd 375
Picture Wear Originals 129
Pilgrim by Post 54, 489
Pine Candle Box 270
Pine Cupboard, The 527
Pinks by Post 190
Plantiflor 294
Playring Ltd 527
Plumbs 270
Poppers by Post 129
Poppy 37, 130, 348
Portable Computers Ltd 167
Portable Office Direct 167
Portsmouth Golf Centre 502
Posh Pots 294
Postcript 55
Pozzani Pure Water 440
Pranks Unlimited 528
Present Perfect 441
Presents for Men 349
Primavera 393
Princess Pleaters 393
Pringle of Scotland 130
Public Domain & Shareware Library, The 167
Puffin Book Club 55
Pull The Other One 349
Purple Fish 254
Purple Flame Aromatics 376
Purves & Purves 441, 455

Quinessence 376

Rachel Grimmer Ltd 131
Rachel Riley 131
Racing Green 132
Radiator Cover Company, The 177
Rainbow Fairweather Decorative Furniture 441
Rainford House of Elegance 442
Rannoch Smokery 232
Raydek Safety Products Ltd 467
Readicut Ridings Craft 393
Readicut Wool 394
Ready-made Centre Ltd 442
Real Life Toys 528
Real Meat Company, The 233
Record Corner 489
Red House Books Ltd 56
Red Letter Days 350
Rediscovered Originals 132
Reid & Waterers Ltd 350
Reid Wines (1992) Ltd 233
Reject China Shop 443
Remember When 351
Renahall Ltd 376

Riancraft Stationery 517
Richard Kihl 234
Richard Wade Etchings 27
Richard Woodall 234
Rickitt Educational Media 168
RNLI (Sales) Ltd 71
Robert Mullis Rocking Horse Maker 529
Robert Norfolk 133
Robson & Sons, L 223
Rocking Horse Shop, The 529
Rockingham Fender Seats 270
Rohan Designs 133
Romantic Garden Nursery, The 295
Rosie Nieper 134
Rosie Pockett 134
Rowan Yarns 394
Rowland's 134
Royal Academy of Arts 351
Royal Mint Coin Club 156
RSPB 71
RSPCA Trading Ltd 72, 313, 351
Running Heads International 56
Rural Crafts Direct 352
Russell House Tapestries 395

Safe Products Group 443
Sally Grafton Design 17
Sally Small 254
Samuel Dobie & Son Ltd 295
Sandridge Farmhouse Bacon 234
Sara Davenport Tapestries 395
Sara Jayne's Truffles 235
Sarah Deem 38
Sarah Meade's Special Occasion Cakes 235
Save The Children 72
Saxon Leather Upholstery 271
Say It With Hours 352
Scent Direct 191
Scent to You 377
Schmidt Natural Clothing 38
Scholastic Book Clubs 57
Science Museum 464
Scope Central Trading Limited 72, 353
Scope International Ltd 57
Scotch House, The 135
Scotland Direct 157
Scottish Gourmet, The 236
Scottish Tea Selectors 236
Scotts of Northwich 503
Scotts of Stow 443, 456
Scroll Names 353
Secret Looks 135
Sedlescombe Vineyard 236
Selectdirect 168
Selective Marketplace 136

Selfridges Selection 136
Seventh Heaven 271
Severn & Wye Smokery 237
Seymours of Bradford 137
Shaker Kitchens 444
Shallots 137
Shankara Limited 509
Shareware Publishing 169
Shellys International 255
Shetland Knitwear Associates 138
Shire Books 58
Shirley Price Aromatherapy 377
Shirlina Ltd 255
Shore Thing 509
Signs of the Times 445
Silk Shades 395
Silver Direct 17, 353
Silver Editions 354
Simble & Sons, J 175
Simply Salmon 237
Skillls for Kids 530
Skipper Yachts 530
Slendertone 378
Smallcombe Clocks 542
Smitcraft 27, 396
Snowbee Uk 503
Snowchains Europroducts 458, 539
Sofas and Sofa-Beds 271
Softback Preview, The 58
Software Source, The 495
Soled Out 256
Sorcerer's Apprentice, The 396
South Down Trugs & Crafts Ltd 296
South Kensington Museums Catalogue 355, 464
Sparklers Shirts 138
Special EFX Ltd 355
Spencer Thorn Jewellers 18
Squidgy Things Ltd 39
Squires Gate CD 489
St Andrews Woollen Mill 138
St James's Teas Ltd 238
Staffordshire Enamels 157, 356
Stamping Ground, The 177, 445
Stamping Heaven 397
Stanley Gibbons 397
Start Smart 139
Steamboat Food & Drink Ltd 238
Steamers 356
Stencil Essentials 28, 446
Stencil Factory, The 29, 446
Stencil Store Company, The 398, 446
Stevenson Brothers 530
Stevensons of Norwich 447
Stockbag Company, The 458

INDEX

Stockingfillas 531
Stone Marketing 517
Stop Shop by Mail 177
Stork Talk (Midlands) Ltd 39
Storyline 490
Stroke Association (Trading) Ltd 73
Structured Wholesaling Ltd 277
Sue Foster Fabrics 447
Suffolk Herbs 296
Sulis 139
Summerbee Products 378
Sundaes Sandals 256
Supernova Cycles 503
Susan J 139
Sutton Seeds Ltd 297
Swaddles Green Farm 239
Swaledale Woollens Ltd 140
Sweet & Maxwell Ltd 58
Sweet Pea 356
Swimshop 510

Talking Book Club, The 59, 490
Talking Book Shop, The 59
Tall Ships Playframes 471, 531
Tandy by Mail 181
Tanners Wines Ltd 239
Tapeworm 491
Tarquin 140
Tartan Landscapes 141
Tavernors 240
Taylor Nash 240, 357
Tea House, The 241
Tecno Retail Ltd 478
Teddy Bears of Witney 157
Teleflorist 191
Tensor Marketing Ltd 278, 357
Terrace & Garden 297
Tesco Floral Express 192
TFH 461, 532
Thai House Co, The 297
Thanet Business Supply Shops 468
Thimbelina 39
Thimble Guild, The 158
Thiz Bags 40
Thomas Pink 141
Thompson & Morgan 298
Ticklemore Cheese Shop 241
Tiles of Newport and London 448
Timney Fowler 448
Tiny Computers 169
Toast by Post, A 241, 315
Toddler toys 533
Toffee Shop, The 242

Tomas Seth & Company 29
Touch Design 448
Town & Country Manner 143
Tuf Clothing Company 144
Traditional Garden Supply Company, The 298
Traidcraft plc 314
Travellers' Tales 491
Travelling Light 143
Treasure & Heirlooms 533
Treasure Chest 533
Trefriw Woollen Mills 398
Treske 272
Tressilian Flower Farm 192
Tridias 534
Truggery, The 299
Truprint 478
Tulleys of Chelsea 272
Tupperware 456
Turnstyle Designs 178, 449
Turquaz Ltd 449
Twining and Company, R 232
Two Wests & Elliot 299

Unicef 73
United Cutlers of Sheffield 449, 456
Universities Federation for Animal Welfare (UFAW) 74, 357
Unlimited Colour Company 144
Unmera Smoked Products 242
Unwins Seeds Ltd 299

Valley Clematis Nursery, The 300
Van Meuwen 300
Vernon Geranium Nursery, The 301
Victoria Dolls 158, 534
Video Plus Direct 492
Vigo Vineyard Supplies 242
Village Bakery, The 243
Village Cakes 243
Vincemeros 244
Vital Foods Ltd 379

Waitrose Direct 192
Waitrose Direct Wines 245
Wallace & Barr Ltd 301
Wansbeck Dolls' Houses 535
Wards of Adisham 245
Warren & Son, W T 244
Watermill, The 245
Waterstone's Mailing Service 60

Weald Smokery, The 246
Wealth of Nations 144
Wearite 145
Weleda (UK) 379
Wellerwear (RGH Ltd) 145
Wentworth Collection 158, 535
West Clothing 146
Westminster Collection Ltd 159
Wetherall Ltd 146
Which? Books 60
Whisky Connoisseur, The 246
White Company, The 450
White Horses 535
White House Coffee Roasters (Nottingham) 247
White Knight Technology 169
Whittard of Chelsea 247
Wholesale Kitchen Appliances 450
Wholistic Research Company 380, 451
Wicker & Box 248
Wigglets 146
Wildsounds 492
Wilkes & Weaver 40
William Grant & Sons International Ltd 248
Willow Fabrics 398
Windows Mail Order 493
Windrush Mill 302
Wine Finds 249
Womankind Worldwide 74
Wood Floor Sales 178
Wood Green Animal Shelters 75
Wooden Horse Stables 536
Wooden Tops 273
Woodpecker Gifts 536
Woods of Morecambe 147
Woods of Windsor 380
Woolpit Interiors 451
Wootton Vineyard 249
World of Learning 493
World Wildlife Fund UK Ltd 75
Worldwide Flowers 193
Wrangle Point Kites 399
Wright & Logan 479

Yateley Industries for the Disabled Ltd 399
York Excel 479
York Photo 479

Zena Cosmetics (UK) Ltd 381
Zig Zag Designer Knitwear 147
Zorbit Babycare 41